THE HISTORY OF HUMAN POPULATIONS

Volume II
Migration, Urbanization,
and Structural Change

THE HISTORY OF HUMAN POPULATIONS

Volume II
Migration, Urbanization, and Structural Change

P. M. G. Harris

PRAEGER

Westport, Connecticut
London

Library of Congress Cataloging-in-Publication Data

Harris, P. M. G.
    The history of human populations : v. 2. migration, urbanization, and structural change /
P. M. G. Harris.
        p.   cm.
    Includes bibliographical references (p.   ) and index.
    ISBN 0–275–97191–0 (alk. paper)
    1. Population—History. I. Title.
    HB851.H286   2003
    304.6'09—dc21   00–061110

British Library Cataloguing in Publication Data is available.

Library of Congress Catalog Card Number: 00–061110
ISBN: 0–275–97191–0

First published in 2003

Praeger Publishers, 88 Post Road West, Westport, CT 06881
An imprint of Greenwood Publishing Group, Inc.
www.praeger.com

Printed in the United States of America

The paper used in this book complies with the
Permanent Paper Standard issued by the National
Information Standards Organization (Z39.48–1984).

10 9 8 7 6 5 4 3 2 1

For Lois Green Carr,

scholar, colleague, friend

—distinguished in each.

Contents

Illustrations

FIGURES

TABLES

Preface

This is the second volume of a three-part study of the role of certain forms of change in human population history. The first discovered a few mathematically related patterns of growth and decline for the size of populations in publications on historical demography that, over the last half century or more, have covered many kinds of societies and smaller communities on all continents, save Antarctica, from the time of the Roman republic and the Han Dynasty forward to the present time. Some of these six shapes of demographic expansion and atrophy have been roughly perceived in the literature. They are not totally unfamiliar. Volume I of this new study, however, has specified precisely these few types of trends that are both necessary and sufficient to model sustained growth and decline all across the spectrum of recorded human experience. It has demonstrated how each form is closely mathematically related to the others. And it has identified typical historical settings or conditions in which they have appeared, implying certain connections between each form of demographic change and the history of social, cultural, and economic developments.

Populations expand or contract as the result of births, deaths, and net migration. Once a population is relatively well established, migration becomes the least significant of the three in determining population size. How migrations accumulate and peter out, how migrants are absorbed into receiving populations, large or small, and how the compositions of both the new home population and the migration itself alter over time, nonetheless, offer invaluable insight into the nature of structural change in populations.

This present, second volume of the study culls three large and rich historical literatures to explore the relevance of the types of universal trends that are found in population growth and decline for demographic changes in migrations and in the populations receiving them. The first topic concerns relatively free migrations, in which people have chosen to leave one part of the world for another or, more locally, one region of a society for another. The second is the robust record of that most involuntary migration of all, the international slave trade from the 15th into the 19th century. The third literature with valuable insight for our analysis involves, in relatively modern times at least, the most people of all. This is urbanization, the movement from countryside to town or city—sometimes quite locally, sometimes over great distance. To discover common forms of adjustment that have been shared by each of these types of much-discussed migration since about 1500, shapes that are identical to those found for expansion and contraction in population size in Volume I, pinpoints and illuminates patterns of change that must somehow be generated by the innate behavior of births and/or deaths in the process of continuous demographic renewal, the topic to which Volume III turns in order to bring our search for the source of certain widely relevant historical universals to its ultimate fruition.

This second phase of the ongoing study, too, could not have been accomplished without the work of many investigators in many parts of the world who have published fruitful population history over the past half century or more. Such valuable findings continue to appear, including several since Volume I was being finalized in 1999 and 2000. I have tried to incorporate some of these new or previously overlooked results here and there in the current writing. Other relevant findings have come out even as this second part of the study was prepared for production. Some of that most recent work has been noticed and employed, too; other contributions have been called to my attention or actually supplied in draft by generous colleagues. I fear, however, that still further relevant and valuable inquiry has simply still been missed. In part that is a risk of ingrained, undisciplined overreaching; in part it results from the Piaget system of organization that pervades my half of an academic household in contrast to the Hannoverian Palladian form of the other. Apologies are offered in advance for oversights that surely still persist.

In the end, however, hopefully there are not too may omissions—or errors—in what is offered here. Clearly, improvements will be made, both in data and in interpretation. That is the nature of collective progress in research. Perhaps, though, what is published here will be sound enough and clear enough to entice others to grasp and to pursue what seem to be significant and far-reaching implications of what is presented, to be for others what the work of so many previous scholars on populations and their societal settings have been for me.

Some of the first ideas developed in this study were identified, refined, and applied to northern American colonial population growth and migration under support from the Center of the Study of the History of Liberty in America at Harvard University in the 1960s. Several faculty study leaves from Temple University over subsequent years facilitated work on the various international slave trades and the regional development of population, its diverse components, and its socio-economic setting in the colonial Chespeake. Seminal to ideas about the connections between demographic and economic change (a relationship so close that I sometimes term it "demonomic") was research with Lois Green Carr, Russell R. Menard, and Lorena S. Walsh for the St. Mary's City Commission on pre-revolutionary Maryland and Virginia under grants in the 1970s from the National Science Foundation and the National Endowment for the Humanities. Occasional "spousal leaves" and cooperation in scheduling from Temple history colleagues made substantial subsequent work on the project possible until the "golden years" of full-time research and writing finally arrived. The past decade has been a period through which support and friendship from the Department of History at Indiana University, Indianapolis, and stimulation from both the "usual suspects" and visiting scholars at the Economic History Workshop and Population Institute for Research and Teaching at Bloomington made inquiry both enjoyable and better.

Besides being a stimulating and sharing research colleague over the years, Lorena Walsh graciously, patiently, and perceptively read and commented upon rather more than half of this volume in draft—three chapters, bless her, more than once. The critical application to the manuscript of her skill and experience on the slave trade, colonial slave populations, and the life of early colonial migrants has much improved what is offered here. Some of the most exciting intellectual activity in which I have ever engaged was in brainstorming issues of the population and economy of the American colonies with Russell Menard. Lois Carr, to whom this volume is dedicated, has for decades caught me out at things I should not be doing (including the "GI" in line 22 of page 8 of Volume I, which should simply be "G"), explained why elements were unclear or over-stated, stimulated my research through the richness of her own inquiry into Chesapeake history and her dedication to the subject, and fed and hosted us splendedly through the years—a hospitality, at once both alimentary and intel-lectual, that all who have worked in Annapolis know well.

Hans-Jürgen Grabbe, a friend since the dark days when rather more strike than scholarship was taking place, besides filling an important gap in the record for early American migration has broadened my perspective by inclusion in international conferences and providing the better part of a year in Halle (Saale), where much of Chapters 3 and 4 were drafted. That writing on urbanization was heavily based upon the work of one of two well-known investigators whose achievements inspired much of the present study and without which it could not have been constructed. Only far too late in life have I had the opportunity to meet each.

The sweeping analysis by Jan de Vries of European urbanization between 1500 and 1800 (as well as his 1997 book with Ad van der Woude on the blossoming and fading of the early modern Netherlands and E. A. Wrigley's seminal 1985 article on comparative urbanization) set the challenge and provided the key material for analyzing the growth of cities in the new terms of demographically based change that I was developing. Comparably, years before, as soon as it was published the slave trade *Census* of Philip Curtin demanded that an interpretation of migration and population development apply to his magnificent overview of many sources and many destinations in this distinctive form of relocation. His picture has been somewhat altered and considerably enriched by subsequent research; but it is upon Curtin's shoulders that so many of us stand.

David Eltis, author of much of the best recent slave trade analysis, not only has put forward in his extensive and continuing publication a model of careful and thought-provoking research. He generously allowed me to work in Chapter 5 with data on slave prices from research that was still on its way into print. This opportunity hopefully has reduced my fumbling around in someone else's area of expertise—at least on that particular topic. To a considerable extent, a study like this one involves repeatedly traversing vaguely sensed minefields in many scholarly areas for which the knowledgeable in fact have accurate maps. A little professional help goes a long way in reducing the amateurish blow-ups along the way. Any remaining disasters, on this topic or others, are of course my own responsibility.

My wife, Marianne Wokeck, has over the years taught me the particulars of much colonial immigration, has shared her research files and conference experiences, and has of late put up good-naturedly with a retiree intently focused on his comfortable, if messy, study.

Cynthia Harris of Greenwood Publishing Group saw the potential of this project and got it under way before moving up to other responsibilities. It all would not have happened without her experienced and supportive editing. Heather Staines, promptly and informatively addressing all issues and queries, has for the present volume been everything that an author wants in an editor. John Donohue of Westchester Book Services has patiently and professionally overseen production from a complicated and not always well-disciplined manuscript.

Indianapolis, May 2003

Introduction

An inquiry, begun some time ago, into how the population of one part of the Western Hemisphere increased historically led to the discovery that a few simple and closely related patterns of expansion and contraction have been followed by recorded human populations of many types (Harris 2001, Volume I of this study). To find such regularities immediately raised questions about how those few repeated and closely connected forms of trend might be generated.

Change in the size of populations is recognized to be determined jointly by rates of births, deaths, and migration. In most situations, migration is quantitatively the least significant of these three dynamics of demographic change. Developments in fertility and mortality make more of a difference. Nevertheless, the ways that migrations accumulate and dissipate, alter in composition, and merge into their receiving populations provide invaluable insights into the manner in which demographic structures change as fertility and mortality interact, with some people dying off and being replaced by others. A comparative study of migrations and how they have been digested into populations reveals much about the manner in which the workings of such renewal guide or filter the way that change of many types passes through demographic structures.

THE INSIGHTS AND CHALLENGES OF REPEATED PATTERNS OF GROWTH AND DECLINE IN HUMAN POPULATIONS

The previous stage of this historical and comparative study, which is presented in three volumes, has shown how populations—large and small, ancient and modern, in both sophisticated and simple societies—most commonly have expanded in just one repeated form (Harris 2001). This very general pattern of *growth*, called the G curve for short, entails constant proportional deceleration toward zero increase (Figure I.1a). With time the upward trend becomes steadily flatter and flatter. For representing this kind of asymptotic demographic behavior, the G function improves upon the "logistic" curve that was developed by Pierre-François Verhulst in the 1830s and popularized by Raymond A. Pearl and Lowell J. Reed and Alfred J. Lotka in the 1920s (Verhulst 1838, 1845, 1847; Pearl and Reed 1920; Lotka 1925, 83, 289–92, 122–27, 328–29, 369).

In a relatively small minority of instances, demographic increase takes other shapes. To capture any extended trend of growth, however, only three further patterns seem to suffice. Each of these is mathematically a very close "relative" of G.[1]

In conditions of population *explosion*, a popular but not very well understood demographic topic of the later 20th century—which has often erroneously been considered a modern "Third World" phenomenon—the E curve accelerates proportionally in the persistent way that G decelerates (Figure I.1a). Expansion starts slowly but continually picks up speed, progressively multiplying pressures to support a population.

The F curve of constant proportional growth, meanwhile, neither decelerating nor accelerating (Figure I.1b), takes the same 3 percent exponential slope that was approximated by Benjamin *Franklin* in 1751 and incorporated into the argument of Thomas Robert Malthus a half century later (Franklin 1751, 4: 228, 233; Malthus 1798, 20, 23). The present historical record indicates that such log-linear increase has occurred only among frontier populations in relatively modern societies (as Franklin, and Malthus after him, contrasted New World demographics of their respective eras to Old World outcomes) or among peripheral (in a different sense also "frontier") zones of modern economic development. Simple exponential increase at no *other* rate than 3 percent appears, contrary to what is predicted by theories of stable populations, from their invention by Leonhard Euler (1760) to their exposition by 20th-century demographers.

There is also evident from the historical survey of demographic growth and decline reported in Volume I a third, not very frequent, alternative to G-type demographic increase that is based on G. In this *half-speed* form of proportionally decelerating growth, called H (Figure I.1b), G's rate of slowing is divided by the constant e, the base of the natural logarithm. This kind of more slowly slowing expansion has appeared historically where societies have "developed" economically, allowing the stronger drag of G upon further expansion in population size to be weakened. According to presently available evidence, the earliest examples of demographic increase in this form emerged across northern Europe during the 16th century—in the maritime provinces of the Netherlands and then slightly later in Sweden (the valuable Baltic trading partner of the Dutch), England (soon to provide the main global rivalry for Dutch commerce),

Figure I.1a
Six G-Based Curves: G and Its Transformations D, E, and C

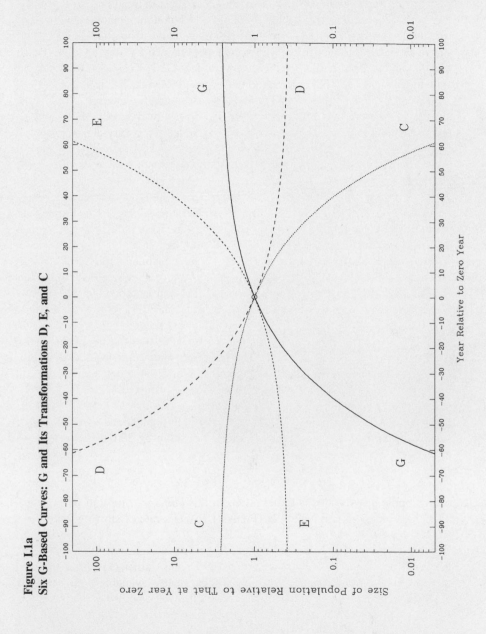

Figure I.1b
Six G-Based Curves: G, H, F, and G'

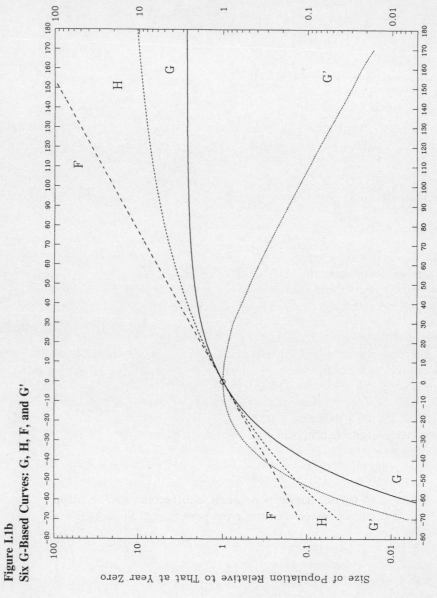

Size of Population Relative to That at Year Zero

Year Relative to Year Zero

Table I.1
G and Related Formulas

G $P_{(t)} = P_0(e^{1-e^{-.03t}})$

 or $\ln[1-\ln(P_{(t)}/P_0)] = -.03t$

D = 1/G

C $P_{(t)} = P_0(e^{1-e.03t})$

F $P_{(t)} = P_0e^{-.03t}$

 or F = G/G'

H $P_{(t)} = P_0[e^{e(1-e^{-.03t/e})}]$

 or H = G/G'$^{-2}$

G' $P'_{(t)} = -.03P_0[e^{1-.03t-e^{-.03t}}]$

E = 1/C = G^I

t = time t minus time 0 ($t - t_0$). For C and E, time is reversed ($t_0 - t$) by change from $-.03t$ to .03t.

and Germany (before that part of Europe was devastated by the Thirty Years War). Since that time, the populations of several—though by no means all—European countries and regions have for at least a while grown this way, as have several peoples in North America and southern South America and, much more recently, in eastern and southern Asia—except for China, where a series of H trends began as early as the 1740s (Harris 2001, 243–44).

These three accelerating, constant, and more slowly decelerating E, F, and H alternatives to the more general G pattern of demographic growth, it should be remembered, all share certain characteristics: (1) They are all relatively infrequent. (2) They are all closely and simply based upon the mathematical structure of G, as Table I.1 indicates. (3) They are all comparatively modern, not being observed in available historical data for populations before the 1500s.[2] (4) Generally none of them appear in small, local populations—only in regional or societal aggregates. G is the universal shape of growth for the first-level "building blocks" of which larger peoples are composed (Harris 2001, 382).

At times, of course, human populations also become smaller. Happily, the effects of even very severe *disaster* progressively tend to decelerate after the opening shock. They do so in D form, which is nothing but 1/G. This is a shape of decrease that Sherburne F. Cook and Woodrow Wilson Borah encountered repeatedly three decades ago in their demographic studies of colonial Spanish America, though they failed to specify it properly and to understand the significance of what they had found (Cook and Borah, 1971, 1974, 1979; Harris 2001, 101–9). It applies also to demographic declines recorded during the era of republican Rome, to several stages of dynastic atrophy in China, to the inroads of the Black Death in medieval Europe, and to more modern phenomena such as the impact of the Irish diaspora of the 19th century and the decay of inner cities in America and Europe across the later 20th century.

Occasionally, however, populations shrink in a different form. That alternative to D in sustained atrophy is even more rare than the E, F, and H exceptions to growth in the basic G shape. In this sixth and least frequent member of the little family of G-related curves for population size, loss starts slowly but *accelerates* with time toward total *collapse*, an ultimate eventuality not seen yet among peoples who have left records. Still, several historical populations whose niche or way of life seems to have been failing have started to shrink along such a C route for a substantial period before their circumstances altered. Examples run from floundering, would-be sugar islands of the colonial Caribbean to rural departments of France, as in the late 19th and early 20th centuries the country was said to "face depopulation" from falling fertility—and urbanization increased (Harris 2001, 123, 199, 203; Spengler 1938).

To summarize, Figures I.1a and I.1b graph the six curves in semi-logarithmic or ratio scale to show how their shapes both resemble and differ from each other. Table I.1 provides the formulas for comparison. It demonstrates how closely the six functions are related to each other mathematically.[3]

HOW DO SUCH REGULAR AND RELATED FORMS OF DEMOGRAPHIC CHANGE OCCUR?

To find that the growth and decline of populations over and over again take just a few closely connected forms immediately poses fundamental questions about how such regularities come about. In demographic thinking there are three places to look. Births add people. Deaths subtract them. The difference between in-migration and out-migration pulls in or pushes out some additional persons.

In most circumstances, even quite small variations in fertility or mortality are considered to change population size more readily than net migration. The processes of migration, nevertheless—especially in "settler" societies like colonies—often reveal vividly how the *structures* of populations alter. Change in age distribution, in particular, though reflecting prior trends in births and deaths, in turn feeds back to shape significantly the way that fertility and mortality contribute to the future growth or decline of populations. To analyze how migrations wax and wane, and how they simultaneously affect the receiving population while being absorbed into it, unveils an underlying guidance system for change in demographic structure that in turn helps explain how birth and death rates behave as they do across time and generate expansion and contraction for populations in just the few repeated patterns observed. A third volume of this comparative and historical study presents that final phase of analysis.

Likely connections of migration with G-based forms of growth already present themselves in the pages of Volume I. There, many of the most obvious, marked, and unquestionable fits of G trends with demographic increase appear where populations have been significantly fed by migration. The sizes of *new* settlements—colonies, frontier areas, and comparable units—have regularly expanded demographically along steep, sustained segments of the G curve. *Cities*, which in order to grow notoriously depend upon in-migrants rather than an excess of birth over deaths, likewise uniformly and definitively display long stretches of increase in the fundamental G pattern (Harris 2001, ch. 8). Meanwhile, regions or locales of known *economic development*, other demographic entities for which net in-migration is known to be crucial, are seen to enlarge regularly in G-related fashion, though sometimes via H or E rather than G itself. From this global evidence, we can already suspect that migration in turn likewise unfolds via G-connected patterns—in how its numbers come and go, in how it affects the composition of the receiving and also the sending population, in the way that the typical imbalances of relocating peoples by sex and age are digested and smoothed out in the demographic structures of the new home society.

What, then, are the shapes that migration takes through time, both in size and in composition? How are these related to the ubiquitous G form of population growth? For what reasons do such trends occur? What do those movements of in-flow or out-flow contribute toward molding population increase or decline into G-related patterns? What changes in demographic structure are embedded in and revealed by the dynamics of migrations and their new and old home populations? These are the issues for the chapters of this second volume of our inquiry. They are pursued in available histories of both free and forced migrations, in international relocation but also in internal movements including urbanization. Usable records or estimations stretch from the Middle Ages to the present time and concern both the New World and the Old.

THE STEPS OF INQUIRY

Chapter 1 begins by exploring trends through time in the size of several kinds of historical migrations whose particulars are known. It first analyzes the familiar big, long-distance transoceanic transfers of the 19th and early 20th centuries to (and sometimes from) North America, South America, southern Asia, and Australasia. Then it examines certain internal movements from region to region that are traceable within the modern United States. The third step is to explore how various peoples contributed toward establishing European populations in British North America and the Caribbean across a considerably earlier span of history, during the 17th and 18th centuries. Finally, the shapes of diverse migrations in other parts of the globe at other times are determined. Included are immigrations to French Canada in the 1600s, the Dutch East Indies between 1680 and 1792, Australia up to 1865, and Asiatic Russia between 1855 and 1949. So are emigrations out of some German principalities between the 1680s and 1869, Spain (to Argentina) between 1858 and 1913, later-disgorging Portugal between 1863 and 1972, four major regions within Italy between 1878 and 1913, and departures of Jews from Russia from the 1880s through the 1910s. The last set of examples in Chapter 1 patterns intakes of indentured laborers to the British

Caribbean, French colonies of the Indian Ocean, Australia, some U.S., British, and French islands of the Pacific, British Africa, and Dutch Guiana—and also the outflows from India and other sources that provided labor in this form to replace slavery from the 1830s down to World War I.

Such a comparative survey of some of the available data indicates that— transcending many different kinds of historical contexts, during four centuries and across most parts of the globe—the general pattern for migration flows has been G', the first derivative of G. The shape of this curve, which entails a positively or rightward skewed rise then fall in number, is included in Figure I.1b. Exceptions to this ubiquitous pattern come (as for population growth in Volume I) chiefly where broad *aggregates* of various narrower contributing migrations are considered. These compounded departures from the simple norm can take the form of G or H, perhaps even F.

A principal significance of having migration repeatedly follow the derivative of G is that its accumulation in the receiving population will tend over and over again to channel growth there into a G trend (mathematically, via the integration of G'). The more important immigration is for a population—for instance, early in a colonial settlement—the greater the effect of this shaping force upon the development of demographic size will be.

Chapter 2 then demonstrates how from the 1400s through the 1800s tributaries of the notorious international slave trade flowed and ebbed similarly. This most coerced type of relocation repeatedly followed the same trending as the migration of totally free individuals and families—or bound servants, soldiers, and convicts who enjoyed only intermediate freedom of movement. Major importing regions—from Europe and the Atlantic islands to the Americas, North Africa, or Arabia and India—repeatedly consumed black slaves in G' or related aggregate G or H form. Varied exporting zones along the African coast everywhere loaded captives on slave ships according to successive G' trends through time. Quite local details of where slaves were collected and put on board—by assembly point, by carrier, by ethnic source—over and over again display G' patterns. So do records of Africans shipped by vessels of the principal European powers that were engaged in the slave trade, and even by ships based upon certain ports within these leading slaving nations. Similarly, slave sales to particular local markets of the New World—this French sugar island, that British mainland colony, one segment of the Brazilian coast, a particular watershed within Dutch Guiana or Virginia—all are patterned by G'. From slave-taking in the African interior to ultimate disposal to consumers of the New World, wave after wave of G' shape characterized the flow and ebb of activity from various sources, by various middlemen and shippers, and at various locations of ultimate purchase and use.

However large the African slave trade was, or the intercontinental relocations of the 19th and early 20th centuries that followed it, probably by far the greatest migration of the past few centuries was to cities. As less and less human effort had to go into producing food, more and more people shifted to urban centers and the activities conducted there. What shape did trends of urbanization take?

Chapter 3 examines the growth of cities. Their demographic expansion—like that of historic slave populations—under typically poor conditions for natural replacement must continually be fed with new residents. How people come to individual cities in flows of G' shape is demonstrated internationally with examples from England and the Netherlands across the 16th, 17th, and 18th centuries down through illustrations from German centers for the middle 1800s to the late 1900s. How the compositions of city peoples altered in G-related fashion as they grew with migration is shown with evidence from Batavia and Edo, Rouen and Geneva, and even the little centers of the Danish West Indies. How the *collective* urban populations of *societies* or *regions* also expanded in G-connected form—the proportions of people dwelling in cities, the role of different kinds of cities—is evident in data from modern Sweden, Ireland, New Zealand, and the United States and from England and various provinces of the Netherlands before 1800.

Building upon the path-breaking analysis of E. A. Wrigley (1985), it is next possible to track, compare, and contrast urbanization and some of the demographic and economic shifts connected with it between 1500 and 1800 in three societies that led the development of modern Europe: the Netherlands, France, and England. The size of the urban, agricultural, and rural non-agricultural populations in all of them can be seen to have unfolded in G-based patterns. So did the proportion of each total population that was composed of the three types of residents. English developments and the likely reasons for them can be even more finely analyzed exploiting the work of Ann Kussmaul (1981)—and Wrigley's treatment of London (1967; Wrigley and Schofield 1981)—while the Dutch experience extends and clarifies some of the interpretation of Jan de Vries and Ad van der Woude (1997; also de Vries 1985). A sense emerges of the G-related forms taken historically by at least some regional or national urban networks and various forces that shaped them, an analysis that one would hope could be extended to societies with many and great cities such as China, India, and Japan, to various parts of South and Middle America, or perhaps back into at least a few centers of the Middle Ages.

Chapter 4 examines some of the things that are known about interational urban *systems*. How did cities that interacted with each other and competed with each other evolve as a consequence of these dynamics? What can be learned about the paths along which complex and far-reaching geographical networks of cities grew and changed?

The rich analysis of de Vries (1984) for Europe between 1500 and 1800 offers a foundation for better understanding that additional data and interpretation can fruitfully extend into other times and other regions. His generalizations, however, benefit from re-trending and regrouping the evidence. Identifying the G-based curves embedded in the growth of cities of various sizes and in the changing proportion of populations dwelling in them demonstrates how regional urban systems in fact moved together or apart through time in ways rather different from his categorizations and conclusions. So does reexamining the fortunes of individual centers across the three centuries that he studied. The shift of urbanization to northern Europe, the periodization of urban change (especially relative to economic developments), and the international influence and succession of super-centers from Naples and Venice progressively northward to London emerge more cleanly and more clearly when their likely G-related patterns are perceived. Such new trendings of urbanization can be extended—employing the work of W. Abel (1962), Paul Bairoch (1988, 1990), and others and various findings from both volumes of this present study—to analyze profitably at least some international urban developments from the 1100s to the 1900s. It also links insightfully urban population increase, city founding, and urbanization in proportional terms to total population trends in countries, some historical movements in the agriculture that fed cities, the deveopment of alternative employments for people, and the flows of Europeans and Africans to New World societies that are patterned in Chapters 1 and 2.

The concluding portions of this volume probe how the compositions of migrations and the structures of the societies that they entered altered through time. Clues as to the likely G-related shapes of such changes, too, appear in all of the preceding chapters.

For the early modern period, records of slaves, because they were valuable property, sometimes provide better demographic information than what survives for the bulk of European settlers. Chapter 5 looks at how African American *populations* emerged progressively out of various local imports via the slave trade. The data extend from the tobacco plantations of Virginia and Maryland across the Carolinas and the Caribbean to the cane farms and sugar mills of Bahia and the hinterland of Rio de Janeiro.

In plantation societies, blacks uniformly took over populations from whites along G paths. Early quirks of importation might generate another kind of pattern for a few years (mostly reflecting the G' of the initial local wave of slave arrivals itself). Universally, however, the trend soon converged to follow a G trajectory—though later local enthusiasm for fresh Africans, as from a change in crop mix, might replace the original G segment with a second, successive and steeper pattern of the same underlying form. Then, as slavery ended, from the Ohio Valley to the West Indies and the Atlantic shores of South America, the proportion of persons having African descent within local populations generally *shrank* in C form, the downwardly accelerating relative of G.

What is known about the regional non-white populations of the British, French, and Dutch West Indies—and closer inspections of developments within particular colonies from southern Maryland to Bahia—then demonstrates how the rate at which slaves failed to replace themselves, their net natural *decrease*, generally improved (declined) with time in D-shape trends. This softening of the harsh demographic imbalance of most slave populations (and even positive natural increase in some, from the Chesapeake and the Carolinas to Cuba) was accompanied by shrinking rates of importation of further Africans in the same D shape of trend. In short, slaves became more self-replacing with time even as most non-white New World populations continued to grow vigorously. Such expansion less and less depended upon further deliveries.

A falling rate of importation was widely accompanied by changes in the *composition* of the slave trade. The weight of females and the young among those transported frequently altered. Such changes very generally took G-based patterns. Sometimes they swung up and down in temporary G' fashion. This happened most often in distribution by sex as localities that were developing new plantations or switching from less labor-intensive operations to cultivating and processing sugar or extracting metallic riches from undergound particularly wanted additional men. Or the composition of imported Africans could shift in G or D trends of more substantial duration. The weight of children in the trade, up or down in proportion, typically altered that more long-term way.

G-related movements in what slaves were worth, both in America and in Africa, throw further light upon how slave populations evolved. Prices in America tended to increase via G trends that were related to changes taking place in local demographic regimes for slaves. Robust and less gradual price increases along the African coast, meanwhile—as slave-catching stretched farther and farther inland—forced shippers of slaves to cope with falling crude profit margins, which declined along G-connected paths. One effect of such shifts appears to have been rates of mortality among their coerced "passengers" that rose for a while in G' fashion during the 1700s in all the main national trades.

In the end, though, it can be seen how it was something in the way that the composition of New World African *populations* altered, not the content of later shipments, that steered the normalization or nativization of slave peoples into G-type trends. No matter how skewed things were at the start (and imports often were significantly lopsided), G was the form according to which women and children increased as a proportion in these populations. Such developments could occur at different levels. Some African American populations attained significant net natural increase surprisingly soon; others continued to fall far short of replacing themselves right down to the era of abolition. But demographic improvement was widespread; and such stabilization very generally took the D (1/G) shape in natural decrease or the corresponding G shape in natural increase.

Chapter 6 then proceeds to show how the same patterns of normalization or stabilization have characterized other historical populations. Adjustments in these shapes have not been exclusive to the extraordinary circumstances of slavery. As European peoples of various origin, arriving in a variety of manners (free, servant, convict) "naturalized" in colonies from Newfoundland and the St. Lawrence to New Mexico, and across the Caribbean to Guatemala and Surinam—sometimes blending with native peoples, sometimes mixing with Africans—their compositions altered in the same G-connected patterns as those observed among slaves. The proportions of continuing arrivals by sex, age, and legal standing, also changed this way, shows evidence from the Chesapeake, the West Indies, and the Delaware Valley across the 1600s and 1700s, travelers from Extremadura to the New World in the 1500s and early 1600s, and immigration to French Canada during the 1600s and early 1700s.

At other times and other places before the most recent era, similar trends of transformation seem also to have been the rule. Examples of these ubiquitous patterns of normalization come from America's Old Northwest in the 19th century, from the migrations and resultant populations of Australia and New Zealand in that same era, from immigrant marrying-in that has been identified in 18th-century South Africa, from the staffing of the Asian operations of the Dutch East India Company in the 1600s and 1700s, and from the makeup of the much-discussed 19th-century Irish diaspora. Very long-range examples with movements of the usual shapes appear in the rate of immigration to the Netherlands since 1531 and the age structures of England 1541–1871, Sweden 1750–2000, and France 1740–1951. These demonstrate how long-established societies, not just newly settled colonies, have repeatedly and continually experienced structural change of G-based shape in their populations. That Europe and European colonies do not alone share histories of demographic development in these forms is made clear by evidence from rural Liaoning Province in northeastern China 1774–1873.

Finally, a sample of more recent data illustrates trends of the same G-based types in how immigrants have been digested and the way that other alterations in the composition of populations have evolved. In the wake of the great modern era of immigration to the United States, in one national group after another across the first half of the 20th century, those who had been born in America swelled in G form as a proportion of total people from that particular foreign "stock" as the group "naturalized" in their new home. Comparably, the aggregate proportion of the foreign-born, their native-born children, and their second-generation native grandchildren among the people of the United States rose and fell between 1850 and 1970 in G-based trends. Meanwhile, the relative weight of various age groups within the American population likewise expanded and contracted in G-related paths. Such age movements appear for the native-born and for the foreign-born and pertain state by state across the country between 1800 and World War II, as do changes in the proportion of females for once sex-imbalanced frontier areas that were normalizing demographically.

Changes of demographic composition in these few closely related shapes, furthermore, were not limited to the United States. From the early 1800s past World War I, trends for altering sex and age compositions took G-based shapes not only among those coming to America but also in total flows of people exported everywhere by various European countries, say the classic studies of 19th- and early 20th-century migration. Movements inside modern Europe, not just out of it, also display such forms. Within Germany, across the middle of the 19th century, accumulating migrants into the Düsseldorf region as a whole— and its agicultural, industrial, and mixed areas separately—all composed percentages of the local population that increased in G form. Within Russia, between the emancipation of the serfs in the 1860s and World War I, the average proportion of villagers receiving passports that authorized them to seek lives elsewhere in that vast and changing society also swelled in G shape in 6 of 8 regions of the country—from the Baltic to the Urals and the Caucasus. In the famous agricultural areas of the Central Chernozem and the Ukraine, departures instead crested close to 1910 in the more wave-like G' manner. Across the late 19th and early 20th centuries, meanwhile, death rates for imported indentured Indian and Pacific Island workers declined in G-related trends as their populations in the Caribbean, Guyana, Assam, Fiji, and Queensland normalized. Similarly, in the trades that shipped such indentured workers across this ocean or that, the proportion who were female and death rates on the voyage shifted in G-connected patterns that are familiar from previously examined traffic in slaves, convicts, and free passengers.

All in similar G-related ways, Africans from the Atlantic slave trade accumulated in and transformed plantation societies of the New World, 19th-century European immigrants flooded into agricultural then industrial areas of the United States, fresh settlers across several centuries added their number to the populations of various continental frontiers, and new arrivals enlarged cities and permeated their existing populations The patterns in how people came, how their weight in the local population increased, and how they became part of normal demographic replacement follow the same few, closely related types of trend in all these historical contexts. Better understanding of the ways that migrations build up and taper off, how their makeup alters, and how they affect or respond to demographic changes in the societies that they help form opens up useful insight into how births and deaths, too, might repeatedly take trends in similar G-based forms. That becomes the topic of the third and final volume of this study, in which the most fundamental origins of such pervasive G-related patterns are uncovered.

NOTES

1. After some experimentation in comparing the goodness of fit of the G curve with data thought to be moving through time in this form against other familiar modelings for trends (Harris 2001, 32–36, 398–99), the procedure has been the following. First is to place a template for the G or other G-related curve indicated over the semi-logarithmically graphed range of data suspected of taking a given shape. Second is to fit (via the method of non-linear regression employing the Marquardt-Levenberg algorithm) the hypothesized shape of trend in terms of *proportional* error (making percentage deviations in small populations count as much as errors to scale in big ones). The third step, after the fitted curve has been graphed through the selected data, is to reexamine the scatter around the proposed trend line to identify (and probe possible reasons for) outliers if and when they occur and to re-examine expansions or contractions in the chronological range of data that might improve collectively the fit for this segment of

time, any preceding it, and any following it, and perhaps show how another member of the little G-based set of curves might be more appropriate. A reason for limiting the attempted models all just to "relatives" of the G curve is the potential simplicity and power of interpretation to be gained by representing all sustained trends with just one pattern of bend or a minor modification of form that retains the same fixed .03 coefficient of change. In finally choosing and interpreting trends, their suitability to what is known of the history of the studied population is also considered.

2. Including very early possible manifestations of the E curve in four provinces of Ming China beginning in the 1490s (Harris 2001, 266).

3. E is not only C turned upside down; it is the inverse function of G, or G^I. F, meanwhile, is equivalent to G divided by its first derivative, G', and H is G divided by the square root of G', being halfway between G and F in that sense. The logarithmic version of G emphasizes how the rise of the curve decelerates via the constant $-.03$.

Chapter 1

The Nature of Trends in Migration

Net migration works with births and deaths to determine the size and composition of populations. Patterns of movement in or out of a population must be assessed in order to comprehend properly by what means and to what extent fertility and mortality account for demographic growth and decline. This is a point sometimes passed over too lightly by demographic theorizing that assumes that populations are "closed" (dimensioned by birth and death rates alone). Besides, to determine how migration movements build up, peter out, alter in composition, and change the populations to which people go and from which they come reveals much about the underlying demographic dynamics, including how fertility and mortality evolve and in turn affect the size and makeup of populations.

In the first volume of this inquiry several indications have already appeared that G-based trends characterize migration. First of all, new societies or settlements have seen their early populations, which clearly grew principally from migration, expand in G form. This has been observed for mainland North America (both in first settlement and across three centuries of subsequent frontier expansion), in the Caribbean, Brazil, Australia and New Zealand, and in the borderlands of Russia—eastward into Siberia and southward across the Steppes (Harris 2001, chs. 1–4 and 6). In addition, cities, which tend to enlarge more from migration than from natural increase, have grown demographically almost entirely via just G paths (ibid., ch. 8). Likewise, "developing" societies or economically advancing regions within them, which also are noted for attracting people, have all around the globe expanded in G-based forms.

Migration reflects adjustments between and within populations whose numbers in most instances (excepting for a while in new settler societies) are nevertheless primarily still determined by movements in birth and death rates. Some further addition or deletion of people appears as the terms of life (be they economic, social, political, or spiritual)—and information about them—improve or deteriorate "here" as opposed to some alternative "there." Such dynamics of "push" and "pull" include excessive or insuffcent natural increase in one population or the other and some form of divergence of opportunity (more exactly, *perceived* disparity) between the two settings.

Among historically documented cases of relocation, most familiar to contemporary readers are the much-discussed transoceanic migrations of the 19th and early 20th centuries. Aided by railroad traffic overland in both giving and receiving countries and also by steam-powered transport at sea, millions of people changed residence decade after decade—often traveling thousands of miles. Because for the most part they left from and arrived at a limited number of transportation centers during an age of better developed record-keeping, more is understood about their changing numbers than about the chronological shape of other massive historical resettlements, except perhaps the much-studied Atlantic slave trade. These large and often long-lasting but only dimly outlined migrations include the inter-provincial movements of Chinese that are known to have kept cropping up across at least two millennia, the attraction, flight, or forced transplantation of Russians to various borderlands from the time of Ivan the Terrible through the age of Stalin, and even the relatively modern phases of *Drang nach Osten* for German-speaking peoples since the 17th century into Prussian frontiers, the Baltic, Poland, Austria, Hungary, and Russia—let alone the medieval precursor of this thrust.

What patterns through time, then, did the best-recorded (if still imperfectly measured) great overseas movements between Waterloo and World War II follow? How did those trends relate to the G-based shapes of demographic growth and decline that Volume I has observed in all the major sending and receiving countries?

Modern data also offer insight into the nature of migration *within* certain societies. Such evidence shows that comparatively short-distance internal movements, at least in some historical contexts, have taken the same form as the most famous intercontinental ones. Those findings provide more insight into how observed regional trends of population increase have unfolded, for instance as part of the continental filling out of the United States.

Earlier in time, good examples of how peoples from several different origins were drawn to, and contributed to, growing "new" populations come from colonial British America. European migration to West Indian colonies and to those of the mainland both repeatedly took the same G-related shape found in modern international and internal movements. So, separately and differently, did the successive waves of English, Southern Irish, Northern Irish, and Germans, who between the 1630s and the 1770s began to make North America a "melting pot." A common pattern of how migrations wax and wane emerges.

Other historical cases demonstrate that migration in this form prevailed well before the modern era and was no more limited to Anglo-American settings, or even the New World, than it was after 1800. French immigration to colonial Canada and the West Indies in the 17th century, emigration out of several German regions in the 18th and 19th centuries (mostly eastward within Europe, not across the Atlantic), and the early European peopling of Australia all followed trends of the same shape. So did the global movements of the indentured laborers, principally Indian, who replaced slaves—especially where sugar was cultivated—after various countries espoused abolition in the early 1800s. Certain specific flows out of Spain, Portugal, and Italy illustrate the prevalence of similarly shaped movements at more local levels of origin or destination during modern times as well, while Russian migration to Asia and departures of Russian Jews add further insightful perspective.

The few exceptions to the up-and-down G' pattern of migration that is so ubiquitous occur where mixed, aggregate migration is being observed. Examples include all European immigration to the United States, interchange between Britain and a whole range of colonies (both before 1800 and after), or the internationally diverse supply of Europeans recruited by the Dutch East India Company to man its far-flung Asian operations during the 1600s and 1700s.

These recurring historical patterns of relocation, both between and within societies, have been shared by quite different kinds of migrants. The flow and ebb of free families and individuals, contract laborers, bound servants, and convicts has taken a single set of repeated G-based paths. Legal status has not much affected the patterns that these otherwise distinctive migration waves have followed through time. How peoples of every standing have left supplying populations, been transported by passenger or servant or convict trades operated under a variety of national flags, and been absorbed into new home societies have, it can be shown, each—over and over again—taken the same few trends based on the familiar G formula.

THE G-RELATED SHAPES OF MODERN TRANSOCEANIC FLOWS

Records for the millions of persons who left Europe for an array of "New World" destinations between 1815 and 1939 and from 1945 onward toward the present vary considerably by country of origin and by the jurisdiction within which these people chose to make their new home. The same applies to movements *within* the Americas or from colonies or erstwhile colonies in Africa, the Americas, and Asia back to "mother" countries in Europe. In grouping national sources, even moving from one era to another within the migration history of a single country, different types of evidence often must be mixed—most notably, all travelers with immigrants or emigrants and those who remained in new locations with those who at some later time returned. The standard sources are replete with qualifying notes.[1] Thus, any patterning has to be rather approximate and must be understood to be such. Still, it seems possible to demonstrate how a certain standard pattern kept recurring among these famous intercontinental transfers of people and to identify the conditions under which a few exceptional shapes of trend seem to have occurred.

Figures 1.1 through 1.6 illustrate patterns for average annual emigration from European countries. Graphed are total emigration, those who came to the United States, and others. Tables 1.1 and 1.2 put together results for all modern trans-oceanic migrations that have been analyzed (based upon graphings and curve fittings whether or not the given case appears in a figure). These concern total emigration from particular European countries or groups of them, flows into the United States from various specific or aggregated sources, and certain other recorded migrations—including ones back into Europe from abroad and some other New World national intakes regardless of origin—into Australasia and southern Africa as well as North and South America.

The best-known intercontinental movement of the 19th century is the Irish diaspora. Super-charged by disaster to the potato crop in 1845 and 1846, this thrust saw millions leave home to seek tolerable conditions of life. As a starting point for international analysis, estimates for migration per year from Ireland to the United States constitute the middle plot of Figure 1.1. From 1842 through 1927 the solid squares reflect quinquennial annual averages from the U.S. Bureau of the Census (1975), *Historical Statistics* (1: 105–6, Series C 92), omitting the unusual years of World War I. From 1786 through 1815 they represent yearly averages from the decadal computations of Hans-Jürgen Grabbe for Irish coming to the United States, including those arriving via Canada (1989, 194, Column B). From the 1827–1833 period Charlotte Erickson provides an estimate for 1830 (1981, 179). Added to her average yearly numbers from Irish ports are, as per her advice, 20 percent of American immigrants who had left from English and Welsh points of departure (ibid., 181). My U.S. estimate for 1830 further includes two-thirds of those who typically went to Canada in this period by her reckoning. It is well established that the large majority of Irish who landed in the Maritime Provinces soon moved on south to New England, while perhaps half who came via Quebec and Montreal also ended up across the border (Handlin 1972, 50).

The long G' model curve for the data represented by solid squares in this portion of the graph is fitted to Grabbe at 1815, my modification of Erickson at 1830, and the conventional data of *Historical Statistics* thereafter. The high symbols at 1847 and 1852 (for 1845–1849 and 1850–1854), of course, reflect the notorious emergency emigration of the potato famine years. The hollow, downward triangles from 1816 through 1843 that generally run alongside this plot are based upon the classic analysis of William Forbes Adams (1932, 413–26). In order to obtain estimates for all Irish coming to the United States, I have added 0.8 of those arriving in the Maritime Provinces and 0.5 of those who disembarked at Quebec or Montreal to the numbers that Adams gave for direct travelers to the United States.[2] Experts on this migration can adjust the assumed

Figure 1.1
Emigration from Ireland

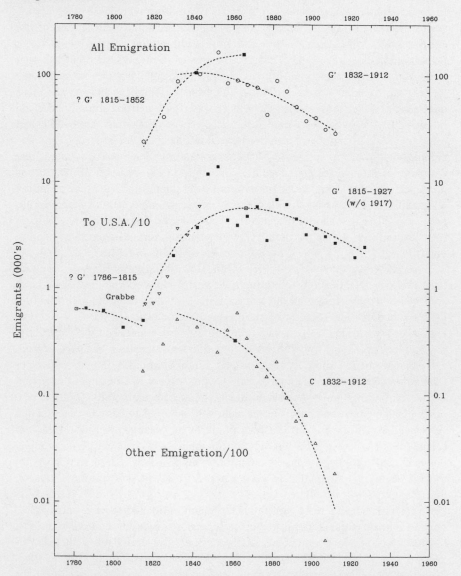

Sources: *Historical Statistics* 1: 105–6, Series C 92; Mitchell 1992, 125–38; Grabbe 1989, 194, Erickson 1981, 179, 181; Adams 1932, 413–26, Vamplew 1987, 4: Handlin 1959, 42, 50

proportions and see if their results differ enough from what Figure 1.1 proposes to conclude that the shape offered, with peak at 1866, fails to capture well the long-term movement of the data. Among other insights, this fitted curve suggests that the famine temporarily exaggerated a rise in Irish emigration to the United States that had been building since the peace of 1815. It did not *initiate* the large wave observed or break its pattern in any lasting way.

The rightward-skewed, humpbacked form of this surge between the 1810s and the 1920s makes the quantity of migration climb then fall away in G' form. G' is the first derivative of G. Thus, this pattern of migration represents the *rate* of growth for a population that increases in G fashion. This is what the derivative means: the speed of change in some function (velocity, as the calculus was developed for physics). Migration, in other words, by surging up then tapering off in G' form moves in a way that would promote or feed growth of G shape in population size but then becomes increasingly less important as demographic expansion in G form levels out. This is not to say that natural increase, the excess of births over deaths, does not contribute to the shape of growth that is going on. The point that we begin to demonstrate here, rather, is that migration repeatedly, in the overwhelming majority of cases encountered in an international and historical survey of considerable scope, by taking a G' path behaves in a fashion that would promote or reflect decelerating, G-shaped population growth.

In such a G' pattern, as Figure 1.1 accentuates, the pace of Irish immigration to America soared from 1815 through the early 1840s, climbing steeply from well *before* the potato famine to a level typical of the second half of the 19th century once the crisis years were past. The abortive Irish politics of the 1790s, British economic depressions that followed Waterloo and recurred even more painfully in the 1830s, troubles of the pivotal linen industry in Northern Ireland, and changes in the practices of absentee English landlords together had put emigration onto the general course that it would follow for over a century well before the potato famine, terrible as it was, burst onto the scene. A better grasp of the underlying trend raises some questions about how the causes and the consequences of this famous diaspora ought to be assessed. Earlier on, the estimates of Grabbe for 1786 through 1815 suggest a prior G' surge that topped out in the early 1780s, capping another, previous wave of Irish migration during the 18th century to a smaller receiving population, which is examined later in this chapter.

The top plot in Figure 1.1, meanwhile, depicts estimated average annual *total* emigration from Ireland, not just people coming to the United States. From 1852 through 1912 the data come from Mitchell (1992, 127–30). Prior to that (1815–1842) I have combined what seem to be reasonable possibilities for departures to the United States, Canada, Australia, and Britain.[3] In this top series of Figure 1.1, too, there stands out a sharp thrust of Irish out of the homeland that was well under way before the famine. This starts—from 1815 through 1852—to follow a G' pattern very parallel to that for Irish coming to America (with t_0's at 1865 and 1866, respectively). The bottom plot of the figure indicates how the numbers of Irish headed to destinations other than the United States (Canada, Australia, and Britain) shot upward in parallel fashion from 1815 through 1832. What happened, then, however, was that removals to these other sources simply dried up from 1832 through 1912 (Mitchell's total emigration less entrants to the United States), along a C curve. This proportionally accelerating form of contraction (G reversed in time) has been associated historically with populations that have lost their niche (Harris 2001). Faster and faster they go out of business. This is what apparently happened to Irish emigration to Britain, Australia, and Canada beginning in the 1830s, before the famine, and pushing right through those horrible years almost without imprint of that crisis upon the trend.

The famine emigrants instead went in droves to the United States. Perhaps this is not so surprising. In Britain, conflict between Irish and native workers grew more and more bitter with the collapse of early trade union efforts and the severe depression of the 1830s. Travel to Australia, though often conducted courtesy of the British government, involved convict status or invoked the imagery of resettling in a prison society under British domination.[4] Canada wanted small farmers to occupy the land; but she did not have the demand for laborers, construction workers, and jacks-of-many-trades to be found in the larger nation that lay to the south across a long and weakly regulated border.[5] The result of the C-shape collapse in the emigration of Irish everywhere else except the United States, beginning already in the 1830s and 1840s, was an earlier and more steeply descending G' trend for total Irish emigration from 1832 through 1912 than the comparable path for just arrivals in the United States (with base year for the curve at 1841 rather than 1866).

The middle plot of Figure 1.2, which concerns migration to the United States from England, Wales, and Scotland for the century 1822–1922 (actually 1820–1924, taken by annual averages for successive quinquennia but omitting 1915–1919), shows that another large international flow of people across the Atlantic clearly took G' shape. This wave peaked later than the U.S. immigration of the Irish. The crest of the fitted curve comes at 1883 rather than 1866 (part A of Table 1.1).

So many people participated in this flow to the United States that the top plot in the figure, which graphs *all* emigration from Great Britain according to Mitchell, could from 1822 through 1897 be represented by a G' curve with t_0 only slightly earlier, at 1876.[6] Such a G' hump or wave, however, is not the only type of trend that underlies the data for English, Welsh, and Scottish emigration. Though there is considerable variability from quinquennium to quinquennium, it seems likely that from 1822 through the remainder of the 19th century outmigration to all places *other* than the United States followed a G path instead, as the bottom plot of the figure indicates.[7] It should be realized that this represents a *composite* flow, not one just between two populations—as in the middle plot for the United States alone—but from Britain to Canada, the West Indies, India, Australia, New Zealand, Southern Africa, and other less frequent

Figure 1.2
Emigration from England, Wales, and Scotland

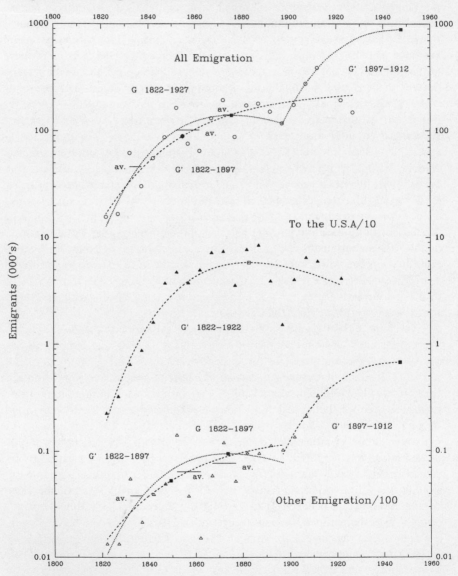

All Emigration

G 1822–1927

G' 1897–1912

av.

av.

av.

G' 1822–1897

To the U.S.A/10

G' 1822–1922

G 1822–1897

G' 1897–1912

G' 1822–1897

av.

av.

av.

Other Emigration/100

Emigrants (000's)

Sources: Mitchell 1992, 125–38; *Historical Statistics*, 1: 105–6, Series C-91.

destinations. Then, a new burst of British emigration to non-U.S. locations that appeared early in the 20th century may, as plotted, have reverted to take the more usual G' form.

When combined with the British flow to the United States, these movements elsewhere tend to make total British emigration from the 1820s perhaps all the way into the 1920s take a G path rather than one of G' (the top plot of Figure 1.2). While this overall emigration from England, Wales, and Scotland contains some shadow of the G' curve for the substantial flow to the United States, it could be said that from the 1820s through the 1920s the total number of people leaving Britain, while fluctuating considerably, rose along a G path with its base year at 1855. Working from the population sizes and birth and death rates of Wrigley and Schofield (1981), their critics, and the censuses, it is estimated (in Volume III of this study) that net emigration from *England*, as a proportion of the current population, climbed from the early 1800s through 1926 along a G curve. The readily identifiable shifts up and down across these underlying trends of G or G' shape, meanwhile, have long been noted and discussed. They have formed one important aspect of the Kuznetsian "long swings" observed in the U.S. and international economies.[8] In the end, it seems from evidence concerning Ireland, on the one hand, and England, Scotland, and Wales, on the other, that we can fruitfully and safely approach other migrations with the hypothesis that simple movements from one population to another single destination tend to take the G' form, while transfers involving more than one source or destination tend to compound into G trends instead.

Emigration from Germany (graphed and fitted from Mitchell but not presented in a figure) rose from 1822 through 1892 along a G' trend quite similar to that possible for Britain across this period, as part A of Table 1.1 indicates. From the middle 1890s to World War I, however, while continuing that same bend, the numbers—though parallel—are markedly lower than before. Judging from a similar drop-off in Germans arriving specifically in the United States during these years, there took place a real downward shift in the numbers, not just some change in who was being counted. Did the rising nationalism that soon featured so significantly in the coming of World War I hold more people at home? Did the social supports initiated by Bismarck now relieve more potential movers of pressures to emigrate? Perhaps most importantly in this modern context, Klaus J. Bade shows how a sharp rise in German real wages between 1891 and 1900 accompanied the drop-off in emigration (1992, 134). The German G' for those coming to America between 1822 and 1892 was, nonetheless, almost exactly parallel with the comparable flow from England, Wales, and Scotland between 1822 and 1922 (the middle column of part A of Table 1.1).

Though the numbers are much smaller, for Switzerland 1867–1927 and for France from the 1850s through to World War I, G' curves with base years in the 1880s also underlie the movements of recorded emigration.[9] For Denmark and Norway fitted G' humps peak just a little later, at 1893 and 1897. Briefly, as Table 1.1 also indicates, Belgium and Austria experienced emigration curves

Table 1.1
Approximate Overseas Emigration from European Countries, 1822–1927

A. By Country

Country:	Total			To the U.S.A.			Elsewhere		
Ireland	1812-1852	G'	1865	1815-1927	G'	1866	1832-1912	C	1861 C
"	1832-1912	G'	1841						
Britain I	1822-1897	?G'	1876	1822-1922	G'	1883	1822-1897	?G'	1874
"	1822-1927	?G	1855 G				1822-1897	G	1849 G
Germany	1822-1892	G'	1886	1822-1892	G'	1883			
"	1897-1912	G'	1886						
Switzerland	1868-1927	G'	1889						
France	1855-1915	G'	1888ᵂ						
"	1857-1892	G'	1898						
Norway	1847-1927	G'	1893						
Denmark	1867-1927	G'	1897						
Belgium I	1847-1867	G'	1883						
Austria I	1842-1877	G'	1891						
Belgium II	1872-1902	G'	1909						
Netherlands	1847-1902	G'	1908						
"	1847-1986	?G	1896 G						
Sweden	1852-1892	G'	1915						
Portugal	1867-1927	G'	1916						
Italy I	1877-1897	G'	1920				1877-1902	G'	1918
Britain II	1892-1912	G'	1947				1897-1912	G'	1947
Belgium III	1902-1912	G'	1937						
Spain	1865-1922	G'	1938ᴼ						
Austria II	1877-1912	G'	1936						
Hungary	1872-1912	G'	1947						
Italy II	1897-1912	G'	1940	1867-1912	G'	1939	1902-1912	G'	1949
Russia	1877-1912	G'	1938	1867-1912	G'	1944			

B. Waves in Groups of Countries

Countries:	Total			To the U.S.A.			Elsewhere		
I:									
Ireland	1832-1912	G'	1841	1815-1927	G'	1866	1832-1912	C	1861 C
II:									
Brit. & Germ.	1827-1902	G'	1877	1822-1927	G'	1883			
Switz. & Fra.	1867-1922	G'	1884						
Nor. & Den.	1867-1927	G'	1890						
....									
Six Countries	1822-1927?	G'	1882						
III:									
Swed., Bel.,									
Neth., Port.	1857-1927	G'	1906						

Table 1.1 (continued)

Countries:	Total	To the U.S.A.	Elsewhere
IV:			
A-H, Russia			
Spain, Italy	1877-1897 G' 1924		
	1897-1912 G' 1943		
ALL Europe	1867-1897 G' 1892		
	1897-1912 G' 1939		

C. Waves in U.S. Record Groupings of Countries

Countries:	Total	To the U.S.A.	Elsewhere
Ireland		1815-1927 G' 1866	
Brit., Germ., Other NW Eur.		1827-1927 G' 1883	
Scandinavia		1827-1912 G' 1905	
S & E Europe		1877-1912 G' 1931	
Southern Europe w/o Italy		1852-1882 G' 1890	1852-1892 G' 1907
		1887-1912 G' 1952	1897-1927 G' 1946

^{W} = from Woodruff; $^\circ$ = omitting 1897 and 1902; G = takes G trend; C = takes C trend.

Sources: Mitchell 1992, 124–38; *Historical Statistics*, 1: 105–7; Woodruff 1966, 106–7; Figure 1.1
(for Ireland).

of G' shape in comparable timing; but by the 1870s they both shifted into new, stronger, and later surges.

The people of Sweden, as depicted in Figure 1.3, participated in a rather later G' wave of emigration. The t_0 for the fitted curve of 1852–1892 comes at 1915. As in Germany, though, the number leaving the country according to Mitchell dropped for the quinquennia of 1900–1904 through 1910–1914, as the figure indicates. The decadal calculations of Woodruff, on the other hand—presented as the second plot in Figure 1.3—suggest that this G' pattern instead persisted up to 1910 without breaking. Who is correct, and why? The arrival of Scandinavian immigrants in the United States (including Norwegians and Danes with Swedes), which is plotted at the bottom of Figure 1.3 from *Historical Statistics*, supports the longer G' trending of Woodruff's data. Out-migration from Portugal between 1867 and 1927 took a G' path of comparable timing, as Table 1.1 shows. A second 1872–1902 surge from Belgium and a first recorded wave from Italy between 1877 and 1897 did so as well.

For the Netherlands, a G' for 1847–1902 with base year at 1908 is also a possibility; but the simplest modeling there is probably a single G trajectory all

Figure 1.3
Some Emigration from Scandinavia

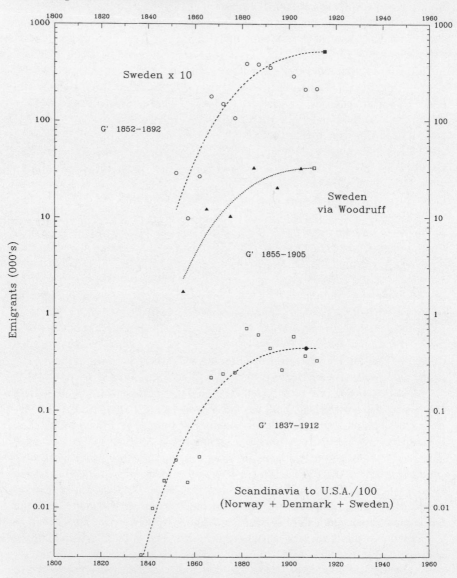

Sources: Mitchell 1992, 128–38; Woodruff 1966, 106; *Historical Statistics*, 1: 105–6, Series C-93.

the way from 1847 to 1986. Although its curvature is timed from a t_0 four decades later, 1896 rather than 1855, this is the same exceptional trend form followed by total emigration from Britain between 1822 and 1927. What distinguishes both of these countries for most of the period in question is having populous overseas possessions or former colonies. The traffic out to and back from these diverse and substantial territories, which tends to aggregate several narrower flows that did not have the same timing, seems to have taken different shape from that of most transoceanic migrations.

For the early years of the 20th century, however, emigration from Britain—in particular to destinations other than the United States—took G' shape with t_0 at 1947 (Figure 1.2). This timing of surge characterized relocations from several other European countries, too (part A of Table 1.1). Such patterning is seen in Spain between 1865 and 1922 (disregarding the very low quinquennia of 1897 and 1902, during which colonies were lost through war), Hungary 1872–1912, and Russia 1877 and 1912 and is accompanied by second waves of G' emigration for Austria 1877–1912 and Italy 1897–1912—and a third spurt for Belgium 1902–1912. Figure 1.4 employs Italy to illustrate how the great 1867–1912 surge to the United States was part of a shift in the total national pattern of leaving for 1897–1912 from a preceding 1877–1897 G' that had been driven by migration to other new homes. Figure 1.5 presents the simpler case of Russia. "Other Central Europe" in U.S. immigration totals designates primarily arrivals from what was at the time the Austro-Hungarian Empire.

The comparable timings of G' curves for so many of these national patterns suggest how certain *clusters* of countries participated in successive waves of emigration out of Europe. Part B of Table 1.1 outlines these aggregates and their collective migrations. The categories are not the same as the geographical groupings that are conventional in the literature. Ireland stands alone as a first wave, with her total emigration declining from the 1830s along a G' path with its t_0 as early as 1841 (vs. 1866 for movement to the United States alone). Britain and Germany, Switzerland and France, Norway and Denmark all compose paired out-flows whose composite G' curves crest on average four decades later, astride the early 1880s.[10] As shown in Figure 1.6, all six countries together (Group II) produced an aggregate out-migration whose G' topped at 1882—certainly for the data of 1822–1907, perhaps onward to 1927, though the 1897–1912 G' surge for England, Wales, and Scotland leaves a mark upon the compounded evidence. Collectively, then, Sweden, Portugal, Belgium, and the Netherlands produced a third wave of emigration from Europe. For all 1857–1927 evidence this Group III category of transoceanic movements followed a G' pattern with its peak at 1906.

Across the last quarter of the 1800s aggregate out-migration from Austria-Hungary, Italy, Spain, and Russia took a G' path with t_0 at 1924. The first wave of departures from Italy did most to determine this first pattern for that bloc of Group IV countries, as part A of Table 1.1 and Figure 1.4 indicate. From the

Figure 1.4
Emigration from Italy to the United States and Elsewhere

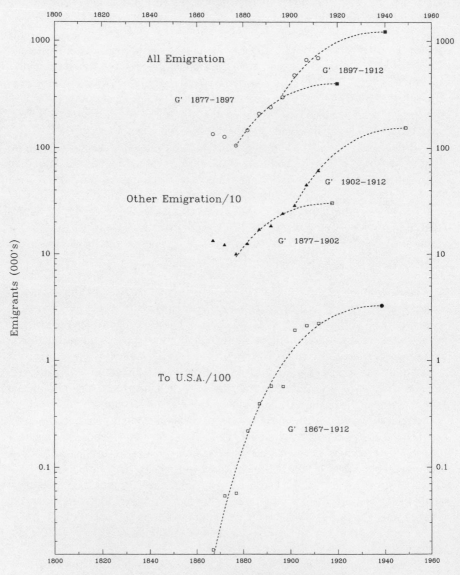

Sources: Mitchell 1992, 127–38; *Historical Statistics* 1: 105–6, Series C-100.

Figure 1.5
Emigration from Other Central Europe and Russia

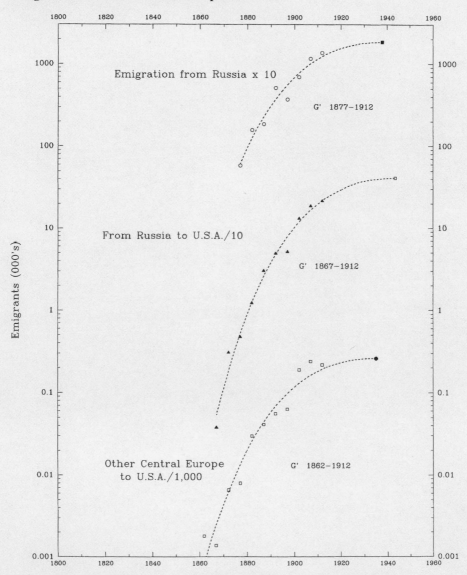

Sources: Mitchell 1992, 125–38; *Historical Statistics* 1: 105–6, Series C-98 and C-99.

Figure 1.6
Successive Waves of Modern European Emigration

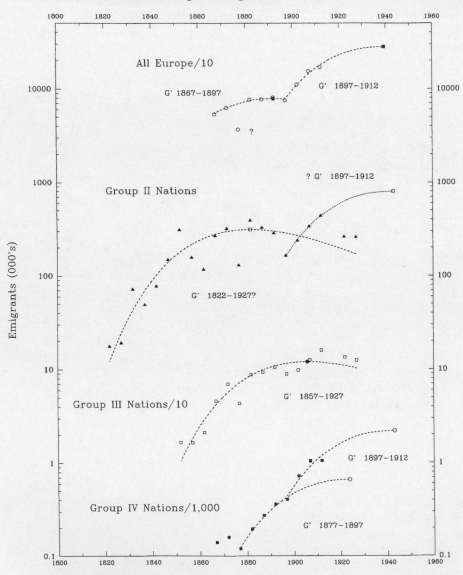

Source: Mitchell 1992, 125–38.

1890s to World War I, however, later spurts from Italy and Austria joined the trajectories of Spain, Hungary, and Russia to compose Group IV's second G' trend with t_0 at 1943.

One thing to note about these international waves is their spacing. The aggregate G' curves for Groups II and III and the two successive surges of Group IV peaked 24, 18, and 19 years apart. The lag between emigration from Ireland (I) and the Group II surge is about twice as long: 41 years. Just over every 20 years, in other words, except for a crest in the early 1860s—though Irish migration to *America* did follow such timing—from one part of the continent after another, starting with Ireland and moving eastward and southward, wave after wave of Europeans were sucked up to be deposited overseas. The great migration pump powered by comparative transoceanic conditions regularly reached out further and further across Europe for a new frontier of supply. Each of these successive waves crested in G' fashion.

Another important point is that the collective surges of the Group II aggregation (especially from Britain and Germany) and Group IV were quantitatively stronger than that of Group III (from Sweden, Portugal, and the Low Countries).[11] Thus, looking at approximate *total* emigration from Europe, at the top of Figure 1.6, only two G' surges appear: first for 1867–1897, with peak at 1892,[12] then for 1897–1912 with t_0 at 1939.

Viewing the great transoceanic movements of the 19th and early 20th centuries from the perspective of countries that *received* people, similar shapes of trend not surprisingly emerge, as part C of Table 1.1 and Table 1.2 summarize. Unfortunately, the usual groupings of immigrants by source, as for the United States in *Historical Statistics*, have obscured the actual timing of some flows and ebbs. The ups and downs of arrivals to America from Britain and Germany, as part C of Table 1.1 summarizes, were similar enough from 1822 all the way through to 1927 (without the years of World War I) to follow jointly a clear G' pattern with peak at 1883. The Netherlands and Belgium, however, sent sufficient people abroad over the same century-long period to override the earlier G' patterns for France and Switzerland within "Other Northwestern Europe," a category that has conventionally been forced upon the American evidence by the prejudices of those seeking to restrict entry to the United States to "old" sources, keeping out less desirable immigrants from "new" areas of southern and eastern Europe. Instead, numbers for Belgium, the Netherlands, France, and Switzerland together for the period 1822–1927 probably fluctuate around something like a G trajectory that has its base year for the formula in the early 1850s. This trend for in-flow to the United States from those other countries of northwestern Europe closely resembles the G path that is likely for total emigration from England, Wales, and Scotland (given in part A of Table 1.1 and plotted in Figure 1.1). The whole aggregated immigration to the United States from this more acceptable zone of Europe, however—including Britain and Germany—followed closely a G' curve with a peak at 1883.

Table 1.2
Comparing Patterns in Other Modern Migrations

A. Intercontinental Flows to the U.S.A.

Total	From Europe	From Elsewhere	From the Americas
1822-1897 G' 1884	1827-1897 G' 1886	1822-1867 G' 1866	
1892-1912 G' 1947	1847-1912 H 1848	1867-1882 G' 1911	
1847-1912 H 1850		1892-1912 G' 1962	1892-1927 G' 1965
1935-1975 G' 1988			1937-1967 G' 1996
1975-1994 G' 2014			1975-1994 G' 2017

B. Overseas Immigration into Certain European Countries

Britain	Belgium	Netherlands	Sweden
1857-1912 H 1902	1842-1912 H 1893	1867-1932 H 1903	1872-1907 G' 1918
1857-1912 G' 1904			
1902-1912 ?G' 1943	1937-1967 G' 1982		1927-1977 G' 1977

C. Immigration to Other "New World" Destinations

Brazil	Argentina	Canada	Mexico
1842-1962 G' 1912	1857-1952 G' 1919	1862-1932 G' 1911	1917-1932 G' 1976
		1952-1986 G' 1964	1947-1982 G' 2009

Australia	New Zealand	Zimbabwe	South Africa
1847-1922 G 1853	1859-1917 G 1863	1917-1982 G' 1966	1927-1982 G' 1977
1932-1972 G' 1992	1932-1986 G' 1989		

U.S.A.	Canada, Brazil, Arg.	U.S.A., Can., Brazil, Arg.
1847-1912 H 1850	1862-1972 G' 1916	1857-1962 G' 1907
1822-1897 G' 1884		

Sources: *Historical Statistics* 1: 105–7; Mitchell 1992, 124–38; 1993, 90–97; 1995, 85–86; Woodruff 1966, 106–11.

"Scandinavia" in the U.S. classification is dominated by the greater numbers for Sweden relative to Denmark and Norway. Hence, the curve-fitting for the C section of Table 1.1 produces an intermediate G' with t_0 at 1905, more like what was found for Swedish emigration as a whole (1915) in part A of the table (and Figure 1.3) than for Norway and Denmark (1890). Migrants from Spain and Portugal compose the bulk of the U.S. category "Other Southern Europe" up to World War I, while the large majority of those originating in "Other Central Europe" (Figure 1.5) came from one part or another of what was once Austria-Hungary.

For all their shortcomings, these rough matches of territory make it possible to estimate the form taken by European overseas emigrations to destinations other than the United States in addition to the ones that part A of Table 1.1 covers. In the case of Austria-Hungary or "Other Central Europe," so much of the flow came to America that the residue is not worth modeling. From Portugal and Spain or "Other Southern Europe" pairs of G' curves for both U.S. and non-U.S. transoceanic migration for the most part closely resemble each other, distinguished only by a little lag in timing for the non-U.S. flow before the 1890s. For "Other Northwestern Europe" (Belgium, the Netherlands, France, and Switzerland), however, immigration to the United States up through 1927 took an appreciably earlier-based and flatter G path (t_0 at 1843) than migrants going elsewhere overseas (t_0 at 1885). This latter surge, dominated by the Netherlands and Belgium, which held colonies that were large relative to the size of the homelands, was substantial enough to determine the shape of all out-migration for these four countries in aggregate.

Figure 1.7 and part A of Table 1.2 summarize recorded immigration *into* the United States from the 1820s to World War I. The total might be said to have moved upward in two successive G' surges of 1822–1897 and 1897–1912 with zero years at 1884 and 1947, respectively. These reflect the large clusterings of migrations from particular European countries in Group II and IV timing already noted in discussing Figure 1.6. On the other hand, as Figure 1.7 shows, movement from the late 1840s up to World War I tended to swing back and forth in historically familiar variations around an H trend with t_0 at 1850. What this alternative conceptualization does is to indicate that total immigration to the United States across this substantial period in effect rose parallel with the growth of the American *population*, which increased from the 1850s through the 1930s along an H curve with base year at 1853 (Harris 2001, 17). On the whole, this swelling continental population added immigrants in constant proportion to its current size, though the familiar Kuznets cycles of the nation's development elevated or depressed the numbers in approximate 20- to 25-year swings around the underlying trend.

Most immigrants came from Europe. The alternative trendings for these are much the same, as the middle plot of Figure 1.7 shows. More distinct was the patterning for immigrants from other sources. After the exclusion of Asians in the later 19th century, most of these people came from elsewhere in the Western

Figure 1.7
Approximate Modern Immigration to the United States

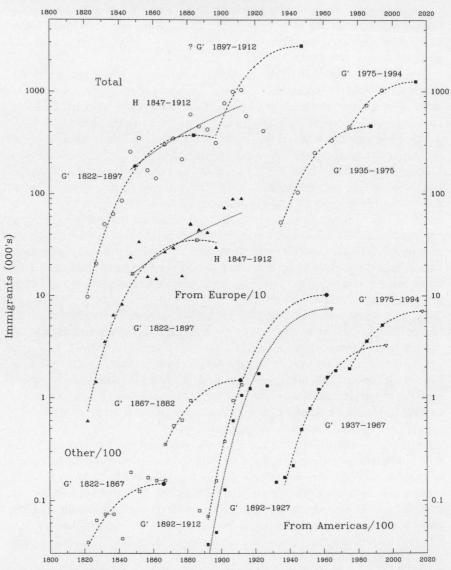

Sources: *Historical Statistics*, 1: 105–6, Series C-89 and C-90; *Statistical Abstracts* (U.S. Bureau of the Census, 1998), 11.

Hemisphere. Waves of such non-European entrants to the United States crested three times: (1) at about 1866, along with the Irish flow to America, though not with *total* emigration from the Emerald Isle; (2) at 1911, supplementing the relatively small surge from Sweden, Portugal, and the Low Countries (Group III) at this time; and (3) at 1962, some two decades after the potential second and bigger crests of the Group IV national waves from southern and eastern Europe, which were cut off legally by the politics of prejudice in the 1920s. The legally registered non-European G' surge from the 1890s forward was almost all from the Americas, as the bottom portion of Figure 1.7 indicates. A new, second upward trend of that shape from neighbors of the Western Hemisphere began out of the Depression, while a current third surge of likely G' shape from sources in the Americas took off in the 1970s. Students of recent U.S. immigration ought to find further analyses in these G-based terms to be useful. Do estimates of illegal immigration, for example, conform to the same G' patterns, or do they alter the trends proposed here?

Some countries in Europe are known to have *received* substantial numbers of people as well as sent them out. Once again, the data are frustratingly fuzzy. Many recorded entrants were returning from sojourns or tours of duty in overseas possessions; others came to Europe to stay—or to try their best to stay. The imprecise evidence, however, at least gives some sense of traffic patterns back and forth; and, historically, frequency of travel has not been irrelevant for ease of migration. Figure 1.8 shows how an 1857–1902 G' surge into Britain is timed (with peak at 1904) about a typical Kuznetsian wave span later than emigration outward from England, Wales, and Scotland (Figure 1.1; part A of Table 1.1). What may have been another G' movement just before World War I, in contrast, was synchronous with the current G' push of outward movement. Yet entry to Britain all the way from the 1850s to the 1910s, as the figure depicts by a light trend line, could also be captured by an H trend with its t_0 at 1902. Unlike the parallelism just observed in the United States as a receiving country, this represents a much steeper path than the H tracks that growth in the populations of England/Wales and Scotland was taking across that era (with t_0's at 1794 and 1779, respectively) (Harris 2001, 148, 151).

What *did* resemble closely this H trend for entry into Britain were arrivals in Belgium between 1842 and 1912 and the Netherlands between 1867 and 1932 (Figure 1.8 and part B of Table 1.2). In effect, across the latter half of the 19th century and the early 20th century several countries with colonies and/or dominions, not just one nation, received people in chronologically parallel H fashion. It would be of interest to see if the same kind of trend has characterized entry into many diverse European countries since World War II (e.g., adding Italy, France, Portugal, and Spain to the list) from peripheral areas once under their control—mostly in Asia and Africa but also the West Indies and Oceania. What may be at work, in other words, is a very general way in which shifts in development, from country to country or within nations, move people to where economic growth and jobs are expanding in their once-colonial spheres of in-

Figure 1.8
Modern Immigration into Certain European Countries

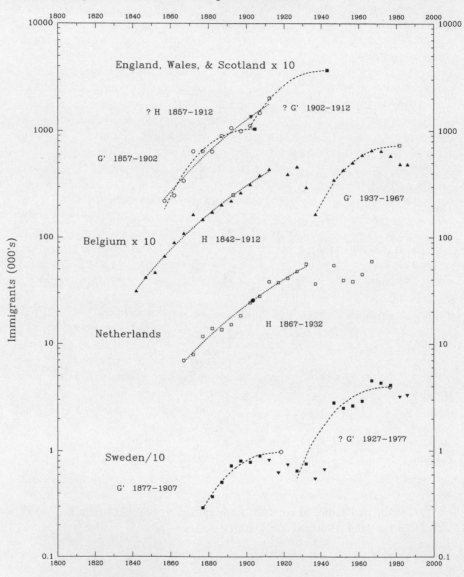

England, Wales, & Scotland x 10

? H 1857–1912   ? G' 1902–1912

G' 1857–1902

Belgium x 10   H 1842–1912

G' 1937–1967

Netherlands   H 1867–1932

Immigrants (000's)

? G' 1927–1977

Sweden/10

G' 1877–1907

Source: Mitchell 1992, 125–38.

fluence and connection. Evidence for Sweden, however, demonstrates that migration into *every* European society did not take this form. Here, two G' surges seem most likely, separated by a decline, perhaps of D shape, from the early 1900s to World War II. Sweden did not have colonies and so has not possessed the same kinds of networks for migration with the less developed parts of the world, either in or out. This difference would seem to strengthen the developmental hypothesis proposed to account for the H patterns observed.

Other "New World" societies besides the United States have, of course, also received substantial modern immigration. Part C of Table 1.2 summarizes trends that seem to fit some of the major movements. In Brazil and Argentina, as illustrated by Figure 1.9, G' waves with base years in the 1910s capture the data from the middle 19th century even past World War II. Canada (not pictured) probably also saw entrants rise between 1862 and 1932 via a G' pattern with t_0 at 1911. Movement into these three other major receiving countries of Western Hemisphere immigration, in other words, provides an important New World complement to parallel and bolster the smallest and weakest Group III surge of European entry to the United States (Figure 1.6).

After World War II, however, a new G' curve appears between 1952 and 1986 in Canada. This extra surge offset noticeable drops that occurred in South American immigration as the socio-political climate of Brazil and Argentina soured in the 1960s. The extra Canadian intake made in-migration for all three countries together (top of Figure 1.9) flow and ebb until the 1970s quite tightly around a G' curve with its crest at 1916. To add the United States (part C of Table 1.2) makes entry for the four biggest importers of population to the Western Hemisphere, omitting the years of World Wars I and II and the Depression, collectively rise then fall from 1857 through 1962 closely via a G' with t_0 at 1907 (because the flow into the United States pushed upward rather earlier than the other three). In all, migration to the Americas since the 1850s—with one country progressively taking up weight from others (recently including Mexico with a G' surge of in-migration 1947–1982 that has been heading for a top at 2009)—has balanced out into what looks like one G' trend with familiar Kuznetsian developmental swings shifting across it. Nowhere outside the United States, though, has immigration possibly increased along a trend parallel to the growth of the receiving population, in either H or G form. Did the nature of U.S. economic development shape immigration there this way? Or did the relationship work the other way around?

In the southern Pacific, in contrast, immigration to both Australia and New Zealand in the later 19th and early 20th centuries shows a tendency to have expanded in G rather than G' fashion (Figure 1.10). The t_0 for the 1857–1917 G trend in New Zealand falls at 1863; the one that is possible for the more wavering Australian data of 1847–1927 comes at 1853. For the two countries together, a G curve with its base year at 1842 is indicated for 1852–1927. Both national curves are flatter than the G trends for the growth of the receiving populations during this era (Harris 2001, 82). Immigration and population

Figure 1.9
Modern Immigration to Other Leading New World Destinations

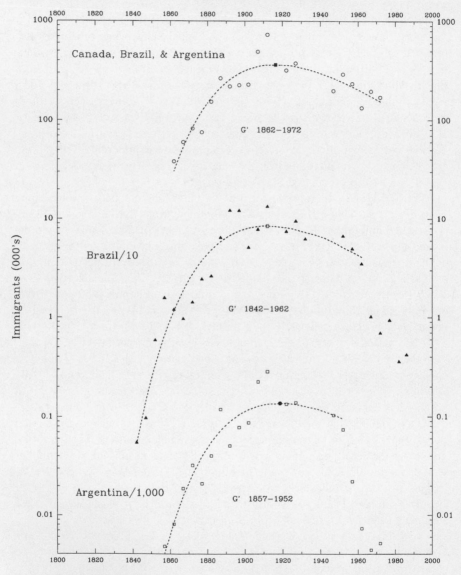

Source: Mitchell 1993, 90–97.

Figure 1.10
Immigration to Australia and New Zealand

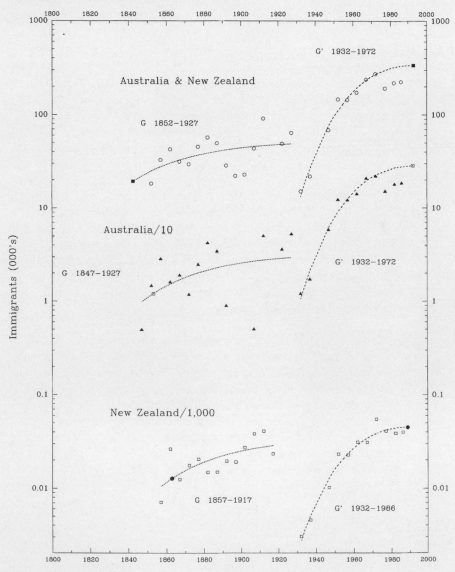

Source: Mitchell 1995, 86.

growth once again are not parallel, contrary to what has been found for the United States across the same period. Rather, these antipodean trends (though fed by migrants from more than one country of origin) mimic the G curve seen likely to underlie all emigration from England, Scotland, and Wales in Figure 1.2 and part A of Table 1.1. They even more tightly resemble the pattern for all British emigration going to destinations outside the United States, of which Australia and New Zealand were major components, though clearly not the whole tide.

The parallelism of particular intakes to Australia and New Zealand with the home-country out-flow suggests that British dynamics shaped that shared pattern. In contrast, the parallelism of all European migration to the United States with the growth of that receiving population suggests mechanisms dominated by the receiving country instead. Those hypotheses appear to merit careful exploration. For Canada, meanwhile, population size from 1824 through 1901 took G form with base year at 1851 (Harris 2001, 65–66). This trend paralleled the out-flow of *all* migrants from Britain over the same period, much the way that the demographic growth of the United States accompanied a possible H for all European migration there, except that the relevant Canadian source was British rather than European. The two likely G' curves that are probably preferable for representing widely fluctuating Canadian immigration from the 1860s through the 1980s, furthermore, follow each other in a way not incompatible with an alternative G trending between 1862 and 1972. Elsewhere in the Southern Hemisphere, European migrations into South Africa and Zimbabwe (formerly Southern Rhodesia) up until the early 1980s seem to have swelled in G' form, the first cresting a little later than the other.

In sum, flows of national transoceanic emigration and immigration across the past two centuries that are commonly documented and much discussed in the literature of the social sciences overwhelmingly took the form of G', the lopsided, wave-like derivative of the G function. The few exceptions that followed H or G paths appeared where special developmental relationships existed between European home countries and colonies or dominions or in the aggregate shape of entry to or departure from geographical *groups* of populations whose individual migrations diverged considerably in timing. G' has been the shape of almost all one-to-one migration flows. G and H alternatives have usually involved a compounding of sources or destinations.

THE FORMS OF INTERNAL RELOCATION

Well-known migrations *within* countries have taken shapes similar to these famous transnational, often transcontinental movements. Data from the United States serve to demonstrate that point. Illustrations come from what is known about the demographic development of the Old Northwest, the numbers of persons in certain clusters of U.S. states who had changed districts of residence as of successive censuses, and the transfer of slaves westward between the Revolution and the Civil War.

Studies of the Old Northwest (Ohio, Indiana, Michigan, Illinois, and Wisconsin) throw light upon migration within the United States. They have the advantages of capturing what happened in the earliest years of settlement for a region, not just later decades, and of considering all in-migrants, not only the foreign-born. Figure 1.11 presents some of the major outlines from this research. First of all (top of the graph), the population of the region as a whole increased in familiar G form from 1800 to 1860 (with t_0 at 1858), though the individual states display some variation—in part because of boundary changes when they were still territories (Vedder and Gallaway 1975, 161). The estimated number of residents produced by natural increase followed a quite parallel G path of growth from 1805 through 1855 (with its t_0 at 1860). Meanwhile, net in-migration for this region bounded by the Ohio and Mississippi Rivers and the Great Lakes rose, then fell via a G' pattern with its peak at 1847, whether as calculated decadally 1805–1855 in the original 1975 study or via 20-year time segments as in the follow-up paper of a dozen years later (Vedder and Gallaway 1987, 306). These calculations are plotted by hollow squares and filled circles, respectively. Then from the late 1800s through the middle of the 1900s a new surge of G' shape probably appeared in regional in-migration, with its top in the early 1920s.[13] The number of foreign white male immigrants who resided in the five-state region, meanwhile, fluctuated from 1875 through 1915 in Kuznetsian 20+-year rhythm around a G' trend with t_0 at 1907 (Parker 1987, 262, note 14). This underlying pattern compares with the 1898 of the G' curve for 1850–1900 and 1911 for 1900–1970 in the geographically more extended North Central zone of which the Old Northwest formed the eastern part (fitted but not presented).

The interaction of these two movements, meanwhile, resulted in a declining *rate* of in-migration for the region relative to its current population. The pace fell off sharply, along a D path, between 1805 and 1855, according to both the 1975 and the 1987 analyses of Vedder and Gallaway (the bottom plots in Figure 1.11). The data of the latter study suggest, in addition, that a second decline of D form in the in-migration rate of the Old Northwest occurred from 1850 through 1950. Across the first half of the 19th century, perhaps again later over a second era, the rise of local natural increase made further in-migration less attractive and less important, an insight into the way that demographic structures change that is pursued in subsequent chapters.

Thus, several reported aspects of population increase in the Old Northwest take G-based forms. The G' curve captures surges in the numbers of in-migrants. The G pattern characterizes the demographic growth with which this in-flow was associated. The D shape is taken by the shrinking relative importance of further arrivals for the existing population. These are fundamental, insightful findings that will recur in other historical settings.

Figure 1.11
Migration to the Old Northwest, 1800–1950

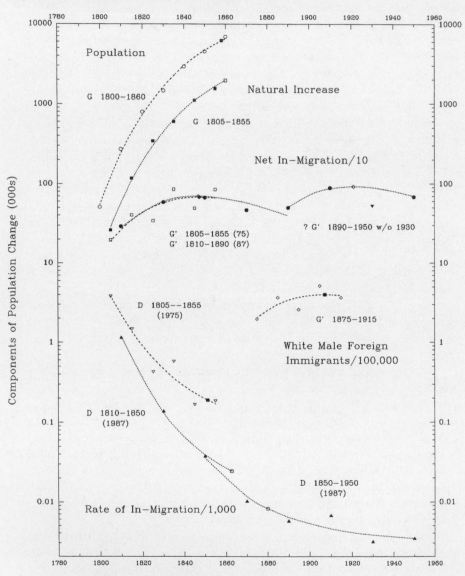

Sources: Vedder and Gallaway 1975, 161; 1987, 306; Parker 1987, 262.

It is possible to extend some of this kind of analysis to other regions of the United States, though more crudely. Instead of current in-migration, as for the Old Northwest, the limits of easily accessible data require working with the numbers of persons born in an area relative to the population residing there. Table 1.3 displays trends in the amount of such accumulative in-migration and out-migration for whites and for non-whites among districts of the country. Figures 1.12 through 1.14 illustrate some of the evidence visually (*Historical Statistics*, 1: 89–92, Series C 15–24).

Across the third quarter of the 19th century, outward surges of white population in G' form are evident from all five districts of the United States east of the Mississippi as settlement pushed westward (Table 1.3, part A). To derive these numbers, those both born and currently residing in a particular area are subtracted from all living white persons in the country who were recorded by the census in question to have commenced their lives in this region. For New England, the Middle Atlantic, and the South Atlantic (and therefore all territory east of the Appalachians) these G' curves topped out around 1870. For the East North Central district (the Old Northwest), the G' between 1850 and 1900 headed toward a t_0 at 1906. In the East South Central district (the states of Kentucky, Tennessee, Alabama, and Mississippi) out-migration of whites seems also to have expanded in G' form from 1850 to 1880 toward a crest at 1881 (with a dip in the years following "the War") before it increased in an accelerating E trend with t_0 at 1914 from there to World War I. This subsequent curve is virtually parallel to the rise in number of foreign-born persons residing in the South 1860–1920 (with t_0 at 1921).[14] Replacement of departing native whites by those born outside the country is indicated for a region that, whatever the reservations about foreigners, was even more reluctant to accept non-whites in many roles. White out-migration in E form was then also picked up by the three easternmost Atlantic districts from the 1870s on to 1960 (the aggregate trend is presented in the top plot of Figure 1.12). This movement was matched (with t_0 also at 1958) by a second, 1910–1960 E surge for the East South Central states, which once again paralleled increase in the number of foreign-born in the South. The absolute amount of relocation out of the Old Northwest (the East North Central district of the census), meanwhile, increased rapidly from the mid-1800s into the mid-1900s, but along three successive G' curves.

These three outward surges, with tops at 1906, 1925, and 1969, not surprisingly are echoed in white *in*-migration for the West North Central (1850–1940, 1899), Mountain (1870–1930, 1927), and Pacific (1870–1900, 1914; 1920–1940, 1954; 1940–1960, 1975) districts as shown in Figure 1.13 and part B of Table 1.3. Even nearer movement into Louisiana, Arkansas, Oklahoma, and Texas (the West South Central zone) displays G' curves with peaks at 1905 (1870–1890) and 1923 (1890–1940). Likewise, relocation of whites into the East North Central district between 1850 and 1890 with peak at 1868 reflects out-migration with similarly timed G' shape from all states east of the Appalachians (part A of the table). Mid-20th-century white in-migration into the Mountain, West

Table 1.3
Migration among Divisions of the United States

A. Numbers of Whites Who Had Moved Out of Various Geographical Divisions

New England	Middle Atlantic	South Atlantic	East of Appalachians
1850-1880 G' 1871	1850-1880 G' 1867	1850-1880 G' 1860	1850-1870 G' 1872
1900-1960 E 1952	1880-1960 E 1960	1890-1960 E 1953	1870-1960 E 1958

East North Central	East South Central
1850-1880 G' 1906	1850-1880 G' 1881
1900-1940 G' 1925	1860-1910 E 1914
1940-1970 G' 1969	1910-1960 E 1958

B. Numbers of Whites Who Had Moved Into Certain Divisions

Pacific	Mountain	West North Central	West South Central
		1850-1940 G' 1899	1870-1890 G' 1905
1870-1900 G' 1914	1870-1930 G' 1927		1890-1940 G' 1923
1920-1940 G' 1954			
1940-1960 G' 1975	1930-1960 E 1954	1940-1960 ?E 1997	1940-1970 ?E 1961

East North Central	East South Central
1850-1890 G' 1868	1850-1870 G' 1847
1890-1910 G' 1905	
1910-1940 G' 1942	1880-1960 E 1955
1950-1970 G' 1979	

C. Numbers of Non-Whites Who Had Moved Out of Various Divisions

South Atlantic	East South Central
1870-1920 E 1959	1880-1930 E 1918
1920,1930 ?E 1907	1910-1940 G' 1943
1940-1960 G' 1969	1940-1960 G' 1975

D. Numbers of Non-Whites Who Had Moved Into Certain Divisions

Middle Atlantic	East North Central
1870-1900 E 1869	
1900-1930 E 1902	1870-1910 E 1909
	1910-1930 G' 1962
1940-1960 G' 1970	1940-1960 G' 1977

Source: *Historical Statistics* 1: 89–92.

Figure 1.12
Whites Leaving U.S. Areas East of the Mississippi

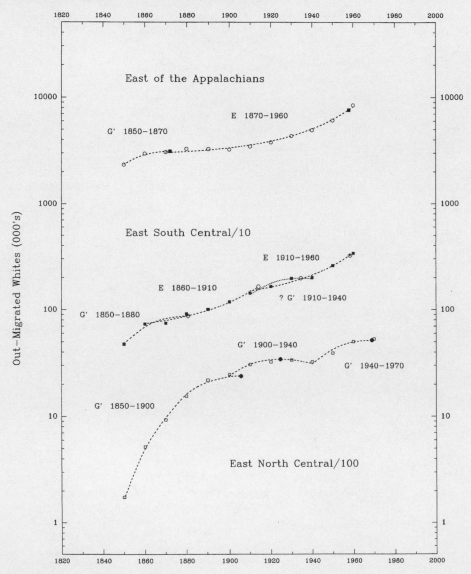

East of the Appalachians

E 1870–1960

G' 1850–1870

East South Central/10

E 1910–1960

E 1860–1910

? G' 1910–1940

G' 1850–1880

G' 1900–1940

G' 1940–1970

G' 1850–1900

East North Central/100

Out–Migrated Whites (000's)

Source: *Historical Statistics* 1: 89–91.

Figure 1.13
Migration into Western Regions of the United States, 1850–1960

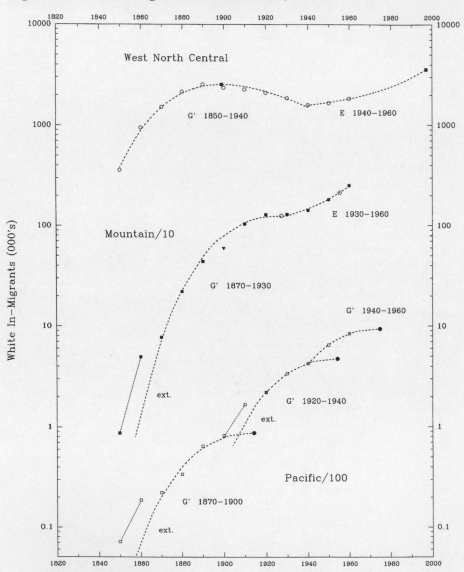

Source: Historical Statistics 1: 89–91.

South Central, and East South Central areas once more paralleled outward movement from more eastern districts in that era, though now taking E form, while
the East North Central cluster of states acted like a revolving door, with whites
entering and leaving in similar successive G' patterns across the middle 1900s.

The numbers of *non-whites* who relocated from region to region within the
United States also mounted along G' and E paths, as Figure 1.14 indicates.
Movement out of Alabama, Mississippi, Tennessee, and Kentucky for several
decades following the Civil War closely paralleled the E trend of their *in*-
migration into Ohio, Indiana, Michigan, Illinois, and Wisconsin (parts C and D
of Table 1.3). Again, following World War II, such largely reciprocal trending
between the East South Central and East North Central states was repeated,
though in between, from 1910 through 1930, migration into the Old Northwest
increased far more steeply than the other flow. Since the Depression, similar G'
curves also connect non-white emigration out of the South Atlantic and into the
Middle Atlantic. Before about 1930, however, the numbers leaving the South
Atlantic, though also taking E form, climbed very modestly relative to the 1870–
1900 and 1900–1930 surges of non-whites into the Middle Atlantic. In all, for
non-whites as for whites, the numbers of people relocating from one part of the
United States to another throughout have followed G-related patterns since the
records begin.

Looking over the trends summarized in Table 1.3, it appears that the numbers
of people moving in and out of the examined districts of the United States took
just two patterns. Most frequent (26 of 41 cases) was some segment of a G'
curve. This was the universal shape in early stages of settlement and population
growth. The other third of the trends observed took E form; but this pattern
appeared only between the Civil War and 1960, and not all regions had it.[15] No
other kinds of trajectories are necessary.

It is suggested that two different sets of dynamics were at work:

1. The G' pattern seems to represent a marginal utility for bringing new people into an area, which first rose as the opportunities there developed, then fell
as demands for workers and settlers weakened with the stengthening of natural
increase in the local population and intensified competition for whatever openings were available. Such a waxing and waning "pull" scenario implies that
fertility developments and economic growth, not just migration, followed G-
based paths.

2. The E pattern among U.S. whites following the Civil War (and some non-
whites between 1870 and 1930), in contrast, appears associated with a "push"-
like net flow westward out of the eastern seaboard and into the East South
Central, North and South West Central, and Mountain regions. This E-type
movement is reminiscent of the shift of surplus British population out of the
countryside and older cities to the new sites of the Industrial Revolution (Harris
2001, ch. 8).[16] Have structural changes of the economy, especially falling requirements for labor in agriculture, to some extent recently pushed people
around the same way regionally within America? If so, this has happened un-

Figure 1.14
Some Migration of Non-Whites within the United States

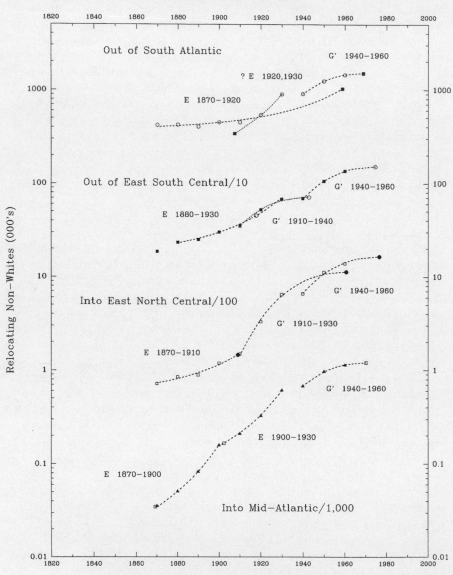

Source: Historical Statistics 1: 91–92.

derneath an overall pattern of national population increase in H form as opposed to the *nationwide* E growths of countries like modern Mexico or 18th-century England (Harris 2001, chs. 4 and 5). The E pattern, it should be remembered, is the upside-down image of C, a trend of population decline found historically where certain ways of life seem to have been losing their niche. Under those conditions, are people exported in E form (a topic to which Chapter 3 returns in examining urbanization)? What does it mean that Ohio, Indiana, Michigan, Illinois, and Wisconsin have, in contrast, not apparently been involved in such movements, in or out? Or California, Oregon, Washington, Hawaii, and Alaska? Have their agricultures, unlike other regional ones, remained competitive? Is E-type migration generally a phenomenon of redistributing and exploiting surplus, and cheap, labor? How have recent local E movements within the United States been related to E forms of population increase that appear in developing countries to which much American work and investment has migrated during the development of a more integrated international economy in recent decades?

Pushing our understanding of non-white migration back further in time, something is known also about the movement of enslaved African Americans within the United States across the *first* half of the 19th century. Fogel and Engerman (1974, 45–47) provide calculations for the volume of slaves relocated from east of the Appalachians into the Mississippi watershed for each decade between 1790 and 1860. The second plot on Figure 1.15 shows how the average annual numbers hovered around an underlying G' trend with its peak at 1850. What this means is that through the first half of the 19th century slaves were transferred across the mountains into the New South in a pattern almost exactly parallel to the influx of mostly white population into the Old Northwest (above the Ohio) with its t_0 at 1847 in Figure 1.11. The undulations across this trend, furthermore, reflect the same "long swings" that characterized the development of northern Trans-Appalachia.

Expressed as a percentage of all slaves currently in the United States (the top plot in Figure 1.15), this migration also followed a G' pattern with comparable fluctuations; but the surge crested rather earlier, near 1835. Kulikoff (1975, 208) has added estimates for the proportion of slaves each decade who were moved *within* eastern states. These percentages take very much the same trend as those for interregional transfers estimated by Fogel and Engerman, also peaking around 1835. Not only did free whites and slaves migrate westward between the Revolution and the Civil War in virtually identical patterns, into territories both north and south of the Ohio River, but slaves also were shifted around *within* the states of the Old South according to much the same G' pulse of the early 1800s. Not surprisingly, the combined interregional and intrastate flows also rose and fell via G' with t_0 at 1835.[17]

Since the slave-using New South interior imported people in the same pattern as the slave-free Old Northwest, was some general growth of opportunity across the U.S. interior inducing Old South slave owners to value and encourage re-

Figure 1.15
Slave Movement within the United States, 1795–1855

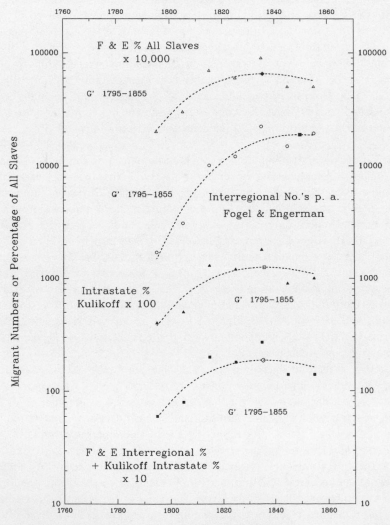

Sources: Fogel and Engerman 1974, 1:46; Kulikoff 1975, 208.

production among their bound laborers to move or sell in the newer territories? Or was surplus population somehow being generated in parallel fashion by the internal demographic dynamics of both white and black people, north to south, who lived east of the Appalachians? Regional parallelism for the latter reason seems more likely than any economic orchestration. In any case, the G' form of internal migration was at least as general across the first seven decades of U.S. history as has been found to be the case for transoceanic immigration and interregional migration during the century thereafter.

SIMILAR MOVEMENTS IN EARLY BRITISH AMERICA

Data from the 17th and 18th centuries indicate that G' was the predominant shape for migration also before 1800. To begin, the top plot in Figure 1.16 shows how the average annual number of headrights granted for European settlers and servants in Virginia from the 1630s through the 1690s swung up, then down around a G' curve with peak or zero year at 1645 (Craven 1971, 15–16). The five-year groups 1640–1644 and 1645–1649—extremely low because of the British Civil War—are graphed with a different symbol and not included in the curve-fitting. The average annual number of settlers for 1619–1621, which a burst of energy by the Virginia Company's treasurer Sir Edwin Sands produced during the years preceding the great Indian attack on the settlements, does, however, fit this pattern and is included in its calculation (Morgan 1975, 98).

Russell R. Menard has provided comparable estimations of European immigration to Maryland between 1634 and 1680 based upon a sample of headrights there (1988, 104). Sitting lower, at the middle of the figure (plotted with hollow squares), these rise later and more steeply than Craven's data for Virginia. While also following approximate G' shape, they increase along a curve that heads for a top only near 1695, about 50 years later. Menard's calculations for European migration to Maryland and Virginia *together* between 1635 and 1695 (the second level of plot, with solid squares) then can be summarized by a G' trend with its t_0 at 1671, midway between the timings for the two colonies separately (ibid., 105).[18] Table 1.4 displays these particulars for trends of immigration to the Chesapeake and relates them to comparable movements elsewhere in colonial British America.

Maryland, it turns out, in the timing of her 17th-century G' surge of European immigration was typical of a larger group of colonies. Estimates from Galenson for four regions—New York and New Jersey and the two Carolinas—first collectively crest in 1701 (the solid triangles) compared with Menard's 1695 for Maryland. In Figure 1.16 an average for the 1700s and the 1710s is included to underscore the suitability of the proposed underlying curve for these calculations of Galenson. His estimations indicate, moreover, that white immigration into New York and New Jersey combined and into each of the Carolinas for the most part also moved in such a manner separately, though these local trends are not fitted or graphed independently here (Galenson 1981, 216–17).

Figure 1.16
European Migration to Mainland British North America

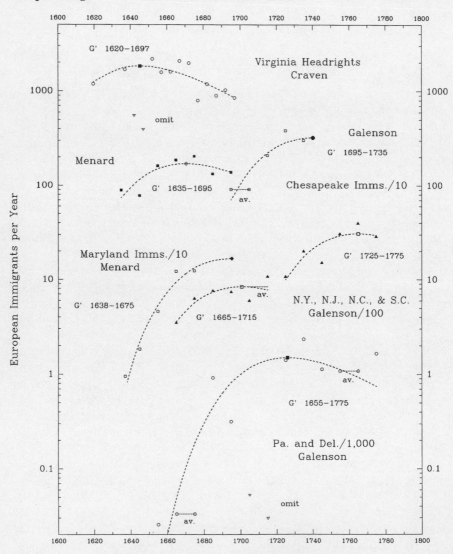

Sources: Craven 1971, 15–16; Menard 1988, 104–5; Galenson 1981, 216–17.

Table 1.4
Comparing Some Trends in European Migration to British America through 1775

A. To Mainland British North America (w/o Canada)

New England	peak 1630s			
Virginia	1620-1697 G' 1645[a]			
Md. & Va.	1635-1695 G' 1671[b]			
Maryland	1638-1675 G' 1695[b]	1665-1715 G' 1701[c]	1695-1735 G' 1740[c]	
NY, NJ, NC, SC		1655-1775 G' 1726[c]		1725-1775 G' 1765[c]
Pa. & Del.				
ALL MAINLAND	1645-1705 G' 1668[d]		1705-1775 G' 1746[d]	
New Estimates	1645-1685 G' 1670[e]		1695-1725 G' 1732[e]	1725-1786 G' 1762[e]

B. To the British West Indies

Barbados	1655-1685 D 1677[c]	1675-1775 G' 1698[c]
Antigua	1655,1665 ?D 1672[c]	1675-1755 G' 1694[c]
Nev., Mont., St. K.	1655-1695 D 1669[c]	1685-1775 G' 1700[c]
Jamaica	1665-1735 D 1674[c]	1675-1755 G' 1693[d]
ALL B.W.I.	1635-1695 G' 1632[d]	1735-1775 G' 1774[c]

C. To All Known British American Colonies (w/o Canada)

Gemery	1635-1705 G' 1643[d]	1705-1775 G' 1744[d]
Galenson (approx.)	1655-1705 G' 1640[c]	1715-1772 G' 1734[c]

Sources: [a] Craven 1971, 15–16; [b] Menard 1988, 104–5; [c] Galenson 1981, 216–18; [d] Gemery 1980, 215; 1984, 303, 342; [e] Figure 1.20.

For Pennsylvania and Delaware, finally, omitting the extreme low estimations for 1705 and 1715 and averaging for 1665–1675 and for 1745–1755, Galenson's numbers swing back and forth around a G' trend that tops out about 1726. Figure 1.16 and Table 1.4 show how this surge was timed rather earlier than the G' trends that underlie Galenson's *second* waves of European immigration for certain regions: 1695–1735 into the Chesapeake (with its t_0 at 1740) and 1725–1775 into New York, New Jersey, and the Carolinas (t_0 at 1765). These later movements contributed toward generating the 18th-century G' surge in white migration to *all* of Britain's 13 mainland colonies of North America collectively that the calculations of Gemery (1984, 303) produce for 1705–1775 with peak year at 1746 (Figure 1.18, below)—a finding generally mirrored in Galenson's estimates for 1705–1765 (with t_0 somewhat earlier, about 1734). Both Gemery and Galenson make very slim calculations for the 1740s, even considering that this was a period of chronic warfare and risky travel.[19] This lowness is probably, in part at least, a consequence of their technique for deriving net migration indirectly from population growth and natural increase.

In the West Indies, meanwhile, Figure 1.17 demonstrates how the first visible tendency as of the 1650s is for white immigration to decline locally roughly in D form (Galenson 1981, 218). Such patterning reflects the way that free and servant European populations on these islands soon began to shrink and be replaced by African slaves. The number of white settlers and bound laborers fell away in D fashion on island after island—and not only in British colonies (Harris 2001, 71, 74–75). Here in Figure 1.17 we see the *arrivals* of new Europeans shrinking that way, too. The demographic decline for whites was not just the effect of high mortality; a closing spigot for further immigration played a large role as slaves became more desirable relative to servants. Each of these D-type trends of contraction in immigration to the British West Indies that Galenson's data outline had its t_0 around the early 1670s, according to Figure 1.17 and part B of Table 1.4.

By the 1680s, however, later surges of white in-migration loosely in G' shape are indicated for Barbados, Antigua, and three other British Leewards—all peaking from 1694 to 1700. In contrast, the volume of white immigration to the big island of Jamaica continued to shrink in decelerating D fashion into the 1730s before a late-18th-century wave appeared there. This last roughly approximated G' form with a maximum in the middle 1770s.

Collectively, estimates for the British West Indies by Gemery not surprisingly echo for the period 1675–1755 the G' movement found for component islands by Galenson (Figure 1.18 from Gemery 1980, 215, and 1984, 342 "hybrid" variant).[20] What is distinctive about this aggregate, however, is that rather than declining across the 17th century in D form like white migration to particular islands, the *overall* flow to the British West Indies, according to the calculations of Gemery, took a G' trend with an early t_0 at 1632. It was from this temporary opening wave, many of whose participants shortly died or relocated to other colonies, that European settlement gave way to African slavery. The bottom plot

Figure 1.17
European Migration to Some Parts of the British West Indies

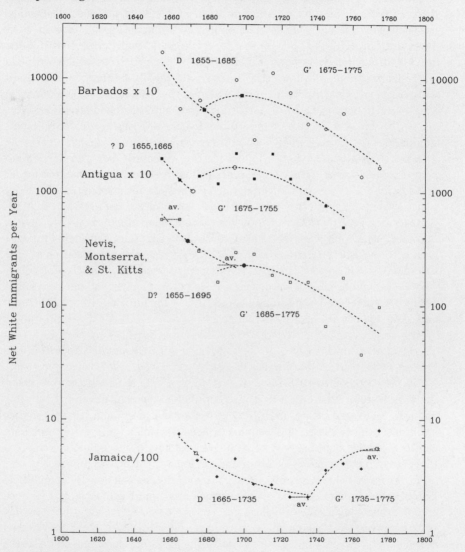

Source: Galenson 1981, 218.

of Figure 1.18 displays Gemery's version of the numbers and successive G'
curves fitted without the extremely low data of the 1660s and the 1700s (which
are marked with filled triangles rather than diamonds).

For the future Thirteen Colonies of the *mainland*, meanwhile—Figure 1.18
and Table 1.4—Gemery's calculations indicate a G' surge for 1645–1705 with
t_0 at 1668 (for Galenson, it comes in the early 1670s). According to Gemery,
then, British immigration to America as a whole (mainland and West Indies
together, part C of the table and the top plot in the figure) took a G' form from
1635 through 1705 that peaked at 1643 (compared with about 1640 for the
1655–1705 data of Galenson). For the 18th century, Gemery's mainland data
suggest a G' surge with top year at 1746 with the 1705–1765 estimations of
Galenson approximating such a trend with t_0 near 1734, again each without the
very low number for the 1740s. With the mainland now the dog and the West
Indies the tail—the reverse of the middle 1600s—this makes total British migration to America via Gemery's numbers (without the low 1740s) tightly follow
a G' curve with peak at 1744. (For Galenson, the top of the 1705–1765 trend
arrives a little sooner.) The exaggerated dip that both sets of estimations appear
to have for the 1740s seems to reflect their method: the population base from
which they begin the decade is probably too high (*Historical Statistics* 2: 1168,
Series Z-1). Sutherland's estimation for the mainland colonies at 1740, it will
be noted, stands out above the steady .03 trend of increase found in Volume I
of the present study (Harris 2001, 17). It constitutes the greatest proportional
deviation from that path between 1680 and 1850 and may simply be wrong.
Minor changes in growth rates, death rates, or birth rates for the population
being considered can significantly affect the technique employed by Gemery
and Galenson for estimating net migration.

Another, less indirect method for establishing the trends of European immigration coming to early America has been employed more recently (Grabbe
1989, 194–95; Fogleman 1991, 27; 1992, 698; 1996, 2). Rather than working
downward from overall growth in the population and speculations about rates
of birth, death, and natural increase that for the era must be based upon rather
scant and localized data, this technique primarily builds upward from separate
estimates of the main national or ethnic transatlantic flows of the colonial era
that successive generations of historians have put together and refined.

While Fogleman (1992, 693) has compared his calculation for *cumulative*
European migration to the mainland colonies in the pre-Revolutionary 18th century with the conclusions of Galenson, Gemery, and others before them, he has
been strangely silent about the comparative distributions of these movements
across time. Decade by decade, his results for 1705–1772 are often very different
from the computations of Gemery and Galenson that he cites; but he never takes
note of this or asks why such discrepancies in timing appear. In the bottom half
of Figure 1.18 his calculations for the Thirteen Colonies collectively can be seen
to climb steeply, perhaps via a G' trend that tops out as late as 1773. In proposing

Figure 1.18
Migration Estimates for Europeans to British America

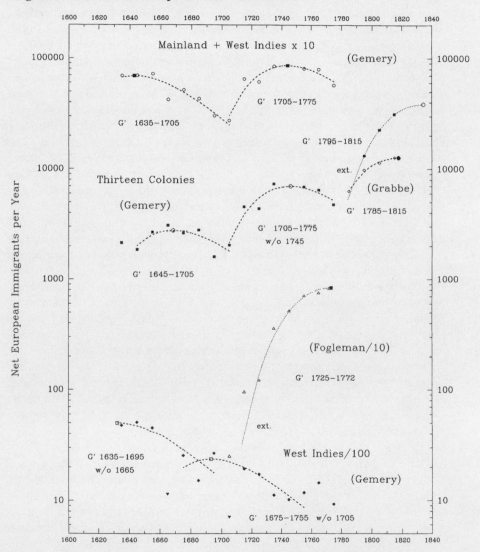

Sources: Gemery 1980, 215; 1984 "hybrid," 303, 342; Grabbe 1989, 195. Fogleman 1996, 2.

this representation through time, however, Fogleman identified only some 12 percent of the total European immigration that was calculated by Gemery and Galenson for the 1700s, 20 percent for the 1710s, 24 percent for the 1720s, and 46 percent of their modeled numbers for the 1730s. Neither Fogleman nor his American and European readers seem alert to how different his estimations are from former contributions to the literature, let alone question why they might depart so much from previous calculations that he cites. He does, however, offer less extremely low numbers for the 1740s than Galenson and Gemery.

Previously, applying a similar additive approach, Grabbe (1989, 195) came up with calculations much lower than those of Gemery for the following years from the 1780s through the 1810s (the second plot in Figure 1.18). Among all these so widely divergent results across the first 180 years of European migration to America, who has gone wrong, and where—and for what reasons? The marked differences observed here raise some basic issues about what the best estimates really are, the optimal way to resolve the discrepancies, and the historical implications of what in the end seem to be the most dependable calculations.

For European immigration in the 18th century Fogleman constructed decade-by-decade estimations for six major groups: Southern Irish, Northern Irish, German-speaking peoples, Scots, Welsh, and English. In attempting his own amendations and projections, for the first three of these flows he could draw upon substantial work already available in the literature. For the Scots and Welsh there was much less on which to build. For the English, Fogleman failed to take advantage of one of the most important and best-known products of modern historical demography, whose data might have guided him as to the reasonableness of the numbers that he proposed. Table 1.5 offers—in terms of average immigrants per year for successive decades—suggested revisions of his estimates. These are explained forthwith. Underneath them for comparison in part B of the table appear the annual levels that Fogleman's calculations imply. The period 1770–1775 is averaged for six years. It should be remembered that "Northern" and "Southern" Irish mean only those whose ships came from ports within and outside Ulster, while "German" includes German-speaking peoples of several different sorts.

To estimate *Southern Irish* migration, Fogleman started with the data of Marianne S. Wokeck on arrivals to the Delaware Valley from non-Ulster ports.[21] To begin his 1730–1775 calculations, Fogleman apportioned persons from unknown points of departure, including those whom Wokeck found landing in Delaware, according to the ratio of Southern to Northern immigrants among the knowns for each decade. This is a reasonable and frequently employed approach to handling unknowns when there is no guidance from another source. The left panel of Figure 1.19 demonstrates how, based upon the ultimate findings of Wokeck (1999, 172–73), such decadal Delaware Valley computations for 1725–1772 take a G' path with t_0 at 1754 (perhaps going back into the late 1600s, as the projected extension of the curve hints).

Table 1.5
Estimated Annual European Migration to the Thirteen Colonies, 1700–1775

A. New Estimations

Years	So. Irish	No. Irish	"Germans"	Scots	English	Welsh	Other	All Europeans
1700-09	[80]	[60]	4	52	2,696	363	[10]	3,265
1710-19	214	128	298	131	2,762	372	[20]	3,925
1720-29	467	278	480	210	2,598	350	[20]	4,403
1730-39	616	524	1,673	524	2,748	370	[80]	6,535
1740-49	1,481	995	2,407	813	2,778	374	[110]	8,958
1750-59	964	1,539	4,808	970	3,501	471	[120]	12,373
1760-69	894	2,667	934	1,800	3,133	422	[160]	10,010
1770-75	872	2,872	835	4,500	2,202	297	[117]	11,695
Total 1700-75:	52,392	79,142	111,050	72,000	215,372	29,002	[5,900]	564,860

B. Fogleman's Annual Numbers

Years	So. Irish	No. Irish	"Germans"	Scots	English	Welsh	Other	All Europeans
1700-09	80	60	10	20	40	30	10	250
1710-19	170	120	370	50	130	90	20	950
1720-29	300	210	230	80	220	150	20	1,210
1730-39	740	440	1,300	200	490	320	80	3,570
1740-49	910	920	1,660	310	750	490	110	5,150
1750-59	810	1,420	2,910	370	880	580	120	7,090
1760-69	850	2,120	1,450	1,000	1,190	780	160	7,550
1770-75	650	2,200	867	2,500	1,183	767	117	8,284
Total 1700-75:	42,500	66,100	84,500	35,300	44,100	29,000	5,900	307,400

[ ] Estimate from Fogleman.

Sources: Fogleman 1991, 340–59: 1992, 698–709; Wokeck 1999, 45–46, 172–73, 180–81, and unpublished calculations: Smout, Landsman, and Devine 1994, 98, 104; Wrigley and Schofield 1981, 528–29.

Figure 1.19
Estimates of Irish and German Migration to the Thirteen Colonies

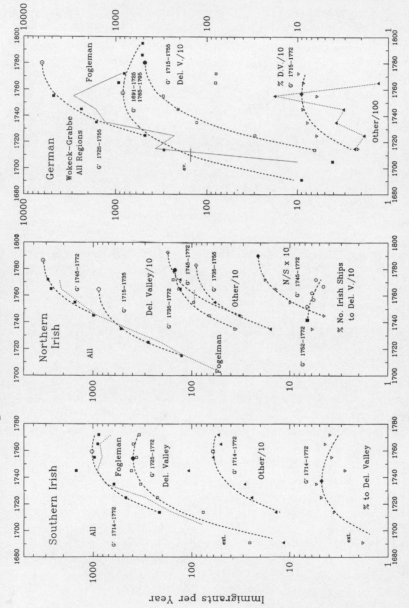

Sources: Wokeck 1999, 172–73 and 45–46; Wokeck 1981, 1996, and unpublished data; Fogleman 1992, 698–708; Grabbe 1989, 194.

Then, to estimate arrivals to *all* the Thirteen Colonies out of Southern Ireland from the numbers for just the Delaware Valley, Fogleman divided for each decade by .45, the proportion he found overall arriving there among Audrey Lockhart's *ships* from 1730 to 1775 (1992, 705–06). My own reckoning[22] is that more like .38 of Lockhart's ships from Southern Ireland (1976, Appendix C) came to the Delaware Valley. Any difference of that scale is less important, however, than the *variation from decade to decade* that Fogleman ignored. The ratios range from .28 to .54, doubling how totals for the Thirteen Colonies as a whole should be adjusted when projecting from the Delaware Valley from one period to another. To make estimates of Southern Irish coming to the colonies before 1730, finally, Fogleman (1992, 706) apportioned what he saw to be the number of earlier in-migrants according to the decadal distribution among the 13 percent of Lockhart's incomplete record of ships arriving during that time span.

In fact, Wokeck's immigrant estimations of 1730–1775, from which Fogleman projects, include many ships that she identified from American records of Irish arrivals that were not evident to Lockhart from sources on the other shore (Wokeck 1996, 115; 1999, 180–81). The proportion of vessels arriving in the Delaware Valley from Irish ports outside Ulster among ships that were actually covered by Lockhart ranges from 25 to 46 percent for the discussed year groups between 1730 and 1775, 38 percent for all ships of the whole period together. From Lockhart's Delaware Valley ships before 1730, Wokeck[23] estimated regional immigrant numbers that yield an annual average of perhaps 28.3 persons for 1711–1718 and 83.2 for 1719–1729 (also 9.5 for 1681–1699, with no ships from the pertinent sources identified from 1700 through 1710). Dividing these annual estimates by .38 produces the "Southern Irish" calculations for the Delaware Valley before 1730 that I include in the left panel of Figure 1.19. To estimate arrivals to all the colonies, those numbers are in turn divided by the percentage of Lockhart's ships known to have come to this region of the colonies in each time period.[24]

These suggested corrections alter the overall picture substantially, especially through time. The new summary estimate for 1700–1775—in the top half of Table 1.5—is that some 52,400 persons came from Southern Ireland rather than the 42,500 of Fogleman. His likely 19 percent deficiency in the total, furthermore, masks annual averages for the 1720s and the 1740s that are 35 to 40 percent below more precise projections from Wokeck's work. The 1720s and the 1740s are known to have been hard times in Ireland (Daultry, Dickson, and Ó Gráda 1981, 626; Wokeck 1983, 263–69; 1996, 119–21; Cullen 1994, 128–30; Ekirch 1987, 25). Notably, the current of Southern Irish immigration in the 1740s to ports outside the Delaware Valley spiked in the 1740s after a couple of years of famine in Ireland (the next to bottom plot—solid, upward triangles—in the left panel of Figure 1.19).

Finally, each of these more accurately estimated 18th-century flows—to the Delaware Valley, elsewhere, and all colonial destinations together—rose and fell in G' fashion with t_0's in the later 1750s. Most smoothly adhering to such form are the best-documented numbers, for Philadelphia and Delaware; fluctuating most around any underlying trend are the numbers to ports outside this region of regular and vigorous trade with Ireland. The 1740s, in particular, witnessed an unusual number of extra arrivals from Southern Ireland beyond the reach of the Delaware Valley. The *proportion* of ships that came to the Delaware, though, apparently crested in the 1730s as the "best poor man's country" of the early 1700s began to lose attraction for pioneering settlers and merchants alike relative to western Virginia and the Carolinas while New York and Baltimore competed more strongly with Philadelphia in trade with Ireland.

In turning to arrivals from *Northern Ireland*, Fogleman (1992, 705–8) likewise rooted his calculations in estimates from a draft of Wokeck's *Royal Academy* paper (1996). To her data, with arrivals from unknown ports distributed North and South like the knowns, he applied a multiplier based upon the proportion of Robert J. Dickson's Ulster ships that came to the Delaware Valley between 1750 and 1775 rather than some other colonial destination (Dickson 1988, Appendix E). For the years 1700–1729 he estimated Northern Irish from Southern numbers according to the ratio of the two for the 1730s (1992, 707). These calculations, too, can benefit from improvement.

Most notably, his numbers for the 1720s, 1760s, and early 1770s seem 20 to 25 percent too low, as the center panel of Figure 1.19 and the second column of Table 1.5 portray. This happens, first of all, because Fogleman—as for Irish from southern ports—applied a constant (in this case .57) proportion of Delaware Valley arrivals among Dickson's ships 1750–1774 to estimate total immigration to the Thirteen Colonies whereas (according to notes supplied by Wokeck) the share actually ranged from .46 for the early 1760s to .67 for the early 1750s. In fact, these regional percentages of arrivals from 1752 through 1772 appear in the bottom plot of the center panel of Figure 1.19 (the hollow circles) to follow the same G' form topping out near 1735 that underlies the proportion of colonial *Southern* Irish coming in through the ports of the Delaware, which is displayed at the bottom of the left graph. It would seem not unreasonable to conclude that mainland colonial trade with Ireland as a whole shifted first toward then away from Philadelphia and its environs this way. My estimates for 1715, 1725, and 1735 apply this hypothesis to derive Ulster numbers from what is known of the ports of the South. Out of these new calculations emerge a G' curve for Northern Irish coming in through the Delaware Valley 1735–1772 (hollow squares) that peaks about 1780 and a G' type underlying trend for Ulster arrivals at *other* colonial ports that is roughly parallel across the 1730s, 1740s, and 1750s (solid triangles in the center panel of Figure 1.19). Then, however, those *other* numbers break well above such a pattern. Though the data points are too few and too close together for establishing a meaningful trend, any G' curve for 1755, 1765, and 1772 would be likely (as approximately illustrated) to peak only in the 1790s. It is this fresh surge preceding the Revolution, now flowing more frequently to ports like New York and Baltimore and to the Carolinas, that Fogleman most significantly underestimates.[25] His figures appear 21 percent low for the 1760s and 23 percent low for the early 1770s. These shortfalls contribute the most toward making his aggregate from Northern Irish ports about 13,000 less than the more precise estimates in the top section of Table 1.5.[26]

In calculating the immigration of *German*-speaking peoples to 18th-century colonial America, Fogleman strangely did *not* start from estimates provided a decade before by Wokeck (1981, 260–61). Instead, he chose to base his computations upon the percentage of people with German surnames in the 1790 census (Purvis 1984) and his own construction of German immigration through Philadelphia from older sources (he cites Strassburger-Hinke 1934; Sachse 1895, 1–10; and Brumbaugh 1899, 54–70). Having culled some numbers from various secondary works that dealt with German-speaking immigration to other parts of the colonies (1992, 701–2), Fogleman then made a projection from the distribution of German names in the 1790 census to derive a multiplier that would estimate the total number of persons arriving outside the Delaware Valley and then distributed them by decade. Both of these procedures seem seriously flawed.

On the one hand, Fogleman dived in to recompute Philadelphia entrants from Strassburger-Hinke all over again; (1) He did not explain (1992, 700–704, 695) why he chose to ignore the comparable calculations of Wokeck (1981, 260–61; 1983, 111), targeting only—to demonstrate his "improvement"—her overall approximation from a demonstrably less technical publication (Wokeck 1985). (2) The reader is not told how he made crucial decisions, such as estimating the women and children who accompanied the more frequently listed men of the ship lists, or how these methods followed or departed from those that had been explicitly set forth by Wokeck (1981).[27] (3) He displays no curiosity about how his results by time period differ so much from those of Wokeck. For instance, already in their intial 1981 presentation her numbers for the Delaware Valley in the 1740s represented some 20 percent more than his, from 10 to 12 percent extra in the 1750s and early 1770s, while he estimated somewhat more than she for the 1760s. These discrepancies might have provided insightful signals as to how to work the two versions together in order to obtain the best ultimate understanding, from whoever's research it came.

Especially during the peak years, Wokeck found more German immigrants, even for Philadelphia, because she did more with shipping (the database of Stassburger-Hinke was not complete) and with other sources like occasional lists of servants (in the 1740s and preceding the Revolution).[28] For similar reasons, the likely shortfall of Fogleman's conclusions has grown with continuing research that has expanded command of the "Trade in Strangers" that transported German-speaking peoples to America (Wokeck 1999). This work now raises the 1700–1775 Delaware Valley total to about 81,000 in contrast to the 67,000 of Fogleman, a not insignificant gap of 21 percent. His computations are particularly far off the mark in certain years: Wokeck now finds 47 percent more than he in the 1740s, 37 percent in the 1720s, and 22 percent additional German immigrants to Philadelphia in the 1750s. These findings significantly subvert the impression that Fogleman conveys of both the scale and the timing of this important, first substantial, non-English-speaking migration of Europeans to British North America.

Where Fogleman's calculations most poorly depict the apparent reality, however, is for Germans coming to American ports outside the Delaware Valley. He correctly recognized that this set of his measurements and projections was less certain. But even allowing for his extrapolation that, on the basis of two groups of German American populations as of 1790, the numbers located in the sources that he does identify ought to be roughly trebled,[29] he captures perhaps only 10 percent of the immigrants outside Philadelphia estimated by Wokeck for the 1730s, some 16 percent in the 1750s. Her data are based upon an understanding of the various settlement projects of the era and the trade of German-carrying ships. This comprehension is built upon the usual business sources of the 18th century (newspapers, customs-house records, notarial evidence, and the correspondence of merchants in the colonies, England, and the Netherlands over agency, interest, insurance, and other commercial matters). The consequence for German immigrant numbers outside Philadelphia is about 12,500 more arrivals than Fogelman guessed, or 71 percent above his estimate. Meanwhile, in spite of his glance at the Rotterdam shipping records, Fertig (1994, 201) buys into Fogleman's indirect, census-based method for calculating arrivals outside the Delaware Valley and the substantial undercount that results from it.

The right panel of Figure 1.19 shows across its middle (the plot with hollow squares) how the number of German-speaking migrants to the Delaware Valley swelled in G' fashion from the 1710s to the 1750s. Then the trend broke back to about a quarter of the level of mid-century. A more abrupt surge into the early 1750s, meanwhile (bottom of the graph, solid triangles), characterized the in-flow of Germans to other colonial regions and their ports. Together, *total* likely in-migration by Germans consequently pushed upward via two distinct G' patterns. Across the second quarter of the 18th century, from the 1720s through the 1750s, the wave crested along a path with t_0 near 1780. Preceding that era but also *following* it—from 1715 (perhaps earlier) to 1725 and then from 1765 through 1795—an underlying G' pattern with t_0 more like 1755 was the track followed. The data for the later 1780s and for the 1790s come from Grabbe (1989, 194).

In effect, an exceptionally strong supply of migrants for a while, the ability of Dutch, British, and American merchants to fit them profitably into their business plans, and the capacity of various kinds of colonists in America to make the immigrant influx work to their advantage, too—in land sales, tenancy, and labor—collapsed like an economic "bubble" back to the level of about 1730 with the Seven Years War, effective competition from Prussia, Russia, and Austria-Hungary to obtain German settlers (relocations that did not require ocean travel), and a tendency for opportunity for new arrivals in America to dry up—

especially in Pennsylvania as settlement squeezed up against the Allegheny Mountains, the increasingly hostile remaining native population, and English plans to restrict access to the interior after 1763.

The fourth plot on the right-most graph of Figure 1.19 (near the bottom with hollow, downward-pointing triangles) shows how, among Germans estimated to have come to the colonies, the percentage who arrived through Philadelphia swung upward in a G' path that reached its apogee in the 1750s, something like two decades later than the greatest weight for Philadelphia within the flood of Irish immigrants. Then the relative pull of the Delaware among Germans kept strong as the second G' trend of arrivals to the colonies between 1727 and 1757 broke. In contrast, the Irish went elsewhere more readily, and their total numbers surged while the significance of the Delaware for their migration waned. The role of Philadelphia merchants in providing transportation and the importance of having previous fellow ethnic settlers in the Greater Pennsylvania hinterland to "consume" new German immigrants (two main thrusts of Wokeck's interpretation) were more crucial for attracting and absorbing Germans than were comparable dynamics for the Irish.

After the Revolution, Grabbe's computations for 1795 through 1815 suggest a new G' trend in German migration to the United States (fitted but not graphed). This headed toward a top for the curve in the 1830s at about 1,800 per year, more than twice the underlying "natural" G' peak indicated by data for the years 1715–1725 and 1765–1795 together, but only about a quarter of the height to which the extraordinary G' surge from the 1720s through the 1750s aspired had it continued to the 1780s.

To get numbers for *Scots*, Fogleman (1992, 707–8) mined the figures of Ian C. C. Graham (1956, 185–89) and Bernard Bailyn (1986, 92) for the 1760s and early 1770s and estimated arrivals across the preceding part of the 18th century according to what he thought was the chronological distribution for the Irish. Subsequent analysis by Smout, Landsman, and Devine (1994, 98, 104) agrees that the greatest concentration of this migration did indeed come in the period 1760–1775; but it more than doubles the numbers of Scots likely to have made the move (72,000, not 35,300), with 45,000 coming in the last 15 years rather than 25,000, and 27,000 between 1700 and 1760 rather than 10,300. The main reason for such a distinction between the two sets of estimates seems to be a much larger flow of Lowlanders, many of whom came through Irish or English ports.[30] Since Smout et al. offer no guidance on the matter of distribution through time before 1760, I leave the six decadal proportions for 1700–1760 the way that Fogleman estimated them, applying them to the higher total. Table 1.5 reports the new results.

Fogleman acknowledged being least sure about his estimates of *English* migration to the colonies. Indeed, that is where his greatest problems with assumptions and numbers lie. He concludes that about 44,000 English persons came to the Thirteen Colonies between 1700 and 1775 on the basis of Bailyn's data from the list of the years 1773–1776 (1986, 92), the ratio of English to

Scots therein, a speculation by Richard S. Dunn for English servants coming to the mainland 1700–1775 (1984, 159), and an assumption that the number of English increased steeply across the decades of the 18th century proportional to what he had calculated for the Scots (1992, 708—which, in turn, was based upon his distorted view of the Irish). All of these are doubtful moves.

In the first place, while citing calculations from Wrigley and Schofield for a total of 423,000 net emigrants out of England for the whole span of 1700–1775 (1981, 528–29), Fogleman does not question whether his estimate that only 10 percent of that number came to the Thirteen Colonies (in a century when very few English now went to the West Indies) makes sense. It doesn't. Then, decade by decade his assumption of constant English/Scottish (therefore Irish) ratios leads him to make the English numbers increase aggressively over the 1700–1775 span whereas the Wrigley-Schofield calculations for total emigration from the country are largely level for the hundred years beginning in the 1670s (compare Gemery 1986, 35). The marked difference in these two tendencies has raised no warning flags for Fogleman (or his editors, reviewers, and readers) about data that he has presented repeatedly without further consideration (1991, 27; 1992, 698; 1996, 2; 1998, 71). Nicholas Canny (1994a, 58–59, 64), on the other hand, considers the numbers of English to have been rather evenly distributed over time other than an exceptional burst that is caught by Bailyn's pre-Revolutionary records. By joining Fogleman in estimating only some 50,000 total coming to mainland British North America between 1700 and 1775, however, Canny, too, makes the pattern of the English numbers implausible.

Figure 1.20a illustrates another approach for exploring what a better assessment might be from the kinds of insights that are available. First of all, let us assume that Wrigley and Schofield were approximately correct in estimating net emigrants for England, both by total and by decade. Second, let us hypothesize that half of these people came to the Thirteen Colonies, once the big flows of the middle 1600s to Ireland and the West Indies were over. The solid squares of the top series of the figure portray these assumptions from the 1670s through the 1860s. At the left end of the plot, meanwhile, the hollow circles represent 90 percent of Gemery's computations by decade for *British* coming to the mainland settlements in the 17th century (1980, 215) in order to derive *English* numbers from his data. For this operation, which assumes for want of more specific evidence constant proportionality across the decades, I borrow Fogleman's estimates for 17th-century Irish and Scots and speculatively withdraw another few thousand Welsh from the English with whom he lumps them (1998, 68). Such derivations from Gemery's data are averaged for the 1680s and the 1690s in order to observe their underlying height better. For the 1670s and in their averages for the 1680s and 1690s, as the figure indicates, the levels of my adjustment of Gemery for English alone and the hypothesized movement to the Thirteen Colonies as one-half the national emigration reckoned by Wrigley and Schofield are almost identical.

A century later, there is an even more direct way of verifying the assumption

Figure 1.20a
Estimates of Some Migrations from England and from Europe between the 1630s and the 1900s: English to the Thirteen Colonies, the Caribbean, and Elsewhere

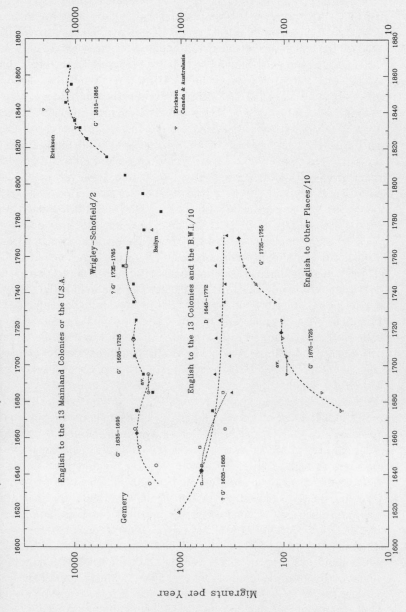

Sources: Gemery 1980, 215; 1984, 342 "hybrid"; Wrigley and Schofield 1981, 528–29; Bailyn 1986, 92; Erickson 1981, 179, 181; 1989, 352.

that about half of English emigrants came to mainland America. In the registers researched by Bailyn, from December 1773 through March 1776 some 4,513 English individuals (including 298 convicts) were found headed for a new life in the Thirteen Colonies (1986, 92). That is equivalent to 1,865 per year. For the 1770–1775 period half of the Wrigley-Schofield annual emigrants would be 2,202. The 85 percent of them captured in Bailyn's registers makes the half-of-Wrigley-Schofield number seem very much like a reasonable hypothesis, since the official records that Bailyn employs are recognized not to be complete.[31]

The figures of A. Roger Ekirch (1987, 73, 23) for convicts likewise support the reasonableness of the new estimates for English immigrants to the Thirteen Colonies that are offered in Table 1.5. The average annual numbers of such criminal transportees to Maryland (where most, but not all, of them went) amount to 6.2 to 8.3 percent of my calculations for all English who migrated across the era 1746–1765 compared with 6.6 percent convicts found by Bailyn in the registers for the years 1773–1776. Ekirch, however, identifies twice as many convicts coming to Maryland annually in the period 1766–1775. These amount to 20.7 percent of my estimates for all English to all the Thirteen Colonies in the years 1770–1775. This altered ratio, however, may do more to signal the increasing popularity of the judicial practice involved (which soon expanded to populate New South Wales and Van Diemen's Land, now Tasmania) than call into question the lowness of the half-of-Wrigley-Schofield estimation on the eve of the Revolution since the frequency of transportations in the area around London approximately doubled after 1765 from what had been the average since 1725 (ibid., 23). The long-term tendency of transported convicts to hover around 250 per year from the early 1720s through the early 1760s, furthermore, provides still another suggestion that to project the generally steady level of English migrants to the Thirteen Colonies in Table 1.5 across most of the 18th century is the right approach.[32]

Later, in the second quarter of the 19th century, Charlotte J. Erickson has found 11,487 English and Welsh persons emigrating to America in 1831. Reduced by the 13.5 percent proportion of Welsh in this total that she identified a decade later at 1841, this makes for 9,931 English as compared with 9,029 estimated as half of Wrigley-Schofield total emigration at 1831 and 10,150 at 1836, as the upper right corner of Figure 1.20a indicates. As of 1841, however, following the deep English depression of the late 1830s, her total suggests that well more than half of total emigrants probably came to the United States— 20,050 rather than the 12,368 halved from the *Population History* for 1846 (Erickson 1981, 179; 1989, 352). While the hypothesis of half English emigration coming to the territory that became the United States breaks down in the migration boom of the second quarter of the 19th century, widely spread independent computations by Gemery, Bailyn, and Erickson indicate that it is a wise choice from the later 1600s to the 1830s.

For the *Welsh*, meanwhile, Fogleman estimates a 1700–1775 total of 29,000 based upon the weight of Welsh names in the 1790 census and an immigrant-to-population ratio and distribution by decade that rely upon his conclusions about the Irish (708–9). Interestingly, this figure makes the Welsh total 11.9 percent of my revised English and his Welsh numbers combined for the years 1700–1775 compared with 13.5 for 1841 in Erickson's analysis. In short, the 29,000 total that Fogleman advances may be about right but should be distributed—as my revisions do—across the decades like the English, not the Irish. It is accepted in Table 1.5, finally, that there was a trickle of various other European immigrants, beyond the six listed groups, of about the scale proposed by Fogleman.

What are the implications of these new estimations? Most basically and importantly, contrary to the frequent emphasis in the literature on non-English, "ethnic" ancestral migrations and Fogleman's very low calculations, the English must be recognized as a much more important component of European migration to America north of the Rio Grande before 1800. Their numbers, furthermore— in contrast to other groups who mostly came later in the colonial era—increased, as Figure 1.20a shows, only very gradually from the 1630s to the 1770s. Their inflow, furthermore, probably rose in three successive G' waves that crested near 1663, 1714, and 1755 (with the 1740s being low and the 1750s relatively high). Decline into the 1780s, begun *before* the Revolution as Britain pushed back France on three continents to enhance its standing as a world power, was followed by recovery to mid-1700 levels in the early 1800s. This thrust upward continued to the middle of the 19th century, though after about 1830 it apparently took a higher and higher proportion coming to the United States to sustain that numerical pattern as total English emigration, according to Wrigley and Schofield, peaked and perhaps started to decline in a G' trend from 1815 into the 1860s.

For the conclusions of Fogleman, in total and especially over time, these results are devastating. In all, about 10 times as many English people came as he estimated for 1700–1775, and their numbers were much more evenly distributed from one end of this period to another than he proposed. In consequence, he may miss something like 98 percent of the English migrants of the 1700s, 95 percent for the 1710s, 92 percent in the 1720s, and 82 percent in the 1730s, improving only to a 62 percent shortage in the 1760s and 46 percent by the years 1770–1775. His English figures severely distort several important perspectives on European migration across this era.

The new estimates offered here, in contrast, help generate several useful insights into the broader pattern of European relocation. For example, by adding the calculations of Gemery for the British West Indies—reduced by 10 percent to separate out Scots, Irish, and Welsh roughly according to the same ratio as estimated for the 17th-century mainland (based on Fogleman 1998, 68)—patterns can be obtained for all English migration to the Americas and, by subtraction, movement elsewhere. Do these other potential trendings, also plotted in Figure 1.20a, make sense?

First, while the early G' surge of migration to the West Indies (compare the bottom plot of Figure 1.18) casts its shadow—lightly delineated—on the totals for English coming to the Americas, the data from the 1630s through the 1770s generally take the path of a D curve of decelerating decline. Dragged down by the negative experience of Europeans in the West Indies—and, for a while, retarded by reduced natural increase at home—generally fewer and fewer English people came to the Americas across the 17th and 18th centuries.

Next, if this number is subtracted from the total English emigration per year derived by Wrigley and Schofield, then an approximation for those going *somewhere else* can be hazarded. The result is the bottom plot on the figure. The people involved probably went to Ireland, Scotland or Wales, India, Canada and the Ceded Islands after 1763, and various military forces. Not graphed are the many English persons who apparently left for such non-American destinations annually in the 1640s, 1650s, and 1660s. This movement amounted to more than twice the annual average for the 1750s, the next highest decade between 1630 and 1775, when the population of England was much larger. The oft-repeated assertion that the flood of English into Ireland in the 17th century frequently equaled or outnumbered the combined out-flow of English and Irish to all the American colonies (Cullen 1994, 117; Canny 1994a, 61 citing the 1674 comment of C. Reynal) can be more precisely stated. Between 1640 and 1670 from 5,300 to 6,000 net English emigrants per year who were implied by the analysis of Wrigley and Schofield did *not* come to the American colonies of the mainland or the Caribbean (subtracting Gemery 1980, 215). Given the known history of the time, it seems safe to assume that the vast bulk of these went to Ireland. Their total for 30 years would be about 113,000 or more (almost all in the two decades between 1650 and 1670, given Irish events) compared with Reynal's contemporary estimate of 200,000 gone to Ireland. In the 1650s and 1660s they did apparently exceed Gemery's British annual averages of 5,560 and 4,870 coming to the New World, though this was no longer true in the 1670s. The high level implied for the 1640s by subtracting Gemery from Wrigley and Schofield seems problematic, given the immigration-discouraging Irish uprising that took place at the beginning of the decade and subsequent revolution in England. One possibility is that the method of the *Population History* somehow undercalculated English deaths in the Civil War, which Reynal estimated to have come to 300,000, and thereby projected too much net emigration at this time. Perhaps this is a hypothesis that the Cambridge group will test, encouraged to do so by the fact that otherwise their estimations of emigration can be so well bolstered by independent evidence based upon perspective from the receiving territories.

Having fallen through the 1670s and 1680s well below this early Irish-driven crest, the numbers of English people going elsewhere than to the Americas then rose into the early 1700s approximately in G' fashion, largely driven, it would seem, by the new Irish operations of William III and the long period of war and military recruitment between 1687 and 1713 in which England engaged. Then from the 1730s into the 1750s a new series of wars and the exploitation of India probably did most to drive the fresh G' trend of that era. In the 1760s and early 1770s the non-American numbers then fell off significantly. The plausibility of these residual movements after English people going to America are deleted from estimated total emigration out of the country would seem to strengthen still further the judgment that the flows to the Thirteen Colonies and the British West Indies proposed here have been calculated reasonably well. At the same time, it supports a likely appropriateness of G-based modeling for English migration to other places, too.

Turning, finally, to estimated *total European* immigration to the Thirteen Colonies and the early United States, the upper plot in Figure 1.20b shows how between the 1640s and the 1850s the numbers rose in five successive G' curves, which peaked at 1670, 1731, 1762, 1816, and 1883 respectively. For the 17th century, Gemery's British estimates for the mainland are supplemented by the number and timing of Dutch, French, Swedish and Finnish, and German immigrants argued by Fogleman (1998, 68–69). The 1705–1772 data come from the summary column of part A of Table 1.5, the new estimates that I propose for the 18th century. Calculations from 1786 forward are those of Grabbe (1989, 194–95). Overall, a quite gentle rise in immigration numbers was the norm through 1815, in spite of a population that was doubling every 23 years (Harris 2001, Figure 1.1).

An important consequence of this patterning in the scale of European immigration is depicted in the second, lower plot of the figure. Here, estimated incoming Europeans per year are displayed as a *proportion* (per 10,000) of the white population of the receiving society at the beginning of each decade. The rate quickly dives and (excepting a low number for the 1690s) in doing so declines very tightly along a single decelerating D curve from 50 percent in the 1630s, a clearly unsustainable figure, to about 1 percent per annum across the second quarter of the 18th century. This D trend has its t_0 at 1678. What the pattern signifies is how a population that grew in G form between 1607 and 1670 with t_0 in the mid-1670s, then via the constant $e^{.03}$ F path (Harris 2001, 17) progressively normalized and reduced its dependence upon immigration—a process that Chapters 5 and 6 probe in depth. A further D-shape trend of nativization appeared after a spurt of foreign-born persons (especially Germans) raised the percentage slightly in the 1750s. In a process well under way before the Revolution, the white population of the Thirteen Colonies, thereafter the new Republic, continued to grow at 3 percent per year while reducing its intake of immigrants from something like 1.3 percent yearly to more like 0.2 percent (21.7 per 10,000) by the end of the Napoleonic Wars.

The well-known subsequent burst of European arrivals in the 19th century, it should be noted, failed—except briefly in the 1840s and 1850s—to return the immigration *rate* to the non-slave plateau of the mid-1700s. The absolute numbers were now indeed large; but they could not sustain even a level of 1 percent of the existing white population of the United States. There would seem to be two ways of trending what happened after 1815. On the one hand, the data for

Figure 1.20b
Estimates of Some Migrations from England and from Europe between the 1630s and the 1900s: Numbers and Rates of European Immigration to the Thirteen Colonies and the United States

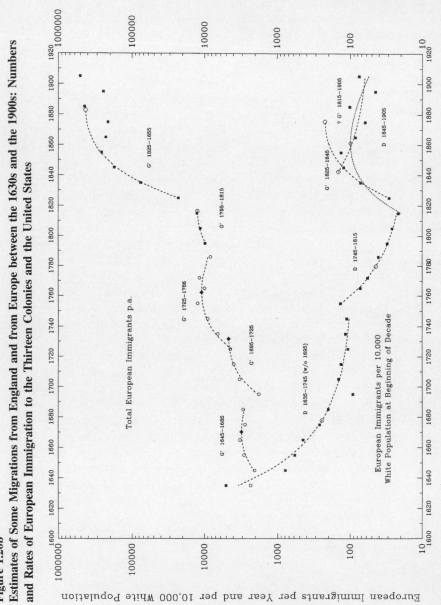

European Immigrants per Year and per 10,000 White Population

Sources: Table 1.5; Gemery 1980, 215; Fogleman 1998, 68; Grabbe 1989, 194–95; *Historical Statistics* 2: 1168, Series Z-1.

1825, 1835, and 1845 take a clear G' path headed toward a peak around 1875. From 1845 through 1905 the intake ratio, while fluctuating substantially, then swings back and forth around a new D curve with base year at 1842. Alternatively—more crudely and less justifiably, it would seem—the rate per 10,000 existing white population might be roughly modeled from 1815 through 1905 with a single G' track that tops out around 1861. Both patternings are shown on the graph. Either way, the rate of European immigration to this society from the middle 1600s to the middle 1800s moved over and over again in G-based patterns.

Figure 1.11 has already demonstrated D-shape trends in the rate of in-migrants into the Old Northwest region of the United States from the early 1800s to 1950. Thus, the process of normalization or nativization in the composition or structure of populations that have had substantial immigrant components is now indicated to have repeatedly taken G-based D form. By such movements, furthermore, it is implied that changes in the makeup of populations by age and sex that are connected with nativization likewise followed G-related paths. Such possibilities are the topics of Chapters 5 and 6.

Fogleman and those who have uncritically accepted his numbers have grossly distorted the peopling of the Thirteen Colonies in the 18th century. First of all, including his estimate for Africans, something like 840,000 migrants came between 1700 and the Revolution, not the 585,000 that he proposes. Slaves remain the largest group at 278,000 (now some 33 rather than 48 percent of the total),[33] but the English come close behind at 215,000. They amount almost to the Irish (126,000) and the Germans (111,000) put together, exceeding those much-discussed non-British groups if the 29,000 Welsh are included. By themselves, the English amounted to 38 percent of all Europeans, almost three times the 14 percent that Fogleman portrays. He has encouraged exaggeration precisely where hyperbole sprouts all too easily—in "ethnic," generally filiopietistic history.[34]

Looking at the in-flows over time, finally, the total intake of Europeans to the British colonies of the North American mainland in the 18th century must be understood to have been much more substantial in the early decades than has been argued, much higher during the first half of the 1700s. A consequence of that re-estimation is that relative to the size of the existing population, further arrivals from Europe in relative terms became substantially and systematically less important even as they became more varied in composition. The reality of migration to colonial British America appears to have been quite different than what has recently been presented and, along with its implications, must be better comprehended.

THE CHARACTER OF SOME OTHER HISTORICAL MIGRATIONS

While space and time prohibit mounting an exhaustive demonstration here, it can at least be illustrated how a wide variety of other migrations historically have taken the same few G-based patterns as have been observed in our largely British-American explorations so far. Evidence is available from populations that range greatly in size and complexity. Some of this movement can be traced back for several centuries. The kinds of people migrating vary from free families of means to single young people in search of work, to exiles, to convicts, to slaves. In the end, a fairly clear picture emerges concerning what patterns of relocation occur under which historical conditions. This means normally just the G' curve, with occasional G and D exceptions for certain flows that aggregate discrete movements into broader and more complex streams.

Figure 1.21a opens this stage of inquiry by depicting patterns for Spanish migration to the New World in the century before the English transatlantic flow outlined in Figure 1.20a began. Estimates that include sailors who probably did not return to Europe (Mörner 1992, 212) rise from 1550 through 1612 in a G rather than a G' trend.[35] This suggests a broadly cumulative migration like those between Britain and her Commonwealth daughters in the 19th century (Figures 1.2. and 1.10; Table 1.1). Iberian material from another type of source, however, indicates quite a different pattern. Records of emigration to America by region of origin within Spain (Nadal 1984, 61, citing Martínez, who calculated from Boyd-Bowman 1976) swing up and down substantially from period to period; but from the years 1493–1519 through the years 1580–1600 they do so around a G' curve that peaks at 1549, which is also the t_0 for the contrasting G curve of Mörner's calculations. Do the latter perchance rely on the amount of *shipping*, thus measuring such traffic more than migration itself? Or is there some other explanation for the significant divergence of the two series, such as a decline in Spanish record-keeping that shows up especially when origins of emigrants are sought?

Ida Altman (1989), meanwhile, has provided information about migrants to America from two areas of Extremadura, an inland region of Spain. Though timed somewhat differently, from both Carceras and Trujillo the numbers of emigrants between 1501 and 1575 rose in two successive G' spurts interrupted by a drop in the 1540s. The dip around 1550 in the broad time periods of Boyd-Bowman (the next to top plot on the graph) may, in fact, reflect the kind of sequence of G' trends evident in the observations of Altman, while by the 1580s competitive recruitment for the Armada (or competitive participation by Portuguese, as of 1580 under the Spanish Crown) cut into the flow to Spanish America, as evident in the series from Martinez and Altman's data for Trujillo. Reported local departures in all do seem to have repeatedly followed G' paths.

Turning to American enterprises of still other European powers, Figure 1.21b plots probable trends of migration to the French West Indies and to New Netherland. Decadal averages for indentured servants shipped out of La Rochelle to the Caribbean (Mauro 1986, 99, after Debien 1952) fluctuated substantially. For the whole recorded period from 1640 through 1715, however, the way that numbers fell away in the long term can be roughly summarized by a G' trend with t_0 at 1641. This makes the French flow to the West Indies parallel the G'

Figure 1.21a
Some Immigrant Flows to Spanish America, New Netherland, and the French West Indies between 1505 and 1715: To Spanish America in the 1500s

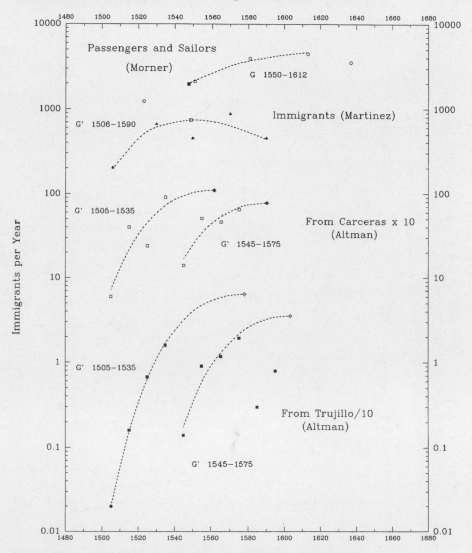

Sources: Morner 1992, 212, 216; Nadal 1984, 60; Altman 1989, Tables 8 and 9.

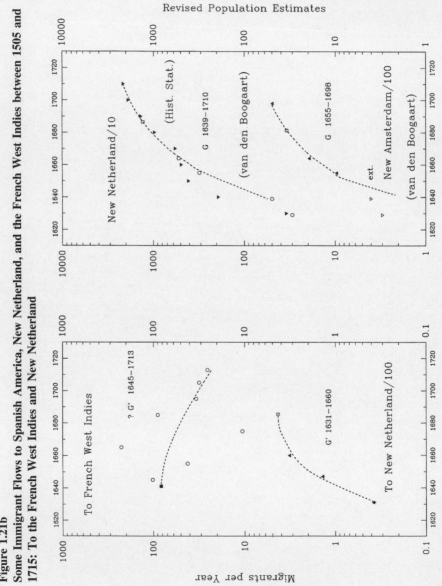

Figure 1.21b
Some Immigrant Flows to Spanish America, New Netherland, and the French West Indies between 1505 and 1715: To the French West Indies and New Netherland

Revised Population Estimates

New Netherland/10

(Hist. Stat.)

G 1639–1710

(van den Boogaart)

G 1655–1698

ext.

New Amsterdam/100

(van den Boogaart)

To French West Indies

? G' 1645–1713

G' 1631–1660

To New Netherland/100

Migrants per Year

Sources: Mauro 1986, 99; van den Boogaart 1986, 61, 77–79: *Historical Statistics* 2: 1168. Series Z 12.

pattern of estimates by Gemery (and by Galenson) for white migrants to the *British* American colonies in general according to Table 1.4 and Figures 1.16 and 1.18. Meanwhile, the G' crest for the Virginia headrights of Craven peaked at 1645, the flow to the British West Indies at 1632. These simultaneous surges in such diverse contexts are unlikely to have reflected the kinds of distinctive events in England and France that have been invoked to interpret them. Something more general was at work.

The average annual number of migrants from Europe (many not Dutch) to New Netherland—modern New York, New Jersey, and Delaware—rose from the 1620s to the 1660s along a G' path that headed toward a peak at 1686 if the flow had not been cut off by the English conquest (van den Boogaart 1986, 61). This makes immigration to New Netherland, shows Table 1.4, follow a timing somewhat before G' surges to Maryland, to the Carolinas, and to New York and New Jersey (including post-1664 English data), and somewhat after the peaks around 1680 characteristic of Barbados and the Leewards. In sum, Spanish, French, and Dutch patterns of migration to the New World (1) took the same type of G' shape found in modern migrations and (2) tended to accompany contemporaneous waves of settlers coming to British America.

The right panel of Figure 1.21b presents trendings for the populations of New Netherland and New Amsterdam (van den Boogaart 1986, 77–79) that correct, clarify, and confirm judgments made in the first volume of this study. The additional data make the people of New Amsterdam along with little Haarlem (in other words, Manhattan Island) expand in G fashion from 1655 through 1698 almost exactly like computations for New York County (Manhattan) previously based upon Rossiter (Harris 2001, 297)—with t_0's at 1681 and 1683, respectively—a surge that seems to have taken off following the Freedoms and Exemptions offered settlers in 1639 and Governor Kieft's War of the early 1640s. For the colony of New Netherland without South River (Delaware), on the other hand, the calculations of van den Boogaart substantially reduce previous estimates from *Historical Statistics* (2: 1168, Series Z 12) for New York at 1640, 1650, and 1660 but at the same time make the growth of this bulk of New Netherland's population (few Europeans as yet lived in what is now eastern New Jersey) line up with the G trend for New York's demographic expansion from 1670 through 1710 (ibid.). Thus, for the computations of van den Boogaart for 1639–1664 (hollow circles) and *Historical Statistics* for 1660–1710 (filled downward triangles) together, one gets the kinds of single G pattern with t_0 at 1686 that is presented in the upper plot of the right panel of Figure 1.21b. The new data simplify the growth of New York population into a single G trend from 1639 to 1710, eliminating the extra 1640–1670 G pattern proposed in Volume I (Harris 2001, 42). Once again, it is a pleasure to have better information that was previously not available, or that I just missed, strengthen and simplify the interpretation that has been offered.

In the colonization of French Canada in the 17th century, meanwhile, according to a recent revision of the estimates (Charbonneau et al. 1987, 15), which is plotted in the lower left area of Figure 1.22, the total for recorded immigrants from France per year—military personnel, *engagés* (indentured servants), women, and others (including male and female religious)—rose and fell between the time block of 1608–1639 through that of 1680–1699 in a manner that approximates a G' curve with peak at 1670. This G' curve matches in timing exactly with the pattern of population increase for New France, which is estimated to have taken G shape between 1650 and 1670 with t_0 at 1670 (Harris 2001, 65–66). The migration curve, in other words, is a constant times the derivative of this particular growth curve with this particular base year. For the St. Lawrence River region of "Canada," which with British conquest became Lower Canada and then the modern province of Quebec, the opening growth G between 1625 and 1706 had its base year rather later, about 1687 (ibid.). That, however, is precisely when the G' derivative curve for arrival dates between 1632 and 1672 of people living in families by 1680 has its t_0 (Charbonneau et al. 1987, 19)—the lowest plot in the left side of Figure 1.22. Were these identified family members residents primarily of what is now Quebec Province? If they were, once again the t_0 of the local migration curve has an exact match of date with the peak for the derivative of the growth curve for its population. In the same fashion, the original 1645–1685 G' surge of European immigration to what would become the Thirteen Colonies of British North America (Table 1.4 and Figure 1.20b) crested at 1670, almost precisely at the t_0 for the opening G-shape growth trend of the society into which these people moved (Harris 2001, 17).

Very little of total emigration from the Netherlands, meanwhile, ever came to America. Instead, most disappeared across the 1600s and 1700s into a notorious sinkhole for unfortunate, discontented, or ambitious population that was provided halfway around the world from the Americas by European operations in southern Asia. The Dutch East India Company (VOC), in particular, sent out about 475,000 Europeans from the early 1600s to the end of the 1700s, an emigrant flow almost equal to all non-African migration to the Thirteen Colonies of British America between 1700 and 1775 (Lucassen 1994, 172–73 vs. Table 1.5 here). Some 255,000 never returned, and only very small European populations ever appeared in the Dutch East Indies.

The top part of Figure 1.22, first of all—in hollow circles—plots average annual numbers of employees sent out by the VOC (de Vries and van der Woude 1997, 439, 432). Only about half of these were Dutch in origin. The company tapped a broad northern European base of manpower (Lucassen 1987, 157). That probably has much to do with why the trends for 1606–1675 and 1695–1765 take G rather than G' shape. Complex and widespread destinations, stretching from the Cape of Good Hope to the Pacific, were involved along with mixed European origins. At about 4,000 per year across the span from 1650 to 1690 this flow almost doubled current European migration to the British North American colonies and just failed to match the peak of the shorter-term surge to Cromwellian Ireland. In the third quarter of the 18th century the eastbound

Figure 1.22
Some Dutch, French, German, and Australian Migrations, 1570–1870

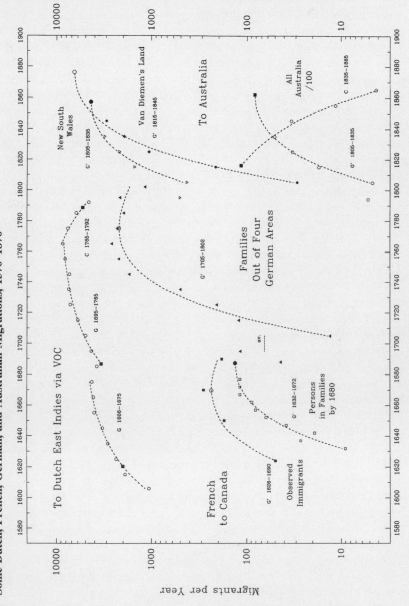

Sources: Charbonneau et al. 1987, 15, 19; de Vries and van der Woude 1997, 439, 432; Fogleman 1991, 71; Vamplew 1987, 4.

numbers (now about 8,000 per year) came to more than twice the flow from England and Wales (a much bigger society) to America, were more than sufficient to have sated the appetite of London's depressing demography (see Chapter 3), and equaled the current totals for all the much-discussed non-English European ethnic and national groups that came to North America combined!

When the company undertook its operations, moreover, migration was already a common phenomenon in the Netherlands and neighboring territories. Jan Lucassen (1994, 161) has estimated that across the two centuries from 1675 through 1875 (probably beginning sooner) on average 30,000 long-distance migrant workers a year came to the northwestern coast of Europe, stretching from Flanders northeastward through the Dutch maritime provinces as far as German Oldenburg, to engage in a wide variety of seasonal employment, both agricultural and industrial. As in Britain, the familiarity of one kind of migration was there to encourage the stranger, longer overseas leap that provided still one more option (Kussmaul 1981; Horn 1979).

Since most of them went to poorly documented populations of central and eastern Europe (not to the New World, as Americans might be tempted to think), the substantial 18th-century flow of *emigrants* out of various parts of Germany cannot be linked to the growth trends of the peoples that they augmented. For these flows, more than one recent scholar has mined the research of Werner Hacker to establish total numbers and patterns through time. In the center of Figure 1.22 are plotted the number of families per year known to have legally left Baden, the Breisgau, the Bishopric of Speyer, and the territories of the imperial city of Ulm (Fogleman 1991, 71–72, who cites the relevant publications of Hacker). These generally follow a G' curve that peaks at 1775. Previously, as Fogleman acknowledges, Wolfgang von Hippel (1984, 37, citing several other sources) had plotted from Hacker the annual numbers legally departing for southeastern Europe from Upper Schwabia, the Upper Neckar, Hohenzollern, the southern Black Forest, and the northern shores of Lake Constance. What Fogleman did not realize was how much the timing of these other waves that he cited departed from his own regional selection from southwestern "Germany." A background graph for the present discussion, which is derived from von Hippel, shows a 1687–1802 G' surge out of Upper Schwabia that peaked as early as 1738, not the 1775 of Fogleman's families, while the 1697–1802 G' curve for the other regions examined by von Hippel has a t_0 at 1763. Perhaps Fogleman felt comfortable in making all European emigration to the Thirteen Colonies climb so steeply between 1705 and 1775 and peak so late because his particular regional selection for discussing *out*-migration from Europe rose this later way. Even within southwestern Germany, however, out-flows from different areas display quite different timing, though the immigrations seen in composing this study have all taken G' paths.

Besides British America, Spanish America, the French West Indies, New Netherland, and New France there is a very different "New World" society in whose forming the crucial role of immigration can also be patterned. From the

1800s through the 1830s total immigration to *Australia*, convict and free, rose along a G' curve that headed for a crest at 1862, as the lower right corner of Figure 1.22 indicates (Vamplew 1987, 4). As shown in the upper right corner of the graph, the 1805–1835 G' path for immigration to New South Wales, the original area of settlement, had its t_0 slightly earlier, at 1857; the curve for arrivals at Van Diemen's Land (Tasmania) was later and steeper, headed for a peak only at 1876, about two decades later. In other words, immigration into different parts of Australia, like emigration out of different areas of southwestern Germany or into various colonies of America, followed distinctly timed waves that each bore the stamp of the G' pattern. While the first, very early growth curve for the European *population* of Australia, for 1790–1815, takes G form with t_0 at 1834, the second, for 1810–1830, has its base year at 1858 and the third, for 1830–1911, has a t_0 at 1881 (Harris 2001, 80, 82). Though not as simply as for New France or mainland British North America, complicated by the delay in how soon convict migrants could have children, the connection between G' waves of early immigration and G-form population increase is present for early Australia, too. After the 1830s, however, total migration there dropped off in accelerating C fashion. This is a form of decline found in populations whose niche has failed. The transportation of convicts to Australia had fallen out of fashion—first in areas that had been colonized earliest, then elsewhere (and at home).

Figure 1.23 then presents illustrations of other 19th- and 20th-century migrations in G' form. The left side of the left panel begins with two sets of numbers from von Hippel (1984, 139, 218) for emigration from Württemberg. The data swing around the underlying trends; but his information for five very specific locations (top) and for all of Württemburg (bottom) both hover around underlying G' trends that peak close together, respectively, at 1865 and 1871, reinforcing the impression that each separately gives of the path taken. Second, in one of several significant 19th-century streams of modern immigration outside of North America, the flow of Spaniards to Argentina rose twice via G': first loosely in the years 1856–1893 and then more tightly in the years 1893–1913 (Nadal 1984, 177). Also outbound from Iberia, total Portuguese emigration took G' shape 1863–1928 almost exactly parallel before the 1890s to the Spanish movement to Argentina. It did not, though, experience the second G' surge of that transatlantic migration, continuing instead on the old path through the 1920s. After the Great Depression, however, a new surge of Portuguese emigration from 1938 through 1972 followed a new G' path toward an anticipated top at 2001 (Magalhães Godinho 1992, 21).

The last two plots of the left panel of the figure deal with Russia. On the one hand, approximations of annual migration into Asiatic regions of tsarist Russia and the U.S.S.R. (the downward-pointing, hollow triangles—from Woodruff 1966, 108–9, omitting the 1920s and considering only the years 1910–1914 in the previous decade), after a short possible G' trend for the years 1855–1875, rise afresh from 1885 into the 1950s or later along a likely G' curve with t_0 at

Figure 1.23
Some Other In- and Out-Migrations since 1800

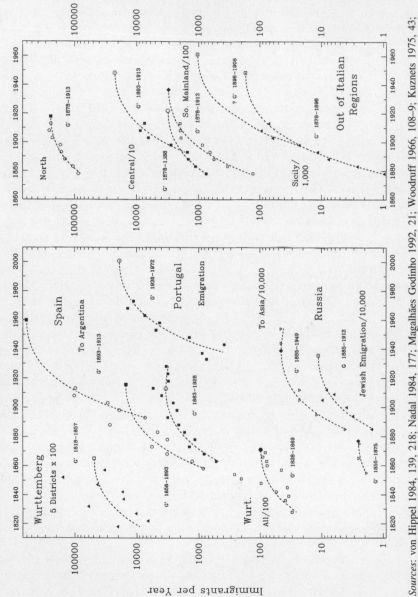

Sources: von Hippel 1984, 139, 218; Nadal 1984, 177; Magalhães Godinho 1992, 21; Woodruff 1966, 108–9; Kuznets 1975, 43; Martellone 1984, 402–3.

1939. Meanwhile, the population of the three economic districts of West and East Siberia and Far East together swelled via a G trend from 1926 through 1970 that had its t_0 at 1926 (Harris 2001, 222, 227). This provides another close timing between a G' of migration and a G of total resulting demographic increase. Such patterning also makes movement into Siberia and Central Asia rise parallel with Russian immigration to the United States (Table 1.1 and Figure 1.5), another historical instance in which a pool of potential movers spilled out in more than one direction simultaneously. The last plot in this side of the figure (the solid, upward triangles) fits the G' model to the Jewish component of emigration to America from 19th-century Russia (Kuznets 1975, 43). The curve for 1885–1912 headed toward a peak at 1937 until it was cut off by U.S. legislation in the 1920s.

The right-hand panel of Figure 1.23 displays differently timed surges of emigration from broad regions of Italy between the 1870s and World War I (Martellone 1984, 402–3). From the North, departure to various foreign destinations—though substantial—increased only a little across the period, along a G' curve topping out at 1918. Relocation from Central Italy apparently followed a parallel course until the 1890s. Together these regions fueled the 1877–1897 G' pulse for all of Italy seen in Figure 1.4. The later G' wave of total Italian emigration in that figure, cresting at 1940, and the pattern for Italians going to the United States from 1868 to World War I, in part then reflect the new G' path for emigration from Central Italy that began as of the early 1890s (t_0 at 1948). Most of that new wave, however, is well known to have come from farther south. Tracks of this broadly parallel G' nature (with t_0's at 1937 and 1948) were shared by those who left the Southern Mainland between 1878 and 1913 and Sicily from 1878 to 1896. The Sicilian out-flow, though, exhibits what may have been the start of a new, still steeper spurt between 1898 and 1908 headed for a top at 1961 before starting to collapse on the eve of World War I.[36] As seen in other parts of the world, the different regions of Italy all produced emigration in G' shape, though their flows display different timing—and also sometimes went to different places (ibid., 398–404).

Figure 1.24, finally, plots through time the international traffic in contract laborers that, as slavery was abolished by one nation after another during the 19th century, replaced it in the canefields and comparably unpleasant work sites of the globe. Over half of these indentured workers came from the Indian subcontinent; but substantial numbers of Chinese, Japanese, Africans, Pacific Islanders, Javanese, and—for a while—Europeans were involved (Northrup 1995, 158–60).

The left panel of the figure plots the *intake* of these laborers for certain areas. The half-million (a quarter of the total) who came to the British Caribbean clearly arrived between 1840 and 1920 according to a G' pattern with its crest at 1872, as the top plot in the left panel of the figure indicates. The 7,000 to 8,000 migrants a year involved roughly equalled the number of British citizens coming to the United States at the time, whose G' curve peaked about a decade

Figure 1.24
Global Indentured Migrant Workers from the 1830s to World War I

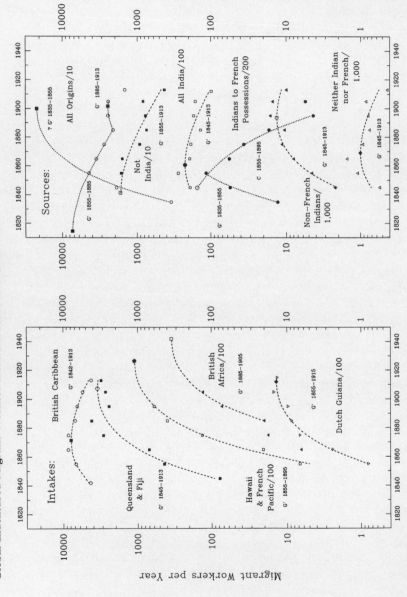

Source: Northrup 1995, 158–60.

later (Figure 1.2); it clearly exceeded the number of Irish who annually moved to America, except for a few years following the Great Famine (Figure 1.1). Queensland and Fiji, also British possessions, absorbed large amounts of the new labor supply, jointly along a later G' track with its t_0 at 1907.[37] Almost as many went to Hawaii and several French islands in the Pacific along a still later G' path that until the 1890s climbed toward a maximum year for the formula at 1926. The flow into British-controlled Natal, Transvaal, and East Africa, however, in aggregate equalled the number of indentured workers going to all those Pacific destinations. After a slower start, it crested steeply in G' fashion between 1885 and 1905 toward a t_0 in the 1940s before being cut back during the years just preceding World War I. Meanwhile, the 57,000 contract laborers headed for Dutch Guiana spread out across time in a G' pattern that had a top contemporaneous with that for Queensland and Fiji.

In addition, Cuba and Peru garnered substantial numbers of indentured workers, most of them Chinese from a spike of out-migration that occurred during the three decades that followed the disasters of the Taiping Rebellion. The biggest short-term engagement in the flow of 19th-century indentured labor, however, involved the French. Their possessions, especially Mauritius in the Indian Ocean, took about 650,000 contract workers during the century recorded—or 31 percent of all of them. These were mostly Indians and were recruited principally just in the 1840s, 1850s, and 1860s. The filled circles halfway down in the right-hand panel of Figure 1.24 follow a G' trend that, if completed, would have topped out at 1896 closely parallel to the global total for this type of labor. Soon after the Mutiny, however, France's employment of Indians for her sugar islands collapsed along the displayed C path between 1855 and 1895, as more and more Indians went to other destinations—all controlled by the British—in a G' pattern between 1845 and 1913 with its peak at 1894 (the plot with solid triangles that cuts *across* the C-shape downturn for French-recruited Indians). As a consequence, the total of Indians migrating globally as contract workers, while the annual rate peaked around 1860, did not collapse like the French recruitment from the subcontinent but continued an underlying G' pattern on until World War I (the hollow squares across the middle of the right panel of Figure 1.24). That the G' curve for average numbers for contract workers who were *not* Indian peaked at 1841, two decades ahead of the comparable trend for Indians, underscores how the people of the subcontinent poured out to supply the labor of the world's sugar industry, displacing other sources.

If one looks at the annual totals for *all* workers of this sort around the world (the top plot in the right panel of Figure 1.24), one G' trends appears between 1855 and 1885 with t_0 at 1815, then a second between 1885 and 1905 with t_0 at 1902. If, however, one takes out the brief but substantial French incursion into the trade during the 1840s, 1850s, and 1860s, what remains looks much like a single G' from the 1840s to the 1910s (not graphed). The French pioneered the use of indentured workers, with energy and success. Indians going to their Indian Ocean islands of Mauritius and Réunion alone amounted to half of all contract workers globally in the 1840s and 1850s. But, following the Mutiny, the British progressively took over the Indian source of supply to provide labor for a succession of their own colonies around the world. Whether the French through the natural increase of their early wave of indentured workers had enough labor without further recruitment (repatriation from Mauritius was not especially high—Northrup, 1995 132) or the British saw a good thing within their grasp and after securing imperial control of India could cut the labor-seekers of other powers out of the subcontinent will have to be decided by someone who knows the local details.

   Though there are competing modelings and interpretations for such patterns that might be offered for some of these examples, the overall impression is that as far back in time as usable records go and wherever in the world they exist, historically migrations have overwhelmingly taken just the G' shape. Flows of free migrants; those bound by indenture, convicts, and slaves; and relocations of white, black, yellow, and brown peoples all have built up then dwindled in this way. The form has characterized movements of persons seeking new lives in North America, the Caribbean, South America, southern Africa, the Indian Ocean, Indonesia, Australasia, Oceania, southeastern Europe, and Asiatic Russia. It captures the pattern of out-migrations from nations or regions of Europe, the Americas, India, Oceania, and equatorial Africa.

   Indeed, G' is as dominantly the most frequent form among migrations as G has been shown to be for population growth and D for demographic decline in the first volume of this study (Harris 2001). In new settlements, moreover, the G' and G curves tend to share the same t_0, G' being the derivative of G and migration at this point in the history of a population being the predominant source of growth. Once significant natural increase begins, however, the marginal utility of additional immigration begins to decline. Further entrants must compete with children of the already established, and the benefits of relocation become less compelling.

   The implication is that the mechanisms by which a native population appears control the tap of subsequent immigration. Such processes of nativization or naturalization are the topic of Chapters 5 and 6. This phenomenon, it must be recognized, can hold just as true within an *established* population—for instance, where the niche for new labor in the British West Indies after the emancipation of slaves in 1834 opened the door for Indians alongside people of African and European origin. While the children of those newcomers soon help fill up openings, the numbers involved in such later migrations to established populations and consequent generational transitions are no longer so directly reflected in the growth of the *total* population as are intakes of migration and their replacement processes during early years of settlement and naturalization. They constitute a much smaller portion of the total demographic scene; but they are nevertheless still there and behave the same way.

   Of the infrequent alternatives to G' in the historical patterning of migrations, the most common is the G curve of constantly decelerating growth, itself the dominant shape for population increase. This form of trend has been observed generally for 19th-century emigration from Britain that did not go to the United States and specifically in movement to Australia and New Zealand (Figures 1.2 and 1.10 and Table 1.2); in out-migration of the 19th century from the Netherlands and Belgium, which also possessed large colonial holdings, and in the 17th- and 18th-century exports of various excess European humanity by the Dutch East India Company (Table 1.2 and Figure 1.22); and in migration from Spain to all her varied holdings in the New World during the 1500s (Figure 1.21a). Each of these historical settings entailed flows into populations that needed constant—not peaking, then declining—additions to sustain their growth. An aggregation of people from complex sources going to scattered destinations was also generally involved in movements of this exceptional shape.

A very few migrations have even taken the more slowly decelerating H form of expansion. This shows up in the underlying path of total immigration to the United States from the late 1840s to World War I, which parallels the H trend of demographic growth in that much-discussed receiving population (Figure 1.7). This country for several decades drew in a proportionally constant additive from abroad, a process that must not be lost sight of behind the up-and-down Kuznets cycles around the underlying trend. Immigration *into* Belgium, the Netherlands, and Britain (mostly from their colonies) also assumed H form for a while, though with the t_0's late in the 1800s rather than at the middle of the century. The United States, magnet for so much of Europe, and these three powers with substantial colonies to feed them all seem to have drawn immigration in the H manner for several decades starting in the middle of the 19th century. In the United States the flow paralleled the growth pattern of the total society; in Britain, Belgium, and the Netherlands the H of population increase was appreciably flatter than the H of immigration. Hence, the in-flow seems to have been feeding some *part* of the whole, not its entirety—most probably the industrial sector with the economic growth that transpired between about 1850 and World War I. Examining the employments and places of residence for immigrants in those countries during this era should readily define just what that sub-societal magnet was.

Another small group of exceptions to the predominant G' pattern of migration involved the D curve of constantly decelerating decline. This is most noticeable as the white *populations* of British West Indian islands contracted in similar paths (compare part B of Table 1.5 with Harris 2001, 71, 99). The curves of atrophy in this form for European peoples on Nevis, Montserrat, St. Christopher, and the Bahamas had t_0's in the 1670s right along with those for declining white immigration, though the D curves for Barbados and Jamaica were timed rather earlier and therefore flatter through the later 1600s and early 1700s. As servants were replaced by African slaves, European migration dwindled, thus doing much to bring about the loss of white population. Aggregated, this island-by-island phenomenon stamps its D-form imprint upon the more slowly declining total

number of migrants from England who came to the West Indies and the mainland colonies together after the middle of the 1600s (Figure 1.20a). Overall, the
attractions became less compelling for them, though other nationalities stepped
in to bolster the numbers—especially in flows to the Thirteen Colonies of the
mainland (Figure 1.20b); and estimated total emigration from England generally
rose from the later 1600s through the pre-Revolutionary 1700s (Wrigley and
Schofield 1981, 528–29). The D curves across the bottom of Figure 1.20b, on
the other hand, concern *proportions* of the populations being considered that
were constituted annually by migration. This is one of the G-based patterns of
structural demographic change or altering composition that is discussed in later
chapters.

In four cases among the many illustrations of migration trends that are presented in this chapter, the downwardly accelerating C pattern appears. In a global
survey of changes in population size, this pattern has been the mark of socio-
economic systems failing to maintain a niche, like unsuccessful, would-be sugar
islands (Harris 2001, ch. 3). That the flow of Dutch East India Company manpower sent to Asia should drop off in C fashion 1765–1792 as the VOC approached failure at the end of the century seems consistent with such an
interpretation. So does the 1835–1865 dive of immigration to Australia as the
transportation of convicts fell out of favor at both ends of the process of transportation (Figure 1.22). Why French shipment of indentured workers, mostly
from India, collapsed in similar accelerating manner after Mauritius and Réunion
had opened up this globally popular substitute for banned slaving in a big way
(Figure 1.24) must be left to those who know the details. But failure to compete
with the British for Indian labor—perhaps after a British change of policy—
seems fortified as an explanation in contrast to local satiation of supply through
rapid natural increase of the new workers on the Mascarene Islands in the face
of the fact that such trends of transition from immigrant to native in most known
historical contexts have for their decline taken D, not C, shape. In the end—as
so often the case in the study of migration—we come back to the Irish diaspora,
whose flow to destinations other than the United States drained away ever faster
in C form from the 1850s to World War I. Possibilities of how this happened
have been raised in discussion of Figure 1.1.

Finally, a little evidence of migration in upwardly accelerating E shape has
appeared. This emerges so far in our survey only after the 1860s in the movement of people, white and non-white, across the regions of the United States
and the accumulation of foreign-born population in the South and the West of
that country (Figures 1.12, 1.13, and 1.14; Table 1.3). More work is needed to
understand the reasons for this pattern; but it may well be linked to the E-type
demographic increases associated in several parts of the world, both historically
and currently, with cheap mass labor stages or forms of industrialization.

In conclusion, G' has been the overwhelmingly most frequent trend for migration historically, while reasonable hypotheses come to mind for where and
how a few kinds of similarly G-based infrequent exceptions occur. G' migrations

would seem to predominate (and repeatedly foster demographic increase in G form) at least in part because of the way that the renewal of migrant populations or sub-populations works—how native children progressively take over and make further in-migration less appealing from the perspective of both the giving and the receiving peoples. How renewal might repeatedly take this shape, a next level of excavation as our analysis digs deeper and deeper, is taken up in Chapters 5 and 6.

So far, however, the discussion has been largely silent concerning the most notorious and one of largest historical migrations of all, the Atlantic slave trade. According to what patterns did this filthy business that was so vital for so much of the Americas obtain and distribute its "product"? How did these movements differ from trends for migrants who enjoyed various degrees of freedom?

NOTES

1. For the general discussion here the basic sources have been B. R. Mitchell 1992, 124–38; 1995, 85–87; and 1993, 90–97 along with U.S. Bureau of the Census (*Historical Statistics*) 1975, 2: 105–9, Series C 89–119 and Woodruff 1966, 103–11.

2. For 1825–1845, including separating out the Maritime Provinces from all of Canada, his corrected departures from Ireland to the United States and to British North America are employed (413–15). For earlier years, the same fractions of his numbers for New Brunswick and Quebec are added to Young's U.S. estimates (Adams 1932, 418–22) or—for 1816–1819—developed from Adams's numbers for the United States and British North America and, within the latter, the weight between Quebec and the Maritime Provinces among emigrants sailing from Belfast 1818–1819 (426, 420).

3. For the first two, data from Adams for the United States and British North America are taken, with no need to apportion Canadian arrivals for eventual residence south of the border. Half of all immigrants to Australia in these early years, convict and free (Vamplew 1987, 4), are considered to have been Irish. The 420,000 Irish resident in Britain (especially London, Manchester, Liverpool, and Glasgow) by 1841 (Handlin 1972, 42) are estimated here to reflect about 7,000 immigrants a year in the 1810s, 9,000 in the 1820s, 11,000 in the 1830s, and 14,000 in the early 1840s. Again, those who may have better numbers can test the consequences of these for the overall trending proposed.

4. If half the convicts were Irish, something like 8,000 per year were shipped Down Under in the 1810s, 16,000 in the 1820s, and 25,000 in the 1830s (Vamplew 1987, 4; Figure 1.22).

5. Entry to the United States by *land* was not measured much until the 1850s.

6. Levels for England, Wales, and Scotland before 1850 are estimated by subtracting Irish arriving in the United States (*Historical Statistics*) from total emigration recorded for the United Kingdom (Mitchell 1992).

7. To estimate this, British immigration to the United States is subtracted from calculations for all emigration out of England, Wales, and Scotland. In addition to the quinquennial symbols, averages are presented for the years 1832–1837, 1852–1862, and 1867–1877 in order to indicate the more likely G nature of the underlying trend. What would be the best G' fit for the same time span is presented as well, by the curve with the lighter line.

8. For one discussion of these historical phenomena and their literature, see Harris 1969, 248–93.

9. For France, the 1855–1915 data from Woodruff 1966 show this bend more clearly than the shorter 1857–1892 series from Mitchell 1992. Both results are summarized in the first column of part A of Table 1.1.

10. At 1877, 1884, and 1890, respectively.

11. Though the first spurt of emigration from Italy in Group IV to countries other than the United States took similar timing and would somewhat raise the total European out-flow that followed this third stage of G' path.

12. The low number at 1877 is not included in the curve-fitting. Since Ireland, the nations of Group II, and—to a lesser extent—the migrations in Group III and Group IV all show a dip at this point, it seems probable that something in how people were pulled overseas sagged at this time, not some push dynamic within Europe.

13. This tentative trending ignores the differently symboled low for 1920–1940, which would seem to be a temporary product of the Depression.

14. Fitted but not graphed.

15. The exceptions without any likely E trend were emigration from the East North Central region, in-migration into these same Old Northwest states, and movement into the Pacific zone.

16. More English detail appears in Volume III and other subsequent publication.

17. Kulikoff's further effort (1975, 210) to estimate percentages of slaves emigrating by generation (rather than year of movement) smooths out the actual decadal swings in numbers and proportions. For interregional shifts and for all slave migration alike, the increases for those born 1772–1823 follow G' paths that peak around 1820. The birth cohorts of 1823–1833 and 1833–1843, however, for some reason then tail off below such a trend.

18. Galenson's estimates for Maryland and Virginia together (1981, 217), which are based upon certain assumptions about demographic processes in the colonies (ibid., 212–16), suggest via inspection a G' curve rather earlier than that of Menard, peaking in the early 1650s (closer to Craven's Virginia headrights) rather than 1671.

19. Compare the new estimates offered in Table 1.5 and Figure 1.20a.

20. Galenson's total for the West Indies is rather less stable across the decades and somewhat lower than that of Gemery.

21. He cited (in 1992) "very recent work"—in actuality a draft that Wokeck shared with him of what appeared, after long publication delay, as her 1996 *Royal Academy* article. He made no acknowledgment, however, that the basic pattern of this migration had been presented in her dissertation almost a decade before (Wokeck 1983, 267–68), though Wokeck kept refining the numbers as better information about certain ships became available in her continuing research. In trending her results for Figure 1.19, Wokeck's most recent and complete evidence (1999, 172–73, 180–83) is employed.

22. From Wokeck's computations out of Lockhart, which have been made available by her.

23. In unpublished calculations made available by her for this discussion.

24. That means 18.2 percent for 1681–1699, 35.7 for 1711–1718, and 48.1 for 1719–1729.

25. The data of Dickson (1988, 282–87) show the proportion of vessels going to Maryland and South Carolina rising from 0 to 21 percent across the year groups studied and the New York portion at 21 percent from 1750 through 1769. The New York share

dipped in the early 1770s; but through the 1790s and early 1800s more and more new Americans from the Emerald Isle entered via New York, which by 1815 had captured "the lion's share" of the Irish immigrant trade (Grabbe 1997, 386).

26. More recently, L. M. Cullen (1994, 126, 128, 140) has also built 18th-century estimates upon Wokeck. These are significantly low (for instance 1,000 per annum total North and 500 South 1751–1775) mostly because he underweighs the proportion of the total who probably went to ports outside the Delaware Valley.

27. Fertig (1994, 199) somehow was convinced that Fogleman's "improvement" and the reason for his different Philadelphia numbers derived from the fact that Fogleman varied the ratio for projecting total passengers from men across time. So did Wokeck, as a more careful reading of her work would have revealed (1981, 264–65, especially note 3). While Fogleman may have decided to *change* the ratios across time differently, his method is not disclosed to readers of his dissertation or his 1992 article. He is also silent about how his use of the lists compares with that of von Hippel (1984, 31–36), who in turn did not address Wokeck's discussion of the imperfections of the data and procedures for getting from the listed names to an estimate for total passengers.

28. Fertig (1994, 200–201) paid better attention to Wokeck's ongoing work and is aware of both recording defects in the Stassburger-Hinke lists and the existence of ships that were not covered in these sources. His non-Philadelphia estimates, however, rest like Fogleman's mostly on backward leaps from German names in the 1790 census, not the kind of collection of information on shipping and settlement projects that was compiled by Wokeck (1999). While he appears to have seen some of the Dutch records that Wokeck has mined, he does not *use* these to break free of Fogleman's undercounting. Even Wokeck's amateur research assistant, paid in 5:01 P.M. beer and genever as the Rotterdam archive closed (and dinner on the way back to Amsterdam), has read the English versions of contracts that arranged shipping for "charter parties" not going to Philadelphia. Records like this in the Netherlands, London, and America provide better sources, for those willing to work them, than back-projections from names in the 1790 census.

29. Fogleman says that he distinguishes the 1790 "German" population that had come through Philadelphia ("Group 1") from those who had arrived elsewhere ("Group 2") among those alleged to have German names in the 1790 census. What areas does he conclude were fed by Philadelphia, and how did these *change* over time? Then, how safe is it to assume a similar ratio of immigration to 1790 German population from regions that were settled in quite different periods (with significantly different time spans over which to produce descendants before the first census)? The reliance on 1790 name distributions itself seems a risky basis for making reliable calculations about prior migration, often several decades and more than one generation before. For instance, by then Heinrich Müller has frequently become Henry Miller (especially outside his church).

30. The registers employed by Bailyn capture about 1,500 Scots per year going to the Thirteen Colonies for the months of 1773–1776 that are covered rather than the 4,500 annual total implied by Smout et al. 1994. This is a large difference that could raise questions about the new, higher estimate for 1770–1775. But Bailyn (1986, 76–80) recognizes that the administrative system for locating and reporting the Scottish evidence was weak, including the Clyde (Glasgow etc., through which most Lowlanders came). Whether it was so poor as to register only one-third of out-bound Scots could stand some further research.

31. Bailyn found 5, 12, and 39 percent of arrrivals in Virginia, Maryland, and New York, respectively, to be missing from the exit registers (1986, 93) even among debarkations that were predominantly English rather than generally less well recorded Scots.

32. In his 1986 treatment (35), Gemery confusingly lists estimates per decade for *all white* immigrants to British America from Galenson (1981) alongside his own calculation of *British* emigrants to the colonies and *English* migration from Wrigley and Schofield. Still, the ultimately relatively level trend for numbers coming to the Thirteen Colonies between 1650 and 1775 stands out.

33. Chapter 2 reexamines the migrations of the international slave trade.

34. Even the usually careful Cullen estimates the Irish to have been weightier in the 17th-century New World total than they were. If all the 400 Irish per year whom he calculates had gone to the Caribbean (1994, 139—I assume all traveled after 1625), they would have composed only about 8 percent of the 4,900 annual British flow there according to Gemery for the 1630s and 1640s; and 16 percent for the 1650–1700 era. It is hard to see how the Irish made the largest single European contribution to the islands (Cullen 1994, 113). Meanwhile, the *rate* of total Irish emigration that his population figures and emigration estimates imply around 1625, 1675, 1725, and 1762 (1994, 139–40) is consistently well below the rate for these time periods for total English emigration according to Wrigley and Schofield 1981—51, 63, 83, and 82 percent of the English proportion per annum, respectively (much of that early flow being *into* Ireland, as Cullen fully understands). The rate of *out*-migration for Ulster that he stresses (139–40) indeed was exceptionally high, though about 0.69 percent annually (assuming a regional population of approximately 400,000 around 1770) rather than the 1.00 percent level that he estimates.

35. Actually 1541–1560 through 1601–1625. (The first line in his table reads "1506–1560" whereas the end of this period was at 1540, as indicated by the next line and his sum for 1506–1560.) The t_0 for passengers and sailors together comes at 1548. The curve for passengers alone (who outnumbered non-returning seamen by more than two to one) came slightly earlier, and that for sailors rather later; but both also apparently took G form separately from 1550 to 1612 (judging by averages for three time periods between 1540 and 1625).

36. Martellone (1984, 401, 404) cites military service for the Italo-Turkish War, a short recession in the United States, and a dispute with Argentina over the health inspection of immigrants as reasons for the drop-back that began in 1911.

37. Though, alternatively, a steeper and later-timed G' trend is possible for 1845–1885, followed by a drop in level for the 1890s, 1900s, and 1910s.

Chapter 2

The International Slave Trade, 1450–1850: Further Perspective on Familiar Movements

Upon first consideration, slaving—the forced relocation of captives in chains from one part of the world to another—might seem a form of migration immune to demographic influences, just a matter of business dynamics. Do the G-related movements observed in more voluntary migrations then simply not apply to flows of slaves? Upon further thought, though, how many new laborers were desired in various regions of consumption and available for enslavement in a variety of African sources can be seen to be sensitive to demographic developments on both sides of the Atlantic.

One of the most thoroughly and expertly worked topics in the recent historical literature has been the Atlantic slave trade. This early modern commerce in forced labor collected and shipped millions of persons to the New World and other destinations from the 1400s through the 1800s. The traffic of western European powers in Africans has been quantified across time more informatively than many other historical migrations. Do these slaving activities follow the same patterns that have been observed among the movements of free and only temporarily bound peoples who were mostly of European extraction?

The nasty commerce in forcibly obtained and held humans can be viewed through several steps of its operation. How did the demand for Africans wax and wane in various parts of the world? How did the roles of certain regions of Africa in supplying slaves change with time? What happened to the parts played in the business of transportation by slavers from different countries? Did both obtaining slaves and delivering them to consumers of labor unfold at the local level along the same patterns as the larger, aggregate flows; or did they instead display their own trends through time? Answers to these and related questions significantly extend our understanding of how migration has worked historically, comparing its most coerced form with what has been learned from the historical movements of free families and individuals, servants, indentured workers, and convicts. What is general and what has been exceptional in this most notorious form of migration?

SLAVE IMPORTS TO MAJOR REGIONS OF CONSUMPTION

Figures 2.1a, 2.1b, and 2.1c plot trends for the numbers of slaves imported into various consuming regions: to Europe and the Atlantic islands off Africa in the early years, then to various parts of the Americas. Table 2.1 compares and contrasts these trend shapes and their timing. The information comes from several sources and summations available in an active literature that has been growing and maturing for half a century.[1]

Many of us, though chipping away at it and refining it, have for more than 30 years been fruitfully employing the path-breaking "*Census*" of Philip D. Curtin (1969). My own perceptions concerning the nature of the trends in the slave trade and confirmations of the chronological patterns involved originally developed with the resources provided by that splendid seminal work. The analysis of this chapter to a great extent reinforces once again just how good Curtin's study was. Herbert S. Klein's handy recent summary of the numbers (1999, 210–11) mostly draws upon Curtin but blends in subsequent findings by David Eltis (1987) for the later decades of the trade. In dealing with British North America, further calculations from Eltis (2000, 48) and Russell R. Menard (McCusker and Menard 1991, 136) provided additions and corrections that I knew to be important while I was pulling together past explorations to draft this chapter back during the twilight years of the last millennium.

Then out came the magnificent source represented by the CD-ROM database of *The Atlantic Slave Trade* (Eltis, Behrendt, Richardson, and Klein 1999) followed by a summary of some of its key evidence through time by Eltis (2001). On top of everything else involved in this present study, it did not seem feasible to delve anew in this rich data set for the very latest evidence, as several scholars of the trade have already done most productively. Eltis's summary, however, makes possible insightful comparison of the trends that are indicated by the new—sometimes more complete, sometimes still quite incomplete—evidence based upon shipping records that the CD-ROM provides (this database is still a work in progress) with the patterns previously derived from Curtin and others. These blend the best business data available at their time with contemporary estimates of this or that part of the trade and historical knowledge of the growth of slave populations, areas and eras of illicit or otherwise perhaps unrecorded traffic, and so forth. As Eltis has pointed out (2001, 17), few revolutionary divergences appear in the trends observed. Nevertheless, departures of one kind of series from the other are significant at certain times and places. Perhaps a third of all slave voyages between 1527 and 1866 are not covered in the CD-ROM, and many calculations depend upon inferences (Smallwood 2001, 257, 259). The discrepancies between the new database and older published evidence raise some intriguing issues that still must be addressed.

European slaving from Africa[2] first took labor to Europe: to Portugal, Spain, Sicily, and Italy. Then the labor desires of sugar-growers and other colonists drew the trade to the islands of the eastern Atlantic: to Portuguese Madeira, the Azores, and the Cape Verdes and to the Canaries controlled by Spain. Table 2.1 and Figure 2.1a show how the flow to Europe probably took a G' form that crested about 1478 then fell across the 1500s and 1600s as such a pattern would dictate. The table indicates how undisplayed graphing for the aggregate intake to the Atlantic Islands without São Tomé apparently rose in a G' path between 1463 and 1513 with its t_0 near 1497. Slave imports to these ocean outposts were held close to that level by a second G' surge that crested about 1540 but then declined down this familiar shape of track through the later 1500s.[3]

Far to the south, São Tomé sits closely but safely offshore in the right-angled joint where the west-to-east coast of the hump that forms western Africa encounters, past modern Nigeria, the north-to-south shore that runs down along the Congo and Angola. The Portuguese plunged aggressively into cane cultivation here toward the end of the 15th century, drawing upon coerced labor extracted from mainland sources. Slave imports surged from 1488 (1475–1500) forward along a G' trajectory with peak year at 1546 before tapering off along this track to 1588, as Table 2.1 indicates. Joseph C. Miller (2002, 24–25) has recently summarized how slave shipments from Luanda and Benin (until the rulers of the latter region terminated slave exports in 1516) fed this flow to São Tomé. After 1580, when the kingdoms of Portugal and Spain were merged, Portuguese slavers began to divert cargoes to Spanish America. The combination of these movements for São Tomé with the generally smaller numbers for the more northern Atlantic Islands produces a G' curve for the years 1488–1588 with t_0 at 1533 in Figure 2.1a. Then, a second G' pattern with base year at 1591 temporaily broke the decline in the imports of São Tomé across the 1600s. Along with the beginnings of a slave trade to the Spanish New World—where colonists, among other activities, dared to cultivate sugar cane in the face of opposition from entrenched Andalusian growers—these differently timed G' waves of regional importation added up to yield what was probably a G trend for the Atlantic slave trade as a whole for the years 1488–1563 (between 1475 and 1575). This curve had its t_0 at 1498, as the right-most column of Table 2.1 indicates.[4]

Slaving to early Spanish America, which carried westward across the Atlantic practices that had been developed in the Canaries as well as Portuguese holdings off the African coast, is one part of the historical record where data seem to be elusive and erratic. Curtin's estimates of three decades ago (Klein 1999, 210–11) at 1538, 1563, and 1588 (1525 through 1600 in 25-year groupings) suggest a G-shaped rise in annual intake with base year at 1549. If projected forward,

Table 2.1
Trends of Slave Imports into Various Atlantic Regions, 1450–1850

G' Type Regional Surges		G Form Regional Expansions		All Atlantic Imports
Europe	1463-1663 G' 1478			1488-1563 G 1498
Atlantic Islands I	1463-1513 G' 1497			
Atlantic Islands II	1538-1588 G'			
Sao Tomé I	1488-1588 G' 1546	Spanish America I	1538-1638 G 1549	1560-1638 G 1569
Sao Tomé II	1588-1688 G' 1591	Brazil I	1560-1688 G 1593	
		Spanish America II	1663-1785 G 1650	1638-1785 H 1645
Dutch West Indies I	1663-1738 ?G' 1671	British Caribbean I	1638-1730 G 1670	1663-1763 H 1677e
		French Caribbean I	1636-1730 G 1691	
		Brazil II	1688-1785 G 1691	
Brit. Mainland America I	1645-1705 G' 1704em			
Danish West Indies	1688-1795 G' 1725c	British Caribbean II	1730-1770 G 1720	
		French Caribbean II	1730-1770 G 1724	
		"	1713-1763 G 1734e	
Dutch West Indies II	1738-1788 G' 1753			1785-1838 D 1752
Brit. Mainland America II	1710-1785 G' 1757			
Guianas	1713-1813 G' 1760			
		Brazil III	1785-1845 G 1781	
Spanish America III?	1785-1859 G' 1828	Spanish America III?	1785-1835 G 1804	

e Eltis 2001. em Combination of Eltis 2000 and Menard numbers (see text). c From Curtin.

Sources: Klein 1999, 210–11; Eltis 2000, 48; Eltis 2001, 45; McCusker and Menard 1991, 136; Curtin 1969, 119, 216.

Figure 2.1a
Imports from the Atlantic Slave Trade 1463–1865: Total, Europe, the Atlantic Islands and São Tomé, Dutch Caribbean, and Spanish America

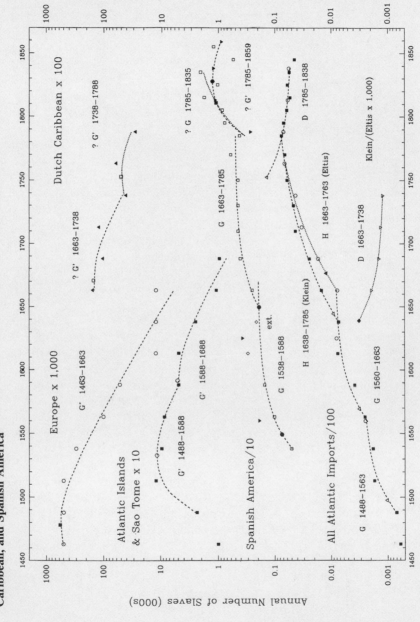

Sources: Klein (Curtin, etc.) 1999, 210–11: Eltis 2001, 45. See text for which data are fitted.

this curve almost exactly hits his estimate at 1638 (hollow diamond), though for the time period 1600–1625 his calculation somehow rises well above this trajectory. Drawing upon the new database, meanwhile, Eltis (2001, 45) gives comparably higher annual averages for 1519–1600 and 1600–1650 (represented by the solid, downward triangles above the fitted curve). The high levels for these very broad data groups around 1560 and 1625, however, would conform to an elevated G pattern of only slightly later timing than that for Curtin's lower numbers. The new perspective suggests that long-term development in deliveries to Spanish America may have grown the same way—though there was a decided spike of activity in the later 1590s (Eltis 2001, 24, drawing upon Vila Vilar 1977)—but at a higher level (unless, of course, the CD-ROM database includes importing territory that Curtin did not cover). This is one place where some further analysis by those who best know the data and its historical setting seems called for.

By the second half of the 1500s, however, the big story was Brazil, to which in the early part of the century the Portuguese transplanted both sugar and African slavery. Imports there surged upward into the later 1600s, as Figure 2.1b suggests, along a G path with base year at about 1590. The stronger curve presented on the graph extends a fit to the older Curtin data of just 1563–1638 on toward 1688, where the estimates of Curtin and Eltis from the new database lie close to each other. Indeed, the two series (symbolized by solid squares and hollow circles, respectively) are for the most part close enough to each other to fit the lighter G curve for the years 1560–1688 (1519–1700) with base year at 1593 rather than 1590 to their combined annual averages—with one exception. The problem is a very low number for the third quarter of the 17th century from the CD-ROM database (hollow circle) in contrast to a rather high average for the period from Curtin's analysis (filled square). Certain, possibly incomplete, regional imports to Bahia and to northeastern Brazil (Pernambuco, etc.), meanwhile, according to the wide groupings of time employed by Eltis (2001, 45), may have risen and fallen off between 1519 and 1675 in G' fashion as indicated in Figure 2.1b. Much of the Portuguese trade, though, is apparently not covered in the CD-ROM database (Eltis 2001, 23; Smallwood 2001, 259).

Recently, Miller has been more specific about the data problems of this era. He sees, after the early 1600s, "growing (but unrecorded) shipments to Pernambuco and Bahia" (2002, 26, note 10). He considers between 1650 and 1699 a "barely documented" period. His own estimates for the Portuguese trade of this era are 50 percent higher than those of scholars relying on the CD-ROM database. In his words, "The late seventeenth-century shipments from Central Africa of Brazil—mostly Pernambuco—remain one of the least satisfactorily documented periods in the entire Atlantic slave trade" (ibid., 65, note g). The database comparisons for 1651–1675 and 1676–1700 in Figure 2.1b, moreover, suggest that most of the shortfall resides in the *third* quarter of the 17th century, when Portugal regained independence from Spain and northern Europeans pushed their way into the Atlantic slave trade on a large scale.

Figure 2.1b

Imports from the Atlantic Slave Trade, 1463–1865: Brazil and Its Major Regions

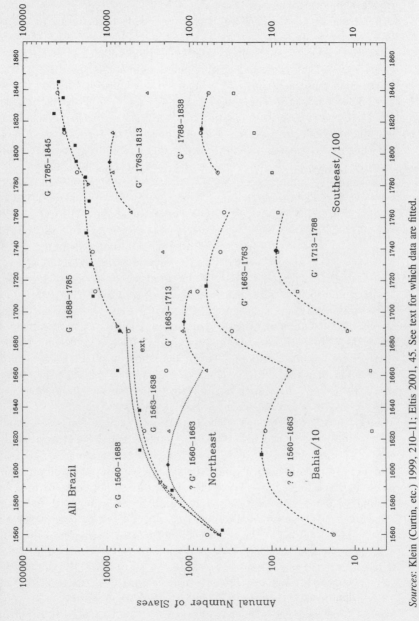

Sources: Klein (Curtin, etc.) 1999, 210–11; Eltis 2001, 45. See text for which data are fitted.

Later discussion in this chapter attempts to hold various perspectives on slaving to Brazil up against each other in order to identify what trending for the later 1600s is best and what further analysis is needed. The database calculation for slave imports to the tiny Dutch Caribbean islands (Figure 2.1a)—which were largely conduits to mainland colonies—for example, displays a hump, possibly of G' shape, from 1650 through 1750 while deliveries to the Guianas (Figure 2.1c), next door to northeastern Brazil, likewise entail a high number around 1663 (1650–1675) in the recent summarization by Eltis (2001, 45). How many slaves from these delivery points, recorded or unrecorded, ended up in Brazil as well as what is now Venezuela? The Dutch had held northeastern Brazil from the 1630s into the 1650s, running the slave trade to the region and capturing key trading stations in Africa. Did all transactions just stop with Portuguese reoccupation—especially at a time when recorded Portuguese slave deliveries, according to the database at least, may have dropped substantially, and plantations had to be rebuilt after Dutch withdrawal? Or is a substantial portion of Portuguese slave-trafficking simply not covered in the surviving shipping records of this period? Eltis (2001, 24–25) employs analogy with the establishment of sugar production in the British Caribbean to justify lowering older estimations of Brazilian imports. Yet he stresses how much more efficient the British were in business; and, almost certainly, by his own calculation (2000, 48—see Figure 2.1c here) the database significantly underrepresents slave intake to the British Caribbean during the third quarter of the 17th century.

The comparatively small figure of the current CD-ROM for Brazil does much to pull the total for the Atlantic trade below Curtin's earlier estimate at 1663 (for 1650–1675). Still, from 1560 through 1638 (Curtin via Klein 1999) or 1663 (Eltis 2001) recorded deliveries out of the whole business—fading in Europe, the Atlantic Islands, and São Tomé but expanding in Spanish America and especially Brazil—rose approximately in G fashion with base year at 1569 if both series are trended together, as in Figure 2.1a.

Again, from 1688 through 1785, the annual averages for Brazil from Curtin (Klein 1999) and from Eltis (2001) are similar enough to fit as a single series with a G curve based at 1691, though the evidence around 1710 from both sources is somewhat high. Figure 2.1b also shows how, according to the record of the database, successive G' waves of imports to northeastern Brazil, Bahia, and the Southeast (Rio de Janeiro, etc.) probably contributed to the G shape of the whole huge colony. According to Curtin, a second surge of slave trading into Spanish America between 1663 and 1785 accompanied this total Brazilian movement, though with an appreciably earlier base year for the flatter G curve segment, at 1650 rather than 1691. Table 2.1 and Figure 2.1a show this. What are not graphed are the very low estimates of Eltis from the CD-ROM database for Spanish America across this period: no evidence for the years 1650–1675 where Curtin calculated about 2,500 annually, 280 per year rather than 4,100 around 1688, 1,280, 570, and 720 across the first three quarters of the 18th century as opposed to more like 4,500 estimated by Curtin for 1700 through

1760 from various historical perspectives, and even more in the years 1760–1780. As of the middle 1600s the supply of slaves to Spanish America switched to Dutch and English control from the Portuguese, who apparently never got back into this particular trade (Eltis 2001, 24). Transshipments from Curaçao, Barbados, Jamaica, and other bases of inter-American slave trading are not yet included in the CD-ROM. As many as 85 percent of Dutch Caribbean imports went quickly to Spanish America. Numerically, transfers from Jamaica were even more substantial (ibid., 35, 36; Introduction to *Database*, 23; see also Figure 2.10a for Jamaica, below). Re-shipments to Spanish America from Curaçao, Barbados, and Jamaica in the 17th century are especially difficult to calculate. Curtin's old estimates seem preferable until more information on transshipments is available in the new data set.

During the early 1600s, meanwhile, the French and the British in turn introduced slave-cultivated sugar to their West Indian possessions. Labor imports for these scattered holdings in the Leeward and Windward Islands, Jamaica, and St. Domingue (modern Haiti) likewise developed in G form, as Figure 2.1c and Table 2.1 indicate. The French Caribbean surge paralleled the second G for Brazil with t_0 at 1691; the G for the British Caribbean came between the Brazilian and Spanish patterns in timing, with base year at 1670. This opening British trend is calculated using as one series recent computations by Eltis (2000, 48), the solid, upward triangles, and Curtin's estimates for 1638 through 1730 (Klein 1999, 210–11), the solid squares.[5] The hollow circles represent annual averages from the CD-ROM database (Eltis 2001, 45). At 1625, 1688, and 1713 these lie with or somewhat above the fitted trend. (In the early 1700s, substantial reexports from Jamaica are not taken out of the total.) At 1663 (for the years 1650–1675) the number is very low, amounting to less than 40 percent of the curve for the other data at this point. Such a cut in the slave trade for this quarter of a century makes no substantive sense. The British at that time were aggressively expanding sugar cultivation with bound African labor, and slave populations on their islands were exploding (Harris 2001, 72, 74–75).[6] Reproduction was very limited, so this growth came from imports. Something substantial appears to be missing in the CD-ROM, though Eltis captured the likely numbers in his 2000 estimations. As Eltis has warned (2001, 17–18), while a splendid source for many purposes, the database is not an infallible foundation from which to quantify slave importation in certain places at certain times. This especially appears to be true in the 17th century, when northern European and Iberian powers were jockeying with each other for control of the Atlantic, seizing each other's colonies and shipping, and not always trading the way that government policy and current international alliances or enmities prescribed.

There is, Figure 2.1c shows, also substantial divergence in calculating imports into the French Caribbean. According to Curtin (Klein 1999), annual numbers surged in G fashion from 1638 through 1730 along a G track with t_0 at 1691. From the current CD-ROM database, in contrast, while estimates around 1625 and 1660 start upward in much the same way (hollow diamonds), the increase

Figure 2.1c
**Imports from the Atlantic Slave Trade: British and French Caribbean, British
North America, and the Guianas**

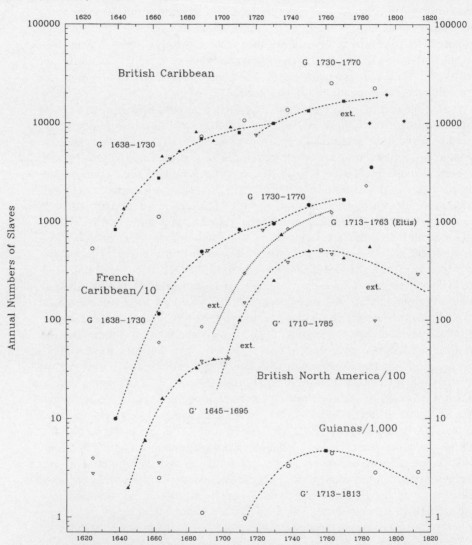

Sources: Klein (Curtin, etc.,) 1999, 210–11; Eltis 2000, 48; 2001, 45; McCusker and Menard 1991,
136, 154.

breaks back for the quarter century around 1688 and then takes G form from about 1700 through 1775 with the delayed base year of 1734. The late 17th century was *not* a slow period for the development of French sugar cultivation, as the rapid growth of African *populations* on Martinique, Guadeloupe, St. Croix, and St. Domingue across the late 1600s indicate (Harris 2001, 72, 74). Once again the database is significantly short. Eltis (2001, 37) agrees with Curtin that in the 17th century slaves for the French islands were mostly not carried by French vessels. Also the editors of the database (Introduction, 4–5) have concluded that "much of the seventeenth-century French traffic is missing."

From the perspective of the database, low numbers for both the British and the French Caribbean colonies during the later 1600s join a Brazilian drop and the incomplete evidence for Spanish America in this era to lower or to postpone expansion in average slave consumption for the Atlantic as a whole in the manner shown near the bottom of Figure 2.1a. That is, while from 1638 through 1785 the numbers as estimated by Curtin (Klein 1999) rise in H form with base year at 1645, the trend for the yearly averages from the CD-ROM records, though also taking H shape, swell along a trend of this sort that begins only at 1688 and that has an appreciably later t_0 of 1677, as Table 2.1 summarizes. The very bottom plot in Figure 2.1a shows how the ratio of aggregate numbers based upon Curtin's calculations (Klein 1999, 210–11) to Atlantic totals from the database (Eltis 2001) shrank systematically in D fashion from 1.91 (almost double) around 1663 (1650–1675) to 1.22 by 1738 (1725–1750)—continuing then to 0.95 at 1763 and 1.09 at 1788, or roughly equal. Overall, this trend seems to reflect progressive improvement in the commercial organization and governmental supervision of the international trade—essential foundations for relatively full and reliable accounts—which are unlikely to have been comprehensive all at once. As put by the editors of the CD-ROM (Introduction, 4), "later in the slave trade era . . . everyone kept better records."

Further, fresh and quite parallel, G trends for the British and French colonies that commenced around 1730 contribute, according to the estimates of Curtin (Klein 1999, 210–11), to such overall expansion of New World slave consumption in H form across the 18th century. For the British Caribbean, averages from the database for the years 1725–1750 and 1775–1800 (hollow circles, Eltis 2001, 45) run about as much higher as the number for the years 1700–1725. More deliveries have been uncovered since Curtin's effort three decades ago; but at the same time substantial reexports have not been extracted to estimate regional consumption properly. In the end, however, the trending probably remains parallel. The high database exception at 1763 (1750–1775) would seem to reflect shipments inspired by seizures of French plantation holdings during the Seven Years War, which added new cane-producing areas under British control. For French colonies, meanwhile, the database numbers (hollow diamonds) run lower than Curtin's older estimates, though they similarly shoot up with the drive of the 1780s to pack slaves into St. Domingue, which contributed to the hemisphere-shaking revolt of the early 1790s. Some part of the difference in level comes from the fact that Cayenne appears with the islands in the Curtin plot but with the other Guianas from the CD-ROM database.

The other historical cases of an H shape of trend in immigration that have been encountered in this study were into the United States from about 1845 to World War I (Figure 1.7), as that country industrialized with the help of immigrants from many European origins, and into Britain, Belgium, and the Netherlands over the same 19th-century period of Western economic development (Figure 1.8), drawing in large part upon the relatively populous overseas dependencies of these nations. The implication here is that across the later 17th century and almost all of the 18th century the forced migration of Africans fed the economic growth of the European colonies of the New World and their motherlands in much the same way. This adds new insight as well as new support to the classic thesis of Eric Williams (1944) about the significance of African slavery for the growth of both the Americas and Europe.

In U.S. immigration of the 1800s, the H path for the increase in incoming people paralleled in timing, and therefore slope, the growth of the *population* of the United States. It is difficult to aggregate the populations of all slave-based colonial societies to compare with total imports of Africans—primarily because of incomplete information for relevant parts of Spanish America. Still, Tables 2.1, 3.2, and 4.4 in the first volume of this study (Harris 2001) have identified H trends in the *total* populations of Virginia 1670–1710 (with t_0 at 1671), Cuba 1700–1792 (1693), Jamaica 1710–1770 (1698), Brazil 1690–1823 (1710), St. Domingue 1720–1780 (1723), and South Carolina 1720–1770 (1768). These suggest that the H pattern of demographic increase was a familiar one in *plantation societies* of the Western Hemisphere during the era in question. Using McCusker (1970, 2: 712) and McCusker and Menard (1991, 154, 136, 172), furthermore, it is possible to aggregate the slave population at least of the French West Indies and the British colonies of America (including the mainland). These numbers (not shown here) swelled along a rapidly decelerating G path from 1650 through 1700 whose base year came at about 1686, in between the t_0's of 1670 and 1691, respectively, for the G-shaped English and French slave imports of that era. Then, from 1710 through 1780 the total slave population of British America and the French Caribbean together multiplied in H form with base year at about 1726, approximately where French and British *G* trends for slave imports after 1730 had their t_0's (1724 and 1720). In other words, up into the early 1700s for the major northern European colonial powers, at least, it took G-shaped imports of Africans to produce G-shaped growth in the slave population. Thereafter, at least up to the new surge of the French trade at the end of the century, G-type trends in slave intake produced a stronger, more slowly decelerating *H* pattern of expansion in the slave numbers. The implication is that some degree of replacement via reproduction, though mostly not yet amounting to positive natural increase, was now occurring in the African American populations of the French Caribbean, the British West Indies, and the mainland colonies of British North America.[7] Since $H = G/G'^{-2}$, some way that migration naturalizes or normalizes involving G-based movements is again indicated.[8]

Imports to lesser or newer peripheral zones of slave employment—to the mainland colonies of British North America, to the Danish and Dutch West Indies, to the Guianas—continued, however, to take just the G' shape, like other regional footholds or market expansions for African slavery preceding them that are listed in the left portion of Table 2.1.[9] The first wave into British mainland North America, with t_0 at 1704, is based upon calculations by Eltis (2000, 48) and—for the 1640s—Menard (McCusker and Menard 1991, 136).[10] For the years 1650–1675 the average from the new data base (hollow downward triangles) is once again substantially lower for some reason, though at 1688 the two series match and continue to do so through the next G' surge for the region, which crested around 1757—a trend that may have extended into the first quarter of the 19th century, as up-and-down evidence from the two sources suggests. It is often difficult to separate colonial or early U.S. vessels from British ones (*Database*, Introduction, 25); and in the waning years of the trade the American flag could be carried on vessels in fact belonging to Spanish or Portuguese owners (Eltis 2001, 25). In the Guianas, a G' wave of slave imports from 1713 through 1813 topped out in the vicinity of 1760, while a new G' maximum for the Dutch Caribbean (Figure 2.1a) may have arrived near 1753, according to the database computations of Eltis (2001, 45). Better detail on Dutch deliveries is presented shortly in Figures 2.5a and 2.5b.

As international opposition to slavery gained momentum, from the 1780s into the 1840s, average annual numbers of slaves received from the Atlantic slave trade declined, probably in the kind of D form indicated in Figure 2.1a by estimates both from Curtin and from the database. The Dutch trade collapsed in the last several years of the 18th century; the French one was decimated by the revolt on St. Domingue, though it struggled along for a while. British slaving and imports into the United States were abolished in the early 1800s. Portuguese, Brazilian, U.S., and French ships, however, continued to serve 19th-century demand—primarily for the plantations and mines of Brazil and for the Spanish islands of the Caribbean, where sugar cultivation was aggressively expanding. Average annual numbers entering Brazil probably rose in G fashion from the 1780s into the 1840s (Figure 2.1b). Imports into the United States continued to drop off reluctantly, in spite of the constitutional ban, from a G' peak in the late 1750s into the early 1800s (Figure 2.1c). Traffic into the Spanish Caribbean, primarily Cuba, from the 1780s rose to an all-time maximum in the 1830s. Figure 2.1a indicates that this dying spurt may have taken either G shape between 1785 and 1835 or G' form if one follows the flow through to 1859 (1851–1867).

These regional shifts in consumption brought about the D trend of decline in the Atlantic slave trade as a whole from the 1780s into the 1840s. British naval patrols and the discovery of willing contract workers, principally from India, then fairly much finished it off by the middle of the century.

Both local G' waves of importation and slowing, but not reversing, G trends of expansion for wider and more complex segments of Atlantic imports of Africans tended to follow each other about every two to two-and-a-half decades apart, as Table 2.1 shows, though some gaps appear in the sequence. These successive G' waves or more durable G-shape surges upward in the volume of recorded or estimated deliveries appear to reflect Kuznetsian "long swings" in the international slave trade that reach back three to four centuries before the U.S. data of the 1800s from which the theory of such fluctuations was developed.[11] The spacing resembles that for the series of crests in European immigration to the United States that appeared in the first section of Chapter 1 (especially Table 1.1 and Figures 1.6 and 1.7).

In all, across four centuries of Atlantic history the rise and the fall of slaving in its major markets took G-based forms everywhere. Humpbacked G' was typically the shape of penetration into new, local, or marginal territories, where a maximum was attained in response to fresh opportunities or a change in circumstances but then could not be sustained. Slowing but more lasting and not declining G trends were the form for persistent, well-capitalized, broad, and compounded regional expansions of the business. During its inglorious prime the Atlantic trade as a whole even magnified for a century and a half between the 1630s and the 1780s along the kind of H path associated elsewhere with inmigration during major, lasting, and accumulative economic development, as in the United States between the 1840s and the 1910s (Figure 1.7).

G-BASED TRENDS IN PROVIDING HUMAN CARGOES

It is one thing for imports of slaves into the major consuming areas to take G' and G forms. But do such patterns also appear in how coerced laborers were *supplied*? Chapter 1's analysis of European movements has shown that *emigration* as well as immigration repeatedly took the basic G-related shapes. Does the same apply to the regions of Africa that provided the miserable cargoes of the slave trade?

Figures 2.2a and 2.2b and Table 2.2 demonstrate that it does. Less is known about the number of Africans embarked and the loading points of slave voyages than about how many were delivered and where. The *Database* (Introduction, 9) currently includes the former information outbound for just 7,437 and 15,493 of a total of 27,237 voyages compared with 15,778 and 20,403 arriving in the Americas. Informed inferences by Eltis (2001, 44), however, allocate the partially known or contextually indicated in ways that significantly enrich our previous understanding of the trends in supplying slaves from various coasts of Africa.[12]

The newly adjusted and synthesized evidence, and Eltis's deft and sensible handling of it, fill out gaps and clarify patterns in what was previously visible from gradually accumulating published sources. The new estimations on this

Figure 2.2a
Estimated Annual Slave Exports from Various Parts of Africa: All to Atlantic Trade, West Central Africa, Bight of Benin, Bight of Biafra

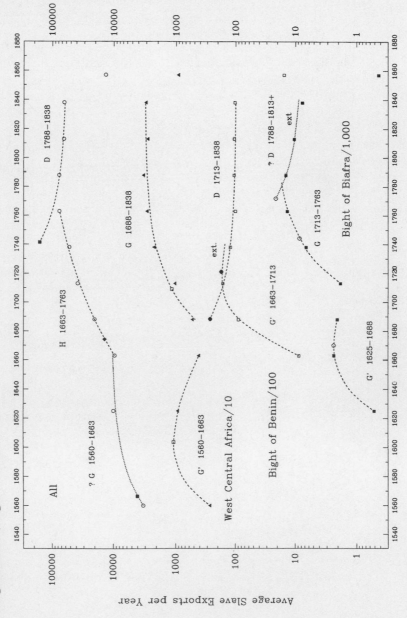

Source: Eltis 2001, 44.

Figure 2.2b
Estimated Annual Slave Exports from Various Parts of Africa: Senegambia, Sierra Leone, Windward and Gold Coasts, Southeast Africa

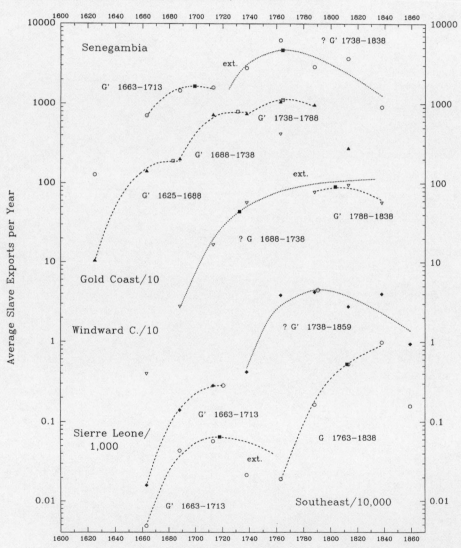

Source: Eltis 2001, 44.

Table 2.2
Estimated Regional Trends of Slave Exports to the Atlantic

Region	Entry Phase			Phase II			Phase III		
West Central Africa	1560-1663	G'	1604	1688-1838	G	1709*			
Bight of Biafra	1625-1688	G'	1670	1713-1763	G	1744*	1788,1813+	D	1772
Gold Coast	1625-1688	G'	1683	1688-1738	G'	1731	1738-1788	G'	1765
Senegambia	1663-1713	G'	1699	1738-1838	?G'	1715			
Southeast Africa	1663-1713	G'	1718	1763-1838	G	1812*			
Bight of Benin	1663-1713	G'	1721	1713-1838	D	1688			
Sierra Leone	1663-1713	G'	1721	1738-1859	?G'	1791			
Windward Coast	1688-1738	G	1733*	1788-1838	G'	1803			
Total to Atlantic	1560-1663	G	1566*	1663-1763	H	1674	1788-1838	D	1742
American Imports	1560-1638	G	1569*	1663-1763	H	1677^e	1785-1838	D	1752
				1638-1763	H	1645^f			

* = G rather than G' growth; ^{e} = Eltis 2001; ^{f} = with fuller estimation from Figures 2.1a and 2.1b
for the later 1600s.

Sources: Figures 2.2a and 2.2b.

topic, though it must be remembered that much inferring is involved, do more
to change what over the years I had surmised from Curtin (1969), Richardson
(1989), Miller (1992), Klein (1999), and other sources than my conclusions on
any other major aspect of the slave trade. Still, the fresh data and new projections
that are now made available, rather than weakening the G-based patterns of
export trends perceived in former stages of analysis, have thankfully clarified
and strengthened them.

First of all, as Table 2.2 summarizes, in seven of eight regions of Africa the
initial export trend recorded for a particular section of the coast took G' form.
The one exception is found for the Windward Coast (between Sierra Leone and
the Gold Coast), where from the later 1600s into the middle of the next century—perhaps all the way into the early 1800s, as Figure 2.2b indicates via a
light curve line—increase for some reason appears to have followed a G path
instead. This portion of the African coast was a small source of slaves (except
for a sharp spike in the 1751–1775 period, attaining only several hundred a year
in contrast to the 4,000 to 32,000 annual levels reached by the seven other
regions examined). There also seems to be some ambiguity about the way voyages to this portion of the African coast were identified by contemporaries. The
total exported to all New World destinations, meanwhile, rose between 1560
and 1663 in G fashion with t_0 at 1566, very much like the somewhat smaller

number of slaves eventually delivered annually to the Americas (zero year at 1569).

A major point made across the past three decades—by commentators from Curtin to Eltis—is how, through time, slavers shifted across a sequence of fresh or renewed coastal sources to obtain their cargoes. The seven opening G' curves in the first column of Table 2.2 support that view. They also display, however, the same kind of "long-swing" patterning as observed in Chapter 1 for other immigrations and emigrations. Two potential waves of such a timing are missing in the long early gap between West Central Africa and the Bight of Biafra and the Gold Coast; but it is then 20 to 25 years from there to the crest from Senegambia, and a comparable span from that G' peak to the cluster of opening spurts topping out in Southeast Africa (around the Cape of Good Hope into the Indian Ocean), the Bight of Benin (sometimes called the "Slave Coast"), and Sierra Leone. Secondary regional waves of slaves with G' shape with crests at 1715, 1731, 1765, 1791, and 1803 were extracted from Sengambia, the Gold Coast (two of them), Sierra Leone, and the Windward Coast, respectively. The geography of these movements is not so simple or uni-directional as it has sometimes been portrayed. Captains of slavers probed wherever there might be fresh markets or weakened rivals.

Along three coasts, however, the sources were complex enough and/or the competition diverse enough for exports to increase for substantial periods in continually, if more slowly, expanding G form rather than up-and-down G' shape. "West Central Africa" covers a vast zone of heavy slaving from modern Cameroon southwards through Congo and Angola. Whereas the Portuguese largely controlled the southern majority of this extensive region, Dutch, British, and French intruders seriously cut into their claimed monopoly in the north and also to some extent at the southern extreme.[13] The result was apparently a mix of G' trends in local African supply and for particular groups of European carriers that summed up as a G pattern for the huge slave-rich region of West Central Africa as a whole. "Southeast Africa" included, in modern terms, territory all the way from eastern South Africa to southern Kenya. Particularly as antislavery and suppression cut into more northern traffic across the Atlantic, vessels of more than one flag went there to load Africans, about 10,000 annually from 1826 through 1850. The G trend out of the Bight of Biafra between 1701 and 1775, meanwhile, took annual exports to some 14,000 a year. Perhaps a new look is appropriate, *pace* disparaging remarks about the nature of slaves from there and the popularity of loading there, at the different kinds of vessels that acquired slaves along this part of the coast in the 18th century. What kind of mix of sellers and buyers was involved? On the whole, multiple traders and multiple loading points seem to have generated G rather than G' out-flows of Africans for certain sections of the coast.

For estimated total exports into the Atlantic trade, these regionals G' and G trends compounded still further to shape an H trend from the 1660s into the 1770s (top of Figure 2.2a). This, of course, paralleled closely the H pattern shown in Figure 2.1a for total imports out of the Atlantic trade according to the recent estimations of Eltis (2001, 45). The fact that a rather different H curve represents aggregate imports when information in addition to the database is taken into account, however, serves as a reminder that export records, too, may be more incomplete in the later 17th century than current interpretations allow. Where and when do likely shortfalls lurk?

The D shape of decline in total exports during the twilight of the Atlantic slave trade, on the other hand, closely follows a similar trend in estimated New World imports. That loadings in the Bight of Benin started to atrophy this way as early as the 1710s and in the Bight of Biafra perhaps along a *later* D track from the 1780s forward raises issues about local participation in slaving that a later section explores a little further.

In gathering and shipping slaves, as much as in disposing of them through various Atlantic markets, the path for annual numbers through time consistently took the humpbacked G' form or it compounded multiple local G' surges into broader regional G trends. How did the G' pattern keep recurring in the generation of slave exports? The implication is that any extension of slaving to fresh sources picked up steam from small beginnings, hit some maximum, then found it more and more difficult to obtain usable bodies. The possibilities for slave-gatherers in an African region came and passed by in G' fashion just like the window of local opportunity for free immigrants to make a home in particular parts of the New World. In that other, freer case, discussed in Chapter 1 (and further in Chapter 6), the establishment of a native population seems to have given the G' trend its shape, encouraging then discouraging further migration. How did comparable demographics work in reverse for the local supply of potential slaves, through the siphoning off or devastation of a people? Data on the sex and age of the victims should help in understanding these processes. So should the prices that various types of captive labor brought in various places at various times. But one can already envisage dynamics through which a population was thinned out and simultaneously learned how to avoid or to resist the once-new menace, passing on the consequences from generation to generation via who was left, how vulnerable the survivors were, and how attractive this particular residual population remained for slavers.

Second and third G' surges for a given coastal area of supply would seem to entail the penetration of new hunting zones, mostly deeper and deeper into the interior as slaving violated and corrupted more and more of Africa.[14] The way that both initial and subsequent local G' increases in slave exports tended to be spaced out at about 20- to 25-year intervals, among regions and within them (Table 2.2), reiterates the existence of Kuznetsian "long-swings" in Atlantic history that go back centuries in time. These apparently affected several aspects of life not only in the New World but also in the Old World zones of Europe and Africa that were tied to Atlantic development.

THE CHANGING ACTIVITY OF VARIOUS POWERS IN AFRICAN SLAVING: TRADES TO THE MEDITERRANEAN, THE AMERICAS, AND ASIA, 1550–1861

For the main slaving groups, from the late 1500s or early 1600s onward it is possible to discern the general trends for their sector of the trade through time. First of all, long before the Portuguese entered the business of black bodies in the 1400s, Arabs had brought slaves northward from sub-Saharan Africa toward the Mediterranean. This commerce did not stop when Europeans took up sea-borne trade in slaves. It continued alongside it. The top plot in Figure 2.3a shows that about 5,500 victims a year in the 1500s, rising to about 7,150 by the 1700s—in what may have been a G curve with base year around 1506— were transported from equatorial Africa across the great desert to Morocco, Algeria, Tunisia, Libya, and Egypt (Austen 1979, 66). This means that the trans-Saharan volume amounted to three times that of Atlantic slaving during the first half of the 1500s and about twice the European competition between 1550 and 1600 and roughly equaled traffic to all the Americas together as late as 1650 (compare Figure 2.1a). It was through the later 1600s and early 1700s that European involvement began to dwarf the Saharan commerce: surpassing 3 times its size by 1700 and 6 times across the next few decades, and reaching a peak of 10 times that competition toward the end of the 18th century. What made the difference are the successive European national surges into slaving that are graphed in Figures 2.3a and 2.3b. The trans-Saharan trade, nevertheless, itself later grew afresh, doubling between 1750 and 1840, possibly in a proportionally accelerating E manner.[15]

The big, regular Atlantic slaving power of the 16th and 17th centuries was Portugal. Her aggregate exports from West and West Central Africa—and, later, Southeast Africa (mostly Mozambique)—probably expanded from the middle 1500s through the early 1800s in a series of G-type surges that took the average annual number of persons carried on Portuguese ships from about 3,200 in the 1500s, to 10,000 in the later 1600s, to about twice that during the later decades of the 18th century, and to 43,000 yearly for the second quarter of the 1800s before the trade began to fade. Figure 2.3a and Table 2.3 show the duration and spacing of four successive G curves between 1560 and 1838 with base years at 1604, 1666, 1729, and 1795, respectively. Of these numbers, many were transported on ships based in Portugal's great slave-consuming colony, Brazil, rather than in the metropolis, Lisbon—though most of those vessels apparently had Portuguese owners.

From 1700 forward the quarter-century database evidence from Eltis (2001, 43)—the hollow downward triangles in the Portuguese plot—sits at very much the same level as decennial calculations that I had made previously from published sources (the solid squares).[16] As in imports to Brazil (Figure 2.1b), however, the database numbers are very low for the later 1600s. What calculations from Miller (1992, 109) indicate, instead, is about 10,000 a year in Portuguese

Figure 2.3a
Known Traffic Volume of the Major Slaving Powers: Trans-Sahara, Portuguese, and Dutch Traders

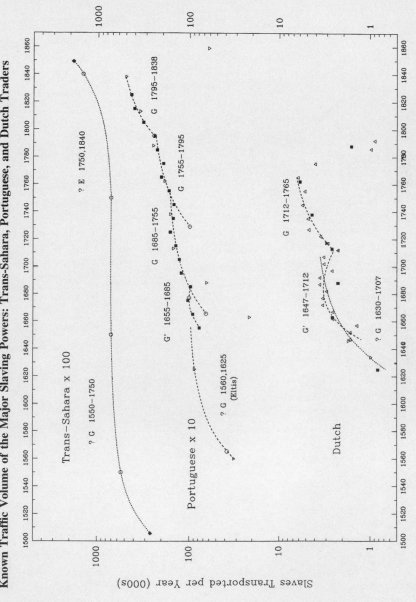

Sources: Austen 1979, 66; Eltis 2001, 43; Miller 1992, 109; van den Boogaart and Emmer 1979, 369, Postma 1990, 110, 115, 121, 295.

Table 2.3
Comparing Trends for the Leading Slaving Groups

A. Successive G Growths

Trans-Saharan	Portuguese/Brazilian	Dutch	British	French
1550-1750 G 1506	1560-1685 ?G 1604	1630-1707 ?G 1645	1625-1725 G 1668	1663-1713 G 1706
	1685-1755 G 1666		1725-1795 G 1719	1715-1775 G 1719
	1755-1795 G 1729	1712-1765 G 1717		
	1795-1838 G 1795			

Asian
1815-1845 ?G 1806

B. Surges of G' Shape

Portuguese/Brazilian	Dutch	North American/Spanish	Danish
1655-1685 ?G' 1677*	1647-1712 ?G' 1684*	1713-1788 G' 1763	1688-1713 ?G' 1691
		1785-1813 G' 1838	1763-1788 ?G' 1804

C. Possible Accelerating Trends

Trans-Saharan	Asian
1750,1840 ?E 1849	1815-1861 E 1854

* Alternative to G also fitted.

Sources: See Figures 2.3a and 2.3b.

traffic during the 1660s, 1670s, and 1680s, perhaps rising and falling between 1650 and 1690 in the kind of G' hump that Figure 2.3a depicts. The database averages for 1519–1600 and 1601–1650, on the other hand, would fit the kind of G curve with t_0 near 1604 that the figure also proposes. Projected forward, such a trend—as is shown—hits the typical level found from other sources for the later 1600s. Perhaps, with the same kind of short-term fluctuations that appear elsewhere, this was indeed the pattern in which the Portuguese slave trade actually evolved between the early 1500s and about 1690.

In the middle of the 1600s the Dutch, who with the English had been inter-loping here and there in Iberian spheres of commerce, entered the Atlantic slave trade in force. Previously, Sephardic Jews based in the Netherlands had "in-truded" into the areas of the Portuguese slave trade from 1580 to 1630, picking up cargoes in areas sufficiently remote from the central Portuguese base at Lu-anda (Miller 2002, 26). The shipments of their West India Company, which got going only in the later 1620s, were bolstered by the temporary occupation of sugar-growing northeastern Brazil. Merchants of the Netherlands then compen-sated for Portuguese reacquisition of that region by new colonization along the Guiana coast and trade to the settlements of other powers.[17] Dutch participation in the slave trade rose rapidly from the later 1640s to crest in the early 1680s but then dropped off in continuing G' form, according to the calculations of Postma (1990, 110). Those computations (hollow, upward triangles) vary widely—through three wars with the English and other interruptions—around the underlying trend that is fitted in Figure 2.3a to include broader chronological averaging for 1636–1657, the 1660s, the 1670s, and 1685–1694 in order to make the underlying trend more readily visible. Estimation from the database record (Eltis 2001, 43) fits this Dutch pattern in the periods 1651–1675 and 1701–1725; but for 1676–1700 the average annual intake derived from the CD-ROM is once more significantly low.

If, moreover, Dutch traffic to their temporary holdings in Brazil is considered (the hollow, *downward* triangles in the 1630s and the 1640s from van den Boogaart and Emmer 1979, 369), one could say that the Dutch trade in slaves perhaps developed from the 1630s through to the early 1700s according to a G trend instead, with its base year near 1645. This alternative conclusion is sup-ported by the database average for the half-century surrounding 1625 (the solid square) and probably by what Miller has to say about interloping from the 1580s through the 1620s by Sephardim relocated in the Netherlands (2002, 26). The data of Postma, it should be remembered, are at this stage just for the West India Company. Such an alternative trending, probably the preferable one, then requires an explanation of how Dutch traffic dropped in the early 1700s from about 3,500 annually, on average, before the new G trend evident for the year 1712–1765 took off from a level of just two-thirds that high. Perhaps weakness in the West India Company's system, which opened the door to "Free" traders in the 30-year charter renewal of 1730 (Postma 1990, 201), was the cause of this downward shift before the new G path carried the national traffic to about

6,000 per year in the third quarter of the 18th century. Printed sources and the database then agree on the collapse of Dutch slaving, for various reasons, that commenced in the 1770s.[18]

While the Dutch carried about a third as many slaves as the Portuguese at the beginning of the 18th century and again in the 1760s, the British proved to be more formidable competitors in trade with Africa. English slaving was probably already expanding rapidly in G form from small beginnings considerably before the Company of Royal Adventurers in 1660 and its more effective successor, the Royal African Company of 1673, were formed by Stuart insiders after the Restoration in order to corner its profits. In fact, real monopoly forever eluded these official ventures. There existed too many ways to work around the claim (Curtin 1969, 151; Galenson 1981, 216, 218; 1986, 13–21). The ready availability of data for the Royal African Company, as a consequence, seems to have somewhat distorted the historical picture of British slaving during its early decades. New entries from the CD-ROM database (solid squares), recent calculations by Eltis (2000, 166—shown as hollow downward triangles), and the old estimations of Curtin (1969, 211—the hollow circles after 1700) together all hug a 1625–1725 G trend with t_0 at 1668 (Figure 2.3b). Lagging about 20 to 25 years after the initial G-shaped expansion of the Dutch, this curve parallels the second Portuguese trend of 1685–1755, as part A of Table 2.3 indicates. As a result of this pattern of expansion, by the early 1700s British bottoms already carried about the same annual number of slaves (around 15,000) as Portuguese vessels.

Then, a robust second G-shaped increase in British slaving occurred, as estimations from Curtin (hollow circles), Anstey (1975, 13, shown as hollow triangles), and the database (filled squares) indicate.[19] Parallel to the Dutch second surge of 1712–1765, this brought British traffic to almost twice the volume of the Portuguese in the third quarter of the 18th century before the fourth, 1795–1838, G-form expansion for the Portuguese restored their carriers to preeminence in the Atlantic slave trade. In the first quarter of the 19th century they matched the British 35,000 average for 1751–1775; in the second, their typical annual numbers exceeded that level by over 40 percent (reaching about 50,000 per year) before their business, too, was eventually curtailed after Brazilian independence and with the establishment of British naval patrols.

In the 17th century, the French had mostly purchased the slaves desired by their Caribbean colonists from European competitors. Curtin estimated that of some 5,000 individuals a year imported into the French West Indies from 1676 through 1700, only about a quarter were supplied by the slavers of La Rochelle and other ports of France's Atlantic coast (1969, 119–21). Figures that he cited as high points—1,000 annually for 1670–1672 and 1,500 for 1682–1684—indeed fall (as two hollow squares) above the G trend for the period 1651–1725 that emerges from the evidence of the CD-ROM database (filled squares) at 1663, 1688, and 1713, as shown in Figure 2.3b. This G had its t_0 around 1706,

Figure 2.3b
Known Traffic Volume of the Major Slaving Powers: British, French, American/ Spanish, Danish, Asian

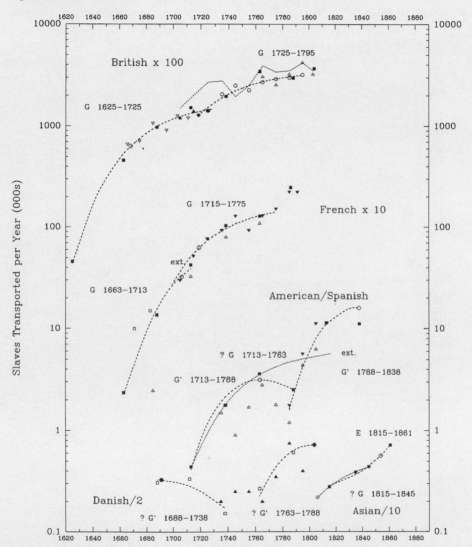

Sources: Eltis 2000, 166; 2001, 43; 1987, 248; Curtin 1969, 211, 121; Anstey 1975, 13; Richardson 1989, 10; Geggus 2001, 135; Lovejoy 1998, 150.

about 40 years later than contemporary Portuguese and British trends, as Table 2.3 shows.

With extensive French occupation of St. Domingue (the western half of originally Spanish Santo Domingo, subsequently called Haiti) in the late 1600s, fresh demand for Africans arose. In the 18th century, shipowners of Nantes and other Atlantic ports entered slaving substantially, carrying on average some 10,000 Africans annually by the second quarter of the 18th century and 13,000 between 1751 and 1775 in a trade that swelled along a G trend with base year around 1719. This was almost exactly parallel to contemporary, G-type expansions for Dutch and British competitors, as Table 2.3 indicates. Geggus (2001, 135—the hollow upward triangles) estimates rather lower numbers around 1713, 1738, and 1763. In movement, however, these closely mimic the bend of the database curve. The solid downward triangles display the annual averages argued by Richardson (1989, 10). These hold to the same G path. In the 1780s a new surge in French slaving took off, attaining a briefly lead-sharing level with the Portuguese of about 25,000 Africans a year (as the British pulled out of the trade) before being broken off by the great slave revolt in St. Domingue. Thereafter, much more modest supplying of Africans to Windward Islands retained by the French after the peace of 1763 and to the Mascerenes (in the Indian Ocean, from Southeast Africa) continued into the 19th century but is not graphed.

In the 17th century whatever slave trafficking was conducted by British colonists, in the West Indies or from the mainland, is hard to distinguish from homeland operations. Across the 18th century, according to the new database (Eltis 2001, 43—shown as solid squares), such trade surged upward in something like a G' manner from a few hundred in the early 1700s to crest in the 1760s at about 3,500 a year, approximately one-tenth of the volume handled by British carriers at that point. Decade by decade Richardson (1989, 10) calculated lower numbers (the hollow upward triangles); but these, for all their fluctuations, tend to parallel such a G' path. Whether the level was lower because Richardson categorized colonial traders differently, because he did not cover exports from Southeast Africa, or for some other reason will have to be decided by the experts. So will a decision on the shape of trend actually being followed. Did the American trade take G' form because it was a smaller, more localized business? Or did the little disruptions of the 1770s and early 1780s just carve a dip from what was really a G path of development (an alternative possible trend that Figure 2.3b includes in a lighter line)? Following the Revolution and the prohibition of slave imports to the United States as of 1808, the U.S. trade becomes blurred with the revived Spanish traffic to stock West Indian holdings (especially huge Cuba), where the cultivation of sugar burgeoned and the Bolivarian independence movements did not reach. Aggregate U.S. and Spanish slaving swelled from 1,000 or 2,000 to over 11,000 a year on average between the 1780s and the first quarter of the 19th century before leveling out in the next 25 years. Figure 2.3b displays the kind of G' curve that approximates this later movement.[20] Alternatively, one could fit a G pattern to the same truncated evidence. That option, though, projects an enormous volume of mid-19th-century traffic to which this trade would have been headed, a level unlikely in the prevailing historical conditions of limited territory now open to new slave labor.

The Danes more clearly did run a small slave trade that mostly focused narrowly on their own minor holdings in the Virgin Islands. From 1688 through 1738 and again from 1763 through 1788, their traffic seems to have crested in successive G' waves. The hollow squares are from the database (Eltis 2001, 43); the solid upward triangles derive from Richardson (1989, 10). From 1763 through 1788 both are included in the fitting. This second G' wave tends to compensate for the dip of American slaving in the 1770s and 1780s. Even at their peak in the 1780s, however, Danish vessels carried only about 1,200 Africans per year. (The Danish averages are divided by 2 to fit the graph.)

In the end, as slaving (not yet slave-owning) became illegal for country after country and New World imports declined, accelerating increase of the E pattern may have appeared as the slave trades of the Indian Ocean and also the great sand sea of the Sahara expanded to exploit the decline in competition among buyers and the momentum of slave "recruitment" that had become so ingrained in the life of black Africa. By 1840, the trans-Saharan trade (Figure 2.3a) probably doubled to reach about 14,500 annually (Austen 1979, 66) while traffickers across the Indian Ocean—to Arabia, Persia, and India (Figure 2.3b)—carried another 7,000, compared with more like 2,500 at the beginning of the century (Lovejoy 1998, 150). An alternative trend for this Asian trade up through 1845 might be a G that somewhat resembles the last Portuguese expansion of that shape (Table 2.3). Jointly the *gains* of about 11,800 more now going to North Africa and southwestern Asia replaced the disappearance of legal American carriers from slaving after 1808 or amounted to twice what the Dutch had transported annually before giving up on the trade—or the scale of French slaving as late as 1750. The approximate 21,500 per annum *total* of these two still-growing non-Atlantic trades around 1850 exceeded what either the Portuguese and Brazilians or the French had carried before the 1780s.

Quite generally, then—as Table 2.3 summarizes—between the middle 1500s and the middle 1800s the participation of leading European groups of shippers in the Atlantic slave trade over and over again expanded along G paths. Typically, these national businesses acquired cargoes along more than one part of the African coast and disposed of slaves in more than one region of the New World. That the G shape for total European businesses results from such aggregation is bolstered by the G' form previously observed in the supply centers of Africa (Table 2.2) and in localized consumption at various Atlantic destinations (Table 2.1)—a pattern that is also evident in more limited national trades like the Danish one or the last Spanish-American burst to Cuba.[21]

Trending in G and G' patterns this way clarifies who prospered in the business at what time, intimates G-related shapes of change in market share among competitors (which should be a useful insight for economic analysis), and focuses exploration of the reasons for these movements on the right time and place and participants. Succession in the Atlantic trade from one slaving power to another is a familiar topic; but the new patterning clarifies some of its issues.

SOME FINER PATTERNS IN HOW SLAVES WERE OBTAINED, SHIPPED, AND SOLD: POINTS OF COLLECTION AND LOADING, THE HOME PORTS OF SHIPS, AND LOCAL VENUES OF DISPOSAL

Further details about the flow and ebb of various parts of the slave trade enhance insight as to how a few basic patterns kept recurring across time, especially the repeated G' form of local operations. Information is drawn from Patrick Manning's work on international operations in the Bight of Benin (1979, 1982), coastal analysis by Eltis and Richardson (1997) for the Bights of Benin and Biafra, and a variety of studies dealing with the ways that the Dutch, French, Portuguese, Spanish, and British and their colonists obtained, transported, and marketed Africans.

Manning's detailed analysis of slaving in the Bight of Benin and its hinterland (modern Dahomey/Benin and western Nigeria) offers two helpful perspectives. The first, in Figure 2.4a, delineates the surges of participation in the region's slave trade by nationals of several leading Western powers (1979, 117). No information is available before the 1640s. For one thing, local rulers had shut off slave exports in 1516. From when they were evicted from Angola by the Portuguese in the 1640s forward, however, the Dutch led the way with exports that crested in G' form for 1655–1735 around 1691 at about 1,500 a year. The English, though, opened their trade right behind the Dutch in a G' surge between 1675 and 1805 that peaked at 1722. As of then, they typically shipped some 3,800 slaves annually out of the Bight of Benin. Still stronger became the presence of slavers for the northern, sugar-growing territories of Portugal's great holding in Brazil. They exported about 6,200 slaves per year from this part of the African coast as their G' trend peaked out along with British traffic of some 60 percent that size in the early 1720s.[22] Simultaneously, French entrepreneurs generated a slave trade from the Bight of Benin that also initially maximized in the 1720s.[23] At about 1,900 annually this amounted to half the scale of the British flow.

The Dutch then virtually disappeared from the Bight of Benin as British, Brazilian, and French slavers all harvested cargoes from this portion of the African coast in very parallel fashion to mid-century or beyond. It was the Portuguese/Brazilians, though, who generated a new, comparably large and lasting surge in their business across the late 1700s and the first half of the 1800s, as Figure 2.4a shows. This G' curve once more peaked at some 6,100 slaves a year near 1811. Meanwhile, French slavers, enticed by the burgeoning demand of St. Domingue, expanded their exports from the 1740s through the 1780s along

Figure 2.4a
Some Details of Slaving in the Bights of Benin and Biafra: Slave Exports by Various Powers Out of the Bight of Benin

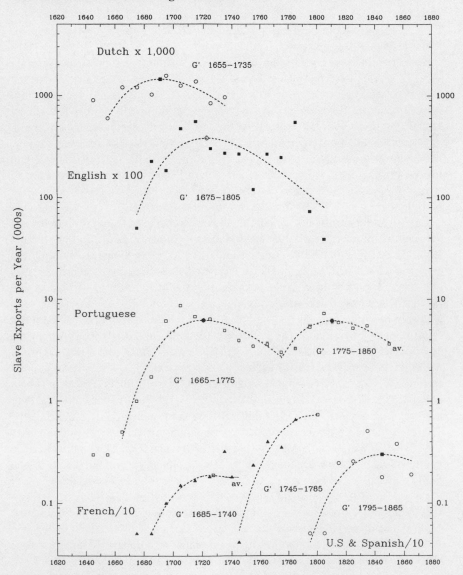

Source: Manning 1979, 117.

a G' path that would have produced even more—approximately 7,400—"recruits" annually from the Bight of Benin simultaneously in the early 1800s; but the great revolt cut off this business abruptly before it could top out. It could be said that, after a drop in their trade, British slavers also enlarged their Bight of Benin traffic in something like a G' path with t_0 near 1802 (not unlike the French and Brazilian patterns); but this path (not graphed), which would have reached a level of about 6,000 a year at its summit, broke by 1790—and the data generally continue to waver around the earlier, long-lasting G' curve for 1765–1805. Perhaps there was just a temporary push in the 1780s to beat anti-slavery mobilization. Spanish slavers and U.S. operators, who also significantly served Cuba and the rest of the Spanish Caribbean, then stepped in to market Benin slaves along a G' trajectory for 1795–1865 that peaked around 3,000 annually in the 1840s as finally slave-shipping progressively became illegal country by country in the Western world and was actively interdicted at sea.[24]

Enough international parallelism for the rise and decline of these various trades out of the Bight of Benin appears in all periods, however, to suggest that the patterns of local numbers significantly reflected *African* determinants, to which shippers of all Western powers adjusted. There are two sets of trends that help in beginning to probe that interpretation.

On the one hand, Figure 2.4b demonstrates how slave loadings shifted from one part of the coast to another, both along the Bight of Benin and around the Bight of Biafra (Eltis and Richardson 1997, 26). Data for Calabar (Old Calabar) in the middle of the Bight of Biafra suggest that an early G' wave of exports may have occurred there in the 17th century, with its crest at 1679 reaching about 570 slaves per year whose places of shipment are identified. There is only a hint of pattern here; but all exports from the Bight of Biafra (Figure 2.2a) seem to have crested in G' fashion in the 1660s (says the CD-ROM database). Meanwhile, Dutch traffic as a whole perhaps peaked in G' fashion about 1684, the Portuguese trade near 1677 (Table 2.3 and Figure 2.3a), while Dutch exports from the nearby Bight of Benin surged in a G' path with maximum at about 1691 (Figure 2.4a). Further research should divulge how Calabar took part in such regional and national patternings of the 17th century.

The earliest 18th-century surge in exports along this substantial Benin–Biafra segment of the African coast took place at Whydah, somewhat west of Lagos in the Bight of Benin. Running all the way from 1674 through 1824 (if one thinks in terms of an average for a low in 1799 and high in 1824), this G' trend peaked near 1725 at about 2,600 slaves annually. Figure 2.4a shows how English, Portuguese, and—to 1740—French vessels all sucked up cargoes along the Bight of Benin in G' waves of this timing.

Supply then shifted back to the Bight of Biafra. Calabar and Bonny (between Calabar and the delta of the Niger) from the 1720s to the 1820s produced G' waves of slave exports that crested near 1770. At maximum, Bonny provided about 2,600 captives per year on average—to equal the maximum loaded at Whydah half a century before—Calabar around 1,900. Then a last pair of re-

Figure 2.4b
Some Details of Slaving in the Bights of Benin and Biafra: Exports from Particular Parts of the Coast

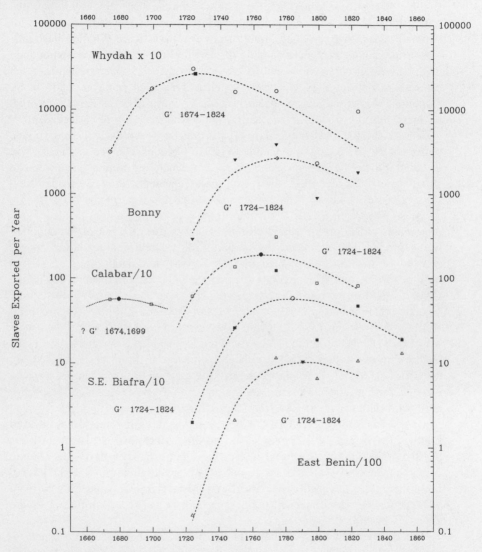

Source: Eltis and Richardson 1997, 26.

gional flows, with a crest near 1787, surged out of the eastern portion of the Bight of Benin (Badagry, Porto Novo, and Lagos) and Southeast Biafra (from Bimbia through the Cameroons and Gabon down the coast to Cape Lopez), attaining lesser levels of approximately 1,000 and 600, respectively, as new zones of supply were sought for cargoes. This last set of G' waves is contemporaneous with surges of that shape for French and Portuguese slaving from the Bight of Benin as a whole (Figure 2.4a); the somewhat earlier up-and-down trends for Calabar and Bonny are less easily connected with the behavior of national trades. In Bonny and Southeastern Biafra, as from Whydah, for some reason the quarter century around 1799 provided noticeably fewer slaves than the long-term G' curve would call for. An educated guess, which further research can test, is that the massive setback to the French trade from the revolt in St. Domingue was at least a significant part of the cause. Did the French do more business with these sources than with Calabar and the ports of eastern Benin?

Scholars of the slave trade have long noted how supply shifted from one portion of the African coast to another. Figure 2.4b adds finer geographical detail to the evidence of Figures 2.2a and 2.2b that, when any limited section of the shoreline can be identified, these out-flows repeatedly took G' shape. New sources of slaves, however, not only swung back and forth along the shoreline; they also penetrated further and further inland.

Manning's data on the ethnic origins of slaves exported out of the Bight of Benin, graphed in Figure 2.4c, throw some further useful light upon how supply evolved across first coastal then interior regions. During the more than two centuries from 1640 through 1870 this one limited zone, often called the "Slave Coast" of Africa, provided close to 2 million slaves, about one-fifth of the total Atlantic trade (Manning 1982, 9; Klein 1999, 208–9).

The Aja lived mostly within 200 kilometers of the coast, along the lower watersheds of rivers from the Volta eastward to the Ouémé (Manning 1982, 23). Before about 1740 they supplied some 90 percent or more of the persons caught up in the slaving of the Bight of Benin. The number of these Aja people who were sucked into the European trade (as opposed to any trans-Saharan dealings northward within Africa) rose from about 1,000 per year to more than 10,000 along a G' path topping out in 1717. It was this surge in supply that allowed English, Portuguese, and French slavers to elbow into this part of the African coast right behind the Dutch, all in G' waves that crested in the 1720s (Figure 2.4a). Somehow Aja numbers then fell off somewhat, abruptly, in the 1740s. From there, they declined systematically in fresh G' fashion from 1745 through 1855, dropping back to about 1,000 a year once more, as the top plot in Figure 2.4c shows (ibid., 335–36, 343).

British, French, and Portuguese slavers all saw their businesses expand simultaneously in G' form to a peak about 1720 because that is how the supply of Aja grew. According to Manning, the slave-catching system of Dahomey was developed between 1640 and 1670 (1982, 9). The Dutch, as Figure 2.4a indicates—who were temporarily in possession of large sugar-cultivating areas of

Figure 2.4c
Some Details of Slaving in the Bights of Benin and Biafra: The Ethnic Origins of Slaves Marketed via the Bight of Benin

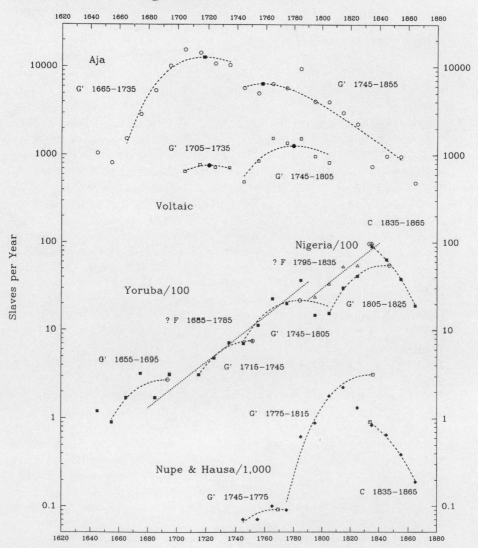

Source: Manning 1982, 341–43.

Table 2.4
Shifts in the Ethnic Origins of Bight of Benin Slaves

Dahomey		Western Nigeria	
Aja	Voltaic	Yoruba	Nupe & Hausa
		1655-1695 G' 1693	
1665-1735 G' 1717	1705-1735 G' 1721		
1745-1855 G' 1758		1715-1745 G' 1751	
	1745-1805 G' 1780	1745-1805 G' 1784	1745-1775 G' 1769
		1805-1825 G' 1847	1775-1815 G' 1836
		1835-1865 C 1833	1845-1865 C 1832

Source: Manning 1982, 341–43.

northeastern Brazil from 1632 through 1654 and also marketed slaves to early
New World planters of other powers—were the main purchasers of Benin labor
during these "years of decision" for Dahomey. They garnered about 70 percent
of the regional stock during the 1640s, 1650s, and 1660s (Manning 1979, 117).
The evolving system "could supply a large number at low cost to slave export-
ers." The relevant institutions that emerged in this critical period "included warfare, raiding, kidnapping, judicial procedures, tribute, and sale of persons by
destitute families." These "reinforced a willingness to tolerate or justify the
enslavement of one's enemies or even one's own." State power facilitated the
collection and sale of slaves as various principalities (especially Danhommè)
warred upon and raided each other. The majority of slaves, however, were handled by the "mercantile sector." While some captives were kept in Dahomey,
only royalty built up their retinues this way. Until the 1830s, the profit to be
had from selling overseas far exceeded gains from any domestic use of the labor.
Warfare evolved as a purposeful technique for gathering human property; increased slavery was not a by-product of conflict but its purpose (Manning 1982,
9–11).

    According to Manning, by the 1730s slave procurers were running out of
suitable Aja bodies (1982, 10). The drop in trend level around 1740 in Figure
2.4c would seem to reflect this. New sources were needed to keep up the profits
and to meet the scale of demand that had been established for the "product."
Figure 2.4c shows how various Voltaic peoples of the deeper interior north of
the Aja (ibid., 23) during the early 1700s supplied another several hundred
slaves a year in a G' pattern parallel with the 10 times as large a flow that came
from the Aja. As the level of available Aja dropped in the 1740s, however, a
new G' surge in the Voltaic supply appeared, raising annual numbers from that
inland region by up to 50 percent. The timing of this trend, though, now lagged
behind that of the Aja by about two decades rather than paralleling it (Table
2.4). Captured by the 1745–1805 Voltaic pattern is a new effort to replace absent
Aja with people from the deeper interior, not just a marginal geographical expansion of the system of slaving that was operating among the Aja.

Of greater consequence for the long run, however, was the extension of Benin slaving *eastward* from the homelands of the Aja into the territory of the Yoruba, in what is now western Nigeria. An early spate of "recruitment" here had added just 100 to 300 persons annually to Benin's supply across the late 1600s. The numbers may have followed the kind of G' path proposed from 1655 to 1695. (There are no Yoruba data for the decade of the 1700s.) Peaking in the early 1690s, this opening spurt seems to reflect the pioneering activity of the Dutch in the Bight of Benin, as comparison of Table 2.3 with Table 2.4 indicates. It would represent about one-fifth of the supply of the Dutch if they were the only traders to take Yoruba in this early era. For the time being, vessels of other later-entering powers seem not to have done much in western Nigeria.

Then a later G' surge in Yoruba victims of Bight of Benin slaving becomes quite clear. From the 1710s through the 1740s the numbers approach a modest peak of about 750 annually along a curve with its t_0 around 1751. As Table 2.4 shows, this G' movement resembles that for Aja slaves from 1745 through 1855. That makes this second move into the Yoruba a geographical extension of that core region's operations, compensating for some of the drop in the Aja level. Subsequently, as a second wave of Voltaic victims supplemented falling Aja numbers along a G' curve peaking at 1780, a new contemporaneous surge of Yoruba in that same trend shape and timing, now netting some 2,000 slaves per year on average, topped out in the 1780s. Meanwhile, a modest preliminary probe for "fresh blood" for the regional slaving system among the Nupe and Hausa of Nigeria's interior, north of the Yoruba (Manning 1982, 23), appears from 1745 through 1775 at the bottom of Figure 2.4c.

More substantial are the roughly parallel G' surges that next produced some 2,000 Nupe and Hausa slaves annually for Bight of Benin export markets by about 1820 along with some 4,000 Yoruba. Now the bulk of the regional business depended upon Nigerian rather than Dahomeian supply as Aja numbers had declined to 1,000 per year and inland Voltaic peoples had for some reason disappeared as sources for coastal exporting. While British trade in the region spiked upward from the 1750s through the 1780s in a manner parallel with the G' curves for Portuguese and French slaving along the Bight of Benin with their t_0's at 1811 and 1800, it was these two other national groups who apparently consumed the bulk of the offerings as slave-catching shifted eastward and inland into Nigeria. Could they pay better prices? Did they develop better political connections with slave-making principalities? Did the British simply pull back, starting in the 1790s well before their trade became illegal? Or did the wars of the French Revolution for some reason pose more of an impediment to their business than to that of other powers?

Finally, as Atlantic slaving was curtailed in the 19th century, annual numbers of both Yoruba and interior Nupe and Hausa peoples declined in accelerating C form, each with base years in the early 1830s (Table 2.4).[25] A propping up by U.S. and Spanish end-players in the 19th century (Figure 2.4a) could not reverse the decline of slaving from the Bight of Benin.

There is, however, perhaps another way of looking at the historical extension of the "Slave Coast" trade into what is now western Nigeria. This region seems to have behaved as a "frontier" for the Dahomeian slave system. Roughly, that is, from as early as the 1680s through the 1780s numbers acquired from the Yoruba rose in approximately F form—constantly proportional expansion at a .03 rate. Then from the 1790s through the 1830s all Nigerian slaves per year shipped out through the Bight of Benin (Yoruba, Nupe, and Hausa together— the hollow triangles in the plotting) again multiplied in the log-linear path of the F function. Insights into how slaving worked as it spread across contiguous populations arise from this alternative long-term, multi-local patterning as well as the sequence of G' spurts that contributed to it.

In sum, early arrangements among the coastal principalities of the Aja in the middle of the 17th century to provide slaves to the Dutch were soon expanded to serve Portuguese, French, and English competitors in the Atlantic trade. In the early 18th century the Aja *population* began to fall as a result of this stripping for export. A D-shape trend of decline for 1695–1775 with t_0 in the early 1670s is indicated by Manning's estimations.[26] The demographic density of potential additional Aja slaves fell off this way. Faced with significant local depletion of its prunable stock, the slave-obtaining system of the Bight of Benin was extended into neighboring regions, first the Dahomeian interior to the north and then eastward into what is now Nigeria. In this process of evolution and adaptation, each new wave of regional involvement seems to have taken the familiar G' shape, though the compounded, overall extension into western Nigeria could alternatively be modeled in the F form for substantial stretches of time.

The stage-by-stage penetration of the Benin interior this way across the 1600s and 1700s closely resembles the picture that Miller paints for an earlier epoch in Central Africa (2002, 39–45). There, early Portuguese arrangements with Kongo kings led, after about 1520, to "civil war" in this area just south of the Zaire River—much of it conducted by Christian elites. The hunt for slaves continued to spread outward until by the 1670s raids for captives were penetrating well into the plateau of Central Africa. Whether in Dahomey or in Central Africa, such extension of the catchment area further and further out to obtain victims clearly involved trends in things like the costs of getting slaves and gains to be had from slaving. Given the repeatedly observed movements in the numbers of captives "produced" by this business, many economic aspects of the industry are likely to have experienced G'-related behavior.[27] The universality of G-based change in all sorts of historical developments in *populations*, not just slaving, however, indicates that at bottom the determinants of such ubiquitous shapes are demographic rather than economic.

Other insightful patterns emerge from further details that various scholars have published about the leading national slave trades. Though this information was mostly made available before the CD-ROM database was distributed, that collection in fact heavily draws upon the evidence of these studies. In addition, a few recent investigations that have employed the database can also be utilized. In all, the trends encountered in the remaining figures and tables of this chapter should stand up quite well as the database is mined in new research and should pose challenges for such further work and provide some guidance for going about it.

Among the various European trades of the Atlantic, that of the Dutch provides good insight concerning both from where slaves were shipped and to what areas of the New World they were sold. In part, this is because the West India Company theoretically held a monopoly for the relevant business among Dutch maritime interests until the 1730s. Figure 2.5a shows how from the 1660s into the first decade of the 1700s—after the Portuguese drove them out of the coastline south of the Zaire River—Dutch traffickers drew Africans from the Loango area in a G' pattern that paralleled the cresting then receding trend of their business on the Slave Coast 1665–1735 (Bight of Benin; compare Figure 2.4a). Loango was the region stretching northward from the Zaire or Congo River past Cabinda to Cape Lopez through modern Congo and Gabon. Meanwhile, some early slaving along the Gold Coast, where the Dutch overwhelmed Portuguese presence in the early 17th century, for some reason dropped off markedly, as the bottom plot of Figure 2.5a indicates. For the time being gold, not captive humans, was apparently the main interest for the Dutch in this part of western Africa. Likewise, significant slave flows of the 1658–1674 era from Senegal, the Ivory Coast, and the Bight of Biafra, which had emerged as operators from the Netherlands shouldered their way into Portuguese business in many parts of Africa, dwindled in the next decade and a half, and disappeared totally from the records by the 1690s as Dutch concentration on the Slave Coast and Loango evolved (Postma 1990, 57–61, 115)—and competition from other European powers increased.

By the 1720s, however, substantial Dutch slaving from the Gold Coast (over 1,000 annually) had reemerged, equalling current flows from Loango and from the Slave Coast. Resuming as if the average level of the 1660s and 1670s had long ago initiated a G' pattern, without regard to the collapse in between (are there, perchance, missing data?), the underlying trend for this business from the Gold Coast topped out at 1713 as Figure 2.5a and Table 2.5 indicate—about a quarter century after the early Loango and Slave Coast trades, as these faded. Loango slaving was not over for the Dutch, however. Across most of the 1700s a new G' surge appeared there, carrying the average annual level to twice where it had been in the late 1600s. Meanwhile, Dutch traffic from the extended Guinea Coast of West Africa became important for the first time since some experiments of the 1670s as free traders replaced the West India Company from the 1730s forward. By the 1770s they averaged some 3,200 Guinea slaves per year along a G' curve that peaked in the middle 1770s, not quite two decades after the 1758 t_0 for the second G' spurt from Loango. As of the 1770s, total Dutch slaving, except for remnants from the Gold Coast, fell off drastically, as Figure 2.3a shows.

Figure 2.5a
Details of the Dutch Trade: African Sources of Slaves

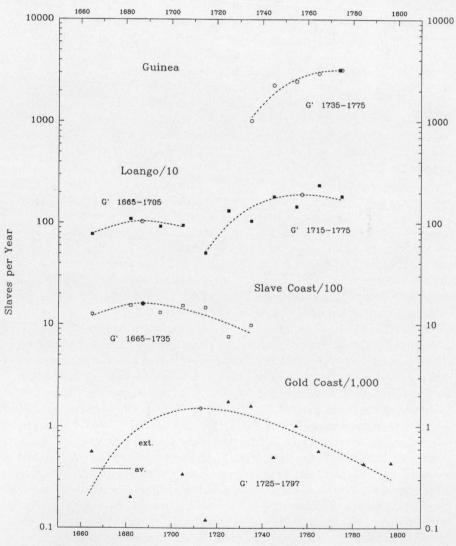

Source: Postma 1990, 115, 121.

Table 2.5
Movements of the Dutch Slave Trade

Sources			Deliveries		
			Brazil, Curaçao, St. Eustatius I	1629-1732	G' 1658
Slave Coast	1665-1735	G' 1687			
Loango I	1665-1705	G' 1687	All Guyana I	1665-1685	G' 1696
Gold Coast	1725-1797	G' 1713	Surinam I	1660-1717	G' 1709
			Surinam & Guyana I	1665-1715	G' 1710
			Essequibo & Dem. I	1675-1742	G' 1721
			All Guyana II	1695-1742	G' 1730
Loango II	1715-1775	G' 1758	Berbice I	1705-1735	G' 1754
			Curaçao & St. E. II	1732-1777	G' 1756
Guinea	1735-1775	G' 1774	Berbice II	1742-1772	G' 1781
			Essequibo & Dem. II	1742-1772	G' 1793
			Surinam II	1717-1772	G 1739
			Surinam & Guyana II	1715-1772	F -

Source: Postma 1990, 115, 121, 14, 21, 35, 186, 191, 195, 212, 218, 220–21, 223–25.

Each of these local African surges of the Dutch trade generally took the G' shape. So did almost all of the principal intakes to markets through which Dutch slavers disposed of their cargoes in the New World.

Figure 2.5b shows, first of all, the 17th- and early-18th-century sweep of initial Dutch imports to their Caribbean bases—often for resale, licensed or illegal, to nearby Spanish colonies like the territory of modern-day Venezuela— and to parts of northeastern Brazil that the West India Company held for a while as "New Holland." Though evidence begins in the 1590s, that early it records just experimentation in the trade by individual captains and some capture and resale of Portuguese cargoes. But the West India Company (WIC) generally avoided slaving during its first decade (beginning in 1621). It was the capture of parts of Brazil and some Portuguese bases along the Gold Coast (notably, little Mori as a start and then, in 1637, the crucial stronghold of Elmina) that brought the Dutch into slaving in a significant way (Postma 1990, 10–22). The top plot of Figure 2.5b presents average annual estimates for captures at sea and WIC shipping 1623–1635 (Postma 1990, 13–14), the Dutch Brazilian trade of 1636–1651 (ibid., 21, originally quantified in van den Boogaart and Emmer 1979, 368–69), and the Caribbean activities of Curaçao and St. Eustatius, which supplied slaves to the Spanish American colonies under *asiento* agreements as well as feeding the labor appetite of Dutch possessions (Postma 1990, 35, 54, 199, 223, 224). This G' trend with its peak traffic around 1665 at some 2,700

Figure 2.5b
Details of the Dutch Trade: Consumption in Various Places

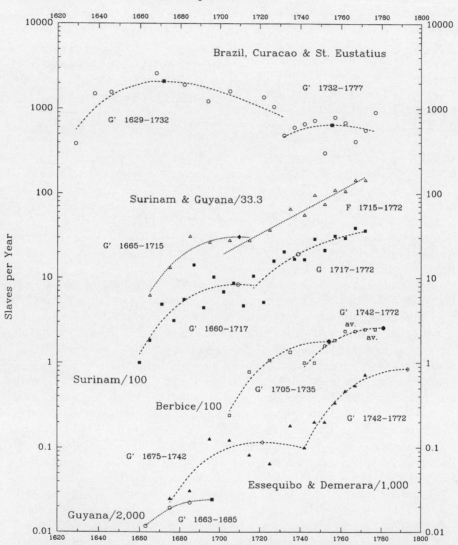

Source: Postma 1990, 14, 21, 35, 186, 191, 195, 212, 218, 220, 221, 223–25.

imported Africans captures the significant entry of the Dutch into Atlantic slaving, including supplying most of the slaves for the takeoff of English Barbados as a sugar colony (Curtin 1969, 55; Handler and Lange 1978, 25).

By the 1660s, as the second war with the English ended, which gave Guyana and Surinam to the Dutch by conquest and in exchange for New Netherland, a visible slave trade developed to this section of the northern mainland coast of South America. The very bottom plot in Figure 2.5b indicates a small initial G' trend heading toward some 50 slaves annually at a t_0 near 1696 for the group of settlements that later became British Guyana. In timing, this little initial mainland surge reflects the Slave Coast and Loango G' curves of Dutch slave-loading that topped out just before 1690 (Table 2.5)—though as yet the overwhelming majority of Dutch cargoes were delivered elsewhere. To Surinam, next door along the Caribbean coast of South America, the pull for black labor was much greater—along a G' track for 1660–1717 that topped out at about 840 slaves annually near 1709. While the quinquennial data fluctuate substantially, the decennial combination of these Surinam estimates with calculations for the Guyana settlements (Essequibo and Demerara can be seen crudely to follow a 1675–1742 G' path with t_0 at 1721 in the figure) produces a cleaner 1665–1715 G' trend with peak at 1710 for all the Dutch plantations of the mainland (Surinam and Guyana together), which collectively by then consumed about 1,000 new Africans per year.[28] This total mainland pattern parallels the activity of Dutch slavers along the Gold Coast 1725–1797, as Table 2.5 indicates. Did colonial demand draw out such renewed regional supply; or did the recovery of Gold Coast loadings for Dutch vessels provide additional labor on terms that enticed the planters of Surinam and Guyana to expand their plantation development?

In 18th-century Guyana new G' trends of slave imports appeared. For Berbice, spurting 1705–1735 consumption along a curve headed toward a high at 1754 temporarily in the 1710s and the 1720s drove the numbers for the two other regions of Guyana, Essequibo and Demerara, visibly below their joint G' trend. This was followed by another G' surge for the Berbice plantations 1742 through 1772 with t_0 at 1781. For that pattern, annual numbers for 1760–1764 and 1765–1769 and 1770–1774 and 1775–1779, respectively, are averaged in order to capture the underlying track behind the sharp swings in imports that resulted from the slave revolt of 1763 and the robust restocking of Africans that followed. In Essequibo and Demerara, intake also rose strongly from the 1740s forward. This G' trend headed toward a crest that would have come as late as 1793 if Dutch slaving had continued to be significant past the 1770s, which it was not (Postma 1990, 215–21).

In Surinam, just to the east along the northern coast of South America, a rather different patterning characterized the slave intake of the 18th century. From 1717 through 1772 the trend is G, not G', as Figure 2.5b indicates. How might that be so? First of all, Surinam was a much bigger enterprise than the three Guyana settlements. Supporting a diverse agriculture, it imported about four times as many slaves, reaching a level of some 4,000 annually in the early

1770s rather than the 1,000 for all Guyana—and 600 or so for Curaçao and St. Eustatius at their 18th-century peak in the 1750s (Postma 1990, 212–13). Further, the colony had a contemporary reputation for devouring slaves (ibid., 184). While Postma stresses high mortality, elsewhere he notes a significant presence of escaped slaves or maroons (213). Whatever the true weight of these different detractions, the growth of the slave *population* of Surinam in the 18th century was unusual in that it required continuing parallel import expansion in G form; a G' spurt did not suffice to get G growth going and keep it in pattern.[29] Continually increasing replacement was required. Another interesting insight of Figure 2.5b is that the mainland Dutch colonies together, both Guyana and Surinam, perhaps imported Africans in the constant proportional F manner from the 1710 through to the early 1770s. This is an exceptional finding. It needs to be related carefully to the pattern of settlement and the nature of economic development for this group of Dutch colonies.

A fresh surge of Dutch slaving out of the Loango region of northern West Central Africa from 1715 through 1775 took a G' path, peaking at 1758, that resembled the import trends for Berbice between 1705 and 1735 and the Dutch Caribbean islands between 1732 and 1777 (Table 2.5). Then a substantial return of Dutch ships to the Guinea Coast of western equatorial Africa helped significantly in supplying the slaves consumed in the labor-intensive growth of Surinam and Guyana that continued into the 1770s. It looks as though Dutch entrepreneurs, now free of West India Company restraints, may have gone back to Guinea in response to the growth of these mainland South American plantations of the Netherlands. Or did some opening of Guinea to Dutch participation make the New World expansion supply-driven? It would seem that further research could fruitfully tease out the nature of these and earlier dynamics in the Dutch slave trade of the 17th and 18th centuries.

When in the 1700s the French took up shipping slaves to their colonies on a large scale rather than mostly buying them from international competitors (counter to the prevailing principles of mercantilism), they sent vessels to coasts that were already well established in supplying slaves to Europeans. Primarily their cargoes drew from the Bight of Benin along a G' curve, apparently under way already in the 1690s, that reached a level of some 5,300 a year by the 1720s, as Figure 2.6a indicates (Richardson 1989, 14; Manning 1979, 117, for before 1700). Recent calculations by Geggus (2001, 135)—the hollow, upward triangles—at 1688, 1713, and 1738 show fewer exports for the periods 1676–1700, 1701–1725, and 1726–1750; but the rising movement basically curves the same way. A parallel G' trend, also with t_0 in the 1740s, characterizes the expansion of French slave exports from Senegambia, that part of black Africa closest to Europe and to the West Indies, from the 1700s right through to the 1790s. During the 1720s, 1730s, and 1740s this traffic reached about 1,300 persons a year.[30] Table 2.6 summarizes these trends.

Hollow squares toward the bottom of the figure demonstrate how, during the

Figure 2.6a
Some Particulars of the French Slave Trade: African Sources of Slaves

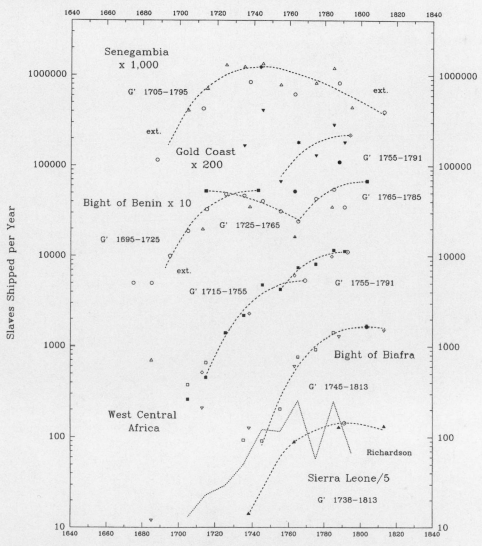

Sources: Richardson 1989, 14; Manning 1979, 117; Geggus 2001, 135.

Table 2.6
Comparing Trends of Purchasing, Shipping, and Consumption in the French Slave Trade

Origins in Africa

Bight of Benin	1695-1745	G'	1743
Senegambia	1705-1795	G'	1744
West Central Africa	1715-1755	G'	1769
Sierra Leone	1738-1813	G'	1791
West Central Africa	1755-1791	G'	1793
Gold Coast	1735-1813	G'	1794
Bight of Benin	1765-1785	G'	1803
Bight of Biafra	1745-1813	G'	1803

Port of Ships

Nantes	1714-1780	G'	1743
Other Ports	1714-1767	G'	1760
Other Ports	1767-1791	?G'	1812
Nantes	1774-1791	?G'	1825

Area of Consumption

Guadeloupe	1638,1663	?G'	1680
Martinique	1638-1710	G'	1699
St. Domingue	1663-1730	G'	1725
Guiana	1688-1795	G'	1735
Guadeloupe	1688-1816	G'	1739
Martinique	1730-1828	G'	1758
Louisiana	1710-1770	G'	1760
St. Domingue	1730-1770	G'	1767
St. Domingue	1770-1791	?G'	1817

Sources: Figures 2.6a, 2.6b, and 2.6c.

first two decades of the century, French captains also plumbed the possibilities of the Bight of Biafra, east of Benin, harvesting some 650 slaves per year there in the 1710s. But apparently they then gave up on the region until the second half of the century. Another temporary expansion of the French slave trade probably occurred along the Gold Coast in the 1730s and especially in the 1740s, according to Richardson. What this did, apparently, was to supplant falling numbers from nearby Benin, for a G' curve for these two regions *combined* would carry the 1695–1725 trend found in Benin forward into the 1740s. Approaching mid-century, these two contiguous regions together sold some 6,000 captives a year to French vessels. The shift of origin within the area resulted in a retro-actively timed G' decline for the supply from Benin alone, as if the base year of the formula had been pushed back from 1743 to 1715 (the second fitted trend for the hollow circles in the graph). Richardson (1989, 12) reiterates how imprecise coastal allocations of the slave trade remain, even after considerable refinement in their study. While, for example, Geggus separates out the Windward Coast (still further west of the Bight of Benin, between the Gold Coast and Sierra Leone), Richardson does not.

The future of French slaving, however, was in fact shifting considerably further southward along the Atlantic shore of the continent. From small beginnings at the end of the 17th century, more and more French vessels visited West Central Africa. At first, they did not directly challenge the hegemony that the Portuguese claimed for Angola through their bases at Luanda and Benguela. Instead, they probed north of the Zaire (Congo) River, along the Loango Coast, which later became French Congo and Gabon. Dutch and British ships had for some time been intruding effectively here contrary to Portuguese claims. Between 1710 and 1760 the average numbers of persons loaded annually by French slavers along this part of the littoral rose in G' form from some 300 to more than 4,500, replacing the Bight of Benin (Slave Coast) as the leading French source of black bound labor.[31]

Then, principally to satisfy the appetite of the planters of St. Domingue, French slaving surged anew across the late 1700s until the fateful revolt took place against France's greatest consumers of slaves.[32] By the 1780s and early 1790s no less than 11,000 captive laborers a year on average were being extracted by French shippers from West Central Africa, as Figure 2.6a indicates. To obtain this burgeoning supply, French captains now probed south along the coast into estuaries between the Congo River and Luanda and, even further, down the ineffectively controlled southern Angolan shoreline between Benguela and the Kunene River, the artery into the eastern hinterland of southern Africa. From this remote littoral they smuggled a few thousand slaves annually before their trade collapsed in the early 1790s (Miller 1988, 227)—perhaps enough to make the difference between the 1715–1755 and 1755–1791 curves for West Central Africa in Figure 2.6a.

From mid-century to the eve of the French Revolution, however, French slave exports from the Bights of Benin and Biafra, the Gold Coast, and Sierra Leone also increased in fresh G' fashion. Figure 2.6a and Table 2.6 show how these trends mostly resembled the increase from West Central Africa in timing and, therefore, in proportional gain.[33] From Southeast Africa, mostly from Mozambique for delivery to the Mascarene Islands, Stein (1979, 121) indicates numbers for French slaving that from 1705 through 1765 might also be roughly captured by a G' curve, with peak at about 950 annually in the 1750s. Then they, like exports from other regions, follow a fresh, higher trend of that shape that attained about 5,000 a year by 1791. Geggus (2001), however, shows only about 1,200 French slaves from Southeast Africa on average between 1776 and 1800. While numbers from Southeast Africa, West Central Africa, the Bight of Benin, and the Gold Coast collapsed after the great revolt in St. Domingue in the early 1790s, French slave acquisitions in the Bight of Biafra, Sierra Leone, and Senegambia continued to follow G trends that had been running for years. The latter trades seem to have conducted most of their business with the Windwards and Cayenne, which continued to want bound labor after 1792, while in the second half of the 18th century over half of St. Domingue's Africans came from West Central Africa alone and another quarter from the Bight of Benin (Eltis 2001, 46).

In sum, the numbers of slaves purchased by French shippers from every region in Africa that they tapped display G' patterns of growth and decline—and probably no other form of trend. Modeling exports this way, furthermore, clarifies how French slavers were pushed or enticed to operate in various sources of African labor, while it elucidates just what those underlying regional trends really were in an environment of often imprecise data. The French evidence, furthermore, affords one of those happy experiences of inquiry in which the more recent improved and more complete information (first from Stein 1979 and Richardson 1989, and most recently from Geggus 2001) fits the offered argument (here, the universal G' shape of the local French trends) better than the original evidence (Curtin 1969 and 1975) with which this type of analysis of the slave trade was first made years ago.

Something is also known about the ports whose shipping carried these captive cargoes. While some averaging is necessary to even out short-term variability, it is clear from Figure 2.6b that the number of vessels that were based on Nantes—now the leading base of the business, which mounted 45 percent of all identifiable French slaving voyages from 1700 through early 1793—rose then fell around an underlying G' trend between 1714 and 1780 that peaked at about 18 ships per year near 1742. Several other ports, however, began to push themselves into the trade approximately parallel to the 1715–1775 G' surge in French traffic from West Central Africa (Table 2.6). By 1760 they outfitted some 19 slaving ventures annually, on average—a number rising via the G' shape from 1714 through the 1760s, it appears. For the 1750s, 1760s, and 1770s these competitiors then significantly outweighed Nantes in the business—about 1.5 to 1. As their slave trades surged anew from the 1760s through 1792 (along a G' path with t_0 near 1812), these other ports now handled twice as many Africans

Figure 2.6b
Some Particulars of the French Slave Trade: The Home Ports of Ships

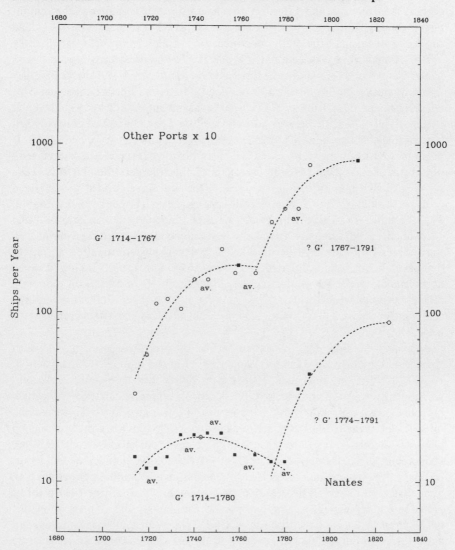

Source: Stein 1979, 207–9.

as Nantes, though the Nantes trade, too, rose strongly before the door of St. Domingue was slammed shut by Toussaint l'Ouverture (Stein 1979, 207–9).

These shipping data that move through time in G' patterns suggest at a still finer level how "market share," even within national industries, changed historically in G-based paths. The Atlantic slave trade *in toto*, French involvement in it, the regional operations of French vessels along the African coast, and the participation of particular French ports all unfolded in G' patterns. The implications of population trends in G-connected form for economic analysis extend further and further as our study proceeds.

It is also possible to outline flows of slaves into particular French possessions in the New World. As shown in Figure 2.6c (summarized in Table 2.6), Martinique displays the first clear and sustained G' surge in imported Africans. This curve from the 1630s through 1710 peaked at about 1,800 per year at 1699 (Curtin 1969, 119, 216). It was accompanied by early, tentative growth in imports to Guadeloupe between 1625 and 1675 (midpoints at 1638 and 1663). If these 25-year averages were taking a G' path, they would have topped out temporarily at about 140 in 1680. It was the later, much larger 1688–1816 G' wave for Guadeloupe that brought as many as 3,000 new slaves a year to the island at its crest around 1739. Along with this movement occurred a smaller 1688 to 1795 G' influx of Africans to French Guiana (Cayenne) that maximized near 1735 at about 440 annually. It was for St. Domingue, however, that the annual introduction of slaves in this era of the early 18th century forged to the fore. In that likely G' surge the average for the period 1675–1700 (1688) is high (denoted as a diamond on the graph); but the data for 1663, 1710, and 1730 fall smoothly along the familiar curve with a peak of about 4,000 at 1725. Henceforward, the assets and wishes of St. Domingue would do most to shape the French slave trade.

A second G' surge for Martinique carried imports there to a maximum of some 3,400 annually in 1758 for the period 1730 through 1828 (at least from 1730 to 1770 if the later swings should instead be fitted separately). Accompanying this was the introduction of slaves to Louisiana 1710–1770, which probably peaked at about 500 annually near 1760. Once again, however, the most slaves went to the large half-island of St. Domingue. Here the second wave of imports, from 1730 through 1770, topped out at close to 10,000 per year around 1767. Then, from 1770 to the great revolt the number of new slaves coming to St. Domingue soared afresh, reaching over 30,000 a year along a G' track that would have crested at about 54,000 imports annually at 1817 if it had not been cut off violently. Finally, after St. Domingue (and Louisiana) passed out of French hands, slave imports to Guadeloupe and Guiana swung upward again (graphed but not fitted), breaking from past G' trends and surpassing the local maxima for previous annual averages. While these late shifts were significant on the scale of previous comparable imports to those two colonies, they did not make up for the loss of St. Domingue. The flow to Guiana reached only some 1,000 annually in the 1820s, and the new intake for Guadeloupe perhaps

Figure 2.6c
Some Particulars of the French Slave Trade: Imports by Specific Colonies

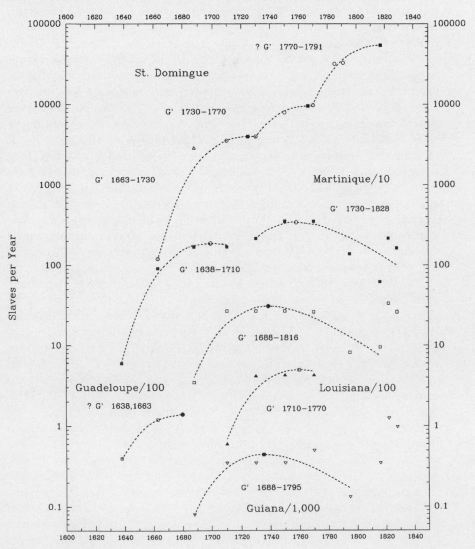

Sources: Curtin 1969, 119, 216; Eltis 1987, 247.

3,000, while the change in Martinique did no more than average out the low numbers around the turn of the century roughly to continue the G' curve that had begun by 1730.

Table 2.6 relates these trends in the importation of slaves to the patterns observed for exports acquired by French ships from various portions of the African coast and the role of certain French ports in providing the vessels that carried this trade. Insightful observations and fruitful questions arise from these comparisons.

First of all, the adoption of sugar cultivation or its robust expansion, initially on Martinique then upon St. Domingue and Guadeloupe, supported average annual slave purchases that reached 1,800, 3,500, and 2,700 by the 1710s, respectively, most recently and steeply rising on St. Domingue and Guadeloupe after the 1670s. Such burgeoning demand seems to have enticed ships from Nantes into the business. These vessels opened up or expanded French operations of the early 1700s in Senegambia, the Bight of Benin, the Loango region of northern West Central Africa, and—temporarily before 1720—the Bight of Biafra. Previously, across the later decades of the 1600s, slave imports to the French Caribbean had been transported mostly in foreign bottoms, with La Rochelle serving as the leading home port among French carriers (Curtin 1969, 121). If the aggregate level for French colonial imports from French vessels was indeed about 1,250 a year during this early phase, Manning's estimates for French activity in the Bight of Benin (Figure 2.6a) suggest that about half of early French cargoes came from this section of the African coast alone.

The new 18th-century trade of Nantes, drawing upon not one but many sections of the African coast, grew to a temporary peak in the 1740s, fostering the expansion of plantations on Guadeloupe and in Guiana while continuing the robust development of St. Domingue, as Table 2.6 next shows. The success of this business apparently attracted more and more competition from ports other than Nantes. The slave trade of these rivals surged upward in G' form from the 1710s to crest temporarily in the 1760s, catching up with and surpassing the activity of Nantes. It was the growing (and cheaper) slave supply in West Central Africa, also rising in a G' path that headed for a peak in the 1760s, that made room for these new entrepreneurs in the French trade to find "product." It was the doubling of consumption on St. Domingue, meanwhile, in a G' trend likewise topping out temporarily in the 1760s, that primarily expanded New World markets for their cargoes.

In the lower levels of Table 2.6, however, the relationships among movements in French sources, shipping, and colonial consumption at first glance seem to behave in a noticeably different way. Whereas likely G' trends for sales to St. Domingue and French slave shipping—both from Nantes and from other ports— approximately match, the curves for loading on French ships in West Central Africa, Sierra Leone, the Gold Coast, and the Bights of Benin and Biafra do not rise as much, heading for peaks in the early 1790s or early 1800s rather than around 1817.

In analyzing the patterns, it first seemed as though the reason for this discrepancy might lie in the extent to which interlopers of other nations cut into the great marketing opportunity provided by the French Caribbean, especially St. Domingue. Suppliers from Britain, the Netherlands, Denmark, and North America are known to have delivered substantial shares of the Africans arriving in the French West Indies. Curtin estimated some 38 percent for the 18th century as a whole (1969, 219). Summing the trends of Figure 2.6a (which employ more complete data from Richardson 1989, 14) against those of Figure 2.6c indicates, however, that while Curtin's calculation might be about right for the first half of the century on average (using his 15 percent adjustment for loss on the voyage), in the 1760s, 1770s, 1780s, and early 1790s the non-French proportion among deliveries dropped almost in half, to more like 22 percent. Increasing intrusion by competitiors does not account for the discrepancy in the late-18th century pattern between French slave-loading in certain parts of Africa and the data for shipping and West Indian arrivals. Other factors seem to bear instead.

For one thing, across the later decades of the 18th century, an increasing proportion of French slaving in West Central Africa was taking place illicitly in areas not only claimed by the Portuguese but recognized diplomatically to be theirs by the French government—south of the Congo River at the top of Angola and below Benguela at the bottom of that sprawling region (Miller 1988, 226–28). Under these circumstances, actual French loadings from West Central Africa may well have risen more steeply (via a G' path of rather later timing) than the available data indicate.

Overall, in purchasing along the African coast, in committing shipping to the trade, and in the consumption of slaves by various colonies, the French evidence further expands our understanding of how the Atlantic trade again and again developed via successive G' waves of local activity. That was the way that flows of even forced migration first developed and then declined.

Earlier, larger, and more gradually growing than the slaving of the Dutch or the French, the trade of Portugal—which increasingly became a business operating out of her great colony, Brazil—was also composed of segments that followed G' patterns. Figure 2.7a presents some trends in the African sources of Portuguese or Brazilian cargoes. The comparable movements for the Costa da Mina (the Bight of Benin or Slave Coast) have already appeared in Figure 2.4a.

The port of Luanda, the administrative center for Portuguese presence in West Central Africa, was (is) situated about a quarter of the way from the northern to the southern border of modern Angola. Benguela lies about two-thirds down that stretch of coast. "Angola" in the era of heavy Atlantic slaving was a loosely applied label that at times included embarkations from Cabinda, north of the mouth of the Congo River, or even locations all the way up to Cape Lopez in modern Gabon. In these northern regions, however, the Portuguese could not control the trade and had to put up with dominating activity by British, Dutch,

Figure 2.7a

Specifics of the Portuguese–Brazilian Slave Trade: Exports from West Central and Southern Africa, Including the Traffic of Competitors

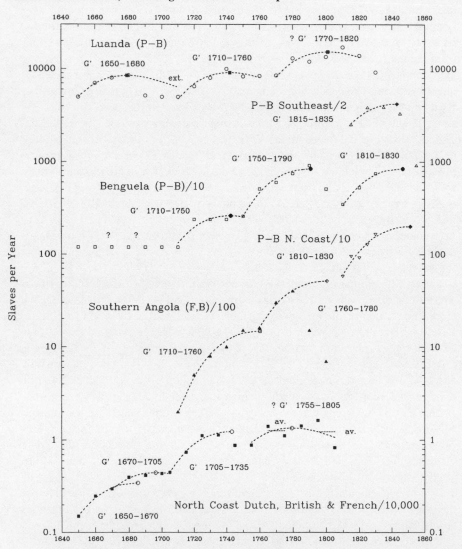

Sources: Miller 1992, 109; Richardson 1989, 13, 14; Postma 1990, 115, 121; Eltis 1987, 98, 250–52. See Figure 2.4a for Portuguese–Brazilian exports from Benin.

and French shipping. I follow Joseph C. Miller (1992, 106–7) in attributing exports from this part of the coast to Dutch, British, and French operations until the French pulled out of the trade with the Revolution and the slave revolt of St. Domingue, after which Brazilian operators moved in to exploit the void.[34] Around Luanda, the Portuguese and Brazilians maintained better control, though some British and French interlopers sneaked in south of the Congo River during later years of the 18th century. (The Dutch apparently stayed more focused upon Loango.) In the southern end of Angola (Miller 1992, 109), Portuguese admin- istration was weaker, and it was tempting—and feasible—to sidetrack supply from the interior to quiet river-mouths further down the coast or even to French and British agents in Benguela itself, though this shadowy traffic is difficult to quantify. In the most extreme reaches of Angola, from Benguela down to the Kunene River, it was the French and the British who led the trade that diverted slave delivery coming from the southern African interior away from Benguela. This export collapsed in the last two decades of the 18th century as the French pulled back in slaving after the debacle of St. Domingue and the British moved toward making it illegal. From Southeast Africa (primarily Mozambique), fi- nally, some 76 percent of slave vessels with known nationality that had loaded in this region but were caught by British naval patrols between 1811 and 1867 were Portuguese (Eltis 1987, 98). The estimates for Portuguese-Brazilian exports from this area of origin that are used in Figure 2.7a take that portion of Eltis's totals for Southeast Africa (ibid., 250–52).

Graphing in Figure 2.7a of these regional origins of Portuguese or Brazilian slaves indicates, first of all, the usual ubiquitous surges with G' shape. There are occasional gaps in the trending; and approximations of the numbers still tend to be quite rough or incomplete (especially before about 1720). It would seem advisable, however, to assume as a working hypothesis for the time being that the G' form was just as general here as among the regional sources for the Dutch and French trades. These G' patterns, furthermore, provide additional insight into how Portuguese slaving evolved.

From the central base at Luanda, following the Portuguese recovery of north- eastern Brazil from the Dutch, exports rose from 1650 through 1680 along a G' path that topped out in 1679, according to Miller's estimates (1992, 109). His calculations for 1690 and 1700 then drop off substantially below a projection of this curve. But if carried forward, it would converge upon his conclusions for the early 1700s, as Figure 2.7a illustrates. This is one of several places in the historical record where more information would be especially helpful. Up the coast to the north, meanwhile, Dutch and British vessels were extracting more and more Africans from the Loango area and its environs. A first G' growth in business there between 1650 and 1670 had its t_0 at 1685, as Table 2.7 sum- marizes. This made the trend quite parallel to that for Portuguese shipments from Luanda. This early, the Loango trade was dominated by the Dutch, whose G' trend for exports from there between 1665 and 1705 crested at 1687, as Figure 2.5a and Table 2.5 have shown.

Table 2.7
Developments in Portuguese–Brazilian Operations and Some Locally Competing Trades

African Exports			Colonial Imports		
			Bahia from Luanda I	1724-1763	?G' 1661
Luanda I	1650-1680	G' 1679			
x North Coast I	1650-1670	G' 1685			
x North Coast II	1670-1705	G' 1696			
B. of Benin I	1665-1775	G' 1721	Pernambuco from Luanda	1724-1738	G' 1718
Luanda II	1710-1760	G' 1742	Rio de J. from Luanda I	1724-1773	G' 1750
Benguela I	1710-1750	G' 1743			
x North Coast III	1705-1735	G' 1744			
x South Coast I	1710-1760	G' 1760	Bahia from Luanda II	1768-1820	G' 1760
x North Coast IV	1755-1805	G' 1779			
Benguela II	1750-1790	G' 1791	Rio de J. from Benguela	1784-1828	G' 1790
Luanda III	1770-1820	?G' 1801	All North of Bahia	1738-1838	G' 1793
x South Coast II	1760-1780	G' 1801	Rio de J. from Luanda II	1773-1820	G' 1804
B. of Benin II	1775-1850	G' 1811	All South of Bahia I	1783-1848	G' 1809
			All Bahia	1758-1848	G' 1810
Southeast Africa	1815-1835	G' 1843	All South of Bahia II	1808-1848	G' 1844
Benguela III	1810-1830	G' 1847			
P-B North Coast	1810-1830	G' 1852			

× = not Portuguese–Brazilian.

Sources: Miller 1992, 91–93, 100–101, 109; Manning 1979, 117; Eltis 1987, 98, 243–44, 250–52.

A renewed surge in slaving from the north coast of West Central Africa followed from 1670 to 1705. This topped out over a decade later than the preceding G' movement and seems to reflect the increasing activity of the British along that shore in the late 17th century (see Figure 2.9a, below). Meanwhile, ships from Bahia poured into the Bight of Benin (Elmina, the Slave Coast) seeking human cargoes. Their exports rose from some 500 a year in the 1660s to over 8,000 in the first decade of the 1700s (Manning 1979, 117, 135–38) along a G' trajectory that topped out at about 1721 (Figure 2.4a). This surge increased to equal the volume of the Portuguese trade from Luanda. Out of that Angolan base, though, the dip of traffic in the late 1600s, which—if real—may have pushed Brazilians to go get slaves themselves, gave way to new G' expansion from 1710 to 1760. This trend, around its peak at 1742, lifted Portuguese Luandan volume back above Brazilian loadings from the Bight of Benin, from which coast exports declined until the 1770s. Meanwhile, as Bahians helped themselves in the Bight of Benin, Lisbon operators at Luanda seem to have developed some modest compensatory business at Pernambuco, to the north of Bahia, that reached about 850 slaves per year.[35] This G' expansion peaked parallel at 1718 with Brazilian exports from the Slave Coast, as Figure 2.7b and Table 2.7 indicate.

The atrophy of known shipments from Luanda to Bahia from the 1720s through the 1760s—from about 3,000 annually to more like 1,000—that is shown in Figure 2.7b suggests that demand for bound labor from this sugar-growing part of Brazil was tapering off (perhaps with some appearance of natural replacement among slaves) in a manner that reduced imports there from both Luanda and the Bight of Benin (Figure 2.4a) across the middle of the 1700s. To the south around Rio de Janeiro and into that port's rich interior, however, the middle of the 18th century was a boom time for fresh African labor. The annual numbers swelled in a G' wave between the 1720s and the 1770s, attaining 4,500 around the crest at 1750. Benguela probably loaded slaves through the middle of the 18th century along a G' path that resembled that of Luanda in this era, reaching a level of some 2,600 (Figure 2.7a). But the international competitors of West Central Africa's northern coast also expanded exports in parallel G' fashion with t_0 at 1744 right along with the Portuguese operatives of Luanda and Benguela. It was not demand just from southern Brazil that supported this mid-century surge of outbound traffic in captive labor.

What were the dynamics of supply from the African interior at this time? Miller presents a vivid picture of how in West Central Africa a "slaving frontier" moved inland from the Atlantic coast, decade by decade and century by century from the 1500s through much of the 1800s (1988, chs. 4–7). Coastal dwellers became used to, and dependent upon, imported goods. These could be obtained by providing slaves. On the edge of this spreading zone of cultural and economic change, militaristic polities made a profitable business of warfare for the purpose of taking people. The men and boys were sold into the Atlantic slave trade; women captives mostly enhanced the wealth and power (and by their fertility the domestic production of slaves) for these "warlord" states, whose rulers prospered and became stronger until another inland surge of Portuguese military might crushed them as competitors and impediments to trade, rather than useful partners, and the frontier once again rolled further inland, starting the process all over. The Kongo kings had operated this way as early as the late 1500s, conducting war for slaves around the edges of their area of control and building economic consolidation within the nuclear kernel. The Portuguese out of Luanda adopted this strategy in the 1650–1680 period, which is reflected in their estimated slave exports (ibid., 143; a valuable mapping of successive "frontier" zones from the 1570s through the 1870s appears on page 148). Apparently, the Dutch and their suppliers had learned to play the same game north of the Congo River in Loango and were expanding output in parallel fashion, as Table 2.5 and Figure 2.5a indicate.

In the 1740s and 1750s, the next wave of labor exports from Luanda crested, the first G' expansion out of Benguela maximized (Table 2.7), and a new con-

Figure 2.7b
Specifics of the Portuguese–Brazilian Slave Trade: Brazilian Regional Disposition of Slaves

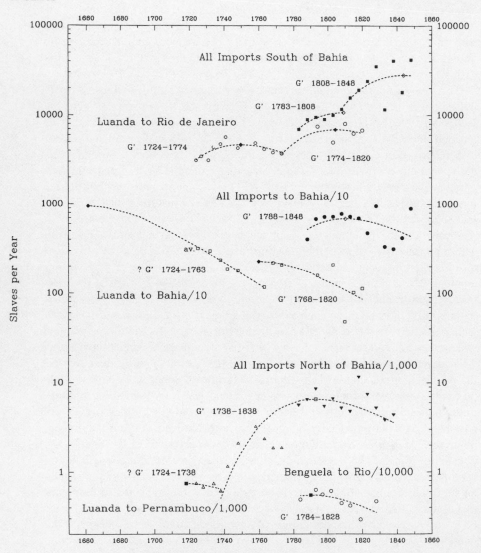

Sources: Miller 1992, 96–97, 100–101; Eltis 1987. 243–44.

temporary surge also occurred along the North Coast. At this time, increased warfare for slave-making, currently led by the Lunda, was convulsing the Kwango and Kasai Valleys, two of the most populous areas of the hinterland (Miller 1988, 145–46, 216). Captives from this interior could be marketed not just west to Luanda but southwest to Benguela or northwest across the Congo River to the Loango or North Coast. All three loading zones thus prospered simultaneously in the fashion shown by Table 2.7. Later G' waves of slave exports—which, as Table 2.7 summarizes, crested around 1760, 1780, 1800, and 1845, respectively, in West Central and more southern Africa—presumably reflect similar dynamics as the "slaving frontier" strode further and further afield from its origins in the 1500s.

Such successive geographic penetrations of African societies by a way of life relying heavily upon slaving would seem to have involved—in each wave— economic, political, military, cultural, and demographic changes whose consequences did not disseminate all at once. Rather, people (or at least their leaders) became used to, perhaps virtually addicted to, a new economy of international trade and its goods, progressively developed slaving systems with which to purchase or produce what they desired, experienced shifts in political and military power that evolved from their current positions within the division of labor of the complex inter-societal network of slaving, and absorbed consequent demographic losses, gains, and rearrangements (like altered sex ratios). Typically, such fundamental social changes are significantly influenced by the succession of generations, whether today one is talking about learning to work with a computer or, earlier, considers adapting to fighting and hunting with guns. Thus, we can expect that the absorption of a new "recruitment" zone or method for otherwise producing slaves (such as a debt-based social structure) diffused across populations in ways resembling how various "New World" sites have been exploited or how people in various parts of the world have taken advantage of urban development. The first book of this study has found each of these types of openings to accumulate population in G-shaped trends. Chapter 1 of the present volume demonstrates how such growths have, among other resources, been fed by migration in the shape of G', the derivative of G, as notably exemplified by 17th-, 18th-, and 19th-century waves of people coming to North America who were recruited from progressively wider and wider territorial rings that spread outward with time from the original center of supply in northwestern Europe. Catchment areas for future Americans spread from southeastern England to the west and north; to Ireland, Germany, and Scotland; and still later from there across Scandinavia and southern and eastern Europe.[36]

We may never know the historical trends in the size of African societies that were harvested or looted for slaves, though the D-shaped decline of the Aja in Dahomey provides a valuable clue (Manning 1982, 343). But the *emigration* extracted from them by slave-catching clearly rose and fell in G' fashion just like the immigration that has been attracted more freely to settlement frontiers and developing cities throughout the historical record. The rate of change in these seemingly remote, exotic societies of "Darkest Africa," therefore, seems to have been steered into the same standard paths as the experiences of closer, more familiar instances of historical metamorphosis.

Table 2.7 shows that for the Portuguese-Brazilian trade, slave exports from the Bight of Benin followed G' curves that peaked near 1721 and 1811 (Figure 2.4a), not with but *between* the waves drawn from West Central Africa (Figure 2.7a). For the international slaving of this other more northern and western region of the continent, Manning's data have been seen to sketch out a similar step-by-step involvement of successive parts of the interior of Dahomey and western Nigeria and even D-shape decline in the population of the Aja, the people whose ominous "hearth" experience gave the Slave Coast its name (Figure 2.4c and Table 2.4 and their discussion). In other words, the same kind of processes took place in two key areas of African slaving, but in alternating phases.

Meanwhile, Brazil, the destination of these captive Africans, pulled in more and more slaves between 1676 and 1700 and the 1780s in G rather than G' fashion. The successive, somewhat differently timed G' waves of exports headed for Brazil from various parts of West Central Africa, on the one hand, and the Bight of Benin, on the other, summed up to fill out this composite import pattern of G shape for the whole huge colony (Figure 2.1b). This suggests that it was changing demand from the growth of the slave-consuming, sugar-cultivating and mining regions of Brazil that set the outlines for Portuguese-Brazilian slaving, not supply in Africa. Trading from one specific part of the African coast or another, that is, took advantage of local opportunities of supply or price or power to help itself to a piece of the pie of profits currently being offered for delivering slaves to Brazil. In comparable fashion, leading New World segments of slave consumption—which, whether Spanish, Portuguese, British, or French in control, in aggregate each followed G-shape trends across the 18th century—have been seen collectively then to meld into an H curve for the Atlantic trade in its entirety (Figure 2.1a), indicating that the development of the plantation sector of the New World as a whole in turn set that overarching pattern within which national slaving activities then jostled against each other in G-shaped surges of competition (Figure 2.3) to secure the "correct" or "desired" supply of Africans.

The presence of G' local trades *within* a national business furthermore, suggests that when work in progress turns back to reconnect demographic change with economic processes in other historical contexts, specific industries or other sub-categories of activity within a national economy may likewise wax and wane in G' form as opposed to the G patterning of broader developments. On the other hand, some G-shaped economic processes may further aggregate into H or F trends of change, as local population growths have been seen in Volume I to compound to form such broader patterns, like the F for U.S. total population between 1670 and 1850 or an H twice thereafter (between 1850 and 1930 and from 1940 to the present).

For the Spanish slave trade, two kinds of specific records survive: one very early and one very late. The first covers, from the 1550s to the 1630s, activity under licenses by which the Spanish government authorized—first for Seville investors, later for foreign carriers—the transportation of Africans to the New World. The second concerns the shipment of slaves, principally to Cuba, from the late 1700s into the middle of the 1800s.

Across the early years, records exist for ships permitted to carry slaves from certain sources, both in vessels from the official New World port of Seville and then via *asiento* agreements begun with foreign suppliers in 1595, as the Spanish gave up trying to break the hold of the Portuguese upon the trade of the African coast (Curtin 1969, 21). From these data, as presented by Huguette Chaunu and Pierre Chaunu (1955–1960, 6: 402–3), Curtin (1969, 105–8) generated estimates for the number of slaves exported from various regions in terms of *piezas de India*, an equivalency in adult males that weighted women and children as partial units. In doing this, he distributed the licensed human cargoes of ships of unknown or mixed loading according to the knowns. Figure 2.8a plots the average number of *piezas de India* that he calculated per year as coming from three broad zones of the African coast.

Distinct geographical stages of the trade for the Spanish colonies before 1640 emerge. First, slaves were shipped mostly from Cape Verde—actually, the "Guinea of Cape Verde" or the coast from the Cape Verde peninsula to the Sierra Leone River. As this surge began to flag, three dozen voyages from the Canary Islands, Spain's somewhat closer-to-home outpost in the Atlantic, were authorized between 1596 and 1605. In Figure 2.8a these have been grouped with the larger flow from Cape Verde because, according to Curtin (1969, 103), they tapped the same original sources: slaves from the interior of Cape Verde brought overland to the coast of Mauritania and from there across to the Canaries. Collectively, however, this northern traffic from sub-Saharan Africa was soon declining. While approved exports from the region vary substantially from one five-year period to the next, they hover around an underlying G' curve with t_0 at 1563.

What made total *imports* to Spanish America take instead the probable G form evident for the years 1538–1638 in Figure 2.1a and Table 2.1 was how the trade soon spread to draw upon other sources. By the 1570s, the Spanish turned further along the African coast for slave cargoes.[37] Initially, most were authorized from "Guinea," at this early time a loose label for the whole West African coast from Sierra Leone through the Bight of Benin. The bottom plot in Figure 2.8a (hollow squares) shows how the numbers from this region shot up roughly along a G' path that would have topped out at 1641 if it had continued to its maximum rather than collapsing after 1610.[38] It was from still further south that the *asiento* trade of the early 1600s was to pull its forced labor.

The annual numbers from Angola and São Tomé rose almost exactly parallel to those of Guinea through the late 1500s, but on past 1595 as Portuguese

Figure 2.8a
The Early and Late Spanish Slave Trade: Piezas de India Licensed from African Sources, 1553–1638

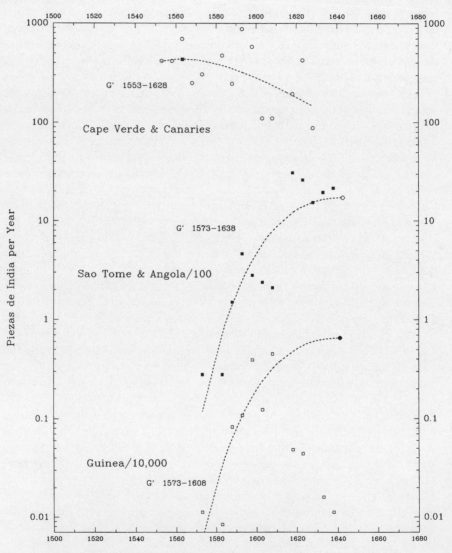

Exceptionally low data from 1578 and 1613 omitted.

Source: Curtin 1969, 106–7.

carriers exploited the *asiento* system.[39] For them, all the African coast was readily accessible; and this is where the supply lay. The beginnings of new trends for shipments from beyond Sierre Leone had indicated this even before 1595. But the roughly G' growth toward a peak at 1643 from the most southern, Angolan regions of Africa continued right into the 1630s rather than breaking at 1610 like the G' for Guinea.[40] Thus, as Curtin noted long ago in different terms (1969, 108–10), the sources of slaves for Spanish America first shifted down the coast away from the Canaries and Cape Verde and then under licensed Portuguese agency in the early 1600s moved still further southward to focus on Angola at the expense of Guinea. Each of these geographical waves, we now learn, followed underlying G' shape.

Such was also the pattern for deliveries by Spanish slavers and their collaborators and competitors to the Americas from the 1770s through the 1860s as progressively the trade in Africans became more and more an international target for reform. Figure 2.8b trends data for imports to Cuba, Puerto Rico, and other Spanish colonies.[41] The Caribbean, which had long been a backwater for Spanish colonialism, in the later 18th century turned into a booming frontier of development. The growth of the West Indian sugar industry, which in the 17th century had been led by the relatively small islands of the English but in the 18th depended for expansion chiefly upon French possessions (particularly large St. Domingue), now reveled in the spacious Spanish tropical holdings of Cuba, Santo Domingo, and Puerto Rico, and expanding sugar planters hungered for slaves.

According to the data of Eltis (1987, 245), captive Africans surged into Cuba from the late 1780s through the early 1860s along a G' path that peaked at about 11,000 per year around 1828. A projection of this curve backward in time suits both an estimate of Curtin (1969, 35) for 3,500 per annum on average 1774–1807 (midpoint 1791) and Deerr's number of 1,400 at 1776 (1949, 1: 278–81). These are denoted by "C" and "D" symbols on the figure.

For Puerto Rico (Curtin 1969, 44, 35), the data are less ample. Still, the average annual numbers of arrivals rose in G' form from 1810 through 1837 toward a t_0 at 1848. This trend, furthermore, connects with the level estimated by Curtin for 1774–1807 at the end of his time span (presuming that average annual slave imports for Puerto Rico in this preceding era were for the time being flat, rather than increasing vigorously like those of Cuba). Then deliveries to Puerto Rico somehow shrank for the 1846–1859 and 1860–1865 periods. Meanwhile, if a sudden high but brief spike to 850 per year in the 1820s is excepted, the very modest residue of traceable deliveries of slaves to all Spanish colonies of the New World other than Cuba, Puerto Rico, and the Rio de la Plata also rose from 1805 though 1835 in something like G' fashion with t_0 at 1843 before collapsing in the 1840s and 1850s following the Bolivarian revolutions.[42]

These import movements for Puerto Rico and other Spanish American colonies excepting Cuba and the Rio de la Plata parallel the G' trend for Spanish

Figure 2.8b
The Early and Late Spanish Slave Trade: Imports to Cuba, Puerto Rico, and Other Colonies*

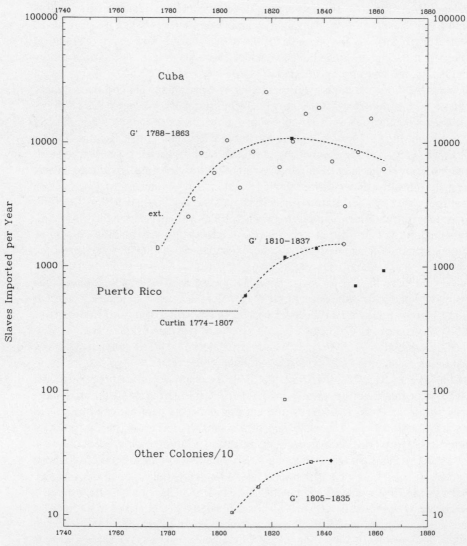

* Not including Rio de la Plata. C Curtin; D Deerr.

Sources: Eltis 1987, 245, 249; Curtin 1969, 35, 44; Deerr 1949, 1: 278–81.

and U.S. exports from the Bight of Benin in Figure 2.4a. (With importation illegal at home, U.S. carriers turned to feed the growing appetite of Spanish America.) This Slave Coast pattern also peaked in the middle 1840s. Thus, activity for at least one source of slaves for Spanish America confirms the shape of change in imports to at least some of these colonies, though the much larger wave coming to Cuba crested about two decades earlier. What more do the relationships of the G' curves involved say about the way that African sources and Spanish American consumption were linked?

In sum, for imports to particular parts of Spanish America toward the end of the Atlantic slave trade, as for Spanish-authorized deliveries from Africa at its beginning, the G' curve once more generally captures the trends of increase and decline. Additionally, it assists in framing further inquiry about how the trade worked, from the source of its cargoes to the disposal of its commodity in the New World.

For much of the time, between periods of early and then late domination by the Portuguese, the most substantial segment of the international slave trade was conducted by the British, who transported some 20,000–40,000 Africans across the Atlantic yearly during the 18th century (Figure 2.3). Discussion of this hefty portion of the business has on purpose been saved for last. On the one hand, probably most is known about it. The detail becomes quite fine, though at some cost in increasing variability as smaller and smaller parts of the whole are considered. On the other hand, these British particulars can, as nowhere else, be linked to various insights concerning local slave and owner populations that make it possible to explore just how the forced migration of the Atlantic slave trade took on the so ubiquitously observed G' shape and in turn left imprints of this pattern upon the development of local society and economy in the Americas.

Figures 2.9a and 2.9b begin by plotting the average annual numbers of slaves extracted from various parts of the African coast by British carriers. As early as the 1660s some 3,500 slaves annually were coming out of the Bight of Biafra (the plot with the hollow squares at the bottom of Figure 2.9b). But these numbers fell off to about 1,000 as the focus of "recruitment" shifted elsewhere. The next earliest surge in supply, topping out around 1703, was drawn from the Bight of Benin (the Slave Coast), whence up to 4,000 chained men, women, and children per year were being transported in British bottoms by the late 1600s and early 1700s (Figure 2.9b). Soon behind this came a wave out of Senegambia, the most northwestern coast of black Africa. The underlying G' curve for this long-lasting movement—all the way from 1666 to 1775—crested at 1721 (Figure 2.9a). The left portion of Table 2.8 facilitates comparison of the duration and timing of these surges. In early increases that did not last for long, British exports from West Central Africa rose in similar fashion from the 1660s through the 1690s, and slave loadings from the Gold Coast appear to have climbed comparably across the 1660s and 1670s.

In the Gold Coast, after being set back in the 1680s, shipments swelled then

Figure 2.9a
African Sources of the British Slave Trade, 1662–1808: Senegambia, Sierra Leone, and the Windward Coast

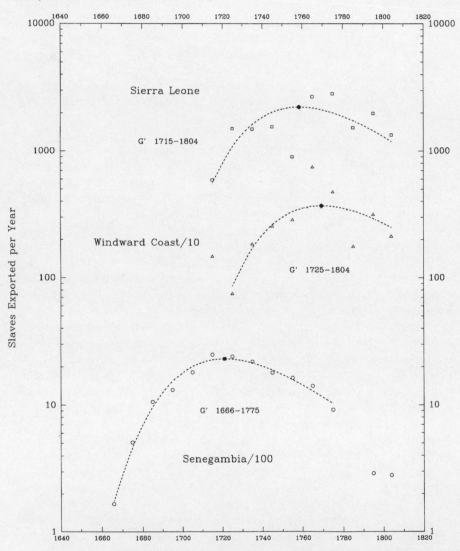

Sources: Eltis 2000, 166 (17th century); Richardson 1989, 13; Curtin 1975, 114, 116, 118.

Figure 2.9b
African Sources of the British Slave Trade, 1662–1808: Gold Coast, Benin, Biafra, and West Central Africa

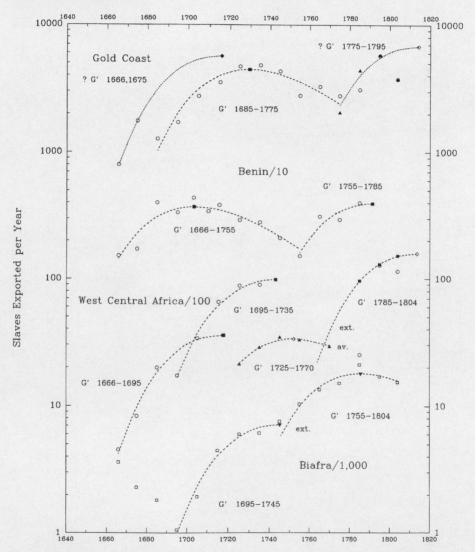

Sources: Eltis 2000, 166 (17th century); Richardson 1989, 13; Curtin 1975, 123, 126; 1969, 150.

Table 2.8
Pulses in the British Slave Trade, 1643–1806

African Sources

Biafra I	1655-1695	? decline
Benin I	1666-1755	G' 1703
Gold Coast I	1666,1675	?G' 1716
W. Central I	1666-1695	G' 1717
Senegambia	1666-1775	G' 1720
Gold Coast II	1685-1775	G' 1730
Biafra II	1695-1745	G' 1745
W. Central II hi	1695-1735	G' 1743
" " II lo	1725-1770	G' 1752
Sierra Leone	1715-1804	G' 1758
Windward Coast	1725-1804	G' 1769
Biafra III	1755-1804	G' 1786
Benin II	1755-1785	G' 1792
W. Central III	1785-1804	G' 1814
Gold Coast III	1775-1795	G' 1814

Slaving Group

London	1710-1750	?G' 1637?
Royal African Co.	1675-1705	G' 1678
London	1735,1755	?G' 1699
Bristol	1710-1775	G' 1714
Liverpool I	1735-1775	G' 1780
London II	1755-1788	G' 1792
Liverpool II	1755-1806	G' 1818

Colonial Consumption

Barbados I	1655-1685	G' 1648
St. K. & Nevis I?	1655-1685	?G' 1665?
Chesapeake	1637-1695	G' 1693
Virginia H-Rights	1643-1692	G' 1695
No. Carolina I	1675-1695	G' 1700
Barbados II	1681-1741	G' 1707
Jamaica I (total)	1666-1711	G' 1709
Montserrat	1655-1775	?G' 1712
Antigua	1655-1775	G' 1717
All Leewards	1666-1775	G' 1717
Pa. & Del.	1685-1775	G' 1722
St. K. & Nevis II	1685-1775	G' 1724
Virginia II	1699-1770	G' 1741
Jamaica II (tot.)	1711-1771	G' 1742
Jamaica (retain)	1721-1771	G' 1754
Jamaica (trans.)	1706-1731	G' 1752
No. Carolina II	1695-1755	G' 1761
Maryland & S.Pot.	1731-1772	G' 1768
So. Carolina I	1708-1737	G' 1773
Other Brit. W.I.	1730-1795	G' 1774
James River	1738-1767	G' 1775
So. Carolina II	1752-1770	G' 1791
Georgia	1745-1775	G' 1798

Sources: Figures 2.9a, 2.9b, 2.10a, 2.10b, 2.11a, 2.11b, 2.12, 2.13, 2.14.

shrank in G' form for 90 years along a curve that topped out a little later, near 1730. The second trend in West Central African exports surged more strongly. This G' curve crested in the 1740s at about 9,000 per year according to Richardson (1989, 13). Curtin's older estimates (1969, 150)—the solid, upward triangles in Figure 2.9b—perceived many fewer British slaves to be coming out of Angola (even including others from as far away as Mozambique). Their G' curve from the 1720s through the 1750s nonetheless peaks at 1752 compared with the 1743 for the 1695–1735 calculations of Richardson. A G' of approximately this timing, in other words, seems to represent the nature of *change* through time in British slaving out of West Central Africa across the middle of the 18th century, though there are some questions about who is included in this category by the two differing authorities. (Some work with the new CD-ROM data should readily settle the divergence.) This sequence of G' trends is summarized and compared with others in the left side of Table 2.8.

Curtin's data (1975, 116, 118) delineate rather later G' curves for British slave exports out of Sierra Leone (t_0 at 1758) and the Windward Coast (t_0 at 1769), as Figure 2.9a indicates. The annual averages vary more about the underlying trends; and the maxima of the curves reach only 2,200 and 3,700 per year, respectively. Still, the general underlying G' patterns seem evident. Then, beginning in the 1750s, British slaving from the Bights of Benin and Biafra, further east along the coast, experienced fresh G' surges toward peaks at 1792 and 1786 and typical annual exports that reached 4,000 from Benin but as many as 18,000 yearly from the Bight of Biafra (Figure 2.9b). Even later locally renewed waves of British shipments occurred across the last years of the 18th century from the Gold Coast and from West Central Africa. Each followed, before Britain terminated the trade, G' paths aimed to crest in 1814. The first reached an average annual level of about 6,000 before breaking.[43] From West Central Africa, however, Curtin (1969, 150—the solid squares in Figure 2.9b, contrasting with the hollow circles for Richardson)—calculated as many as 15,000, approximately matching the peak rate of extraction from the Bight of Biafra some quarter-century before.

The British slave trade had shifted southeastward down the African coast in a major way before it became illegal in 1808. But in this and every prior stage of its development, along all the principal coasts where cargoes were purchased and loaded, the business of this nation's carriers had prospered and declined consistently in surges of G' form. Indeed, this has been shown to be true for all the leading national slave trades of the Atlantic. Such recurrent patterning, though not perfect, should help clarify further, in sources that continue to improve, how to resolve differences among the conclusions of various scholars and further enrich insight as to how Africans were swept up into the net of Atlantic slaving.

Trends of G' shape similarly frame the history of how slaves were *consumed* in various parts of British America. Figures 2.10a and 2.10b present some examples from the Caribbean; Figures 2.11a and 2.11b contain illustrations from

Figure 2.10a
Slave Imports to Some British West Indian Colonies: Jamaica's Total,
Reexported, and Retained Arrivals

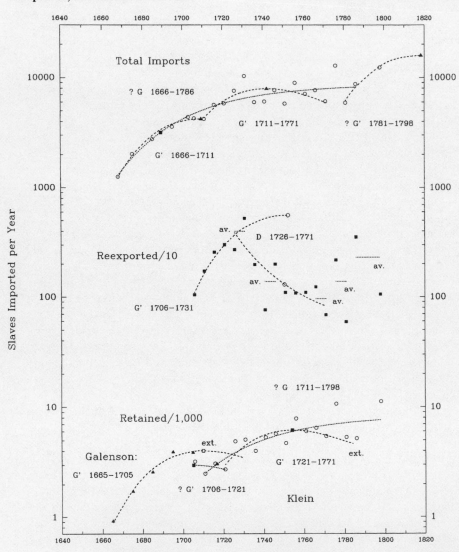

Sources: Eltis 2000, 208; Klein (Sheridan) 1978, 154; Galenson 1981, 218.

Figure 2.10b
Slave Imports to Some British West Indian Colonies: Barbados, the Leewards, and Certain Other Islands

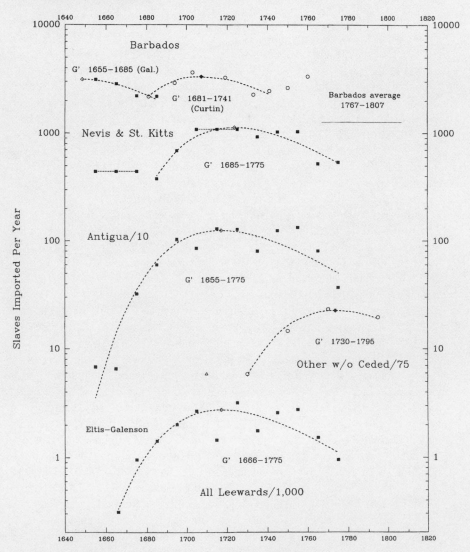

Sources: Curtin 1969, 55, 140; Eltis 2000, 208; Galenson 1981, 218.

mainland settlements of North America. The right side of Table 2.8 lists more fully how wave after wave of slave imports became part of British colonial life.

Barbados led the British march into plantation slavery as the island turned from other crops to sugar around the middle of the 17th century. This early in local development, direct records of slave imports there are lacking. The Dutch, in fact, supplied the bulk of slaves to this colony until 1663 (Curtin 1969, 55). Galenson's estimates (1981, 218) from population numbers and certain assumptions about demographic processes, though, produce the kind of G' pattern shown from the 1650s through the 1680s in Figure 2.10b. This has its t_0 at 1648, right in the middle of the local shift to sugar (Dunn 1972, 59–69). The net growth of the slave population of Barbados, once the "carrying capacity" of the island for sugar plantation life had been encountered, and both European settlers and their slaves dispersed to seed settlement on Jamaica, in the Leewards, and in the Carolinas, settled down to follow a G path from 1670 to 1710 with base year at 1636 (Harris 2001, 72, 74). Galenson's estimated immigration curve for Africans closely resembles the derivative of that trend. With little if any natural increase this early among Barbadian slaves, it should.[44] Meanwhile, comparably estimated slave imports to St. Kitts and Nevis averaged across three decades jointly more like 400 a year than the 2,800 of Barbados.[45]

Following these intitial G' surges of slavery onto Barbados and perhaps the English end of St. Christopher (St. Kitts) and Nevis, African bound labor took hold on the mainland. Headrights awarded for blacks in Virginia from 1643 through 1692, according to Craven (1971, 86), and estimations for slave imports into Virginia and Maryland together by Galenson for 1655 and 1665 (1981, 217), then Eltis for 1675, 1685, and 1695 (2000, 208) tell the same story (Figure 2.11a): slave migration into the Chesapeake swelled in G' shape with t_0 around 1695 probably from the 1620s (say Donnan's earliest data in *Historical Statistics* 2: 1172—the hollow circles between 1620 and 1640) to the end of the 17th century, reaching approximately 350 per year.[46] This was not much by West Indian standards; but by the 1670s incoming slaves were a visible feature of Chesapeake life. The handful per year who, Galenson estimates, trickled over into North Carolina between 1670 and 1700 (Figure 2.11b) increased along a largely parallel G' track. Table 2.8 relates the duration and timing of these mainland trends to each other and to early intakes into Caribbean colonies.

Peaking several years later, in the early 1700s, a second wave of slave importation to the British West Indies appeared, as the table also summarizes. The identifiable new surge of Africans into Barbados between 1681 and 1741 (Curtin 1969, 55) took a G' path of this phasing (Figure 2.10b). So did both the delivery and the incorporation of slaves into local life that followed English seizure of Jamaica in the 1650s. Eltis's arrivals 1666–1711 (2000, 208), the retentions cited by Klein for 1706–1721 (1978, 154, from Sheridan 1974, 503–4), and estimates of net imports by Galenson 1665–1705 (1981, 218) take G' paths that crest at 1709, 1705, and 1710, respectively. Figure 2.10a depicts these patterns, and the right portion of Table 2.8 summarizes them. Of the surge of slave arrivals, which

Figure 2.11a
Slave Imports to Some British Mainland Colonies: Virginia and Maryland, and Delaware and Pennsylvania

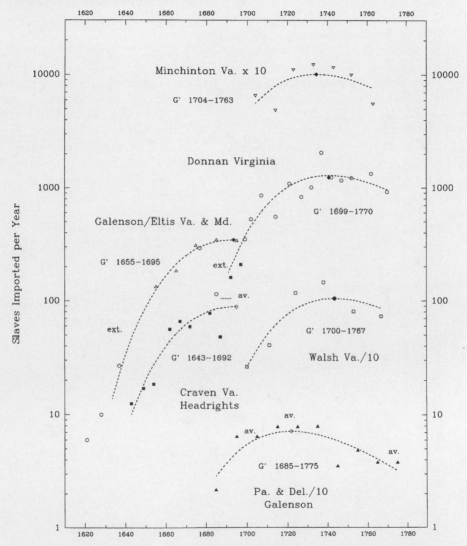

Sources: *Historical Statistics* 2: 1172; Craven 1971, 86; Galenson 1981, 216–17; Eltis 2000, 208; Minchinton 1976, 44; Walsh 2001, 166–69.

Figure 2.11b
Slave Imports to Some British Mainland Colonies: South Carolina, North Carolina, and Georgia

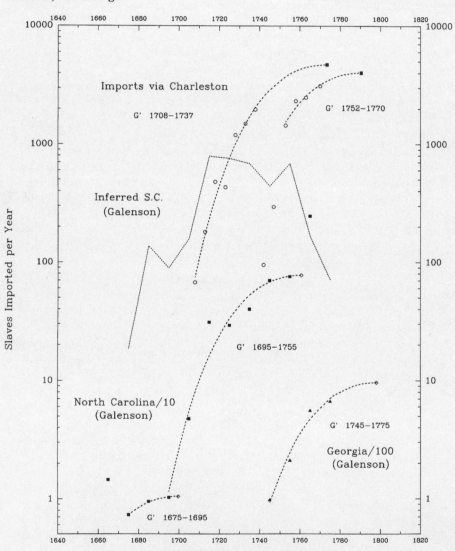

Sources: Historical Statistics 2: 1173–74; Galenson 1981, 217.

reached a level of about 4,200 per year in the early 18th century, some 3,000 (Klein) to 4,000 (Galenson) remained on the island. The rest were transshipped to other ultimate destinations, a practice that was just beginning to gain momentum. This is the way that Jamaica began to develop a slave population. That population began to grow across the late 1600s in a G path with its own base year at 1710 (Harris 2001, 72, 75), which—as previously observed for Barbados—makes importation simply a multiple of the derivative of the local demographic growth curve, rising and falling with it.

Behind this wave of slave imports to Barbados and Jamaica arrived G' flows of Africans into the Leeward Islands (Figure 2.10b; Galenson 1981, 218). Island by island, these curves peaked between 1712 and 1724 (Table 2.8). For all the British Leewards together, the crest came at 1717 with some 1,700 new arrivals per year (combining the 1666–1685 calculations of Eltis 2000, 208, with the 1695–1775 estimations of Galenson 1981, 218). Coincident with this movement into the Leewards, which for a while were rather marginal in West Indian development relative to Barbados and Jamaica, the introduction of slaves into Delaware and Pennsylvania, on the northern mainland fringe of the Chesapeake plantation region, also took G' form from 1685 through 1775. This maximized at 1722. It reached just about 70 additional slaves per year, however, and considerable averaging is needed to reduce the swings that occurred from decade to decade (Galenson 1981, 216).

Some two decades later crested the second G' wave of slave imports into Virginia. Whether computed by Donnan 1699–1770 (*Historical Statistics* 2: 1172), Minchinton 1704–1763 (1976, 44), or Walsh 1700–1767 (2001, 166–69), the flow takes the familiar up-and-down form of the derivative of G and tops out between 1735 and 1744.[47] Whereas it peaked at just over 1,000 imports per year on average, this trend ran parallel with the G' pattern for much larger slave deliveries to Jamaica. These topped out at 1742 with about 8,000 arrivals annually (Klein 1978, 154). The D-shaped crash in reexports off the island that occurred after 1733 made the G' curve for slaves *retained* in Jamaica peak rather later—in the early 1750s, as Table 2.8 and Figure 2.10a show.

This decisive downturn in Jamaica's reexport of Africans from the 1720s to the early 1770s probably resulted from the growing commercial tensions with Spanish America that led to the War of Jenkins's Ear. Whereas transshipments to the colonies of mainland British North America fell away as of the 1720s or sooner (panel b of Figure 2.12), the loss amounted to just a few dozen imports per year, not the 3,000 Jamaican annual reexports that disappeared by the late 1740s. The shift of the French to provide slaves for their own colonies, which has been discussed with the slaving history of that nation, undoubtedly was also a factor. The precise dynamics of the observed likely D-shaped decline in Figure 2.10a would seem to merit some further research.

Then in the later 1760s and early 1770s would have crested G' curves for imports to Charleston, South Carolina, for the period from 1708 through 1737 (*Historical Statistics* 2: 1173–74), certain other British colonies of the West

Indies from 1730 through 1795 (Curtin 1969, 140), and probably North Carolina 1695–1755 (Galenson 1981, 217). Before a new rush of plantation development in the 1760s, North Carolina seems to have taken in only some 750 slaves a year on average (Figure 2.11b). Neighboring Charleston was importing close to 2,000 annually before the scare of the Stono Rebellion broke the G' trend there around 1740. (The growth trajectory was headed for close to 5,000 a year at 1773 when it was interrupted.) Beyond Jamaica, Barbados, and the Leewards, other British possessions in and around the Caribbean, without the islands ceded by France in 1763, came to consume on average about 1,700 new Africans per year by the eve of the American Revolution (Figure 2.10b). Table 2.8 also samples how several local G' trends of slave importation in the mainland colonies also peaked in the later 1760s and early 1770s: into Maryland and the neighboring South Potomac naval district of Virginia 1731–1772; into the James River watershed 1738–1767 (perhaps, too, into the York and the Rappahannock during the early 1700s before breaking by 1730); in the delivery to Virginia of slaves by vessels from Liverpool and from other British American colonies from 1700 to 1767; and in shipments to Virginia and to South Carolina by Bristol slavers until their role in this mainland slave trade collapsed after about 1730.[48]

Finally, a few mainland British colonial regions across the later 18th century imported slaves along G' paths that headed toward peaks that would have been achieved—had the trends continued past the American Revolution—only in the 1790s. That was the case for Charleston 1752–1770 once the Stono scare was over (*Historical Statistics*, 2: 1173–74), for neighboring Georgia 1745–1775 (Galenson 1981, 217), and for deliveries to the rapidly developing James River watershed of Virginia by slavers based on Bristol and Liverpool for several decades after the 1720s (Walsh 2001, 168–69; plotted in Figure 2.14 below).[49]

In short, slave sales or consumption in the British colonies of the New World—from a central hub of distribution like Jamaica to a marginal region like the lower Delaware Valley, from Barbados in the beginning to Georgia near the end of the British and American Atlantic trades—developed and spread in repeated manifestations of the G' trend. What has been observed in Dutch, French, Portuguese, and Spanish colonies of the Western Hemisphere is most frequently and most firmly evident in this best-documented and explored, and much of the time the largest, of all the European ventures in transporting bound Africans to forced labor in the New World.

Even more clearly than among the operations of other nations in Atlantic slaving, furthermore, it is possible to follow the roles played by key ports in certain segments of the British trade. Figure 2.12 trends average annual tonnage from London, Bristol, and Liverpool that cleared for West Africa (Lamb 1976, 91–92, 98–99), the number of slaves transported by the Royal African Company during its years of dominance in the later 1600s (Galenson 1986, 30), slave deliveries by Bristol ships to Virginia and South Carolina, both direct from Africa and from the West Indies (Minchinton 1976, 44), and total Virginia imports from Africa and from other colonies (Klein 1978, 124). Together, these

Figure 2.12
The Roles of Leading English Ports in the West African and Slave Trades

a. English Shipping to West Africa   b. Slaves to the Mainland Colonies

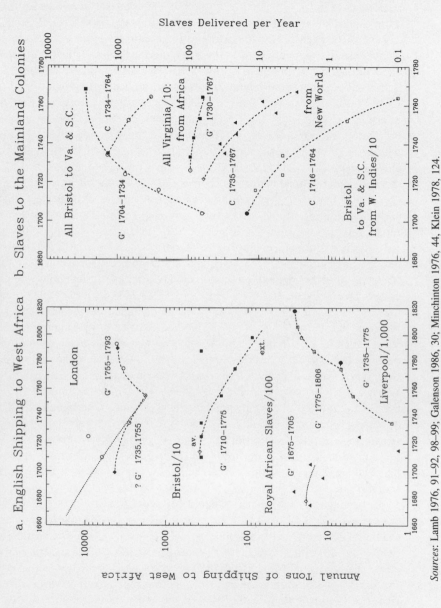

Sources: Lamb 1976, 91–92, 98–99; Galenson 1986, 30; Minchinton 1976, 44, Klein 1978, 124.

data throw considerable light upon how the flows of Britain's slave trade evolved and how G' pulses in African supply were connected with G' waves of black in-migration into the colonies. Table 2.8, in its central section, presents particulars of some of these slaving trends for comparison with movements in exports out from various parts of Africa and imports into various colonies.

Panel a of Figure 2.12 was created by multiplying the typical number of vessels cleared annually for West Africa from leading British ports between 1710 and the early 1800s (Lamb 1976, 91–92) by the average tonnage of ships in this trade that were out-bound from these particular commercial centers during successive periods of time (ibid., 97–98). For London, at the top of the left side of the figure, right away there arises a question of how to model the evidence. First of all, the exceptionally large number of ships reported for the individual year of 1725 seem to constitute an aberration. Without 1725, the data for 1710 and the decades of the 1730s and 1750s might be said to align with a G' trend that falls from a hypothetical peak of about 22,500 tons a year at 1638. This (the lighter line), however, seems to project too much West African trade too early. For example, while the average *tonnage per vessel* out of London in this traffic also declined from 1705 through 1725 (ibid., 98), a G' path to fit it would have its crest at a point more like 1695, not back in the 1630s. Lower down in this left-hand panel of Figure 2.12 appears a more plausible insight into early activity out of London: the average annual number of slaves known to have been loaded between 1670 and 1710 by the Royal African Company implies a G' trend with t_0 at 1678 (Galenson 1986, 30). If one plots a G' curve just for the averaged tonnage data of the 1730s and the 1750s for London clearings to West Africa (at the top of the graph), meanwhile, the kind of G' pattern indicated has its maximum at 1699. This suggests that, as the trade of the Royal African Company collapsed in the 1710s and 1720s, independent competitors out of London jumped into commerce with West Africa. The volume of traffic that they first attempted in the early 18th century (the era of the South Sea Bubble), however, could not be sustained—partly as investors from other ports, especially Bristol, carved out a portion of this promising business for themselves. The G' trend fitted to the data of the 1730s and the 1750s suggests a trend for the hold that London shippers could *keep* on this trade during the first half of the 18th century.

The average annual tonnage cleared for West Africa out of Bristol, for example, trebled from 1710 to 1725 (the two years are averaged for part a of Figure 2.12) before settling down into a G' path into the 1770s (perhaps on to the 1790s, if 1798 is typical of that decade while 1786 is exceptional). This curve had its t_0 at 1714, lagging some 15 years after the G' that is hypothesized for London. Later in the century, as Liverpool pushed into West African trade from the 1730s through the 1770s, average annual tonnage from this port also increased in G' fashion, with t_0 at 1780. A later G' surge from the 1770s to 1806 headed toward a crest at 1818 as this burgeoning port of northwestern England cleared 16,600 tons of *slavers* annually from 1789 through 1795 compared with

3,900 from Bristol and just 3,250 out of London.[50] In between these successive waves from Liverpool, West African clearances from London revived somewhat in G' form from the 1750s into the 1790s, cresting at 1792, according to panel a of Figure 2.12.

Table 2.8 shows how these movements in the West African trades of the leading English ports related in time to comparably G'-shape patterns of exports from various parts of the African coast and imports into specific colonies of the Americas. The London trend from the 1730s through the 1750s (t_0 at 1699) basically parallels G' timings for loadings off the Bight of Benin (1703), on the one hand, and, on the other side of the Atlantic, contemporary deliveries to the Chesapeake (1693), Barbados (1707), and Jamaica (1709). The G' curve for activity from Bristol that fitted in behind that of London peaked around 1714, or approximately parallel to the role of Senegambia as a source of supply (and what had been temporary opening G' paths of British exports from the Gold Coast and West Central Africa) and the introduction of slaves into the Leeward Islands. How far can vessels out of London or Bristol be tied directly to the development of new African sources of slaves or new areas of consumption in the New World? This would seem promising ground for further cultivation with the CD-ROM database. Did merchants generate or merely follow these movements? Was it a demand- or supply-driven system of intercontinental business? Earliest of all, the fragmentary pattern for export of British slaves out of the Bight of Biafra from the 1650s through the 1690s (Figure 2.9b) and the rise then fall of Royal African Company traffic would seem most likely to reflect the involvements of London merchants in the development of a slave population on 17th-century Barbados. But the details will have to be worked out elsewhere.

The vigorous entry of Liverpool into the Atlantic slave trade during the second quarter of the 18th century undoubtedly had much to do with second waves of importation for Jamaica and, less importantly, for Virginia. Merchants could use cargoes of slaves to establish themselves in what were for them new or weak plantation markets. This traffic, which kept sugar imports to Liverpool growing from the 1660s right through to the 1750s along a G curve with base year near 1717 (Harris 1992, Figure 18,b), apparently effectively drew fresh supply from slave providers in the Gold Coast, the Bight of Biafra, and West Central Africa as the trades of London and Bristol both declined. The suggestion of Table 2.8, however, is that Liverpool slaving ventures between 1735 and 1775 unfolded most like the third, 1755 to 1804, G' wave of British exports from the Bight of Biafra while the resurgence of London in the trade from the 1750s into the 1780s most resembles the 1755–1785 G' reassertion of British slave loadings in the Bight of Benin. Subsequently, the amount of Liverpool tonnage cleared for West Africa swelled afresh from the 1770s into the early 1800s along with third waves of British exportation from West Central Africa and the Gold Coast in this era. Meanwhile, the history of slave imports to the Carolinas, Georgia, and later-developing locales within the Chesapeake are associated by the timing of their G' curves with these later pulses of Britain's traffic in bound Africans in which Liverpool began to play a significant role. How do the available records for ships of particular ports support such hypotheses about connections that arise from the resemblances in trends among shipping, slave supply, and sales?

Even within the traffic of a given port or the intake of a specific colonial region, furthermore, the evolution of the slave trade proceeded along G-based paths. Panel b of Figure 2.12 shows, first of all, how deliveries to Virginia directly from Africa for the recorded era between 1730 and 1767 (solid squares from Klein 1978, 124) took G' shape with maximum for the curve at 1726, rather like the trade into the Leeward Islands in the right segment of Table 2.8. Meanwhile, however, Virginia imports from the West Indies and other parts of the New World declined precipitously in C fashion, falling off faster and faster along the kind of trend found in the first volume of this study for populations unable to hold their niche. This kind of accelerating collapse from a t_0 at 1722 had been previewed by the also C-shaped decline of deliveries on Bristol ships from the West Indies to the mainland colonies of Virginia and South Carolina (the bottom plot in the right panel of Figure 2.12, from Minchinton 1976, 44). This curve had its base year at 1704. Clearly, the shipment of slaves into the plantation areas of mainland British North America from the West Indies had seen its day by the years following the Peace of Utrecht of 1713. A collapse in Jamaican reexports after 1731 (Figure 2.10a) is confirmed by these data from one lesser destination to which they were sent, the British zones of the North American mainland.[51] In a similar accelerating shrinkage, *all* Bristol slave shipments to Virginia and South Carolina, which had been multiplying robustly across the first third of the 18th century in a G' path headed for a high at 1768, abruptly fell away from the 1730s forward, along a C curve with base year at 1735, though the left panel of Figure 2.12 shows that Bristol clearings for trade with West Africa, while lessening in G' fashion, did not decline at all this steeply. Either Bristol merchants saw better promise in slave deliveries elsewhere or the mainland colonies no longer needed their business, perhaps because of mounting natural increase in their African American populations, perhaps because of mounting competition to dispose of slaves on the mainland, notably from Liverpool merchants.

The right-hand or b portion of Figure 2.13 plots the trends for slave deliveries to Virginia by various merchant groups (Walsh 2001, 168–69).[52] As presaged by what has been seen already, after rising for the first quarter of the century along a G' curve with its t_0 set well ahead, at 1770, the slave traffic of Bristol vessels into the colony dropped away rapidly from the 1730s through the 1760s via an accelerating C trajectory with its base year at 1740. This is almost exactly what *all* Bristol imports to the mainland did in Figure 2.12b. Slave shipments to Virginia on London ships, however, which had changed only slowly across the first few decades of the 18th century along a G' path with t_0 at 1710, had gone into this kind of dive considerably earlier, shortly after 1720, along a C curve based at 1720—two decades before the path of the Bristol trade. Then as

Figure 2.13
Some Particulars of the Chesapeake Slave Trade

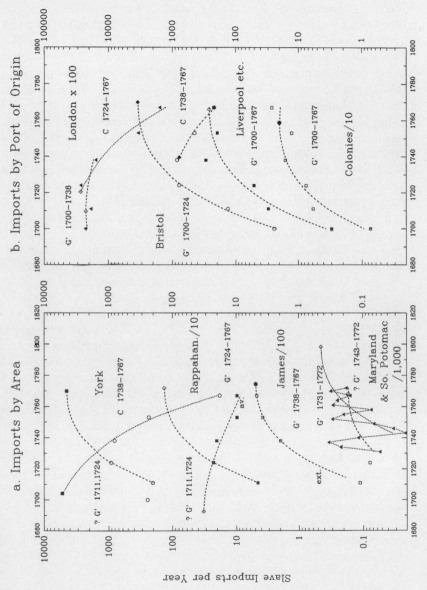

a. Imports by Area

b. Imports by Port of Origin

Slave Imports per Year

Sources: Walsh 2001, 168–69; Kulikoff 1976, 15.

Bristol had displaced London, Liverpool (which dominated the slave trade among other British outports) kept up to the eve of the Revolution what Bristol did not sustain—Virginia slave deliveries that rose in G' form toward a crest near the end of the 1760s. Slave imports to Virginia on ships based upon the colonies (the West Indies, other plantations, and Virginia herself) rose in very much the same timing. Since Bristol merchants kept up their only gradually declining G' pattern of trade with West Africa across the 1700s (part a of Figure 2.12), it seems more likely that they diverted their slave deliveries to the West Indies, where more profit was to be had from sugar than could be obtained from tobacco, than that they were pushed out of the mainland market by competitors based upon Liverpool or the colonies. Slave deliveries were used to establish colonial connections in the tobacco trade. Once those transatlantic channels of doing business were established, engaging in the unattractive and risky slave trade—or encouraging other vessels of one's home port to do it—became less important or appealing. There is also the possibility that the places where Bristol operatives traditionally sold their slaves in the Chesapeake were zones especially advanced in the transition to natural increase among African Americans. Some further research on these dynamics appears profitable.

It would seem that changes in slaving to Virginia were shaped by an evolving geography of demand that Liverpool and colonial merchants, the newer participants in the trade, could particularly exploit to advance their business. The evidence for local slave arrivals to various zones within the Chesapeake during the pre-Revolutionary 18th century shows what happened within the overall flow of this substantial forced migration to the Upper South.

Panel a of Figure 2.13 displays average annual slave imports at various stages of the 18th century into the York, Rappahannock, and James watersheds of Virginia (Walsh 2001, 168–69) and into Maryland together with the South Potomac naval district of northernmost Virginia right across the river from Maryland's lower Western Shore (Kulikoff 1976, 15). Deliveries on the York River, the heartland of the Chesapeake's best tobacco cultivation and earliest slavery, rose sharply during the 1710s and 1720s from 200 to almost 1,000 annually, perhaps along the kind of G' curve with t_0 near 1770 that characterized Bristol, Liverpool, and colonial shipments to Virginia in the right side of the figure. Then slave imports in the York region plummeted into the 1760s in C fashion. With its base year at 1704, this downwardly accelerating curve resembles the trend along which Bristol merchants stopped shipping slaves from the West Indies to Virginia and South Carolina (the right or b side of Figure 2.12). In the next rivershed northward, the Rappahannock, which also grew profitable, sweet-scented leaf and indulged heavily in slavery, the same type of G' as in York characterized growing imports of Africans in the early 1700s. The pattern likewise broke in the 1720s from its maximum of about 225 per year; the curve that replaced it in the Rappahannock, however, was probably not a C but a more gradually declining G'—one that had its base year back in the 1690s, when the first wave of imports to Virginia crested. The pattern is similar to the G' curve along which London deliveries to Virginia moved before the 1740s (part b of Figure 2.13). Interpreting these locally contrasting declines, however, is complicated by the way that both of the rivers served as highways to the interior. Did York and Rappahannock planters stop importing as many slaves by the 1720s because the natural increase of their existing workforce sufficed to provide the labor that established plantations needed (and fewer new plantations were being formed in these regions)? There is some evidence in this demographic direction (Menard 1975; and Chapter 5 of this present volume). But it is also clear that the development of Virginia's interior was shifting during the 18th century. Not as many of the new slaves for new plantations entered via the York anymore.

Though the Rappahannock interior of northern Virginia continued to expand, if more modestly, it was in the south of the colony that the promise of the later 18th century lay. The kind of G' path headed for a peak around 1770 that slave imports to the York and Rappahannock regions abandoned in the 1720s was followed all the way across the pre-Revolutionary 18th century by the intake of Africans along the James (the Upper and the Lower James naval districts together), which reached about 500 a year in the 1760s (the hollow squares in the left panel of Figure 2.13). The large, James-fed interior of southern and southwestern Virginia had become the leading zone for developing new plantations. Even at its zenith on the eve of the Revolution, however, only about half the number of Africans per year entered to serve this region as had been brought in through the York area in the 1720s and 1730s. What was happening was that throughout the Chesapeake there were more and more creole slaves to be moved by their owners, or sold, to new areas of settlement. That is how Virginia slave imports as a whole were declining in G' fashion as of about 1740 (Figure 2.11a). What panel a of Figure 2.13 reflects is a geographical reshuffling of the intake of additional Africans according to the growth experience of Virginia regions within the overall pattern of declining demand for imported labor that was being pared back by vigorous African American natural increase even as the population of Virginia continued to grow rapidly and its slave proportion held steady.

Another area of continuing plantation development with a role for fresh slaves lay northward long the Virginia shore of the Potomac and in Maryland across the river. Triennial data for imports there (Kulikoff 1976, 15) swing up and down substantially, especially before the 1750s. It would seem as if the best standardized trend for them might be a G' from 1731 through 1772 with peak at 1768, rather than the steeper alternative omitting the 1730s that is also offered at the bottom of panel a of Figure 2.13. In short, the marginal regions of the James and Maryland finished out the kinds of G' trends for slave imports that the York and Rappahannock watersheds commenced in the early 1700s but soon abandoned as appetites for fresh Africans were satiated by increasing local reproduction. The role of improving replacement deserves careful attention in other local and regional markets for slaves.

Merchants who shipped slaves had to operate within these shifting regional parameters of demand across the Upper South. It was Bristol traders who pushed larger and larger numbers of new slaves into the York and the Rappahannock during the first quarter of the 18th century, reaching 800 per year along a G' curve headed toward a top at 1770 (the solid squares in panel a of Figure 2.14). At this point those rivers served hinterlands in which plantations producing good-quality tobacco were being extended significantly. Then it was the Bristol carriers who upped anchor and slipped away, delivering *no* slaves at all to this once-promising zone of Virginia from 1761 through 1774. Meanwhile, in contrast, merchants from other English ports (at first chiefly London, but then increasingly Liverpool) continued to supply the York and the Rappahannock with an only gradually shrinking flow of slave imports at a level of about 300 per year along a G' curve cresting at 1716.[53] In a virtually total regional shift within Virginia, shown at the bottom of the graph, from the 1720s forward slaves flowed into the James in Bristol ships along a G' curve aimed at 1798 that would falter only after it exceeded 300 annually in the 1750s. Liverpool operatives, a rising force in the West African trade as Bristol gradually faded, were not to be outdone. They attacked the market of the James for Africans in a G' path parallel with the growth of Bristol's business, though they attained only about half of Bristol's so geographically focused level of deliveries there by the eve of the Revolution. Many of Liverpool's slave imports, as noted, continued to go to the York and the Rappahannock. Bristol's did not.

Even within the James watershed, groups of merchants left G' imprints in their slave imports, as the right or b panel of Figure 2.14 indicates. In the poorer agricultural zone of the Lower James naval district, traders from the three big British ports did not dispose of many slaves. Their business grew modestly and erratically around a G' trend that capped at something like just 30 arrivals annually at 1748. Three or four times as many new Africans were brought to the Lower James by ships based in Virginia, the West Indies, and other colonies, and the growth of their trade was steeper, swinging around a potential underlying G' path with t_0 near 1760. In the fast-growing and more agriculturally promising Upper James, in contrast, it was operators from Bristol and Liverpool, and occasionally London, who dominated the slave trade. Their deliveries climbed toward 400 annually along a G' curve headed for a crest at 1781.[54] Meanwhile, traders based in the colonies, though their much more modest activity rose in the Upper James in G' parallel with advances in the Lower, at most contributed about 20 new slaves a year and even lost that little toehold in C fashion after the 1730s.

At the expanding *northern* margin of the Chesapeake, meanwhile, slave deliveries into Maryland upon colonial ships (not graphed), though reaching just a few dozen a year, apparently grew from 1711 through 1767 along a G' path headed toward a crest near 1760, much like the increasing colonial role in the Lower James. While Liverpool imports rose (in some yet indeterminate pattern), the big change was the C-type collapse in the number of new slaves arriving on London vessels between 1700 and 1738, then a G' resurgence in such deliv-

Figure 2.14
Local Virginia Imports by Port of Origin of Slave Vessels

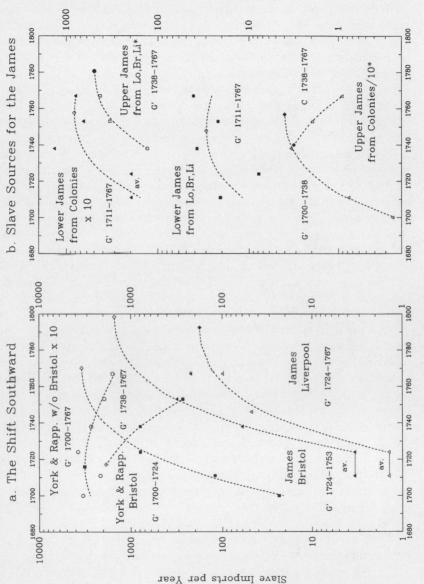

a. The Shift Southward

b. Slave Sources for the James

*West Indies for 1767 with London, Bristol, and Liverpool (Lo,Br,Li).

Source: Walsh 2001, 168–69.

eries from 1738 through 1767 that headed for what would have become a maximum near 1780. This is not unlike the path followed by London trade with the
West African coast between 1755 and the 1790s (part a of Figure 2.12).

In the British portion of the Atlantic slave trade, as in other national segments
of this notorious early modern business, obtaining slaves in Africa, shipping
them across the ocean, and disposing of them in New World markets each
evolved in sets of G' trends. Though some local collapses in C or D form were
evident, and the whole Atlantic trade or some large, complex portion of it that
embraced several differently phased local parts could in aggregate approach G
or even H patterns of growth, change in the G' shape was virtually universal
across this famous, widespread, and long-lasting historical case of forced migration.

In export region, shipping group, or area of consumption, G' movements of
specific operations interacted to fit into and help generate G patterns of broader
or more general scale. In obtaining slaves, this pyramid of G' steps in commerce
rose from particular loading place, to hinterland, to European national trade or
African tribal supplier in the area, to total numbers from a major region of
Africa. In transport, it aggregated from the business of particular groups of
carriers with specific loading zones or points of sale to the role of certain ports
across the business to whole national Atlantic trades. In marketing, the hierarchy
of G' components ascended from disposal at given river mouths or specific
islands to sales throughout substantial colonial regions or the consumption of a
nation's whole set of slave-demanding New World possessions.

How could the G' form be so ubiquitous in developments across four centuries
of history for this much-studied forced migration? It seems unlikely that in every
context of acquiring, transporting, and selling slaves the economic dynamics
could be identical for endogenous reasons. That possibility appears even more
remote when we have seen, in Chapter 1, how general G' change has been in
many diverse settings of free migration as well. What economic input could
leave just this one imprint over and over again in so many and such diverse
historical situations? Instead, it seems more likely that inherently *demographic*
processes for some reason keep making the addition or subtraction of people
likely or attractive, whether they are being compelled to move by others or are
relocating of their own volition. Movements of production, price, trade, labor
market, and so forth then must adapt to the tendency of certain inputs from
population dynamics to alter in this repeated pattern.

Thus, inquiry must turn to exploring demographic changes that take place
within migrations and the societies that receive and produce them. How do these
shape and reflect the flow of people from place to place so regularly in just a
few G-based forms? First, though, it must be recognized that, however well
known they may be, both free and forced transoceanic or otherwise transnational
relocations compose just a fraction of the history of human migration. What
patterns have movements of less distance and less historical drama followed?

NOTES

1. Indeed, while writing this chapter (and a later one that also deals with slaving) over the last several years, as a non-specialist I have not been able to keep up consistently with all the good discussion coming out. Apologies are offered for relevant contributions that are not employed.

2. As opposed to its Arab predecessor, competitor, and partner.

3. The curves for the Atlantic Islands and São Tomé separately were—like that for Europe—fitted to the data of Curtin (1969, 119) but are not presented here.

4. Of these early trades, the CD-ROM database covers only the beginnings of deliveries to Spanish America.

5. The solid upward triangle for 1,380 in the early 1640s assumes all arrivals for the years 1601–1650 in the CD-ROM came between 1630 and 1650, not before. From McCusker and Menard (1991, 154), meanwhile, one also gets an annual intake of somewhat over 1,000 per year on average around 1643, assuming that 15,000 Africans that appeared between 1640 and 1650 were all imports since 1635, though other arriving slaves had died.

6. Many Jamaican slaves of Spanish planters successfully ran away during the British conquest of the late 1650s and had to be replaced.

7. Menard (1975) has estimated this phenomenon into the early 1700s for the Upper South. Here it is suggested that this was not the only region of increasing slave reproduction (though often not full replacement). Chapter 5 presents some details.

8. The *halfway* nature of H between G and F turns out to be as follows: $F = G/G'$; $H = G/G'^{-2}$; $F = H/G'^{-2}$ where G'^{-2} is the square root of G', the first derivative of G.

9. The older data of Curtin (1969,119, 216) are used for the Danish West Indies. The British and the French provided the bulk of the imports, many from the Leeward Islands. Then, for the 1790s, the Danes—headed toward abolition in 1792—threw open the trade to all comers (Hall 1992, 23), producing the spike for the 1790s seen in Klein's more updated numbers (1999, 211). The literature on the Danish trade is cited in Eltis 2001, 21–22.

10. Decadal gains for slave numbers in British North America before 1700 are assumed to come overwhelmingly from importation, not natural increase. The small additions of slaves in the Carolinas this early (McCusker and Menard, 172) are considered roughly to offset the as yet limited portion of Chesapeake slaves who were native-born.

11. See Harris 1969 for one treatment of this literature.

12. It should be remembered that in this analysis only the loading zone of slaves is identified, not the location of their original homes, though there certainly existed some significant connection between the littoral of export and the hinterland that was accessible therefrom. Miller (1992, 78–84), for example, succinctly and aptly depicts and explains such coast-inland dynamics for the great supply zones represented by Congo and Angola.

13. See discussion of Figures 2.7a and 2.7b and Table 2.7.

14. Useful discussion of this transitional process can, for example, be found in Manning 1982, 9–12, 22–49; Miller 1988, 105–69, 207–44; and Lovejoy 1998 (1983), 66–158.

15. Support for that hypothesis would seem to come from the pattern of the 19th-century trade to Asia, which is discussed shortly.

16. My version sums calculations for the Portuguese-dominated trade from Angola

(Luanda and Benguela) offered by Miller (1992, 109) and Manning's conclusions (1979, 117) about Portuguese/Brazilian loading from the Slave Coast (Bight of Benin or Costa da Mina) and allocates 76 percent of slaves estimated to have been shipped from East Africa from 1811 to 1867 (Eltis 1987, 250–52) to the Portuguese according to the proportion of vessels headed for Brazil among ships of known destination that were detained by British patrols during that era (ibid., 98).

Portuguese exports from the northern end of West Central Africa, Loango, to which they laid claims that were hard to enforce against Dutch, English, and French intruders, became truly substantial—consistently 10 percent or more of all Portuguese operations—only in the 1810s and 1820s (up to 9,600 and 13,000, respectively, on average), though back between 1700 and 1720 at 2,300 and 2,700 they may temporarily have equaled 15 percent of Portugal's current market share in the Atlantic slave trade Miller (1992, 109).

17. Postma (1990, 4) has argued that at times in the 17th century the Dutch replaced the Portuguese as the main group of carriers. Up until 1663, according to Curtin (1969, 55, 117), the Dutch supplied most of the slaves imported into the booming English colony of Barbados. Cutting them out of this and other English commerce was, after all, what the first Navigation Acts were all about—and the foundation of the Royal African Company. Van den Boogaart and Emmer (1979, 371–72, especially note 48) have presented a contrary conclusion. Unfortunately, evidence provided from the CD-ROM database by Eltis (2001, 43, 45) does not readily allow one reliably to compare British traffic in Africans with slave consumption in British colonies in the 1651–1675 period as a perspective on these differing points of view.

18. The series of wars that began with the American and then the French Revolutions "weaned the Dutch away from the slave trade" as merchants found other uses for their shipping and their money. Abolition followed in 1814, accompanied by an agreement with the British to suppress slaving (Postma 1990, 289–90). Postma's annual averages (295) had already fallen drastically for the period 1780–1795. Thus, his starting date for this disengagement at 1795 (289) seems to be too late.

19. High calculations by Anstey for the 1790s and from the database for 1751–1775, the era in which sugar islands were taken from the French in the Seven Years War, provide the main variation around the proposed trend. Even apparently elevated estimates by Richardson (1989, 10), which the database evidence has lowered (the light line above most of the other data after 1700), tend to parallel the G trend offered for 1725–1795 in Figure 2.3b.

20. Included in this fit with information from the database and the estimates of Richardson are earlier calculations from Eltis (1987, 248)—the solid downward triangles.

21. And perhaps early efforts by the Portuguese and the Dutch to establish African labor in the New World.

22. A plotting of the data of Schwartz for traffic from Mina to Bahia (1985, 344) produces the same G' trend as Manning for all Portuguese exports out of the Bight of Benin.

23. For this curve, the data of 1735 (high) and 1745 (low) are averaged.

24. Averaging 1835 and 1845 and 1855 and 1865 in the figure would make this pattern most clear.

25. A sudden drop in Nupe and Hausa numbers accompanied by a lift for the Yoruba around 1830 suggests a shift in how slaves from the Nigerian interior may have been classified.

26. (1982, 343; not graphed). It perhaps extended through 1815 at a rather lower level.

27. A sample of evidence, concerning how regional trends in slave prices and price differentials across the Atlantic both took G-based forms, appears in Chapter 5.

28. The numbers are multiplied by 3 relative to Surinam alone simply in order to see the trends separately for comparison.

29. Data from Postma 1990, 212 and 185. The population numbers, though not shown here, have been graphed and fitted by eye. Chapter 5 contains further discussion of slave demographics in Surinam.

30. Data from Geggus (2001, 135) again entail somewhat lower annual exports from the region but bend in a similar way from the late 1600s into the early 1800s.

31. The curve is fitted to the data of Richardson (solid squares). The hollow diamonds show how closely the recent calculations of Geggus lie to such previous trending for French exports from West Central Africa.

32. Data for the 1790s as a decade are averaged in my calculations as if all transactions had occurred in 1790, 1791, or 1792 since the loss of St. Domingue and the fright that it generated cut back French slaving drastically—though some continued to the Windward Islands and to Cayenne.

33. The data of Richardson for Sierra Leone from 1735 through 1795 (the light vacillating line at the bottom of Figure 2.6a) follow a somewhat earlier G' path than the fitted trend shown, which is based upon Geggus. In the Gold Coast and the Bight of Biafra—and to some extent the Bight of Benin—the French were returning after earlier efforts that had not been sustained.

34. To subtract calculated exports from Loango or West Central Africa by the Dutch (Postma 1990, 115, 121), British (Richardson 1989, 13), and French (ibid., 14) from Miller's (1992, 109) estimates for the "North Coast" (from the Congo/Zaire River up to Cape Lopez) leaves—on average—almost no residue for Portuguese or Brazilian carriers between 1700 and 1800 (though in certain decades the number runs from 600 to 2,700, in others it is negative). Over the next 30 years, however, Brazilian activity here became substantial, as the Portuguese-Brazilian North Coast plot in Figure 2.7a (downward-pointing hollow triangles) demonstrates.

35. Miller (1992, 103) considers the Luanda to Pernambuco data arround 1770 to be deficient. Though graphed they are not included in the curve-fitting which, instead, picks up the calculation of Eltis for all imports north of Bahia (1987, 243–44).

36. But never diffused much within France, with telling consequences for Canada and Louisiana.

37. For all sources, exceptionally small numbers for 1571–1575 are omitted in curve-fitting, as are data for 1611–1615 for the same reason.

38. The number of *ships* permitted to draw upon Guinea, with or without adding in the unknowns, climbed in parallel G' fashion (plotted and fitted but not presented here). That lends support to the rather scattered distribution around this curve for Curtin's estimates in *piezas de India*.

39. The small number of shipments from "São Tomé" included slaves from the nearby Bight of Biafra mainland, according to Curtin (1969, 104).

40. Again, *ship* numbers from São Tomé and Angola also expanded via a G' curve with t_0 at a comparable date without any allocation of licenses for "mixed" or unknown sources.

41. Except deliveries to the Rio de la Plata.

42. The Rio de la Plata trade served not only the area of modern Argentina and Uruguay but—via overland trade—Bolivia and even Chile and Peru. To obtain my es-

timates, the calculations of Eltis (1987, 249) for "Other Spanish Americas" are reduced by the trend for Puerto Rico fitted in Figure 2.8b from Curtin (1969, 44). The data for the 1840s and 1850s from this procedure, however, produce negative values for the residue.

43. The solid triangles in Figure 2.9b represent the estimates of Curtin, and the hollow circles the data of Richardson (1989, 13). At 1795 and 1804 the two Gold Coast estimates are equal.

44. Calculations for early Barbados by Eltis (2000, 208) generally support computations by Galenson (1981, 218) for the 1660s and the 1670s and by Curtin (1969, 55) for the 1690s. He comes up with an average for the 1680s, however, that rises well above estimations from both Galenson and Curtin. The annual data upon which Eltis's average for this decade is based seem to rely upon a heavier proportion of imputation and estimation than other calculations that he makes (Eltis 1996, 196).

45. And swung from positive to negative and back with the vicissitudes of competitive Caribbean colonization and warfare in this era.

46. As a confirmation of this pattern (rather than what Galenson computes for the 1680s and 1690s for Virginia and Maryland together), decade-to-decade gains in black population for the Chesapeake as a whole that were calculated by Menard (McCusker and Menard 1991, 136) rise from 1640 through 1700 in G' form as if they, much like Donnan's Virginia imports and Craven's Virginia headrights, would crest near 1700. At this early stage, increase in slave population came overwhelmingly from imports.

47. Galenson's estimations of African migration to the Chesapeake after the 1660s display no intelligible relationship to what direct sources concerning slave deliveries indicate and seem to be based upon fallacious demographic assumptions.

48. Particulars for all but the first two of these cases are given as Figures 2.12, 2.13, and 2.14 are discussed.

49. The lightly marked line for net African migration to South Carolina from Galenson's inferences that is superimposed in Figure 2.11b upon direct data for slave entries via Charleston serves two purposes. On the one hand, it illustrates how calculations based upon assumptions about natural increase constitute a very rough method for assessing net migration. On the other, it reminds us of how slaves (or servants or free immigrants) entering through a particular place did not necessarily live out their lives there. Of the jump in net intake that Galenson estimates for North Carolina in the 1760s or the 1745–1775 surge for Georgia, how many new slaves came via Charleston? How to weigh the apparent discrepancies in this particular set of data will have to be undertaken by someone who knows the region well. Menard's estimates for South Carolina imports (1989, Table 10) closely follow the Charleston numbers, at a slightly higher level up through the 1730s and at a somewhat lower level for the 1750s, 1760s, and 1770s—though in both periods along quite parallel paths.

50. Of all ships cleared for West Africa in this era, an appreciably lower percentage out of London were slavers: more like 55 percent than the 90 for Bristol and 95 for Liverpool (Lamb 1976, 93).

51. They also went to the Spanish American colonies, principally what is now Venezuela, and a few to French possessions (Curtin 1969, 25–26). What form did decline for traffic to these other destinations follow? Figure 2.10a suggests D rather than C. Why might such divergences in pattern of decline among colonies occur?

52. Dr. Walsh generously shared a draft of her analysis before it was published.

53. Separately, Liverpool deliveries swelled from 1711 through 1767 along a G' curve

with crest near 1750, while slaves arriving in London bottoms dropped away ever more rapidly in C form (fitted, but not graphed).

54. Exceptional arrivals of about 150 per year on average in West Indian ships from 1761 through 1774 are classified with the business of these major players unlike the preceding trickle on such vessels.

Chapter 3

Going to Town: Urbanization and the Demographic Development of Cities

Throughout the long historical epoch of the early modern and modern eras that is being examined, neither the much-discussed transoceanic movements of the 17th, 18th, 19th, and 20th centuries explored in Chapter 1 nor the four-century-long slave trade examined in Chapter 2 composed the largest share of human, even just Western, migration. Century in and century out, many more people went to cities. Often staying within national or other political boundaries, these movements are for the most part poorly recorded. Bureaucracies were not inspired to keep careful track. Supplementing quite recent demographic accounting on urbanization, nevertheless, several scholars have provided insights for particular cities or groups of them back as far as the 16th century.

Did these movements take the same forms that have been found to be so general among the international migrations of free persons, servants, convicts, and slaves? Or has urbanization entailed something different, something special?

The possibilities are examined at three levels. First, in the development of individual cities, what trends did incoming numbers take, both absolutely and in proportion to already resident population? Within these centers, then, how did demographic structures change both with regard to the role of former immigrants and in other respects? Second, how did *urbanization*, taking not one but many cities at a time into consideration, affect the populations of societies or broad regions within them? Finally, in what ways did urban development evolve on a comprehensive international scale? How do the increasingly familiar G-based set of curves help in understanding better the way that cities developed in a more comprehensive fashion across several or many societies?

IN-MIGRATION AND DEMOGRAPHIC CHANGE IN CITIES

Figure 3.1 depicts trends in migration to and the significance of migrants within four European towns or cities between the 1510s and the 1790s. The largest is Dutch: Amsterdam 1535–1795. Two are English: Norwich 1515–1685 and Nottingham 1702–1797. The fourth is Spanish Cuenca 1625–1775. Rather different things are known about migration into each. In all cases, however, the oberved demographic change seems to have followed familiar G-related forms.

The information for Amsterdam comes from Jan Lucassen and Rinus Penninx (1985, 162–63). From 1575 through 1603 the number of new *poorters* who were foreign-born is given. This index of immigration from those admitted to citizenship seems to have risen in G' fashion between the 1570s and the early 1600s, an era that saw Amsterdam lead the break of the northern Netherlands from Spain and rise to surpass Antwerp as the trading hub of northern Europe. It seems possible, too, that from the 1530s into the 1570s as part of the empire of the Spanish Hapsburgs Amsterdam also saw immigration surge in G' form as the city took advantage of the new political opportunity to link its extensive Baltic and North Sea operations with the markets of Iberia and the Mediterranean. This early spurt brought only some 15 new foreign *poorters* into city citizenship per annum, however, compared with the 125 annually attained by the first years of the 1600s.

The second series for Amsterdam in Figure 3.1 (with hollow circles) represents the number of foreign-born women and men among brides and grooms in weddings that were registered in the city. Unlike new *poorters* who probably tried to get citizen status as soon as they could after arrival, there is no telling how long foreign-born brides and grooms had been around. Some may have come as children in refugee families; others may have been engaging in second or third marriages after many years of residence. This likely greater spread across the life cycle helps give the trends for this index of immigration based upon marriages G and D rather than G' shape. Also, from 1575 to 1603 was a period of well-known shock and vigorous growth, whereas across the subsequent two centuries Amsterdam settled down—first to thrive as Europe's leading entrepôt and then largely to coast along on its early 17th-century achievements as English, French, Hamburg, and Danish competitors whittled away much of the city's global business. Over the last years of the 1700s fewer weddings with foreign-born participants were registered annually in Amsterdam than in the 1640s and 1650s. The D-type decline from the 1640s into the early 1700s reflects an era during which the maritime provinces of the Netherlands began to lose population, and even mighty Amsterdam just about stopped growing, riding a dwindling G trend of expansion onward from the first half of the 1600s (Harris 2001, 200–201, 304–5). Why the shorter alternating G and D trends in the number of foreign-born brides and grooms appear between 1715 and 1785 will have to be investigated by someone who knows the local details.

Figure 3.1
Average Annual Migration into Four European Cities between 1500 and 1800

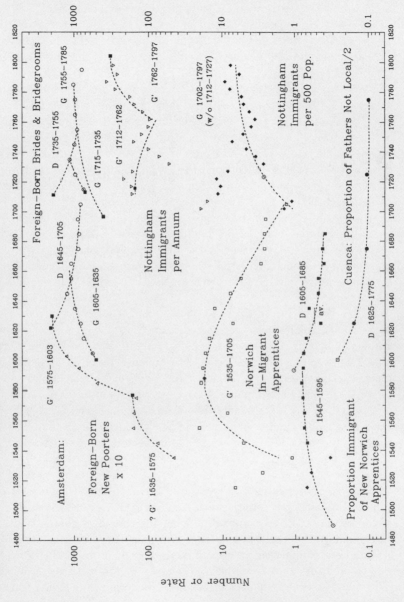

Sources: Lucassen and Pennix 1985, 162–63; Chambers 1965, 351; Patten 1987, 89; Reher 1990, 265.

For Nottingham in England, too, the number of immigrants (hollow, downward triangles) appears to have taken G' trends—fairly clearly 1762–1797 and perhaps also 1712–1762 before that, though the 1730s display a marked temporary drop (Chambers 1965, 351). If, however, one takes the early evidence for 1702 and 1707 as firm and regards the evidence for 1712–1727 as the temporary aberration instead, then the data indicate that immigrants to Nottingham as a *proportion* of the current population of the city rose around an underlying G trend across the 18th century (the solid diamonds in the lower right portion of Figure 3.1).

In Norwich, a leading center for textiles and other crafts in East Anglia, what is known are the local or external origins of youths who were admitted to apprenticeships (Patten 1987, 89). The annual numbers of immigrant apprentices to all trades (hollow squares) rise, then fall via a G' trend from the 1530s all the way into the early 1700s. As a *proportion* of all new apprentices, however— shown as solid squares—outsiders increased instead in G fashion from the 1540s (perhaps earlier) to the 1590s then declined via a D trend across the succeeding century (especially if the 1620s and 1630s are averaged). Here in Norwich, as in Nottingham, change in proportion, a structural dimension, adheres to the longer-lasting, constantly decelerating form (G or D), while the numbers of the current migration follow G's up-and-down derivative, G'. The relative presence of immigrants among apprentices involved a longer-term process of adjustment than the economic stimulus that opened a window for more apprentices in general.

For the Spanish city of Cuenca in New Castile (Reher 1990, 265) the origin of parents of children who were being baptized was recorded. The proportion of fathers who had at some time come from places 50 kilometers or more away from Cuenca (from the same province, other provinces, or abroad) atrophied from 32 percent during the first half of the 1600s to 20 percent over the second half of the 1700s via a D trend. Across these two centuries, the population of Cuenca first contracted markedly from a much higher level through 1597, then remained relatively stable—bracketing some demographic decline around 1700 (Harris 2001, 346). With such stagnation, the role of in-migrants apparently systematically declined.[1]

Figure 3.2 addresses the striking role of early modern London. The top plot, with solid squares, first estimates that the population of London steadily, though ever more slowly, rose as a proportion of the people of all England between 1562 and 1737, from about 4 to more like 15 percent. That increase followed an H curve, a pattern rarely observed so far for migrations or their impact upon demographic structure. To derive this trend, which is in reality an indicator of relative demographic activity rather than a direct ratio of the two populations, I have averaged the percentage of all English baptisms found for London with the percentage of English burials recorded in the city (Wrigley and Schofield 1981, 167). London consistently provided more of the burials than it did of the

Figure 3.2
The Role of London in the Urbanization of England, 1562–1825

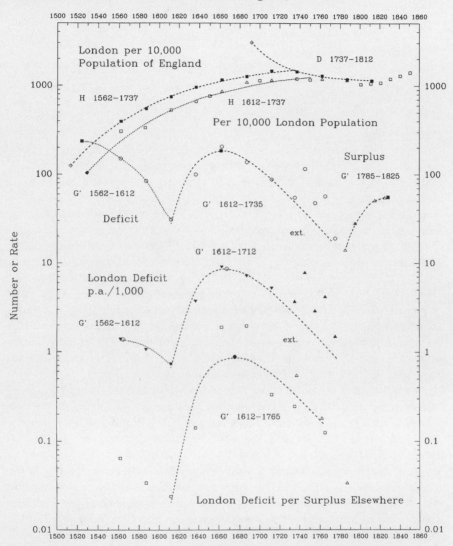

Sources: Wrigley and Schofield 1981, 167–69; Schwarz 2000, 651; Harris 2001, 304–5 328, note 5.

Table 3.1
Trends for the Weight of London in the Population of England

Av. Baptisms & Burials			Population (Direct Data)			Burials		
1562-1737	H	1513*	1612-1750	H	1529	1587-1737	H	1512
1737-1812	D	1692*	1750-1821	D	1691	1737-1812	D	1706
			1821-1851	?H	1728			

	Population (All Estimates)			Baptisms		
	1587-1637	G	1581	1587-1637	G	1576
	1650-1762	G	1626	1662-1737	G	1632
	1762-1821	D	1704	1737-1812	D	1696

*Curve fitted (others are approximations).

Sources: See text.

baptisms, as one would expect for a large urban magnet. Over the long haul, however, the two ratios and their average all mostly moved up together in the pattern indicated.

Table 3.1 summarizes the various movements. The trends with asterisks have been fitted; the others are approximated by eye via template.

There is some tendency for London's share of baptisms to fall lower relative to burials moving backward in time before 1687 (1675–1700). This makes G trends for 1587–1637 and 1662–1737 likely for the proportion of English baptisms taking place in London, though these succeed each other in such a way as to parallel quite closely the H-shaped average trend for burials and baptisms together in Figure 3.2. London's share of English burials, meanwhile, displays less distinctive movement of its own. The pattern for 1587 through 1737 is another H, and one almost identical in timing (t_0), Table 3.1 shows, to that for movement in the average for baptisms and burials.

Actual available estimates of the population of London are before 1801 more widely and irregularly spaced through time than the city's baptisms and burials reported in the *Population History* (Russell 1948, 298; Finlay 1981, 60; Wrigley 1967, 37, 44–51; Wrigley and Schofield 1981, 528–29; Schwarz 2000, 651; Harris 2001, 150–51, 304–5, 328 note 5). It is nonetheless possible to take these numbers directly as a proportion of the Wrigley-Schofield computations for the size of England's population. This operation produces the ratios represented by hollow squares and hollow triangles in the upper portion of Figure 3.2. The squares are for estimates of London's proportion where the population of the city has been independently calculated elsewhere. The triangles denote interstitial approximations based upon interpolation that has been made between the more reliably known London points in time. The H trend of lighter line that runs through these symbols is fitted only to the calculations that do not involve interpolation. This curve for 1612 through 1737, while lower than that for just the averaging of baptisms and burials, is close to its timing—with base year at

1529 compared with 1513. The estimate for 1700 is a little high, also pushing up somewhat interpolations to the left and to the right that are based upon it. Backwards in time, meanwhile, the curve runs through what would be an averaging of ratios involving old estimations for the population of London by Josiah Cox Russell for 1563 and 1580–1593. In all, by either method of estimation, the H shape of London's rising significance within the total English population seems clear, expressing numerically classic points that have been made by Wrigley (1967).

Then, from the 1740s to the early 1800s, as Table 3.1 summarizes, baptisms, burials, their average, direct comparisons of London and England with only the surest data, and a more frequent series including interpolations between scattered estimations for London all say the same thing. Namely, London declined as a proportion of the total population of the country along a D-type trend with base year in the 1690s or early 1700s. The city did not stop growing. Other centers and their hinterlands, particularly in the industrializing North and Midlands, just expanded faster (de Vries 1984, 270–71). Then, from 1821 through 1851 London's share of the English population began to enlarge once more, in what may have been another H trend, one with its t_0 near 1728.

Across these historical movements, the population of London displays from the 1560s up into the 1770s a substantial deficit of baptisms relative to burials (Wrigley and Schofield 1981, 168). The next-to-bottom plot in Figure 3.2 (with filled trangles) shows how the average annual size of this shortfall swung up and down through time. Such a gap between current baptisms and burials implies generally parallel movements for migration into the city, since the population of London grew quite regularly across the era covered (Harris 2001, 304–5).

First the deficit declined between 1562 (1550–1575) and 1612 (1600–1625) as if coming down from a G' crest at about 1565. A much greater G' surge, though, followed from 1612 through 1712 or later. This pattern implies that at the top of the curve near 1667 something like 9,000 net persons were joining the population of the city annually. Decadal data from Schwarz (2000, 561) for 1735 through 1775 (the *upward* solid triangles) then run appreciably higher than a forward projection of this curve would call for (as do ungraphed 25-year averages from the *Population History* centered at 1737 and 1762). Though at quite a different level, those later 18th-century estimations, while fluctuating, nevertheless decline approximately parallel to an extension of the G' curve fitted to the data for the years 1612–1712. Are different measures being applied to the same phenomenon?

The plot just above this one, whose symbols are hollow circles, trends the average annual demographic deficit for London as a *proportion* of the city's current population. In the smaller city of Henry VIII and his children, the G' wave of demographic loss implied by the evidence between 1562 and 1612 may in fact have crested higher than the well-publicized, subsequent disasters of the notorious 17th-century sinkhole of the Stuarts, embellished though that urban cesspool may have been with both fire and plague. The rate of the later surge reached about 1.85 percent per year at 1661 compared with some 2.35 percent implied for the early Tudor years by the previous curve. Again, the computations for 1745, 1755, and 1765 lie well above a forward projection of the extended second G' pattern. In these proportional terms, however, the curve hangs close to calculations employing the deficits of Schwarz at 1735 and 1775. Then from the 1780s across the 1820s, in contrast, London produced a *surplus* of baptisms over burials (Schwarz 2000, 561). While the proportion for the 1800s is slightly negative, the ratio of the positive excess for the 1780s, 1790s, 1810s, and 1820s takes a G' shape just as much as the two preceding surges of deficit. Whether in deficit or in surplus, the demographic balance of London between 1550 and 1830 swung back and forth via the derivative of the basic G curve, implying the net in- and out-migration in this form that is now so familiar for human relocations.

The bottom plot in Figure 3.2, finally, depicts the average annual demographic deficit for London between baptisms and burials as a proportion of the comparable surplus from the rest of England as the total population of the country continued to grow. In terms of the differences, between 1650 and 1700 (midpoints of 25-year groups at 1662 and 1687) London consumed almost twice as many people as the rest of England produced, contributing enormously to a few decades of outright decline of population for the nation (Harris 2001, 148, 150). The city's relative drag on the demographic system shot up during the first half of the 17th century from as little as 2 to 3 percent to as much as 195 percent before receding toward 10 percent as of the 1760s. This striking swing tended to follow G' shape with peak at 1675, as the fitted curve in the figure suggests. (The hollow squares employed for the fitting are from the calulations of Wrigley and Schofield through 1712, then Schwarz at 1735 and 1765; the hollow triangles at 1737 and 1762 are based upon the data of the *Population History*).

Wrigley, of course, long ago (1967) called attention to this marked effect of London upon the English population. Besides the new quantitative trendings for key elements of his argument that are presented in Figure 3.2, some inter-city and transatlantic insight can be added to his analysis.

First of all, the 1535–1705 G' surge for in-migrant apprentices in Norwich (Figure 3.1) peaked at 1588 just as net migration to London, if correctly inferred from the deficit of births in the city relative to deaths (Figure 3.2), approached its *lowest* point in the early 1600s. Previously, moreover, the number of arrivals in Norwich had dropped markedly from the 1510s into the 1530s just as implied immigration for London may have crested (1524 by proportion of the population). Later, also, as London immigration probably shrank through the early 1700s, the number of migrants to Nottingham attained a maximum in the 1710s (Figure 3.1).[2] Then, as Nottingham experienced another wave of inward migration that crested in the early 1800s, London began to *export* people, judging by the balance of burials and baptisms, along a G' track that topped out in the 1820s. Throughout the long period between 1510 and 1830, in other words, there is a repeated tendency for London to draw people when other English cities did not—and vice versa.

Such an offsetting relationship between a metropolis and secondary cities should not be too surprising logically. There is also a long historical record of such competing pulls. Lawrence Stone (1947) wrote about how in the 16th century London soaked up the business of Boston, Winchester, and other once-prominent medieval ports. Without making the historical connection, Bailyn subsequently (1955, 94–98) showed how the growth of colonial Boston in the 17th century dominated and reduced the activity of New England competitors like Portsmouth, Ipswich, Plymouth, and New Haven. Then Benjamin Labaree (1962) and Stephan Thernstrom (1964) discussed how Boston subsequently lost ground (also, population growth there ceased) in the later 1700s as places like Newburyport—and Middletown, Providence, Marblehead, and Salem—thrived, only to have Boston's early 19th-century renaissance undercut them again. Two centuries of New England history confirm the processes observed between London and her outports in the 1500s. Much of 18th-century British transatlantic commerce, meanwhile, is a story of how once-leading London gave ground to the likes of Bristol, Liverpool, and Glasgow.[3] Between 1500 and 1800 Madrid's expansion appears to have been inversely related to the demographic fate of surrounding Spanish cities (de Vries 1984, 277–78, discussed in a later section of this chapter).

English migration overseas, both to America and elsewhere, also bore a relationship to London's need for extra people. Wrigley (1967) noted that 17th-century London absorbed as many English as the colonies. Beyond that well-taken point, several insightful timings for overseas relocation and domestic urbanization can be observed.

For one, emigration from England followed G' curves that tended to peak when the demographic deficit for London receded and shrank as the metropolis required more fresh blood to compensate for negative natural increase. Migration to places other than the Americas (including Ireland and Scotland), which crested at 1718 and at 1770 (Figure 1.20a), and to the West Indies, which peaked at 1632, 1693, and (for Jamaica) 1774 according to Table 1.4, like demographic intake into Norwich and Nottingham, tended to *complement* the implied G' flows into London, not competing in timing but filling out the niches in between. In marked contrast, English migration to the Thirteen Colonies of the mainland in the 17th century took G' form with peak at 1663 (Figure 1.20a) very much *like* the surge of net negative natural increase calculated for London (t_0 at 1661 for the rate relative to the size of the city; 1667 for the 1612–1712 G' trend of absolute numbers in Figure 3.2). This should not be so startling as it has been shown that men and women of this era often tried first for a better life in the city; then, when hopes were frustrated, they signed on for the colonies (Horn 1979, 66–74; Souden 1979).

An independent perspective for patterning is more difficult to establish after 1700. Gemery's analysis shifts from English to a broader group of Europeans;

and the G' movements in Figure 1.20a, it should be remembered, are themselves derived as half of the Wrigley and Schofield estimates for all English emigration and thus obviously rise and fall with their timing. That includes relocation to the West Indies, Ireland, Scotland, and other destinations such as service in the military or with the English East India Company. The general level of this plot for English emigration to the North American colonies in the era 1695–1775 is therefore more certain than the timing of its two G' surges, which peak in the 1710s and the 1750s.

Figure 1.20b, however, shows that the new calculations of Table 1.5 for *all* European immigration to the Thirteen Colonies took G' tracks in the years 1695–1725 and 1725–1786, with t_0's at 1732 and 1762, respectively. The first of these curves, the weaker one, topped out as the volume of immigration to London as implied by demographic deficit dipped to a low point in the 1730s before bouncing somewhat during a long-term pattern of decline (Figure 3.2). The second and stronger G' trend for movement to America that took off from the level of the 1720s reached its maximum as apparent migration into London moved toward still lower levels in the 1770s, even though this later surge of Europeans to British North America contained proportionally fewer English (Table 1.5). Thus, from about 1700 down to the Revolution, emigration to the Thirteen Colonies now flowed and ebbed *inversely* to London's thirst for new inhabitants. As noted, in the 17th century London was markedly England's center of growth and activity. Thus, those who did not catch on to an acceptable way of life in the metropolis served as the leading pool for American migration. In the 18th century, other British centers—provincial ports and also foci of the new industries—competed better for business and people with London. Migrants for the New World more often derived directly from other parts of the country, recruited and shipped by the merchants of Bristol, Liverpool, and Glasgow.

In absolute numbers, however, London devoured far more in-migrants than mainland America. Some 6,000 per year coming to the city in the period 1750–1775 represents probably twice as many English as were drawn to the Thirteen Colonies in that period (Wrigley and Schofield 1981, 168; Table 1.5 in Chapter 1 of this present volume). The ratio for 1725–1750 was about 3 to 1. Those for 1700–1725 and 1625–1650 approximated 2 to 1. For 1675–1700, however, the pull of London out-powered the attraction of the mainland colonies more than 3 to 1; and for 1650–1675, which colonial historians consider the apogee of appeal for the colonies in an era of hard times at home, the ratio reached almost 4 to 1 (about 9,100 annually on average compared with 2,500). Particularly in the early years, the colonies lived on London's leftovers, so to speak.

These are minimum estimations since over the period in question London more than just replaced her deficit of births versus deaths. The city grew significantly, most rapidly in the 17th century (Harris 2001, 304–5). In general, moreover, whether London sat in command or gave ground relative to provincial centers in Britain, American colonization ebbed and flowed as a spin-off of the geographic mobility of urbanization at home that Wrigley has so classically analyzed (1967, 1985).

Figure 3.3, on the other hand, employs some data on the rate of migration into German cities to illustrate how the development of urban centers in much more modern times, too, has followed the same G-based paths established for the earlier Dutch, English, and Spanish cases of Figures 3.1 and 3.2. A generation ago, Wolfgang Köllmann pioneered the way by establishing some consequences of migration for the Wupperthal city of Barmen (which was later merged with neighboring Elberfeld). The top plot in Figure 3.3 (hollow circles) shows how net migration into the city in absolute number crested near 1880, probably along something like the G' path that is fitted through his data (Köllmann 1965, 589). Evidence from the origins of marriage partners at 1815 and 1855 and from censuses for 1895 through 1907 (ibid., 594, 596–97) indicate, however, that from about mid-century to World War I the *accumulation* of former in-migrants became less and less significant within the population of Barmen along a D trend with base year at the end of the Napoleonic Wars. Köllmann's calculations for current flows, meanwhile, showed increase in the rate of *net* in-migration from about 8 per 1,000 existing inhabitants per year around 1809 to almost 23 per 1,000 by 1871. Thereafter, the pace dropped away drastically, to less than 2 per 1,000 on the eve of World War I. While these rates are not readily trended and represent net migration rather than just in-migration, they display an upward movement from 1809 to 1871—from Napoleonic occupation to the Franco-Prussian War—that becomes increasingly familiar with data from other German cities.

In recent work on Düsseldorf—located not far from Barmen on the Rhine between its Wupper and Ruhr tributaries—Steve Hochstadt (1999, 83) has presented *rates* of in-migration.[4] Over the long haul, these rise around an underlying G path based at 1822. The calculation for 1840 is unusually high; estimates for 1817 and 1860–1870 are low. The kind of G' trending added to the graph for evidence just through 1870 is also a possibility. Still, the G-shape summary seems most appropriate until the emergence of a new trend after 1870 can be demonstrated. Data that Hochstadt depicts for Berlin—the Prussian then German capital—for instance, rise (the hollow squares beneath Düsseldorf) from 1837 though 1880 in a movement quite parallel with the current trend for that Rhineland city and for net migration into Barmen (ibid., 83, 234).[5] The difference is that the drop below trend for Berlin came not between 1860 and 1870 but between 1850 and 1860, the decade following the abortive European revolutions of 1848. For many, America was a friendlier place to go to than the Prussian capital. Why the slump for Düsseldorf comes later than that for Berlin is something that will have to be explored by local historians. Although evidence does not resume after 1880 until the 1920s, by that point the rate of migration into Berlin relative to the current size of the city had significantly declined—as is also evident with proportional net migration into Barmen.

Figure 3.3
Migration into German Cities, 1817–1988

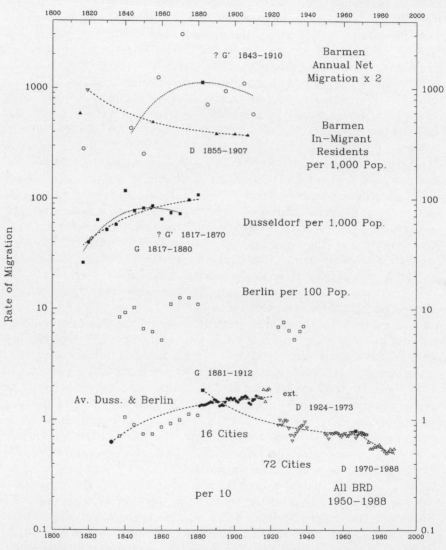

Sources: Köllmann 1965, 589, 594, 596–97; Hochstadt 1999, 83, 117, 223, 234, 246.

The bottom area of Figure 3.3 graphs from Hochstadt trends for groups of documented German cities in aggregate through 1939 and then all migration for the Bundesrepublik Deutschland (BRD) up to the *Wende*, assuming that in recent years the draw of cities has dominated trends of migration for West Germany. The early hollow squares, to which no trend is fitted, represent average rates of in-migration for just Düsseldorf and Berlin from 1827 through 1880.[6] Generally these two-city averages rise quite parallel to a G trajectory with base year at 1833 that trends average rates between 1881 and 1912 for Barmen, Berlin, Breslau, Cassel, Chemnitz, Dortmund, Düsseldorf, Elberfeld, Erfurt, Essen, Frankfurt an der Oder, Görlitz, Halle, Köln, and Krefeld (Hochstadt 1999, 116–17). These are represented by solid circles. Reaching out further into the 20th century along this G path, the hollow, upward triangles denote averages for 19 cities that kept records during the years of World War I (ibid., 222–23). On average, they seem to extend the same G trajectory.

As of the 1920s, however—in the stark conditions that followed World War I—a major shift downward in urban immigration rates appears for Germany. This has been presaged by the evidence for Berlin. The *downward*, hollow triangles represent average rates for 72 cities (Hochstadt 1999, 220, 222). Together with the overlapping *upward* hollow triangles that commence at 1950, these form a 1924–1973 series that takes D shape with t_0 at 1883. The hollow upward triangles stand for annual rates for all migration for the BRD or Federal Republic of Germany (ibid., 277). It is assumed that these overall national rates of migration in the 20th century were mostly determined by what happened to cities. Subsequently, from 1970 or so to the collapse of the DDR (German Democratic Republic), migration rates for Germany subsided still further—perhaps along a new D track based at 1967. On the eve of the *Wende* they reached just 5 per 100 compared with some 7.5 in the early 1970s, 10 in the 1920s, and 16 just before World War I.

In diverse historical contexts from 16th-century England and the Netherlands or 17th-century Spain to Germany on the eve of the *Wende*, in-migration to specific cities has apparently tended to take G' form. Meanwhile, in contrast, *rates* of arrivals compared with current population and the *relative* significance of former migrants within given urban entities have both instead risen via G or fallen via D. They reflect a longer-term process by which new people are digested by and take root in city populations.

Besides the proportional rate of current migration into cities and the accumulative weight of former migrants within their inhabitants, other things can be determined about the structural change of urban populations. Historical examples can be drawn from the colonial Caribbean, France, Switzerland, Java, and Japan.

Figure 3.4 displays some trends of urbanization in two small islands of the Danish West Indies (N. Hall 1992, 88–90). On St. Croix, the proportion of the population that lived in the two centers of Christiansted and Frederiksted (filled squares) probably swelled from the 1750s into the early 1800s in a G pattern

Figure 3.4
Some Aspects of Urbanization in the Danish West Indies, 1758–1838

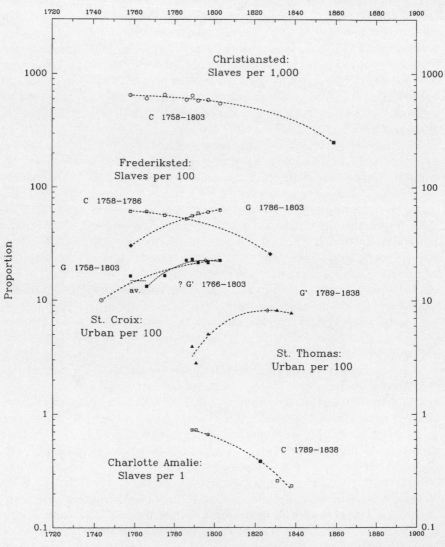

Source: N. Hall 1992, 88–90.

that reached about 23 percent in 1803 from a low of about 13 percent in the 1760s. A G' curve, however, for some reason seems more likely from 1789 through 1838 for Charlotte Amalie within the total population of St. Thomas, peaking at 1826 as high as 82 percent (filled upward triangles). What was behind such an abrupt and overwhelming concentration of population on this particular island?

It is also possible to trace what proportion of each town's population was composed of slaves. For Christiansted and Charlotte Amalie bound Africans made up a smaller and smaller portion along C trends, dropping away from levels of 65 to 75 percent when the local records begin. The trend for Charlotte Amalie falls more aggressively—in part, presumably, because being later it encompasses an era in which the slave trade and slavery were under international pressure. By 1838 less than 24 percent of the town's population were slaves as the center grew to double the size of once-dominant Christiansted. For Christiansted, on St. Croix, at 1803 still 55 percent of residents were bound Africans. For Frederiksted, also located on St. Croix, the proportion who were slaves first declined somewhat more steeply, along a C path more parallel with that of Charlotte Amalie than the one for Christiansted. In the 1780s, however, for some reason slaves began to become a *more* important demographic element in this littlest town of the group, probably along the kind of G trajectory offered in Figure 3.4. Scholars of the Danish West Indies (now the U.S. Virgin Islands) will have to elucidate the social and economic, and perhaps legal, changes connected with these trends. It seems, however, that both the pace of urbanization and the composition of urban population in this cluster of small West Indian islands can be insightfully summarized in terms of G-based movements.

In the large central place of the Dutch East Indies, Batavia (now Djakarta) on Java, in contrast, the size of the population rose from about 23,000 in the 1670s to more like 140,000 in the 1780s before the Dutch East India Company (VOC) expired. Quite a little is known about change in the composition of the population (Spooner 1986, 37, 41, 43–49, 52–54).[7] Figure 3.5a begins by depicting trends in the ethnic composition of the population of Batavia. Europeans, Eurasians, and Portuguese-speaking Christian Mardijkers (the last as of the 1690s represented about 12 percent of the whole) all constituted shrinking portions of the demographic total, each along a pair of C trends. Each decline was interrupted by the riots of 1740 and their aftermath, during which the numbers of residents in these three groups held their ground while others atrophied for the time being. The weight of slaves, a much larger sub-population that commenced the 18th century with more than a third of the total inhabitants of the city, likewise dropped away in accelerating C fashion. For slaves, however, no lift appears after 1740, though between 1760 and 1780 the percentage did for some reason rebound significantly before dropping off still further by 1790.

In contrast, as the right-hand panel of Figure 3.5a shows, four other types of inhabitants of the city flowed and ebbed twice in relative number between 1691 and 1790—in each case in G' patterns—and ended the 18th century with about

Figure 3.5a

The Demographic Development of Batavia, 1691–1790: Ethnic Composition

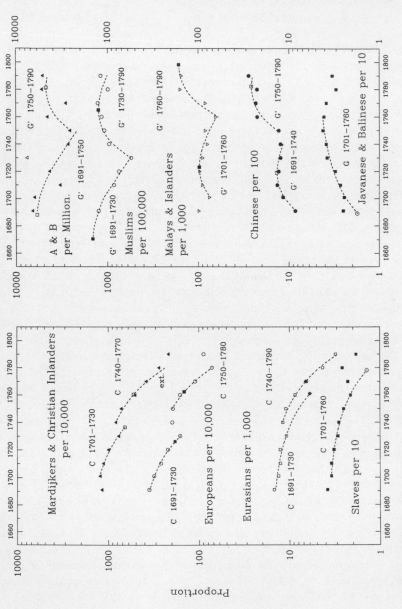

A & B = Amboinese and Bandanese.

Source: Spooner 1986, 44.

as big a share of Batavia's population as they had composed in 1691, or even appreciably more. Muslims and non-Muslim Jentiven, with whom they mixed because these people came from much the same parts of India, Southeast Asia, and the Indonesian Archipelago as they, probably attained a maximum relative demographic weight within Batavia about 1670, hit bottom around 1730, then probably rose a second time in G' form to crest in the 1760s. Next in timing came the small group from the islands of Amboina and Banda. Their proportion topped out at about 1690, troughed in the 1740s, and finished the 18th century with a G' peak near 1780. Considerably behind them, the much larger Chinese community of Batavia rode one G' curve to a crest near 1720, then—after a low during the troubled 1740s—a second trend of that shape to a maximum in the 1780s. On the eve of the termination of the VOC, Chinese composed about a quarter of the city's population. A still slightly later pair of G' waves characterized the percentage composed by the middle-sized element of Malays and various scattered islanders (often Muslim and mostly from parts of what had been the empire of Macassar). This residual group peaked first in the 1720s around 10 percent and then at the end of the century probably constituted over 16 percent of Batavia's people. Meanwhile, in contrast, Javanese and Balinese swelled continually in G fashion to rise from 24 to 42 percent of the inhabitants of the city between 1701 and 1760, though their representation dropped back somewhat thereafter.

Some of the underlying data for the patterns of Figure 3.5a may be sensitive to changing groupings in how various peoples were classified. The available evidence, however, suggests that the ethnic composition of Batavia during its last century under the VOC repeatedly shifted in G-based forms, and the way that some groups took one kind of patterning, and others took another, would seem to offer further insight into the way that particular peoples fared and competed with each other as Batavia grew and confronted various challenges. The big populations of slaves, on the one hand, and Javanese-Balinese, on the other, followed C and G trends, respectively, along with small but privileged sub-populations of Europeans, Eurasians, and Mardijkers/Christian Inlanders. The significance of other groups in the city rose and fell in more temporary G' fashion.[8]

One element in competition involved the way that various peoples reproduced. For these processes, measures appear only every 30 years in Spooner's presentation, compared with every 10 years for ethnic composition. Still, some likely trending emerges that fruitfully distinguishes the demographic behavior of one group from another.

Figure 3.5b begins with the proportion of women among adults, the foundation for much of the process of demographic replacement. Here it can be seen that Eurasians, Europeans, and Chinese over long periods of time gave up women relative to men in an ever faster C fashion (though for Europeans and Chinese something of a bounce stopped this erosion near the end of the century). For Europeans and Eurasians these downward trends had much to do with how

Figure 3.5b
The Demographic Development of Batavia, 1691–1790: Proportion of Adults Who Were Female

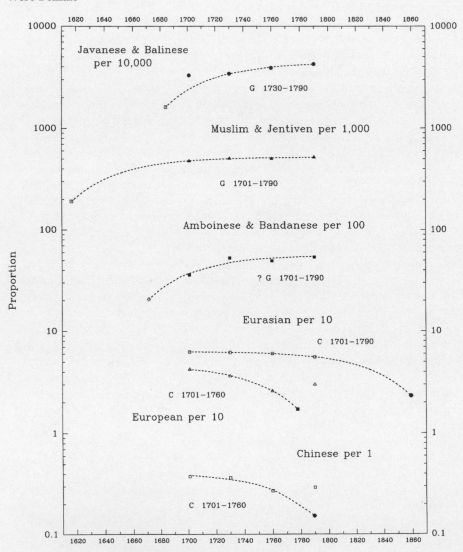

Source: Spooner 1986, 41, 45–49, 52, 54.

their share of the city population shrank in Figure 3.5a. The Chinese, in contrast, even after they had fewer women relative to men, managed to swell in G' fashion significantly as a portion of Batavia's people. This happened even while females among them (as among Europeans) ran at a level of less than 30 percent of adults compared with a minimum of 56 percent for Eurasians. European and Chinese males came to the city in considerable surplus. Apparently, for Europeans at least, extra Eurasian women largely made up the deficit. What did Chinese men do?

For the large group of Javanese and Balinese, meanwhile, a mix with about a third who were women at 1701 and 1730 shifted to more like 43 percent by 1790, apparently taking a G path of increase as this portion of the population normalized demographically in significant, if not complete, fashion.[9] Such increased feminization helped their relative numbers rise, also in G shape, across most of the 18th century (Figure 3.5a). The small group of Amboinese and Bandanese, on the other hand, normalized quite completely, likewise probably in G pattern, reaching 54 percent women among adults by 1790. For Muslim and Jentiven residents, meanwhile, already by 1701 women composed 48 percent of adults. Still, their proportion kept slowly increasing in even flatter G fashion to 52 percent toward the end of the century. While coming from all sorts of places from India eastward, these people appear to have been demographic veterans of the long-standing Portuguese colonial operations that the Dutch took over in the 1600s. Mardijkers and Christian inlanders were even more female by the early 1700s (about 57 perent) but show no systematic trend through 1790. Like Eurasians, their city population contained extra females who presumably offset shortages in other groups. For slaves, too, the proportion of women among adults remained generally flat across the 18th century. Their level, however, was only about 43 percent. For Malays and miscellaneous island peoples, information does not extend across much of the 1700s.

Beyond having relatively more women in their midst, some groups in the city produced more children, and the number of children relative to women changed with time across the 18th century. Figure 3.5c demonstrates two, possibly three types of trend for such developments.

For Europeans, Eurasians, and Mardijkers with Christian inlanders, as the left panel of the figure indicates, from 1701 through 1790 or 1760, ratios began at 1.4 to 1.8 children of all ages per woman but steadily fell off in accelerating fashion along C curves headed toward base years around 1790. By the end of the century Europeans and Eurasians had only about 0.6 children per woman. In contrast, among slaves (the bottom plot in the graph) the ratio of children per woman may have been accelerating upward. By 1790, however, it reached only 0.44 from a base level of 0.33; and the curve fit is just a rough one. More evidence is needed to be confident about any trend.

Meanwhile, the ratios for children under 14 for Chinese and for Amboinese/ Bandanese displays G' surges that peaked at 1716 and 1730.[10] Among Muslims and Jentivan the ratio of all children per woman may have followed a similar

Figure 3.5c
The Demographic Development of Batavia, 1691–1790: Children per Woman

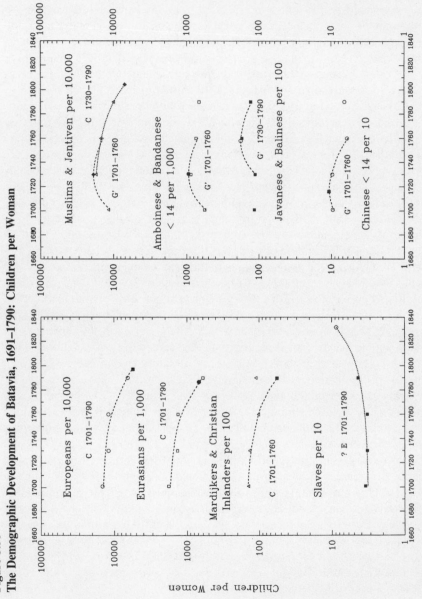

Source: Spooner 1986, 41, 45–49, 52, 54.

trend from 1701 through 1760. From 1730 through 1790, however, a C curve comparable to those in the left panel of Figure 3.5c is probably most accurate. This had its t_0 just slightly later (1804) than the other three trends of this type in the other panel of the figure. For the Javanese and Balinese, a delayed G' surge probably occurred. This peaked at 1758 rather than 30 to 40 years before. By the end of VOC rule, in spite of the downward slope of their G' trend, Javanese and Balinese had about 1.3 total children per woman compared with 1.2 for Amboinese and Bandanese and—thanks to an infusion of youths over 14—1.5 among Chinese. This contrasted to 0.4 among slaves and 0.6 among Europeans and Eurasians, with ratios for Mardijkers/Christian inlanders and Muslim/Jentiven sub-population falling in between at 1.0 and 1.1.

In all, several aspects of demographic competition and adjustment in this Asian colonial city of Batavia—the sheer numbers of various sub-populations, their respective structural normalizations, even implications for sex life and intergroup relations—appear to have taken familiar G-based forms. Such trends throw further light upon how the different processes unfolded in parallel or contrasting manner from group to group in an 18th-century melting pot that sometimes merged and sometimes erupted in racial and ethnic mania, as Djakarta has also done in much more recent times.

A G-shape transition toward a normal sex balance also apparently occurred in Edo (Tokyo) during the decades preceding the Meiji Restoration, says the trending in the top right corner of Figure 3.6a (Saito 1990, 215). There are not many observations or a long period of covered time; but that seems to be the pattern. Meanwhile, the proportion of the population who had migrated into the city probably peaked near 25 percent around 1848 in a G' surge. How did this phenomenon relate to the fundamental changes in Japanese society, economy, and population that took place in the middle of the 19th century?[11]

Longer series for French Rouen and Swiss Geneva (Perrenoud 1990, 247), though they entail rather widely spaced evidence, make it possible to detect historical movement in how fertility occurred in the experience of urban females. On the one hand, the hollow symbols depict how in both cities the proportion of women who had been married before they were 25 fell twice along C paths between the middle of the 1600s and the early 1800s. A new curve of that shape replaced the old one approximately in the 1720s. Remarkably parallel C trends appear in the size of completed family for the women of each of the cities. This is not surprising since before modern contraception age of marriage did much to shape a woman's lifetime fertility. The dynamics are rather more complex than that, however, as Perrenoud's analysis shows. These more detailed and sophisticated findings are taken up along with fertility movements for modern populations in the third volume of this study.

Bardet, meanwhile, has provided further insight with regard to changes in the vicinity of Rouen, beyond just that city (1990, 267–68). His data show how in Rouen, its suburbs, three local villages, and the other Seine watershed centers of Barentin, Vexin, and Meulan the average family size for women married

Figure 3.6a
Reproductive and Related Trends in Several Cities and Their Environs, 1635–1867: Some Demographic Developments in Rouen, Geneva, and Edo

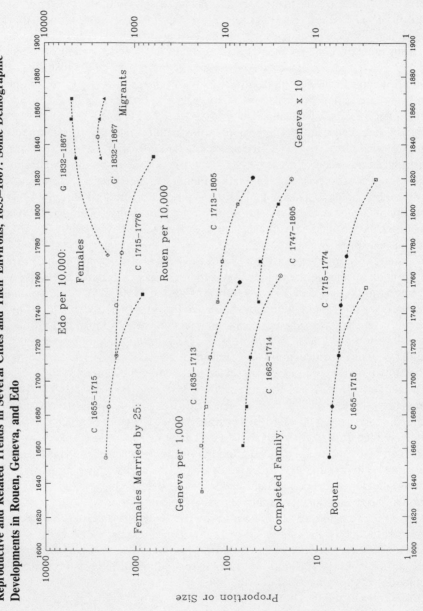

Sources: Saito 1990, 215; Perrenoud 1990, 247.

between the ages of 15 and 49 all fell in C patterns during the period between 1680 and 1800. When and how much the number of children decreased differed. That distinction set one place somewhat apart from another. The C shape of change, however, was shared everywhere. This was true, furthermore, for the families of both manual and non-manual workers. A single form of adjustment was apparently very generally experienced across the Seine Valley below Paris.

Using more indirect and less precise insight into underlying movements in fertility, it is possible to sketch out trends of change in the English city of Nottingham, 12 parishes westward across the Midlands in Worcestershire, and the Flemish city of Ghent along with some surrounding territory. Figure 3.6b and Table 3.2 demonstrate how in the 18th century the patterns in western Belgium and central England took different shape from those of francophone Geneva and the centers of the lower valley of the Seine.

Rather than repeated C shapes of fertility reduction, G-form increase, decelerating D-type decline, and even "exploding" or accelerating E-mode advance in reproduction appear. The gain of fertility in E manner emerges in the crude birth rate of Nottingham after about 1740 (Chambers 1965, 351), in the ratio of baptisms to marriages in the dozen Worcestershire villages studied by Eversley from 1710 through 1820 (1965, 404), and in births relative to marriages in areas of poor soil around Ghent (including le Vieuxbourg) but also in a zone of fertile soil in northern Flanders (Deprez 1965, 620).

Together, the data and what is said about them in the secondary sources suggest that Nottingham as it moved into the era of the Industrial Revolution and the poor soil areas of Flanders with their rural industry saw reproduction expand in E form without reversal. The Worcestershire parishes and the fertile area of northern Flanders illustrate a rather different phenomenon. Each experienced an E-shape tendency for births to increase; but also in each case movement of that type was broken back and started over again, thus not achieving as much net change during the 18th century as in other places that were examined. It is as if the demographic dynamics that generated E-shape increase in fertility occurred in these locations, too; but the strictures of successful agricultural life (such as not dividing farms excessively generation after generation) fought back the process. Meanwhile, non-agricultural work provided families of the poorer areas some leeway for marrying sooner and having more children. Such contrasting conditions have been attributed by Rudolf Braun (1978) to the agricultural as opposed to the proto-industrial upland settlements of Canton Zürich in Switzerland in about the same period.

Meanwhile in Ghent, its central and peripheral parishes, Nottingham before the 1740s and the surrounding agricultural and industrial villages for a longer period, and the Belgian areas of Alost and Schorisse, gain in reproduction took G form instead. There was demographic expansion; but the opportunity was used up fairly quickly, and further increase began to approach a halt rather than grow greater and greater. The central parishes of Ghent and the agricultural villages of Nottinghamshire, furthermore, began the 18th century with declines

Figure 3.6b

Reproductive and Related Trends in Several Cities and Their Environs, 1635–1867: Estimated 18th-Century Movements in Some Localities of Flanders and England

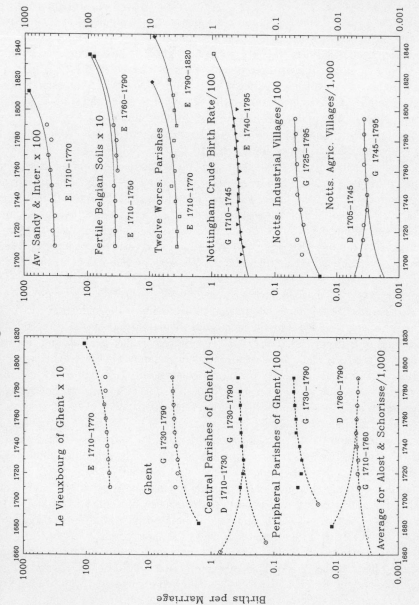

Sources: For sources and particulars, see Table 3.2.

206

Table 3.2

Parallels and Contrasts in 18th-Century Trends of Reproductive Change for Certain Localities of Switzerland, Normandy, Flanders, and Central England

Accelerating Increase

Le Vieuxbourg of Ghent[i]	1710-1770	E 1815
Sandy and Intermediate Soil[i]	1710-1770	E 1812
Twelve Worcs. Parishes I[a]	1710-1770	E 1819
" " II[a]	1790-1820	E 1848
Nottingham (CBR) II	1740-1795	E 1838
No. Flemish Fertile Soil I[i]	1710-1750	E 1837
" " " II[i]	1766-1790	E 1835

Decelerating Increase

All Ghent[i]	1730-1770	G 1683
Central Parishes of Ghent II[i]	1730-1790	G 1669
Peripheral " Ghent[i]	1730-1790	G 1698
Alost & Schorisse I[i]	1710-1760	G 1643
Nottingham (CBR)	1710-1745	G 1668
Notts. Agricult. Villages II[a]	1745-1795	G 1683
" Industrial Villages[a]	1725-1795	G 1691

Accelerating Decline

Geneva I[c]	1662-1714	C 1762
" II[c]	1747-1805	C 1820
Rouen I[c]	1655-1715	C 1755
" II[c]	1715-1774	C 1820

Decelerating Decline

Central Parishes of Ghent I[i]	1710-1730	D 1662
Alost & Schorisse II[i]	1760-1790	D 1681
Notts Agricult. Villages I[a]	1705-1745	D 1674

[a] = baptisms/marriages.
[i] = births/marriages.
[c] = completed family per woman.

Sources: Deprez 1965, 620, 622; Eversley 1965, 404; Chambers 1965, 333, 352; Perrenoud 1990, 247.

of reproduction. These followed comparably decelerating D shape, events whose impact petered out. As rural industry began to falter in the unpromising agricultural settings of Alost and Schorisse, across the later decades of the 1700s the ratio of births to marriages there, too, began to fall off in D fashion.

A window into urban mortality, not just fertility, is provided by the work of Reher on Cuenca (1990, 83; not graphed). As the population of this Spanish city contracted drastically between the end of the 1500s and the 1640s and then gained back only some of its population slowly from there into the early decades of the 19th century (Harris 2001, 347), the proportion of recorded marriages in which one or both of the participants was widowed rose from under 10 percent around 1626 to almost 30 percent around 1826 along a G path with t_0 near 1627. The implication is that this pattern reflects how mortality for adults rose in a relatively stagnant population center like this.

These local patterns for the proportion who married young, for average size of completed family, for ratios of local births or baptisms to marriages, for crude birth rate, and for the significance of re-marriage among all unions suggest that for individual cities or towns—as for some other populations examined in previous chapters—still more basic demographic changes than urban growth, numbers and rates of migration, ethnic composition, age distribution, sex proportion, and child/woman ratios altered repeatedly in G-related forms. The most elemental demographic behavior, it is implied—fertility and mortality—followed such trends as well.

REGIONAL AND SOCIETAL PATTERNS OF URBANIZATION

Next, questions arise as to how trends of these kinds affected the development of cities in aggregate, the broader process of *urbanization*. Evidence from mighty London's position within early modern England, in-migration to documented groups of 19th-century German cities, even the small-scale collective town development of the colonial Danish West Indies, the extensive and complex catchment area for the peoples of Batavia, and close parallels in structural demographic change among widely separated places such as Rouen and the lower Seine Valley, Geneva, Flanders, and England's Midlands (Figures 3.2, 3.3, 3.4, 3.5a, 3.5b, 3.6a, and 3.6b) indicate that the same type of G-based trends are likely to apply to regional or national urbanization.

Historical information on urban development for several countries demonstrates how that has in fact been the case. Figure 3.7 begins by trending some data for Sweden, Ireland, and New Zealand.

In Sweden, from 1810 through 1850 or 1860, relatively little increase took place in the proportion of the population that lived in cities and boroughs (*Historisk statistik*, 66, 52–53). At most, the fraction expanded along the kind of flat G segment fitted to the evidence for 1810, 1830, and 1850. From 1870 through 1940, then, the urban segment of the Swedish population swelled robustly and

Figure 3.7
Trends of Urbanization in Sweden, Ireland, and New Zealand

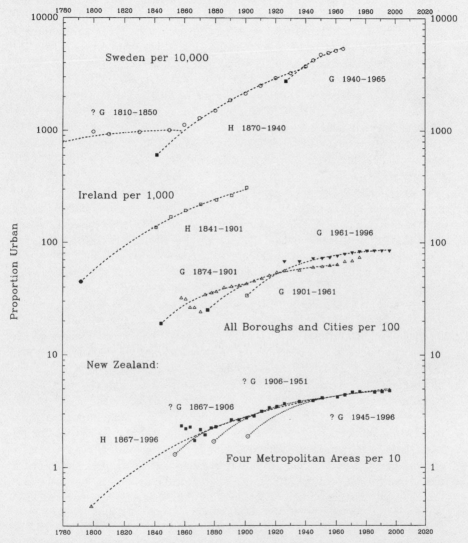

Sources: *Historisk Statistik* 52–53, 66; Smyth 1992, 61, Bloomfield 1984, 56; *New Zealand Official 1998 Yearbook*, 89.

enduringly in H form—from 10 to 37 percent of the total population. Evidence for 1940 through 1965, however suggests that in the later 20th century Swedish urbanization shifted over into a more rapidly decelerating pattern of increase— along a G trend that was newly steepened in the 1940s but began to flatten out through the 1950s and 1960s as it exceeded 50 percent. Students of Swedish population can easily determine if this trend continued or was replaced by another form across the later decades of the 20th century.

In Ireland, as the Famine and its aftermath drove hundreds of thousands overseas, domestic cities nonetheless grew, albeit not so dramatically. Between 1841 and 1901 the share of the population that was urbanized expanded—rather earlier than in Sweden—also in H fashion, from 14 to 31 percent. The H pattern, connected so widely in Volume I with the demographic growth of economically developing countries and regions, appears to be common in northern European urbanization in the later 19th and early 20th centuries, though more swiftly decelerating and less persistent G trends are found at other times. Interested readers can readily explore what the Irish movement across the 20th century became.

A first glance at New Zealand—a different, colonially birthed kind of society—suggests that the share of the population living in cities and boroughs instead of following a long H trajectory may have expanded between 1874 and 1996 along three successive, G-shape paths: 1874–1901, 1901–1961, and 1961– 1996 (the next-to-bottom plot in Figure 3.7). The first two trendings in this part of the graph involve data for boroughs and cities (Bloomfield 1984, 56). The third, for 1961–1996, works with numbers for those living in urban areas and towns with over 1,000 inhabitants (*New Zealand Official 1998 Yearbook*, 89)—a somewhat larger sub-population, as the comparative levels for overlapping years indicate. The bottom plot in Figure 3.7, however, shows that if just the four historically largest metropolitan centers of New Zealand are considered (Auckland, Wellington, Christchurch, and Dunedin),[12] their inhabitants increased as a proportion of the population of the country from 1867 through 1996 closely via an H trend with t_0 at 1799. This timing makes the H curve for New Zealand almost exactly contemporaneous with that between 1841 and 1901 for Ireland (t_0 1794), a fellow periphery of British hegemony. Table 3.3 displays this relationship. Also discernible (with faint trend lines) for the four largest centers are three successive G trends. In timing these closely resemble patterns in the plot above for the broader "urban" population of the country as the four cities stretched to embrace about 48 percent of New Zealand's residents by 1996 compared with 85 percent for all communities containing 1,000 or more persons. Yet inspection of the graph shows that since between about 1870 and 1961 this more inclusive series moves parallel with that for just the four largest centers, a comparable H trend is also quite suitable there. On the whole, Sweden, Ireland, and New Zealand all urbanized in H fashion for long stretches of time, as Table 3.3 recapitulates.

The United States has been another "New World" society growing out of

Table 3.3
Trends of Modern Urbanization in Four Populations with Divergent Growth Patterns

Country	Proportion Urban			Total Population Growth		
United States	1830-1930	H	1835	1850-1930	H	1854
Sweden	1870-1940	H	1842	1848-1943	H	1757
New Zealand	1867-1996	H	1799	1858-1881	G	1895
				1881-1901	rG	1878
				1901-1945	G	1901
Ireland	1841-1901+	H	1794	1851-1961	D	1826

+ = May extend later.

Sources: Figures 3.7 and 3.8a; Harris 2001, 27, 82, 148–49.

European colonization. Beginning about 1830, as the top plot in Figure 3.8a demonstrates, the proportion of the population there who dwelled in communities of over 5,000 inhabitants increased for a century in H form with zero year at 1835, from about 8 to more like 52 percent. That makes urbanization in a fourth modern country in a fourth kind of historical context proceed via the same type of pattern. Table 3.3 shows how the H path for the United States through the later 19th century was parallel with that for Sweden. With later zero years around 1840 these two countries urbanized more robustly than Ireland and New Zealand, which show base dates for their H trends near 1795.

The populations of these four societies underwent quite different historical experiences during the periods examined. Ireland and Sweden were old European countries; the United States and New Zealand were 17th- and 19th-century colonizations across the ocean. Immigration was central in the demographic development of New Zealand and the United States, not for Ireland and Sweden in the periods considered. To the contrary, they supplied other societies with people. Ireland and New Zealand were secondary societies under British control; Sweden and the United States were independent. The form and degree of industrialization, a major factor in urbanization, varied substantially across these national examples. Finally, four different relationships appear between urbanization and how the total population was expanding.

In the United States, Table 3.3 (Figures 3.7 and 3.8a; Harris 2001, 27, 82, 148–49) shows that the proportion of people with urban residence grew for decades along an H path close to parallel with total demographic increase, with t_0's at 1835 and 1854, respectively. In Sweden between 1848 and 1943 the size of the national population also swelled in H fashion, but much more flatly than the pace of urbanization—with base years at 1757 and 1842 for the two H curves. Aggregate Swedish town and city development moved parallel to that of the United States; population increase for that country did not. In New Zea-

Figure 3.8a

Growth of Cities and Density of Settlement in the United States, 1790–1990: Urbanization and Non-Agricultural Employment

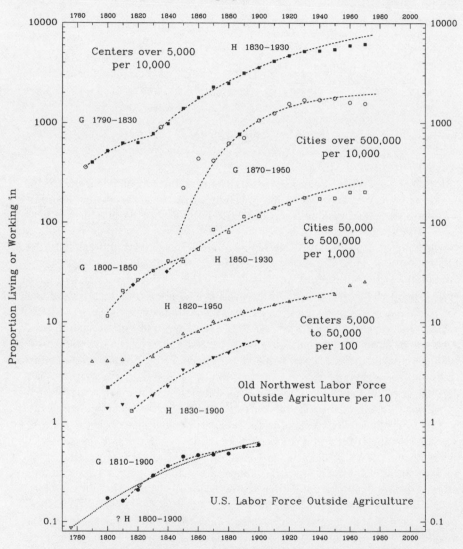

Sources: Historical Statistics 1: 11–12; von Ende and Weiss 1987, 113; Gallman 1975, 37 (from David 1967, 196, revised series).

land, meanwhile, as urbanization took H shape from 1867 into the 1990s, from 1858 through 1881, and again from 1901 through 1945, the population increased instead via two G trends based close to 1898 while a retrogressively flat third G phase of expansion intervened from 1881 to 1901 as growth in settlement temporarily stepped back from initial over-enthusiasm.[13] In Ireland, of course, drastic D-type population *decline* was taking place as the country urbanized in H form. Clearly, populations became more urban in a variety of historical and demographic settings. Also clearly, they did so in H fashion in spite of substantial differences in context.

Modern census data offer the opportunity for readers to test this interpretation in many populations with adequate records. Here two national cases, one since 1800 in the United States and the other in the Netherlands across three centuries before 1800, illustrate some particulars about the parts played in this urbanization process by centers of different sizes, room for expanding settlement, and changes in economy and employment. Further inquiry might want to keep these apparent connections in mind.

Figure 3.8a introduces some of the relevant questions. After showing how the percentage of the U.S. population dwelling in all towns and cities with over 5,000 residents steadily swelled in H fashion across the hundred years from 1830 through 1930, rising this way from 7.8 to 52.3 percent of the population, it demonstrates how the Great Depression set back this trend. From 1950 through 1970, however, it looks as though urbanization by this definition may have resumed its upward movement in a path parallel to the H for 1830–1930. More recent data can test whether this was the case or if further increase in the weight of towns and cities in America took a different type of trend, perhaps the kind of G found in Sweden after 1940 (Figure 3.7). G probably *was* the pattern for increasing urban concentration in the Jeffersonian, preindustrial United States of 1790–1830.

If one separates out only the biggest centers, however, quite a different picture emerges. The proportion of the U.S. population living in cities of over 500,000 inhabitants rose from 4.2 percent at 1870 to 17.7 percent at 1950 via a G trajectory, not an H path (the second plot, with hollow circles, in Figure 3.8a).[14] From 1950 to 1970 the proportion then began to shrink, perhaps according to the kind of D curve seen to characterize the decay of so many U.S. inner cities in the later 20th century.[15]

The fraction of the U.S. population residing in towns or small cities of 5,000 to 50,000 persons, in contrast, after swelling via an H trend from 1820 through 1950 actually shifted *upward*, thereafter taking share away from the biggest cities in the much-discussed process of postwar suburbanization. Intermediate cities with from 50,000 to 500,000 inhabitants, meanwhile, first proportionally expanded in G fashion from 1800 through 1850 (their growth does most to give expansion for all centers of over 5,000 the early G shape in this period). Then they gained population share in H fashion—rising from 4.1 to 17.7 percent of the U.S. total from 1850 through 1930. Set back by the Depression, their expansion may nonetheless have resumed a parallel H course thereafter, as Figure 3.8a indicates.

From epoch to epoch—both as metropolises with half a million or more inhabitants came onto the scene in the later 1800s and early 1900s and well before, when from 1800 through 1840 "big" just meant breaking above 50,000—aggregate population in U.S. cities of the largest size tended to gain demographic share via the more rapidly decelerating G trajectory. They came on faster, but then also lost their momentum more swiftly. It was urbanization at lesser levels of concentration, not the most central places, that so persistently took H form over long periods of time. This finding would seem to hold some further implications for the way that the H shape of demographic change is related to certain types of economic development, a relationship that the first volume of this study has posited and begun to explore by identifying the world-wide historical contexts in which the H trend of population increase has appeared compared with the settings experiencing G and other G-based forms (Harris 2001).

The growth of smaller urban units has centrally involved economic change away from agriculture. Moving to town in American history has meant leaving the farm. One does not have to be writing in Indiana to understand that. A little American literature suffices. Along these lines, changes in the proportion of the labor force engaged *outside* agriculture in the five states of the Old Northwest (Ohio, Indiana, Illinois, Michigan, and Wisconsin) indicate how the population of a region that first developed on the basis of promising farming shifted to other activities in H fashion between 1830 and 1900 (von Ende and Weiss 1987, 113). This H trend pushed upward from a base year in the 1810s that is located partway between those for national urbanization into communities at the 5,000 to 50,000 level and for the H-type shift toward larger centers of the 50,000 to 500,000 range (t_0's at 1816, 1800, and 1839, respectively). That the percentage of the *national* labor force not engaged in agriculture instead increased via a more swiftly decelerating G trend from 1810 through 1900 (Gallman 1975, 37, drawing upon the revised series of Paul David 1967, 196) would seem to reflect the way that in the continental expansion of the United States, beyond change within one region or another, agricultural territory as a whole was first aggressively added to the nation but then annexations became increasingly less suitable for farming.[16] Meanwhile, steam power allowed manufacturing to move to the largest centers of population, which were expanding collectively in G form. On the other hand, if one looks at all the data from 1800 through 1900, there is some tendency for an H alternative to emerge (as indicated by a fitted trend with lighter line in Figure 3.8a). It would be of interest to know what comparable calculations would say about the shape of movement forward into the early 1900s—and also, 35 years after David's computations, what the best estimates for the composition of the U.S. labor force across the 19th century currently are.

The reorganization of agriculture to support a higher and higher fraction of a population not absorbed in the production of food is one of the major themes of modern economic development. The indication is that this process, if not universally, has at least frequently taken the H shape—a hypothesis that will be taken shortly to the European analyses of Wrigley and de Vries.

First, however, recent study of the density of settlement across the history of the United States makes it possible to trend certain developments that underlie urbanization, especially where societies have an open end for expansion.

Figure 3.8b begins by showing in its top plot how from 1870 through 1990 the proportion of U.S. territory (without Alaska and Hawaii) that contained at least two persons per square mile rose from 41 to 86 percent along a G track from a base of 32.9 percent at 1857 (Otterstrom and Earle 2002, 68). Before then, the level shifted up and down according to how much new total territory was being added. Between 1840 and 1850, for example, rather generous slices of Mexico and the contested Oregon region were appropriated and the proportion of total square miles that was "settled" instantly plummeted.

Yet even as "Manifest Destiny" tried to justify seizing chunks of whatever could be had, the amount of territory actually settled climbed systematically. The second plot of Figure 3.8b (solid squares) shows that since 1870, with no more contiguous continental land added on, the *total* area settled and the *proportion* of all territory occupied rose together—as one would expect. From 1810 through 1870, however, as the quantity of available space expanded with one acquisition after another, the area actually settled to a density of 2 persons or more per square mile grew in H fashion with t_0 at 1800. This is what the proportion of the population living in urban centers of 5,000 to 50,000—the foundation of urbanization in America—did for over a century beginning in 1820 (Figure 3.8a). Are these parallel H trends in urbanization and spread of settlement related? And how? What was their role in letting the U.S. population expand in H fashion for almost a century after 1850? Some interesting research possibilities are framed by the trends identified.

Even closer to the phenomenon of urbanization itself, meanwhile, the proportion of settled U.S. territory with a density of 90 or more residents per square mile, after rising in what was probably G shape across most of the 19th century, expanded from 1890 to 1940 along an H path with base year at 1858 (the third plot, with hollow squares, in Figure 3.8b). This compares with the H curve for total U.S. demographic increase 1850–1930 with zero year at 1854 (Table 3.3) and G trends with t_0's at 1857 and 1861 for proportion of total territory settled and amount of land occupied, respectively. How might these movements have been connected? Later, from 1940 through 1990, the percentage of the continental U.S. that was settled to a density of 90 per square mile or more grew again in H fashion, with base year at 1910—as opposed to the 1881 for the H of total population increase estimated for 1940–2050 (Harris 2001, 27). Once again, what might these relationships indicate?

The bottom plot of Figure 3.8b trends the number of square miles being added annually to the settled area of the country. Though the numbers swing about,

Figure 3.8b
Growth of Cities and Density of Settlement in the United States, 1790–1990:
Trends in Total and Dense Settlement

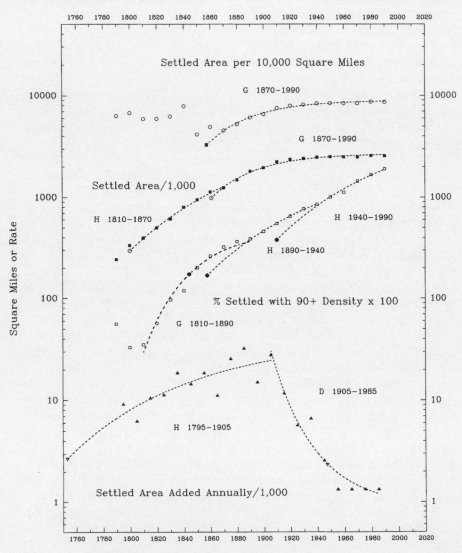

Source: Otterstrom and Earle 2002, 68.

from the 1790s into the first decade of the 1900s they hover around an H path with base year at 1753. This was about the time that conquest of French mainland North America opened up the trans-Appalachian interior for British colonial settlement, though the home government tried hard to keep that invasion from happening, contributing significantly to the loss of the Thirteen Colonies. As of 1905, however, the number of new square miles of settled area per year achieved in the United States dropped off sharply—probably in the kind of D fashion illustrated.[17] In these terms, Frederick Jackson Turner's "closing of the frontier" can be trended—but beginning after 1910, not as of 1890, as the land-sale data of Gates (1960, 71) indicated a generation ago.

Another view of the end of the American frontier is presented by the middle plot of Figure 3.8c. Here the amount of wilderness territory holding fewer than two persons per square mile that was contained in the boundaries of the United States is seen to expand from 1790 through 1870 fairly much in log-linear fashion with exponential rate of .0296. From the 1670s into the 1850s the population of the Thirteen Colonies and the United States that they became increased via the F relative of the G curve—constant proportional growth at .03 percent, a phenomenon noted by Benjamin Franklin as early as 1751 (Harris 2001, 16–20). In other words, over the long haul the wilderness area controlled by the United States and the country's population expanded in constant relationship to each other. The drop of wilderness growth well below this underlying trajectory around 1840 provides another insight into what "Manifest Destiny" was all about: to hell with the neighbors; the tie between population and space must be maintained. In the 1880s the pattern began to break, and since 1890 or so the amount of land not occupied by two or more persons per square mile has systematically shrunk via a D trend with base year at 1894. This movement displays Turner's choice of timing rather better than the pattern for new area actually being settled annually (in Figure 3.8b).

A D path, as the top plot in Figure 3.8c indicates, also underlies how from the 1840s into the 1970s the *rate* at which territory settled to a density of 90 per square mile or more enlarged (Otterstrom and Earle 2002, 76). With its zero year at 1855, this trend offsets vertically G movements from 1870 forward in total settled area and proportion of all territory settled that Figure 3.8b has presented, with t_0's at 1861 and 1857. The growth rate for *all* settled areas, however, followed quite a different pattern. From the 1790s right into the 1940s the pace fell off in increasingly faster C form around a base year of 1906. From this perspective, the reality behind the American dream of open frontier died off like a species going extinct, a slow-starting but accelerating process that persisted throughout a century and a half. Such a trending makes for a rather different interpretation from that offered by Otterstrom and Earle (84–85).

This exploration in the United States presents insights into pre-urban coagulation of settlement and urbanization in societies with geographical frontiers, a framework of analysis that could be applied to places like Canada, Australia, Brazil, and perhaps Siberia. In contrast, most societies do not live in such a

Figure 3.8c
Growth of Cities and Density of Settlement in the United States, 1790–1990:
Amount of Wilderness and Growth Rate of Settlement

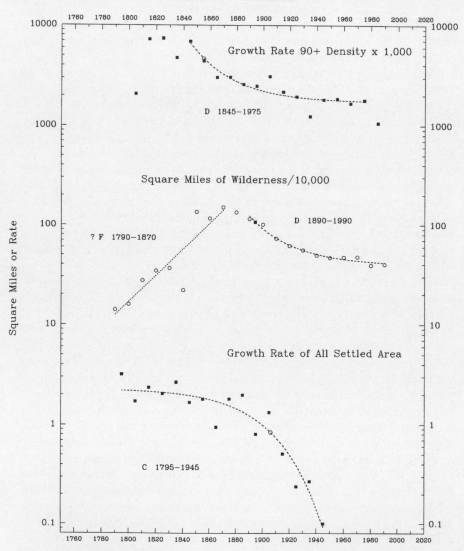

Source: Otterstrom and Earle 2002, 68, 76.

fluid setting. While the experience of the Netherlands between about 1500 and 1800 does not present itself via regular decadal census data, the kind of evidence available for many more recent countries, rich accumulating scholarship on this early modern nation nonetheless permits some valuable perspective on urban growth and change in a dynamic (eventually not so dynamic) society whose boundaries were not continentally elastic.

The changing role of cities and non-agricultural activity in the cutting-edge economic development of the Netherlands in the 16th and 17th centuries has for some time been a fascinating topic in early modern history (for example, in English: de Vries 1974; Wallerstein 1974, 1980; Wrigley 1985; de Vries and van der Woude 1997). What does this striking Dutch historical case say about the part played by H and other G-based trends in the processes of urbanization?

Figure 3.9a plots the aggregate size of urban populations for several parts of the Netherlands between 1514 and 1815 (de Vries and van der Woude 1997, 52–54, 58–61, 67–68). In the coastal province of Holland and independently in its two subsequent divisions north of the IJ and from Amsterdam southward, the number of people living in cities apparently climbed collectively in H form from the early 1500s into the early 1600s. The hollow data circles represent 18 voting cities of Holland plus The Hague (ibid., 52). Serving as a check for trending, the solid, upward triangles cover just some larger cities with populations estimated at 1550, 1600, and 1650 (de Vries 1984, 271). Together, the two series indicate urban growth of the H shape in both northern and southern Holland from 1514 through about 1620. At this point, after the brunt of the struggle for independence from Spain had been borne, it seems as if the cities of South Holland, led by the key ports of Amsterdam and Rotterdam, shifted into a fresh but G-shaped additional surge of expansion while urban growth in North Holland kept to its slowing H trajectory until about mid-century. Separately, fresh G trends for the expansions of Amsterdam and Rotterdam after 1600 with base years at about 1613 have been identified, and The Hague, the capital of the country, enlarged in tandem (Harris 2001, 304–7).

After about 1680 in South Holland, perhaps a little sooner in North Holland, the aggregate urban population began, however, to *shrink* as the early modern European leadership of the Netherlands in commerce, industry, and the cultivation of industrial crops was battered by competition and boxed in and drained away on land and at sea by war. Urban decline in South Holland and for all Holland followed a D trend from about 1680 right through to the end of the Dutch Republic in the 1790s. In North Holland, whose cities were not such mighty centers of trade and finance, D-shape shrinkage of the urban population began rather sooner (probably around 1660) and cut deeper. For the other provinces of the Netherlands besides Holland, meanwhile, though the evidence is widely spaced, it would seem that total urban population *increased* in a rather flat segment of the G curve from 1525 all the way through 1750 (de Vries and van der Woude 1997, 61). In inland Overijssel, in particular, appreciably more vigorous G-type growth occurred after 1675, a pattern continued by the three

Figure 3.9a
Some Trends or Likely Trends in Dutch Provincial Urbanization, 1514–1795: Urban Population Growth

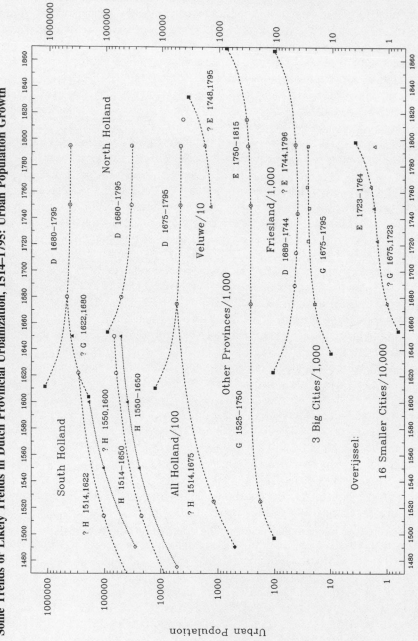

Source: de Vries and van der Woude 1997, 52–55, 58–61, 67–69.

largest cities of the province until the end of the 1700s. While not rising as much and decelerating rapidly already by the middle of the 16th century, the aggregate growth of cities in other parts of the country held level across what was a long era of decay for urban population in Holland. It was the lesser centers of this once-proud province that bore the burden, since Amsterdam, Rotterdam, and The Hague managed to sustain long trends of growth in very flat G trajectories across the 17th and 18th centuries (Harris 2001, 304–5, 307).

Between 1750 and 1815 a different form seems to have characterized urban expansion in the Netherlands outside of the no longer so glorious province of Holland. It appears as if the urban population now grew slowly but at steadily increasing speed via the accelerating E relative of the G curve. There are only three data points to indicate this for all other provinces together; but a parallel trend would fit the 1744 and 1776 evidence for Friesland while urban population in the Veluwe and 16 smaller cities of Overijssel may have expanded in slightly earlier and steeper E trends, as the lower portion of Figure 3.9a shows. This conclusion is based upon sketchy information. The Belgian cities of Bruges and Evergem, however, quite clearly grew contemporaneously in E fashion over the second half of the 18th century, while the population of the Netherlands as a whole expanded this way in the years 1759–1839 and likewise the peoples of the provinces of Utrecht, Overijssel, Friesland, Groningen, and Drenthe across comparable periods (Harris 2001, 198). In the Duchy of Brabant, mostly left in the southern Netherlands (now Belgium), the population of the countryside increased via an E trend from 1693 through 1784 with t_0 around 1802. In the cities of this region, an E trend for demographic expansion is also possible between 1755 and 1784 (the zero year would be near 1824), but only after loss of population in the early 1700s (Helin and van der Woude 1997, 416).

The E form of demographic increase, moreover, was common across other European nations and regions as industrialization began to spread across Europe, notably England 1726–1806, Ireland 1725–1791, Scotland 1755–1821, Denmark 1735–1801, briefly France 1792–1837 (Harris 2000, 148–49)—also in the 19th century, through various regions within Belgium and France, central Europe, and Russia (ibid., 199, 206–7, 208–29, 212–13, 216, 220–23). Taking everything together, it would seem that the expansion of lesser cities in E form (as in Nottingham across the 18th century) constituted an integral part of such demographic growth—that the Dutch evidence of Figure 3.9a, though sparse, was part of a broader international pattern. The contraction of cities of the Netherlands in the earlier part of the 1700s, meanwhile, was more than a distinctive national phenomenon; it was shared at this time primarily by certain nearby centers in the Hapsburg domains of what is now Belgium.

Figure 3.9b looks at the growth of cities as a *proportion* of the total population of various parts of the Netherlands. The most outstanding feature of the graph is how in region after region the share of people dwelling in cities began in the 1600s and early 1700s to shrink in D form. Roughly parallel decline in this pattern began in North Holland as of the 1620s, in the Veluwe and Overijssel

Figure 3.9b
Some Trends or Likely Trends in Local Dutch Populations, 1514–1795: Urban Population as a Percentage of the Total

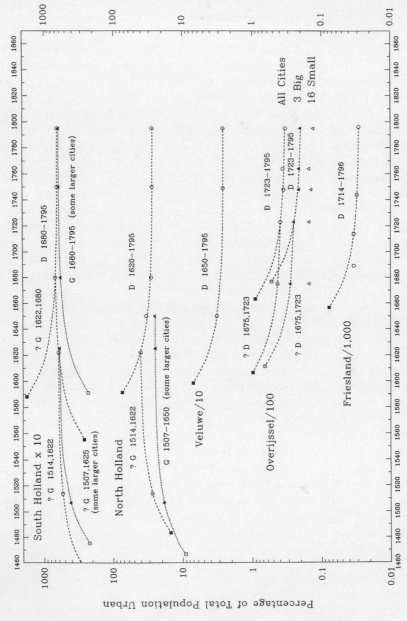

Source: de Vries and van der Woude 1997, 52–55, 58–61, 67–69.

probably near mid-century, and at about 1680 in South Holland. Later, quite parallel D trends commence around 1715 or 1720 in the lesser maritime province of Friesland and as a second stage of de-urbanization for Overijssel—especially if one looks at the 3 largest cities of this interior province, but probably also with regard to 16 smaller ones (de Vries and van der Woude 1997, 53–55, 58, 61, 67–69). In this period of Dutch urban weakening, as inland regions gained ground relative to once-dominant maritime zones, a few big cities of South Holland nevertheless continued to garner a slightly higher proportion within their provincial population by cannibalizing smaller neighboring centers (Amsterdam, Rotterdam, and The Hague at the expense of Leiden, Gouda, Delft, Haarlem, and the like). This gain is shown by the G trend for the solid, upward triangles from 1680 through 1795 at the top of Figure 3.9b.

Earlier, between the early 1500s and 1625 or 1650, a few larger cities had embraced greater and greater proportions of the population in both the northern and the southern zones of Holland (de Vries and Van der Woude 1997, 52; de Vries 1984, 271; Israel 1998, 114, 328, 332, 621, 1007). They appear to have done this along the kinds of quite parallel G curves fitted to the solid, upward triangles in the upper left quarter of Figure 3.9b. Rather less parallel G patterns would fit data at 1514 and 1622 for all urban residents of North and South Holland (the hollow circles). The latter then again increased as a percentage of the local population between 1622 and 1680 (possibly via the kind of G path suggested in the figure) before shrinking back across the next 115 years to the end of the Dutch Republic.

That during the rise of the Netherlands to its Golden Age of the 17th century the cities of Holland, the economically leading province—both all urban centers and a few leading central places—swelled as a proportion of the regional population in G form opens up some interesting questions. Between 1562 and 1737, as Figure 3.2 has demonstrated, London—the big rival of Amsterdam as England became first challenger then surpassor of the Netherlands—expanded to embrace a larger percentage of the national population in the less quickly slowing, more durably growing H path instead. So did cities and towns in general in Ireland, Sweden, New Zealand, and the United States from about 1850 into the early 1900s during a modern era of economic development.

The Netherlands of the 16th and early 17th centuries was a leading industrializing and commercializing power of the Western world that has been characterized as "the first modern economy." Probably a better clue as to how Dutch urbanization leading into the Golden Age took G rather than H form proportionally (it did enlarge via H in absolute size, as Figure 3.9a has shown) lies in the G-shaped behavior of *big* cities in the United States. These collectively swelled in G fashion as a proportion of the total U.S. population from 1870 through 1950 before starting to contract (Figure 3.8a), much like the cities of Holland from the early 1500s into the 1620s. In America since World War II, big cities that had developed in the 19th century have become less competitive places in which to work and live. As noted, many urban cores there have fairly much hit a ceiling for size or actually begun to shrink in D form (Harris 2001, 297, 299), like the Dutch urban population of the later 1600s. The difference would seem to be that while in the contemporary United States room existed for new residences and new businesses, both with favorable terms for growth, sometimes just a mile or two away across an old political boundary during the process of suburbanization, that was less of an option for the Netherlands of the 17th century, the most highly urbanized country of the West. While both economic and population growth did move inland to some extent (de Vries and van der Woude 1997), the human and material resources could not be expanded to further diversify and support continuing growth, in spite of the significant—if proportionally declining—in-migration noted in Figure 3.1, especially as international competitors sliced into the maritime and colonial operations that had brought the republic resources and had made the Netherlands great. As American capitalism shifts investment and employment abroad in our present era, will more than just the population of the biggest inner cities, perhaps even some of the so recently voracious and invincible suburbs, comparably fall into D-type decline?

In all, not only the demographic experience of individual cities but also the history of collective urbanization at the level of country or region have followed familiar G-based shapes of trend. As is so evident in the present era of globalization, however, urban systems have an international dimension, in which one country's growth promotes another's decline—or vice versa.

CITIES, AGRICULTURE, AND OTHER RURAL ACTIVITIES IN THE CORE COUNTRIES OF EUROPEAN DEVELOPMENT

The growth of urban concentrations and networks in Europe during the early modern period has long been of great interest to historians, sociologists, and economists. Debates about how "modern" society, "capitalism," and other elements of our present world evolved grasp and exploit whatever fragments of information exist concerning urbanization. Data are firmest for parts of northwestern Europe. Even here, however, the pieces of evidence scatter widely and thinly over time. With caution about the slimness of the data and the tentativeness of conclusions that can be drawn from them, it is nonetheless possible to employ insights from the new type of trending offered in this study to carry our understanding of the historical development of urban systems in the West somewhat further, especially regarding the era from the 1500s into the 1800s.

Figure 3.10 starts the analysis by exploiting the perceptive and provocative work of Wrigley and de Vries to trend how cities drew into themselves a larger proportion of the populations of France, the Netherlands, and England across three or four centuries after 1500. Though these societies are often linked together as primary engines of early modern development (for example, Wallerstein 1974, 1980), the expansion of cities within their populations unfolded in

Figure 3.10
Comparing Urbanization in France, the Netherlands, and England

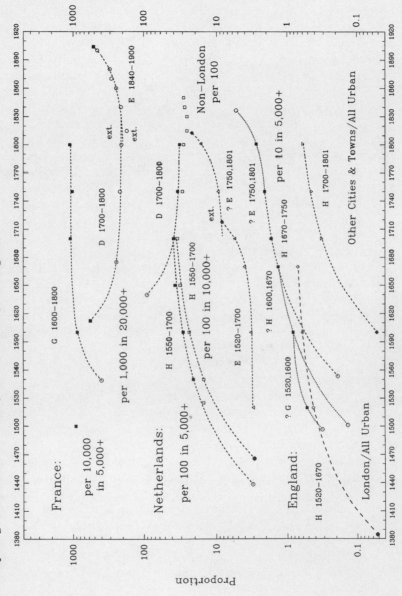

Sources: Wrigley 1985, 718, 714, 688; de Vries 1985, 662.

quite different patterns, trends whose sometimes parallel and sometimes diverging shapes help explain how the three countries jostled and to some extent supplanted each other as the life of Europe evolved across the 16th, 17th, 18th and 19th centuries.

After receding slightly between 1500 and 1600, from 9.1 to 8.7 percent during a century of civil strife, the proportion of the people of France who lived in cities and towns of 5,000 or more inhabitants (Wrigley 1985, 718) apparently then expanded modestly in G fashion between 1600 and 1800 to reach a level of about 11 percent during the 18th century. This gradual movement contrasted markedly with the urban vigor of the northern (Dutch) Netherlands in the 16th and 17th centuries. Here the fraction inhabiting cities of 5,000 or more expanded in robust, only slowly slowing H form (the solid squares on the graph) from 1550 through 1700 (ibid., 714). From an already elevated level of 21 percent at 1550, about twice what France would see at any point before the 19th century, Dutch urbanization by this definition came to embrace no less than 39 percent of the nation's people by 1700, almost four times the proportion in France. If one trends only rather larger centers, those with 10,000 or more inhabitants (de Vries 1985, 662), a rather steeper contemporary H trajectory emerges (the hollow squares). This second fit indicates that the era of strong urbanization began for the Netherlands in the middle of the 16th century, because the level was 15 percent at both 1525 and 1550.

As of the end of the 1600s, however, Dutch urbanization—as already suggested by Figure 3.9b—began to atrophy substantially as a share of the total population. The percentage for those living in centers of 5,000 or more and persons resident in cities of over 10,000 dropped off in parallel D manner from 1700 through 1800, as data every half century suggest. For the more inclusive category of communities, the level receded from 39 to 33 percent. A slightly flatter D segment captures the shrinking of the proportion of the population inhabiting cities of 20,000 or more (de Vries 1985, 662). Then, across the 19th century, Dutch urbanization grew once more—now in accelerating E fashion, taking the percentage in cities of 20,000 or more from 20.8 to 45.6 percent. The dip to 17.5 percent at 1815 would seem to reflect a temporary effect of a decade and a half of French domination.

In England, meanwhile, still different patterning seems probable. First, the proportion of the population in all communities with 5,000 or more inhabitants increased between 1520 and 1600 from a level of only 5.25 percent of the national population—barely more than half of the French 9.7 percent level of 1500, just one-quarter of the 21 percent for the Netherlands—to 8.25 percent at 1600, close to the current French fraction of 8.7. As France de-urbanized somewhat during the 16th century, England caught up from a very low starting point. The informed guess of Figure 3.10 is that this change took G shape like expansion in France after 1600, but along a somewhat earlier G path as during the 1500s England passed through her Tudor religious shifts without engaging (yet) in full civil war, which the French experienced in the 16th century. From 1670 (following the Restoration) to 1750, though, it seems likely that English urbanization picked up the kind of H trend seen in the Netherlands between 1550 and 1700, though involving a t_0 at 1554 in contrast to the much earlier Dutch 1438. This 80-year H path carried the share of English people who lived in centers of 5,000 or more from 13.5 to 21.0 percent, doubling the largely unchanging French level but still reaching only some two-thirds of the Dutch proportion, even though the latter had been coming down appreciably from its 1700 high. Between 1750 and 1801, however, the English proportion rose still further as the Dutch level continued to decline and the French percentage stayed put. As of 1801, some 27.5 percent of the population of England lived in communities of 5,000 inhabitants or more, finally rivaling (though still not catching) the 33 percent of the Netherlands.

Across these successive stages of English urbanization, as the bottom plots of Figure 3.10 indicate, from 1520 through 1670 the percentage of city dwellers who lived just in the metropolis, London (the hollow diamonds), increased in H fashion from 43 to 70 percent of all urban residents (Wrigley 1985, 688). Thereafter, the momentum of urbanization shifted elsewhere; and the share of the urban population living in places *other* than London between 1700 and 1801 expanded, also in H form, from 32 to 60 percent (the hollow, downward triangles). The H pattern, in other words, seems to characterize the shifting roles of distinct types of centers within the total as well as the increase of urbanization in general, a kind of change to which we return shortly.

It is hypothesized that as a whole the English expansion in urbanization across the later 18th century took the accelerating E form. Though based upon just two observations, at 1750 and 1801, this particular shape of trend is posited for good reason. First, the well-documented city of Nottingham has been observed to have grown demographically in E fashion between 1750 and 1800 (Harris 2001, 308). That E trend had its t_0 in the 1790s. Meanwhile, the population of England as a whole increased from 1726 through 1806 via an E track with t_0 at 1822 (ibid., 148). Figure 3.10, furthermore, shows how an E trend with its base year not far away at 1813 would fit the 1750 and 1801 percentages of the English population living in all centers of more than 5,000 except London (the hollow, upward triangles across the middle of the graph, from Wrigley 1985, 688). It was the proportionally shrinking role of London 1737–1812 (Figure 3.2) that made the likely E for all of English urbanization somewhat weaker (follow a later E path through the same years).

In addition, as the total population of the Netherlands expanded from 1750 through 1839 in E fashion toward a base year at 1866, the percentage residing in all cities of 20,000 or more, as Figure 3.10 demonstrates, rose in an E trend between 1840 and 1900 with a zero year at 1904. Though the large centers of Amsterdam and Rotterdam display no such tendency (Harris 2001, 305), 16 smaller cities of the Dutch province of Overijssel do, at least across the middle of the 1700s (Figure 3.9a). Southward, in what is now Belgium, the populations of Bruges and Evergem likewise expanded in the E pattern across the last decades of the 18th century (ibid., 308), though a national population trend is difficult to establish before 1800 for what was then the southern or Austrian Netherlands. While the people of France multiplied only briefly from 1792 through 1827 via an E track with base year at 1876 (ibid., 152), the populations of departments containing major cities—Seine (Paris), Rhône (Lyon), Bouche du Rhône (Marseilles), Nord (Lille), and Gironde (Bordeaux)—expanded in ways that are also captured by E trends, with t_0's approximately at 1847, 1854, 1880, 1886, and 1894, respectively (ibid., 199). Urbanization in later-18th-century England and in the Netherlands, Belgium, and France during the early 19th century, it seems, quite generally involved ever faster expansion of cities within national populations whose overall size increased simultaneously in E form.

Other trend fittings of Figure 3.10 that are proposed on the basis of few and widely spaced data are also not unrelated to better-documented patterns of the same era for the national populations in which these movements of urbanization took place. For example, the population of England expanded in H form between 1685–1726 and 1561–1656, setting the context for the H trends of proportional urban growth that are posited for, 1670–1750 and 1600–1670, respectively (Harris 2001, 148–51). In each case the H for urbanization was rather steeper through the period (had a later t_0) than that for overall increase in the population. Earlier, the G suggested in Figure 3.10 for the two data points of 1520 and 1600 would have a base year at 1497 compared with one of 1507 for the quinquennially calculated G pattern of growth in the population of England between 1541 and 1566 (Wrigley and Schofield 1981, 528). Curves fitted on the basis of scant information in Figure 3.10 receive support from the fact that in one period after another urbanization and total population growth were closely connected in early modern England.

Comparably, as urbanization in France increased only very little in late G-curve fashion across the 17th and 18th centuries, the population of the country expanded very slightly between 1675 and 1792 (Harris 2001, 152). Though this small change actually took successive D, G, and G paths, each of those trends was almost flat, so that the net result looks very much like the 1600–1800 G trend posited in Figure 3.10 for change in the French urban proportion. In the Netherlands, the H of urbanization between 1550 and 1700 and the D between 1700 and 1800 that followed are not the patterns for the Dutch population at large. They do, however, closely resemble trends through the 1500s and 1600s and then the 1700s for the size of the population in *Holland*, the great maritime province wherein the "action" of the Dutch economy first exploded, then atrophied as the Golden Age of the Netherlands first came, then went (ibid., 198, 200). In not only England but France and the Netherlands often thinly documented curves of Figure 3.10 are supported by their very general relationship to movements in the overall populations of the countries considered from the 1500s into the 1800s. Across this long time span of development in the Western world, total demographic increase was accompanied by, perhaps powered by, increasing proportions of people who lived in substantial towns and cities.

Figures 3.11a through 3.11e reexamine growth in the urban, rural agricultural, and rural non-agricultural segments of the Dutch, English, and French populations between 1500 and 1800 (Wrigley 1985). They cast further light upon the relationships between urbanization and national expansion and frame analysis of the economies that were connected with these demographic developments (the topic of a study that follows the present one). Figure 3.11a, 3.11b, and 3.11c present, respectively, what appear to be likely or possible G-related trends in the Netherlands, France, and England for the size of three elements of each population: urban dwellers (living in centers of 5,000 or more), rural residents engaged in agriculture, and rural persons not involved in agriculture (ibid., 1985, 714, 718, 700).

The number of people in agriculture hardly increased at all between 1550 and 1750 in the Netherlands or between 1500 and 1700 in France (11 and 21 percent in Figures 3.11a and 3.11b, respectively). Expansion in France probably started out along very much the kind of G path pertaining in the Netherlands 1550–1650, with t_0 in the 1430s (Table 3.4 facilitates comparisons). For the 17th century, however, French rural growth took the somewhat later G path evident for England between 1520 and 1670, with base year in the 1490s. By starting out on such a more active track already by the early 1500s, though, the peopling of English farming increased by 65 percent between 1520 and 1670, three to six times as much as agricultural growth in France and the Netherlands.

English agriculture, on the other hand, *lost* people (12 percent) between 1670 and 1750, seemingly along the kind of D track presented for the bottom plot in Figure 3.11c. While the Dutch agricultural population hardly changed at all before 1750, the French one seems to have expanded a little (about 11 percent) across the early 1700s, possibly along the kind of G path offered tentatively in Figure 3.11b. Then, through the second half of the 18th century all three agricultural populations are hypothesized to have expanded in E form. The Dutch trend for 1650 through 1800 is based upon four data points, is supported by comparable movement within several provinces, and seems highly likely. Besides, the total Dutch population expanded in such an E pattern from 1750 through 1839 (Harris 2001, 148, 151). That information at just two dates, 1750 and 1800, would fit an E trend of almost identical timing for the agricultural population of France (Figure 3.11b) is likewise supported by the way that the people of that country, too, increased in E form between 1792 and 1827 (ibid., 148–52). The E trajectory for England, again documented only at 1750 and 1801, nevertheless is likewise in line with expansion of the total English population in such a shape between 1726 and 1806. With t_0 at 1822 this made E growth for the agricultural segment in England (base year at 1851), while comparable to that for France and the Netherlands (1861 and 1857), considerably less aggressive than the trend for the total population. Other, not agricultural, elements drove accelerating overall demographic expansion in the 18th century

Figure 3.11a
Urban and Rural Components of the Dutch, French, and English Populations, 1500–1800: The Netherlands

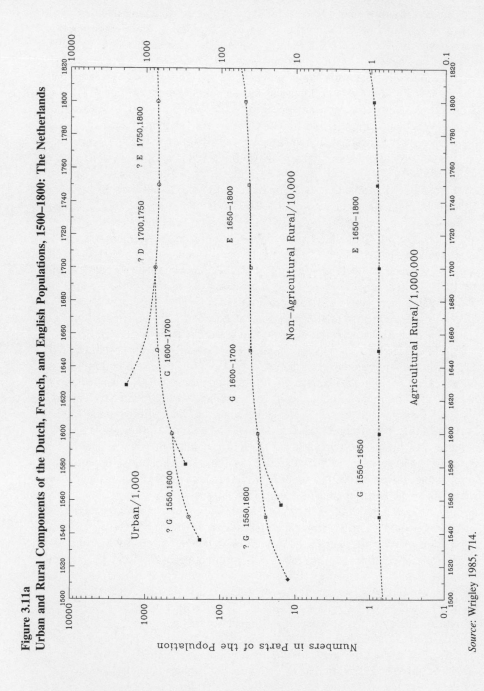

Source: Wrigley 1985, 714.

Figure 3.11b
Urban and Rural Components of the Dutch, French, and English Populations, 1500–1800: France

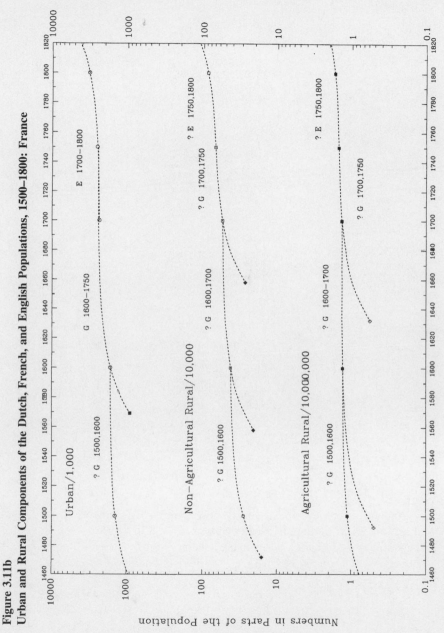

Source: Wrigley 1985, 718.

Table 3.4
The Growth of Agricultural and Non-Agricultural Population in the Netherlands, France, and England, 1500–1800

Netherlands	France	England

Rural Agricultural:

Netherlands	France	England
1550-1650 G 1435	1500,1600 ?G 1439	1520-1670 G 1497
	1600,1700 ?G 1492	
	1700,1750 ?G 1632	1670-1750 D 1606
1650-1800 E 1857	1750,1800 ?E 1861	1750,1801 ?E 1850

Rural Non-Agricultural:

Netherlands	France	England
1550,1600 ?G 1512	1500,1600 ?G 1472	1520-1670 H 1452
1600-1750 G 1559	1600,1700 ?G 1558	
	1700,1750 ?G 1658	1700,1750 ?H 1575
1650-1800 E 1858	1750,1800 ?E 1839	1750,1801 ?E 1816

Urban:

Netherlands	France	England
1550-1650 H 1508^d	1550,1600 ?H 1430^d	1550,1600 ?H 1518^d
1550,1600 ?G 1536^w	1500,1600 ?G 1441^w	1520,1600 ?H 1477^w
1600-1700 G 1582	1600-1750 G 1569	1600-1700 H 1538
1700,1750 ?D 1629	1600-1750 H 1475^d	1700,1750 ?H 1594
1750,1800 ?E 1902	1700-1800 E 1838	1750,1801 ?E 1805

Total Population:

Netherlands	France	England
1500-1620 G 1471	1500,1600 ?G 1450?^{w}	1561-1656 H 1461
1620-1750 G 1574	1600,1700 ?G 1520?^{w}	
	1675,1700 ?D 1566	1656-1686 D 1587
	1700-1752 G 1650	1686-1726 H 1492
1750-1839 E 1866	1752-1792 G 1702	1726-1806 E 1822
	1792-1827 E 1876	

^{w} = 5,000+ from Wrigley.
^{d} = 10,000+ from de Vries.

Sources: Wrigley 1985, 714, 718, 700; de Vries 1984, 30; Harris 2001, 148–52.

for England in contrast to the much more parallel E trends of total and agricultural populations for the Netherlands and France. In those two countries, population actually increased in somewhat more tardy E form than its agricultural segment (1866 vs. 1857; 1876 vs. 1861; in contrast to 1822 vs. 1850 for England).

As Joan Thirsk (1978) demonstrated so vividly and convincingly, the rural population of England turned to many profitable, small-scale non-agricultural pursuits in the 16th and early 17th centuries. Figure 3.11c and Table 3.4 show how this allowed the non-agricultural rural population of England to expand

Figure 3.11c
Urban and Rural Components of the Dutch, French, and English Populations, 1500–1800: England

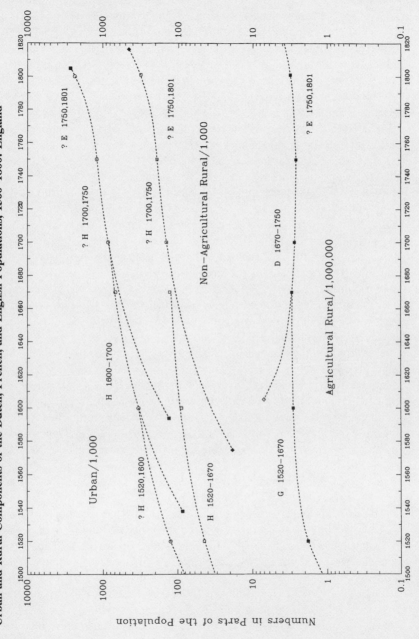

Source: Wrigley 1985, 700.

robustly (by seven) between 1520 and 1801. From 1520 through 1670 an almost tripling of this group took H form with base year at 1452, which resembles very closely how the much more frequently documented total population of England enlarged in H fashion between 1561 and 1656 with t_0 at 1461 (Harris 2001, 148, 150–51).[18] From that point to 1750 there was some further expansion (about 50 percent), perhaps along the kind of second H path offered in Figure 3.11c. This now, however, would have entailed much steeper H-type increase than for the population as a whole in the period (t_0 near 1575 rather than the 1492 for English people of all types 1686–1726, following D-shape demographic loss between 1656 and 1686).

From 1750 to 1801 growth in the non-agricultural rural population of England, while now probably taking E shape, went back to just paralleling total population increase as it had up through 1670. The suggested E trend for 1750 and 1801 would have its zero year at 1816 compared with 1822 for the overall population of England (Table 3.4). In other words, from 1520 through 1670 and again from 1750 to 1801 the number of people living in the English countryside who did not engage in agriculture increased along with the total size of England's population. Between 1670 and 1750, in contrast, their number enlarged appreciably faster than the national pattern of demographic growth.

A 1650–1800 E trend for the rural non-agricultural segment in the Netherlands, too, paralleled increase in the total population over the same period. In France, however, what may also have been E-form expansion in this part of the society in the 18th century was rather steeper than growth for all residents of the country. In contrast, across the 17th century and perhaps also the 16th, increase in rural population not engaged in farming seems to have taken G shape, making Dutch and French developments of this sort largely parallel each other—and also barely exceed national demographic expansion.[19] The result was that non-agricultural rural population in the Netherlands, for all the reputation of that country as an early modern economic innovator, multiplied by only 1.7 between the early 1500s and 1750 in contrast to about 2.5 in France and 4.2 in England.[20] Which country would one expect to produce an "industrial revolution" in the later 18th century?

Urban population, meanwhile, expanded in England between 1600 and 1700 along an H track that made its size multiply by 2.5 (Figure 3.11c). This change took place while both the agricultural and the total population of the country saw some decline (Table 3.4). Across the same period it looks as though urban residents in the Netherlands (Figure 3.11a) and France (3.11b) increased via generally parallel G trends instead and were enlarged by only 1.7 and 1.4, respectively.

Previously, from the early 1500s to 1600, very little expansion (just 14 percent in a century) had taken place collectively in centers with more than 5,000 inhabitants in France, according to Wrigley (1985, 718), perhaps along the kind of G path hypothesized in Figure 3.11b. In contrast, just between 1550 and 1600, a time span half as long, urban population in the Netherlands using the

5,000 plus categorization climbed robustly (67 percent). This change may have taken the steeper (later) G trajectory with zero year at 1536 that is posited in Figure 3.11a and Table 3.4. A more restrictive "urban" classification by de Vries (1984, 30) that starts only at 10,000, on the other hand, indicates an H trend for the Netherlands from 1550 through 1650 with zero year at 1508 and would allow a substantially flatter H segment for France across the reduced span of 1550–1600, with t_0 near 1430. Table 3.4 reports both sets of possible trends, for centers above 5,000 people and for just those with 10,000 or more residents. In England, the inhabitants of towns and cities with 5,000 or more multiplied by 2.6 (increased 160 percent) between 1520 and 1600. These two data points would fit an H curve with zero year at 1477 (compared with 1518 for cities of 10,000 and more residents in England for the span 1550–1600, according to de Vries—very parallel with the comparable track for the Netherlands in this shorter era).

From 1700 through 1800 French urban population next increased in E fashion, first slowly and then progressively more rapidly. This trend augmented that segment of the French people by 37 percent in the 18th century. The numbers of Dutch living in centers of 5,000 or more, meanwhile, actually *shrank* 9 percent between 1700 and 1750. Growth across the second half of the 18th century only restored urban population in the Netherlands at 1800 to 95 percent of what it had been a century before. Previously noted information on Dutch provincial populations and shifts from the big maritime cities to inland centers makes the two-point D and E trends proposed in Figure 3.11a and Table 3.4 more than guesses. In England, however, what was perhaps a third H trend raised the number of urban residents 44 percent between 1700 and 1750. Then—the general context suggests in E form—the numbers almost doubled between 1750 and 1801 (up 95 percent) to make the urban population of England multiply by 2.8 in the 18th century as the nation moved to industrialize.

Figure 3.10 has portrayed trends in the *percentage* of the population that was urban in the Netherlands, France, and England across the 16th, 17th, and 18th centuries. Figures 3.11d and 3.11e examine movements in other aspects of the composition of these "core" countries of Western development during the early modern era.

In Figure 3.11d and Table 3.5 it first of all stands out how little the total number of persons supported by agriculture in France increased relative to numbers actually engaged in agriculture across three centuries between 1500 and 1800—just from 1.38 to 1.70, or a change of 23 percent in 300 years. For the latter two centuries of this long epoch, a very flat segment of an H trend—based all the way back in the 1340s—perhaps captures the movement. Previously, a G with base year near 1400 would fit the ratios at 1500 and 1600. A G curve segment only slightly steeper than the latter, with t_0 at 1439, is a pattern that would also represent change in England between 1520 and 1600, as part A of Table 3.5 indicates. In addition, the levels are virtually equal: from 1.32 to 1.43 in England, from 1.38 to 1.45 in France. For the Netherlands, in contrast,

Figure 3.11d
Urban and Rural Components of the Dutch, French, and English Populations, 1500–1800: Total Population per Person in Agriculture

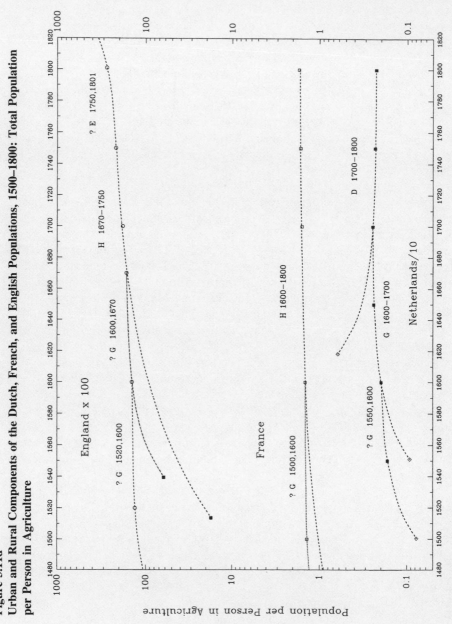

Source: Wrigley 1985, 700, 718, 714.

Figure 3.11e
Urban and Rural Components of the Dutch, French, and English Populations, 1500–1800: Share of Rural Population Not in Agriculture

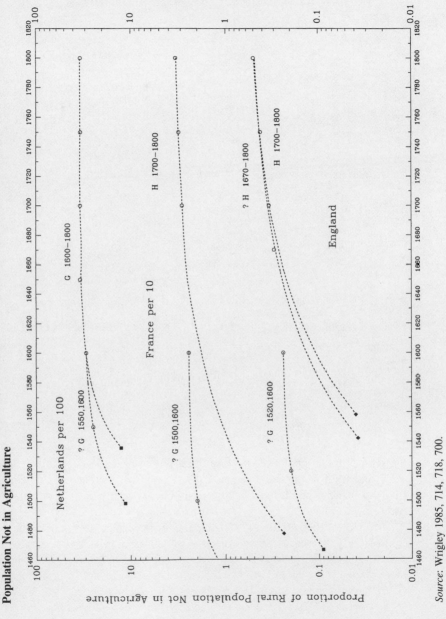

Source: Wrigley 1985, 714, 718, 700.

237

Table 3.5
Changing Proportions of Non-Agricultural Population in England, France, and the Netherlands, 1500–1800

A. Population per Person in Agriculture

England		France		Netherlands	
Ratios:					
1520	1.32	1500	1.38	1550	1.67
1600	1.43	1600	1.45	1600	2.00
1670	1.65	1650	?	1650	2.42
1700	1.82	1700	1.58	1700	2.47
1750	2.19	1750	1.63	1750	2.33
1801	2.76	1800	1.70	1800	2.27

Possible Trends in Ratios:

1520,1600 ?G 1439		1500,1600 ?G 1402		1550,1600 ?G 1500	
1600,1670 ?G 1540				1600-1700 G 1551	
1670-1750 H 1514		1600-1800 H 1345		1700-1800 D 1618	
1750,1801 ?E 1834					

B. Proportions of Persons Not in Agriculture

% Rural Pop. Not in Agriculture: *% Total Population Urban:*

Year	England	Netherl.	France	Year	England	Netherl.	France
1500-50	20	25	20	1500-50	5.25	21	9.1
1600	24	29+	24+	1600	8.0	29	8.7
1650-70	30	34	?	1650-70	13.5	37	?
1700	34	34	29	1700	17.0	39	10.9
1750	42	34	31+	1750	21.0	35	10.3
1800	50	34	34	1800	27.5	33	11.1

Source: Wrigley 1985, 700, 718, 714.

the ratio of total population to those in agriculture by 1550 had aready attained 1.67; and by 1600 it had risen to 2.0, pulling still further above France and England in what might have been a G trajectory with t_0 near 1500 as opposed to 1402 or 1439.

Then, from 1600 through 1700 the Dutch ratio increased still further in G form, from 2.0 through 2.5. Across this middle century of the three studied, in contrast, the French ratio lifted only from 1.45 to 1.58. Between 1600 and 1670, meanwhile, total population per English person in the agricultural sector rose rather more, from 1.43 to 1.65—probably via a second G path. Subsequently— from 1670 to 1750, however—the English ratio enjoyed visibly more robust increase, in the H pattern, while the French relationship remained level and the Dutch ratio as of 1700 began a D-type *decline* that lasted until 1800. As of

1750 the English ratio had climbed to 2.19, at last coming close to the slipping Dutch one (2.33), while in France the result of continuing minimal change was a ratio of still just 1.63. Between 1750 and 1800 the French figure probably improved at an increasing rate, while the Dutch ratio atrophied still a little more. The E-shape surges in urban and non-agricultural rural population seen in Figure 3.11c, however, by 1801 took the number of English supported on average by each person in agriculture to 2.76, rather higher than even the Dutch maximum during the Golden Age of the 1600s.

In sum, across three centuries France supported relatively very little more population by her agriculture than she had in 1500. This very limited advance in efficiency accompanied the demographic parsimony for which France is historically famous, especially via early reductions in fertility. The Netherlands, as is well known, in the later 1500s and the 1600s created (along with Flanders just across the border) the most productive agriculture recorded for pre-modern Europe. But the country did not sustain the non-agricultural population growth achieved in the Golden Age. It was only after 1800 that modern development in these respects took hold in the Netherlands. After a start no stronger than that of France, however, English agriculture (toward the end of the era supplemented somewhat by Irish and colonial production) managed to more than double the mouths fed per individual engaged in domestic agriculture. From 1600 forward, particularly after 1670, this provided the manpower and womanpower, first for Thirsk's "projects" and then for the factories that let England supplant the Netherlands and outrun France to come to lead economic development in the Western world.

Figure 3.11e and part B of Table 3.5, finally, sketch out the role of rural non-agricultural activity in these historical changes. As of the early 1500s, Wrigley has estimated (1985, 718, 700, 714) that of the rural populations of France and England 20 percent were not engaged in agriculture compared with 25 percent in the Netherlands. While increase occurred in all three countries during the 16th century—perhaps via the kinds of G trajectories proposed in the absence of indications for some other form of trend—the steepest change in this period, the G with latest zero year, was taking place in the Netherlands, where by 1600 slightly under 30 percent were in activities outside agriculture compared with 24 percent in France and also England.

In the 17th century, however, non-agricultural development in the countryside in these three "core" countries of European modernization parted ways. The Dutch proportion rose to 34 percent by 1650, the apogee of the Golden Age; but the G path that it was taking—and continued to follow all across the 18th century—took the proportion no higher by 1800. In France, fresh increase—now in H shape—seems to have begun in the age of Richelieu and extended to 1800. This brought the percentage of the rural population of France who were active outside agriculture to 34 percent by the time of the Revolution, catching up with the Dutch in this respect. In England change in the H form also appeared—possibly by 1670 and possibly only after 1700, as Figure 3.11e illustrates alternatively. Either trend, however, was far more robust than the H-type movement in France. By 1800 no less than *half* of the rural population of England was not participating in agriculture. Thus, while between 1500 and 1800 England rose from being 0.58 as urban as France to 2.48 times her larger competitor in this respect, the share of the rural population in England who were engaged in activities outside agriculture climbed from equaling the French proportion to exceeding it, and also that for the once-leading Netherlands, by half. The population shifts that made England rather than France or the Netherlands the cutting edge for the era of industrialization occurred not only in movement to cities but within the life of rural society. Underlying and supporting both, as Wrigley (1985) has demonstrated, was more productive agriculture.

Whether or not packaged under the once-catchy label "proto-industrialization," these developments in the early modern European countryside have attracted considerable interest during the past few decades and have been the subject of much fruitful and provocative research. The extensive economic implications of the demographic trends noted in Figure 3.10 and Figures 3.11a through 3.11e are explored in another study in progress. But one example concerning change in the forms of labor in rural England illustrates the kinds of "demonomic" interactions involved.

Figure 3.12 draws upon the work of Ann Kussmaul (1981, 12–13) to estimate trends for certain changes that took place in populations of the English countryside between about 1600 and 1830. The evidence for successive dates come from an ever-changing sample of parishes. Therefore, patterning is only approximate. Even from these tentative operations, however, some insight emerges as to how the composition of rural populations in England altered with time, a perspective that adds profitably to what has been learned from Figures 3.11c, 3.11d, and 3.11e and Tables 3.4 and 3.5.

According to Kussmaul, farmers and their servants and laborers composed about 21 percent of parish populations (which included not only men in non-farm activity but women and children who often worked without being recorded as "labor") fairly consistently at 1599, 1688, 1695, 1697, and 1705 in computations gleaned from 11 different parishes scattered across England from Middlesex to Westmoreland and from Kent to Wiltshire. The likelihood is that this level was characteristic of the long-undocumented gap from 1599 through 1688 as well as across later, better-recorded years of the era. Then, from about 1750 to 1830 the proportion declined to some 13 percent or about two-fifths of its previous level. This change roughly followed a D curve with base year at 1733, which is offered in the top plot of Figure 3.12.[21]

The weight of just the farmers themselves in parish populations, meanwhile, seems more likely to have shrunk instead in accelerating C fashion from the 1770s—or perhaps as early as the 1690s—into the 1830s, as the second plot in Figure 3.12 indicates (the hollow squares). From the 1680s into the 1790s the trend might have been one of D shape; and by the end of the 17th century farmers had already in some form declined from 11 to 7 percent of parish

Figure 3.12

Farmers and Their Workforce in Some Parishes of England, 1599–1831

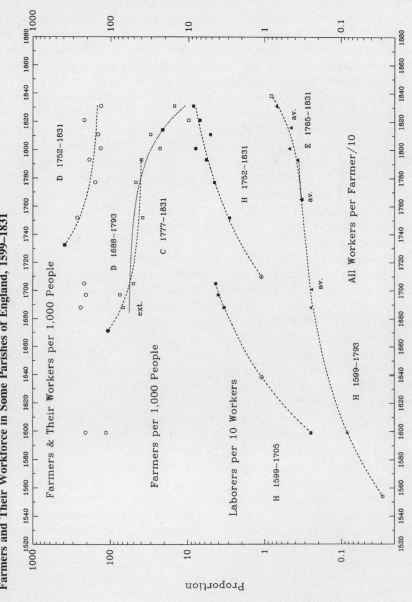

Source: Kussmaul 1981, 12–13.

populations, on average, compared with further atrophy to just over 1 percent by the 1830s. To have the weight of farmers decline in C fashion across the late 1700s and early 1800s with t_0 at 1814, however, mirrors vertically the way non-agricultural rural population in England is implied in Figure 3.11c and Table 3.4 to have grown between 1750 and 1801 via an E trend with zero year at 1816. The two data sets support each other.

One thing that happened between the middle of the 18th century and 1831 was that farmers, as there were relatively fewer of them in the rural population, on average took on more labor while the size of the rural agricultural population also enlarged in what probably was E form (Figure 3.11c)—which is how the total population of England clearly grew. In Kussmaul's communities, workers per farmer—servants and laborers together—multiplied between the 1760s and the 1830s from 3.2 to 6.9 in E fashion with t_0 at 1838, as the bottom plot in Figure 3.12 indicates. That makes this change parallel to the hypothesized E-type increase in the ratio of total population to persons in agriculture for England as a whole between 1750 and 1801, with zero year at 1834, as shown in Figure 3.11d and Table 3.5.[22] Having more workers per farmer, in other words, increased in the same way that English agriculture during this period produced the food to support more and more population not engaged in farming. Meanwhile, as Peter Clark (2000, 744, 746) has recently summarized, demographic surplus from three different size categories of towns (starting at just 500 residents) and in all the major regions of England swelled in comparable accelerating E fashion, helping provide more persons simultaneously for agricultural work, non-agricultural activity, and urban employment, which have all been estimated to swell in E form like the total population of England, though not equally steeply (Table 3.4).

An important part of the much-discussed "Agricultural Revolution" of the 18th century seems to have been an aggressively enlarging farm work unit. Enough extra population was being produced to have sufficient workers for this change at the same time that additional people were being drawn to cities and engaged in non-agricultural pursuits in the countryside. There would seem, in short, to be support here for the argument of Ester Boserup (1965) that demographic increase in certain conditions can facilitate economic growth, not just devour it and hinder it. Ironically, the E-type demographic engine that in more modern appearances has been feared as "population explosion" seems to have done this in 18th-century England. In what other historical settings, then, might this form of demonomic dynamic also have appeared? One candidate is certainly Japan, whose population grew in repeated E trends between the early 1870s and the 1930s (Harris 2001, 249) as the national economy modernized and industrialized following the Meiji Revolution.

Earlier in England, from about 1600 up into the middle or later 1700s, the number of combined servants and laborers per farmer in the parishes studied by Kussmaul seems to have grown along an H path with t_0 at 1554. This trend closely resembles the H trajectory along which the proportion of the rural residents of England who were not in agriculture mounted from approximately the 1640s to 1801 (Figure 3.11e), somewhat steeper than the 1670–1750 rise in the ratio of total population to those in agriculture for England as a whole (Figure 3.11d and Table 3.5). In other words, up to about 1750—as in the several decades thereafter—farmers typically took on more workers in a manner very parallel to the pattern in which the activities of rural England shifted away from agriculture and the population of England in general expanded beyond farm employment. In this earlier era, though, the crucial and connected trends took H rather than E shape. While, as they did later, the number of farmers in the rural population declined in this earlier era between 1599 and the early 1700s, the shape of this trend is unclear.

In these processes of change across the countryside, furthermore, less and less of the labor force for farmers was composed of servants. More and more were laborers. The share of workers for farmers who were laborers perhaps increased from as little as 2.5 percent at 1599 to 44.0 percent in the early 1700s. After dropping off somewhere and in some unknown form during the early 1700s, it swelled from 29.0 percent at 1752 to 86.2 percent by 1831. Rural service had virtually disappeared. Each of these trends took H shape, it seems. The first had its zero year at 1638; the second at 1710. Neither pattern has an obvious parallel in other movements observed in Figures 3.10 through 3.12. Both trends of change seem to be internal to the shifting nature of how farms operated—and did not directly affect or reflect, like total labor employed per farmer, the pattern according to which agriculture supported more and more English people per person in farming or the rate at which the rural population, not just the urban one, turned to non-agricultural pursuits. It can be expected, however, that shifting from servants to laborers made employment more flexible and geographical mobility more fluid in ways that simultaneously fostered agricultural productivity, the advantages of scale to be had from larger farms, and also urbanization— particularly at centers of new commercial and manufacturing development that were crucial for the "Industrial Revolution."

A similar shift to more flexible relationships between farmers and their work- force, at the expense of servitude, within a context of increased rural activity in non-agricultural pursuits is evident in the late 18th and early 19th centuries in part of Britain's American colonies (Clemens and Simler 1988). In Chester County, Pennsylvania, between 1750 and 1820 the share of both servants and slaves in household labor forces dropped off rapidly. The percentage who were inmates—non-family members who lived within the household property but were not bound to the owner (many were cottagers with short-term agree- ments)—in contrast increased from 16 to 51 percent along a G path with t_0 near 1747. A series of rich studies of rural occupational change both within and outside of agriculture across much of Europe, furthermore, have appeared since the early 1970s. The trends of these developments and their relationships to demographic change are explored elsewhere.

To summarize, flows to particular towns or cities seem to have swelled and shrunk historically in G' manner just like the free and forced migrations whose more numerous details were available for Chapters 1 and 2. In similar fashion, too, such intakes in G' form—pushing up, then weakening urban growth—have contributed to shaping the G trends that are encountered so ubiquitously in the population growth of towns and cities from Europe to Asia to the Americas and Africa (Harris 2001, ch. 8, 295–330, and 342–58).

One consequence of these patterns in going to cities has been that the *composition* of urban populations has altered in G, or likewise constantly proportionally altering D and C forms. Evidence to that effect comes from Amsterdam and Norwich across the 1500s and 1600s, Cuenca, Rouen, and Geneva during the 1600s and 1700s, 18th-century Batavia, Ghent, and Nottingham, and on into the 19th century both in rapidly industrializing Barmen of the booming Rhineland Wupperthal and in the small, more tranquil towns of the Danish West Indies. The proportion of current or former migrants in the urban population, its racial or ethnic mix, the weight of females in the total, the percentage of them married by a certain age, children per woman present at a given time, completed family size, and ratios of births or baptisms to marriages are all elements of demographic composition that the history of one city or another has been shown to have altered in G-based trends.

Does structural change in these same forms comparably characterize the much more numerously recorded free and forced migrations previously examined in Chapters 1 and 2 and the ways they interacted with the populations that received them? Is there here, in other words, the beginning of very *general* insight into the way developments are channeled into G-related shapes as they are digested by or pass through populations? An important agenda is established to take back, in subsequent chapters, from these tantalizing perspectives via urbanization to structural change that accompanied the other kinds of migration that have been introduced.

First, however, it must be noted that—as in the Atlantic slave trade or in the freer transoceanic relocations of the 17th, 18th, 19th, and 20th centuries—specific urban migrations *in aggregate* tend to add up to flows of people that take G or D forms rather than the G' up-and-down shape. An example is provided by migration into German cities between the 1830s and the 1980s (Figure 3.3). Such collective movements in turn can foster growth in total urban populations for societies, or large parts of them, that take H as well as G shape. As a consequence, some aspects of broad national and regional *urbanization* follow similar patterns.

It has been seen how the *proportion* of urban residents in the populations of Sweden, Ireland, New Zealand, and the United States across long stretches of the 19th and 20th centuries expanded in H form. Before about 1840 in Sweden and the United States and also after 1940 in Sweden, in contrast, such increase took G shape instead. What distinguishes the historical era with H trends is an epoch of modern economic change—even in blighted Ireland, whence country people emigrated overseas in droves, driving up the proportion of people living in cities this way along with actual urban relocation.

Earlier, as the Netherlands—led by its rising maritime province of Holland— from the 1500s into the middle of the 1600s became "the first modern economy" on the basis of her efficient agriculture and fishing, new industry, and aggressive trade, collective urban population in the coastal heartland of Dutch achievement apparently also expanded in H form, though that was not the case in the towns and cities of other provinces (Figure 3.9a). What did not apparently occur, however, was *proportional* H-type increase, even in preeminent Holland. How did such failure to keep urbanization, for all its high level in the Netherlands, moving forward more persistently than in the rapidly decelerating G pattern reflect or affect the way that stagnation pervaded the Dutch economy for many decades after about 1650 and how the population of several documented parts of the country (Figure 3.9b) visibly de-urbanized in D-type trends?

Some of the patterns emerging for the New World society of the United States naturally involve conditions peculiar to a nation that for generations enjoyed an elastic continental frontier: for instance, the pace of new settlement, expansion of the accumulative area occupied, wilderness that was left to settle. Gains of G then H shape in the proportion of inhabited land that was *densely* settled, however, help in understanding how urbanization in this country took H form through the later 19th and early 20th centuries. Similarly, the way that the proportion of the employed who were engaged in activities outside agriculture, even in the farm-rich states of the Old Northwest, also increased in H fashion points to connections between agricultural change and urbanization that have been probed insightfully in other historical contexts, notably, northwestern Europe between 1500 and 1800.

An application of the new analytical tool-kit of G-related trends to the classic work of Wrigley (1985) on the Netherlands, France, and England first of all reveals marked differences among the urban histories of these countries. The percentage of the Dutch population living in cities increased in H fashion from the middle 1500s to about 1700, before dropping off in D form with the passing of the Golden Age. The urban share of the English population (especially centers other than London) likewise enlarged via H—but later, from the middle 1600s to the later 1700s, as Britain challenged the Netherlands and became the leading economic power of northern Europe. Such an H pattern, however, never appeared in France, where the proportion living in cities at 1800 was barely higher than it had been at 1500.

Underlying more robust English urbanization from the later 1600s into the later 1700s, furthermore, was a basically parallel H-shape increase in the productivity of English agriculture, in terms of how many people were provided for per person engaged in agriculture. This is the kind of pairing observed a century later in the workforce composition and urban growth of the United States (Figure 3.8a). Kussmaul's (1981) research on rural communities, meanwhile, has shown how the number of workers per farmer and the proportion of those workers who were wage laborers also rose in H fashion as the productivity of English agriculture increased via H. The scale and flexibility of agricultural employment, in other words, likewise altered in the H manner during the crucial period of development. Would an examination, say, of technological and organizational change in U.S. farming in the 19th century indicate trends similarly linked with agricultural productivity, urbanization, and H-type population increase there?

Based upon the historical socio-economic contexts in which it has appeared, Volume I has hypothesized that the H pattern of population growth has been associated with some form of economic development that did not occur where the more usual, rapidly decelerating G trends of demographic increase have occurred. The details of urbanization and agricultural change in H form that have been encountered here provide insight into just what may have been involved in this mode of population increase. Do they, or comparable contributing movements, appear when one examines other historical settings where the H form of demographic expansion has occurred?

The list includes the United States since 1850 (Harris 2001, 27), Canada briefly in the 18th century (66), the big plantation colonies of Jamaica and St. Domingue in the 18th century (70), Brazil between 1690 and 1940, Argentina most of the time between the 1770s and the 1970s, and Mexico from 1831 through 1910 (114).

In the Old World, besides England, the Dutch province of Holland, and probably Sweden from the 1500s to about 1700 or a little later, Spain and Portugal from the middle of the 17th century to the middle of the 18th century, and 17 European countries for some span of time in the 19th century or early 20th century, including Russia, Serbia, Iceland, and Ireland (before 1841) display substantial H-shape overall demographic expansion for sustained periods of time, but never France (148–49). This H form of population growth did, however, appear for a while during the 19th century in the French departments of Seine and Nord (around Paris and Lille) and, at one time or another, across a web of *regional* European populations spun from the Netherlands and Germany and northern Italy (and perhaps some areas of Spain during the later 1600s and early 1700s) eastward across parts of Austria-Hungary into areas of Russia that stretched from the western borders to the North Caucasus and, after the 1950s, to Central Asia (186, 190–91, 198–99, 206–7, 213, 220–22).

Increase in the population of China, too, switched to three successive H trends of growth, beginning in the 1740s; and several provinces show demographic patterns of this type across various stretches of time between there and the present (244, 258–59). In Japan and her regions, in contrast, such movement *never* appears (251, 271). But in several societies of southern Asia the H trend of population increase has emerged in modern times, often recently as the accelerating demographic expansion of "population explosion" has come under control, as in India since 1960 and several of her states (250–51, 274–75). In Africa (280–81), the H form of population growth has emerged so far only in

Egypt (1882–1927 and then, after a period of "explosion," again from 1960 to 1990 or later) and perhaps briefly in Kenya and Tanzania around the middle of the 20th century. Did the contributing H-type movements in urbanization and agricultural change that have been observed in northwestern Europe and the United States for certain periods since 1500 also play a role in these historical cases of exceptional population increase in H form as opposed to the much more frequent, rapidly slowing G pattern?

It seems likely, meanwhile, that upward-accelerating E trends for workers per farm in England between 1765 and 1831 (Figure 3.12) and for total population supported per person in agriculture there (Figure 3.11d), for the pace of urbanization in the Netherlands and England following about 1750 (Figure 3.10), and for the growth of cities like Nottingham, Bruges, and Evergem in the later 1700s (Harris 2001, 308) and some Asian and African centers more recently (ibid., 319–22, 326) begin in turn to identify dynamics that comparably help understand the way that many populations have experienced E-type expansion or "population explosion." Far from being a phenomenon of just the recent "Third World," demographic increase in this ominous, speeding-up form diffused across Europe, starting with England and Ireland in the 1720s—in this case as it spread including France briefly after the Revolution (ibid., 148–49 and the tables of Chapter 6). This form of demographic change seems intimately associated with early, labor-intensive phases or forms of economic development, as it probably was in 20th-century Asia and Latin America as well, from Japan and India to Mexico and Venezuela (ibid., 250–51, 114).

Dutch data on the urbanization patterns of different kinds of cities (Figures 3.9a and 3.9b), meanwhile, and Wrigley's analysis of the fate of London against its English urban competition (Figure 3.2) already reveal how some centers gained at the expense of others in certain places and times. Such shifts in the hot spots of urban plate tectonics have been a fruitful element in the broad-thinking literature about international patterns of urbanization and their role in the creation of the modern world. What part, then, did demographically shaped, G-related patterns of change play in these sweeping interregional developments?

NOTES

1. Data for the origins of mothers display less change. The proportions of fathers from foreign countries, adjacent Spanish provinces, other provinces, and more than 50 kilometers away in the same province all came down separately from 1625 through 1775, though not so smoothly in D fashion as they did together.

2. If, furthermore, London's demographic deficit (strength of attraction) truly hit another high in the 1730s, as might be read from Figure 3.2, this was where a short, sharp cut in immigrants to Nottingham shows up.

3. Harris 1992 illustrates and trends some of the shifts documented by Jacob Price (1973 and other works) and historians of West Indian shipping and trade.

4. To roughly trend his evidence, Figure 3.3 estimates 1817, 1820, and every fifth year thereafter from his Figure 3.

5. For Berlin 1837, 1840, and every fifth year through 1880 are estimated from his graph; then, 1924, 1927, 1930, 1933, 1936, and 1938 from his Figure 19.

6. But include the Barmen rate at 1860 as given by Hochstadt (1999, 115).

7. Regrettably, I omitted Spooner's useful work as it is relevant to Chapter 8 of the first volume of this study (Harris 2001). The city generally expanded along a G path from 27,000 at 1673 to about 140,000 in the 1780s. This approximate curve had its zero year near 1686. The numbers fall below this trend at 1740 and 1750 following the riots of 1740, which not only decimated the substantial Chinese element of the population, especially in the inner city, but also brought about significant temporary reductions in the size of all other groups except the small European, Eurasian, and Muslim/Jentiven elements (Spooner 1986, 51, 43). While the recovery of 1750–1790 that followed this crisis might be said to take G' shape with crest at about 1776, the G proposed probably better captures the movement right acrosss the 117-year record of the city's population under the VOC.

Someone willing to take the proportion of Batavia's population residing in the outer as opposed to the inner city as a surrogate for the weight of urban in-migration would find that this percentage rose and topped out in G' fashion from 1673 through 1720, then followed a G path from 1730 through 1790 (Spooner 1986). The interested reader could further pursue the changing demographic significance of several sub-zones within the inner and outer areas of Batavia as an insight into how G-related trends might represent the shifting neighborhood sands upon which cities so characteristically grow.

8. Lest it be thought that such G-related change in urban ethnic composition was an exotic Asian phenomenon, among migrants to Geneva between 1625 and 1727 persons of French origin composed more and more of the total via what seem to be movements of G shape. For men the proportion rose from 20 percent of the total in the years around 1635 to 58 percent by 1726 along a G path with t_0 around 1639. (Most of the rest came from local sources within 25 kilometers of the city of Geneva or from the Pays de Vaud, and only a few from the remainder of Switzerland or elsewhere.) For women in-migrants, in contrast, those originating in France climbed from just 1 percent to 48 percent via a G with a much later zero year at 1682. Apparently French men had been drawn by the attractions of the city for some time; for French women, it seems, 20 years of building pressure by Louis XIV on the Huguenots, which culminated with the revocation of the Edict of Nantes in 1685, was more important in the motivation to migrate. The data come from Poussou 1997 (285), who draws upon Perrenoud. Similar distinctions between family migration in periods of pressure and a larger role for single men in more normal times are identified in other migrations in Chapter 6.

9. A combined average for Javanese and Balinese (as Spooner 1986, 49, gives them separately at 1760 and 1790) is weighted by their current numbers.

10. In the later decades of the 1700s, among the Chinese, older children somehow came to outnumber younger ones, a phenomenon worth further inquiry.

11. Compare the population shifts in Japanese regionalism and local development that are patterned and discussed in Harris 2001 (268–72, 319–325, 340–42, 356–58, 373–74).

12. Though Hamilton surpassed Dunedin as of the 1980s.

13. None of these G patterns of demographic growth paralleled the alternative G trends possible, but not preferred for urbanization.

14. The aggregate *number* of people living in U.S. cities of over 500,000 inhabitants has previously been seen to have increased from 1890 through 1970 along a G path with

base year at 1915 (Harris 2001, 30–31). This finding was hypothesized to presage a relevance of G-related trends for urbanization beyond the level of individual cities.

15. Harris 2001, 296–302.

16. Even increase in the total acreage of public sales, including timber and desert land, had begun to slow down appreciably by the 1850s (Gates 1960, 71).

17. Small negative numbers for *loss* of settled territory in the 1950s, 1960s, and 1980s are averaged with some gain in the 1970s (Otterstrom and Earle 2002, 68).

18. An alternative trending would be an H for 1600, 1670, and 1700 with t_0 around 1480. That, however, would change the general picture only slightly.

19. The annual pattern for French baptisms between 1500 and 1600 that Dupâquier (1997, 447) cites from Biraben and Blum seems to support the kind of G trend for French population size that is hypothesized from just the two turn-of-century estimates by Wrigley.

20. By 1.6, 1.7, and 2.9 as of the middle of the 1600s.

21. While data for 3 Westmoreland parishes in the later 1690s fall in line with evidence from other locales in the period, the distributions for 31 parishes of this county at 1787 (whose population total is unknown) show exceptionally little labor of any kind per farmer and very few laborers among servants and laborers together compared with ratios for parishes in other parts of England. The reasons for this difference could be either 18th-century regional divergence for a northern county located not far from exploding textile centers or the manner in which the data were collected. This 1787 Westmoreland material is not included in the trending presented in Figure 3.12.

22. Some averaging of Kussmaul's data for 1752 and 1777, on the one hand, and of 1811 with 1821, on the other, clarifies such an underlying E shape of change.

Chapter 4

The Growth and Change
of Extended Urban Systems

Cities do not serve just single societies. They form focal elements in international networks that exchange things, people, and ideas. If individual cities evolve in G-based forms (Harris 2001, ch. 8) and individual countries urbanize in similar patterns (Chapter 3 in this volume), according to what shapes do broader, interlocking urban systems develop? How do such trends unfold?

The extensive collection of data and framework of analysis presented by Jan de Vries (1984) and Paul Bairoch (1988, 1990) make it possible to pursue insights just obtained from mapping out urbanization during three or four centuries following 1500 in the three seminal countries of the Netherlands, France, and England into an even wider and more modern international context. Re-examining the available evidence in terms of the G-based patterns that are entailed reinforces some of the periodization and regionalization of how cities evolved in Europe that have been advanced and explanations made for them. Other aspects of that eye-opening and challenging literature seem to require some reconsideration. Our review provides some fresh insight and probes, at least preliminarily, how the new kind of G-rooted interpretation might be applied to global urbanization well beyond the confines of early modern Europe.

THE EXPANSION OF CITY POPULATIONS IN EUROPE
AFTER 1500

Figure 4.1 summarizes estimated trends in the numbers of persons living in certain sizes of cities in broad European regions between 1500 and 1800 (de Vries 1984, 72). From these patterns it would appear that the framework of

Figure 4.1
European Population Living in Cities of Certain Sizes

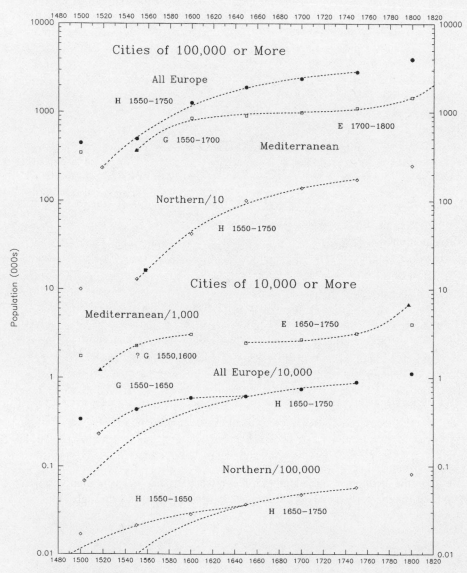

Source: de Vries 1984, 72.

place and time chosen by de Vries for his analysis—Northern versus Mediterranean, the "long" 16th century verses the era that followed—has tended to
obscure some simple movements in his data. For example, as the top plot in
Figure 4.1 demonstrates, the total number of people who resided in the largest
cities of the 300-year epoch that he studied—those with 100,000 or more inhabitants—in fact increased for Europe as a whole all the way from 1550 to
1750 along one *continuous* H trend. This aggregate multiplied by 5.7 as the
number of cities with that many dwellers expanded from 3 to 12. The implication is that a *single* process of development among the most central of all
central places was at work across these two centuries for Europe as a total,
overarching economic and demographic system. At this capstone level, the time
spans of 1500–1600/1650 and 1600/1650–1750 were *not* distinctive phases for
aggregate growth in the leading centers of Europe, as de Vries says. Earlier,
between 1500 and 1550, collective expansion in the largest hubs of trade, finance, and empire for the continent was hardly discernible. Later, as de Vries
correctly states, a new trend of growth for the biggest cities appeared beginning
in the later 18th century. His data for 1750, 1800, 1850, 1890, and 1979 in fact
suggest accelerating E-type expansion for 1750–1850, then H growth for 1850–
1979, trends that as the discussion proceeds can be put into a compatible context
of other things that are known about the modern history of European and global
urbanization.

The number of Europeans inhabiting places with 5,000 to 40,000 residents,
meanwhile, remained virtually flat from 1500 all the way to 1800 (not graphed).
While the total living in all cities of 10,000 or more persons (the plot with solid
circles in the lower section of Figure 4.1) increased first in G form 1550–1650
and then in more slowly decelerating H style 1650–1750, this happened because
the population of Europe as a whole swelled in different ways from one of these
periods to the next, not because a new trend appeared in the relative weight of
urbanization across the continent. The increase in numbers resident in cities with
10,000 or more inhabitants over the second hundred years (1650–1750) was in
fact slightly greater than during the first (1.44 vs. 1.40), though de Vries (257)
leaves the impression that more "selective" later urban development involved
less urban growth in general—which was not the case.

Reinforcing the conclusion that the urban system of Europe as a whole, despite familiar internal geographical shifts, developed quite seamlessly right
through the economic and demographic crisis that has conventionally been
stressed for the early 1600s are unbroken H trends from 1550 through 1800 in
the *percentage* of Europe's people who resided in communities of 5,000 or more
inhabitants and from 1550 through 1750 in the proportion who lived in centers
containing 40,000 or more (not graphed, but founded upon de Vries 1984, 76).
The next section of this chapter takes up such patterns in the *proportion* of
Europeans (and other peoples) who resided in cities during various eras.

Within a framework of mostly continuous, long-term urban development for
Europe as a whole, however, lie significant *regional* variations. The lead—as

has been well comprehended by de Vries and by others who have studied the early modern competition of Europe's nations—was seized by the preeminent cities of the *North*.[1] Together, as the top half of Figure 4.1 indicates, their collective populations increased along an H trend from 1550 through 1750 that was appreciably steeper than the H for residents of all European cities over 100,000, multiplying by 13.5 rather than 5.7.

Paris, already reaching 100,000 in the 1500s, was joined in this topmost classification by London as of 1600, Amsterdam by 1650, and Vienna and Lyon by 1750. More significantly, by 1650 Paris and London had pushed Naples and Venice off the top of the list as the largest urban centers of Europe; and as of 1750 the biggest five were London, Paris, Naples, Amsterdam, and Vienna, in that order (de Vries 1984, 269–78). Even more striking was the increasing *size* of northern Europe's leading cities. By 1750, London and Paris alone held about 1,251,000 people between them. Along with the 210,000 inhabitants of Amsterdam, these three biggest cities of northwestern Europe contained as much population as all the other 12 urban centers over 100,000 combined, and more than one-tenth of the size of Europe's total urban population (places of 5,000 inhabitants or more) as of 1750 (ibid., 72).

While the biggest cities of the northern portion of the continent in aggregate increased strongly and persistently in the slowly slowing H form, population in the comparable preeminent centers in the Mediterranean regions of Europe grew, in spite of their greater number, only in the more rapidly decelerating G pattern from 1550 to 1700, as the top portion of Figure 4.1 also shows (via hollow squares). This trajectory made their aggregate rate of expansion fall further and further behind that of northern metropolises after 1600. Later, the E pattern of increase in the leading cities of the Mediterranean that seems to appear 1700–1800 brings to mind the kind of demographic expansion observed in modern conditions of "population explosion" as has been observed in certain large centers of recent Asia and Africa (Harris 2001, 320–22, 326). Inspection of data from de Vries (1984, 72, graphed but not fitted) suggests that from 1750 through 1850 the biggest cities of northern Europe also gained population in accelerating E form. Then, however, from 1850 through 1890 to 1979 this aggregate number went back to increasing in H fashion. E-type total population growth has been observed (Harris 2001, 148–49) in many countries of Europe, principally northern Europe, between about 1725 and 1850: England, Scotland, Ireland, Denmark, Iceland, the Netherlands, and France (and rather later in Germany, Austria, Portugal, and Spain). It has been hypothesized that demographic increase in this pattern has historically been associated with early stages of industrialization that were especially dependent upon mass labor. What was happening in and around the leading centers of Mediterranean Europe—Naples, Lisbon, Rome, Venice, Milan, Madrid, and Palermo—between 1650 and 1750 that produced E-type population increase (albeit less gain than via the contemporary H for cities of 100,000 and over in northern Europe)? Why did they, unlike their northern competitors, fail to precede or follow such E-form change with a phase of expansion in H shape?[2]

A sequence of similar G, then E growth appears in the lower section of Figure 4.1 for all cities of 10,000 people or more in Mediterranean Europe from 1650 through 1750, not just the biggest centers. If one starts calculating upward from what de Vries sets as the very bottom of the "urban" scale—all populations in towns of 5,000 people or more—the same E for 1650–1750 and possible G for 1550 and 1600 (followed by some loss of urban residents before 1650) show up for Iberia and Italy. Looking at all northern urban populations of 10,000 or larger (the bottom plot in the figure), in contrast, one sees aggregate growth to have taken place in two successive H trends: the first 1550 through 1650 and the next 1650 through 1750. In the initial surge, northern urban population multiplied by 1.7 over a century; in the second, it grew by a factor of 1.6, hardly any less. In all, for northern Europe 2.7 times as many people lived in cities of 10,000 and more in 1750 as in 1550, compared with 1.4 times the earlier number in the Mediterranean zones of Europe, where urban population multiplied by 1.3 in G form from 1550 to 1600, then fell back almost as much during the familiar crisis period of the next half century, and finally re-enlarged 1.3 times 1650–1750 by E acceleration (the third plot from the bottom of the figure).

The result, as these two regional patterns occurred together, was that the loss between 1600 and 1650 in Mediterranean areas dragged total urban growth for Europe between 1550 and 1650 into a G path of rapid deceleration, as the figure shows—but not decline. The increasing weight of northern cities within European urbanization as time went by, however, brought about multiplication of 1.44 during the H trend over the years 1650–1750 for all European centers with 10,000 people or more, compared with 1.55 growth in H form for northern areas alone. In all, the urban population of Europe almost precisely doubled in the two centuries between 1550 and 1750.

From this re-trending in G-based terms, it seems that by the periodization that he borrowed and the regionalization that he imposed, de Vries missed some key developments in the numbers of people who lived in early modern European cities. Instead, some tentative application in Table 4.1 of G-related curves to broad-interval national data that he provides suggests the following.

Most parts of Europe may have shared H growth in the aggregate size of their urban populations for some time after 1550. This was an age of robust expansion for the nations and peoples of Europe (and a much-discussed era of economic inflation). That form of increase for city dwellers was shallowest (had the earliest base years, around 1400) in Germany between 1500 and 1600 and probably Northern Italy between 1550 and 1600 and steepest in the Netherlands and also probably Switzerland, England and Wales, and Scandinavia (with t_0's in the early 1500s, more than a century later). In contrast, more rapidly decelerating G patterns of urban growth were followed in Austria and Bohemia, Central Italy, and Scotland. An actual contraction of city dwellers in Belgium and Portugal between 1550 and 1600 and Germany, Switzerland, Northern Italy,

Table 4.1

Apparent Trends of Urban Population in Europe, 1500–1800 (in cities of 10,000 or more)

Germany		1500-1600 H 1391	1600,1650 loss	1650-1750 H 1544	
Northern Italy		1550,1600 ?H 1406	1600,1650 loss	1650-1800 H 1512	
Spain		1500-1600 H 1426	1600-1700 D 1571		1700-1800 E 1820
France		1550,1600 ?H 1430	1600-1750 H 1475		1700-1800 E 1842
Southern Italy		1550,1600 ?H 1443	1600-1700 D 1554	?	
Poland		1550-1650 H 1451	1650,1700 loss	?	
Portugal	1550,1600 loss	1600-1700 H 1460		1700,1750 loss	
Belgium	1550,1600 loss	1600-1700 H 1475		1700,1750 loss	
Netherlands		1550-1650 H 1508	1600-1700 G 1583	1700,1750 loss	
Switzerland		1550,1600 ?H 1512	1600,1650 loss	1650-1750 H 1590	1700-1800 G 1678
England/Wales		1550,1600 ?H 1518	1600-1700 H 1550	1700,1750 ?H 1593	1750,1800 ?E 1808
Scandinavia		1550,1600 ?H 1508	1600-1750 H 1584		
Austria/Bohemia		1550-1650 G 1512	1650,1700 ?H 1584	1700-1800 H 1632	
Central Italy		1550-1700 G 1516	1650,1700 ?H 1557	1700-1800 H 1516	
Scotland		1550-1650 G 1516	1650,1700 ?H 1557	1700,1750 ?H 1668	1750,1800 ?E 1797
Ireland			1650-1750 G 1669	1700,1750 ?H 1668	1750,1800 ?E 1798

Source: de Vries 1984, 30.

Southern Italy, and Spain between 1600 and 1650—the eye-catching evidence behind the conventional perception of a period of European urban crisis—made the population in *all* cities with 10,000 persons or more for Europe as a whole grow in G rather than H form between 1550 and 1650, as shown in the bottom half of Figure 4.1.

It was in northern Europe that total national or regional population increase in H shape first occurred, as the evidence of Volume I of this study has indicated—in the Dutch maritime province of Holland, Sweden (Holland's partner in the North Sea–Baltic trade), and England (Harris 2001, 148–49, 200). The location of that pattern of demographic increase—both at this initial stage and later and also in places other than Europe—has been associated historically with certain kinds of economic development, as Volume I of this study has concluded. The current analysis summarized in Table 4.1 indicates that H-type expansion in *urban* population accompanied such early *total* demographic expansion of H shape in Sweden, England, and the most economically active part of the Netherlands. In contrast, for Italy, Spain, and Portugal (ibid., 148–50) and also for France (de Vries 1984, 36, for 1500–1650) G rather than H appears to have been the pattern for general demographic increase in the earliest recorded years forward from about 1500 or 1550. In these countries, in other words, urban expansion took H form sometime between 1550 and 1700, but no trend of *total* population increase via H is evident. (For Belgium, Switzerland, and Poland no general demographic trend can be established this early.)

The other region displaying early expansion of city population in H form in Table 4.1 is Germany. Only after trending the changes of Table 4.1 from de Vries—and also after publishing my assessment of overall population growth patterns for Europe in the first volume of this study (Harris 2001, 148–49) along with an analysis of how the H shapes found in some places tended to be linked with histories of economic development, both nationally and for regions within countries—did I encounter, via Bulst and Pfister (1997, 519) estimates for the population of Germany (borders of 1914) from 1500 through 1618, which Pfister had developed in the early 1990s. These are graphed in the lower panel of Figure 4.2. From 1520 through 1618 their trend is clearly an H curve with base year at 1412. Thus, up to the time of the Thirty Years War, which devastated the region, the area that was to compose modern Germany shared with England, the commercially dominant Dutch maritime province of Holland, and Sweden— eastward along the Baltic—the experience of having *both* total demographic expansion and increase in the size of urban population develop in H shape during the 16th and early 17th centuries. Meanwhile, France, Spain, the Netherlands as a whole, and possibly Northern Italy and Southern Italy witnessed an H trend in the numbers of their people who lived in cities (Table 4.1) but not in the size of their total populations. What does that signify? Did they urbanize without sharing the benefits with the countryside or without developing complementary rural non-agricultural activity?[3] In the end, with the new German evidence the demographic components of the rise to economic leadership by *northern* Europe

Figure 4.2
Urban Development and Population Increase in Central Europe between 1155 and 1800

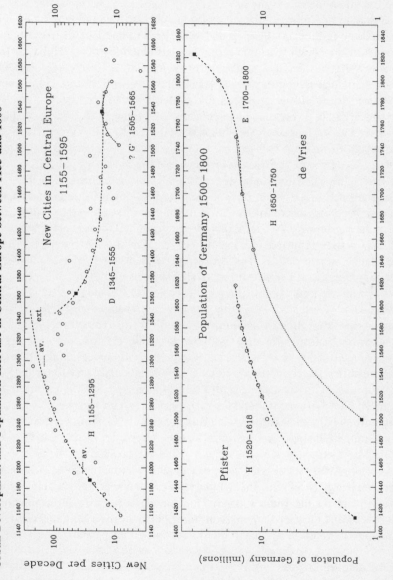

Source: Pounds 1994, 102; Livi-Bacci 2000, 23 (from Abel 1962, 46); Bulst and Pfister 1997, 519; de Vries 1984, 36.

become clearer and more firm via one of those rewarding experiences in which what one did not know turns out to strengthen what one suspected.

While central Europe is being considered, the top panel in Figure 4.2 presents another perspective on the urbanization of that zone up to 1600. It trends the number of new cities being established in the region (Pounds 1994, 102; Livi-Bacci 2000, 23; the origin being Abel 1962, 46). A possible swing up then down in G' fashion, peaking around 1540, may have occurred from about 1500 to 1570. This would have contributed to getting under way the kind of H trend in urban growth observed in Germany after 1520 (Table 4.1). Generally, however, the rate at which new cities appeared through the 15th and 16th centuries vacillated back and forth around a D path of decline that had commenced as the Black Death or bubonic plague devastated Europe in the 1340s. The number of new cities being established fell in very much the same shape and timing as the decline of local and regional populations across western Europe (Harris 2001, 173, 354–55, 360, 363–65). Comparable contractions of D shape for the people of Ming China between 1391 and 1488 and apparently also numbers estimated by Russell for contemporary Mameluke Egypt (ibid., 243–44, 285) extend the impression of the long-term D-form demographic impact of this notorious intercontinental pandemic in the 14th and 15th centuries.

The pace of new city creation in central Europe actually peaked well before the plague struck, as early as the 1290s. Fans of Sergei Eisenstein will recall images of the medieval *Drang nach Osten* replete with crusader crosses and bucket helmets capped with horns (and a visually accommodative score by Prokofiev). Travellers through eastern Germany can enjoy today in even more enduring stone the Romanesque churches of this eastward surge. During the long medieval colonization of East by West the number of new cities founded per decade in central Europe rose from less than 10 in the 1150s to an average of almost 150 for the 1290s and 1300s (nearly 220 for the 1290s alone). The trend took H shape with base year at 1189, as the top panel of Figure 4.2 indicates. While there is some possibility of G' surges from 1155 through 1205 and then 1205 through 1265 along the way, this summary H curve probably best represents the long-term change that was taking place.

For the early 14th century, however, competing trendings offer themselves. With the 1290s and 1300s averaged, there is some case for a G' hump from 1265 through 1375. With the decade of the 1300s taken by itself, a tighter G' would work for the years 1305–1375, segueing into the D curve for the years 1345–1565. An earlier D trend from the 1290s into the 1340s is a third, rough, but possible fit to data for the years 1295–1345. Interpretatively, this has the advantage of being familiar from D-type declines of population in some medieval locales, probably through famine, that may—especially in England in the view of M. M. Postan—have preceded the havoc of the Black Death (Harris 2001, 337, 360–61). In the end, though, the numbers from 1305 through 1325 and perhaps on into the early 1340s remain relatively parallel to an extension of the H trend for the years 1155–1295. There may exist for the early 14th century, in other words, simply some change in the area covered by the available information or for its completeness within the same territory. The ultimate decision as to the best trending for this uncertain period must be left to scholars of medieval central Europe. In the meantime, though, it is fairly clear that the founding of new cities in this part of the continent surged in robust and sustained H fashion from the 1150s into the 1290s and later atrophied in D form from the 1340s toward the end of the 1500s. Until better evidence is presented, these movements might serve as surrogates for the urbanization of central Europe for four centuries before more information comes into play in the later 1500s.

Following about 1600, as the central column of Table 4.1 indicates, Southern Italy, Spain, Northern Italy, Switzerland, Germany, and Poland suffered often-noted urban atrophy across the 1600s (as—beginning a little later—did the cities of certain parts of the Netherlands, Figure 3.9a has shown). In contrast, France, England and Wales, Scotland, Scandinavia, and Austria and Bohemia probably saw their urban populations swell in H form through all or part of the 1600s, while the city population of Ireland expanded in G shape instead and Central Italy held onto its urban numbers along the G trend begun back around 1550.

These offsetting regional tendencies made the number of people living in centers of 10,000 or more for Europe as a whole swell along a fresh, H-shaped path between 1650 and 1750, as Figure 4.1 demonstrates. It was, in the end, principally just the domains of the fading Spanish Hapsburgs in which urbanization was actually set back during the infamous 1600s, a loss that extended to other current or former holdings of this power (Belgium, the Netherlands, Portugal) in the early 1700s. While overall population decline was indeed shared during one period of time or another in the 17th century by France, England, Ireland, and Germany with Italy and Spain (Harris 2001, 148–49; Figure 4.2 here), shrinking *urban* population was not. With respect to the development of cities, it serves little purpose to talk of "crisis" in this era except in the more tightly specified sense of a limited number of familiarly connected territories within Europe, domains whose urban losses were fully counterbalanced by gains elsewhere. Shift in the *location* of urbanization and de-urbanization during this middle epoch of the 1500–1800 era is more important to explore than any misleading notion of general urban crisis in the period.

Going into the 18th century, except for Belgium and Portugal urban growth was the norm for European countries whose data can be trended (the last two columns of Table 4.1). Such expansion took the form of roughly parallel H trends in Northern Italy, Central Italy, Germany, and France (persisting there from 1600 through 1750 with the flattest H pattern of all) and noticeably steeper H paths in Austria and Bohemia, Switzerland, Scandinavia, England and Wales, and Scotland.[4] That group of countries once again constitutes a familiar regional cluster, running mostly south to north through the center of Europe and bending west across the North Sea to Britain, though Belgium and the Netherlands did not in this particular instance participate. What powered H patterns of urbanization across this band of countries at this time? Whereas total population increase in England 1686–1726, Norway 1665–1735, and Germany 1650–1750 took H form, elsewhere across this complex of societies general demographic expansion followed the G pattern instead, whether city growth displays H shape or not in Table 4.1 (Harris 2001, 148–49). In Spain, Portugal, and Ireland, on the other hand, the H trend of total population increase that emerged across the later 1600s and the 1700s did not support urban growth in the same mode.

In contrast, as the accelerating E pattern of increase began to show up in the number of city dwellers in England and Wales, Scotland, Ireland, France, and Spain in the 18th century (the right-most column of Table 4.1), in four out of five countries (France only after the Revolution) general demographic growth also took this form. (In Spain, overall population increase instead continued to hold to its old H trend from the later 1600s.) In the Netherlands, E-shape expansion in overall population was accompanied by some *regional* urban growth in that pattern, as Figure 3.9a of the previous chapter has demonstrated. Starting about 1750 for the country as a whole, growth through 1850 in population centers of 10,000 or more also appropriately appeared in E fashion with base year at about 1880. The initially flat trend just begins too late to show in recorded figures by 1800.[5] For several key countries, in other words, one could say that accelerating total demographic growth and E-shape increase in aggregate urban population went hand in hand, precisely the kind of pairing of total and urban growth patterns that de Vries (1984, 257) says did not happen anymore after his turning "point" of "1600/50."

At the level of the very largest central places, de Vries demonstrated the shift of urbanization to northern Europe in an ingenious way. Attempting to evaluate the ability of particular cities to interact with others as the European urban system grew and changed, he turned to the geographers' concept of "potential." This measure tries to assess the "accessibility of a city to inhabitants of all other cities."[6] Values across time for the eight cities that he found to have the highest potential are plotted in Figures 4.3a and 4.3b.

Figure 4.3a shows how, beginning about 1600, the once preeminent urban centers in Italy—Venice, Milan, and Naples—lost potential in closely parallel D curves across a century or a century and a half. While the 1650 values may be a little low for this path and the data points again are regrettably spread 50 years apart, the similarity of the three trends to each other and to the D pattern indicates that it is well worth investigating carefully with more refined information precisely how loss of potential might have taken a course of this shape in Italy. Between 1625 and 1675 the population of the country, for example, seems (Harris 2001, 150) to have shrunk also in D fashion with t_0 at 1566, only slightly more shallowly than the contraction of potential for the three leading cities (with base years for the D curves at 1583, 1584, and 1591). Earlier, Venice stood at the epitome of possible urban interaction with a value of 100 percent for 1500 and 1550. Naples rose to reach 96 percent at 1600. The fluctuating potentials for Milan—98, 77, and 90 percent from 1500 through 1600—mean-

Figure 4.3a
Potential in European Cities with the Highest Values, 1500–1800: Decline in Italy and Belgium

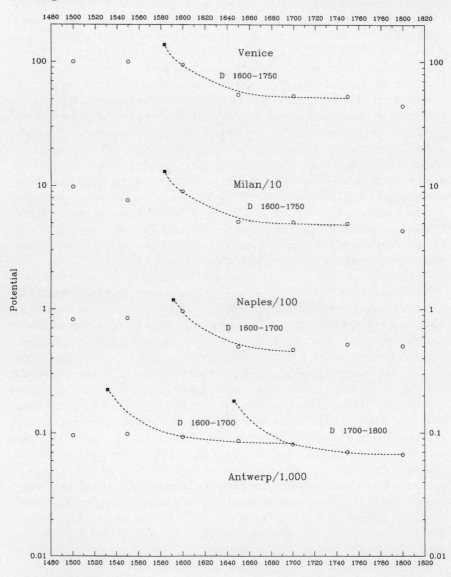

Source: de Vries 1984, 159.

while would seem to reflect the impact of wars of the early 1500s in this contested region. Between 1750 and 1800 further loss of potential appeared for all three Italian hubs, the difference being that Naples somehow saw her value increase between 1700 and 1750 before undergoing new decline.

Antwerp, the early star of northern European urbanization, whose potential had been second only to that of Venice and was still rising between 1500 and 1550, also became somewhat less accessible to other cities from 1600 through 1700 as the northern provinces of the Netherlands won their independence from the Hapsburgs. This is shown in the bottom plot of Figure 4.3a. The D curve here is flatter than in the leading Italian centers, with its base year back at 1532. The breaking away of the northern Netherlands reduced the centrality of Antwerp; but this shift in influence took the potential of the leading Belgian center down only to about 81 percent, not the more like 50 percent level to which the connectedness of Venice, Milan, and Naples was reduced by 1700. Subsequently, however, in a new loss of potential the values for Antwerp fell further still in D shape from 1700 to 1800 to as low as 67 percent as later urban shifts once more realigned connections among the cities of Europe. Table 4.1 shows how the total urban population of the southern or Hapsburg Netherlands (modern Belgium) declined in some fashion between 1550 and 1600 and again between 1700 and 1750 (along with that of her historic trading partner, Portugal, which through Antwerp had supplied northern Europe with desired commodities from Asia, Africa, and her large New World holding of Brazil).

As is well known, Antwerp's loss was Amsterdam's gain. Consequently, the potential for this leading Dutch maritime center rose along a G growth trajectory from 1550 through 1650, as Figure 4.3b demonstrates. Up from nowhere, meanwhile, came Rotterdam—also in the province of Holland but at the mouth of the Rhine River artery of western Europe—to achieve the highest value attainable, 100 percent, in 1600 and 1650. Both leading Dutch cities, however, saw their potential decline thereafter. For Rotterdam, the D for the years 1700–1800 is fairly clear from the three available points with evidence. This curve had its base year at 1653 compared with 1646 for the second wave of decline for Antwerp. While Amsterdam broke this downward pattern with fresh, further disconnection from other European cities between 1750 and 1800, potential there fell from 1700 up to 1750 as if along a D trajectory very parallel to those of Antwerp and Rotterdam—with t_0 at 1644. In the 18th century, the leading centers of the Low Countries were quite generally becoming less significant. Meanwhile, Table 4.1 indicates that the number of inhabitants in all Dutch cities of 10,000 or more also shrank between 1700 and 1750. Until something else is proven, it would seem best to assume that potential faded for the three leading hubs of the Low Countries together starting in the late 1600s (with t_0's all close to 1650), as it had for the preeminent cities from one end of Italy to the other beginning about a century before.

Amsterdam was accompanied by Paris in its rise to interactive significance within the urban system of Europe after 1550. The G curve for the rising po-

Figure 4.3b
Potential in European Cities with the Highest Values, 1500–1800: Trends in the Netherlands, France, and England

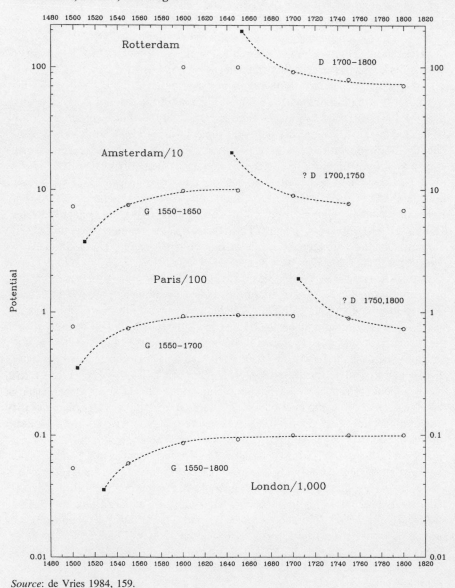

Source: de Vries 1984, 159.

tential of France's capital is based at 1504 compared with 1509 for the leading Dutch entrepôt. Paris, however, apparently retained its high level of connectedness to other European cities longer than Amsterdam, into the early 1700s. If visible decay in the potential of Paris from 1750 or so to 1800 took a D path, that curve would have been based about 1705. That makes it approximately 50 years later than the D's for the decline of potential for the three leading centers of the Low Counties, which in turn lagged behind the D's for dwindling potential in Venice, Milan, and Naples by 50 to 60 years. Was there some rather evenly spaced sequence in how potential shifted from the leading centers of one region of early modern Europe to the hubs of another? The timing of Kondratiev's long cycle for economies comes to mind.

Along a G path based at about 1528, London gained potential approximately two decades behind Amsterdam and Paris. In that process, though, this city became the most accessible center in Europe, with values of 100 percent in 1700, 1750, and 1800 as de Vries calculated them. Water was at that time the easiest surface over which to ship goods and people, and Britannia did indeed rule the waves for many years after three wars with the Dutch helped grind down her chief commercial competition. It would be interesting to apply this kind of analysis after 1800, and outside of Europe (for instance, to include the rise of New York, then Tokyo), as de Vries (ibid., 160) suggests following the broad comparative perspective of Braudel. But within the early modern era of the years 1500–1800 that de Vries examined, the historical inter-connectedness of urban populations to each other seems to be fruitfully structured and simplified by identifying its G-based patterns of change.[7]

A sharper, more simply organized, and more accurate impression of just how urban growth waxed and waned across Europe can be developed with the aid of the periodic data for particular cities that de Vries makes available in his valuable study. Just comparing estimates of size, city by city, in 1650 with numbers for 1550 or 1750, as he provides them for all European centers that at any time between 1500 and 1800 exceeded 10,000 people, serves to clarify which areas in Europe experienced urban growth in each period and which did not (1984, 270–78). That better regionalization improves our understanding of what drove urbanization in these two quite different eras of change.

Together, 61 cities of Scandinavia, the British Isles, the Netherlands, and France whose size is known (or can be confidently approximated) at both 1550 and 1650 became larger over this span of a hundred years. Meanwhile, only three urban centers in these territories lost population.[8] Similarly, four centers that can be followed in eastern Europe and three in Portugal all apparently gained population between 1550 and 1650.[9] Declining or stagnant cities, in other words, were overwhelmingly concentrated in Belgium, Germany, Switzerland, Italy, and Spain.

Systematizing what happened to specific cities within these countries experiencing significant shrinkage helps clarify just where urbanization was retarded and why. In Germany, the western regions generally advanced in urban growth during the hundred years after 1550. A string of 13 cities up the Rhine from Switzerland to the North Sea and the Baltic *all* grew in size between 1550 and 1650.[10] Outside this north–south band in the west, only Danzig and the Saxon capital of Dresden gained population during the period. In contrast, the recorded centers of Germany's once-thriving southern territories of Württemberg, Swabia, and Bavaria all lost inhabitants. Sharing demographic decline with them were several cities located northward toward the Baltic. Of 16 documented centers of the south and east, in other words, only 3 gained population over the century following 1550.[11] Meanwhile, just Soest might be said to insert any sign of demographic decay among western German cities.

In short, it makes little sense to talk of "Germany" in analyzing urbanization between 1550 and 1650. Instead, one must differentiate the territories of the south and east from those of the west. As is well known, Austrian and Swedish armies coursed devastatingly across this eastern and southern swath of cities during the Thirty Years War, taking starvation and disease with them. While there was also fighting in the west, it does not seem to have inflicted the same penalty upon urbanization; either the damage was less or the way that recovery was managed facilitated a stronger rebound already by 1650. Whatever the case, the parts of Germany closest to France and the Netherlands witnessed increase in city populations most like what occurred in these two neighboring countries, while all of the old trading centers of the south and many of those in the east were set back in their growth between 1550 and 1650. Evident are two very distinct "German" zones that each had quite uniform urban experiences internally.

In Belgium, too, about half of the cities reported by de Vries lost population between 1550 and 1650, while the other half gained it. The losers lay across the north of the Spanish Netherlands, nearest to the revolting Dutch provinces. The more southern and eastern majority of the country was dominated by centers gaining population.[12] Similarly, Basel and Zürich, in northern Switzerland, gained inhabitants between 1550 and 1650, while Geneva and Bern did not.

Within the "Northern Italy" of de Vries, meanwhile, it was cities to the west that grew, while among 17 more eastern centers, only Palladio's beautiful Vicenza gained inhabitants.[13] From "Central Italy," meanwhile, Bologna and Ferrara, on the northern slopes of the Appenines, which drain toward the hinterland of Venice in the plains of the lower Po, lost people during the century following 1550 along with Perugia, perched just across the mountains. These three centers filled out a geographical block of 19 contiguous cities of Italy's northeast that shrank in population between 1550 and 1650. Similarly, the cluster of regional centers that *gained* inhabitants extended contiguously southward across most of "Central Italy" from the western area of "Northern Italy."[14] In de Vries's "Southern Italy," moreover, 4 of 6 declining centers sat simply in the eastern half of Sicily.[15] Joining them were little Lecce in the "heel" and Naples, which was big enough by itself to drag down population numbers for "Southern Italy" in aggregate. Thus, de-urbanization in Italy between 1550 and 1650 simply entails what happened to the lower Po drainage area around Venice, to Naples, and to some scattered cities of eastern Sicily. The search to determine why 27 Italian cities may have gained inhabitants between 1550 and 1650 and 25 others lost people is much more clearly and insightfully framed by this alternative geographical classification.

In Spain, finally, declining cities in this era were also mostly concentrated in one region: from just below Madrid northward, mostly within Old Castile.[16] Madrid seems to have grown at their expense, since no other inland center of northern Spain gained population across this century. Another zone of de-urbanization reached up the Guadalquivir Valley from the Gulf of Cadiz into the heart of Andalusia.[17] In contrast, as Seville, the royally designated entrepôt for the Americas, and its market area declined—and did less to smother the business of nearby centers—Aracena and Ecija gained people. Meanwhile, most cities that expanded over the century after 1550 lay along or close to the coasts of Spain, presumably taking some commercial advantage as favored Seville faded.[18]

For the next century-long era, holding population size at 1750 up against that at 1650 city by city shows that zones of de-urbanization during the previous hundred years now were gaining inhabitants (de Vries 1984, 270–78). Most significantly, urban growth predominated in Germany, Switzerland, and Northern Italy, where demographic loss or stagnation had characterized many centers between 1550 and 1650. In all of Italy, only 12 of 58 cities with populations recorded by de Vries shrank or stagnated from 1650 to 1750. Seven of these were in Sicily.[19] The other five losers were strung like a garter across Italy's upper calf, from Genoa to Lucca to Siena to Perugia to Ancona on the Adriatic. Italian historians should be able to discern why these two small groupings of cities atrophied while 46 neighbors expanded.

Like Northern Italy, Germany and Switzerland saw their zones of urban decline between 1550 and 1650 turn into regions of significant city growth between 1650 and 1750. All four centers of Switzerland now expanded. So did 30 of 37 "German" cities. The weak spots were now scattered, not grouped across one large band of territory.[20] Analysis of atrophy becomes a very locally focused task. Meanwhile, all recorded cities of eastern Europe grew.[21]

Scandinavia remained a solid region of urban expansion between 1650 and 1750, as it had across the previous hundred years. So did Scotland and Ireland.[22] In England, meanwhile, only 4 shrinking cities show up among 38 for which estimates for both 1650 and 1750 are available. These included the homes of the two stagnating, conformist universities, Oxford and Cambridge, and also York and Colchester. In all, both the British Isles and Scandinavia remained solid territories of continuing urban growth.

In France, however, rather more cities lost people during the century after 1650 than over the preceding century. The de-urbanization that would pull down the inter-city "potential" of Paris after 1750 and reduce the proportion of city-dwellers within the population of France as a whole was beginning. Six of the 8 identifiable centers that shrank or failed to gain people were located around the Atlantic rim of the country. Other cities also located along this western band of territory, nevertheless, gained inhabitants during the same hundred years.[23] For the most part, local circumstances seem to have been at work, not broad regional shifts in the dynamics of French urbanization.

The one widespread and serious slide into urban atrophy among the countries of Europe between 1650 and 1750 occurred in the Netherlands. Here the ports of Amsterdam and Rotterdam and the capital at The Hague held onto their slowing G trends of population increase (Harris 2001, 307) only at the expense of other centers. Even within their own western province of Holland these magnets diverted inhabitants away from Leiden, Dordrecht, Haarlem, Delft, Alkmaar, Enkhuizen, and Hoorn (as Dieppe, Caen, Le Havre, Cherbourg, Brest, and Nantes appear to have cannibalized some of their French coastal neighbors). Only Zaandam, increasingly an industrial suburb of Amsterdam, added people, while Gouda kept very much the same size. Elsewhere, though Zwolle and Groningen grew, other documented Dutch cities eastward from Middelburg to 's Hertogenbosch and Maastricht and north to Utrecht, Nijmegen, Arnhem, and Leeuwarden all contracted in size. So many lesser centers shrank, while the biggest cities grew more and more slowly, that the Netherlands was the only documented country of Europe to have fewer people living in places with 10,000 or more inhabitants in 1750 than in 1650 (de Vries 1984, 30).

Portugal, too, saw the lesser cities of Evora and Coimbra decline as Lisbon and Porto, the main outlets to the Atlantic, thrived. How much this local change had to do with independence from Spain and a shift of trade overseas rather than with the Iberian interior will have to be sorted out by somebody more knowledgeable. But in Spain, the zone of de-urbanization that had depressed the Guadalquiver watershed during the previous hundred years apparently disappeared after 1650, to be replaced by fresh demographic growth in centers like Seville and Jaen. The hint is that overseas colonial trade, still bound by royal law to Seville, was recovering, based upon more mundane items than the easy metallic pickings of the 16th century. Even within the northern highlands Valladolid gained inhabitants; but loss continued in Avila, Burgos, Medina del Campo, Medina de Rio Seco, Palencia, and Segovia—and several other localities of this 1550–1650 region of urban decay simply lack the necessary later data for determining what happened thereafter. Now, however, Madrid shrank along with secondary centers of her northern hinterland in Old Castile. Around the edges of Spain—on or near the sea—though certain cities continued to enlarge.[24] In all, some of the patterning of growth and decline in cities that had been so prominent in Spain between 1550 and 1650 altered for the next hundred years, though urban decay remained significant for part of the country.

In Belgium, finally, Brussels now between 1650 and 1750 joined Antwerp, Bruges, and Ghent in decline along with Ypres and Mechelen. Sprinkled among these shrinking cities, however, were others—generally lesser competitors—that grew.[25] There was no fairly solid northern region of urban decline within the country as there had been between 1550 and 1650. Meanwhile, as Lille and Tournai and Mons expanded in the south, Valenciennes did not—much as Liège gained population, while Maastricht, just down river in the Netherlands, lost it. The Belgian pattern conforms to what has been seen in several European areas: decaying hubs permitted secondary centers around them to grow, while elsewhere cities of new promise stole action away from their neighbors.[26] In all, between 1650 and 1750 the ebb and flow of European cities was not nearly so regionalized as between 1550 and 1650; but the geographical patterning remains important and insightful.

In all, our understanding of the growth of cities across early modern Europe between 1500 and 1800 is valuably enhanced—clarified, simplified, and strengthened—by identifying the G-based movements that apparently underlie the data. Just how many people through time lived in cities in various zones of the continent, and in particular countries and regions within them, can be fruitfully organized by the familiar G-based curves. Further, since the absolute numbers dwelling in centers of certain scale moved in G-connected forms like this, as did the size of the total populations within which cities flourished or atrophied, it is not surprising that even a complex calculation of urban interactions such as potential, the accessibility of given centers to all other urban places, also followed G-based paths. Such trendings of potential between 1500 and 1800 for key hubs of the continent stand out cleanly and elegantly, making clearer connections within and between the Italian, Low Country, and Anglo-French clusters of serial leadership that so definitively characterized the history of urbanization in early modern Europe.

In addition, simple comparisons of size for individual cities covered by de Vries at 1550, 1650, and 1750 demonstrate how, within the more useful new international framework of periodization and regionalization, urban growth and decline were highly focused geographically during the first hundred years, but then more local and diffuse between 1650 and 1750. For both eras, such details from particular centers confirm and spell out the kinds of regional or national changes that are indicated by G-based trending of city growth, the general pace of urbanization, and shifts in the centrality of leading metropolises, yielding insight beyond the analysis of de Vries into the relationships among rising and falling cities in early modern Europe and the likely reasons for their waxing or waning fortunes.

The years after 1750 or so, as de Vries and others have perceptively proposed, brought a new era of urban and economic history to Europe. Just how marked the geographical differences in urbanization were within Europe during this period stands out best when the data of de Vries (1984, 270–78) and later coverage like that of Mitchell (1992, 72–75) are synthesized to follow growth in a substantial number of individual cities from 1750 to 1800 and then on to 1850. First, although some urban centers expanded both across the later 18th century and the first half of the 19th, others took on significant new population only after 1800. Second, while most observed cities increased somewhat during this span of 100 years, some multiplied vigorously, while others grew very little. These distinctions by timing and degree of urban population increase quite simply and strikingly separate some areas of Europe from others during the era 1750–1850.

To begin, all 12 English, Irish, and Scottish cities for which de Vries and/or Mitchell offers numbers gained population both across the later 1700s and through the first half of the 1800s. Liverpool, Manchester, Glasgow, Bradford, Sheffield, Belfast, and Birmingham multiplied by factors of 10 to 17 between 1750 and 1850 as Britain industrialized. Older centers like Dublin, Edinburgh, Bristol, Leeds, and London enlarged by multiples of 3 to 4. The only other cities in Europe to match the seven most aggressively expanding centers of Britain in growth were five in the Rhineland area of Germany.[27] Berlin and Stettin in the northeast of Germany enlarged not unlike the five older, more moderately growing British centers. Bremen and Frankfurt-am-Main also expanded both in the years 1750–1800 and in the years 1800–1850, but not strongly.

Eastward up the Baltic, Oslo, Göteborg, Riga, Helsinki, and St. Petersburg—like Stettin and Berlin—grew moderately both before and after 1800. Copenhagen and Stockholm also enlarged throughout, but more weakly—like Bremen. Thus, in a swath of 10 recorded cities from the North Sea to the Gulf of Bothnia, only Hamburg did not experience significant growth in both half centuries following 1750; her increase stalled out after 1800. This northern geographical band of centers, which expanded continually between 1750 and 1850, furthermore, extended inland to include not only Berlin but Warsaw, Prague, and Vienna, and Minsk, Moscow, Gorki, and Saratov to the east, joined for some reason by Salonika at the head of the Aegean. Of these eastern and mostly inland cities, growth in Saratov and Warsaw was the strongest, and that in Salonika and Prague more like the minor contemporary change that occurred in Stockholm and Copenhagen. In short, Britain, the Baltic, and inland eastern Europe constituted regions whose cities grew appreciably both from 1750 to 1800 and from 1800 to 1850. In southwestern Europe lay another such cluster. Turin, Marseilles, Barcelona, and Madrid expanded robustly; Seville, Lisbon, and Bordeaux more weakly. Fainter still was growth up the French Atlantic coast at Nantes.

In the rest of the European cities covered by de Vries and Mitchell, significant growth in this hundred-year period did not begin until *after* 1800. That was the case in the Netherlands, Belgium, most of France, almost all of Italy, Switzerland, and southern and most of eastern Germany plus Cologne and Hanover north of the Ruhr.[28]

De Vries provides sizes for still more cities after 1750, though his local evidence stops at 1800. What these more numerous late-18th-century data show confirms the regionalism just discussed. In England, for instance, 40 of 42 recorded centers gained at least a little population, 14 of 14 in Scotland and

Ireland, and 6 of 6 in Scandinavia. In Austria, Bohemia, and Poland 9 of 10 centers grew. This composes a zone of 74 cities from the British Isles across Scandinavia and down into eastern Europe only 3 (4 percent) of which failed to enlarge between 1750 and 1800. At least a little growth took place also during this period in 19 of 21 cities in Belgium. The 1750–1800 sluggishness found in Antwerp and Brussels was not duplicated by the majority of urban centers in their country, though those two largest cities were populous enough to limit Belgian urbanization in aggregate.

In contrast, more than half of the 24 cities documented for the Netherlands and Switzerland definitely failed to expand during the half century 1750–1800— nor did a quarter of the urban centers in France, Germany, and Spain and Portugal, and a third in Italy. Iberia departed from the rest of this zone of weaker growth by not having a single case of actual urban *contraction*, unlike 20 percent of all cities in France, Germany, and Northern Italy and almost 30 percent in the Netherlands and Switzerland. In all, the more broadly detailed picture between 1750 and 1800 provided by de Vries supports the patterning of a narrower sample of more preeminent cities with longer records in showing just how regionalized urban development was in Europe between 1750 and 1850.

The first volume of this study (Harris 2001, 316–18) has already argued how European urbanization after the middle of the 19th century became again geographically more homogeneous, thanks in large part to portable industrialization based upon steam power and railroads that could locate and sustain work at already existing centers of population. Then, the varied growth patterns of a limited number of key centers since World War II hint that more geographical distinctiveness in the development of cities may have returned to Europe in recent decades (ibid., 317–18), as has been observed during the previous approximate epochs 1750–1850 and 1550–1650.

To propose that urban growth in Europe has for several centuries evolved in alternating periods of diversificataion and convergence, each about a century long, may at first seem rather simple-minded. Still, since the middle of the 15th century from four to six distinctive periods of change of roughly 100 years in duration do seem to emerge: perhaps 1450–1550; more clearly approximately 1550–1650, 1650–1750, 1750–1850, and 1850–1950; and probably from 1950 forward.

In the small amount of evidence that is available for the years 1450–1550, what is known of the growth of Amsterdam, London, Frankfurt, Würtzburg, Augsburg, Munich, and Leipzig (Harris 2001, 307, Phases I and II) suggests considerable parallelism in urban growth as Europe recovered from the prolonged devastation caused by the plague of the 1300s and her cities began to prosper from the trades of Venice and Genoa, then Portugal and Spain with Asia, Africa, and soon the Americas. The areas covered are limited, but they represent quite diverse parts of Europe. It would be interesting to see what further data for this early period might do to this impression of interurban similarity.

In contrast, roughly between 1550 and 1650 major *regional shifts* occurred in European urbanization. Urban population shrank during this era in Belgium, Switzerland, and Northern Italy, and also in Southern Italy and Spain, primarily territories of the Spanish Hapsburgs, whose power and prosperity diminished substantially across a century that included the Dutch Revolt, the Thirty Years War, and effective intrusion of northern European powers into Spain's alleged monopoly of New World colonization and trade and Portugal's connections with Africa and the East. The patterning of growth for individual cities (Harris 2001, 307; de Vries 1984, 270–78) has not surprisingly indicated noticeable loss of population also in some centers of southern and eastern Germany (once a financial base for the Hapsburgs) during the first half of the 17th century, the era of the Thirty Years War.

Meanwhile, the biggest cities of northern Europe grew markedly faster than those of the Mediterranean zone; and urban population there in aggregate expanded between 1550 and 1650 in the more robust, slowly decelerating H pattern compared with a more rapidly flattening G for Mediterranean territories. In terms of the potential of the biggest urban centers to interact with other cities, furthermore, Venice, Milan, Naples, and Antwerp lost such interconnectedness in the first half of the 17th century while Amsterdam, Rotterdam, Paris, and London gained it—all apparently along familiar G-based paths. Finally, city-by-city data differentiate *parts* of Germany, Belgium, Italy, and Spain that suffered urban decline during this epoch from those that did not. It becomes possible to delineate without regard to national boundaries regions in which cities prospered from those where they languished. That step sets up more insightful analysis of just how urban fortunes rose and fell.

In sum, as is well recognized, by several different measures the momentum of urbanization shifted from some parts of Europe to others between 1550 and 1650. Northwestern regions in general forged ahead: the British Isles, the Netherlands, France, and Scandinavia. So did adjacent cities of western Germany, though war-worn urban centers of the eastern and southern portions of the territory that became Germany actually lost population (as did combat and contact zones of the Dutch Revolt in the southern Netherlands and northern Belgium). Competitors in the east thrived as well. Dresden, Danzig, Warsaw, Brno, Innsbruck, and Vienna formed a north–south belt across central Europe that, like the urban swath up the Rhine, composed a zone of consistent growth that contrasted with the uniformly gloomier fate for cities of the German regions that lay in between. De-urbanization in Italy, meanwhile, principally involved population loss in the environs of Venice, in and around the Po's Adriatic plains, while the centers of western Lombardy, the Piedmont, and virtually all cities of Italy south of Bologna and Perugia (except Naples and a handful in eastern Sicily) gained size between 1550 and 1650 as the power and influence of Spain in the western Mediterranean and the mercantile might of Venice waned. As for "Germany," the Italian categories employed by de Vries obscure the actual pattern. In Iberia, similarly, it was specifically the northern uplands and the Guadalqiver Valley that de-urbanized (except for the ever-engrossing capital at Madrid), while all around the ocean-oriented edges of the peninsula both Spanish and Portuguese cities continued to grow. These are the preferred geographical groupings with which to try to understand what shaped shifting urbanization in Europe between 1550 and 1650.

In the next distinctive era, in contrast, growth patterns for several leading cities indicate surprisingly *similar* trends in urban expansion across quite different parts of Europe during the century or so after 1650. While the percentage of people living in cities (it will shortly be seen) did fall somewhat during this hundred-year period in the Netherlands, Belgium, Spain, and Portugal, it rose in most territories of the continent. The number of persons dwelling in centers of 10,000 or more inhabitants increased quite generally across both northern and Mediterranean Europe, though via different routes and by somewhat different amounts.[29] While in aggregate the biggest cities of the north expanded more vigorously than those of the south between 1650 and 1750, this meant mostly London and Paris. Amsterdam and Rotterdam did not acquire much more population and also joined Antwerp in seeing their potential for networking with other urban centers start to decline toward the end of the 1600s. What had been zones of urban atrophy between 1550 and 1650 mostly now turned over into areas of growth that contained only a few, mostly idiosyncratically located centers that shrank. Exceptional systematic decay occurred only in the Netherlands, where urban decline was widespread as many gains of the Golden Age were siphoned away.

The century after 1650 as a whole, then, would appear to be a period of very general urban growth across Europe, perhaps driven from country to country by quite common forces, whether domestic or stemming from international commerce. That makes this new epoch depart significantly from the marked regionalism of 1550–1650. Even in the Netherlands, the one country with overall urban decline, the most thriving cities like Amsterdam, Rotterdam, and The Hague started off growing right along with foreign centers that challenged them and stole their business, notably London and Paris. They just did not share in the second wave of expansion across the early 1700s that many other leading cities of Europe enjoyed.

In contrast, the century from 1750 to 1850 seems to have once again been an epoch in which the urban growth of Europe became distinctly regional again. New increases appear around the fringes: across the north from London to Copenhagen to Stockholm; in the east from Warsaw to Vienna; in the western Mediterranean at Rome, Madrid, and Lisbon. Meanwhile cities in between kept following slowing paths of earlier G-shaped growth. In detail, the British Isles, perhaps Belgium, Scandinavia and much of the Baltic, the Ruhr vicinity and some other parts of northwestern Germany, and territories running eastward across European Russia and southward into the Balkans experienced new urban growth already in the second half of the 18th century and more of it between 1750 and 1850. The Netherlands, France, southern and most of eastern Germany,

Switzerland, and Italy began to share in new expansion mostly only *after* 1800 and generally saw less of it by 1850. Some southwestern European centers, principally Turin, Marseilles, Barcelona, and Madrid, grew aggressively all across the hundred-year period; but on the whole Spain and perhaps Portugal fell into the weak rather than the strong zones of urbanization for the era.

Beginning in the later 19th century, though, territorial differences in urbanization commenced to even out appreciably as industrialization spread across Europe. There are signs, nonetheless, that since World War II cities have expanded once again more vigorously in some regions of the continent than in others. That, however, is a history for the 21st century to write.

For the time being, pending further research, it seems that something roughly like alternating centuries of regional convergence and divergence may have been a feature of European urbanization since the 1400s. It would be fascinating to be able to explore the application of that kind of hypothesis to, say, parts of Asia or to the Americas. Clearly developed, meanwhile, however, is the picture that just the demographically ubiquitous G, H, E, and D curves capture the shape of the overwhelming majority of urban changes in Europe since the 15th century. And patterning urban development by such G-based trending fruitfully both confirms and refines or extends several kinds of prior insights concerning how European cities have evolved over the past half millennium or so.

INTERNATIONAL URBANIZATION, 1500–1980: CHANGING PROPORTIONS OF POPULATIONS LIVING IN CITIES

What has been said so far focuses on patterns of growth or decline in individual cities, the fate of urban centers of certain size from one country to another, or trends for the numbers of city-dwellers in certain groups of European societies. Important issues also relate, however, to the *proportion* of people in this territory or that who resided in cities. What forms did *urbanization* or change in the weight of urban residents within regional populations take, and what insights do these patterns provide about how people moved to, or collected in, cities rather than alternative settings for their lives?

Table 4.2 begins by demonstrating how, in spite of data spread out at only half-century intervals, the evidence of de Vries outlines for the long epoch from 1500 through 1800 many informative and readily understandable possible G-connected trends for the *percentage* of people living in various European countries who resided in cities with 10,000 or more inhabitants (1984, 39). The patterns are tentatively estimated by eye and template, not fitted mathematically. When, and if, more frequent data become available, some of these hypothesized movements may need to be respecified or replaced. In the meantime, however, by identifying both familiar and more novel trendings, they extend insight into how European *urbanization* evolved across the early modern era.

To begin with the setbacks, 9 of 16 societies studied experienced proportional

Table 4.2
Percentage of Urban Population in Early Modern European Countries (estimated trends for cities of 10,000 or more)

Declines in Urban Proportion

Belgium	1550,1600	?D 1513		Poland	1650,1700	?D 1623
Northern Italy	1600-1700	D 1540		Netherlands	1700-1800	D 1635
Switzerland	1600,1650	?D 1546		France	1750,1800	?D 1640
Southern Italy	1600-1700	D 1554		Belgium	1700-1800	D 1658
Spain	1600-1750	D 1554		Portugal	1700-1800	D 1664

Urban Percentage Increase via H				Urban Percentage Increase via G		
Spain	1500-1600	H 1404		Germany	1500-1600	G 1461
France	1550-1650	H 1438		England	1520-1640	G 1497*
Netherlands	1550-1650	H 1466		Central Italy	1600-1750	G 1546
				Scotland	1550-1650	G 1550
England & Wales	1650-1750	H 1550		Germany	1650,1700	?G 1585
Switzerland	1650-1750	?H 1556		France	1650-1750	G 1608
Austria/Bohemia	1650-1750	H 1586		Scandinavia	1650-1800	G 1633
				Germany	1700-1800	G 1666
				Austria/Bohemia	1700-1800	G 1683
				Ireland	1650-1750	G 1671

* Wrigley 1985, 5,000+, from Figure 3.10.

Sources: de Vries 1984, 39; Figure 3.10.

urban decline.[30] City after city in the Spanish Netherlands (modern Belgium) lost population during the Dutch war for independence from the Hapsburgs (examples appear in Harris 2001, 307–8). Then, in the 1600s, Northern and Southern (though not Central) Italy, Spain, and probably Switzerland (to 1650) together saw the urban percentage of their people shrink in what seem to be very parallel D patterns, as Table 4.2 shows or suggests. As total population atrophied in D form in Italy between 1625 and 1675 and Spain between 1589 and 1648 (ibid. 2001, 148–51), the city populations of these regions shrank even faster. In short, it appears that decay of the centers of Northern Italy and Switzerland and Southern Italy and Spain did more to drag down overall countrywide populations than the other way around. That should provide valuable perspective on the processes at work behind the observed changes. Meanwhile, the decay of the Spanish branch of the Hapsburgs and their far-flung holdings from the Netherlands to Naples once again captures where, when, and how de-urbanization occurred at this time far better than categories of "Mediterranean," "north-west," "central," and "eastern" as employed by de Vries for century-and-a-half epochs like the years 1500–1600/1650 or 1600/1650–1750, however conventional these long, elastic periods have become for economic historians.[31]

Another group of countries de-urbanized rather later, during the 1700s. Unlike the Spanish Hapsburg holdings earlier on, now no single regime dominated these societies. The Netherlands, Belgium, Portugal, and possibly France (after 1750), however, *did* share the fate of becoming weaker players in the game of European expansion and overseas trade.[32] Thus, European decline in the percentage of population that dwelt in cities during the 18th century also seems to be both more significant and more simply explicable than the analysis of de Vries makes it.

Early modern *advance* in urbanization, meanwhile, took two familiar G-related forms in successive eras: one commencing in the 1500s, and the other in the 1600s. From the 1500s into the 1600s Spain, the Netherlands, and France (according to the calculation of de Vries for cities with over 10,000 inhabitants) became more urban societies via H paths.[33] These changes proceeded from quite different initial levels of urbanization, as de Vries records: 15.5 percent in the Netherlands, 6.4 percent in Spain, and just 4.3 percent in France. But until proven otherwise by data at more frequent intervals, these century-long changes in urban proportion suggest heretofore neglected parallels in H shape whose causes and consequences need to be investigated. While the relative weight of city populations also increased in Germany (up to the Thirty Years War), Central Italy, and Scotland, it did so only in more rapidly decelerating G fashion. Wrigley's calculations for 1520 and 1600 suggest (Figure 3.10) that the urban proportion in England also up to about the Civil War climbed in a G trend that resembles that of Germany, a hypothesis that smaller percentages at 1550 and 1600 for English cities of just 10,000 and more, as computed by de Vries, would seem to support.

Later, after 1650, urbanization swelled in sustained H form in England and Wales, Switzerland, and Austria and Bohemia but expanded only via more rapidly decelerating G in France, Scandinavia, and perhaps Germany. Rather later and steeper G trends would fit the data for Germany, Ireland, and Austria/ Bohemia for the 18th century. Both before and after the middle of the 1600s, that the specified countries urbanized in H rather than G shape for the local time spans identified makes sense against what is known about how prosperity and promise shifted across the map of Europe between 1500 and 1800. H-type population change, as first noted in Volume I of this study, continues to be associated with historical contexts of economic development.

Partially because de Vries worked with evidence at only widely spaced intervals, there exist periods in which urbanization for certain regions occurred that cannot be trended. Still, the patterns suggested in Table 4.2 point to some important alternative conclusions about how European urbanization evolved over the three centuries studied. First, there was more system to change in the percentage of population living in cities than de Vries concluded. Second, more insight into dynamics generating urbanization than he realized can be obtained from these patterns. Some processes that probably underlie the observed movements have already been suggested, such as the interplay of urban, rural agricultural, and rural non-agricultural populations observed from the work of Wrigley (1985) in Figures 3.11a through 3.11e. They are broadly familiar from

Table 4.3
Some Estimated Trends of Urbanization since the 18th Century (percentage in cities of 5,000 or more)

England	1750,1800	?E	1836	1800-1950	H	1750	1950-1980		down
Belgium	1700-1800	D	1676						
"	1800-1890	E	1862^d	1850-1950	H	1748	1950-1980	G	1900
Netherlands	1700-1800	D	1651						
"	1750-1910	E	1942	1910-1970	H	1820			
France	1700-1850	E	1869	1850-1950	H	1786	1950-1980	G	1930
Switzerland	1700-1850	E	1868	1850-1910	H	1813	1950-1980	G	1918
Germany	1700,1750	?D	1620						
"	1750-1850	E	1870	1850-1910	H	1846	1950-1980	G	1930
Scand./Sweden	1700-1800	E	1834	1850,1910	H	1840	1950-1980	G	1930
Italy	1700-1850	E	1887	1880-1980	H	1805			
Spain	1700-1850	E	1887	1850-1950	H	1808	1950-1980	G	1922
Russia/U.S.S.R.	1700-1850	E	1896	1850-1910	H	1796	1950-1980	G	1944
Romania				1800-1910	H	1721	1950-1980	G	1954
Balkans/Yugo.	1800-1950	E	1962				1950-1980	G	1966
Portugal	1750-1950	E	1973	1910-1970	H	1846			
Japan	1800-1950	E	1930				1950-1980	G	1956
United States				1800-1980	H	1810			
Canada	1800-1910	E	1893	1910-1980	H	1834			
Australia				1850-1980	H	1859			
ALL EUROPE	1600-1850	E	1874	1850-1930	H	1802	1950-1980	G	1923
ALL DEVELOPED				1850-1950	H	1801	1950-1980	G	1921

^{d} = de Vries 10,000+.

Sources: Bairoch 1988, 177, 179, 215, 216, 221; 1990, 143; de Vries 1984, 45–46.

the history of social and economic change in modernizing Europe. Other developments should be readily connected with the identified D, H, G, or E trends of urbanization by investigators who know more about particular national histories.

Table 4.3 advances to employ data for the percentage of people living in centers of 5,000 or more for 13 European countries plus Japan, the United States, Canada, and Australia in the *18th*, *19th* and *20th* centuries via data from Paul Bairoch (1988, 1990) in order to extend similar tentative trending into the modern era. Both the similarities and the differences among the nations that he studied are informative.

In the first place, every "developed" country that Bairoch covered except Yugoslavia and Japan for some substantial stretch between 1800 and 1980— from a few decades to a century or more—saw the percentage of its population who lived in urban conditions rise according to the slowly decelerating H "relative" of the G curve. The urbanization of Europe as a whole, furthermore, advanced this way from 1850 through 1930. For all "developed" countries together, such an H trend apparently ran onward to 1950, as the bottom line of the table indicates. The H shape of demographic change that has been seen to characterize the general population increase of developing countries (Harris 2001) and the urbanization of several European nations of rising stature between 1500 and 1750 (Table 4.2, just discussed) consistently applies to the evolution of urbanization for much of the 20th century during modern phases of development in almost all of what are considered as the world's more advanced economies.

After World War II, however, the right-hand column of Table 4.3 shows, in as many as 9 of the 13 European countries and also in Japan, the fresh impetus to further urbanization was by 1980 already visibly flattening out in more rapidly slowing G fashion. In England, the urban proportion of the population, according to Bairoch, actually shrank somewhat between 1950 and 1980. In the Netherlands and Portugal, late-starting H trends, begun only around the time of World War I, lasted to about 1970. In effect, every single European society on the list saw, between 1950 and 1980, any tendency for further urbanization to flatten out one way or the other. In contrast, in the United States, Canada, and Australia long-running H trends continued—in the least to 1980. While the Canadian trend started only around 1910, that for Australia commenced about 1850, and the one taken by U.S. urbanization held to a course that is evident as early as 1800. It should be of some insight that in the United States, at once both a "nation of immigrants" and a contender to displace the economic leadership of Europe, the H trend from 1800 through 1980 was almost precisely parallel to those for Europe in aggregate (without Russia, as Bairoch calculated it) and for all developed countries together (with t_0's at 1810, 1802, and 1801, respectively, as the middle column of Table 4.3 indicates, for curves that have base levels of about 7, 6, and 5 percent). The other great continental country that is covered, Russia, from 1850 through 1910 urbanized along still another H path that is quite parallel with these movements (with t_0 at 1796), though running at a much lower level.

Earlier, however, between the trends of Table 4.2 (which come to an end in the later 1700s) and some time from about 1800 forward, most of the countries of Table 4.3 also shared a common form of movement in their pace of urbanization. For this preceding period, though, the pattern was E, the slowly starting but progressively accelerating transposition of G—as the left column of Table 4.3 demonstrates. In Belgium, the form is observed by using data from de Vries (1984, 45–46) for cities of 10,000 and over about which information at 1890 is also known. In England, data points just for 1750 and 1800 are caught by the E trend proposed; but quinquennially documented, E-type growth for the English *population* from 1726 through 1806 (Harris 2001, 148, 151, from Wrigley and Schofield) fortifies this premise. For Romania early enough data are lacking. Considering all of Europe (without Russia), E-form urbanization by the 5,000-plus criterion is evident from 1600 or even perhaps 1500 through 1850 before the H type of change of the modern era took over. Urbanization in Japan between 1800 and 1950 and in Canada between 1800 and 1910 also expanded in this manner. It would be interesting to put the evidence together for the 18th century in the 13 revolting colonies of British North America, where centers like Philadelphia, New York, Baltimore, and Charleston were aggressively expanding across the later 1700s accompanied by several secondary ports and the first inland cities.

In the 18th century, the first part of the era covered by Table 4.3, exceptional D-shape trends of de-urbanization appear in Belgium and the Netherlands through 1800 and perhaps in Germany through 1750. For the first two, the data of Bairoch (1988) at the 5,000 level, in effect, confirm what Table 4.2 has concluded on the basis of evidence from de Vries starting only at 10,000 inhabitants. By that narrower definition of "urban," however, the sag between 1700 and 1750 for Germany in the percentage of the population that was urban does not appear.

In all, the shared international experience with urbanization that stands out in Table 4.3 trends the way that certain important aspects of the modern world have evolved. Among other things, our interpretation of the early appearance of H-form urbanization in Spain, France, and the Netherlands between 1500 and 1650 and then England, Austria/Bohemia, and perhaps Switzerland between 1650 and 1750 (Table 4.2) as being associated with economic development is strengthened by the later pervasiveness of that pattern in the more modern era, where the diffusion of economic growth is clear. It would be exciting to investigate the comparable patterns in Asia and Latin America, including the years since 1980. Populations on these other continents, too, have clearly been shifting recently from E-type "explosion" into robust but decelerating demographic growth of H form. Has their pace of urbanization done likewise? Or has it instead interacted differently with the general expansion of population that is evident?

The observed mix of national similarities and differences in the relationship between patterns of urbanization and trends of overall demographic increase in Europe and elsewhere from about 1850 to World War I would seem to involve variations in national demonomic inter-workings of economic change and population growth that contrast with the more uniform E-type pairings observed between proportional urbanization and total demographic expansion across the first half of the 1800s. There (as Table 4.5 will illustrate), E trends of population increase quite generally had fed parallel E-type expansion in the proportion of people who lived in cities. In the succeeding phase of H-type urbanization, some populations increased in a similar H way, but some did not. The economic developments involved in such distinctive demographic pairings seem important to identify and are the topic of continuing research.

URBANIZATION, MIGRATION, AND POPULATION GROWTH IN SYSTEMS OF INTERNATIONAL DEMONOMIC CHANGE

Urbanization, to begin with, must be seen as one form of migration among others, both supplementing them and competing with them while all interact with social and economic change. Unsatisfied English men and women of the

17th century could go to London or to the colonies. Discontented residents of Württemberg in the 1700s and 1800s could seek a new life in a developing German city, locally as in Stuttgart or northward as in the Ruhr, or relocate more distantly to the United States—or to Prussia, Hungary, or Russia. Dutchmen failing to find what they sought in 18th-century Amsterdam could chance service in Asia with the East India Company. Such movements helped certain populations grow while skimming off human resources from others. So, of course, did the slave trade. All kinds of migration, meanwhile, both affected and reflected economic changes that were taking place in various parts of the world.

The slowly decelerating H shape of population increase, as every chapter of the first volume of this study has noted (Harris 2001), over and over again has been situated historically in contexts where sustained economic development is known or can reasonably be suspected. The evidence of this present chapter extends further our understanding of such likely "demonomic" interconnections at work via migration and urbanization. Table 4.4 presents some H trends encountered in total demographic expansion, migration to the New World, the growth of population living in cities, and degree of urbanization in order to facilitate considering the relationships of these developments to each other.

In summing up the evidence chronologically, the first insight comes from the way that city founding has been seen to have expanded across central Europe in the Middle Ages, from the 1150s or earlier to the 1290s (or perhaps the 1340s) via a long H trend with base year at 1188. Since the number of new cities established per decade in the region for several generations *following* the Black Death took D form parallel with population decline in that shape that has been identified in many diverse parts of Europe, can our working hypothesis perhaps be that demographic increase throughout much of medieval Europe in this era *before* the plague—a long growth that is well known to have occurred in some type of pattern during the 12th and 13th centuries—also generally paralleled city founding and in continental aggregate took a path of H shape? That would be a far earlier manifestation of population increase in H form than the trends for Sweden, England, and the Dutch province of Holland beginning in the 1500s that currently constitute the first historical signs of demographic expansion in this pattern. Local data from several parts of Europe before the Black Death, however, show only G-type expansion, as do trends for England, China, and perhaps Egypt (Harris 2001, 363, 173, 242–44, 285, 287). Probably it is more likely that the population of central Europe was expanding in G fashion while city-founding and perhaps urban population for the region were enlarging in H form.

For the century and a half or so after the great blow of the Black Death, most demographic evidence for Europe is relatively local—though there is a fair amount of it (including some national and regional examples) to support the D shape of widespread, long-term population loss caused by the pandemic and its social and economic consequences. From about 1500 forward, then, a consid-

Table 4.4
Estimated H-Form Demographic Expansion, Atlantic Migration, and Urbanization

Domestic Population

Holland	1514-1650	H 1445
Germany	1520-1618	H 1413
England	1561-1656	H 1461
Sweden	1570-1720	H 1447
England	1656-1686	D 1587
France	1675-1700	D 1566
Germany	loss	
Italy	1625-1675	D 1566
Spain	1589-1648	?D 1563
England	1686-1726	H 1492
Germany	1650-1750	H 1499
Norway	1665-1735	H 1512
Spain	1648-1768	H 1527
Portugal	1636-1768	H 1547
Ireland	1672-1725	H 1595
United States	1850-1930	H 1853

Migration to New World

Europeans	1513-1588	H 1512
Africans	1538-1613	H 1593
Total	1513-1588	H 1536
"	1588-1688	H 1563
% African Slaves	1538-1710	H 1498
Europeans	1638-1688	D 1637
Europeans	1688-1770	H 1662
Africans	1638-1785	H 1645
Total	1688-1750	H 1663
United States	1847-1913	H 1850

Urban Population

Central Europe   1155-1295   H 1188

All Europe 100k+	1550-1750	H 1519
No. Europe 100k+	1550-1750	H 1558
No. Europe 10k+	1550-1650	H 1441
Germany	1500-1600	H 1391
Spain	1500-1600	H 1426
Poland	1500-1650	H 1451
Netherlands	1550-1650	H 1508
....and probably others*		
France	1600-1750	H 1475
England/Wales	1600-1700	H 1550
Germany	1650-1750	H 1544
Scandinavia	1600-1750	H 1584
No. Europe 10k+	1650-1750	H 1520
All Europe 10k+	1650-1750	H 1503
No. Europe 100k+	1550-1750	H 1558
All Europe 100k+	1550-1750	H 1519

Percent Urban

Spain	1500-1600	H 1404
France	1550-1650	H 1438
Netherlands	1550-1650	H 1466
England/Wales	1650-1750	H 1550
Switzerland	1650-1750	?H 1556
Austria/Bohemia	1650-1750	H 1586
United States	1830-1930	H 1835

* Northern Italy, Southern Italy, France, Belgium, Portugal, Switzerland, England/Wales, Scandinavia.

Sources: Harris 2001, 148-49, 17, 27; Chapters 1 and 2 for European and African migrants: Tables 4.1 and 4.2.

erable amount of reliable evidence exists in Europe for trending side by side population increase, the development of cities, and long-distance migration—at least that across the Atlantic Ocean.

From the 1500s into the 1600s, the pioneering Dutch maritime province of Holland (from 1514 to about 1650), England (1561–1656), Sweden (1570–1720), and Germany (1520–1618) all experienced population growth in H paths with t_0's between 1413 and 1461 (Harris 2001, 148–51, 200; Figure 4.2 in this chapter). Meanwhile, the *urban* populations of *many* countries, not just those four, most likely swelled in the same H form between 1500 or 1550 and 1600 or 1650, as Table 4.1 has indicated: Germany, France, Spain, Northern and Southern Italy, and Poland most flatly; the Netherlands (probably accompanied from 1550 through 1600 or so by Scandinavia), Switzerland, and England and Wales rather more steeply (with later base years for these H trends). This is at least what widely spaced data from de Vries suggest. In England, the maritime port of the Netherlands, Germany, and Scandinavia apparently both total and urban population expanded in H form during the era (though not necessarily in equal amounts). In Italy, Spain, France, and Poland the peopling of cities with 10,000 or more residents shared in taking H shape, but not increase for the total population. Did cities for some reason grow there in this era at the expense of other parts of the population rather than along with them?

In terms of the *proportion* of persons living in cities with 10,000 inhabitants or more (Table 4.2 and the rightmost column of Table 4.4), however, between 1500 and 1650 it was just Spain, France, and the Netherlands (the whole nation, not just the province of Holland) whose populations became more urban along a likely H trend as they expanded overall in more rapidly decelerating G fashion. Before 1650 or so no country displays simultaneous increases in H form of both total population size and the proportion living in cities.

Beginning in the early 1500s, it becomes possible to trend the flow of Old World peoples to the New World. For several reliably outlined flows of Europeans taken together (Spanish, French Canadian, various migrants to British North America and to the British West Indies), an H trend from the early 1500s through the 1590s seems likely, with a base year in the 1510s.[34] The flow of Africans, which is probably estimated upon more complete data than what is available for Europeans, took H form from 1525 through 1650 with t_0 as late as the 1590s. Though following the same H shape of trajectory, it climbed during this era along a considerably steeper segment of the curve. As a result of these two unequal H trends, over the long haul steadily but persistently the proportion of African slaves within total New World migration rose from about 22 percent of the mix at 1538 (for the years 1525–1550) to more like 90 percent by 1710 (for 1700–1720) also along an H path, one with base year at about 1498.

This pattern makes the H trends for approximate European transatlantic migration and for the proportion of all movement to the New World that was African roughly parallel to each other as free colonists—at this stage mostly drawn to tropical plantation settlements and to the mineral riches of Mexico and the Andes—expected slaves to do more and more of the work and produced their own children to the disadvantage of further European immigrants. The rate of Africanization for total migration to the Americas, in other words, over the 16th century increased in direct relationship to the number of Europeans crossing the ocean. Growth in the enslaved proportion of the total Atlantic migration, already at 60 percent by 1600 (without Portuguese in the European part of the denominator), then held to this same H trend also across the 17th century (in spite of a dip for the years 1626–1650), as Table 4.4 indicates, though the trend in European numbers broke back in D fashion with the domestic demographic difficulties of the middle 1600s.[35] A pattern for Africanization in New World migration seems to have been set in the first hundred years. It lasted until a ceiling was hit at about 80 to 90 percent in the 1700s (depending upon the effect of adding in at present unknown numbers of Spanish and Portuguese for various periods of time). These are rough, incomplete estimations of trends; but they should provoke further exploration of how such contemporary H shapes occurred and how they were connected with each other.

The combined system of New World migration during the 1500s and even the numbers of Europeans alone (Table 4.4) grew considerably more steeply than the contemporary H growth of residents in the cities of Spain, which received the bulk of New World wealth and sent the large majority of Europeans across the Atlantic in the 16th century. Meanwhile Portugal, which shipped the most slaves, actually lost urban population between 1600 and 1650. Likewise, the H-type increases of the urban *proportion* within the colonizing Spanish, French, and Dutch populations of Europe in this era were flatter, with base years back in the 1400s, while England before about 1650 (Table 4.2) apparently urbanized in G form, not H. In short, though both generally increased in H shape, attraction to the New World in this era noticeably outpaced urban growth back in Europe. How might this discrepancy provide further insight into the notorious European inflation of the 1500s and the role of New World activity in it?[36]

Moving forward in time, H trends of overall population increase soon subsequently appeared in several parts of Europe. H trajectories of total demographic expansion show up in Portugal 1636–1768, Spain from sometime after 1648 to 1768, England 1686–1726, Ireland 1672–1725, and Norway 1665–1735 (the left column of Table 4.4, from Harris 2001, 148–51). Notably, the Netherlands and France, once strong aspirants for Atlantic power, are missing from this array of nations that stretches up and down the western rim of Europe. European and African migration into the New World, both separately and jointly, seem to have expanded—also in H fashion[37]—more steeply than total population increase of that same shape in Portugal, Spain, and England, which now held the most populous colonies in the Americas.

In this era, the number of city inhabitants in England and Wales 1600–1700, Scandinavia 1600–1750, Germany 1650–1750, Switzerland 1650–1750, Austria/Bohemia (perhaps 1650–1700, more clearly 1700–1800), and possibly Scotland expanded in aggregate via steeper H trends than all cities with 10,000 or more residents in Northern Italy 1650–1800, Central Italy 1700–1800, France 1600–1750, Belgium 1600–1700, and Portugal 1600–1700 (whose zero years sat back between 1460 and 1515 rather than in the middle to later 1500s, as Table 4.1 indicates). At the heart of such national trends was the way that the biggest cities of northern Europe, those with 100,000 or more inhabitants, garnered up more and more population between 1550 and 1750 along an H path with base year at 1558. Meanwhile, however, migration to the Americas—European and African, separately and jointly—swelled via markedly steeper paths of H shape with t_0's in the middle 1600s. After about 1675, going to the colonies increased more robustly than going to the metropolis, for even the grandest cities of northern Europe as well as for urban population on the continent as a whole. To what extent had it become clear as settlements matured that the colonies had more to offer than the dangerous cesspools of humanity that typified Europe's leading urban centers?

Across the hundred years after 1650, moreover, only the rising powers represented by England and Wales and Austria/Bohemia (perhaps also Switzerland) saw the *percentages* of their people who were urban dwellers rise in parallel H fashion. England, furthermore, was the single country with urban proportion, urban numbers, and (more flatly) total population increase all swelling roughly in H trajectories along with H-type expansion in the flow of human capital to the New World between 1650 and 1750. She was taking over leadership in the African and slave trades, in commerce with the Caribbean, and in the peopling of American colonies. Urbanization, migration (not just her own people but many others) to bolster holdings in the New World, and total domestic population increase combined in raising Britain at the expense of Dutch, French, and Iberian competitors. All advanced in H form. As a further insightful perspective, the bottom line in Table 4.4 then shows how, as in a later era the United States in turn grew to challenge Britain for the leadership of development in the West between about 1840 and World War II population increase, immigration, and urbanization there also followed virtually parallel H trends. A confluence of these movements in H shape seems to be a feature of "core" development in the Western world since the 1600s.

From the late 1500s into the 1730s the proportion of the English population that lived in London (Figure 3.2) grew via an H trend parallel in timing to both the increasing numbers of people who resided in all English cities (Table 4.1)[38] and the share of all the English population that these centers of 10,000 or more contained (Table 4.2). Also along H paths with t_0's in the middle of the 1500s expanded the proportion of the rural population of England that was engaged in activities outside agriculture from 1670 or so forward (Figure 3.11e), the average number of workers per farmer in certain documented English parishes perhaps from as early as 1600 through the 1790s (Figure 3.12), and—rather more flatly, with base year for the H in the 1510s rather than in the 1540s—the number of people in England per person in agriculture (Figure 3.11d). Agricultural output in England, meanwhile, swelled between about 1600 and 1700 per acre—per worker and in terms of total output—to a degree that would fit flatter H curve segments with base years considerably earlier—in the 1400s (Harris 1997). With just two points of data available with which to estimate a tentative possible trend, however, the improvements might have commenced considerably after 1600. If these movements in the agricultural economy began about 1650, like the H trend for the proportion of the English population that resided in cities (Table 4.2)—a development that was likely to be connected— they would have been parallel to that urban demographic curve.

It seems as if an increasing scale of units of land being farmed in English agriculture (most operators were tenants, not owners), as it made production more efficient, shifted workers to other pursuits in the countryside and encouraged or forced migration to the nation's cities and a search for opportunity overseas. These processes apparently were stronger and more linked to each other in England during the 17th century than among any of that country's European competitors. Insights like this for understanding the economic development of England as it interacted with the country's demographic evolution can, with the aid of G-based trending, fruitfully be spun out further from the seminal work of Wrigley, de Vries, and Kussmaul and a rich literature on English agriculture and the English economy.

The new H trends in transatlantic migration that ran from the 1680s to the American and French Revolutions had their base year now in the middle 1600s, for northern Europeans and Africans both collectively and separately (the bottom of the second column of Table 4.4). In contrast to previous eras, contemporaneous and parallel H-shape increases (with comparable zero years in the middle of the 17th century) in the number or proportion of persons in European populations who lived in cities, or the size of the whole national populations themselves, now did not appear—with the possible exceptions of aggregate urban inhabitants in Austria/Bohemia and, very briefly, Scotland (Table 4.1) and overall demographic expansion in Norway between 1748 and 1818 and Russia between 1762 and 1815 (Harris 201, 148–49), changes around the northern and eastern *fringes* of the core of European development. Instead, beginning with England, both urbanization and total population increase broke away from the path of Atlantic migration, even though the latter continued to flourish in H form via both free relocation and the slave trade across the 18th century. Industrialization replaced the growth of colonies as the economic companion of demographic and agricultural change in Europe.

The new common path for key aspects of European development, but not transatlantic migration, now took E shape: proportionally accelerating increase. Table 4.5 summarizes trends of that form in the total demographic expansion, city growth, and proportional urbanization of most European countries during this phase of modern demonomic change.

The first column of the table shows how E patterns of national population

Table 4.5
Some Estimated E-Shape Movements in Population Growth, City Dwellers, and Urbanization since the 1700s

	Population[h]	Number in Cities[v]	Percent Urban[b]
Southern Italy	1650-1750 E 1786[v]	1650-1750 E 1778	1700-1850 E 1887[Iv]
Central Italy	1650-1750 E 1799[v]	1650-1750 E 1796	1700-1850 E 1887[Iv]
England	1726-1806 E 1822	1750,1800 ?E 1808	1700-1850 E 1854
Ireland	1725-1791 E 1812	1750,1800 ?E 1798	1750,1800 ?E 1828[v]
Scotland	1755-1821 E 1839	1750,1800 ?E 1797	1750,1800 ?E 1812[v]
Belgium	1650-1800 E 1828[v]	1750,1800 ?E 1837	1800,1850 ?E 1866
Germany I	1700-1800 E 1823[v]	1750,1800 ?E 1823	1800,1850 ?E 1865
Switzerland I	1700-1800 E 1833[v]	1750,1800 ?E 1885	1800,1850 ?E 1864
Denmark	1735-1801 E 1857	?	?
Netherlands	1750-1839 E 1866	very late ?E	1750-1815 E 1869
France	1792-1827 E 1876	1700-1800 E 1842	1700-1850 E 1865
Iceland	1769-1860 E 1890	?	?
Spain	1797-1887 H 1680	1700-1800 E 1820	1800,1850 ?E 1872
Northern Italy	1771-1821 G 1717[I]	1750,1800 ?E 1844	1800-1850 ?E 1872
Portugal	1841-1890 E 1920	1750,1800 ?E 1841	none
Austria I	1850-1880 E 1910	1800,1850 ?E 1850[H]	1750-1850 E 1886[Hv]
Germany II	1864-1910 E 1923		
Romania	1844-1912 E 1918		
Czechoslovakia I	1880-1910 E 1945		
Austria II	1890-1910 E 1934		
Spain	1857-1920 E 1952		
Germany III	1910-1950 E 1977		
Switzerland II	1910-1970 E 1985		
Czechoslovakia II	1910-1930 E 2004		
Hungary	1910-1941 E 1977		
Albania	1955-1990 E 1959		
Japan I	1872-1885 E 1925		
" II	1885-1915 E 1935		
" III	1915-1935 E 1952		
India	1901-1971 E 1972		
Latin America	1920-1950 E 1949		
Asia	1920-1975 E 1974		
Africa	1920-1965 E 1964		
Less Developed Areas	1900-1970 E 1969		
World	1900-1970 E 1975		

I = all of Italy; H = including Hungary.

Sources: [h] = Harris 2001, 148–49, 250–51, 395; [v] = de Vries 1984, 36, 30, 39, 45–46; [b] = Bairoch 1990, 143. Exceptions within columns are noted.

growth marched across most of Europe from the British Isles to Spain and Albania between about 1725 and 1970. Amply documented trends from Volume I of this study (Harris 2001, 148–49) are supplemented with estimates from the more widely spaced computations of de Vries for Germany and Switzerland between 1700 and 1800 and Belgium between 1650 and 1800 (1984, 36). The earliest total demographic expansions in E form (after a local development down the boot of Italy that came to an *end* already by the middle of the 18th century) appeared in England, Ireland, Scotland, Belgium, Germany, and Switzerland. A later phase of E growth spread to Denmark and Iceland, to the Netherlands, and—briefly after the Revolution—to France. Meanwhile, population in Spain and Northern Italy expanded via H and G paths instead. A third era of change beginning in the middle of the 19th century, diffusing southward and eastward across Europe, brought E-type population growth to Austria, Germany (a second round), the Czech regions of Bohemia and Moravia, Portugal, Spain, Austria again, and Romania. A fourth dissemination of E-shape population increase, finally, unfolded only after World War I in Germany (the third trend of this shape there), Switzerland and Czechoslovakia (both second appearances), Hungary, and Albania. Chapter 6 of Volume I shows how many local regions experienced demographic growth of E form according to various sequences within the Netherlands, Germany, Austria, the Balkans, and Russia.

Chapters 7 and 4 of Volume I, furthermore, have demonstrated where population expansion in E shape—accelerating growth or "explosion"—occurred in the 20th century in Asia, Africa, the Caribbean, and Latin America, including state-by-state within Brazil, Chile, and Venezuela (Harris 2001, 126–30). In aggregate, the less developed countries of the world gained people in this E manner from 1900 through 1970, the lowest cluster of entries as the left of Table 4.5 recapitulates, while the inhabitants of Latin America, Asia, and Africa also enlarged separately in such fashion through much of the 1900s. In contrast, Europe was now collectively past change in this form, while America north of the Rio Grande never experienced it (ibid., 385). In all, population growth in the E pattern has been established to have occurred in developing countries or regions (occasionally a boom city) from the 1700s through the 1900s.[39] For better or for worse, as demographic historians of the era following World War II took a while to realize, for ages "population explosion" has historically been a concomitant of certain *type* of economic development, not just a mid-20th-century crisis. An uncomfortable, indeed perilous experience for many it has been, however—and in a few places continues to be. But then this was the case also back in 18th-century England, despite some pastel over-paintings that have been offered by revisionists who, even in the midst of our present "soak the defenseless" culture of crook-and-crony capitalism, would like those "blue books" over which Marx pored in the British Museum simply to go away.

Patterns of city growth and relative urbanization now spell out somewhat further what has transpired during such phases of E-type demographic change, at least in the better-documented European circumstances. The second column of Table 4.5 lists likely and possible E trends for the size of regional populations living in cities of 10,000 or more (de Vries 1984, 30, 45–46, 70). The cases with question marks estimate what timing of E curve, *if* there was one, would fit the two data points available.

For Southern and Central Italy evidence from 1650 through 1750 indicates E trends in aggregate urban population headed for t_0's in the late 1700s.[40] Calculations of total population in these regions across the same hundred years by de Vries would fit E curves with comparable local base years but following numbers for 1800 fall well below such a track (1984, 36). The overall result is no substantial gain in the percentages living in cities for these parts of Italy between 1650 and 1800, regions of Europe that are generally not considered to be leading centers of development during the move to the modern era. Later data from de Vries for Italy as a whole, however, make the urban percentage for the total country rise in late-climbing E form with zero year only around 1887, as the right-hand column of Table 4.5 states.

Two-point data from just 1750 and 1800 on total urban residents in several countries of northern and central Europe would fit E trends for the later 18th century, as the middle column of Table 4.5 indicates, though they of course do not of themselves demonstrate them. Base years for possible E curves would fall near 1800 for England, Ireland, and Scotland, rather later for Belgium, Germany, and most of all Switzerland.

The interplay of total population size and numbers living in cities produces the possible trends in the urban *proportion* offered in the third column of Table 4.5. Two sources are used: unless indicated otherwise, Bairoch (1990, 143) for centers of 5,000 and more and de Vries (1984, 39, 45–46) for cities holding at least 10,000 inhabitants ("v").[41] In Italy, England, the Netherlands, France, and Austria/Hungary one source or the other provides more than two points in time for arguing an E. Elsewhere the estimations are just hypothetical. Still, all six in the cluster of northwestern and central European countries with at least potential E-type total demographic expansion in the era probably or at least possibly saw the *proportions* of their populations also rise in E form into the early 1800s. The E curves likely for the proportions dwelling in cities are timed later (therefore run flatter through the early 1800s) than the trends for the numbers of persons living in cities; but most proposed trends at the 5,000 level via Bairoch have their t_0's together in the 1860s. The percentages inhabiting the somewhat larger centers used as a cutoff point by de Vries rise toward rather later base years for the possible E curves over the first half of the 19th century. These patterns, however, have comparable relationships to preceding E paths for the urban numbers in each country according to his higher threshold for cities.

Such parallels were mostly a northern European phenomenon. While the population estimates of de Vries for 1650, 1700, and 1750 would conform to an E with zero year at about 1795 also for the Spanish people as a whole, more frequent demographic data show an H trend for the years 1648–1768 (perhaps more precisely for 1685–1745) to be the shape of change instead, as for the years 1636–1768 meanwhile in Portugal (Harris 2001, 186, 152). Even though Portugal *could* have an E according to just 1750 and 1800 estimates of urban population, none is likely this early for the urban proportion. In Italy, meanwhile, national population increase from 1771 through 1821 fairly clearly took G rather than E shape (ibid., 151). Separate estimates across the later 1700s and early 1800s for Piedmont, Liguria, Lombardy, and Venetia all take approximately parallel G form (ibid., 190, 192) demonstrating that this was indeed the nature of demographic increase for Northern Italy. Though doing so later, France and the Netherlands[42] did join their northern European neighbors in experiencing E types of trend in total demographic increase, growth of city population, and urban proportion, a triple combination perhaps also occurring in Austria still further along in time.

The parallelism of subsequent national trends in numbers of urban dwellers and their percentage of populations as total demographic increase in the E pattern continued to diffuse across Europe in the later 19th and early 20th centuries must be explored elsewhere. Table 4.5 and regional data from the Netherlands, Belgium and France, Germany, Austria-Hungary and the Balkans, and Russia (Harris 2001, 198–99, 206–7, 213, 216, 220–22) display, however, the many places to which population explosion went. Nonetheless, a hypothesis that these three types of change continued to be related for some time further as aspects of demographic transition and industrialization penetrated eastern and southern Europe and then the so-called Third World seems worth testing.

The ties of these E-shape movements of urbanization (like overall demographic expansion) to contemporary economic developments of the 1700s and 1800s are illuminated, for this era as before, by changes in agricultural population and performance. These now took E rather than H form. The evidence for England is so far the most detailed and the most revealing.

Figure 3.11d hints that the ratio of total population per person in English agriculture *might* have climbed in E form toward a zero year for the curve at 1834 according to data for just 1750 and 1801. Kussmaul's (1981) research (Figure 3.12) has gone further to show how from 1777 through 1831, perhaps from as early as 1700 forward, the proportion of farmers in the population of a group of English parishes declined via a C curve, the upside-down counterpart of E, with t_0 at 1814, while the average number of agricultural workers per farmer in these places accelerated offsettingly upward in E style from the 1760s through 1831 toward a zero year at 1838. In quite parallel developments, farming units grew larger and supported more people per agricultural worker (though not necessarily providing an undiluted lifestyle for them). Quite regularly documented rural wages in England, moreover, rose from the 1750s into the 1810s around an E curve with zero year at 1811 (parallel to how the population of the country increased); and the ratio of urban to rural wages climbed from the 1710s into the 1790s rather more flatly via an E trajectory with t_0 at 1851 (Harris 1997). Did higher earnings to be had in the cities (more and more of them industrial) pull workers out of agriculture this way and force farmers to alter their operations in a manner that favored larger units of production? Estimates at 1700 and 1800 for output per acre from English agriculture and output per worker, meanwhile, *could* support E curves of increase with zero years each around 1840 (ibid.). Did greater efficiency come about because landowners and farmers had to make do with less available total manpower and what appears to have been more costly labor that gave advantage to larger farmers? Some possibilities arise that the development of cities, perhaps especially industrial ones, promoted agricultural change, not just the other way around, though growing city populations did have to be fed somehow.[43]

After the middle of the 19th century urbanization in a cluster of northwestern and central European countries noted for their lead in industrialization continued to be distinctive. The proportions of total population living in cities in these societies, which had risen earliest in E form as that previous pattern of change passed over Europe, now shifted to H shape, while in other European countries later E movements continued to prevail. In Britain from 1800 through 1910 the urban percentage swelled along an H track with base year around 1770, still roughly paralleling total population growth, which now also took an H path from 1816 to 1861 with t_0 at 1758 followed by another H from 1861 to 1939 anchored on a zero year of 1794 (Bairoch 1990, 143; Harris 2001, 148–151). In Belgium, H-type change in urban proportion from 1850 to 1910 paralleled that in Britain. Population growth for the country, while relatively flat from 1815 through 1866, was followed from 1876 to 1910 by a second, steeper H comparable to that for England at this time—with t_0's at 1717 and 1790 for the successive trends (Harris 2001, 148, 165). A surge in urbanization for France between 1850 and 1910, meanwhile, took H form with base year at a rather later date than for Britain and Belgium: in the mid-1790s. The population of France, however, grew very flatly in G rather than the more slowly decelerating H trajectory from 1826 through 1921 (ibid., 148, 152). In the northern departments that contained Lille and Paris, though, total population increase *did* take H shape. For Nord, general demographic expansion first followed an 1801–1851 H with t_0 at 1698, close to contemporary trends for nearby Belgium and for the Netherlands with zero years at 1710 and 1718, respectively. Then an 1851–1911 one with base year at 1764 followed, resembling demographic expansion in later-19th-century Scotland and Denmark, a little flatter than in contemporary Belgium, the Netherlands, and England. For Seine, the department of Paris, there appeared a steeper, longer-lasting H trend for 1831–1931 that had its t_0 at 1823, comparable to a third phase of H-type growth in the Netherlands and Denmark up through the first several decades of the 20th century but commencing several decades sooner (ibid., 199, 148).

Meanwhile, the productivity of agricultural labor in Britain and France, as Table 4.6 shows (from Bairoch 1990, 139), likewise gained according to the H pattern between 1800 and 1880 or 1910, but via appreciably shallower curve

Table 4.6
Yield per Hectare and Agricultural Labor Productivity in Europe and the United States in the 19th Century

	Yield per Hectare			Labor Productivity		
Europe	1800-1910	E	1943	1800-1880	H	1670
United States	mostly level			1800-1910	H	1802
United Kingdom	1800-1880	?G	1762	1800-1880	H	1650
France	1800-1880	G	1762	1800-1910	H	1738
Switzerland	1800-1910	E	1926	1800-1880	H	1705
Belgium	1800-1910	E	1925	1850-1910	E	1912
Germany	1800-1910	E	1918	1800-1880	E	1891
Italy	1800-1910	E	1944	1800-1910	E	1942
Russia	1800-1910	E	1950	1800-1880	E	1943

Source: Bairoch 1990, 138, 139.

segments of this type than contemporary population increase in England or in the areas around Lille and Paris—and more slowly in Britain (t_0 at 1650) than in France (t_0 at 1738), where earlier urbanization and economic development had not proceeded as far by 1800. In both nations, yields for wheat per hectare improved from 1800 to 1880 in G form with base year around 1762 (ibid., 138). That was not the case in Belgium, where productivity per agricultural worker and crop yield both rose instead in roughly parallel E tracks between the early 1800s and World War I. These Belgian patterns resemble movements for both components of agricultural change in contemporary Germany and crop yield in Switzerland, according to Table 4.6—though Swiss labor productivity in raising foodstuffs climbed in H form instead, in steepness intermediate to the trends for Britain and France. The populations of Germany and Switzerland, however, unlike that of 19th-century Belgium, themselves also expanded in E shape quite parallel to these agricultural changes, accompanied by the peoples of Austria, the Adriatic zones of the Hapsburg Empire, Romania, and Portugal.

For Italy and Russia, Bairoch's calculations for agricultural efficiency rise along E paths with noticeably later zero years, in the 1940s (Table 4.6). The population of neither country grew in this form in the 19th century; each took an H path instead. For many regions of Europe, however, population increase according to E trends of this approximate timing is evident, including several *parts* of Russia, though not of Italy. Bohemia and Moravia, Austria (in a second G surge), Slovenia and Dalmatia, Austrian Silesia, Spain, Limburg and West Flanders within Belgium, and several Dutch provinces display E trends of this sort in total population increase across the decades preceding World War I, though France and a sample of her departments, Luxembourg, Hungary, and various parts of the former Yugoslavia join Italy in having no observed national or regional trend of the type in this era. The areas of Russia that display an E trend for total demographic expansion in such timing included the provinces of Livonia, Courland, Estonia, Viborg, Olonets, and Archangel stretching from the Baltic to the White Sea, whose changes resemble E movements in parts of eastern Prussia just to the west; Tver, Smolyensk, Nizhegorod, Vladimir, and Kostrom in the central area around Moscow; Kharkov, Chernigov, Tambov, Orel, Saratov, and Samara to the south; Yaroslav, Vologod, Vyatsk, Kazan, and Perm in the northeast; and the modern economic districts of the Transcaucasus and Central Asia (Harris 2001, 148–49, 198–99, 216, 220–22).

What were the patterns of urbanization and agricultural change in all these other parts of Europe in which E trends of total population growth occurred? One thing that happened is that, as agricultural advance accelerated upward, emigration surged. For example, departures from Russia through the late 1800s and early 1900s rose along a G' path with peak at 1938 (Table 1.1) compared with the estimated zero year of 1943 for the E curve of agricultural productivity shown in Table 4.6 (and a somewhat later base year for the E trend of national crop yields). From Italy, emigration—before being legally restricted by the United States—headed toward a G' peak at 1940 compared with estimated t_0's of 1944 and 1942 for the E-type agricultural changes of Table 4.6 for that country. (The trend for the urban proportion in the population of Italy, however, took H shape like, but much steeper than, population increase for the nation, probably because only certain parts of the country experienced most of the change.) German emigration, too, crested in 1883 relative to an approximated zero year for increasing agricultural productivity also in the early 1890s.

In the United States, meanwhile, yields per hectare remained on the whole quite level across the 19th century. Labor productivity in agriculture, however, rose robustly in H form with t_0 around 1802. Such timing seems to fall between the likely H trends for proportion of the labor force not in agriculture for the country as a whole between 1800 and 1900 and in the later-settled but agriculturally rich Old Northwest between 1830 and 1900 (Figure 3.8a). The proportion of the U.S. population living in sizable towns and small cities with from 5,000 to 50,000 inhabitants meanwhile climbed via H from 1820 through 1950 from a base year for the curve at about 1800, almost exactly parallel with agricultural productivity as more and more of the rural population was not needed in farming and moved to town instead (Figure 3.8a).

Other connections among observed G-based national or regional trends in population increase, city growth, proportional urbanization, migration, and agricultural change will have to be explored in further research. The possible findings look promising, however. Several key issues in how modern populations, economies, and societies have developed already receive fresh perspective from the trending that has been possible, while provocative challenges for extending interpretation further are posed.

The basic movements, furthermore, can be followed down to the present time. Table 4.7 relates regularly documented and systematically fitted trends of population increase from Volume I of this study to patterns of urbanization, the role of industrial activity in total employment, gross national product (GNP) per capita, agricultural productivity, and crop yield that can be estimated from the more widely spaced data of Bairoch (1988, 1990).

In Europe (without Russia, as Bairoch calculates it), urbanization advanced from 1850 through 1930 along an H path a little less steep than that already noted for the United States (with t_0's around 1802 and 1835, respectively). Since World War II, in contrast, the percentage of Europeans living in urban settings has enlarged according to the more rapidly flattening-out G pattern, with a base year in the 1920s. This is the way that the population of Europe has expanded since the postwar baby boom (and also how it grew in the first half of the 20th century). Supporting both urbanization and total increase in population for Europe during the 1800s was an H trend of improvement in agricultural productivity that closely paralleled the trend of the same shape for the United Kingdom alone, as shown in Table 4.6. While labor productivity in farming for Europe in aggregate thus rose like the change in one of the region's long-developed countries, in crop yield European change instead took the E pattern of less developed farming areas like Russia and Italy, with t_0 in the 1940s. The areas under cultivation in Russia and neighboring Eastern Europe were, of course, especially extensive.

In Russia, though two successive H trends of total demographic expansion occurred between 1858 and 1939, no advance of urbanization in this shape emerged in the 20th century as agricultural productivity and crop yield increased only in delayed E form. This patterning contrasts markedly with the H movements found in that other large continental country, the United States, for population growth, expanding urbanization, and agricultural productivity together. In Australia, New Zealand, and South Africa collectively, H-type urbanization also generally expanded in H fashion alongside general demographic growth well into the 20th century. In more recent decades, however, further urbanization in these countries has followed the more rapidly decelerating G shape, even though total demographic increase has taken up a new H path, both patterns much like that for the contemporary United States.

All these "developed" parts of the globe together, as the top line of Table 4.7 indicates, saw their collective urbanization advance via H from 1850 through 1950 like Europe, the United States, and the "other" developed countries of Australia, New Zealand, and South Africa, though their total demographic increase decelerated more rapidly via G—like Europe, not the United States, Russia, or Australia and New Zealand (the large populations within Oceania). Up until World War II, industrialization in these parts of the globe collectively continued to advance proportionally in H fashion, too, though more flatly (with t_0 near 1700, not 1800 or later). Per capita GNP, meanwhile, likewise seems to

Table 4.7

Some Approximate Global Patterns of Population Growth, Urbanization, and Economic Change

Region	Percentage Urban	Population Growth[h]	% Employment Industrial	GNP per Capita	Agricultural Productivity	Yield per Hectare
All Developed Areas	1850-1950 H 1810 1950-2025 G 1923	1920-1950 G 1891 1950-2025 G 1931	1800-1930 H 1700 1950-1980 G 1913	1850-1900 H 1768 1900-1950 H 1875 1950-1980 ?H 1975		
Europe	1850-1930 H 1802 1950-2025 G 1926	1920-1950 G 1880 1950-2025 G 1925			1800-1880 H 1670	1800-1910 E 1943
Russia	1850-1910 G 1838 1910-1930 G 1906 1930-2025 G 1940	1858-1897 H 1821 1897-1939 H 1830 1959-1989 G 1937			1800-1910 E 1943	1800-1910 E 1950
United States	1790-1830 G 1786 1830-1930 H 1835 1950-1970 ?G ?	1670-1850 F 1850-1930 H 1853 1940-2040 H 1939			1850-1910 H 1802	mostly level
Austr./N.Z./S.Africa	1850-1980 H 1850 1960-2025 G 1926	1920-1950 H 1862[o] 1950-2025 H 1922[o]				
Asia Market Economy	1900-1960 E 1972 1950-2000 H 1945	1920-1975 E 1975 1965-2000 H 1945		1850-1900 D 1779 1900-1950 G 1845 1950-1980 H 1920		

Japan	1800-1920 E 1966 1920-1950 G 1926 1960-2025 G 1916	1915-1935 E 1952 1920-1945 G 1902 1945-1965 G 1931 1965-1990 G 1939		
India	1850-1940 E 1957	1901-1971 E 1972 1961-1991 H 1947		
China	1900-1950 H 1813 1960-2025 E 2025	1742-1851 H 1665 1873-1937 H 1741 1950-1990 H 1923		
Latin America	1900-1930 G 1875 1950-2025 G 1942	1920-1950 E 1949 1950-2025 H 1951	1800-1910 E 1937 1900-1980 E 1983	
Africa	1900-1950 G 1903 1950-2025 G 1959	1920-1965 E 1964 1965-2000 F 1990-2025 H 1993	1900-1930 G 1860 1950-1980 G 1938	
Third World		1900-1970 E 1969 1955-2025 H 1945	1850-1900 G 1775 1900-1950 G 1864 1950-1980 H 1922	1800-1880 C 1928 1880-1930 G 1827 1960-1980 H 1930

H = Harris; ° = Oceania.

Sources: Harris 2001, 27, 148–49, 250–51, 385; Bairoch 1988, 290, 302, 389, 400, 414, 428, 430, 459, 461, 495, 513; Bairoch 1990, 138–39, 143.

have risen in H form: once between 1850 and 1900, then again more steeply between 1900 and 1950. Since World War II, however, for "developed" countries in aggregate both total population and the proportion of it living in cities have expanded in the kind of G trends found for Europe and Russia (without the H shape for recent general demographic increase lingering in the United States or Australia and New Zealand)—and evident in the white and "coloured" populations of South Africa (Harris 2001, 83). The significance of industrial employment for "developed" countries, meanwhile, flattened out via G after 1950 generally parallel with further changes in total population and percentage urban. Only in GNP per capita did more persistent, H-type advance continue into the later decades of the 20th century. This phenomenon reflects the much-discussed enlarging role of "post-industrial" components in modern economies. More wealth has come from services and other non-manufacturing activity.

The market economies of Asia,[44] on the other hand, after parallel E-shape expansion of population and urbanization from the early 1900s into the 1960s or 1970s, have seen both these demographic developments shift into parallel H patterns instead. In this they have shared the trending for total demographic increase found in the United States and Australia, New Zealand, and South Africa, collectively, but taken up H-type *urbanization* as those countries no longer sustained it. Meanwhile, beginning after World War II, these Asian economies saw their GNP per capita begin to advance in H fashion, though not as steeply as in the longer-developed territories. Once again the contrasting H, G, and E patterns that are identified capture a well-known modern phenomenon, the emergence of "Little Tigers" and related Asian demonomic developments in recent decades.

Fragments of evidence from Bairoch, however, indicate quite different trendings for Japan, India, and China. Whereas Japan shared the E-type increases in population and urbanization of Asian market economies more generally during the early 20th century, multiple but quickly flattening out G-shape movements have been the pattern since the 1920s. In India, evidence on the percentage living in cities that Bairoch offers for the period 1850 through 1940 (1988, 400) escalates upward along an E trend parallel to that for the population of the country through the 1960s. Thereafter, India's population, ceasing to accelerate in growth via E, took up the kind of H path being followed in the United States and in Oceania since World War II (t_0's at 1947, 1939, and 1922, respectively)— if perhaps with less economic growth to support it in spite of visible development. China, by far the largest population among the planned economies of Asia, displays general demographic expansion since the founding of the People's Republic in comparable H form with zero year at 1923. This, exceptionally, represents the third successive trend of that shape in China, starting from the 1740s. Since the 1950s in Asia's planned economies, according to Bairoch (ibid., 513), urbanization has in contrast proceeded in delayed E manner, though from 1900 through 1950 it rose in H fashion, noticeably more steeply than the H trend for population growth in China from 1873 to 1937. To what extent has the vigor of Chinese society in the later 19th and early 20th centuries perhaps been misunderstood?

In another part of the recently developing area of the world, demographic increase for Latin America as a whole since the middle of the 20th century has been following an H path with base year around 1950, very much like the peoples of India, Asian market economies as a group, and also the United States, Table 4.7 shows. Across the first half of the 1900s, in contrast, an E of population explosion was the movement—as in many less developed societies elsewhere. In urbanization, however, the two successive G trends for the region instead most resemble the experience of Russia. Meanwhile, per capita GNP for Latin America rose only very flatly in E fashion across the 19th century. For the 20th century a second E trend captures the movement, putting most of the improvement in only quite recent years. E patterns in GNP do not appear elsewhere in the data that Bairoch offers. What has been so distinctive about the development of Latin American economies? Do the observed trends help to explain their chronic fragility?

Africa, meanwhile, has been urbanizing like Latin America, via two successive G trends since 1900. GNP per capita there also improved somewhat via one G movement to World War II and another since then, each less robust than the contemporary G for urbanization. The *population* of Africa, however, followed intercontinentally shared E-type explosion from 1920 or sooner into the 1960s followed by non-decelerating, log-linear growth in F form to the 1990s, though since then signs of incipient deceleration are showing. Perhaps by now this deceleration is taking a G shape rather than the H indicated by United Nations projections a decade ago, due in large part to the ravages of AIDS. Hopefully, the African population is not generally entering into the D-shape type of decline found for great medical disasters in history, such as the medieval plague or the exposure of New World peoples to unfamiliar diseases, whether in the Spanish conquest of America in the 16th century or in the invasion of the South Pacific in the 19th.

Fashionable generalizations about the Third World thus must be understood to embrace national or even continental movements that are quite distinct from each other. Considering the less developed parts of the globe in aggregate anyhow, for general population increase between 1900 and 1970, the E form of population explosion already encountered in several regional settings was not surprisingly the pattern. Since the middle of the 20th century, however, Third World demographic expansion as a whole has taken an H pattern almost identical to that for population increase in the United States. How well are that parallelism and its implications understood? To what extent is it the result of the way that large less-developed portions of the globe have become integrated peripherals for the core of the powerful U.S. economy? For instance, Bairoch's data from 1960 through 1980 suggest a current H trend of increase for the proportion of Third World workers engaged in industry, an activity losing momentum within the United States and other developed economies. Per capita

GNP, meanwhile, as of about 1950 began to increase in parallel H fashion, as the last line of Table 4.7 indicates. Previously, into the first half of the 20th century, industrial employment and GNP per person in the Third World had also grown somewhat together—but in G rather than H form.

Clues about the shape of demographic movements and their relationship to economic developments that have appeared in analyses of Europe from 1500 through 1800 prove helpful in delineating comparable processes of population increase, urbanization, and economic change right on into the 21st century. The literature often deals only with quite widely spread evidence; and (aside from population growth from Volume I) the recent patterns proposed here are based upon visual estimates, not actual fits of curves. With more and better data some trendings will change. The outlines that emerge, however, already cast some fresh light upon familiar and vital topics and should inspire research to test out and interpret the suggested connections and differences.

In all, it has been seen not only how individual cities grew and shrank historically almost universally in G and D form, as the first volume of this study demonstrated (Harris 2001, ch. 8), but how several other aspects of historical urbanization have evolved in G-related shapes and interacted with the demonomic environment. Such further perspective began in Chapter 3 with the recognition that the movement of people into cities takes the same G' form as other types of migration, free or bound, surveyed in Chapters 1 and 2. Just a different kind of local destination is involved.

As arrivals in this pattern accumulate in cities, moreover, the share of local population that is composed of former in-migrants increases in the G shape (which is G' integrated), steering local population increase toward the kind of G trend found everywhere in cities and decline into D form. Similarly, if one aggregates migration to several cities rather than just dealing with one, the G and D trends appear when local G' movements of different timing are combined, as in regional or national migration into cities or urbanization in an even broader sense.

Urban populations are noted for attracting and mixing people of many kinds. As one follows the role of particular groups such as ethnic types in a given city, "spot" migrations of a particular time can produce temporary G' impacts in the composition of the residents of a particular center. Once new generations of a "stock" become a factor and demographic replacement comes into play, however, the proportion of a city's population contained in a group waxes and wanes in more long-term, G-based forms: notably G increase and D decline, accompanied by some accelerating atrophy in C fashion here and there as a once-important sub-population is squeezed out by competition.

The records for both whole city populations and particular components of them like ethnic ones, meanwhile, hint that demographic composition, in cities and perhaps far more generally, also alters by sex, by age, and by rate of replacement in G-based forms. These clues from 18th-century Batavia, Ghent, and

Nottingham, Rouen and Geneva between the 1630s and 1800, and Edo (Tokyo) across the middle of the 19th century in Chapter 3 call for some systematic exploration for similar G-related phenomena among populations that are usually better documented in these respects than fluid and elusive urban ones. The challenge is taken up by the two chapters that complete this volume.

Meanwhile, beyond the individual city, collective *urbanization* has been seen to develop (or atrophy) in familiar and insightful G-related trends. Whether in modern nations like Sweden, Ireland, New Zealand, and the United States since 1800 (or a region of them such as America's Old Northwest), in particular provinces of the Netherlands across three centuries before that, in the tension between a London or an Amsterdam and lesser centers nearby, or in the evolution of the three countries that did most to drive the economic development of Europe across the long era from 1500 through 1800, collective city growth and the weight of city dwellers in the total population took G, H, D, and E paths. These patterns help explain how one region surged and another faded historically, as in the famous competition among the Netherlands, France, and England. Trending the part played by agricultural and rural non-agricultural subpopulations in these changes elucidates what urbanization of a given period entailed and how it related to certain much-discussed historical economic developments—for instance, internationally in northwestern Europe during the 16th, 17th, and 18th centuries or, more locally, in some rural parishes of England between 1600 and 1840. New insights emerge from fresh perceptions of the movements that were unfolding and carry still further forward recent fertile scholarship on these topics.

On an even wider stage, insightful G-based trends for how cities of various types and locations have expanded or contracted in different parts of Europe since the later 15th century present a clearer and stronger picture of how *international* urban *systems* evolved on this particular continent across the past half a millennium—and interacted with developments across the Atlantic. The shifting relationships of northern and Mediterranean Europe during various stages of historical change become clearer. So do the timing of comparative urbanization from region to region, the role of particular cities within this change, and shifts within countries as well as between them. Movements in the number of people resident in cities of various types, the proportion of the population of given countries that was urban, the relationships of developments in agriculture or industry with urbanization, the changing access of regional hubs to each other and to lesser centers, and the experiences of different types of cities within particular countries become clearer and better understood when G-related trends of change are recognized and compared. Meanwhile, because of certain movements that are found to be shared internationally, even globally, it has become likely that developments of these kinds have interacted with each other at least somewhat similarly (though in different timing) all around the world—since 1800 as well as before, right into the present time and certain projections that have been made for the future. It will be fascinating to see analysis of the sort explored in these chapters applied to systems of cities in Asia, in the Americas, perhaps in Africa, or wherever the data allow. Hopefully, such endeavors have been stimulated by the evidence and interpretation offered here, sketchy though the suggested outlines have often had to be.

In the meantime, what was it that repeatedly imprinted upon migrations to cities and to other destinations, and on the social and economic consequences of these movements, just a few shapes of change that are related to the G curve? One invaluable type of insight for addressing that question lies in the ways that the *structures* of populations, their *compositions* according to various measures, alter through time—in the processes of generating and digesting migrations but also more generally in demographic replacement.

NOTES

1. De Vries (1984) designates Scandinavia, England and Wales, Scotland, Ireland, the Netherlands, Belgium, Germany, France, Switzerland, Austria-Bohemia, and Poland as "North" and Northern Italy, Central Italy, Southern Italy, Spain, and Portugal as "Mediterranean," as his Table 3.8 reveals (45).

2. Within this southern group, Naples, Venice, Milan, and Palermo contained only about the same number of people in 1750 as they had in 1600 (de Vries 1984, 269–78). Madrid actually lost some inhabitants (Harris 2001, 304–5). Rome and Lisbon, in contrast, saw their populations rise by about half between 1600 and 1750 (de Vries, 1984, 269–78). While Lyon swelled to 97,000 up through 1700, this city's growth was also relatively flat from 1700 to 1800.

3. Compare Figures 3.11c and 3.11e.

4. Though the Swiss H for the years 1650–1750 gave way to a more rapidly decelerating G for the years 1700–1800, it appears. The growth of Zürich, for example, which had expanded 36 percent between 1700 and 1762, turned flat between 1762 and 1812 (Braun 1978, 294, 301).

5. Population increase of the E type also emerged in the other Atlantic rim countries of Iceland and Denmark by about 1730, though for these countries de Vries provides no separate urban data except for Copenhagen.

6. For his calculations, de Vries (1984, 154–59) adjusted the distance ingredient of this measure to reflect crucial advantages of water trade over land transportation during the early modern era.

7. A useful supplement to de Vries's very effective employment of maps (160–66).

8. Strasbourg, exposed to the Rhineland warfare of the early 1600s, and Nijmegen and 's Hertogenbosch, located in regions still being cleared of Spanish garrisons by the Dutch 1590–1604 (Israel 1998, 243).

9. Brno, Innsbruck, Vienna, and Warsaw; Lisbon, Porto, and Coimbra.

10. Freiburg, Heidelberg, Mannheim, Würzburg, Frankfurt, Cologne, Düsseldorf, Barmen, Elberfeld, Hanover, Altona, Hamburg, and Lübeck.

11. Danzig, Dresden, and Leipzig (the last only after major loss in the early 1600s) expanded; Stuttgart, Ulm, Augsburg, Munich, Nuremberg, and Bamberg shrank, as did Chemnitz, Erfurt, Bautzen, Magdeburg, Frankfurt-on-the-Oder, Stettin, and Elbing (near Danzig).

12. Bruges, Ghent, Antwerp, Mechelen, and Leuven (but not little Sint Niklaas) versus Ypres, Lille and Valenciennes (both still Spanish-held), Brussels, and Namur (without Mons and Tournai). Aalst saw no change. Liège and Dunkerque lack information at one of the critical dates.

13. Genoa, Milan, Turin, and Pavia versus Venice and most of its satellites, along with Parma, Piacenza, Mantua, and Brescia.

14. Embracing Florence, Leghorn, Siena, Pisa, Lucca, Rome, and Ancona.

15. Though other cities there continued to grow.

16. Avila, Burgos, Palencia, Valladolid, Salamanca, Medina del Campo, Segovia, Cuenca, Medina de Rio Seco, and Toledo. Volume I (Harris 2001, 304, 306) has demonstrated the robust G-shape expansion of Madrid between 1507 and 1630 with t_0 at 1612. Cuenca, meanwhile, lost much population between 1597 and 1644 via what might have been a D trend with t_0 near 1601 (ibid., 346–47).

17. Jerez de la Frontera, Seville, Cordoba, Jaen, Baeza, and Ubeda.

18. Counterclockwise, these were Cadiz, Antequera (behind Malaga), Murcia, Alicante, Valencia, Barcelona, and Santiago (in the northwest).

19. Palermo, Castelvetrano, and Trapani in the west; Messina, Nicosia, Enna, and Castrogiovanni in the east. Marsala, Girgenti, and Termine, however, gained inhabitants in the years 1650–1750, as did Acireale, Catania, Syracuse, Noto, Modica, and Ragusa along the eastern side of Sicily's triangle and Caltagirone, Caltonisetta, and Mazzarino in the eastern interior.

20. Cologne, Elberfeld, and Soest in the lower Rhine Valley; the North Sea ports of Hamburg and Emden (but not Altona); Freiburg in the southwest; and Danzig on the Baltic.

21. Innsbruck, Klagenfurt, Linz, Salzburg, and Vienna in Austria; also Brno, Prague, and Warsaw.

22. Bergen, Oslo, Copenhagen, Göteborg, Karlskrona, and Stockholm; Aberdeen, Dundee, Edinburgh, Glasgow, Greenock, Inverness, Paisley, and Perth; Belfast, Cork, Dublin, and probably also Waterford and Limerick.

23. Decay from Cambrai near Belgium through Bayeux and Rouen in Normandy to St. Malo in Brittany, Angers on the lower Loire, and the old Huguenot port of La Rochelle versus increase in Amiens, Le Havre, Cherbourg, Brest, and Nantes, and probably also Dieppe, Caen, and Rennes. Arles in Provence and Colmar in Alsace were the other two cities to lose inhabitants.

24. Barcelona, Cadiz, Murcia, and Bilbao. Alicante declined (probably in conjunction with atrophy of western Mediterranean markets in Sicily and Southern Italy), and the size of Valencia cannot be followed.

25. Aalst, Lier, Sint Niklaas, and Leuven.

26. See-sawing between primary and secondary hubs is a familiar historical topic. Lawrence Stone (1947, 103–20) reviewed how the growth of London-Antwerp trade under the Tudors bled formerly active centers of wool export like Boston and Winchester. Bernard Bailyn (1955), examining British colonies a century later, argued how the new Boston in Massachusetts squeezed back competitors like New Haven, Plymouth, Ipswich, and Portsmouth. If one follows the Boston story further, one encounters the 18th-century rise of Middletown, Newport, Providence, Marblehead, Newburyport, Porsmouth, and Falmouth (Portland) as Boston itself then stagnated from the 1740s until after the Revolution.

27. Wuppertal (originally Barmen and Elberfeld) multiplied by 20; and while the

numbers for Dortmund, Duisburg, Düsseldorf, and Essen were so small at 1750 as not to appear in de Vries's lists of leading cities, their rates of growth 1800–1850 (multiplying by more than twice in *half* a century) put them on course with the fast-expanding British dozen.

28. Not much change before and relatively weak growth after 1800 characterized The Hague, Rotterdam, Antwerp, Paris, Strasbourg, Lyon, Toulouse, Geneva, Zürich, Genoa, Milan, Florence, Hanover, Dresden, Gdansk, and Königsberg (the last two lying amid the earlier-starting Baltic zone of modern urban expansion). Somewhat stonger increase between 1800 and 1850 occurred in Brussels, Cologne, Stuttgart, Munich, and Nuremberg, and also in Leipzig and Breslau toward the east. Venice lost population in each half century, and Rome, Bologna, and Amsterdam stayed about the same size from 1750 to 1850—Rome because it lost population during the French occupation (Harris 2001, 305).

29. Urban population, as Table 4.1 shows, increased via the slowly decelerating H pattern up the middle of Europe in Central Italy, Northern Italy, Switzerland, Austria/Bohemia, Germany, Scandinavia, England and Wales, and Scotland.

30. Belgium displays two such downward adjustments.

31. In his conclusion (1984, 255–58), de Vries does note the relevance of problems experienced by the Spanish Hapsburgs in this era. An accessible, brief summary of the literature on periodization appears in Wallerstein 1980, 3–9.

32. Within the Netherlands, several provinces—including sites of the leading maritime centers—have been seen to become relatively less urban (Figure 3.9b), while Holland and Friesland, unlike the Dutch interior, saw even the absolute number of their urban dwellers atrophy between the 1670s and the 1790s (Figure 3.9a). Within France, costs of the Revolution (and the conditions that led to it) hit cities particularly hard in the later 18th century. Unlike de Vries (1984), who focused on cities of 10,000 or more inhabitants, however, Wrigley (1985)—working with all centers of 5,000 upwards—saw no decline in the urban proportion for France between 1750 and 1800 (Figure 3.10). Bigger cities seem to have borne the brunt. Embattled Poland suffered military damage and setbacks in external trade and other aspects of economic life that reduced urbanization in a somewhat earlier period, in the later 1600s, not unlike the Dutch province of Holland, whose merchants had featured so prominently in Baltic as well as oceanic trade.

33. The data of Wrigley (1985), at the 5,000 plus level and lacking an estimate for 1650 or 1550, do not indicate such a French trend (Figure 3.10).

34. Relocations to Brazil cannot currently be included before about 1700. Up through the 1590s, the covered migrations were virtually all Spanish.

35. Numbers relocating to Brazil are lacking for the 1600s in the European part of the equation and may make some difference. The flow to Spanish America, however, was clearly cut way back for the second half of the 1600s (Burkholder and Johnson 1994, 104).

36. A topic taken up elsewhere as part of a broad reexamination of trends in Atlantic prices. (Harris 1996 presents a sample of more local G-form price movements between the 1630s and the 1850s from the colonial perspective.)

37. The European aggregation is once again incomplete. Rough estimates for Portuguese going to Brazil are included: about 3,500 per year during the two opening gold rush decades of the 1700s and some 2,000 or fewer thereafter (Burkholder and Johnson 1994, 247); but now suitable estimates for Spanish America are lacking, though as of the late 18th century European immigration to New Spain and Peru is called "numerically

inconsequential," and the "flood of immigrants" that established Spanish population, especially in the cities, is described as having occurred "in a remarkably short time" after the conquest, which is what the data for 1506–1699 that are available and are included in our trending indicate (ibid., 264, 187, 104).

38. Or places of 5,000 plus 1600–1700 (Figure 3.11c).

39. With a tantalizing possible earlier exception (Harris 2001, 266) in a few provinces of China during the height of the Ming dynasty 1491–1578 and its flourishing material culture (Hebei, Shanxi, and Gansu in the north and Sichuan and Guizhou in the south).

40. Because his category "Mediterranean" combines all three zones of Italy with Spain and Portugal, the evidence of de Vries for that portion of Europe displays an E trend for the total urban population from 1650 to 1750 with a notably later t_0 at 1831 (Figure 4.1).

41. Also for over 20,000 in the Netherlands.

42. For the Netherlands, with a high level of urbanization but delayed population increase in E form, no *contemporaneous* E-shape rise in the number of urban residents appeared. The *proportion* of the Dutch population living in centers of 5,000 or more, however, fairly certainly rose from 1750 through 1815 in E fashion toward the regionally familiar zero year in the 1860s, while the percentage of people who were resident in larger centers of 20,000 or more took a rather later E track with t_0 in the early 1900s (Figure 3.10). The role of *smaller* centers expanded more robustly in Dutch urbanization of this era.

43. By the 19th century the importation of foodstuffs complicates the analysis, as it did in maritime Holland in the 1500s and early 1600s with the rise of the Baltic grain trade. Recent work by Gregory Clark (2001, 496) confirms how from the 1770s (or perhaps earlier) through the first decade of the 1800s all real wages in England (including agricultural ones) gained relative to wages strictly in farming along something like an E path with t_0 in the vicinity of 1845. This, of course, was a period of constant warfare for Britain as well as one of significant economic development. His data from the North and the Midlands and from the Southeast and the Southwest, however, show such movement to be rooted in changes of much longer term. From 1675 to 1805 real agricultural wages in the two largely non-industrial southern regions on average declined via a C trend with t_0 somewhere around 1850. In the industrial Midlands and the North, in contrast, real wages *rose* via an E trend with its zero year also about 1850—a virtually perfectly offsetting movement. (Each series, though, displays a temporary G' hump in real wages between 1725 and 1755 with peak around 1740.) The industrializing part of the country, in other words, shows rising wage pressure imprinted upon agriculture by the demand for factory labor. The largely rural south displays just the opposite. This analysis is carried further elsewhere.

44. As opposed to planned economies. Including Japan and India but not China.

Chapter 5

Stabilizing the Exceptional? Demographic Dimensions of Slavery and Slaving

The numbers of people in various *parts* of populations, not just the total, have previously been seen to increase and decline along trends connected with the fundamental G curve.[1] Preceding discussion here, meanwhile, has demonstrated how various kinds of migration—free or forced, including urbanization—have likewise altered repeatedly in such G-based forms historically. The implication from these findings is that the *compositions* of populations also change via this small, closely related set of G-related patterns, a phenomenon that Chapters 3 and 4 document for a few cities and urban-related developments in several locations. Does the broader demographic record confirm that structural change in populations very generally takes just G-based forms? And what do we learn if this is so? Introduced by Leonard Euler in 1760 and rediscovered and developed by Alfred J. Lotka and R. R. Kuczynski in the early 20th century, how populations "stabilize" as they renew themselves through births and deaths has, for instance, been a central and fertile topic of demography.[2]

There are several perspectives on this kind of internal demographic change that merit examination. On the one hand, how does the weight of various new groups as a proportion of a population alter, say, free immigrants of various types, or perhaps slaves when these have been introduced? Further, how does the rate at which such new entrants come into a population relative to its current size change with time as the characteristics of existing residents evolve? The structures of populations by sex and age are known to have shifted historically, and so has the composition of migration flows. How are these changes connected to each other through the processes of demographic maturity or adjustment? In such dynamics of stabilization or normalization for populations, and what has been called "naturalization" for peoples resettling into them, would seem to lie valuable insights concerning how G-type change keeps recurring throughout so many different aspects of demographic development and related processes of economic and social change.

As valuable property, during the early modern era slaves were often identified more informatively than were free persons of no particular distinction. Work on the growth of black and white populations in Chapter 3 of the previous volume of this study (Harris 2001) and the data upon which Chapter 2 here has been constructed together provide evidence with which to explore and relate to each other the characteristics of slave populations and the composition of the forced migration that continued to feed these often largely non-replacing peoples. How slaves became substantial, frequently overwhelming, parts of certain New World populations can be followed. So can the rate of continuing importation that was needed to attain those patterns of growth and also the inputs of men, women, and children that composed these flows. Paths of change in net natural decrease can be estimated, if only by implication, to show how—while slaves mostly did not reproduce themselves fully—at least a *reduction* in dependence upon further imports occurred as net natural decrease ameliorated.

Evidence on how the demography of slave populations and the slaving that relentlessly kept feeding them interacted comes from the British, French, Dutch, and Spanish West Indies, from the colonies of British North America and the United States to which they gave birth, and from some export flows out of Africa. Together, these insights begin to sketch out a blueprint of how the structures of populations change, a guide for interpretation that can then be applied and tested in other, less unusual historical contexts of demographic development.

GOING BLACK—AND BACK: TRENDS FROM ADOPTING AND ABANDONING SLAVERY

The slave importations outlined in Chapter 2 interacted with the kinds of losses of European settlers that are sketched out in Chapters 3 and 4 of the previous volume of this study (Harris 2001) to alter decisively the composition of populations of plantation colonies of the New World—from their early beginnings with European investors and servants, through the heyday of plantation slavery in the 1700s, then to and past the point where the slave trade began to wind down in the early 19th century. These societies became overwhelmingly Africanized. How that metamorphosis took place across some two dozen colonies is summarized in Table 5.1.[3]

During their opening decades several West Indian colonies plunged into African slavery very abruptly. Jumps in the proportion of the local population that was black between 1650 and 1660 are evident from some examples in Figure 5.1a: for Barbados (from 36 to 59 percent) and Martinique (from 40 to 58 percent) as early European settlers and their servants died or left the islands for better opportunities and increasingly prosperous planters could afford to turn to

Table 5.1

Trends in the Africanization of 25 West Indian Populations and Mauritius (percentage of total who were not white)

Colony	Colonizer	Period	Type/Year	Period	Type/Year	Period	Type/Year
St. Christopher I	English	1670-1730	G 1601	II 1730-1830	G 1678		
Martinique I	French	1660-1710	G 1616	II 1710-1780	G 1656		
St. Domingue I	French	1690-1760	G 1624?	II 1750-1780	?C 1850*		
Guadeloupe I	French	1650-1720	G 1630	II 1720-1780	G 1666		
Barbados	English	1660-1830	G 1625				
Jamaica	English	1700-1780	G 1634				
Guiana	Dutch	1690-1780	G 1625				
St. Croix I	French/Danish	1650-1690	G 1641	II 1690-1730	D 1644#	III 1755-1815	G 1674
Antigua	English	1690-1780	G 1646	II 1690-1780			
Cayenne I	French	1650-1680	G 1651	II 1690-1740	G 1659		
St. Christopher	French	1670-1700	G 1659				
Bermuda	English	1650-1780	G 1657				
Montserrat I	English	1680-1720	G 1657	II 1730-1780	G 1655	III 1780-1830	G 1697
Nevis I	Eng./Fr./Eng.	1660-1740	G 1662	II 1750-1780	C 1846*	III 1780-1830	G 1729
St. Thomas I	Danish	1680-1770	G 1667	II 1770-1815	C 1857*		
Dominica	French/Eng.	1710-1830	G 1668				
Grenada & Grens.	French/Eng.	1700-1830	G 1669				
Tobago	French/Eng.			II 1770-1830	G 1665		
Bahamas I	English	1720,1730	?G 1694	II 1740-1770	G 1695	III 1770-1810	G 1751
British Virgins	English	1700-1830	G 1693				
St. John	Danish	1720-1770	G 1692	II 1780-1815	G 1708		
St. Lucia	French/Eng.			II 1772-1830	G 1706		
Mauritius	French	1767-1817	G 1696				
St. Vincent	French/Eng.			I 1740-1770	C 1817*	II 1770-1830	G 1716
Trinidad	Spanish/Eng.					II 1799-1830	G 1722
Cuba All Non-White	Spanish					1768-1841	G 1730?
Cuba Slaves	Spanish					1774-1817	G 1744?
P. Rico All Black	Spanish					1802-1836	G 1742?
P. Rico Slaves	Spanish					1802-1836	C 1782?
P. Rico Free Black	Spanish					1802-1836	C 1866*
P. Rico All Non-Wh.	Spanish					1802-1836	C 1872*

* = C-type declines; # = D-type decline.

Sources: McCusker 1970, 2: 600–711; Deerr 1950, 2: 278–81; Higman 1984, 77; Hall 1992, 5; John 1988, 40.

Figure 5.1a
Percentage of Non-Whites in Some West Indian Populations: Barbados, Bermuda, Nevis, Martinique, Guadeloupe, and St. John

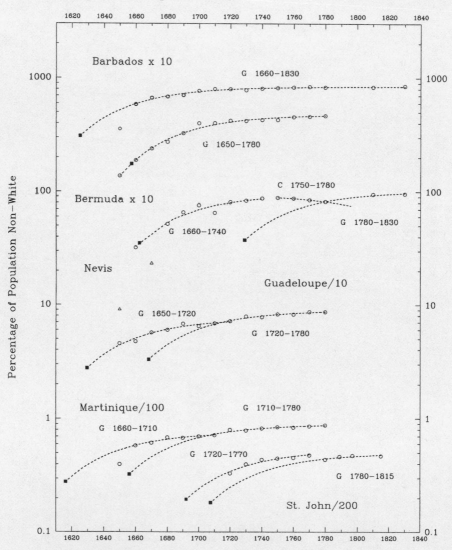

Sources: McCusker 1970, 2: 696, 699, 704, 707, 708, 711; Higman 1984, 77; Hall 1992, 5.

the Atlantic slave trade for their labor. Comparable jumps can be found for Antigua, Montserrat, and both the English and the French portions of St. Christopher in Figures 5.1b and 5.1c. Higman (2000, 230) has just recently reemphasized how abrupt the "sugar revolution" with its shift to slave labor was in some places. Beckles and Downes (1987, 228) have shown how just between 1639–1640 and 1641–1643 slaves jumped from 0 percent of total bound labor on recorded Barbadian estates to 32 percent, and then to 98 percent by 1650–1657. These colonies began in the 1620s and 1630s with virtually no slaves at all.[4] Elsewhere—as on English Bermuda and in St. Croix, Cayenne, and Guadeloupe under the French—gradual, sustained G-shape transitions in demographic composition began as early as 1650. Even in those plantation settlements most abruptly committing to slavery, moreover, within a decade or two of when records begin, local dynamics were channeling change in the proportion of the population that was black into sustained G trends. The initial leap into slavery, that is, however abrupt, was soon stabilized or normalized into a standard form for further change. Across several decades these G trends then took the share of people with African origin progressively from about half to more like 85 to 95 percent. It is important to comprehend how that "steering" into the G path of change came about and how it worked.

G trends for the rising percentage of blacks in the colonial populations covered in Table 5.1 had the earliest base years, and by the later 1600s portrayed most Africanized conditions, in the core colonies for producing tropical crops, especially sugar. The landowners of these territories plunged soonest and most completely into that form of labor. The post-1658 slave workforce of Jamaica was largely brought there by established planters from the seminal English sugar colony of Barbados who transplanted their operations onto the larger island under the leadership of Sir Thomas Modyford (Dunn 1972, 82, 154). Apparently much the same was true for the sugar culture of St. Domingue relative to French beginnings on Martinique and Guadeloupe, once this form of planting began to replace the tobacco growing employing white servants that led the initial agricultural development of that large colony (Price 1973, 1: 77–78). Hence, the further development of the slave populations of these substantial newer holdings tended to follow the G tracks of their "home" islands. Much the same was probably the case for Dutch Guiana. Colonists from the Netherlands had been directly active in the expansion of sugar cultivation and slavery in northeastern Brazil since the 1630s, and indirectly even earlier through the country's smaller but pivotal trading bases in the Caribbean. The first enduring English settlement of all in the West Indies took root upon one part of St. Christopher.

For the French who colonized the rest of the island, in contrast, a significantly higher proportion of the population was black by the turn of the century, more like 90 percent than 70 percent, though via a delayed G path based at 1659. Such later-timed G curves also characterized other French possessions (Table 5.1): St. Croix and Cayenne (French Guiana), where the slave populations, though substantial by the 1650s, took longer to dominate the local scene. Slower

Figure 5.1b
Percentage of Non-Whites in Some West Indian Populations: Other British Possessions

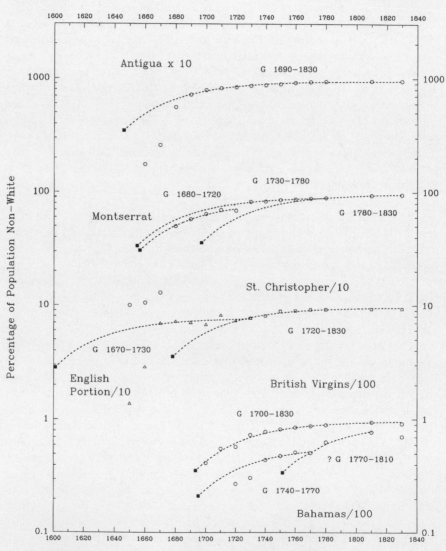

Sources: McCusker 1970, 2: 694, 697, 695, 693, 703; Higman 1984, 77.

Figure 5.1c
Percentage of Non-Whites in Some West Indian Populations: Some Other Sugar Colonies

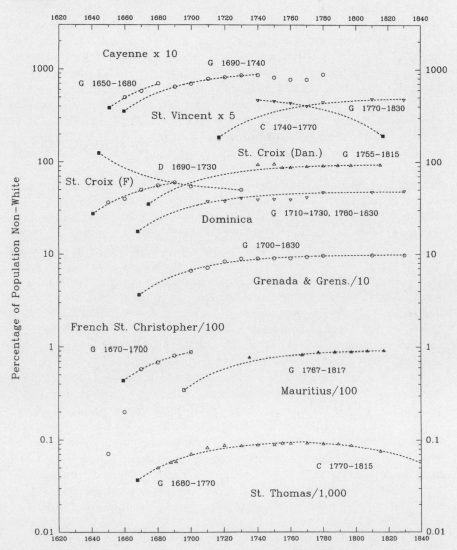

Sources: McCusker 1970, 2: 600, 700, 709, 698, 701, 706, 710; Deerr 1950, 2: 280; Higman 1984, 77; Hall 1992, 5.

transition also was the experience for the British holdings of Bermuda (where, as Figure 5.1a shows, blacks amounted to only 45 percent of the population in the 1700s) and Antigua, Montserrat, and Nevis (where local circumstances delayed, but ultimately did not reduce, a demographic takeover by slaves that approximated 90 percent by 1750 or so).[5] Later, 18th-century increases for the weight of Africans in the populations of Martinique and Guadeloupe, Cayenne, and Montserrat—and St. Croix, now controlled by Denmark—also took G paths with t_0's around the middle of the 1600s, joined by the first recorded trends of Africanization for French Dominica, Grenada, and Tobago and Danish St. Thomas. Still later timing characterized the G-shaped transitions for the Bahamas (where the slave proportion of the population stabilized at just one-half), the British Virgins, St. John, St. Lucia, and Indian Ocean Mauritius, where blacks before long came to more like 90 to 95 percent of the total inhabitants—a timing of G joined by new change on Caribbean Montserrat after 1780.

In a still more delayed G-shaped surge of transition, as Table 5.1 demonstrates, the populations of Cuba, Santo Domingo, and Puerto Rico became more and more Africanized as further expansion for the international sugar industry depended increasingly upon these large Spanish islands. Trinidad, as the British took over, followed a comparable pattern. Sketchy data for Santo Domingo at 1766 and 1794 suggest that both the total non-white population and the slave population there grew in relative importance roughly parallel to better-documented developments on Cuba and the rise of all blacks within the population of Puerto Rico (Deerr 1949, 2: 278–81). The weight of just slaves within Puerto Rican society, however, probably expanded according to a still tardier G trend. In these later-developing and less overwhelmingly Africanized Spanish holdings *all* non-whites amounted to just about half to two-thirds and slaves only one-third or less of the total population even at the height of slave imports and the expansion of sugar production. But the way that the composition of these populations, including various shadings of color and legal status, evolved took G forms as consistently as in the most mono-cultural sugar colonies of the West Indies, whose slaves swelled to 95 percent or more of the local population.

It is also possible in Table 5.1, finally, to distinguish how people of African origin started to become *less* important parts of a few West Indian populations in the later 18th century. Several slowly commencing but downwardly accelerating C trends appear: temporarily for the black proportion on Nevis (from 89 to 82 percent between 1750 and 1780), on Danish St. Thomas between 1770 and 1815 (falling from 91 to 75 percent), and perhaps in parallel timing (at least to 1780) even for notorious St. Domingue (though various combinations of racially mixed sub-populations there may blur the picture). Proportional decline for free blacks and all non-whites on Puerto Rico developed rather less precipitously but is traceable through 1836. Noticeably steeper was the shift away from persons of African descent on French St. Vincent—from 93 to 81 percent between 1740 and 1770, before the new English occupiers began to beef up the island's slave population again. And on St. Croix the share of the population with African origins fell via a D trend from about 60 percent at 1690 to 50 percent by 1730 before the discouraged French sold the island to the Danes, who quickly jacked up the weight of slaves to more than 90 percent in their quest to build a niche in the market for tropical produce.

Uniformly across these 26 populations, however—in evidence stretching from the 1650s to the 1840s—G was the path followed by increases in the proportion of inhabitants who had African origins in some form. In a few places, meanwhile, clues appear that the process could reverse, with the proportion of people of color usually declining via C, G reversed with respect to time.

On the North American mainland, too, slavery first took hold and then weakened its grip in similar G-connected patterns. Table 5.2 and Figures 5.2a, 5.2b, and 5.2c display successive surges of increase in G form as colonies or states most involved in slavery established black sub-populations. Then a sequence of C trends emerges, mostly but not entirely following the Civil War, along which African Americans became a smaller and smaller part of local totals as white in-migration and black out-migration occurred—and also changes in relative fertility and mortality. In the most recent two or three decades, finally—just since 1970 or 1980—there is a hint that the relative atrophy of the black population across the previous hundred years in the former slave states is reversing upward in slow but accelerating E fashion, a shift that may have ominous implications for those who have bet their political futures upon a white South.

At present there still linger some uncertainties about black proportions within the early populations of the plantation colonies on the mainland. On the basis of local data on labor (to be published elsewhere), Menard's assumption that the composition of Virginia's population by race was the same as that for the mostly younger Maryland settlements up through 1730 appears uncertain (1980, 157–66). Still, he and Sutherland are close enough concerning the very small Virginia proportions from 1650 through 1680 (2.1 to 7.0 percent) to plot and trend his estimations for Figure 5.2b and Table 5.2. The result takes a G pattern from 1640 through 1680 with t_0 at 1665 having a level of about 5 percent. This trend indicates that slavery was expanding in Virginia parallel with the proportional Africanization of lesser West Indian colonies (see French St. Christopher through Tobago in Table 5.1, with base years for their opening G curves from 1657 through 1669), but at a much lower *level* even than Bermuda, where the proportion was not 5 but more like 17 percent near 1660. To date, only watered-down Africanization lapped at the distant shores of the Chesapeake. Still, it encroached much in the way that British slavery elsewhere extended its demographic grip.

Figure 5.2a incorporates Menard's recalculations for Maryland through 1730, which reduce Sutherland's excessively high implications (3.4 to 9.5 percent) through 1680 to a more plausible scale (1.7 to 7.3 percent). How to trend the very small Maryland percentages up through 1680, though, is left for further refinement and analysis of local data (which is currently under way). From there

Table 5.2
Changing Proportions of African Americans in Some Mainland Colonies/States

Column:	(1)	(2)	(3)	(4)	(5)	(6)	(7)	(8)
Virginia	1640-1680 G 1665	1690-1830 G 1691			1830-1870 C 1918	1870-1920 C 1946	1930-1970 C 1992	1970-1998 E 2066
Maryland	?	1680-1730 G 1692	1730-1810 G 1716		1810-1860 G 1880	1870-1920 C 1950	1920-1950 C 2059	1970-1998 G 1961
South Carolina		1670-1740 G 1692	1720-1790 C 1812	1800-1890 G 1765		1890-1930 C 1961	1930-1970 C 1988	1970-1998 C 2104
North Carolina			1700-1770 G 1732	1790-1880 G 1756		1880-1920 D 1848	1920-1970 C 2003	1970-1998 C 2128
Georgia		1770-1790 D 1748	1800-1820 G 1771 1820-1840 D 1760	1840-1880 G 1786		1880-1920 C 1979	1930-1960 C 1993	1970-1998 E 2060
Kentucky			1780-1800 G 1744	1810-1840 G 1775	1840-1870 C 1886	1870-1920 C 1931	1910-1950 D 1899	1950-1998 G 1849
Tennessee				1790-1880 G 1788		1880-1920 C 1949	1920-1950 C 1990	1970-1998 E 2081
Alabama				1820-1870 G 1795		1870-1930 C 1964	1930-1970 C 1997	1980-1998 E 2106
Mississippi				1820-1900 C 1779		1900-1920 C 1966	1930-1970 C 1997	1980-1998 E 2070
Louisiana						1810-1930 C 1959	1930-1970 C 2010	1980-1998 E 2049
Arkansas				1820-1900 G 1811			1900-1980 C 1996	1980-1998 ?
Texas				1850-1870 G 1803		1870-1900 D 1858	1900-1990 D 1882	
Florida						1830-1950 C 1956	1940-1980 D 1939	1990-1998 up
Missouri					1830-1870 D 1859	1880-1910 D 1860	1910-1940 G 1888	1940-1998 G 1928

Sources: Historical Statistics 2: 1168; 1: 24–36; *Statistical Abstracts* 1981, 32; 1991, 24; 1999, 34; Menard 1980, 157–66; 1989, Table 1; P. Morgan 1998, 61.

Figure 5.2a
Percentage of Blacks in Some Colonies/States of British North America: Maryland, South Carolina, Tennessee, Alabama, Louisiana, and Texas

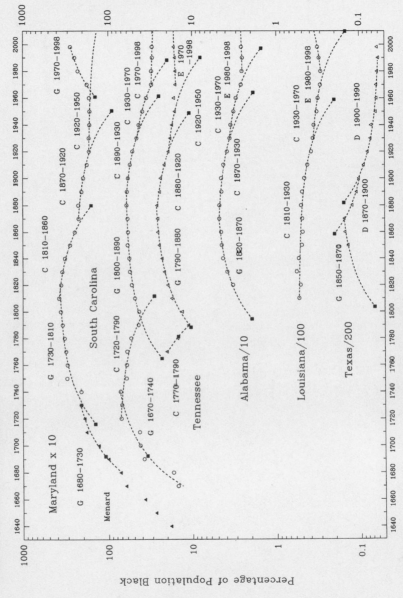

Sources: Historical Statistics 2: 1168; 1: 24–36; Menard 1980, 157–66; 1989, Table 1; P. Morgan 1998, 61; *Statistical Abstracts* 1981, 32; 1999, 34.

Figure 5.2b

Percentage of Blacks in Some Colonies/States of British North America: Virginia, North Carolina, Georgia, and Mississippi

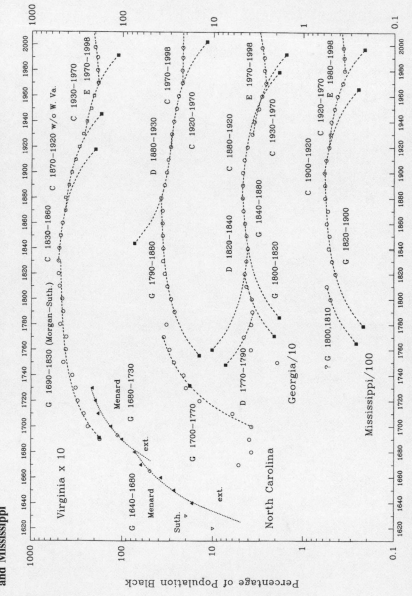

Sources: Historical Statistics 2: 1168; 1: 24–36; Menard 1980, 157–66; *Statistical Abstracts* 1981, 32; 1991, 22; 1998, 34; P. Morgan 1998, 61.

Figure 5.2c
Percentage of Blacks in Some Colonies/States of British North America: Missouri, Kentucky, Florida, and Arkansas

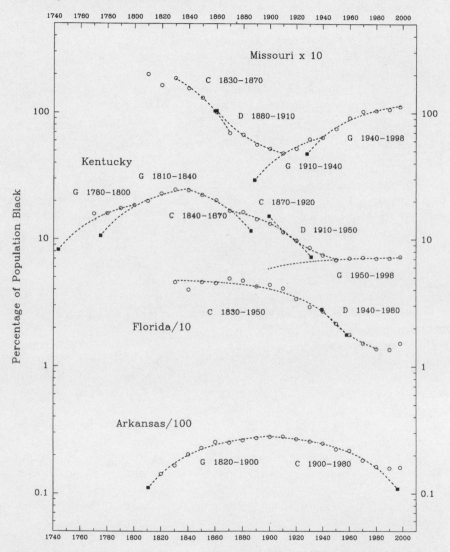

Sources: *Historical Statistics* 2: 1168; 1: 24–36; *Statistical Abstracts* 1981, 32; 1991, 22; 1999, 34.

to 1730, Menard's improved estimates follow the form of a G curve with base year at 1692. That makes the Africanization of Maryland for this half century parallel to changes in Virginia over the long haul between 1690 and 1830 (hollow circles with t_0 at 1691),[6] the difference being that the level in the early 1690s was 11 percent in Maryland in contrast to more like 17 percent in Virginia, the earlier plantation colony of the Chesapeake. Meanwhile, marginal Caribbean settlements that had parallel G trends with t_0's also in the 1690s, such as the Bahamas, the British Virgins, and St. John, had populations that were already 21, 36, and 20 percent black, respectively, at that point. The colonies of the Chesapeake, nonetheless, began to experience along with them a moderately higher level of Africanization. Further G-type gain in the proportion of blacks from 1730 through 1810, whose t_0 came only at 1716 (Table 5.2), then raised the share of inhabitants of African origin in Maryland afresh—to almost 40 percent by 1800, though this still remained below the Virginia level of more like 50 percent (and a weight approaching 95 percent in many of the West Indian colonies).

Further south, meanwhile, the proportion of the population of North Carolina that was African in origin rose in rather later G shape from 1700 to the Revolution, mounting from about 4 to 35 percent (Figure 5.2b). This way it reached the level for Maryland but along a curve dated at 1732 rather than 1716 (the third column of Table 5.2).

As is well known, among the British mainland colonies it was South Carolina that most aggressively packed in slaves. Sutherland's calculations in *Historical Statistics* (2: 1168, Series Z 16, and 1: 34, Series A 195 and A 200) for South Carolina from 1670 through 1700 and from 1740 through 1800 still seem appropriate. In between, the trending of Figure 5.2a employs the recent revisions of P. Morgan (1998, 61). For 1730 and especially 1720 these run somewhat higher than Menard's estimations (1989, Table 1); but both sets of calculations indicate that from 1670 through 1740, along a G curve with t_0 near 1692, about 72 percent of the population there became black by the time of the Stono Rebellion, when coastal rice cultivation most thoroughly dominated the life of the colony. The trend of change for South Carolina, in other words, closely paralleled the decelerating G paths of Africanization identified in Virginia and Maryland in the same period but rose at an appreciably higher level—34 percent at t_0, as if the eventual local maximum would be about 95 percent, the level for the most intense sugar colonies of the West Indies. After about 1730, however, C-shape *decline* in the proportion of blacks occurred in South Carolina as settlers of European stock, who had been migrating down the Piedmont through western Virginia and North Carolina in large numbers, more and more heavily infested South Carolina's interior. The life of the colony was no longer so dominated by its coastal rice plantations. Meanwhile, the weight of slaves in the population of nearby Georgia (Figure 5.2b) also diminished in the era of the Revolution, but in D rather than C pattern. It then rose briefly with the cotton boom of the early 19th century, only to fall off in D shape again with the 1819 crash and as

Georgia's new, enlarged post-Revolutionary interior was energetically settled by land-hungry whites. A level of about 44 percent of African Americans was reached around 1820, approximately the same proportion of slaves that the Georgia population had held in 1770, while the colony in effect was an extension of Carolina coastal plantation culture.

As of 1840 Georgia joined the two Carolinas and several new territories of the South in fresh G-type increase for the share of the population that was black. For the Carolinas the base year of these curves was around 1760 (the fourth column of Table 5.2); for Georgia, Kentucky, Tennessee, and Missisippi it sat around the early 1780s; for Alabama, that kind of trend through the Civil War had its t_0 only at 1795.[7] Arkansas (Figure 5.2c) and Texas (Figure 5.2a), across the Missisippi River, followed along with G's based in the early 1800s. The maximum percentage of the African American population reached in these states by mid-century ranged from 25 in Kentucky, Tennessee, and Arkansas to 30 to 36 percent in Texas and North Carolina, 45 percent in Alabama and Georgia, and 55 to 59 percent in Missisippi and South Carolina.

In the meantime, however—starting well before the Civil War (the fifth column of Table 5.2)—slaves were beginning to amount to smaller shares of the populations of some southern states, as they had in South Carolina across the second half of the 1700s before Cotton became King. The C trend for Maryland began as early as 1810 (Figure 5.2a), a downward trajectory that the composition of Kentucky's population acquired at 1840 (Figure 5.2c). In Missouri (also Figure 5.2c), the decline was steeper, along a C path headed for a base point of the formula at 1859. This lowered the weight of blacks there from 19 to just 7 percent as settlers of European origin poured into the state. In Virginia the decline was flatter, from 50 percent at 1830 just to 42 percent at 1870; but the downwardly accelerating C trajectory headed toward a t_0 at 1918 is clear (Figure 5.2b). Virginia, of course, lost a substantial amount of dissenting population and territory through the formation of West Virginia during the Civil War. Maryland, Kentucky, and Missouri—while each containing strong groups of Confederate sympathizers—frustrated hopes that they would secede from the Union. The structural change of these four populations across the decades before 1861 presaged which way these border regions would be likely to fall with the outbreak of the Civil War. In each location slavery was losing relative importance.

From very early on, Louisiana, too, had experienced a declining weight of African Americans in her population compared with the very high levels (around 55 percent) with which this bottom tip of the Purchase entered the United States at the beginning of the 1800s (Figure 5.2a). More and more whites were drawn to the thriving outlet of the Mississippi Valley, balancing off the early arrival of planters with large slave-holdings who came to grow sugar and cotton in the rich river silt. This C trend continued all the way through the 1920s, bringing the proportion of blacks down to 39 percent in a final rush that sent many north (taking their music with them). Similarly, the percentage of the African American population for Florida (Figure 5.2c) fell in an enduring C pattern from near

50 to just 22 percent between 1830 and 1950 as more whites moved there and many blacks migrated out.

These C trends through the later 1800s and early 1900s toward t_0's in the 1950s had parallels or near parallels in eight other southern states, as the sixth column of Table 5.2 shows. Kentucky, Virginia, Maryland, and Tennessee display C curves of somewhat earlier timing; proportions for African Americans in South Carolina, Alabama, Mississippi, and Georgia run downward rather later. Then another wave of C declines, headed for t_0's near the end of the 20th century and lasting on average from the 1920s to around 1970, appeared in Virginia, Maryland, both Carolinas, Georgia, Tennessee, Alabama, Missisippi, Louisiana, and Arkansas (the seventh column of the table). During these two eras, a few southern states saw their African American proportions shrink in D rather than C form. Such a pattern occurred in North Carolina, Texas, and Missouri across the years just before and after 1900, then in Texas again and Kentucky beginning in the early 1900s and in Florida following World War II. Florida, of course, received a flood of white retirees and other sun-seekers. Texas was boom country both between 1870 and 1900 and for most of the 20th century, likewise drawing in large numbers of whites. What made North Carolina, Missouri, and Kentucky less African American in D rather than C fashion during their respective eras of such change is less obvious, but apparently worth some exploration.

Finally, across very recent decades the populations of most southern states have become relatively *more* black. Only in the Carolina bastions of Jesse Helms and Strom Thurmond have new C-type declines emerged (the last, rightmost column of Table 5.2). In Virginia, Tennessee, Georgia, Alabama, Mississippi, and Louisiana, in contrast, gradual but *accelerating* increase of E shape in the weight of African Americans seems to have developed. In the meantime, the erstwhile border states of Maryland, Kentucky, and Missouri display G-form rises in the percentages of their populations who are black—the type of pattern found in the 1900s in non-southern states like Michigan, Illinois, and California; and upturns of as yet indeterminate pattern have just appeared in Florida and perhaps Texas. New meaning is given to "the South shall rise again."

Looking at the West Indian and mainland data together, it is evident that in 40 American societies in which African slavery achieved importance in the 17th, 18th, or 19th centuries its permeation of the population repeatedly followed G form. In the earliest years, most notably as sugar and slavery were installed during the middle of the 1600s in what were thought to be propitious settings, proportional shifts toward blacks in still small populations took abrupt, often idiosyncratic form. But *everywhere* these original, economically driven decisions soon became subject to a standard regime of G-shaped demographic change. Additional Africanization, on average—even where the most aggressive initial conversion to sugar had occurred—then further doubled the percentage of blacks across several decades of steady change in the G pattern, and *just* the G pattern.

How did this convergence to a universal form of trend take place in the competition of two peoples and the two labor systems in which they engaged? Several slave populations whose inner workings are at least partially known can be employed to dig out some more insight on this point.

Evidence from the erstwhile plantation regions of the United States, meanwhile, confirms in Table 5.2 what the movements of a few Caribbean colonies hinted in Table 5.1: that with declining commitment to slavery (or a subsequent infusion of whites for some reason) *reductions* in the proportion of blacks within a population *also* took G-based forms—most frequently the downwardly accelerating C pattern. The roles of black out-migration and white in-migration and movements in fertility and mortality in mostly generating such C trends, rather than the D-type alternative that occasionally appeared, seem worth careful exploration where the data allow. So do the dynamics that have produced G and E forms of rise for African American proportions in modern times, including improving health and differential fertility as well as migration to find work.

GROWTH, CONTINUING IMPORTATION, AND PARTIAL SELF-REPLACEMENT IN SLAVE SOCIETIES

For several colonies or groups of colonies, at least a few particulars are known about how the size and composition of local black or mixed populations evolved and the way that slave imports fed them. These fragments of insight can be frustratingly incomplete. Nonetheless, they begin to reveal the underlying demographic dynamics that channeled change in the structure of Africanizing populations so simply and so regularly into G-based forms.

Figure 5.3 begins with what is known of the leading territories of the 17th- and 18th-century British West Indies: principally Barbados, Jamaica, and the Leewards. On these islands collectively,[8] from 1650 through 1700 the number of non-whites multiplied in G form with t_0 at 1682 (McCusker 1970, 2: 712; 766, note 658). Then from 1700 through 1760 it grew in H fashion with base year also at 1682. Finally, McCusker's estimates indicate G-form expansion for all non-whites from 1760 to 1780 with t_0 at 1753, while Michael Craton's calculations (1975, 275) suggest a fairly parallel G trend for a somewhat smaller aggregate *slave* population from 1770 all the way to 1830 that has its base year close by at 1760.[9]

With such growth in the non-white population and substantial loss of whites during the later 17th century (Harris 2001, 71), the percentage of inhabitants who had some African origins first surged via a G' curve from 1650 through 1680 with a peak at 1688 as the planters of island after island jumped into slave-powered sugar cultivation during the middle of the 17th century (Figures 5.1a and 5.1b). Then, from the 1670s through 1770s, the proportion of non-whites in the aggregate population of the British Caribbean expanded more gradually and enduringly in a G pattern with t_0 at 1647. The kind of trend sequence that was involved can be seen in the top plot of Figure 5.4 for the French Caribbean,

Figure 5.3

Changes in the Non-White Population of the British West Indies, 1638–1830

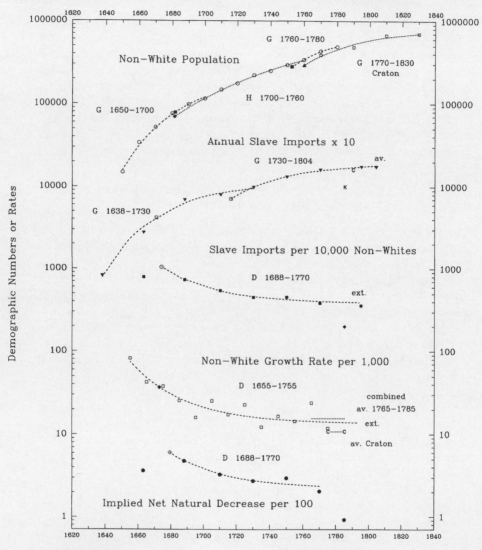

C = Craton; K = Klein.

Sources: McCusker 1970, 2: 712; Klein 1999, 210–11; Craton 1975, 275.

Figure 5.4
Changes in the Non-White Population of the French West Indies, 1638–1785

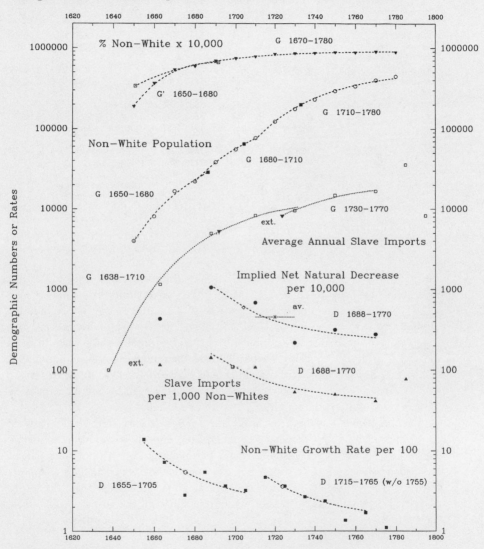

Sources: McCusker 1970, 2: 712; 1: 600; Klein 1999, 210–11.

Table 5.3
Comparing Trends of Growth and Naturalization in the African Populations of the British, French, and Dutch West Indies

Type of Change	British		French		Dutch	
Rate of Net Natural Decrease	1663,1688	rise	1663,1688	rise	1688,1710	rise
	1688-1770 D	1679	1688-1770 D	1704	1730-1770 D	1747
Slave Imports per Non-White Pop.	1688-1770 D	1674	1688-1770 D	1699	1688-1730 D	1690
					1750,1770 ?D	1746
Growth Rate of Non-White Pop.	1655-1785 D	1673	1655-1705 D	1675	1695-1735 D	1711
			1715-1765 D	1724	1745-1765 D	1713
Number of Non-Whites	1650-1700 G	1682	1650-1680 G	1686		
	1700-1760 H	1682	1680-1710 G	1704	1690-1740 G	1717
	1760-1830 G	1757	1710-1780 G	1733	1740-1787 H	1733
Annual Slave Imports	1638-1730 G	1671	1638-1710 G	1693	1663-1770 G	1688
	1730-1804 G	1716	1730-1770 G	1724		
% Population Not White	1650-1680 G'	1688	1650-1680 G'	1691	?	
	1670-1780 G	1647	1670-1780 G	1651	1690-1780 G	1613
					1665-1780 G	1625?

Sources: Figures 5.3, 5.4, and 5.5

the composition of whose overall population evolved in an almost identical form and timing (shown in Table 5.3). Meanwhile, slave imports into the British Caribbean grew via a G path from the early 1600s into the early 1700s and then along a fresh G trajectory from there a little past 1800.[10] The African American population of the British West Indies, by expanding in H fashion, then in fresh G form, kept up a noticeably steeper increase than did further slave imports, as Figure 5.3 demonstrates (the widening gap between the two top plots in the graph). Growth in slave imports, in fact, had begun to fall behind the expansion of the non-white population already by the later 1600s.

What happened was that from 1688 (the quarter-century 1675–1700) forward to the end of the 1700s the *rate* of annual slave imports *per existing non-white population* declined in D fashion from a base year at 1674 (the middle plot of solid squares in Figure 5.3, which does not include the exceptionally low imports of the 1780s in the fit). Though it bounced about somewhat from decade to decade, the growth rate of the non-white population of the British West Indies, meanwhile, was also declining around an underlying D pattern, with its t_0 at 1673 (the hollow squares lower down in the figure).

Subtracting the rate of slave importation from the growth rate for the non-white population, finally, provides a crude estimate for the rate of net natural decrease among the slaves of the British Caribbean. Much attention has been given to the stark evidence that slaves at work in tropical climes did not reproduce themselves; deaths among them chronically outnumbered births. What has been overlooked, though, is how by the 1680s that *rate* of net natural decrease in the British West Indies had begun to *fall*, and such decline generally followed a D path through 1770 from a base year at 1679.[11] This compares with t_0's at 1682 for the first stage of G-shape increase in the non-white population of these colonies and also the H trend of growth that followed (Table 5.3). In all, by the end of the 1670s, though conditions remained too harsh for slaves to reproduce themselves, both the growth of their segment of the population and the trends for further imports reflected the way that natural increase, though remaining negative, was improving (lessening) in D fashion. While still too weak for full replacement, the dynamics of net reproduction were significantly shaping the development of the non-white population and likewise the further importation of slaves.

These demographic processes are not just peculiar particulars from the history of the British West Indies. While Figure 5.4 and Table 5.3 show that the non-white population of the *French* Caribbean enlarged in three successive G trends between 1630 and 1780 rather than the G-H-G pattern of the British possessions (Figure 5.3)—and multiplied over three times more (by 20.9 rather than 6.4 from 1680 through 1780, in large part because the British had more than three times as many slaves already by 1680)—the *percentage* of non-whites within the population expanded almost identically: via an early 1650–1680 G' curve with peak at 1691 and then from 1670 through 1780 along a G path based at 1651. These dates very closely resemble the 1688 and 1647 for the comparable trends for British West Indies, as Table 5.3 shows.

Figure 5.4 further indicates how the annual rate of slave importation per existing non-white population also declined in the French West Indies fundamentally around a D trend from 1688 through 1770. The base year for this curve, however, came at 1699—some 25 years after the 1674 for the comparable trend in the British West Indies. As noted in Chapter 2, the appetite of French colonists for slaves was whetted and then satiated rather later than among their English competitors.

When the annual rate of slave imports relative to the current number of resident non-whites is subtracted from the growth pace for that element of the population, implied net natural decrease for people of African descent in the French West Indies, too, is shown to have ameliorated from 1688 through 1770 approximately along an underlying D—in this case with its base year at 1704.[12] That movement, again, lags behind the British D trend of comparable change by 25 years. The estimated descending curve for net natural decrease among non-whites in the French West Indies, furthermore, levels out at about 2.2 percent per year just like the D for demographic improvement in the British West Indies before it was replaced by fresh decline in the 1770s.

In sum, though in absolute numbers their peoples of African descent—while both following G-based forms—expanded quite differently in time, the British and French West Indies shared two sets of crucial dynamics in their development of slavery: (1) For more than a century after 1670 their transitions from a white to a black population unfolded in parallel G form based at about 1650; (2) In both groups of colonies the rate of net natural decrease softened across 100 years forward from the 1670s in D fashion, trends that bottomed out at the same lower level in the later 18th century. This second movement was accompanied by falling rates of further slave imports that took comparable, largely parallel D shape.

That the first set of adjustments, the proportional shift from white to black population, was almost exactly identical and contemporaneous in these two large groups of West Indian territories, might be attributed to a general manner in which across the Caribbean internationally shared economic conditions encouraged taking up the cultivation of sugar with its preferred labor form, African slavery, in lieu of other possible activity. In contrast, shared (though differently timed) tendencies for net natural decrease in two separate non-white populations to lessen and simultaneously to retard the rate of further slave importation in D form indicate that demographic processes in the New World were the dynamics that shaped the growth pattern of colonial slave populations and trends for regional slave imports so universally in G-connected forms.

Much of what is known about the Dutch West Indies, furthermore, displays similar movements (Figure 5.5). As of 1690, the proportion of the population of Dutch Guiana, the big mainland territory held and developed by the Dutch (especially after the third Anglo-Dutch war gave them also the English slice of the Guianas in the 1670s in exchange for recaptured New Amsterdam/New York), became increasingly African along a G curve based back at 1613 (McCusker 1970, 1: 601). This was a considerably earlier (higher and flatter) trend than the comparable patterns for the English and French holdings, which indicates that, after all even all *northern* European colonies did not simultaneously take up sugar production by Africans in response to the forces of a single Atlantic market. Through their small island bases, especially Curaçao, the Dutch had traded or smuggled slaves for some time into Spanish America and then into English and French territories. By 1690 the populations of these trading stations were too small, relative to mainland holdings in Surinam and Guiana, to much affect the proportion of all Dutch West Indian inhabitants who were of African descent; but the early history of the slave trade through them, like temporary Dutch control of much of sugar-growing northeastern Brazil from the mid-1630s through the mid-1650s (as New Holland), made colonists from the Netherlands even older hands at the transition to black slavery than their English and French competitors. Before 1690, McCusker's data are very low (the solid downward triangles at 1660 and 1680, with no information for 1670). Still, to employ evidence of 83.6 percent for Surinam at 1684 and 71.7 percent of non-whites on St. Eustatius at 1665 (Postma 1990, 197, 185, given as hollow, upward triangles) as surrogates for all the current Dutch West Indies would alter the top G curve of Figure 5.5 only slightly, making it based at about 1625 rather than the 1613 that is projected backwards in time just from McCusker's 1690–1780 estimates.

Figure 5.5
Changes in the Non-White Population of the Dutch West Indies, 1663–1787

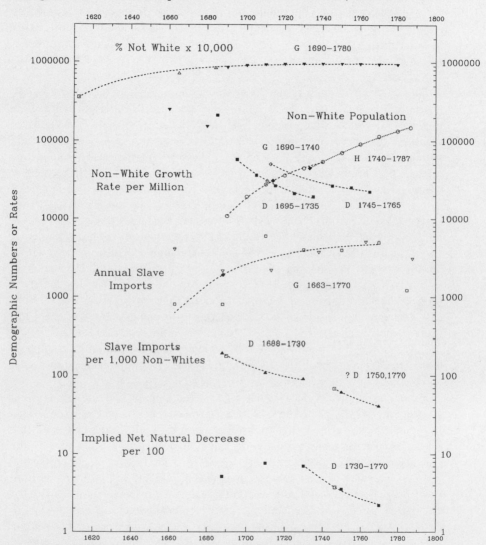

Sources: McCusker 1970, 1: 601; Klein 1999, 210–11; Eltis 2001, 45.

The History of Human Populations

The way that the non-white inhabitants of the Dutch holdings in aggregate increased via G from 1695 through 1740 and then via H from 1740 through 1787[13] made growth rates for this great majority of the population, which had been falling off in D form, revive around 1740. From 1745 through 1765, however, such decline in effect just resumed at a higher level the D curve of 1695–1735 with its t_0 at 1711 (the trends with solid squares in the figure). Thus, for this third national group of colonies, too, the pace of expansion for non-whites took the form of constantly decelerating decline, though—like the French rather than the British possessions—a restarted, upward-shifted curve of this shape seems to have been involved. The Dutch jump, however, occurred around 1740 rather than the French 1710.

For the Dutch colonies of the Americas, slave imports are currently not easy to trend. Figure 2.1a and Table 2.1 fit data from Eltis (2001, 45) that isolate imports to the small Dutch islands. The large slave-hungry settlements situated along the Caribbean coast of South America are lumped, in his categorization, with French Guiana (Cayenne). Figure 5.5 begins by going back to older estimations by Curtin (1969; reproduced in Klein 1999, 210–11)—represented as hollow squares across the middle of Figure 5.5. A G trend fitted to these observations from 1663 through 1770 actually comes close to combined average annual imports from the Netherlands Antilles and the Guianas together according to Eltis at 1688, and then 1738 and 1763 (the hollow downward triangles in this same plot). Such a fitting leaves the computation of Curtin for 1676–1700 (1688) markedly low and that for 1701–1720 (1710) noticeably high, though an average for Curtin and Eltis in the early 1700s would fall just about on the projected curve. The very high level of imports from Eltis for 1651–1675 probably includes large numbers of slaves landed at trading stations of the West India Company but reshipped on to colonies of the Spanish, English, and French during this period of persisting if now dwindling Dutch leadership in Atlantic commerce. Figure 2.3a displays a G' surge in the slave traffic handled by Dutch carriers beginning in the 1640s.

Further work should clarify what are the best patterns. To employ the kind of long-range G curve for 1663–1770 annual slave imports that is hypothesized in Figure 5.5, however, generates familiar types of result. In the first place, the rate of annual slave intake relative to the current non-white population in the Dutch posessions of the New World declined from 1688 through 1730 in D form, then perhaps once more this way between 1740 and 1780 (midpoints 1750 and 1770). These curves had t_0's at 1690 and 1746, respectively, shows Table 5.3. The adjustment first generally paralleled comparable change in relative imports for the French West Indies (t_0 at 1699); a second D-shape drop occurred, however, as the large Dutch slave population of the South American mainland began to normalize. From 1720 through 1780 (1730–1770 midpoints) the rate of net natural decrease implied for non-white peoples of the Dutch colonies fell in a D pattern with is base year at 1747, almost exactly the same as that of the second trend for slowing relative slave imports. This reduction in imports, however, did not begin until net natural decrease was already improving, a further indication that it was better demographic replacement that turned down the tap of the slave trade, not the other way around. Prior to about 1720 worsening natural decrease in the Dutch slave populations had accompanied the aggressive introduction of Africans to plantation holdings in the Guianas.

It is of interest, finally, that as of about 1770 net natural decrease in all three national groups of tropical colonies—British, French, and Dutch—had atrophied from much higher levels to a little over 2 percent. It was a harsh, dangerous life that provided only poor chances to form families; but to some substantial degree replacement, though still negative, had improved, approaching—always in D fashion—what seems to have been a common level of demographic imbalance that pertained across West Indian slavery as of the later 18th century.

Thus, beneath the noxious and depressing—but also somewhat distracting and distorting—pall of demographic devastation that hovered over West Indian slave life, there can be observed at least a certain partial normalization for slave populations that proceeded from the British to the French to the Dutch holdings across the plantation regions of America. As one colonial power after another packed in African slaves to produce desired tropical items for its early modern mercantilist economic system, in particular sugar, its slave trade—which, it will be seen, included many women and children, not just adult men—before long created a population that began to take on dynamics of its own. Growing reproduction relative to the prevailing death rate—though before 1800 it still failed to achieve positive natural increase in most of the non-white populations of the West Indies—nonetheless weakened the pull for further slave imports. Region by region, the trade in Africans to some extent began to generate its own slowdown in growth. All the movements involved, furthermore, took familar G-based shapes.

The demographic experience of several leading individual Caribbean colonies helps confirm and extend this interpretation. From within the British West Indies, from certain preeminent French, Dutch, and Spanish holdings, and from the North American mainland emerge additional insights as to how populations of African descent evolved. The awkward label "non-white" best encompasses the peoples covered. Not all were entirely African; not all were slaves.[14] But all were regarded—and recorded—by contemporary Europeans not to be white.

Among the British colonies, Barbados, Jamaica, and the Leewards all shared certain elements in the development of their populations of African descent. They also diverged from each other in some informative respects. Table 5.4 summarizes the trends. Figures 5.6a, 5.6.b, 5.6c, and 5.6d display graphically the apparent underlying movements that were involved and the shorter-term variability existing around them.

The average annual number of slave imports to all three of these Caribbean regions under British control peaked via a G' curve in the early 1700s. If Galenson's assumptions for the island are close to the mark (1981, 213, 218), on

Table 5.4
Non-White Growth and Naturalization in Colonies of the British West Indies

Type of Change	Barbados			Jamaica			Leewards		
Rate of Net Natural	1655-1685	D	1655	1670-1725	D	1680	1675-1730	D	1680
Decrease	1685-1705	G'	1709	1715-1735	G	1731	1730-1775	G	1718
	1705-1735	D	1716	1735-1800	D	1712			
Slave Imports	1655-1685	D	1663	1670-1725	D	1682	1685-1725	D	1683
per Non-White Pop.	1685-1705	up							
	1705-1745	D	1703	1745-1798	D	1715	1750-1795	D	1724
Growth Rate	1655,1665	?D	1685						
of Non-White Pop.	1675-1705	D	1690	1665-1695	D	1709	1675-1700	D	1694
	1715-1775	D	1681	1705-1798	D	1698	1700-1760	D	1714
Number of Non-Whites	1650-1670	G	1681						
	1670-1710	rG	1636	1670-1690	G	1710	1670-1790	G	1706
	1710-1770	H	1634	1690-1780	H	1704			
				1780-1830	G	1770	1790-1830	?C	1875
Annual Slave Imports	1655-1685	G'	1648						
	1681-1741	G'	1707	1670-1717	G'	1708	1663-1710	G'	1706
	1733-1773	G	1709	1715-1798	G	1719	1710-1770	G	1712
							1750-1795	?C	1854
% Population Not White				1670-1700	G'	1701	1650-1690	G	1672
	1660-1780	G	1625	1700-1780	G	1634	1690-1780	G	1656
% Non-White "Coloured"				1710-1830	G	1733			
% Non-White Free				1750-1810	G	1757			

Sources: Figures 5.6a, 5.6b, 5.6c, and 5.6d.

Barbados, the colony that for the English broke the path into intensive sugar production, a still earlier G' hump in imports also appeared from the beginning of serious introduction of slaves to the colony in the 1640s until the 1680s (Figure 5.6c). On Jamaica (Figure 5.6b) and the Leewards (Figure 5.6d for Nevis, St. Christopher, Montserrat, and Antigua collectively) after about 1710 annual imports rose anew along G paths with base years at 1719 and 1712, respectively (like the British West Indian aggregate intake of Table 5.3—1716 for 1730–1804).[15]

By the end of the 17th century, after early G' movements that reflected the opening surges of the English slave trade, the percentage of local populations that was composed of people with some African descent took up similar but somewhat differently timed G trends across the British Caribbean with t_0's of 1625 for Barbados, 1634 for Jamaica from 1700 forward (after a G' initial hump of stocking up)—many of whose first post-Spanish slaves were transferred by their relocating owners from Barbados—and an appreciably later 1656 for the Leewards.

The patterns for *growth* among these three colonial populations of non-whites,

Figure 5.6a
**Changes in the Non-White Population of the British Caribbean: Jamaica—
Proportion, Number, Growth Rate, and the Weight of Colored and Free People**

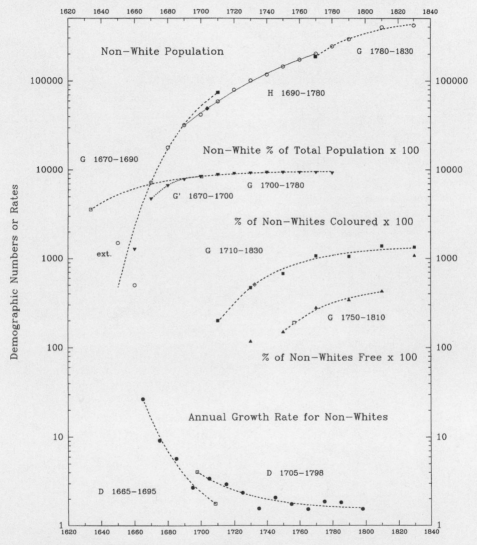

Sources: McCusker 1970, 2: 692; Craton 1975, 275.

Figure 5.6b
Changes in the Non-White Population of the British Caribbean: Jamaica—Rate of Retained Imports, Proportion of Imports Transshipped, and Net Natural Decrease

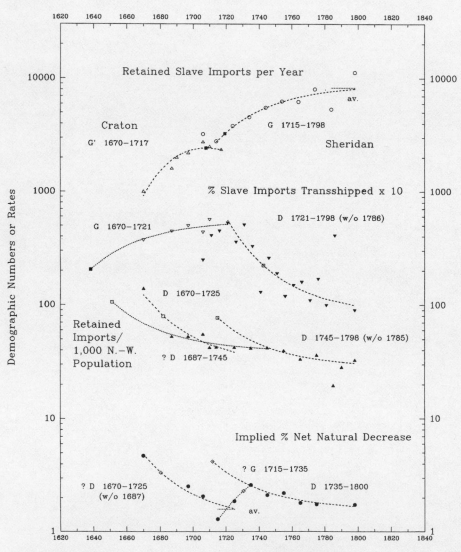

Sources: Galenson 1981, 214–15, 218; Klein 1978, 154; McCusker 1970, 2: 692; Craton 1975, 275, 284.

Figure 5.6c
Changes in the Non-White Population of the British Caribbean: Barbados

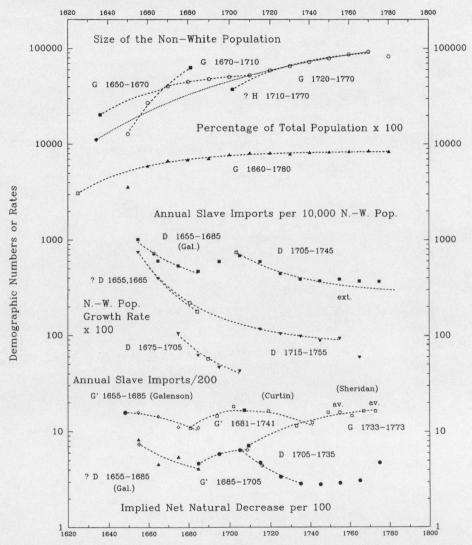

Sources: Figure 5.10b; McCusker 1970, 2: 699; Galenson 1981, 218; Curtin 1969, 55; Sheridan 1974, 505.

Figure 5.6d
Changes in the Non-White Population of the British Caribbean: The Leeward Islands

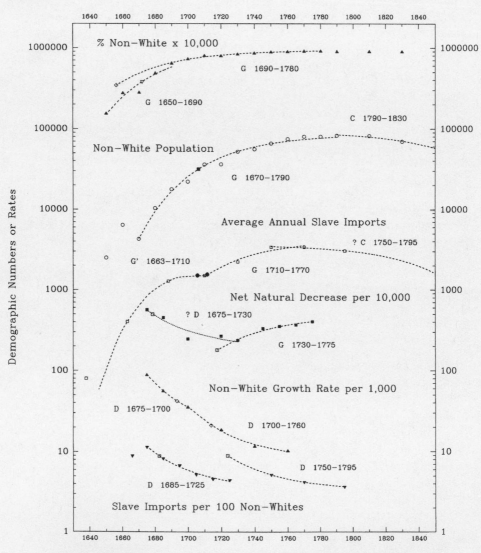

Sources: McCusker 1970, 2: 694–97; Curtin 1969, 119, 140, 216; Eltis 2000, 208; Craton 1975, 275.

however, varied more than that, as Table 5.4 summarizes. Barbados's opening G trend led the way until the 1670s; but then as the island filled up and many planters took their labor elsewhere, the expansion of her slave population largely capped out for a while in a retrogressively timed (flatter) G curve with base year way back at 1636.[16] The Leewards and Jamaica followed along with later, steeper G trends toward t_0's at 1706 and 1710 (Table 5.4). Across the 18th century the non-white population of Jamaica—and probably Barbados—then grew in H shape, the former far more steeply, with base year at 1704 rather than back at 1634. Meanwhile, slaves and other non-whites in the Leewards continued to multiply along a G path anchored on 1706. From 1780 through 1830, however, the slave population there declined, in something like the slow but accelerating C fashion that Figure 5.6d and Table 5.4 suggest. In Jamaica, meanwhile, across this later period a new G trend of increase emerged in the non-white population (top of Figure 5.6a).[17]

The trends in growth *rate* that resulted from these three distinctive histories of expansion in population of African descent typically took D shape, as Table 5.4 summarizes. The way that movements of this form succeeded each other, however, varied markedly from colony to colony. On Barbados (Figure 5.6c), probably no fewer than three D curves shared t_0's near 1680. Such a trend for rate of growth from 1675 through 1705, however, dropped to about half the level of the preceding D path as expansion of the non-white population suddenly flattened out; then it doubled back up to this height as the H-type demographic expansion between 1710 and 1770 began. On Jamaica, too, the early 1700s witnessed a fresh D trend in the growth rate at a higher level as increase of non-white population assumed H form (Figure 5.6a). In this case, though, the preceding D had a base year rather later, at 1709 compared with the 1698 of its successor. In the Leewards, finally, the shift in timing from one D trend of the non-white growth rate to the next worked the other way around: the curve for 1700–1760 was anchored on a later t_0 than its predecessor (1714 vs. 1694, shows Figure 5.6d). Both fed, in succession, a long, G-shaped increase in size for the population of African descent from 1670 through 1790 with just a ripple below the fitted curve at the point of transition in the early 1700s.

Of particular interest for the present discussion is the significance of slave imports relative to the scale of the current population of African descent in the various principal parts of the British West Indies and the net natural decrease that the subtraction of these ratios from growth rates for that part of the population implies. With one exception (in the Leewards), these changes in importation rate and demographic replacement were very parallel to each other within each set of settlements. Table 5.4 summarizes the two types of trends. Figures 5.6b, 5.6c, and 5.6d plot the available data as well as the underlying trajectories.

On *Barbados*, the rate of slave imports relative to the current non-white population was already falling in D form from the 1650s through the 1680s. Net natural decrease seems to have been contracting in this same D-shaped way over this period from a starting level that was not particularly high for a West Indian

slave population (Figure 5.6c). From about 1680 into the first decade of the
1700s, however, the pace for net natural decrease *rose* from about 4.4 percent
to close to 6.4 percent per annum. As of the 1680s a parallel climb in the
proportional impact of slave imports is evident. A mounting loss rate for existing
slaves occurred that kept renewed expansion in the forced immigration of Africans from pushing up the temporarily very flat trend of growth for non-white
population. How much might unrecorded reshipment of slaves from Barbados
to other colonies underlie such a phenomenon at this time?

Across the first third of the 18th century, however, net natural decrease in
Barbados's population with African descent once more improved (fell) in D
form with t_0 at 1716.[18] With net loss of existing slaves ameliorating, the need
for further imports lessened and the impact of the higher mortality levels among
new arrivals became less significant. The import rate, too, declined in D fashion
across the first half of the century, though a little more flatly (with earlier base
year at 1703) than the pace of net natural increase. It would seem that, in spite
of some impact of immigrants upon the death rate, it was primarily improved
reproduction and health among resident slaves that lessened demand for further
imports as time went by rather than the other way around. Other kinds of evidence are introduced shortly to support this reading of what usually happened
in plantation colonies.

For *Jamaica* (Figure 5.6b), there appear to be two ways of applying a D trend
to the rate of current retained imports relative to the existing non-white population. On the one hand, the data from 1687 through 1745 generate a relatively
flat curve segment of that shape with its base year at 1651. But the evidence
from 1670 through 1725 suggests a steeper D path with t_0 at 1682. This second
trending parallels quite well the D curve for implied net natural decrease among
non-whites on Jamaica from 1670 through 1725 (if an exceptionally low calculation for 1687 is omitted).[19] Then a halt in the decline of the relative rate of
slave importation in the 1720s and 1730s accompanied worsening net natural
decrease for the African American population of Jamaica—perhaps via G from
1715 through 1735, perhaps more abruptly—before both shrank in D form
across the bulk of the 18th century.[20] In this phase of local demographic development, net natural decrease began to fall about a decade earlier than the rate
of slave imports. This suggests, again, that improving demographic processes
led the way, not the reverse.[21]

Craton's work on the Jamaican population offers some other confirmation that
the improvement of the demographic regime was mostly an independent variable
in its interaction with the current pace of new slave imports (1975, 284). Figure
5.6a and Table 5.4 show how the percentage of non-whites who were "coloured"
rather than "black" rose in a single G curve from 1710 all the way to the eve
of emancipation at 1830. Though—judging by its issue—it approached a maximum of less than 15 percent, even interracial sex expanded along a G path.
Wasn't this kind of European contact more likely to have occurred with the
creole as opposed to the freshly African element of the slave population? Mean-

while, the percentage of all non-whites ("coloured" and "black" together) in Jamaica who were legally *free* persons also climbed in G form from 1750 through 1810 with base year about 24 years later than for "coloured" among all non-whites. The jump to 10 percent at 1830 would seem to reflect knowledge of imminent legal emancipation in 1834, though Higman (1984, 77) makes the increase start sooner, by 1810. It would seem, within the context of a slave system, that personal involvement with and legal recognition by whites represent further reflections of the course of demographic naturalization among residents of African descent, however limited their own choices might have been in such matters.

In the *Leewards* (Figure 5.6d), up until about 1725 parallel D declines in the rate of slave imports per existing non-white population and in net natural decrease closely resembled the comparable movements on Jamaica (Table 5.4). Much the same was true for the rate of importation across the second half of the 18th century. From 1730 through 1775, however, net natural decrease *rose* (worsened) among those of African descent in the group formed by St. Christopher, Nevis, Montserrat, and Antigua. This G-shaped movement began later than the comparable shift on Jamaica between 1685 and 1705, lasted longer (all the way to the 1770s), and was flatter. What was going on in the Leewards in this period? One possibility is a shift from other uses of slaves to sugar on islands where the cultivation of cane had lagged in the 17th century. Another is the use of the Leewards as a base for stocking other holdings, not necessarily all British, with fresh slaves—including Windward Islands ceded by the French in 1763 and settlements of the mainland. For this purpose, transshipment via the Leewards involved less time at sea than working via Jamaica, further westward into the Caribbean.[22] In nearby Danish St. Croix, between 1783 and 1844 net natural decrease for the slave population declined approximately along a D path with zero year in the vicinity of 1772 (estimated by template from Green-Pedersen 1981, 241). Did a similar pattern of late adjustment subsequently appear in the Leewards?

Other colonies—including settlements of other powers—also witnessed their non-white populations metamorphose through time in ways that resemble these movements observed in the British West Indies. Table 5.5 presents some of the parallel and contrasting trends that are suggested by currently available data. Beyond the leading British colonies and Spanish Cuba forward from the 1770s, for which G-based curves can been fitted and discussed in some detail, the particulars must be regarded as tentative. The patterns at present are estimated here only by template and eye. The limited and sometimes uncertain evidence that exists, nevertheless, seems at least to hypothesize trends and their implications that are worth further exploration as additional and improved information becomes available.[23]

First and foremost, D trends both in net natural decrease and in the rate of annual slave imports relative to current non-white population seem to have occurred (or in the least appear to have been possible) almost everywhere. (Oc-

Table 5.5
Tentative Comparisons of Trends in Net Natural Decrease and Rates of Slave Imports among Selected Non-White Colonial Populations

A. Rate of Net Natural Decrease

Barbados (B)*	1655-1685	D	1655	1685-1705	G'	1709	1705-1735	D	1716	
Jamaica (B)*	1670-1725	D	1680	1715-1735	G	1731	1735-1800	D	1712	
Leewards (B)*	1675-1730	D	1680	1730-1775	G	1718				
Surinam (D)				1700-1744	G	1711	1735-1775	D	1686	
St. Domingue (F)	1710,1730	?D	1680	1730-1750	up		1750,1770	?D	1686	
Martinique (F)	1688-1730	D	1718	1730-1750	up		1750,1770	?D	1731	
Guadeloupe (F)				1663-1710	E	1672	1698-1750	D	1712	
Chesapeake (B)*	1675-1700	D	1728	*1705-1745*	*G*	*1753* INC	*1745-1777*	*D*	*1754* INC	
South Carolina (B)*				*1710-1740*	*?D*	*1751* INC	*1755-1795*	*G*	*1761* INC	
Cuba (S)*							*1774,1791*	*?G*	*1744* INC	

B. Annual Slave Imports as Percentage of Current Non-White Population

Barbados (B)*	1655-1685	D	1663	1685-1705	up	1705-1745	D	1703	
Chesapeake (B)	1675-1725	D	1676	1725-1738	drops	1738-1767	D	1770	
Jamaica (B)*	1670-1725	D	1682	1725-1745	flat	1745-1798	D	1715	
Leewards (B)*	1685-1725	D	1683	1725,1750	up	1750-1795	D	1724	
Martinique (F)	1688-1770	D	1700						
Surinam (D)	1684-1720	D	1714	1720,1730	up	1730-1775	D	1696	
St. Domingue (F)	1688-1730	D	1722	1730,1750	up	1750,1770	?D	1720	
Guadeloupe (F)				1663-1710	E 1685	1710-1770	D	1740	
South Carolina (B)				1710-1730	G 1740	1725-1770	D	1752	
Cuba (S)*				1783-1822	G 1736	1834,1850	?D	1845	

* Fitted and graphed; INC = Net natural increase.

Sources: Figures 5.6a, 5.6b, 5.6c, 5.6d, 5.7, 5.8a, and 5.8b; Postma 1990, 185–86, 212–13; Curtin 1969, 119, 216, 234; McCusker 1970, 1: 705, 707–8; McCusker and Menard 1985, 136; Eltis 2000, 166, Walsh 2001, 168–69; *Historical Statistics*, 2: 1168, Series Z 16; Menard 1989, Tables 1 and 10; Eblen 1975, 216; Eltis 1987, 245, 247, 249; P. Morgan 1998, 81, 84.

casional speculations based upon information for just two points in time are noted as "?D"in the table.) Mostly, for colony after colony between the later 1600s and the later 1700s two declines of this shape were interrupted by a brief period of increase (the middle column of the three listings of possible patterns). There are local variations in the timing of the first and the second D trends of both natural decrease and the proportional rate of slave imports, in their chronological relationships to each other and steepness of decline, in the ways that improving demographic replacement connected with decreasing importation of Africans, and in the precise nature of the intervening reverse movement that temporarily interrupted the downward trending in both variables. Nevertheless, a very general form of population change taking the falling but decelerating D path appears virtually everywhere. Some dynamic following this curve (which simply represents 1/G) seems to have played a central and perhaps universal role in how slave populations normalized and their internal dynamics began to shape the futures of colonial plantation societies through demographic renewal.

Apparent similarities and variations in these movements from one colony to another in Table 5.5 are also insightful. For Barbados, Jamaica, and the Leewards in the British West Indies, Figures 5.6a, 5.6b, 5.6c, and 5.6d have established initial D trends for improvement in net natural decrease and for the rate of slave imports from the later 1600s into the early 1700s that parallel each other in each society. In these pairings, though, Barbados adjusted earlier—with t_0's about two decades sooner and temporary upward reversal of trend starting as early as the 1680s, as Table 5.5 summarizes. Then, in the 18th century, while a new phase of downward simultaneous D-shape movement in net natural decrease and slave importation appeared in Jamaica (with base years for the curve at 1712 and 1715, respectively), the comparable adjustments on Barbados came more in sequence, with the lowering of rates for imports relative to the existing non-white population following a noticeably flatter segment of the D curve than the decline in net natural decrease (t_0's at 1703 and 1716), though change began about 1705. In the Leewards, meanwhile, no *second* D-type decline in net natural decrease occurred before 1780, though a drop-off of this shape that commenced about 1750 in the proportional rate of further slave imports seems to have largely paralleled such movement in Jamaica. In terms of level, meanwhile, estimated net natural decrease for non-whites on Jamaica declined steadily to well under 2 percent along the D trend between 1735 and 1800 (Figure 5.6b), and on Barbados dropped to nearly 2.5 before starting to rise again—gradually in the 1760s, then sharply in the 1770s (Figure 5.6c). In the Leewards, however, it increased continually between about 1730 and 1775, climbing from under 2.5 percent to more like 4 percent, though for reasons apparently affected significantly by elevated transshipment of slaves to other colonies.

How much of these differences or changes from place to place across the British West Indies reflect just how well true, retained imports of Africans have been calculated? How much, in contrast, is the result of shifts in actual mortality and fertility among slaves? Jamaica throughout the 18th century supported considerable mixed agriculture as well as sugar cultivation. Barbados was more mono-cultural; and in the later 1700s planters there led the way in diversifying and intensifying production by making more white sugar and marketing more molasses. After early impediments, the Leewards—especially Antigua—turned aggressively to sugar in the 18th century. Did these economic changes make replacement more difficult for slave populations? While the trends presented here are inferences from data on slave populations and slave imports that are not entirely certain, they point the way to what might have transpired and how to resolve in further research the issues that are raised.

In Dutch Surinam, meanwhile, the sustained G-shaped *rise* of net natural decrease that occurred between 1700 and 1744 (estimated by template and eye rather than formally fitted) closely resembled the 1730–1775 G trend for the Leewards. Surinam, however, had a contemporary reputation for devouring slaves (through disease and hard work, through escape—perhaps also via transfers to Brazil). Thereafter, in contrast to the Leewards, implied net natural decrease for non-whites in Surinam *fell* from the 1730s to the 1770s according to a comparatively shallow D curve that was anchored back near 1686. Meanwhile, the proportional rate of slave imports to this substantial Dutch colony on the South American mainland (part B of Table 5.5) decreased via a D path between 1684 and 1720 then again between 1730 and 1775 (with t_0's at 1714 and 1696), bracketing a brief elevation in the 1720s. In all, the trend sequences in net natural decrease and the relative rate of slave importation for Surinam resemble the patterns found generally in the British West Indies.

In French-held St. Domingue, though the data are scant and widely spaced in time, it is once again possible to discern what may be D-shape trends for net natural decrease and relative rate of continuing slave imports, in each case interrupted by an upward thrust between about 1730 and 1750 (the chronological blocks of 1720–1740 and 1740–1760)—about the same period as in the Leewards. For all the bad reputation of her sugar-growing, St. Domingue—like Jamaica—supported quite mixed agriculture. Therefore, while the colony's flat D trend for improving net natural decrease in the decades preceding the great slave revolt might parallel comparable change in Surinam (both had t_0's around 1686), the *level* for St. Domingue in the later 18th century was something like 2.5 percent compared with more like 6 percent for the expansive equatorial Dutch enterprise on the mainland. On more mono-cultural Martinique, meanwhile, possibly D-shaped decline in net natural decrease "stuck" at about 3 percent, though on Guadeloupe, whose rate had accelerated (for some reason in E form) to an exceptionally high level in the early 1700s, the so widely shared D-type demographic softening of the 18th century continued down to about 2 percent by the 1770s. Such likely colony-by-colony similarities and differences in trend should be explained by local variations in how slaves were used and the conditions under which African Americans lived in these places along with the trends for reexports from particular colonies.

In the Chesapeake—Virginia and Maryland, mainland colonies of England that initially specialized in tobacco (Figure 5.7)—the decline of net natural demographic loss in the late 1600s was appreciably steeper than the likewise D-shaped trend in the rate of continuing importation of labor from Africa (with t_0 at 1728 as opposed to 1676 in parts A and B of Table 5.5, respectively). Unlike what has been found in the British West Indies, however, the replacement rate for non-whites in the Chesapeake then shifted over into natural *increase* ("INC" in part A of the table) that *rose* via G from 1705 through 1745. Morgan's computations for just Virginia in Figure 5.7 (based upon Kulikoff 1977) most clearly indicate this shift—though independent calculations made here for the

Figure 5.7
Trends of Natural Increase in Virginia and South Carolina

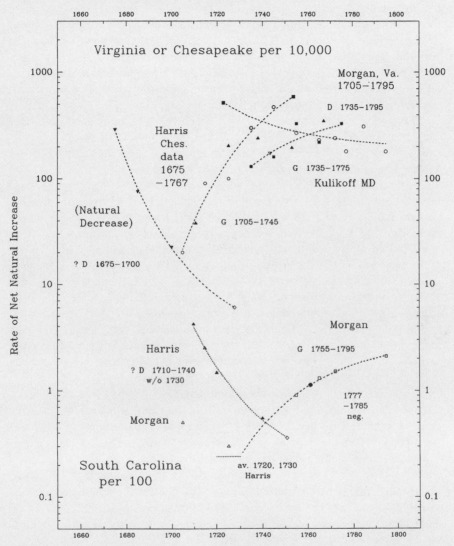

Sources: P. Morgan 1998, 81, 84; Menard 1980, 157–66; Eltis 2000, 48, 208; Walsh 2001, 168–69; Menard 1989, Table 10; *Historical Statistics* 2: 1173–74, Series Z 155; Kulikoff 1977, 413.

Chesapeake as a whole (the solid, upward triangles in the top plot of the figure) fit right in with the same G trend.[24] Having peaked perhaps as high as 4.7 percent per annum in the 1740s, as the hollow circles for Virginia from Morgan indicate, the pace of net natural increase for the slaves of this colony then pulled back in something like D form between 1735 and 1795 to more like 2.3 percent in the last quarter of the 18th century. In neighboring Maryland, however, where there were less new plantation development and slave importation in the later 1700s (Figure 2.13 in Chapter 2), natural increase among slaves, according to Kulikoff (1977, 413) in contrast continued to rise in G form based at 1743 from the 1730s into the 1770s (solid squares in Figure 5.7). The rate of slave importation to the Chesapeake as a whole relative to existing population of African descent, meanwhile, dropped abruptly between 1728 and 1735, where it took up D-type decline once more—now in a steep curve segment with t_0 at 1770 (part B of Table 5.5).

In rice-oriented South Carolina, the proportional pace for adding new Africans to the existing non-white population perhaps increased in G form from 1710 to 1730 or, as implied by data that Mancall, Rosenbloom, and Weiss (2001, 625) have recently presented, crept upward more flatly. Both of these are familiar patterns during the first half of the 18th century, as part B of Table 5.5 shows. Accompanying this move was some type of decline in the relatively high level of net natural *increase* with which the slave population of South Carolina, much of it transferred from the West Indies along with colonizing owners, commenced. My calculations for 1710, 1720, and 1740 from Menard (1989, Table 10) and *Historical Statistics* (2: 1173–74)—represented by the solid triangles in the lower, South Carolina portion of Figure 5.7—fit, along with Morgan's estimate of 2.5 for 1715, a D curve headed toward a t_0 in the early 1750s. Morgan's rates for 1705 and 1725 and my average of 1730 (which had natural *decrease*) with 1740 form an appreciably lower but also declining bound that delineates a range of estimation within which unusual early positive self-replacement by South Carolina slaves weakened as fresh imports from Africa became significant. Morgan's computations for the 1730s and the 1740s indicate that a threshold of neither growth nor decline was reached (actually −0.1 and −0.1 percent).

Thereafter—excluding the late 1770s and the 1780s, when the presence and slave-handling practices of the occupying British army muddied the picture—natural increase for South Carolina slaves grew to over 2 percent again by the 1790s, along a G trend based at 1761. Projected backward in time, this 1755–1795 curve comes close to hitting my calculations for 1740 and for 1720–1730 on average—and Morgan's value for the 1720s, as Figure 5.7 indicates. Mancall et al. (2001, 625), meanwhile, have very recently presented numbers for slave population and current African imports in South Carolina that generate from 1735 through 1805 (without an extreme low in the 1740s in response to the Stono Rebellion) a D trend with estimated zero year around 1753 for the relative pace of importation. This compares with calculations reported in part B of Table

5.5 that produce a D trend from 1725 through 1770 for the ratio of current imports to existing African American population in the colony whose t_0 arrived at 1752. The new data reinforce and extend the previously perceived pattern. Whereas to have more and better evidence on local demographic replacement would certainly help, it seems fairly clear already that the slave population of South Carolina recovered a significant level of natural increase along a G trajectory through the second half of the 18th century, advancing to multiply at about the same rate as the African Americans of the Chesapeake. As was the case in so many plantation societies, better replacement rates once again drove down further slave imports relative to existing black population size according to a complementary G-based path.

On Spanish Cuba, a late stress on sugar production brought an intensification of slave imports between 1783 and 1834 (the middle of Figure 5.8a). This influx helped drive the total number of blacks on the island constantly upward in exceptional log-linear F fashion, as the top plot in the figure indicates (Eblen 1975, 216). By the middle of the 19th century, though, the total for persons of African descent on Cuba began to shrink, perhaps in the kind of D path offered in the figure for the period 1860–1899—or the type of G' track included as an alternative—before growing again (seemingly in G form) during the first two decades of the 20th century. In large part, the 1860–1899 decline reflected the demise of the slave trade, whose imports shrank between 1834 and 1850 and then disappeared. As a consequence of these movements, new slave arrivals per current black population on the island first rose in G fashion from 1783 through 1822, then dropped away in what may have been D form between 1834 and 1850, as the bottom plot of Figure 5.8a indicates. As slave imports rose in significance like this, the foreign-born proportion among black women of childbearing age (15–44) in Cuba enlarged via a G trajectory based at 1780 from just 26 percent at 1791 to 44 percent at 1827 and 1841 (the top plot of Figure 5.8b). Then it fell back via a D curve to just 22 percent by 1877 (ibid., 240).

A simultaneous result of this historical pattern of importation was that between 1817 and 1877 the percentage of Cuba's blacks who were slaves rose and fell along a G' curve with crest at about 76 percent near 1836. This compares with a level of 59 percent at what may have been the top of a previous G' surge near 1776, just 54 percent at 1791, and perhaps even less than that around 1800. By the 1870s, the waning of the slave trade to Cuba made the proportion of blacks who were in bondage contract to only 44 percent (Eblen, 1975, 216).

These levels are very different from—much lower than—those of other Caribbean colonies whose data have been examined. By the 19th century there were many persons of African descent on Cuba not under the restraints of slavery who contributed to the demographic processes of this portion of the total population, which in turn was modest by West Indian standards. Eblen's important work goes on (241, 245) to estimate not only the rate of net natural increase for all the black population of the island but also the intrinsic rates of death,

Figure 5.8a
Changes in the Black Population of Cuba: Size, Percentage Enslaved, Number and Proportion of Imports

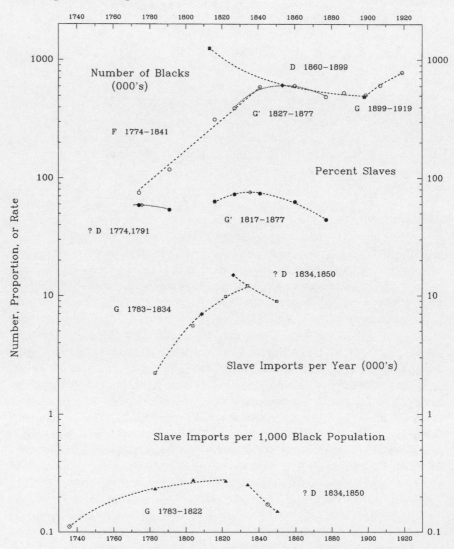

Source: Eblen 1975, 216, 240.

Figure 5.8b
Changes in the Black Population of Cuba: Percentage of Foreign-Born and Rates of Births, Deaths, Growth, and Natural Increase

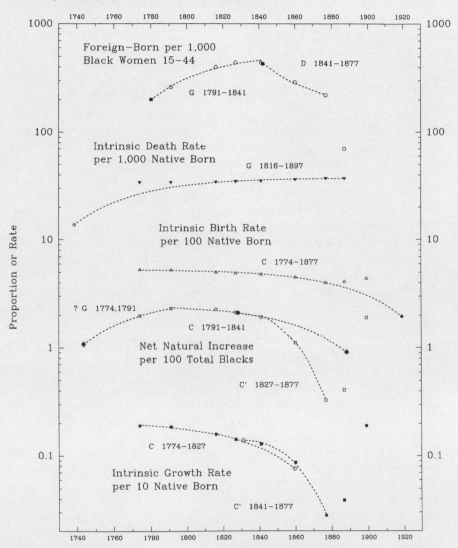

Source: Eblen, 1975, 240–41, 245.

birth, and growth for native-born black women on Cuba across about a century of demographic development (Figure 5.8b).

Net natural increase for the total black population of Cuba probably was rising through the 1770s and 1780s rather parallel to the G trend in the rate of slave importation (with t_0's at 1744 and 1736, respectively). This pace of natural increase, by the way, reached 2.3 percent, the level for the black population of the Chesapeake in the later 1700s and the rate attained by the African Americans of South Carolina in the 1790s (Figure 5.7), and did so in spite of strong importation. That the death rate of the *native* members of the black population rose from 1816 through 1897 in a G path parallel to increase in the rate of slave imports might echo the risk of their exposure to fresh Africans; or perhaps it simply results from an aging of native-born people, children of this substantial wave of immigrants. It may also be just coincidence.

The intrinsic birth rate for the native black population of Cuba, meanwhile, for the hundred years between 1774 and 1877 (before curling upward somewhat in the 1880s and 1890s) fell away—first slowly, but then more and more rapidly—in a C pattern. Considered here is a 19th-century population of the Western Hemisphere. Falling birth rates were now not uncommon in that part of the world. The consequence for net natural increase in the black population of Cuba—and for the intrinsic growth rate among the native-born of African descent—was first of all C type slowing until about 1830 or 1840 as the impact of the slave trade peaked. Then the birth and death rates of the native-born took over, and both net natural increase for all black people in Cuba and intrinsic expansion among those of native birth assumed the so far unusual C' (G' reversed in time) shape. The later-reaching data from Cuba allow us to see how the nativization of the originally slave population of African descent flowed through G-based channels of change into patterns of modern demographic adjustment. What guidance system for demographic change might produce trends of C and C' shape?[25]

Overall, the upper part of Table 5.5 shows how the devastating demographic conditions of slavery began to ameliorate almost everywhere in G-based trends, not only in national aggregates of colonies—as in Table 5.4—but also from settlement to settlement. In certain colonial contexts, like the Chesapeake, South Carolina, and Cuba, net natural *increase* actually appeared, reaching rates not far below those for settlers of European descent. Elsewhere, where slave life was more draining and more dangerous—notably the sugar-specializing islands of the West Indies—it continued to take a proportionally substantial and sustained flow of fresh African imports to keep up the size of the local slave population, let alone make it grow as most of these bound labor forces did. The net natural *decrease* that was involved in these places, nonetheless, also began to change—in this case to *decline* in the G-inverting D form (1/G). Setbacks might occur, as when fresh waves of slave imports were introduced in order to expand or to alter local agricultural operations aggressively or to profit from selling labor to other colonies; but improvement in the demographic system usually soon reappeared in G paths of natural increase or D trends of softening natural decrease.

While one can expect patterns of importing fresh Africans to have left some imprint upon the history of net natural renewal in black populations of the New World, there are reasons that the normalization of these populations might proceed along G-related paths largely independently of the pace of forced immigration. For one thing, modern scholarship has failed to document long-held assumptions about high rates of "seasoning" deaths during the period following arrival in the New World (Klein 1999, 158). For another, in most flows of forced migrants from Africa women and children played a substantial part from the very start. A kernel from which to develop more normal, if not fully replacing, demographic development along G-connected lines was present almost at once. Better demographic conditions could soon reduce the proportional need for additional slave imports (within a given or even rapidly growing demand for labor). Meanwhile, the emergence along G trends of racially mixed and free populations among those of African ancestry on Jamaica and the shift of Cuban black demography from typical reflections of surges of fresh slavery to common patterns of modern demographic transition—all in G-related paths—reinforce this conclusion and provide special insights into the kind of internal processes that might have generated so much population change in just a few repeated and closely related shapes.

THE EVOLVING STRUCTURE OF EARLY AFRICAN AMERICAN POPULATIONS

In particular, how the *compositions* of these slave peoples changed in certain patterns is underscored. Ways that the foreign-born were absorbed via G-related patterns and how populations similarly shifted from white to black have already been observed. Along what lines, then, did other basic demographic developments, as in sex ratios and age structures, unfold during such adjustments? And how might these fundamental alterations in populations have in turn channeled other processes along familiar G-rooted paths?

Occasional evidence about the composition of populations of African descent in several colonies and a few local cases of systematic documentation across time allow some insight into the important question of how slave peoples began to be shaped by the forces of their own demography. Figures 5.9a, 5.9b, 5.9c, and 5.9d present some of the evidence. Most certain are the data from the British colonies of the North American mainland, where relevant time series have been made available by studies of slaves covered in probate. Table 5.6 summarizes the trends that emerge from the figures.

Figure 5.9a depicts movements in the composition of the slave population of the colonial Chesapeake. First of all, the proportion of women among adults aged 16 to 50 in probated estates of four counties (St. Mary's, Calvert, Charles, and Prince George's) along the lower Western Shore of Maryland can be seen to have risen then fallen in G' fashion, cresting at 45.6 percent near 1675 before dropping off into the early 1700s (Menard 1975, 32). Such an early temporary swing toward women has been noted in the opening stages of slavery in several

Table 5.6
Comparing Trends for the Proportions of Children, the Old, and Women in Certain Slave Populations

A. Percentage Who Were Children

Bahia	1632-1788	G	1632					1750-1816	D	1753
British W. Indies	1678-1829	G	1629							
Newton Plant.								1740-1834	G	1703
Grenada								1763,1817	?G	1701
Bermuda	1698-1727	G	1668							
Chesapeake	1675-1715	G	1653 Md	1715-1755	G	1679 Mn		1735-1783	G	1695 K
South Carolina	1688-1775	G	1663 Md-Mn							
Surinam	1705-1754	G	1660							
Trinidad								1811-1822	G	1799

B. Percentage Aged 50 or More

Chesapeake	1664-1705	D	1654 Md	1715,1725	?G	1709 Md		1735-1775	G	1724 K

C. Percentage Women among Adults

Bahia				1632-1739	G	1571		1739-1809	D	1718
British W. Indies	1673-1692	?G'	1676	1692-1834	G	1596				
Newton Plant.								1740-1803	G	1680?
Jamaica*				1682-1772	G	1611				
Bermuda				1698-1756	G	1622		1756-1774	D	1743
Chesapeake	1665-1695	G'	1675 Md	1705-1775	G	1646 Mn		1735-1775	G	1710 K
South Carolina	1705-1735	G'	1719 Md-Mn	1735-1775	G	1691 Mn				
Grenada*								1742-1833	G	1702
St. Croix*								1805-1840	G	1741
Trinidad								1808-1828	G	1762

* = % female all ages; Md = Menard; Mn = Morgan; K = Kulikoff.

Sources: Figures 5.9a, 5.9b, 5.9c, and 5.9d.

Chesapeake localities (Harris 1984). Subsequently, from 1705 through 1775, the regional data synthesized by P. Morgan (1998, 82) produce a G trend with base year back at 1646. To get this series, Morgan blended Menard's 1700–1729 computations for Charles and Prince George's Counties of Maryland (1975, 32, 43) with unpublished data for Middlesex County in Virginia 1700–1749 (supplied to him by the Rutmans), evidence for seven counties of the Virginia "Southside" 1737–1775 (furnished by Michael L. Nicholls), and his own gleaning of inventories for 10 other counties across Virginia.

It is gratifying to see this diverse mix of estimations so closely adhere to the

Figure 5.9a
The Weights of Women and Children in Slave Populations: The Chesapeake

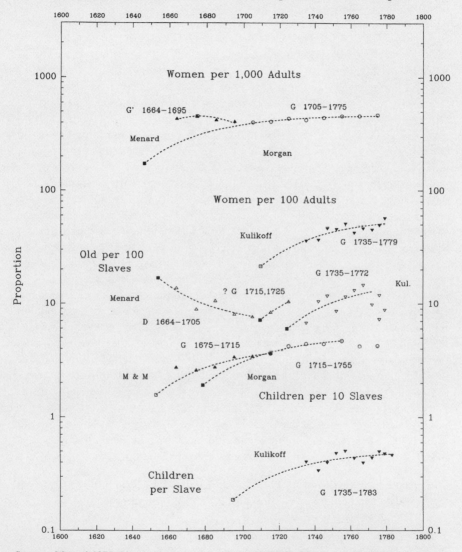

Sources: Menard 1975, 32, 43; Morgan 1998, 82–83, Kulikoff 1975, Appendix, Table 1.

G pattern. What lies beneath this Chesapeake synthesis, however, is illustrated by Kulikoff's data for Prince George's County, Maryland (1975, Appendix Table 1). Here, though fluctuating, the proportion of women among adult slaves (based on inventories and the local census of 1776) also rises along an underlying G path. This however, has its t_0 much later—at 1710 rather than the 1646 of Morgan's composite, region-wide calculations. Prince George's was a secondary, more interior settlement whose development did not take off until the beginning of the 1700s. The lag of the county's G curve for slave sex ratio by 64 years seems fairly proportional to the delay of local settlement there versus St. Mary's, Calvert, Middlesex, York, Isle of Wight, and Northampton Counties right on the bay where regional growth in slavery began.[26]

Increases in the weight of *children* among Chesapeake slaves also followed G trajectories. After dropping off a bit from the 1660s, for 1675 though 1715 percentages of those under 16 among all slaves going through probate rose in G form with base year at 1653 (Menard 1975, 32, 43). Then the geographically more composite calculations of Morgan for 1715 through 1755 (1998, 83)— which include more interior areas in the mix—adhere to a fresh, steeper G trajectory with t_0 at 1679, about a quarter of a century later for this more varied array of local Chesapeake slave populations. Still almost two decades further on comes the base year for the G trend that underlies Kulikoff's results from just Prince George's County, Maryland (the last plot at the bottom of Figure 5.9a).

The proportion of slaves identified by Menard to have been *old* (age 50 and above), meanwhile, fell from the 1660s into the first decade of the next century as imports from Africa first arrived in substantial numbers. This decline, interestingly, took a D shape that in its timing mirrored, upside down, the contemporaneous rise of children within the regional population between 1675 and 1715 (t_0's at 1654 and 1653, respectively). For a while, the slave population became younger from both ends, with relatively fewer older adults at the same time that more children appeared. Subsequently, in Charles and Prince George's into the 1720s, and Prince George's alone thereafter, according to Kulikoff, the percentage of older slaves in the local mix seems to have turned around to grow in G fashion as if it echoed the G curve for children, lagging by 30 years. Gains in both the young and the old now chiseled away together at the proportion of those 16 to 50 as the slave population of the lower Western Shore of Maryland became more normal.

Table 5.6 summarizes those trends to facilitate comparison. It also shows how these G-based movements in the Chesapeake were related to what appear to be similar demographic patterns in other colonial populations of slaves.

For the British West Indies the data are sketchy and scattered. Censuses of Barbados in 1673 and 1676, the Leewards in 1678, a group of Jamaican inventories between 1674 and 1701, records for the island's Bybrook plantation between 1676 and 1709, and censuses from St. Christopher and Montserrat in 1707 and St. Christopher again at 1711 provide the early data for the weight of women among adults (Dunn 1972, 316; Wells 1975, 216, 219, 256). Then, except for a few figures for islands that the British acquired and developed in the later 1700s, there is a long gap until the early 1800s (Higman 1984, 116, 413–16, 462–70; John 1988, 41–42) across which the only published evidence from the older settlements appears to be for the one Barbadian plantation of Newton (Handler and Lange 1978, 68–71).

However limited they may be, these observations and estimations seem to identify a recognizable patterning for the emergence of African women in those plantation societies. The proportion of females among adults in the slave populations of the core settlements of the British West Indies—Barbados, Jamaica, and the Leewards—first was falling from the early 1670s into the early 1690s along something like the post-crest downslope of a G' curve with peak at 1676 (the top plot in Figure 5.9b). That makes this initial change almost exactly parallel to the comparable 1664–1695 movement for women among slaves age 16–50 in the Chesapeake (t_0 at 1675, says part C of Table 5.6), whose 17th-century slaves often were brought in from the Caribbean. Later analysis will show how the proportion of women among adults being *imported* by the Royal African Company (RAC) to Jamaica and the Leewards peaked in G' form around 1680, to Barbados just a little later. At this 17th-century stage, in other words, adult sex ratios in both the British West Indies and the Chesapeake simply mirrored movement in the British slave trade. The difference was that in the West Indies this opening pattern rendered the population even more female among adults (52 percent) than the early maximum of the Chesapeake trend (46 percent). RAC *imports*, however, will be seen to have peaked at merely just over 40 percent women. Was the higher level for the *population* supplied from unoffical slaving competitors (who carried three-quarters of the Africans shipped to the British West Indies in the early years)? Did the RAC, like the Dutch West India Company, particularly stress men for its shipments? Or was a higher proportion of females beginning to evolve out of home-grown sources, in which biology provides a relatively even balance of boys and girls?

Then from around 1692 all the way into the early 19th century available data suggest a possible G trend with its base year at 1596. There are two ways of confirming that such a pattern is not just pulled out of a hat. First of all, evidence from Newton plantation on Barbados (the small filled triangles along the curve, from Handler and Lange 1978, 68–71) indicates that the percentage of females among adult slaves from 1740 into the 1830s (especially from the 1770s forward), though slightly higher, expanded parallel with the trend proposed for the older colonies of the British West Indies in general. Second, calculations by Craton (1975, 284) indicate that the percentage of females among slaves of all ages on Jamaica expanded in G fashion with t_0 at 1611, just a slightly later and steeper G than I estimate for adults in the older British colonies (Barbados, Leewards, Jamaica) collectively. In short, the upper G curve in this top part of Figure 5.9b does seem a highly likely model of the long-term movement being estimated for the older British sugar colonies. These typically contained an adult slave population in which women constituted about 53 percent across the 18th century compared with the more like 43 percent level being attained in the Chesapeake around 1750.

Figure 5.9b
The Weights of Women and Children in Slave Populations: British West Indies and South Carolina

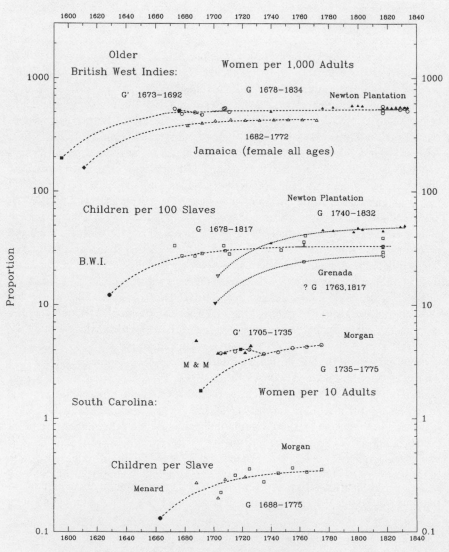

Sources: Figure 5.9a; Craton 1975, 284; Handler and Lange 1978, 68–71.

In South Carolina, part C of Table 5.6 and the next-to-bottom plot in Figure 5.9b also indicate an early G' hump in the proportion of females among adult slaves. This peaked about 44 years later than the early G' surges for the British West Indies and the Chesapeake. As in these other, earlier-developing colonies, though, the temporary early bulge was followed by a longer-lasting G trend of increase. In this colony it was based upon a t_0 at 1691, which—like the opening G' bulge—once again lagged behind the Chesapeake by 45 years but nonetheless preceded the t_0 for Prince George's County, Maryland, by about two decades.

In early-settled little Bermuda, meanwhile, there was a *flatter*, G-type increase for the proportion of women in the slave population across the 1700s (Figure 5.9c and part C of Table 5.6). This rested on a base year back at 1622, some 20 to 25 years previous to the similar trend for the Chesapeake and lagging the British West Indies (1596) comparably. By the middle of the 18th century, however, the female share of adult slaves on Bermuda had attained 58 percent before tapering back to more like 53 percent by 1774. Probably this decline, which started in the 1750s, took a D path. Grenada, on the other hand, originally colonized by the French, became lastingly British only in the later 1700s. Here from 1747 through 1833 the proportion of females among slaves apparently approached 50 percent along a G curve with base year at 1702 (Wells 1975, 256; Higman 1984, 309), rather like South Carolina and Prince George's County, Maryland. Trinidad, finally, was a very late acquisition for the British. Here from 1808 through the 1820s the proportion of females among adult persons of African descent, slave and free colored together, rose along a G path with t_0 at 1762, nearing half as emancipation arrived (John 1988, 40–42; Higman 1984, 415). With some readily comprehensible variations in timing and in the maximum level for women being approached, the recorded African populations of the New World colonies of Britain all, after their initial stocking by the slave trade, settled in to become more female over the long term along G-shape trends.

Following a spike for Barbados of 33 percent at 1673, meanwhile, the proportion of *children* in the slave populations of the West Indies progressively increased via a G trend with t_0 at 1629 from 1678 all the way into the 1820s (Figure 5.9b). The sources are generally the same as for the weight of adult females. The "X" at 1763 represents the average for Grenada, Dominica, and St. Vincent, whose proportions are also given separately. At 1817 the square symbols are for Barbados (highest at 39 percent), Jamaica (lowest at 29 percent), Antigua, and St. Kitts (Higman 1984, 462–64). The level ran at about 33 percent through the middle 1700s compared with about 45 percent in Morgan's Chesapeake sample and almost 50 percent in Kulikoff's probates for Prince George's County, Maryland. Hence, the slave population of the Chesapeake achieved substantial natural increase in the 18th century, and African Americans of the British West Indies, though their demographic condition improved, did not.

Newton plantation on Barbados (the solid upward triangles), however, saw its proportion of slaves who were not yet 15 years old rise from 1740 to 1832

Figure 5.9c
The Weights of Women and Children in Slave Populations: Bermuda, Grenada, St. Croix, Trinidad, and Surinam

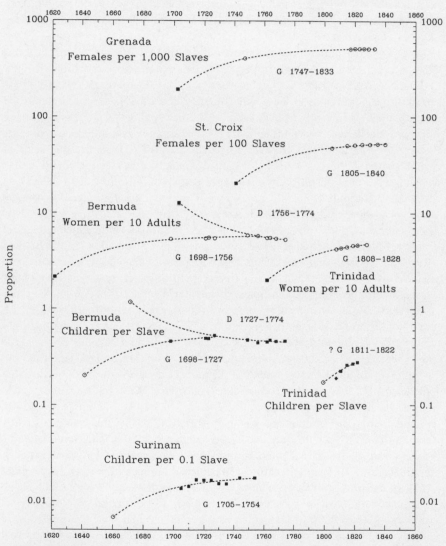

Sources: Wells 1975, 176–77, 256; Postma 1990, 185; John 1988, 41–42; Hall 1992, 85–86; Higman 1984, 414–15, 467.

via a G curve based at 1703 to approximately 50 percent by emancipation. This change generated a local African American population that was as young as the one in Prince George's County, Maryland. Similarly, Bermuda (Figure 5.9c) surpassed the Chesapeake across the early 18th century in the youthfulness of her slaves. On this small, early-settled island complex, those who were under 16 reached half of the population of African descent in the 1720s along a G curve with t_0 at 1668 (compared with the 1653 of the Chesapeake, as part A of Table 5.6 shows) before pulling back a little through the next several decades to about 46 percent. It took the Chesapeake a second increase of G shape (with base year at 1679) to reach this level in the middle of the 18th century (Figure 5.9a). After some fluctuation in the early years before 1708 (the bottom plot of Figure 5.9b), a G curve with base year at 1663 similarly captures the percentages of the young indicated by the South Carolina data first of Menard (1989, Tables 4, 5, and 7—the hollow triangles) and then of Morgan (1998, 83—the hollow squares) and lasts on to 1775. The level for slave children in this colony, though, tended to flatten out around 36 percent, closer to the 33 percent of the West Indies than the 50 percent of the Chesapeake and Bermuda. This was where the slave population of the Chesapeake stood in the early 1700s before its second, 18th-century G-type climb in youthfulness of 1715–1755. That difference held back the surge of net natural increase among South Carolina slaves until shortly before the American Revolution (Figure 5.7).

Data for Grenada at 1763 and 1817, meanwhile, suggest that the share of children in that slave population may have increasd via a G trend based about 1701. That makes for a movement parallel to the more frequently documented weight of females in this group, shown in Table 5.6 and Figure 5.9c. The trend also resembled in timing the G for Newton plantation after 1740 (Figure 5.9b); but that Barbadian curve reached almost 50 percent by the early 1800s in contrast to just 27 percent for Grenada. The few years for which the significance of slave children on Trinidad is known suggest a still more delayed G pattern there, with t_0 for the years 1811–1822 as late as 1799 (John 1988, 40–42). This trend, however, already lifted the local percentage for the young to match that of Grenada as emancipation approached.

Included in Figure 5.9c are plots for sex weights on St. Croix and for children in Surinam. They demonstrate how demographic structures in slave populations other than British ones likewise evolved along G lines. On St. Croix, an island now held by the Danes, a G from 1805 through 1840 that was based at about 1740 carried the percentage of females (of all ages) to slightly over half of the African American population through the first four decades of the 19th century. In Dutch Surinam, the weight of children among slaves also can be followed with some assurance across time (Postma 1990, 185), though the numbers are just for those under 12, which makes comparisons of level with other colonies difficult. Still, the weight of the young in the African population of this Dutch colony increased around a G curve from 1705 through 1754, shows Figure 5.9c. This had its base year at 1660 along with t_0's at 1668, 1653 and 1663 for

Bermuda, the Chesapeake, and South Carolina, respectively (part A of Table 5.6).

The biggest New World consumer of Africans was Brazil. Figure 5.9d plots some information for that country's sugar-growing Bahian region from Stuart B. Schwartz. The female proportions at 1572 and 1591 (marked "I") are for adult slaves who were at this point mostly Indian (1985, 347). The share of females in the total, now African, slave population subsequently rose in G form from the early 1630s through the 1730s (ibid., 347–48). From a top of 47 percent at 1739, however, the representation of females apparently declined in D fashion to less than 30 percent in the 1810s along a curve with base year at 1718. Meanwhile, the proportion of children among Bahian slaves also may have climbed in G form from the early 1630s forward, along a rather later curve—with t_0 at 1632. This makes the weight of children there rise parallel with the comparable composition for the slave population of the older British West Indian colonies from 1678 through 1829 (Figure 5.9b). And both attained a level of about 33 percent. The difference was that with new immigration that was heavily male, the share of children in the Bahian slave population, starting in the later 1700s, probably followed the percentage of females downward in relatively parallel or somewhat later D fashion. The question arises as to which available proportion for 1788 is most correct. The lower, 26 percent, is for slaves in neighboring Pernambuco and also for just slaves in nine parishes of Bahia (Schwartz 1985, 350, 359). The higher, more like 32 percent, is an estimate from Schwartz's data that includes slaves *and* free colored persons in a few Bahian parishes. Both numbers and both G-based trendings in which they are engaged could be simultaneously correct: on the one hand, among all persons of African descent the weight of children may have kept going up to 1788 or later along the G curve begun in the 1630s. On the other, the percentage of children among just *slaves* may have already been falling by 1788 in the D manner proposed. According to Schwartz, the Benedictines had a contemporary reputation for encouraging family development and reproduction on their estates. His average of 20 to 24 percent children for their records from 1652 through 1710, however, does not suggest that they were significantly out of line in that direction from the overall trend for the operation of cane farms and sugar mills (ibid., 355–56).

Some sense of the movements in vital rates for slaves in Bahia is also available from Schwartz (1985, 366). If a 75 per 1,000 estimate for the early 1630s from Engenho Sergipe is representative, the crude death rate (CDR) fell substantially into the 18th century. The next-to-bottom plot in Figure 5.9d fits a D curve to 1633 and 1730 levels from Schwartz along with the Cuban death rate calculations for 1774, 1791, and 1816 from Eblen (1975, 245; compare Figure 5.8b). The estimated local Bahian rate provided for 1750 and a CDR at 1798 from Maranhão (27.0 and 26.7, respectively) lie below this curve (as filled downward triangles) but very much parallel with it. The rate from the inland mining territory of Minas Gerais at 1815 lies right on the line, though the pace

Figure 5.9d
The Weights of Women and Children in Slave Populations: Bahia, Including Vital Rates

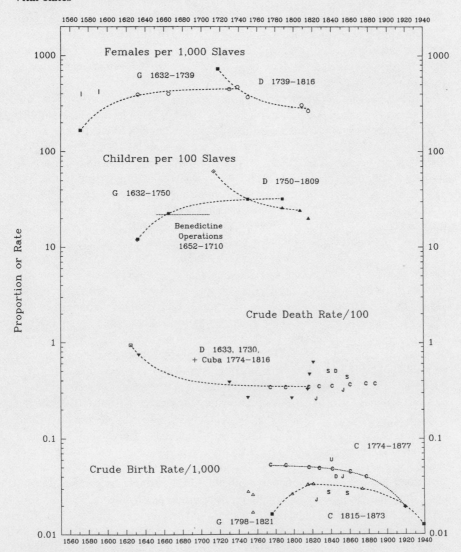

I = Indian; C = Cuba; D = Danish West Indies; J = Jamaica; S = Surinam; U = United States.

Sources: Schwartz 1985, 152, 347–61, 366; Eblen 1975, 245.

of death there seemingly soared in the next few years. The CDR for Cuban blacks also rose, though more gradually, in the 19th century (Eblen 1975, 245). Figure 5.8b has shown how this vital rate increased from 1816 through 1897 along a G curve based in the 1730s. Meanwhile the rate for slaves in Surinam ("S") descended toward this Cuban trend, while that for Jamaica ("J") climbed to meet it (Schwartz 1985, 366). By the 1800s was there a "typical" level of CDR for African American tropical workers to which various local slave populations converged as they worked through their own distinctive historical demographic specifics? (For instance, the Jamaican death rate may have been much lower *before* the emancipation of 1834, which tended to leave former slaves to their own devices.)

Bahian evidence on the crude birth rate (CBR) for slaves—the hollow, upward triangles in the bottom plot of Figure 5.9d—begins only around the middle of the 18th century and varies significantly locally. Across the early 1800s calculations from Maranhão and Minas Gerais rise substantially, possibly along the kind of short G curve offered in the figure. Then available Brazilian birth rates fell across the 19th century, probably along the type of accelerating C curve proposed. One support for that hypothesis comes from how closely the CBR for slaves in Surinam parallels that suggested pattern. Starting from a higher initial birth rate, a C trend was also being followed, meanwhile, by the native-born black population of Cuba from 1774 through 1877 (the "C'"symbols come from Eblen 1975, 245, which are also graphed in Figure 5.8b). The higher reproduction level for Cuba was more like the available spot CBR calculations for the Danish West Indies ("D") and the slave population of the United States ("U"). Plausibly, through the era of emancipation the birth rate for Jamaican blacks (the "J" symbols) rose even more robustly than the death rate to approach the level for native-born Cubans of African descent.

Figure 5.10 presents still another dimension of the demographic development or stabilization of New World populations with African roots. Over and over again, in spite of varying rates of immigration and natural replacement, these peoples became more native-born according to trends of G shape. From the *engenhos* (sugar mills) of Bahia the curve is lowest, barely exceeding 30 percent around 1800. If the slaves of cane farms are included, the 1602–1788 Bahian G curve rises to more like 45 percent native-born, as the second plot in Figure 5.10 indicates (Schwartz 1985, 61, 152, 348).[27]

For other slave populations the available data come closer together. On Jamaica, though the estimate for 1722 is high, the decade-by-decade proportions from 1712 through 1762 generally hover around a G curve with t_0 at 1710. This trend, however, carried the creolization of Jamaican slaves to only about 25 percent, well below the level even for Brazilian sugar-milling estates, let alone the slave population of that colony in general. From 1752 through 1817, however, a second 18th-century G surge made slightly over 60 percent of Jamaican blacks native-born (Craton 1975, 284).

After a relatively high beginning, which probably reflected a demographically

Figure 5.10
The Creolization of African American Populations: Bahia, Jamaica, South Carolina, and Virginia

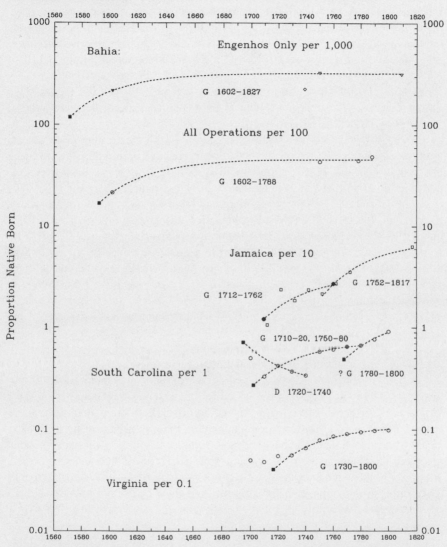

Sources: Schwartz 1985, 61, 152, 348, 352; Craton 1975, 284; Higman 1984, 464; Morgan 1998, 61.

seasoned labor population transferred from the West Indies, for most of the time between 1710 and 1780 the share of South Carolina slaves who had been born in the colony (P. Morgan 1998, 61) built up along a G path parallel to the 1712–1762 trend for Jamaica, as Figure 5.10 shows. These changes toward a creole population were very much taking place together. One difference, however, was that the South Carolina curve was much higher: by the Revolution some 65 percent of slaves there were native. Another departure was that during a surge of imports that led up to the Stono Rebellion, from 1720 through 1740 the percentage of creoles among South Carolina slaves *dropped* significantly, perhaps in the kind of D pattern offered in Figure 5.10 (ibid.). Figure 2.11b of Chapter 2 has shown how sharply imports via Charleston surged up to 1737. Then from about 1780 to 1800 the weight of natives in the South Carolina slave population rose once more, reaching over 90 percent before the slave trade to the United States was officially ended.

In Virginia, by 1700 about half of the slaves were creole, though at present it is impossible to tell how this level had been obtained across the 1600s.[28] From 1730 through 1800, however, a G trend with base at 1717—a little later than the parallel movement in Jamaica—is clearly the pattern (Morgan 1998, 61). This movement (the bottom plot in Figure 5.10) made virtually all of Virginia's slaves native-born by 1800. As a group, then, the British colonies in the New World developed more native slave populations across the 18th century via fairly parallel G paths. In how far creolization had proceeded by 1700 and how high the percentage became by about 1770, however, among the documented colonies Virginia led South Carolina, and Jamaica trailed most behind. Later trends in the latter colonies carried the proportions toward where that of Virginia stood at 1800; but the Jamaican slave population in particular was still noticeably less creole in its composition.

In all, the G shape seems to have characterized over and over again (1) how the age structure of slave populations normalized; (2) how male/female imbalances that arose from locally perceived needs for labor in plantation-building or leverage within the market for slaves worked themselves out; and (3) how slave populations became native-born. As the initial pull to introduce slave labor waned in region after region, some underlying process kept steering into the G shape the most fundamental demographic developments in African American peoples: their composition by age and sex and nativity, their rates of natural renewal (whether more or less than required for full replacement), and dependence upon further migration for growth. And their birth rates and death rates are hinted to have followed G-related paths through time as well.

CHANGES IN THE SEX, AGE, VALUE, AND TREATMENT OF FORCIBLY TRANSPORTED AFRICANS

If the structures of the African American populations that were created by the slave trade so consistently evolved in G-based patterns, did demographic change in such shapes also leave imprints upon what kinds of captives composed the cargoes of this nefarious commerce and other aspects of how the trade in humans worked? One can envision demographic forces coming to bear in several ways. In demand, the developments just observed in receiving New World populations might readily make additional imports of a particular type more (or less) desirable or acceptable. In supply, did the wave- or pulse-like G' pumpings of African peoples from out of one region of the continent after another that are noted in Chapter 2 alter the character of the potential slaves who remained available? In between, in the traffic that purchased slaves on one continent and disposed of them on another, were prices, profits, or procedures altered in G-related fashion by such familiar demographic forms of change in the markets for buying and selling human beings for labor? For decades, scholars of the slave trade have analyzed the sex and age of Africans being delivered, prices in Africa and America, mortality during various stages of the transition from capture to final sale, and the nature and the use of the shipping that was engaged in slaving. Their findings can be at least preliminarily plumbed to see what fresh insight derives from our new perspective on recurrent shapes of change through time.

Trends in the composition of slave traffic by sex and by age can in the least be roughly identified. Fairly precise information exists in print for certain trades at certain times; examples include the British Royal African Company during its short period of effective operation in the late 1600s and early 1700s; the Dutch trade for a century following 1690; aggregate European exports out of the Bight of Biafra between 1770 and 1858, and less confidently earlier, between 1680 and 1770; total exports from other parts of Africa in the late-19th-century stage of the business; and imports into Cuba and parts of Brazil also for the last decades of the trade. These patterns will be examined here. The new database should allow further work by those who possess the necessary knowledge of the sources and how they should be employed. One inquiry based upon the CD-ROM (Nwokeji 2001) suggests that published studies already reveal the basic patterns of change.

Figure 5.11a, drawing upon these past analyses, first plots across its top the proportion that males of all ages constituted in the cargoes of various national slave trades. It then presents the weight of just *adult* males among slaves carried by Dutch vessels—by the West India Company into the 1730s and by free traders thereafter. The bottom plot of the figure, finally, trends the proportion of males of any age among slaves loaded by all recorded trading groups in the Bight of Biafra.[29]

Certain fairly clear impressions emerge concerning how the content of slave cargoes altered across the years. From the 1660s through the 1720s British and Dutch slavers, at least, included rising proportions of males in their shipments. Their symbols represent averages at the midpoint for various time spans summarized by Geggus (1989, 24). The percentages climbed along a G curve from about 53 percent at 1665 to more like 70 percent at 1730, though—as the top

Figure 5.11a
Proportion of Males in the Cargoes of Various Slave Trades

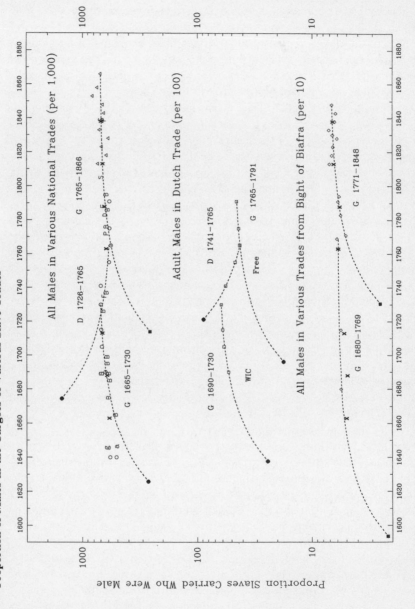

o = Dutch; B = British; D = Danish; F = French; P = Portuguese; S = Spanish; a = Angola; g = Guinea. Triangles = Eltis 1987, all nations; X = Nwokeji 2001.

Source: See note 29.

plot of Figure 5.11a indicates—the British level may have remained a little lower than that of the West India Company (WIC). Recently presented CD-ROM proportions for all African traffic except that from the Bight of Biafra (Nwokeji 2001, 67) predominantly fit such trending from older sources. The departure comes at 1663, where the 1651–1676 proportion is high. To include Biafra—with a significantly lower percentage during this period (49.7 rather than 58.3)—to obtain a comparable *overall* proportion for the Atlantic slave trade, however, brings the level close to the fitted curve.

Meanwhile, just *adult* males expanded even rather more steeply among WIC cargoes to attain 62 percent by the 1730s (Postma 1990, 231). Widely spaced data from the Bight of Biafra (Geggus 1989, 30), in contrast, indicate much less change in loadings there between 1680 and 1769 (from 56 to 61 percent for males of any age). The new CD-ROM data for Biafra suggest rather lower proportions at 1688 and 1713 but fall on the fitted curve at 1663 and 1763. It should probably serve as the working trend until further analysis proves otherwise.

All three of these changes in composition appear to have followed G-shape tracks. The curves for composite international data and for the weight of just adult men within the Dutch trade had base years in the 1620s and 1630s, respectively.

For the Atlantic trade as a whole, and in the Dutch trade in particular, the proportion of males or the proportion of men among adults then declined significantly from the 1720s into the 1760s. Among the assortment of various clues from the international trade, the percentage for males of any age fell from 70 to 57 between 1730 and 1765, declining along what may have been a D path with t_0 in the early 1670s. Coming from what seems to be primarily British evidence, this trend indicates that the weight of males in imports declined parallel with 1688–1770 D-shape softening of net natural decrease in the British West Indies and the shrinking ratio of slave imports to current slave populations there (Table 5.3). For adults alone, after free traders replaced the West India Company in the Dutch trade, the D trend was both clearer and steeper (with base year near 1720 compared with about 25 years later for net natural decrease and the proportional significance of current slave imports in Surinam, shown in Table 5.3). The weight of men in the total dropped from 61 to 42 percent. In the Bight of Biafra, though, there is no evidence of such a sustained shift in the sex compositions of slave loadings, just a short drop around 1770. Why did traffic from this particular region behave differently?

The reason for adjustment partway through the 1700s appears to be African and regional—the kind of dynamic about which Eltis and Engerman have reminded us (1992, 246–57). In the first quarter of the 18th century began a letdown in loading from the Bight of Benin or Slave Coast along a D path that continued to reduce slave exports there from their early G' summit near 1713 right through the first half of the 19th century (Figure 2.2a). In this decline, Dutch shipments from the Benin coast disappeared, Portuguese and British loadings receded by two-thirds to three-quarters from their erstwhile levels, and the fledgling French business of the region suffered a sharp if shorter setback (Figure 2.4a). None of these national trades *as a whole* lost so much momentum this way in the period (Figures 2.3a and 2.3b); it was their Slave Coast source that shriveled. Operations had to shift elsewhere.

Figure 2.4c indicates how it was "recruitment" from the Aja peoples of the Dahomey part of the Slave Coast that plummeted by almost two-thirds from the 1710s and 1720s to the 1750s, though Voltaic tribes of the Dahomey interior also saw their slave sales decline to a low point in the 1740s, if less precipitously. Did something happen to slave-catching, -purchasing, or -exporting in this region at this time that might have significantly reduced the proportion of *men* being shipped across the Atlantic? Did the Aja traditionally provide a high ratio of men, and when their large slave production declined seriously was that enough to affect the weight of men in the Atlantic trade as a whole for a while (or at least the part for which sex has been recorded)? Did the expansion of Danhommè in the 1720s, which has been described as "an attempt by King Agaja to put an end to slave exports" (Manning 1982, 12), fundamentally alter the mix of who left, perhaps retaining men as warriors for the benefit of the state? As more and more Aja were stripped away and the local population substantially shrank (ibid., 10), did the local business perforce turn for supply more to women and children? After decades of slaving wars did men just learn to make themselves scarce? The rate at which Aja population is estimated to have been reduced by slaving peaked at something like 3.25 percent *annually* in the 1710s (ibid., 341–43).[30] Suggestively, this pace of loss declined from its peak in the 1710s to less than half that rate for the 1750s along a D trend with t_0 around 1711, a curve somewhat steeper than the one for all European slaving—Aja and others—from the Bight of Benin (with t_0 at 1688, shown in Table 2.3 and Figure 2.2a). Some interesting possibilities for further investigation into the African dynamics of slaving would seem to emerge here from the way that G-based trends in regional exports and their likely demographic consequences mesh with a temporary reduction in the presence of males in the slave trade as a whole and especially in Dutch traffic. Meanwhile, Figure 5.11a indicates that no such shift in sex composition took place in exports from the Bight of Biafra in this period. Did other loading coasts experience trends like those of Biafra or those of Benin?

Past the middle of the 18th century, all three plots of Figure 5.11a display tendencies for cargoes once again to contain relatively *more* males along new G paths, now anchored near 1720. Thanks to Eltis (1987, 258), all males within the international trade can be followed to 1866; those loaded from the Bight of Biafra to 1848. The series for the Dutch trade ends much sooner, as slavers of this nation went out of business late in the 18th century. But the evidence from 1765 through 1791 seems to move approximately parallel with the other two G trends (it is only slightly flatter). This was an era in which a new wave of plantation settlements developed or expansion within older colonies surged: in

Brazil, the Spanish Caribbean, new tropical territories acquired by Britain, and—for a while—St. Domingue.

This is scarcely the first analysis of the significance of men and males in the slave trade to be offered. It seems, however, to add some new perspective to our understanding. First of all, the movements all appear to have followed G and D patterns. Second, systematic, sustained decline in the percentage of males and/or adult men markedly interrupted the "secular rise. . . . over two centuries" that recent commentators have emphasized (Eltis and Engerman 1992, 257). Virtually *all* of the ultimate increase in the proportion of males, furthermore, occurred early—between the 1660s and the 1710s and 1720s, where the 70 percent masculine level of the 1860s was already attained. Third, some clues are offered as to how both increasing inclusion of males and temporary reversal toward females came about: the first from the conditions of plantation-building or expansion (as opposed to maintenance); the second perhaps from changes in supply as well as New World demographic alterations that shaped demand. Meanwhile, it is necessary to remember that having a general or overall pattern for the Atlantic trade does not mean that consuming localities within America did not *vary* in the proportions of males that they received. Such differential distribution west of the Atlantic will be considered shortly. Finally, it is essential to remember—as previous discussion has shown—that for most slave societies further imports became increasingly marginal as population grew and demographic structure began to normalize (even when it did not achieve full replacement). *Local* dynamics increasingly shaped the weight of both men and children in the resident *population* of African origin, which in turn influenced the desirability of new migrants of various sex and age, a subject that will be taken up as soon as the record for children in the slave trade has been examined.

The top plot of Figure 5.11b shows how the proportion of the young among slave cargoes rose substantially from the 1660s into the 1730s. The international evidence is quite variable, particularly during the last two decades of this era. Still, an underlying G trend with base year at 1654 seems to capture the flow of the assortment of available evidence through time.[31] Recent interregional database calculations (Nwokeji 2001, 67) for quarter-centuries around 1663, 1688, and 1713 (the "X"s in the graph) in net go up roughly the same way, though for some reason they seem to sag in the middle. It should be remembered that these computations omit the Bight of Biafra. Along the fitted underlying G trajectory, the presence of children in the mix roughly doubled from about 9 to more like 17 percent. Substantial national differences are indicated, however. In particular, between 1690 and 1730 vessels of the WIC (the "o" symbols) carried *fewer and fewer* children proportionally along a D track roughly compensatory to the likely rising G for the international trade as a whole. It looks, from this distinctive movement and from the way that males did not decline in the Dutch trade until the WIC was replaced by "free" operators, as if it were company policy, or the kinds of delivery contracts that they undertook, that stressed adult

Figure 5.11b
Proportion of Children in the Cargoes of Various Slave Trades

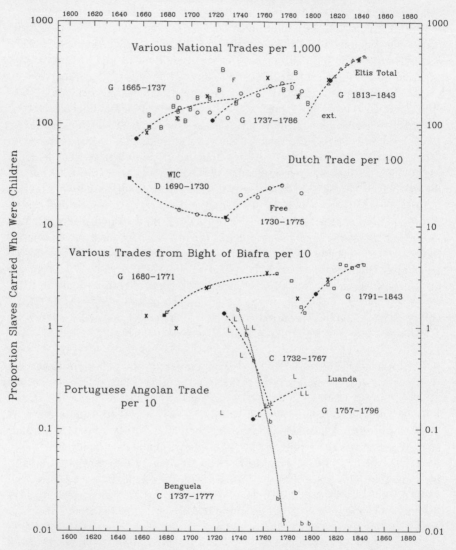

o = Dutch; B = British; D = Danish; F = French; P = Portuguese; S = Spanish; L = Luanda;
b = Benguela; X = Nwokeji, 2001.

Sources: See notes 29 and 31.

men over women and children in a way that departed from what the Atlantic market for slaves typically encouraged over time. That discrepancy might have helped the company go out of business—a possibility of operational error that would seem to merit some further inquiry if the sources permit.

From the 1730s forward for several decades, the weight of children among slave cargoes increased in G fashion again—now from about 17 to over 25 percent and with less variability around the hypothesized trend in the international fragments (though not the CD-ROM perspective for 1751–1775). During this phase Dutch traders, now free of company restraints, followed suit in loading more children. In the Bight of Biafra, meanwhile, from around 1680 or sooner to around 1771 the proportion of children among slaves exported climbed from 14 to 34 percent along what seems to have been an uninterrupted G path.[32] CD-ROM evidence for this region in this era follows the curve of the previously printed information closely (especially if one averages the first two observations).

Both in the international trade as aggregated by Eltis and, less steeply, in cargoes out of the Bight of Biafra (the middle plot of Figure 5.11b), the weight of children climbed a third time in G form across the first half of the 19th century (Eltis 1987, 258). It encourages confidence in the new method of modeling to have these data of Eltis—some of the surest and most regular information that is available on the trade—fit so tightly and so consistently around the G pattern for those 30 years, along with the latest database averages for 1801–1825 and 1826–1850. A projection of the curve backward in time, however, alerts us to the drop in the proportion of children in slave shipments that occurred during the last two decades of the 18th century. The way that such a sharp decline preceded growing reliance of slaving upon children is even more obvious among exports just from the Bight of Biafra. What dynamics reduced the export of children so markedly at this time?

The starkest evidence of all for a sharp setback for the role for children in the slave trade, however, appears rather earlier in Angola. In shipments out of Luanda (the "L"s in the bottom plotting of Figure 5.11b) the percentage of children fell from approximately 10 to only about 1 percent between the 1730s and the 1760s (Klein 1978, 254–56; 1982, 225, 239–40). From the 1760s into the early 1800s this proportion then revived slightly, perhaps along the kind of underlying G path that is fitted. Whereas around 1800 the role of children in exports from Luanda, while recovering, amounted to only about a quarter of the level at mid-century, at Benguela—farther south down the Angolan coast—the young virtually disappeared altogether from slave shipments. Their proportion (denoted by the "b"s at the bottom of the figure) plummeted to less than 1/100th of its former level: from 15.0 to 0.13 percent. An exceptional cargo or two in the 1780s raised the local average back up some, only to fall once more into the 1790s in a fashion very parallel to the C-type curve along which the significance of children in the Benguela trade truly hastened toward extinction, as that particular reversed G-based trajectory typically does. Benguela, even more than Luanda, was drawing supply from further and further away across the interior of Africa, and travel from that heartland to this center seems to have lacked the easier river routes provided by the great tributaries of the Congo further north (Miller 1988, 148, 263; 2002, 57). Were children simply judged unable to make the long and arduous trek to market or not to be worth the transportation cost involved? Were they not captured? Were they killed? Were they sold locally or shipped to traders of the Indian Ocean or the Sahara, the other significant geographical flows of African slavery?

For all these apparent late-18th-century changes in Angola, though, somehow children reappeared strongly in the Portuguese portion of the Atlantic slave trade. The right-hand panel of Figure 5.11c indicates how in the exceptional years of the 1820s and early 1830s the share of the young—mostly boys (Miller 2002, 60)—surged to reach 75 to 80 percent of deliveries to Bahia in northern Brazil and likewise to the southern regions of this great slave-consuming colony. Typically the slave trade of the former was tied to sources in the Bight of Benin, the latter to supply from Angola. What might cause these two upward leaps in youthfulness simultaneously? Miller attributes the rising percentage of adolescent males to a cessation in hostilities among regional African powers that reduced the number of men captives (ibid., 59). On the whole, though, such extreme proportions seems to have represented only temporary upward swings around base trends that more likely followed the kind of G track observed in deliveries to Cuba by Spanish and other, often U.S., slavers. This Cuban trajectory carried the presence of children in cargoes, which apparently had been falling across the 1790s, from about 18 percent to more like 40 percent before a local collapse in importing the young took place in the 1840s and early 1850s. This drop somehow temporarily depressed the percentage of children in the Cuban trade back to its level of 1800 before it regained the preceding G curve of increase at 50 percent in the 1860s, just as the traffic came to an end.

The proportion of *males* in deliveries to Brazil, meanwhile, between 1810 and 1845 dipped in 1/G' shape with troughs in the 1830s at about 60 percent (the left panel of Figure 5.11c)—while the international average (Figure 5.11a) hovered around 70 percent. Alternative to Miller's thesis that peace produced fewer men as slaves (2002, 59), another working hypothesis might be that previously developed zones of plantation and mining in the colony (see the regional trends for Brazil's imports after about 1770 in Figure 2.1b) were now producing enlarged native slave populations, while Cuba's expanding sugar-growers were trying to augment their prime workforce quickly, in the boom around the turn of the century, which produced a G' hump in the proportion of males among new arrivals. Once a slave population became established and began to reproduce itself, then Cuban planters purchased relatively more males in the same steadily and lastingly increasing manner across the last half-century of available slaving as found elsewhere in earlier times among other regional slave trades as these matured (Figure 5.11a). This later, G-shape trend lifted males to about 78

Figure 5.11c
Proportions of Males and Young in the Leading 19th-Century Slave Trades

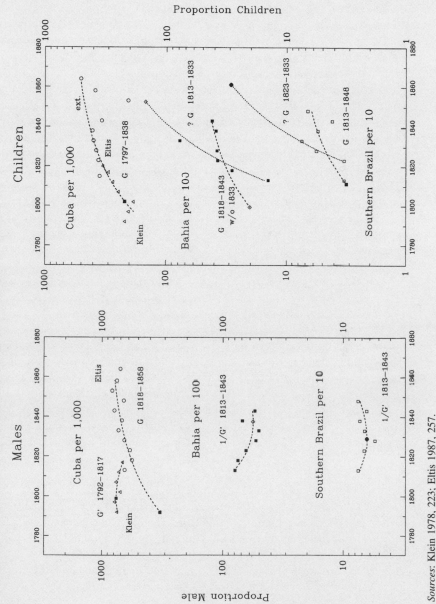

Sources: Klein 1978, 223; Eltis 1987, 257.

percent of all known deliveries to Cuba by the 1850s from the 56 percent that they represented around 1818, even if more of them had to be children.

Further particulars of this type emerge out of shipments by the Royal African Company from the 1670s to the 1720s (Figure 5.12 and Table 5.7). To begin, the records of that business (in spite of supposed monopoly status, it must be remembered that the company carried only about one-quarter of all deliveries to this group of colonies) show that the proportion of adult males among all slaves transported to the British West Indies across the company's half century of activity dipped in a 1/G' pattern, as evident in the top plot of the left or "a" panel of Figure 5.12 (Galenson 1986, 94–96). The share of men in deliveries to Barbados and Jamaica each separately sagged during this period also in 1/G' shape with low points at about 49 and 48 percent at 1694 and 1693, respectively. In contrast, though, the weight of adult males among slaves known to have been delivered by the Royal African Company to the *Leewards* humped *upward* between 1673 and 1723 in offsetting G' form with a peak of 62 percent at 1700. Table 5.7 summarizes these local trends. Collectively, the Leewards were going through agricultural changes to sugar production seen previously on Barbados and Jamaica. Heavy importation of slaves to intensify the cultivation of sugar stressed males of prime age for immediate hard work. In effect, the three different settlement groups of the British West Indies followed each other first into and then past the agricultural shift to stress growing cane.[33]

With extra men emphasized for heavy work, one might expect consequences of elevated mortality and reduced fertility. Interestingly, natural decrease for slaves in the Leewards actually improved (declined) between 1675 and 1730, the era of Royal African operations. The overriding dynamic was that *any* further imports were becoming strikingly less important to the population processes of the islands (Figure 5.6d). The composition of imports, especially for only the fraction carried by the RAC, just did not matter as much for the local demographic regimes as in the early years of plantation development.

As Table 5.7 shows, in all slave imports delivered by the Royal African Company the proportion of females, both among adults and among children (panel b of Figure 5.12 graphs just the former), rose and fell between 1672 and 1725 in G' fashion with peaks of 42 and 34 percent, respectively, at about 1683. This meant that females were relatively most in evidence slightly after the opening G-shape surge of slave imports into the British West Indies went through its zero year around 1670 (Figure 2.1c and Table 2.1). A sequence of more diverse early flow as a migration establishes momentum, giving way to a higher proportion of males as the numbers taper off, is a phenomenon observed also in the history of free migrations.[34] Percentages of females among adult slaves brought by the Royal African Company to the separate leading British colonial areas, moreover, all rose and fell in G' fashion that resembled very closely the track for the enterprise's aggregate (Table 5.7 and the middle or "b" panel of Figure 5.12). The movement was a company-wide one as the RAC diversified its traffic to meet heavy demand for slaves.

Figure 5.12
The Composition of Royal African Company Deliveries to Certain Colonies

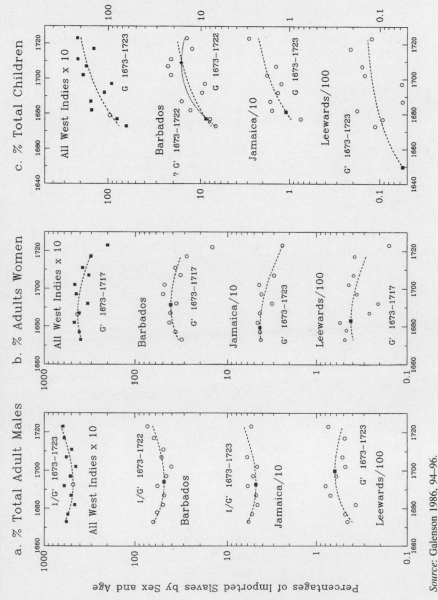

Source: Galenson 1986, 94–96.

Table 5.7
Trends in the Composition of Royal African Company Slaves by Sex and Age, 1673–1723

	All Deliveries	To Barbados	To Janaica	To the Leewards
% of Total Adult Males	1673-1723 1/G' 1693	1673-1722 1/G' 1694	1673-1723 1/G' 1693	1673-1723 G' 1700
% of Adults Women	1672-1725 G' 1682	1673-1717 G' 1691	1673-1723 G' 1679	1673-1717 G' 1682
% of Total Children	1673-1723 G 1680	1673-1722 G 1677	1677-1723 G 1682	1673-1723 ?G 1650
		1673-1722 ?G' 1709		
% of Males Boys	1673-1723 G 1684			
% of Females Girls	1673-1723 G 1686			
% of Children Girls	1672-1725 G' 1684			

Source: Galenson 1986, 94–96.

The proportion of *children* in the mix behaved rather differently, however. For the total documented RAC trade between 1672 and 1725, this percentage rose from 6 to 23 in G form without signs of dropping off again like the share of females, as the right or "c" panel of Figure 5.12 and the third line of Table 5.7 indicate. This kind of G-shaped change applied equally to the weight of boys among males (from 7 to 25 percent) and girls among females (from 4 to 19 percent).[35] All three curves had t_0's in the 1680s. For British West Indian colonies separately, moreover, G was also probably the shape, though a G' alternative for Barbados is a possibility, and the Leewards for some reason purchased very few children in the later 1680s and the 1690s (the right panel of Figure 5.12). Throughout the five decades across which the RAC operated, finally, about half of the Africans that the business forced to migrate to the British West Indies were adult men. Right across the period, in other words, in spite of some shifts up and down, there was an ample supply of women and children with which to build improvements in natural decrease, even though the level of full replacement was not attained.

In all, many particulars of the types of slaves carried to the New World by various trades evolved or shifted back and forth in G-connected patterns. It would seem profitable to pursue in continuing research how such trends related to the structures of the populations both from which and to which the captives were being drawn.

How the slave populations of non-Iberian America developed and naturalized, and what the impact of such changes were, can be mapped out further when viewed along with the perspective of slave *prices*. Figure 5.13, first of all, trends prices obtained for prime male slaves in several New World markets, ranging from the Caribbean coast of South America northward to the Carolinas. The data come from analysis by David Eltis and David Richardson for 242,274 slaves of known price arriving in the Americas on 1,056 voyages: "Markets for Slaves Newly Arrived in the Americas: Price Patterns, 1673–1865" (forthcoming 2003). The authors integrate both published and unpublished primary sources. Prices for prime males arriving at other destinations are standardized on Jamaica, the leading point of arrival, for currency differences relative to sterling via McCusker 1978, for varying lags between arrival and sale, and for comparative transportation costs estimated for certain periods and regions. The last seem just to raise or lower value by 5 to 10 percent throughout long stretches of time and should have minor effect upon the shapes of trending offered in Figure 5.13. Two-thirds of the voyages with recorded prices were British, and most of the remainder were Dutch and French. I am indebted to the authors for sharing the essay prior to its publication.

Figure 5.13 demonstrates how prices in five American regions consistently increased in successive trends of G shape. The plot for Barbados alone at the bottom left of the graph is for men in the first half of Royal African Company sales (Galenson 1986, 56). The alternative G' pattern included in this series for

Figure 5.13
Price Trends for Prime Male Slaves in Colonial Markets, 1673–1808

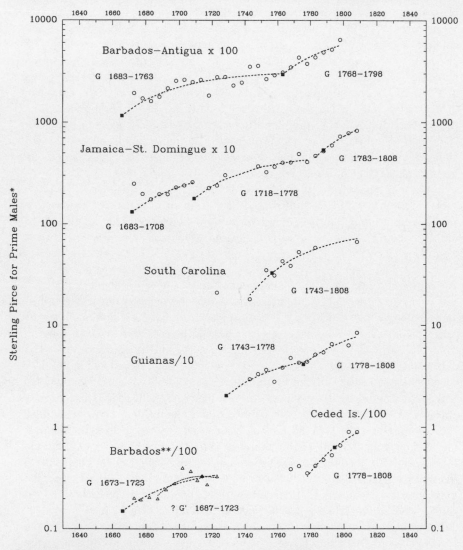

*Standardized on Jamaica (Eltis and Richardson, Appendix Table 2);
**Men in first half of sales (Galenson).

Sources: Eltis and Richardson, forthcoming; Galenson 1986, 56.

Table 5.8
G Trends for Sterling Slave Prices in Various Colonial Markets*

Barbados-Antigua I	1683-1763	G	1666
Barbados Only**	1673-1723	G	1666
Jamaica-St. Domingue I	1683-1708	G	1672
Jamaica-St. Domingue II	1718-1778	G	1709
Guianas I	1743-1778	G	1729
South Carolina	1743-1808	G	1759
Barbados-Antigua II	1763-1798	G	1763
Guianas II	1778-1808	G	1776
Jamaica-St. Domingue III	1783-1808	G	1788
Ceded Islands	1778-1808	G	1795
All Recorded Prices I	1683-1738	G	1655
" " " II	1733-1783	G	1730
" " " III	1788-1808	G	1793

*Prime males standardized on Jamaica by Eltis and Richardson forthcoming;
**Men in first half of sales.

Sources: Figures 5.13 and 5.14a; text.

just the years 1687–1723 is not put forward as a good representation of movement across the whole half-century available but is useful for discussing (later
in this section) relative price patterns for men, women, boys, and girls among
slaves arriving on the island.

Table 5.8 compares the range and the timing of the G trends of Figure 5.13.
Jamaica (there must be few prices for St. Domingue this early) experienced a
first phase of G-shape increase between 1673 and 1708 that lagged just a few
years behind the upward path for Barbados and Antigua (before the 1700s probably overwhelmingly Barbados, as the parallel movement of just RAC prices
on that island tends to confirm). With t_0's at 1672 and 1666, these curves indicate, when compared with Table 5.3, that the price of slaves at this stage in
the development of the British West Indies rose parallel with annual slave imports between 1638 and 1730 (with base year for that G at 1671) but *inverse*
to D trends for the the growth rate of the non-white population 1655–1785, the
rate of importation relative to the current non-white population 1688–1770, and
the softening of net natural decrease for Africans in the British Caribbean 1688–
1770 (with t_0's at 1673, 1674, and 1679, respectively). It took price increases
to expand the number of prime male slaves brought to the region; but these two
movements were each strikingly inverse to the parallel manner in which net
demographic decline lessened and the rate of further African imports relative to
existing slave populations shrank.

In the early 18th century, following a shift of level downward, prices at Jamaica and St. Domingue commenced a new rise in the value of prime male slaves. Though data are lacking between 1730 and 1745, a second trend of G type seems probable. This had its base year at 1709. On Jamaica (Figures 5.6a and 5.6b and Table 5.4), the number of retained slave imports per year 1715–1798 increased via a G track that was anchored nearby at 1719. In the meantime, the growth rate of the non-white population then slowed down in D form between 1705 and 1798 (with t_0 at 1698), while retained imports relative to existing non-white population shifted to pick up decline in D fashion between 1745 and 1798—with zero year at 1715 to follow net natural decrease among those of African descent on the island, whose rate fell from 1735 through 1800 with t_0 at 1712. Once again prices rose inversely to the influx of fresh slaves in proportion to the existing population.

For St. Domingue, the available data do not allow analysis to be so specific. For the French West Indies as a whole, however, the majority of whose slave traffic was in fact devoured by the large French share of the island of Santo Domingo, similar comparisons can be made (Table 5.3 and Figure 5.4). While slave prices as lumped by Eltis and Richardson along with those of Jamaica rose in G form between 1718 and 1778 with base year at 1709, across the 18th century the size of the non-white population and the annual number of slave imports grew along G tracks with somewhat later zero years at 1733 and 1724. Meanwhile, from 1688 through 1770 the rate of imports compared with current slave population and the reduction of net natural decrease both took D paths with t_0's at 1699 and 1704, slightly earlier. While not exactly contemporaneous, these G and D trends make the relevant movements behave generally the same way relative to slave prices as on Jamaica.[36]

Prices for slaves delivered to the Guianas, primarily a Dutch trade, climbed via a still later curve of G shape (Table 5.8). The timing of its base year, 1729, appears to arrive somewhat after that for the D trend in the current growth rate of the non-white population (1713) and rather earlier than the timing for paths taken up by net natural decrease between 1730 and 1770 (1747) and perhaps the rate of imports relative to resident Africans between 1750 and 1770 (1746), as presented in Table 5.3 and Figure 5.5. The data are less informative; but it seems that prices in the Guianas were also rising roughly inverse to the way that the slave population was being taken over by local demographic processes.

In another colonial setting heavily relying upon Africans, South Carolina, a still later G-shape rise in prices appears between 1743 and 1808. It is based at 1759. Recent nominal prices in dollars published by Mancall et al. (2001, 620) appear to rise in G shape from 1747 through 1807 with t_0 around 1760, confirming local calculations made for Figure 5.13 and Table 5.8. Figure 5.7 and Table 5.6 have shown that net natural *increase* appeared between about 1740 and 1795 there in G form with zero year at 1761. Meanwhile, from 1725 through 1770 slave imports to the colony declined as a proportion of the existing African American population in D fashion with t_0 at 1752. In still another historical context, in short, price increases for additional slaves rose inverse to improving demographic conditions and a declining role for fresh imports of labor.

Parallel to price increases for South Carolina, the composite data of Eltis and Richardson for Barbados and Antigua show a new, late upward G trend from 1768 through 1798 with zero year at 1759. For best interpretation, this combination of local markets could profitably be disaggregated. Barbados led the way into slavery for the British West Indies in the middle 1600s, while Antigua, for lack of water, was significantly delayed in taking up sugar cultivation with African labor. For the Leewards as a whole (St. Christopher, Nevis, Montserrat, and Antigua), 18th-century G trends for the size of the non-white population and for annual slave imports and also D trends for the growth rate of the non-white population and slave imports relative to the current resident population of African descent—all with base years in the first quarter of the 1700s—resemble patterns for Jamaica. Unlike the case in other parts of the Caribbean, however, net natural decrease rose via G rather than falling according to D while such movements were at work (Figure 5.5 and Tables 5.4 and 5.5). Barbados, meanwhile, whose price rise for prime males followed a steeper G than the number of slave imports 1733–1773, is known for shifting from muscavado production to claying white sugar and distilling residual molasses during the later decades under consideration. Perhaps the profits obtained by the change in technology made paying relatively more for slaves cost-effective there.

Table 5.8, finally, shows how still later G patterns for rising prices appeared in the Guianas, with zero year at 1776, as a second phase after 1778, and still more steeply (with t_0 at 1788) on the islands of Grenada, St. Vincent, and Dominica, which had been ceded by France to Britain as prizes of war in the 1760s. The latter, later trend was accompanied by a third G movement for Jamaica.[37] The dynamics of those late movements will have to be investigated elsewhere. All these G trends of different timing for prices in particular colonies, however, each separately unfolded in concert with local demographic change, not current general movements of an international market. Apparently demographically shaped colonial demand drove the system.

In one American settlement of the northern European powers after another, as natural demographic processes took over and the importation of further Africans became less significant relative to the number of slaves already present, prices rose inversely. That may at first seem counter-intuitive. As costs for obtaining slaves in West Africa climbed, which will be seen in a moment, it is easy to imagine upward pressure on prices. But why did such a vertical symmetry betweeen G trends for prices and D trends for domestic demographic improvement or normalization appear in this slave portion of the population in colony after colony, often with distinct local chronology?

If one multiplies *rates* of adding on new slaves in D shape by a countervailing G trend in prices that has comparable timing, the result is a constant proportional annual aggregate investment in fresh labor. After a certain period of time, that is, from one chronological and geographical wave of American settlement to the next, what planters collectively paid annually for new Africans relative to the size of their current slave-holdings generally remained *constant*. Their costs for new labor relative to size of operation, in terms of current total manpower, found and held an equilibrium. Sugar colonies might require a higher rate of replacement than those with other predominant crops and labor conditions, like the rice of South Carolina or the tobacco of the Chesapeake. But in each context expenditure on fresh labor established its level and sustained it for a substantial period of time. As a new crop or a new technology altered production, labor requirements, and profits, further changes could appear. For long periods of time, however, in one locality after another the need to add on proportionally less new labor—thanks to improving local demographic conditions—allowed the price that could be paid for slaves in a competitive international market to rise inversely in a colonial region and total costs for new slaves to remain constant to scale.

That is the story from the side of the New World planter who depended on slave labor. What happened from the perspective of his supplier, the shipper of slaves?

It is possible in Figure 5.14a to compare prices paid for slaves in western Africa with what they brought at sale in the American plantation colonies of the British, French, and Dutch. New World prices are for prime males. The New World regional series of Eltis and Richardson (forthcoming, Appendix Table 2) have been averaged from 1673 through 1808 (the hollow circles), weighting by the number of slaves sold at known prices for each market. Prices in Africa for years from 1776 through 1860 are taken from Manning (1982, 332, 334), who adjusted data from Le Veen (1977, 8, 113) for currency and the value of goods given for slaves. From 1638 through 1775 the prices of Bean (*Historical Statistics* 2: 1174, Series Z 168) have been made comparable according to the method adopted by Manning (1982, 334) on advice from Bean and Henry Gemery. These are average prices for all slaves, not just for prime males. Bean made allowances for different transport costs for destinations other than Jamaica (*Historical Statistics*, 2: 1155). Slave trade experts may wish to fine-tune the series somewhat better; but the basic outline—the shapes of trends taken— should remain fairly much the same.

That is, prices in Africa rose markedly between 1675 and 1740, from about 2.8 to 23.8 pounds sterling per slave—a multiple of 8.5. From 1690 through 1740 the path followed was a G curve with t_0 at 1714. From 1675 through 1685 a parallel movement of G form seems to have started but not persisted. Still earlier, from 1640 through 1670, only a few prices are available from Bean. The level for the 10 known values from 1638 through 1667 (the horizontal line depicts the average at about 6.2 pounds) seems to have been rather higher than the dip that is evident for nine prices for the quinquennia around 1670 and 1675.

The prices that *Dutch* merchants and captains paid for slaves along the African coast, however, appear to have behaved quite differently (Postma 1990, 264–65; translated here into sterling via McCusker 1978, 44, 56–60).[38] These rose

Figure 5.14a
Trends in Relative Slave Prices: New World Sales, African Purchases, and Their Ratios, 1638–1865

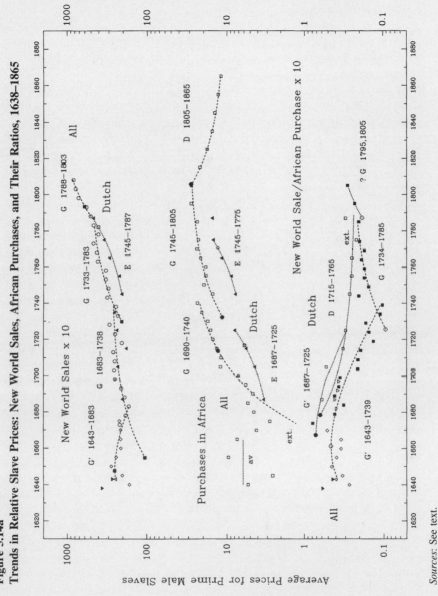

Sources: See text.

in upwardly accelerating, but at first much slower, E fashion from 1687 through 1725 (the solid upward triangles in the middle section of the figure). The bulk of known prices appear to be British. If this is true in Africa as well as America, comparing the "All" trend for purchases there as a surrogate for "British" movements with Dutch levels unveils an intriguing envelope between trends for the early 1700s in which the British price paid soared relative to its Dutch equivalent. Figure 5.14b, which looks at "British" (i.e., "All") prices as a multiple of Dutch ones reported by Postma, shows how what the British paid for slaves along the African coast perhaps jumped from 1.5 times the amount put out by the Dutch as of the 1680s to 2.8 times this international competitor around 1700. Does this relative surge in payment per slave help explain how the Royal African Company soon went out of business? Interestingly, from 1705 through 1725 the gap between British and Dutch buyers then tended to close, behaving as if a G' event had peaked around 1696. What might that have been? Did it have something to do with the protracted warfare of the quarter-century leading up to 1713?

The overall average sale price (two-thirds British) in the colonies of America, meanwhile, from 1683 through 1738 increased along a G curve segment with base year at 1655 (the hollow circles in the top plot of Figure 5.14a), though the averages around 1720 and 1730, an era following financial turmoil in France and England, swing more than usual around the summarizing trend. In this period, prices paid for slaves in the Dutch colonies of the New World (Postma 1990, 264–65, the solid upward triangles in the plot) tended to differ little from the overall average used as a surrogate for prices at British points of sale. Again a G' curve in Figure 5.14b (the top plot) generally captures movement in the relationship of the two trades in this respect; but the differential reaches only about 1.3, not the 2.8 ratio for prices in Africa, as the model curve peaks around 1709—a dozen years later than the G' trend for how much more the British apparently invested per slave to obtain cargoes.

Previously, between about 1640 and 1685, less ample price data suggest that the dip in the consolidated Eltis-Richardson series from 1673 through 1683 for prices in America was in fact the tail end of a G' hump that peaked at about 1648. In the top plot of Figure 5.14a, the hollow circles are from Eltis and Richardson, the hollow diamonds represent average quinquennial "West Indian" prices from Bean (*Historical Statistics* 2: 1174, Series Z 167), the hollow upward triangle at 1643 is a Pernambuco (Dutch Brazilian) average for the years 1641–1645 converted into sterling by Beckles (1989, 117) that covers several thousand deliveries, and the solid downward triangles come from analysis by van den Boogaart and Emmer (1979, 371), also for Pernambuco, averaging values for slaves from Angola and from Guinea for the years 1636–1640 and 1641–1645.[39] The result around the very preliminary point of 1638 is not employed in the curve-fitting; nor are the Bean data for 1640 and 1645 (with only three observations behind each average).

This early surge in the prices that planters would pay for slaves as colonies

Figure 5.14b
Trends in Relative Slave Prices: Movements of British against Dutch Prices

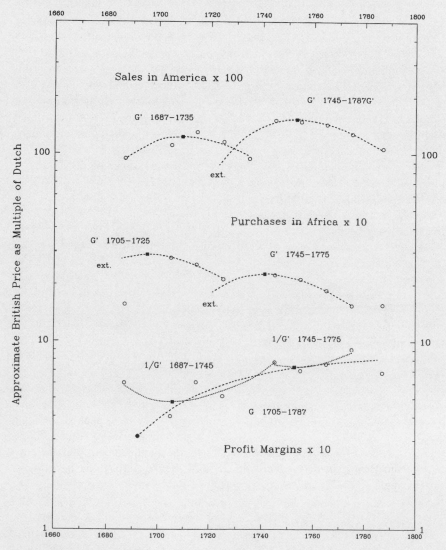

Sources: Figure 5.14a and text.

of northern European powers turned to producing New World sugar in competition with Portuguese Brazil and various Spanish holdings in the Caribbean area generated a G' curve in the ratio of what traders obtained for their cargoes in America relative to what they had to pay for them in Africa.[40] The bottom plot of Figure 5.14a suggests (via the solid squares) that this curve for the ratio peaked at a multiple of about 4.6 at 1661. As the cost of slaves on the African side of the Atlantic for the British surged upward decade after decade following 1675, however, the ratio of sale price in the New World to what had to be paid for cargoes in Africa fell and fell and fell, following the G' path all the way to about 1740. In the Dutch trade (hollow squares), meanwhile, the gross profit margin similarly seems to have peaked in the 1660s and dwindled away in approximate G' pattern to the 1720s. Quite internationally, traders lived with smaller profits or cut other costs as planters in America would buy at only much more slowly rising prices (in trends connected to the demographic normalization of their existing slave-holdings) than were required in Africa.

The volume of sales to British, Spanish, and French colonies, as Table 2.1 indicates, tended meanwhile to follow G patterns of decelerating growth with t_0's at 1670, 1650, and 1690, respectively. Most of the price data are British. Thus, the trade into the Caribbean (Brazil is not covered) seems on the whole likely to have expanded as the integral of the G' transatlantic price ratio curve (G' being the derivative of G).[41] Most evident, British carriers, whose cargoes provide about two-thirds of the known prices in the study of Eltis and Richardson, expanded their traffic in G form from 1625 through 1725 with zero year at 1668—close indeed to being just a multiple of the integral of the price ratio G' curve of 1643–1739 with its t_0 at 1661.

Figure 5.15a and Table 5.9 indicate how from the 1670s into the 1730s or later prices paid in northern European colonies of America for prime male slaves grew in G form, no matter from what region of Africa they had been obtained (Eltis and Richardson forthcoming, Appendix Table 1). There were, however, some differences in the base dates of these G curves and therefore the rates of regional change over the comparable decades from the 1670s into the 1730s. One consequence of these variations (Table 5.10 and Figure 5.15b) was that American sale prices for slaves obtained in Upper Guinea (Senegambia, Sierra Leone, and the Windward Coast), the Gold Coast, and the Bight of Benin rose and fell relative to prices for slaves from West Central Africa and the Bight of Biafra (the more southern and more distant portions of the continent for the colonies concerned—in contrast to the positioning of Brazil) in G' fashion with t_0's around 1701. The differential capped out at about 26 to 28 percent. Insightfully, it has already been seen that it was around 1696 that British slavers paid most relative to the Dutch for African men at the beginning of a G' pattern of change, while about 1706 their gross profit margin was relatively worst compared with that of the Dutch (Figure 5.14b). Meanwhile, Figure 2.2a and Table 2.2 in Chapter 2 indicate how from the 1680s forward the total number of slaves shipped out of West Central Africa rose in G manner based on a t_0 also in the

Figure 5.15a
Prices in America for Slaves from Various African Regions: Trends by Sources

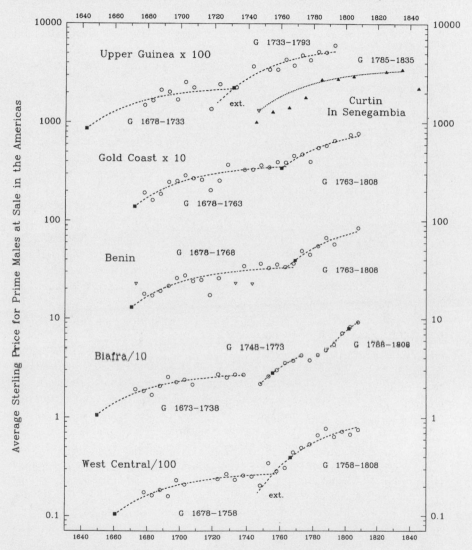

Sources: Eltis and Richardson forthcoming, Appendix Table 1; Curtin 1981, 88.

Table 5.9
G Trends in American Prices for Prime Male Slaves from Various Parts of Africa

Upper Guinea	1678-1733	G	1643	1733-1793	G	1731			
In Senegambia[c]							1785-1835	G	1746
Bight of Biafra	1673-1738	G	1650	1748-1773	G	1756	1788-1808	G	1802
West Central Africa	1678-1758	G	1661	1758-1808	G	1766			
Bight of Benin	1678-1768	G	1670	1762-1808	G	1769			
Gold Coast	1678-1763	G	1672	1763-1808	G	1761			
All Recorded	1683-1738	G	1655	1733-1783	G	1730	1788-1808	G	1793

[c] = Curtin, invoice price in goods.

Sources: Eltis and Richardson forthcoming, Appendix Table 1; Curtin 1981, 88.

early 1700s, providing supply to offset the D-type decline in exports from the Bight of Benin (no longer so much *the* "Slave Coast") from a zero year near 1690. In short, did the Royal African Company get stuck with rising costs in Guinea (including the Gold Coast and Benin), while the Dutch at this point proved more nimble in tapping more distant—and cheaper—sources of supply further down the African shore (at Portuguese expense)?

Figure 2.5a shows how early Dutch exports from the Gold Coast collapsed in favor of G' surges from Loango (the upper segment of West Central Africa) and the Bight of Benin that topped out around 1690, while Dutch shipments from Guinea are absent from the records this early. British slavers, in the meantime, while making their first push into West Central Africa were pulling out of the Bight of Biafra (Figures 2.9a and 2.9b). They dug deeply into the demography of the Bight of Benin along a G' track that crested at 1703 (Table 2.8) and were plunging rapidly via comparable G' shapes of expansion into Senegambia and the Gold Coast, which would top out about 20 years later.

Within the New World, meanwhile, panel a of Figure 5.16 and the right side of Table 5.10 show how prices obtained for slaves at Barbados, though starting lower, rose and fell in G' form between 1673 and 1728 against prices paid at Jamaica.[42] The 1700 date for the peak of this surge suggests that Barbados may have been getting most of its slaves from one or another part of Guinea, while the bulk delivered to Jamaica were from West Central Africa or the Bight of Biafra. Did merchants jumping in to serve the newer colony draw upon what were for the British less familiar—and more distant—sources of slaves? The right or b panel of Figure 5.16 demonstrates how in this era the Barbadians paid extra to have males and adults. Ratios of women to men, girls to boys, boys to men, and girls to women all dipped in 1/G' fashion. The extreme year for each of these preferences, judging by prices paid in the first half of Royal African Company sales (Galenson 1986, 56), came around 1690—as Barbadian planters were achieving their heights of influence before competitors in Jamaica and the Leewards developed to challenge them, apparently aided by labor from new

Table 5.10
Trends for Relative Prices among African and American Regions

From Parts of Africa				In Parts of America			
U. Guinea/W. Central Africa	1678-1733	G'	1702	Barb.-Ant./Jamaica-St. Dom.	1673-1728	G'	1700
Gold C./W. Central Africa	1678-1723	G'	1700	Barbados/Jamaica-St. Dom.	1673-1723	G'	1704
Benin/W. Central Africa	1678-1733	G'	1702				
Biafra/W. Central Africa	flat						
U. Guinea/W. Central Africa	1723-1788	G'	1744	Barb.-Ant./Jamaica-St. Dom.	1718-1763	G'	1733
Gold C./W. Central Africa	1723-1788	G'	1741				
Benin/W. Central Africa	1733-1783	G'	1748				
Biafra/W. Central Africa	1728-1788	G'	1744				
				S. Carolina/Jamaica-St. Dom.	1753-1808	G'	1774
				Guianas/Jamaica-St. Dom.	1748-1808	G'	1777
				Guianas/Ceded Is.	1768-1808	G'	1775
				Barb.-Ant./Jamaica-St. Dom.	1763-1798	G'	1782
Biafra/W. Central Africa	1788-1808	G'	1823				

Sources: Figures 5.15b and 5.16a; Eltis and Richardson forthcoming. Appendix Tables 1 and 2.

Figure 5.15b
Prices in America for Slaves from Various African Regions: Relative Trends for Sources

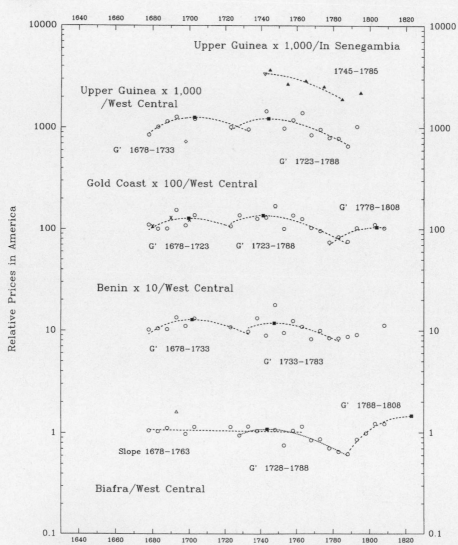

Sources: Figure 5.15a; Eltis and Richardson forthcoming. Appendix Table 1; Curtin 1981, 88.

Figure 5.16
Relative Slave Prices in American Regions

a. Among Various Colonial Markets

b. Within the Barbados Trade

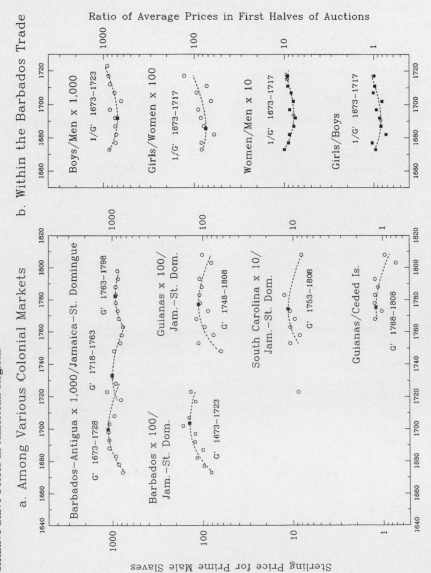

Sources: Eltis and Richardson forthcoming, Appendix Table 2; Galenson 1986, 56.

African sources. As the weight of adult males among total RAC imports to Barbados (and to Jamaica and company deliveries as a whole, but not the Lee-wards) shrank via a 1/G' dip with a bottom in the 1690s (graph a of Figure 5.12), Barbadian planters would pay more for them relative to other types of arrivals.

As of about 1730, the dynamics of the Atlantic slave trade changed. In ag-gregate, prices at sale in the New World and prices in Africa now began to follow each other, rising in parallel, G-shape curves 1733–1783 and 1725–1805 with zero years at 1730 and 1732, respectively (the top two plots in Figure 5.14a). This parallelism, however, began only after a sharp downward shift in what had been robustly increasing African values during the early 1740s. The overall level suddenly dropped about 36 percent from quinquennium to quin-quennium before changing its motion mostly to parallel rather than to vigorously eat away at American receipts. Was there a major increase in the African supply of slaves at this time (especially for the British, who dominate the available price evidence)? Figures 2.2b and 2.2a have indicated that initially very steep G'-type surges in exports *began* around 1740 in Senegambia, Sierra Leone, and the Gold Coast as shipments also climbed vigorously from the Bight of Biafra, though in G rather than G' form. From West Central Africa, traffic also grew, but in a more lasting, G-shape pattern. This curve had its zero year at 1709. Did fresh supply from these regions break back the G trend of ever-higher overall African prices that pertained from 1690 through 1740?

In the Dutch trade, on the other hand, the cost of slaves in Africa remained mostly level from the 1720s to the 1740s, though data for the 1730s are absent. Thereafter, from 1745 through 1775, the price that Dutch slavers paid for men again took a progressively faster E path upward as opposed to the systematically slowing British G. While a similar E curve characterized the rise of values at sale in Surinam (Postma 1990, 264–65, as shown by the solid, upward triangles in the top plot of Figure 5.14a), the difference in timing between the two trends was such that the Dutch ratio for American to African prices leveled out via a D curve from 1715 through 1765 (or, on average, 1785), while its British coun-terpart climbed in G fashion from 1734 to 1785 (with a spike in the early 1740s as the level of African prices sharply shifted downward). The bottom plot of Figure 5.14a displays these comparative movements. Broadly, as shown in the last plot in Figure 5.14b, the result was a G-type increase across the 18th century in the gross profit margin for British traders relative to their Dutch competitors. The levels plotted may be somewhat inexact, given the rough calculations in-volved in plotting them; but the general shape of relative change should hold up to refinements in procedure.

As part of the change that occurred after about 1730, Figure 5.15b and Table 5.10 display a second wave of G' surges in export prices for slaves in other regions relative to West Central Africa. Now the Bight of Biafra joined the Bight of Benin, the Gold Coast, and Upper Guinea in price humps for sales in the New World compared with more southern portions of the continent. These waves all crested in the 1740s. So, as the top plot in Figure 5.15b indicates, did prices in America for slaves acquired out of Upper Guinea relative to their costs in Senegambia (Curtin 1981, 88), a leading region of slave supply within that broad zone of western Africa. This transatlantic comparison would seem to indicate a peak in attractiveness of this source at that time, followed by a long G' decline of interest.

Subsequently, as Figure 5.15a indicates, prices for slaves from all regions were rising in new G trends after about 1730 for cargoes out of Upper Guinea, two to three decades later from other sources; but the increase was enough steeper for slaves from West Central Africa to push down the relative value for those from the Bight of Biafra and Upper Guinea to something like 60 percent of the Loango-to-Angola cost by the 1780s (Figure 5.15b). Arrivals in America from the Gold Coast and the Bight of Benin, meanwhile, slipped to 70 to 80 percent of the price for West Central Africans. Were these shifts driven (1) by planter preferences for one kind of slave over another, (2) by which merchants were delivering the labor, (3) by shifts of supply in Africa, or (4) by competitions with the expanding Portuguese-Brazilian and Spanish trades of the later 1700s? Those who are tempted to consider relative transportation costs determinative for prices in America must explain why all other African regional comparisons went up and down in G' form together relative to the West Central African base.

After the 1780s, from all competing regions prices recovered to equal or exceed those for slaves shipped out of West Central Africa. What impact on these ratios derived from the demise of planter society in St. Domingue, which relied heavily upon West Central African sources for slaves? Naval patrolling to curb the now unpopular slave trade, easier to make effective in regions closer to Europe, also became a factor. Meanwhile, as shown by the left or "a" panel of Figure 5.16, prices for arrivals at Barbados and Antigua, the Guianas, and South Carolina all surged relative to those at Jamaica via G' tracks that crested around the late 1770s (though price in the traffic to the Ceded Islands seems to have closely followed that in Jamaica). In yet a third era, now as the sun started to set on northern European slaving, G' movements of other colonies relative to Jamaica and of other sources relative to West Central Africa tended to follow each other, suggesting once more a pattern in who obtained their slaves from where.

Scholars of the slave trade will doubtless improve upon these comparisons of movements in prices across the Atlantic, between national trading groups (and perhaps official monopolists and free traders within them), among labor-exporting zones of Africa, and among the colonies of the Americas. Hopefully Brazil can be added to the mix. It seems, however, that the trends all tended to take shapes from the G family of curves—as the volume and composition of traffic and demographic changes in the receiving African American societies have been seen to do. The new way of patterning trends, furthermore, seems to facilitate understanding particular developments in the history of this vital if unpleasant early modern business. In the broader analytical arena, meanwhile, economists are put on notice that with both supply and demand embedded in demographic changes that take G-based shapes—a situation that is just as true of spreading settlement, urbanization, and migrating labor in, say, the 19th-century societies of the Western Hemisphere as in the 17th- and 18th-century plantation colonies that preceded them—many familiar interpretations and their equations will be found to be infested with G-based curves.[43]

As slave prices in Africa climbed relative to those in America, how did traffickers in black labor react? General transportation improvements in the size and cost of ships, reductions in the number of sailors needed to handle them, cheaper credit, insurance, and goods desired in Africa (often firearms for war and slave-catching), and more efficient arrangements for disposing of vessels in America or making their return voyages profitable all may have helped slaving merchants keep making money, though not as easily as before. One way to react to a squeeze on profits might have been to take measures (crowding, poorer provisioning, longer stays along the coast to secure more complete loads come to mind) that would risk killing off a higher percentage of the human cargo. What evidence is there of such behavior, and how might it be related to the fundamentally demographic setting of acquiring, transporting, and marketing slaves?

To begin, certain things appear *not* to have happened. The number of slaves carried per ton on average changed very little over the long haul. Analysis by Burnard and K. Morgan (2001, 225) shows no slope of either increase or decline for slavers coming to Jamaica or for British vessels that unloaded Africans elsewhere. While from 1663 through 1788 G curves with base years in the 1620s *might* be possible, virtually all the upward change occurred between the periods 1651–1675 and 1676–1700. In effect, Jamaica-bound ships typically carried about 1.4 slaves per ton, and others 1.2, from 1676 right through 1800. The evidence of Minchinton (1989, 70), meanwhile, indicates that the number of tons per crew member for slavers trading with Virginia, at least, tended to hover around 4.5 from 1726 through 1772,[44] with about 22 hands per ship on average.

This is not to say that merchants who engaged in slaving made no changes. Ships carrying Africans to South Carolina between 1717 and 1765 became bigger—from London, from Bristol, from Liverpool, and from other ports as well. So between 1725 and 1775 did vessels transporting Africans to Virginia (Minchinton 1989, 61). As the top plot of Figure 5.17 indicates, furthermore, less and less of this traffic was conducted in British-built vessels and more and more in prize ships or craft of *colonial* construction (ibid., 66). The pattern by proportion of all vessels employed in this marginal trade (not shown) is virtually identical to the proportion of tons. This trend from 1704 through 1765 took G' form with crest at about 1705. An early 18th-century window pulled homeland shipping into the slave trade for the northern, mainland colonies; but for one reason or another the attraction, and the presence that it inspired, did not last.

British slavers serving Jamaica and other West Indian locations employed

Figure 5.17
Some Illustrative Trends in Slave Trade Operations

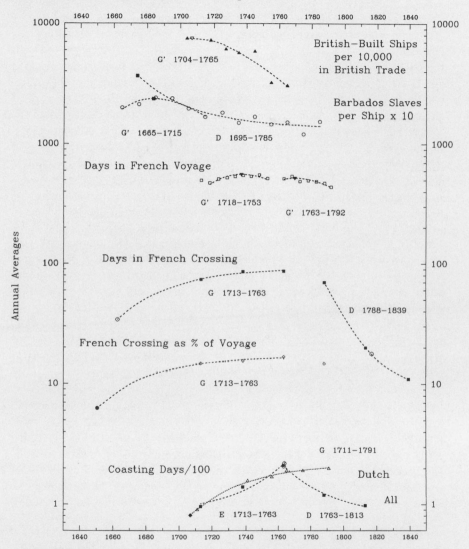

Sources: Minchinton 1989, 66; Behrendt 2001, 195; 1997, 51, Geggus 2001, 136; Klein et al. 2001, 111; Postma 1990, 142.

larger ships than did those supplying the more marginal markets of the North American mainland. Their typical vessel size and number of slaves delivered per ship notably rose after about 1770 as plantation settlements seized from the French (and later from the Dutch) were stocked by their new British occupants. Before then, however, the trends tended to go somewhat the other way (Burnard and Morgan 2001; Minchinton 1989, 62).

Data from Behrendt (2001, 195) most clearly show—in the second plot of Figure 5.17—that the average number of slaves on ships arriving at Barbados between the 1660s and the 1700s first surged upward in G' shape, cresting in the 1680s. From about 1695 through 1785, however, typical slave cargoes then shrank along a D curve with t_0 at 1674. According to Minchinton (1989, 62— weighted average for the two destinations that he gives), the average size of slaving vessels going to Barbados and Jamaica shrank from the 1690s to the 1740s in a manner that is captured by a D trend with base year at about 1672.[45]

These findings make the number of slaves carried per ship and the size of vessels employed in the mainstream of the British slave trade decline parallel with the growth rate of the African American people of the British West Indies between 1655 and 1785, the rate of slave imports relative to the current size of this population between 1688 and 1770, and the rate of net natural decrease estimated for them between 1688 and 1770—with t_0's at 1673, 1674, and 1679, respectively, as shown in Table 5.3 and Figure 5.3.[46] As the delivery of new slaves became relatively less important to the British West Indian system, how much was it simply left to smaller, often colonial operators who wanted to carve out a foothold in Caribbean commerce, using the delivery of labor as an entry, while established British merchants concentrated instead upon marketing the sugar produced?

There also occurred major changes in the duration of various phases of the voyages of vessels engaged in the slave trade. Records for French traffic (Behrendt 1997, 51) indicate that the total length of round-trips for slaving shortened by only about 10 percent between 1713 and 1792 for the total number of days (about 500) from leaving home port until returning to France. Evident, however, are two G' humps that topped out around 1737 and 1770 successively. These patterns and their timing in the third plot of Figure 5.17 seem to reflect how pushes of G' shape to obtain slaves in the Bight of Benin and in Senegambia and to dispose of them in Guadeloupe and Guiana, mostly in ships based on Nantes—all shown in Table 2.6 and Figures 2.6a, 2.6b, and 2.6c of Chapter 2— peaked at about 1740 and were followed by activity from other ports and sales to Martinique, Louisiana, and St. Domingue along G' tracks that crested toward the late 1760s, perhaps acquiring impetus from fresh supply out of West Central Africa.

Evidence from Geggus (2001, 136) shows that for French slavers the length of the Atlantic crossing—the infamous "middle passage"—increased rather differently, in G fashion, from 1713 through 1763 (1701–1775). Thereafter, it shortened markedly, from about 70 days in the 1780s to just over 10 by 1840, apparently in a D path of more effective shipping and also perhaps some haste in order to evade naval patrols trying to suppress trafficking in slaves. The crossing from Africa to the Caribbean, meanwhile, rose as a proportion of the total round-trip from 1713 through 1763 along a slightly earlier and flatter G segment (Geggus divided by Behrendt 1997, 51) before dropping off somewhat for the period 1776–1800.

The most obvious change before the 1800s, however, was an increase in the average time that slavers spent along the African coast gathering their cargoes. According to all such records for the European trade, the duration of this phase of the voyage may have climbed in accelerating E fashion from about 1700 forward to peak in the early 1760s before dropping off along a D trajectory from there into the early 1800s (Klein, Engerman, Haines, and Shlomovitz 2001, 110—the solid squares in Figure 5.17). In these moves the average time along the African coast more than doubled from 96 to 212 days, then dropped back to 98. In contrast, the coasting period for Dutch slavers (Postma 1990, 142— the hollow triangles) while rising through the 1760s not unlike the average for all recorded voyages, kept on increasing along a G path into the early 1790s (when the Dutch abandoned the business). Meanwhile, the daily loading average per day for Dutch slavers (bottom of Figure 5.18a) declined from 1741 through 1791 via a D trend that vertically mirrored the increase in their typical coasting days per voyage, each with t_0's in the early 1700s. Figure 2.2a shows how slave exports for the whole Atlantic business began to decline in D fashion around 1770. A proper understanding of the connection of the observed coasting pattern to volume and sources of exports, however, requires better knowledge of just which European national and African regional trades supply records of times spent operating along the shore. Further analysis should prove a fruitful undertaking, though, especially given the distinctive trend apparent for the Dutch.

Extra time along the coast could cost extra lives—in the human cargo and also in the crew. Figure 5.18a begins by tracing trends for deaths in various phases of the Atlantic slave trade—on the one hand, as crude proportional *loss* of slaves during this or that phase of the overall voyage; on the other, as a more standardized death *rate per month* for the stage under consideration.

In the Atlantic slave trade as a whole as shown by the second plot with filled squares at the top of Figure 5.18a, the death rate for Africans per month of voyage consistently declined between 1688 and 1788 from 97.6 to 46.0 per 1,000 per month (Klein et al. 2001, 113). On average, among sufficiently documented voyages, captains managed to cut mortality in their valuable cargoes per time at sea by more than half. They did this along a D path with t_0 at 1679. It was in the 1680s that alert captains and merchants may have begun to realize that gross profit margins between prices paid in Africa and prices obtained in America were begining to decline (Figure 5.14a).[47] Simultaneously, evidence from the French trade in the very top plot of Figure 5.18a (Behrendt 1997, 51) indicates that mortality in *crews* declined in generally parallel D shape (zero year at 1688) from about 14 deaths per 1,000 per month to fewer than 9. How

Figure 5.18a
Loss Rates and Death Rates* in Atlantic Slaving: For the Whole Trade

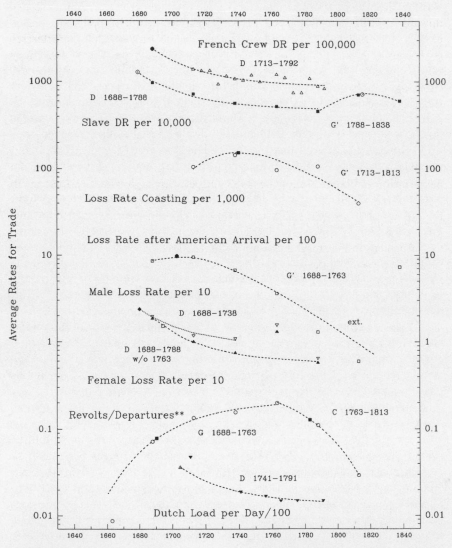

* Death rate per month of voyage; ** = time distribution of revolts divided by time distribution
   of slaves shipped 1651–1867.

Sources: Behrendt 1997, 51; Klein et al. 2001, 113, 111, 116; Richardson 2001, 92; Postma 1990,
   142.

might sanitary and medical improvements have diffused in this pattern? What other kinds of priorities or practices might spread through populations the same way? In other words, do G-based forms of change permeate cultural as well as demographic and economic developments?

Later, between 1776 and 1850 as trafficking in Africans became generally more difficult and sometimes illegal, average mortality rates for cargoes surged upward in G' fashion to exceed 71 per 1,000 per month around 1815 before easing off somewhat. G' waves in deaths even more markedly characterized other phases of the Atlantic slave trade. As time spent coasting along the African littoral in order to fill out loads increased across the first half of the 18th century (Figure 5.17), the proportion of slaves lost to death in this phase of the voyage (regardless of its duration) swelled in G' fashion to peak out at close to 15 percent before falling off all the way to 4 percent in the early 1800s (Klein et al. 2001, 111) as coasting time for some vessels (though not the Dutch) dropped back to the levels of a century before. In America, meanwhile, loss of slaves between arrival and debarkation or sale peaked at just under 10 percent of the cargo near 1703 before following its G' shape of trend down to 3.6 percent in the third quarter of the 18th century (ibid.). Averages around 1788 and 1813 fall below a projection of this line but parallel it, taking the loss rate during this final stage of the passage down to something like 0.6 percent before it jumped to 7.3 percent in the shifting conditions of 1826–1841.

During the middle passage itself, the loss rate for females (without regard to the length of voyage) from 1688 through 1788, without a retrogressive movement for the period 1751–1775 (1763), improved somewhat more strongly than that for males. D trends for solid, upward triangles and hollow, downward triangles about two-thirds of the way down Figure 5.18a indicate this (Klein et al. 2001, 116). These loss rates by sex display a reversal around 1763 that is not evident in the mortality rate per month for both sexes near the top of the figure. Were the average voyages all that much longer during the third quarter of the 18th century? Or do data by sex cover only a smaller, skewed sample of voyages in this era? Further work seems desirable. Only a fraction of the difference can be attributed to the fact that the rate of revolts (and also all violent incidents together) per voyage hit their maximum around 1763. The proportion of revolts per quarter century relative to the proportion of voyages between 1651 and 1867 that took place in the same periods (Richardson 2001, 92) had in fact been climbing since 1675, perhaps 1650, along a G path with base year at 1690. This pattern makes the ratio rise close in t_0 to the G for time spent by Dutch vessels in obtaining cargoes along the African coast. From 1763 through 1813 it then dropped of in a C type of extinction curve that suggests that security was tightened significantly, perhaps abetted by the reductions in coasting time that have been observed in Figure 5.17. Hope for getting home or staying free was greater off the shore of Africa than in the middle of the Atlantic.

Figure 5.18b, finally, depicts trends in average loss rates per voyage and death rates per month as these are known for the leading national slave trades. From

Figure 5.18b
Loss Rates and Death Rates in Atlantic Slaving: Trends in the Leading National Trades

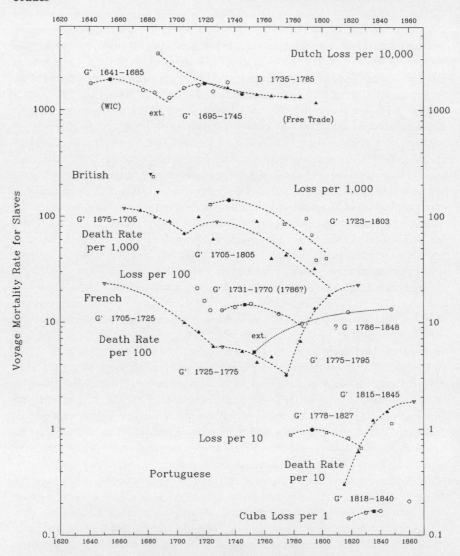

Sources: van den Boogaart and Emmer 1979, 367; Postma 1990, 250–51; Galenson 1986, 38, 184; Anstey 1975, 25; Stein 1979, 209–11; Klein 1999, 139; 1978, 66, 84, 162; Klein and Engerman 1979, 264; Eltis 1987, 272; Haines and Shlomovitz 2000, 263.

the 1640s through the 1740s patterns for crude loss rates per cargo per voyage for Dutch slavers (Postma 1990, 250–51) set out what were basically international patterns—in both loss rate and monthly death rate—across the century and a half before 1800.

That is, from the earliest records available into the 1680s for the Dutch, the 1700s for the British, and the 1720s for the French, G' trends appear that show or imply maximum mortality generally in the 1650s but then carried losses lower and lower as slavers learned to take better care of their valuable cargoes. At first, the Dutch West India Company lost perhaps over 19 percent of its Africans in the voyage during the 1650s (van den Boogaart and Emmer 1979, 367). They pulled this level down to 13 percent by the 1690s. Fragmentary evidence for the English around the 1680s, meanwhile, suggests that a crude loss rate of perhaps as much as 24 percent in the 1680s was brought down to 13 percent by the 1720s (Galenson 1986, 38–39, 184, note 29). Better-documented *death rates per month* recently calculated for the British trade from 1675 through 1705 parallel in G' shape with a slightly later peak year (1664 vs. 1654) Dutch loss rates of 1641–1685, while their French counterparts come down from 1705 through 1725 along a G' path with a peak that projects back to 1650 (Haines and Shlomovitz 2000, 263). Across the 1710s and 1720s, the French loss rate improved from about 21 percent to the 13 percent attained by the Dutch around 1690 and the British around 1705 (Stein 1979, 209). Similarly, by the 1720s the monthly death rate in the French trade caught up with mortality improvements in British slaving (and the one adequately documented Portuguese cargo this early) at around 60 per 1,000 (Haines and Shlomovitz 2000, 263).

This spreading G' pattern of lowering mortality, however, was then reversed in each of the Dutch, French, and British slave trades, as Figure 5.18b then indicates. Crude proportional losses worsened in G' pattern to peak around 1719 in Dutch cargoes, 1736 in British ones, and 1747 for French traffic—retrogressing to levels of 17.7, 14.3, and 14.7 percent, respectively. Dutch achievement in this aspect of the business, now run by free traders in place of the West India Company, grew comparatively worse subsequently as the loss rate in this national branch of Atlantic slaving switched from a G' pattern like those of international competitors to a more level D form of trend. Along such a course, as the top plot in Figure 5.18b shows, deaths on the voyage stubbornly refused to fall below about 14 percent of cargoes carried before the 1790s (Postma 1990, 251), while loss in the British trade came down to about 4 percent by the time the 18th century was over (Galenson 1986, 38; Anstey 1975, 25). For the French (Stein 1979, 209–11; Klein and Engerman 1979, 264), the level of improvement reached along their G' path was about 9 percent before starting to rise again, apparently for some reason in G form, from the 1780s into the 1840s (Klein 1999, 139; actual deliveries compared with total slaves traded between 1808 and 1829 from Stein 1978, 209). Meanwhile, the *monthly death rate* for British traffic between 1705 and 1805, while fluctuating, generally rose in G' fashion to crest at about 89 per 1,000 near 1728 before dropping below 20 per 1,000 in the first decade of the 19th century. The comparable rate for the French trade declined from about 59 around 1731 (noticeably lower wastage than the British 89 of the time) to 32 in the 1770s. The parallel G' path taken sustained the French advantage against the British to this point. Across such a substantial period of time, French captains on average seem to have preserved more of their valuable cargoes.

Then, however, monthly death rates for French slave voyages soared back from the 1770s into the 1790s to pass 135 per 1,000 along a G' trajectory that would, if persisting, have peaked around 1825. A still later sharp G' increase in mortality rate appeared in Portuguese slaving from 1815 through 1845. Reaching 145 per 1,000 for the 1840s, this was headed toward a crest in the vicinity of 1863 (Haines and Shlomovitz 2000, 263). Meanwhile, the loss rate on Portuguese voyages (the hollow squares in the bottom right corner of Figure 5.18b) also rose from the 1820s into the 1840s, though not as steeply. This loss rate for Portuguese (and Brazilian) ventures had from the 1770s to the 1820s risen and fallen in G' fashion with peak at 1793. At that point some 10 percent of the slaves died in transit before improving to more like 6 percent before shooting up in the last decades of the business (Klein 1999, 139; 1978, 66, 84). In between, the Spanish trade to Cuba seems to have seen its loss rate also rise then level out in G' shape between 1818 and 1840, before pushing upward again from there to 1860 (Klein "Spanish" for 1808–1829 in 1999, 139 and Eltis 1987, 272). Deaths per cargo per voyage in this Cuban business ran above the comparatively high level of 16 percent in the second quarter of the 19th century; and the 20 percent that they exceeded around 1860 made this a still more deadly transatlantic run than the last years of French deliveries to St. Domingue or Portuguese traffic to Brazil in the 1840s.

As merchants of northern European nations elbowed their way into the Atlantic slave trade in the 17th century, each documented national group seems to have generated opening loss rates and mortality rates that peaked in G' pattern at levels higher than what was subsequently seen before the waning years of the business in the 19th century. While the French data are insufficient for such analysis, peak years for the Dutch loss curve at 1654 and the British death rate at 1664 make these G' movements virtually a multiple of the derivative of the G trends according to which the volume of these two businesses expanded during their early years, curves with t_0's at 1645 and 1668 respectively (Table 2.3 and Figures 2.3a and 2.3b in Chapter 2). The gross proportional profit margin between what slaves brought in the West Indies relative to what had to be paid for them in Africa, meanwhile, also crested in G' fashion for both national traffics in the 1660s (Figure 5.14a). Inexperienced captains could afford to be careless with their cargoes in this window of golden opportunity. As the margin for profit narrowed, however, each death hurt more and the growth rate in volume to serve proportionally slowing increase in demand was no longer such a scramble. It became an advantage not to lose so many Africans on the voyage.

After western European peace arrived in 1713, however, more slaves were desired to serve developing plantation areas in colonies of America, especially as sugar cultivation expanded in Jamaica, St. Domingue, and Surinam. G curves of fresh growth with t_0's at about 1718 appeared in each of the Dutch, English, and French trades. G' surges of mortality—coming at 1719 for Dutch losses, and 1728 and 1731 in more precise mortality rates for British and French voyages—once again by their close timing generally represent just multiples of the derivatives of the G-type growth curves under way in the respective traffics. In this second phase of expansion, however, profit margins did not simultaneously peak in G' fashion to mask waste. The Dutch trend of this sort was gently but steadily downward in D form; the British G-type improvement of profit margin did not commence until the 1730s. The rate of increase in volume of traffic, not offsetting price margins, seems to have driven the mortality rate for the middle passage nation by nation. Were slaves sicker or more poorly nourished as a consequence of longer coasting in order to fill vessels or the need to strip new sources for captives, both farther along the coast and deeper inland?

As the hunger for labor in St. Domingue called for still further expansion of French slaving beginning in the 1770s (Figure 2.3b and Figure 2.6c), once again mortality rates seem to have followed increase in volume. Meanwhile, Portuguese-Brazilian G' pushes to get more slaves from the Luanda and especially the Benguela areas of Angola (Figure 2.7a) combined with other exports to generate a G-form expansion in the total national trade (Table 2.3 and Figure 2.3a) that had its zero year at 1795, still another instance in which the G' curve for mortality in the trade (Figure 5.18b, with t_0 at 1793) basically represented just a multiple of the derivative of increase in the volume of traffic or change in rate of its growth. Still later G' surges of slave extraction from the Benguela region, the northern end of West Central Africa (formerly popular with the Dutch and the British, who were now both beginning to curtail slaving), and southeastern Africa (Mozambique) entailed longer voyages and also longer overland drives for slaves (Miller 1988) that doubtless weakened their condition and generated, or at least helped create, the G' surge in voyage mortality for the Portuguese-Brazilian traffic that headed toward a G' peak around 1863. Quite generally, mortality in the documented national slaves trades seems to have reflected how the volume of traffic was being increased.

In the history of the slave trade, much attention has been given—without much clear result—to the possible impact upon mortality of crowding during the middle passage in terms of slaves per ton per ship. A better explanation may be suggested instead by the way that high rates of loss among free, servant, and redemptioner Germans of the 1700s appeared as *inexperienced* merchants and captains were attracted by boom periods of elevated supply and demand to try profiting from the business of transporting passengers across the Atlantic. As, after mid-century, the transport of Germans became the domain of fewer merchants and of those who heavily specialized in the business, the loss of life and misery on the voyage declined (Wokeck 1999, 53–54). Among Irish migrants to North America, the worst era was the early surge of the 1720s. By the time of the still larger buildup of the 1760s and 1770s, though conditions did deteriorate somewhat, the experience of the transportation of Germans—and also the slave trade—was known, and techniques and rules of thumb for controlling loss had been widely disseminated (ibid., 207–9). More attention should perhaps be given to the presence and the consequences of comparable degrees of "professionalism"—as opposed to inexperience and opportunistic greed—in the slave trade, if one is willing to dignify its unsavory operations with that term.

From the 1600s into the 2000s peoples of African descent in the Americas have repeatedly increased as a proportion of local populations in G form and declined via C paths. Beginning quite early in the era of slavery, as these black or mixed populations grew, their rate of self-replacement improved—in most colonies through a D-shape diminishing of natural decrease and in the Chesapeake, South Carolina, and Cuba actually via G's of positively strengthening natural *increase*. Meanwhile, the rate of further slave imports relative to the current size of the non-white population likewise declined in D fashion in colony after colony. Both in this measure and in net natural decrease, however, in many places in the early 1720s—with the surging expansion of the Atlantic economy and new plantation development after a quarter century of chronic war—there occurred a temporary reversal of such downward movements.

Improved demographic replacement (whether or not it attained or exceeded par) could come about because, from the very beginning of the surviving record, though males formed a majority—most of all when and where a well-capitalized local expansion or development of plantations was intense—there were plenty of women and children in the mix of slave imports. These persons formed a kernel from which demographic normalization of the African American population could grow—even if such improvement was masked behind terrible conditions for reproduction, parenting, and sheer survival. The weight of women and children increased in G fashion within the non-white populations of colony after colony after colony.

Meanwhile, though males continued to constitute a substantial majority of slave imports, more and more of them were boys rather than men. The role of children in the total traffic repeatedly increased in G trends between the 1660s and the 1840s. The proportions of women and children together expanded for a while against men as new growth in the volume of slave traffic appeared after the 1710s. Looking at particular locations—as in imports to various British West Indian holdings across the half-century starting in the 1670s—G' surges or sags in the proportion of men, women, or children sold in this or that colony seem to reflect where new sugar plantations were being developed as opposed to established ones being maintained. As in most places all incoming Africans together became a lower and lower proportion of the current black population, however, their composition by sex and age mattered less and less for local demographic dynamics.

In the colonies of northern European powers, meanwhile, planters were willing to pay more and more for slaves. These prices rose in G trends everywhere. Those curves tended to parallel in timing and rise inverse to local D trends in the significance of new slave imports relative to the size of the existing African American population. Thus, in aggregate, over a considerable span of time planters paid an amount for fresh labor that was constantly proportional to the size of their slave-holdings.

This equilibrium posed problems for slave traders, for whom the price of captives in Africa was rising much more steeply between the later 1600s and the middle of the 1700s. African price trends, like American ones, took G-based forms. The result of these interfacing transatlantic patterns all rooted in G was that gross margins between America and Africa, between competing groups of slavers, and between one African regional source of slaves and another, or one New World colony and another, all also took G-based shapes, mostly G'. The demographic influences of growth and change in America interacted via these familiar curves through price and quantity with the demographically framed effects of how more and more victims were carved out of a growing list of African populations—though we are likely never to know as much about the African side of the equation as its American counterpart.

How the slave trade operated, finally, was significantly shaped by these demographically guided changes on both sides of the Atlantic. From the 1640s through the 1840s both mortality rates and cruder measures of loss from human cargo turn out to have followed G' trends that simply reflected the rate at which the volume of various traffics was increasing in pervasive G patterns. Inexperienced or greedy operators who jumped into the business as it expanded most probably did the worst at preserving their mortal commodity. Meanwhile, losses as it took longer to fill a ship when people had to be scraped out of more diverse African places, the need to tap more distant sources (overland as well as by sea), greater waste in America waiting to sell a cargo, and even rates of revolt on shipboard all rose and fell in patterns related to G. How, overall, Atlantic-wide death rates per month of voyage, for crew and for slaves in tandem, came down in D form seems to show how the diffusion of knowledge about health and medical practice likewise took G-connected shape, though loss of slaves in a particular trade tended to override this underlying pattern of improvement as durations of various stages of the voyage (and the experience of Africans before they were loaded) changed in the G-related patterns noted.

What kept steering the replacement of slave populations, their regeneration and continuation by births, deaths, and migration, their composition by sex, age, and nativity—even their pricing and their mortality during transportation—into such standard G-based patterns over and over again? It would seem to have been some very fundamental demographic dynamic that kept stamping G-connected patterns upon so many aspects of the development of often originally quite skewed and unusual slave populations. The way that migration flows have repeatedly assumed G-related forms in so many diverse historical contexts points to something, not just about migration itself but more fundamental to the renewal process of populations, that consistently channels change into these forms. It is thus next necessary to probe how potentially universal movements in fertility and mortality might repeatedly embed G-based shapes into so many kinds of demographic developments.

For the most part, this kind of further exploration can be done only with quite modern evidence. Before taking that next step (the business of the ensuing and final volume of this study), however, what can the development of historical populations whose demographic evolution was not affected by the exceptional processes of capturing, transporting, and using slaves add to the insight that has been obtained from the peculiar circumstances of forced African migrants?

NOTES

1. For example, black and white peoples of the Caribbean, ethnic groups in New Zealand, or the racial classifications set by South Africa (Harris 2001, 70–72, 83, 86).

2. The respective contributions of Lotka and Kuczynski are reviewed evenhandedly by Paul A. Samuelson (1977, 109–29).

3. Data are absent or too brief and sketchy to attempt trendings for Santo Domingo or for Cuba and Puerto Rico before the later 1700s. Much of this analysis, which was first explored a quarter of a century ago, employs data collated for many colonies by McCusker (1970); but the literature since does not, for the most part, seem to have much altered patterns for black and total populations in the societies considered (and therefore the black proportion). I have made some changes for colonies of the North American mainland (Virginia and South Carolina) and cited how some more recent estimations elsewhere have mostly tended to confirm the same general patterns or occasionally changed the picture. Experts on particular colonies and their slave populations may still profitably consider how later findings might call for other revisions. Sometimes it is found that the newer and better data demonstrate the proposed kind of trend even better than the old, though undoubtedly some useful alterations might be made.

4. The initial shift, usually accelerating as whites disappeared and more slaves simultaneously arrived, can be followed over two or three decades, from 1650 to 1670 or 1680—surging from 0 to 56, 10 to 50, 9 to 52, 14 to 69, and 7 to 58 percent on Antigua, Montserrat, Nevis, and English and French St. Christopher, respectively. In the 1660s Nevis passed temporarily from English hands to the French, who held the island until about 1690 (McCusker 1970, 1: 546).

5. Antigua was short on water, and the planters of Montserrat for a while had to contend with a population kernel of pesky Irish servants, while Nevis was mountainous and passed to the French for a substantial period (Dunn 1972, 33–35).

6. For this second Virginia trend, data for 1690 (Sutherland) and 1750–1830 come from *Historical Statistics* 2: 1168, Series Z 14, and 1: 36, Series A 195 and 200. Estimates for 1700 through 1740 are taken from P. Morgan (1998, 61).

7. Due to the kind of plowing that was required by its rich but heavy soil, the future Black Belt region lagged behind development in other parts of the state, until not too long before "the War." This might account for a base year of the G curve for Africanization in Alabama which, mixing different parts of the state that developed with different timing, arrives intermediate to the early 1780s and the early 1800s found for neighboring states.

8. Including the British Virgins, possessions ceded by the French in 1763, and other colonies currently under British control, but not Bermuda or the Bahamas.

9. Higman (1984, 77) suggests higher totals for all non-whites, slave and free, at 1810 and 1830, with the latter dropping below the former.

10. The trending of Figure 2.1c is somewhat simplified for Figure 5.3 and extended in time from Klein 1999 and Craton (1975) without including Klein's low value for 1785 in the fit.

11. By the 1770s it was diving again toward the level of actual replacement via reproduction. Calculations by Higman (1984) for 1810 and 1830 indicate a non-white growth rate of −0.26 percent. With the British slave trade closed off, this implies net natural decrease of only 0.26 percent—almost full replacement.

12. A temporarily high rate of loss around 1710 from stalling growth and slave imports rather above the trend is offset by the way that slower importation then accompanied a faster rate of non-white growth around 1730.

13. Trends based upon the combined Guiana holdings of the Netherlands (Surinam along with "Guiana" for Berbice, Essequibo, and Demerara), which constituted the large majority of Caribbean people under Dutch control (McCusker 1970, 1: 601).

14. Native peoples who had survived European colonization were few and also poorly counted.

15. For Jamaica, only "retained" imports are counted. In the 1700s, the numbers come from Sheridan (1974, 504–5) and Klein (1978, 154). Up into the 1710s, the estimates of Michael Craton are employed (1975, 284). These seem to omit slaves transshipped elsewhere from the island. Eltis (2000, 208) appears to cover *all* Africans brought to Jamaica in the period 1666–1710. His source is Eltis (1996, 196–200).

For present purposes, just those arriving captives who stayed in Jamaica are relevant. The plot of hollow, downward-pointing triangles near the middle of Figure 5.6b indicates the way that the differences between Craton's estimates for net imports for the period 1670–1721 and Eltis's average annual numbers, if taken as a proportion of the latter, converge with the share of arrivals who were transshipped that is known to have characterized the early 18th century (the solid, downward-pointing triangles). At this stage, some 40 to 50 percent of slaves imported into Jamaica ended up elsewhere. This was a practice that apparently strengthened in G shape across the later 1600s and early 1700s, as Figure 5.6b shows, before it dissipated in D form across the 18th century, when Jamaica wanted more slaves as planters there tardily turned to intensify sugar production (Eltis 2000, 206–7) and the great nearby Spanish islands built up their own direct slave trades.

Galenson's calculations (1981, 218), meanwhile, *assume* demographic rates that we in fact want to estimate independently here. Further, his computations—which rely upon Gemery (1980, 215)—are based upon the questionable premise that white and black patterns of natural increase were identical (Galenson 1981, 213). The results are excessively high estimations of net natural decrease for Jamaican slaves up into the early 1700s and suspect numbers for net slave immigration. Galenson, furthermore, did not include the demise of new arrivals (in "seasoning," as it was called) as deaths to be subtracted from births in calculating net natural increase. For Jamaica from the 1670s through the 1700s, his indirectly constructed results do not conform well to calculations of arrivals by Eltis from shipping sources.

More direct estimates of imports for Barbados come from Curtin (1969, 55), who built upon the data of Frank W. Pitman (1917) and K. G. Davies (1957). Pitman's annual numbers for most years from 1708 through 1775 are available in Sheridan (1974, 505). While Curtin's calculations for the Leewards (1969, 62–64) utilize some evidence about net natural increase from Jamaica, he verifies his results against independently recorded slave import numbers when and where they are available, a kind of check that Galenson apparently did not perform.

16. Harris 2001, beginning with Chapters 2 and 3, discusses other historical cases of over-ambitious development in which such abrupt ceilings to population growth have been encountered.

17. The data of Higman (1984, 77) indicate a flatter C for the Leewards, with a somewhat higher number for 1830. His lower calculations for 1810 and 1830 also call for a flatter late G for Jamaica.

18. Sheridan (1975, 309) estimated slightly lower rates of net natural decrease for Barbadian slaves around 1688 (approximately what one gets from working with Galenson's estimations of imports), then about the same rate as shown in Figure 5.6c in the vicinity of 1713. Thereafter, however, his calculations around 1738 and 1763 are rather higher than those presented here, making the downward trend of the first half of the 18th century weaker and less clearly of D shape. Some of the difference seems to come from his working with 25-year blocks of time rather than decadal estimates.

19. The estimations for 1715 and 1725 are averaged to show how the curve hits this level.

20. An extremely high figure for the abnormal conditions of the 1780s is not considered.

21. From around 1738 to around 1788 the calculations of Sheridan (1975, 309) fit a D trend with base year near 1714, parallel to but a little higher than the D trend for 1735–1800 (without 1786) at the bottom of Figure 5.6b with its t_0 at 1712. Around 1688 (1676–1700) Sheridan's value is the same. Around 1713 (1701–1725) his calculation is for some reason much higher. This difference may have something to do with how we each handled reexported slaves, whose significance topped out and began to fall in this period. His calculation makes the decline in net natural decrease precede the 18th-century fall in relative rate of importation by even more time than mine.

22. Confirming such suspicion about an effect of transshipment, in correspondence about this manuscript Lorena Walsh has called attention to a growing influx of slaves from the Leewards (particularly from Antigua and St. Kitts) into the Lower James region of Virginia and Maryland (both of which were marginal producers of tobacco and consumers of slaves) beginning in the 1730s. By the 1760s and 1770s the enlarged flows clearly included "new" Africans as well as those who had been "seasoned" in the West Indies.

23. Further progress on this topic can undoubtedly be made with *The Trans-Atlantic Slave Trade* database on CD-ROM (Eltis et al. 1999); but that work is still incomplete in certain respects and should be informed by good knowledge of the varied sources and their limitations and by familiarity with the history and the social context of the populations under consideration.

24. Maryland and Virginia together, from the population reestimates of Menard (1980, 157–66) and the slave imports reported by Eltis (2000, 48, 208) and Walsh (2001, 168–69).

25. Volume III of this study explores very widespread international patterns of this sort in recent "demographic transition."

26. Such local sequencing of Chesapeake settlement and its consequences has been

demonstrated for some time (Harris 1978, 1983, 1984, 1989, 1992). County-by-county details for slave populations of the region are presented elsewhere. Kulikoff (1977, 405) has shown how normalization in Prince George's lagged the decline in sex rations for adults in older St. Mary's and York Counties and how the weight of men relative to women rose between the 1670s and the 1700s.

27. The 1739 percentage for 9 *engenhos* is appreciably lower than the long-range curve for such operations. The 1602 calculation is based upon the proportion of parents who were Negro-criulo or mulatto rather than African among all fathers and mothers of African descent who participated in baptisms at the *engenho* Sergipe between 1595 and 1608 (Schwartz 1985, 61).

28. Subsequent publication addresses this development and its local variations within the general region of the Chesapeake.

29. Postma 1990, 231; van den Boogaart and Emmer 1979, 365–66; Geggus 1989, 24, 30; Eltis 2000, 98, 287; 1987, 258; Nwokeji 2001, 67.

Postma's calculations for the Dutch in the top plot of the figure cover males of all ages; in the middle plot only the proportion who were adult males is taken. The van den Boogaart and Emmer data for the early Dutch trade to New Holland (their part of Brazil) are separated into cargoes from Guinea ("g"—West Africa) and Angola ("a"—which included Congo). In the graphing at 1689, estimates for the Spanish and Danish trades happen to overprint each other; at 1839 Spanish and Portuguese proportions do the same and obscure the 1838 computation of Eltis for all exports from Africa. To get the latter 19th-century series for all trades, I took a weighted average of his regional data (1987, 258, Table B.3).

Recently Philip D. Morgan (1998) has offered calculations of 63 and 65 percent male in the slave trades to Virginia and South Carolina, respectively. Representing time periods with midpoints at 1735 and 1747, these results hug the 1726–1765 D trend in the top plot of Figure 5.11a. Similarly, the 19.0 percent for Virginia that he estimates around 1735 suits the internationally composite pattern in the share of shipped slaves who were children (Figure 5.11b). His South Carolina proportions for children (ibid., 72) of 13.8 percent at 1737 and 20.3 percent at 1767 are a little low relative to the international average; but they parallel its rise across the middle of the 18th century (though the fraction for 1773 breaks below that path).

The "x"s represent proportions for 25-year periods from Nwokeji (there is no information for the years 1726–1750) employing the new database. These symbols were not used in the curve-fitting but are superimposed to show how the latest information, grouped this way in time, mostly follows previously available evidence. (The sources with which earlier analysts worked, after all, have generally been incorporated in the CD-ROM collection.)

30. The next most heavily drained population among the peoples of the Slave Coast, the Voltaic group, never supplied victims at more than one-quarter of that rate.

31. The sources for children are the same as those for males in note 29. Where children under 13 are indicated, 1.15 times that number are estimated for the more usual category of children under 15. Since very small children were not shipped, to put neutral wording on a nasty practice, this procedure somewhat underestimates the weight of the young in the British slave trade around 1737, 1776, and 1796 (Geggus 1989, 24).

32. Geggus 1989, 30. The estimate for 1659–1702 is for British and Dutch vessels; for 1714–1716 and 1765–1778 the loadings are French.

33. Dunn (1972, 28–39, 59–65, 168–77, 188–205) discusses this early agricultural

succession. Eltis (2000, 204–7) highlights rather later stages of the process on Barbados between 1685 and 1705 and Jamaica between 1715 and 1735.

34. For instance, among German and Irish migrants to 18th-century colonial America (Wokeck 1999, and as discussed in Chapter 6 of this volume).

35. The fourth and fifth lines of Table 5.7. Those curves were fitted but are not graphed.

36. How demographic developments in Martinique, Guadeloupe, and Cayenne affect the comparative trending and what happens when prices from St. Domingue are separated from those for Jamaica will have to be explored by the experts.

37. Imports to St. Domingue were cut off by the revolt of the early 1790s.

38. The level for the Dutch trade may not be quite comparable, depending upon just what point in a transaction involving goods and their money value and slaves onshore and on board was captured. But the direction of movement should be basically reliable.

39. Again, guilders have been translated into sterling via McCusker (1978, 44, 53). Contrary to much theorizing about transportation costs, there was virtually no difference in price on average between slaves from nearer Guinea and more distant Angola in the Dutch traffic of this early period to Brazil. It must be remembered, however, that the comparative distances were more equal to Pernambuco, on the easternmost tip of Brazil, than into the Caribbean further north and west.

40. In addition to the symbols already employed for early sales in America, in the top plot of the figure, the hollow *downward* triangles from 1664 through 1698 come from Eltis (2000, 296) by dividing his series of what the Royal African Company *expected* to pay for slaves into the new composite average for New World sales from Eltis and Richardson (forthcoming, Appendix Table 2). Interestingly, around 1703 and 1707 (not graphed) RAC traders expected to pay what would have generated gross profit ratios of 4.6 and 4.0 rather than the falling values of 2.11 and 2.10 for the available data for the Atlantic slave trade as a whole, less than half the margin of their dreams (or unalert accounting?). This may help explain how within a few more years they went out of business.

41. The whole European trade including Brazil and the Atlantic Islands has been seen to expand between 1638 and 1785 via an H trend with base year at 1645 (Figure 2.1a).

42. Slaves of known price coming to Antigua and to St. Domingue this early are unlikely to affect the available aggregate averages much.

43. Inflation and deflation, for example, have historically been elements to move in these G-connected forms (Harris 1996). So has the volume and degree of specialization for a colonial staple trade like tobacco (Harris 1992). Comparable trends appear in international exchange rates up to the 1850s—and in much-studied businesses from English agriculture and the cutting-edge Dutch economy of the 17th and 18th centuries to 19th-century railroads and manufacturing and still more modern enterprise (discussion yet to be published).

44. With understandably slightly fewer tons per sailor in periods of war when there was more armament to handle (69).

45. The data of Burnard and Morgan (2001, 225) suggest that average tonnage at Jamaica and at other points of arrival atrophied more slowly, perhaps in D fashion with zero year around 1630, while slave numbers per ship remained basically level before the late-18th-century surge already noted. Some of the flattening in their patterns may result from using 25-year time blocks rather than the decades employed by Behrendt and Min-

chinton. Another source of difference may derive from how places of arrival were grouped or separated out in the three analyses.

46. Though trends for Barbados alone were rather different (Table 5.4 and Figure 5.6c).

47. The Dutch atrophy in transatlantic profit margin as of 1715 (perhaps as early as 1690) took a D course parallel to that for falling mortality rates for the trade in general. The mostly British overall price gap shrank in G' form instead.

Chapter 6

How Other Populations Have
Normalized or Adjusted

If slave populations have so repeatedly altered historically in composition by sex and age according to G-based trends, does that regularity arise from something inherent in the exceptional circumstances of forced migration and slavery? Or is it indicative of even more general dynamics embedded in how the structures of populations change?

The case for such a broader level of applicability is next examined in three other historical groups of populations and in the migrations that have significantly fed them. First considered are the white or European peoples, or segments of populations, in various colonies of early America. Some of these are the same societies whose slave sectors have just been analyzed; others involve quite different peoples. Next, comparable transformations of composition in certain other early modern settings, from the Old World as well as the New, are explored. Finally, quite modern (and generally more ample, regular, and reliable) data are shown also to display similar G-related trends of change in demographic structure.

GOING NATIVE: THE ESTABLISHMENT OF EUROPEAN
PEOPLES IN EARLY AMERICA

The same populations whose slave elements have provided ammunition for the arguments of Chapter 5 offer an opening insight into movements of demographic adjustment among settling peoples of European stock. Figure 6.1 plots trends in the proportion of white adults in these early American colonies who were women.

Figure 6.1
Proportion of Women among White Adults in British Colonies

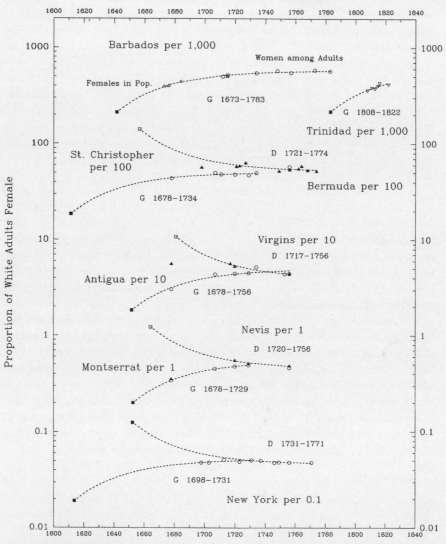

Sources: Wells 1975, 122, 176–77, 216, 219, 242; Beckles 1989, 173; John 1988, 41–42; Pitman 1917, 373, 380.

Most clearly and definitively on Barbados (Figure 6.1) and in Newfoundland (Figure 6.2), but also on St. Christopher, Antigua, and Montserrat and in New York, the weight of women among adults of European origin rose for substantial periods of time in G form across several decades.[1] The earliest G patterns occurred on St. Christopher, which held the first enduring settlement of the English in the West Indies, in New York—also pioneered in the early 1620s, though by the Dutch—and in the seminal fishing outpost of Newfoundland. While no substantial series is available for early Bermuda, another opening foothold for English colonization in the New World, fragments from 1698 and the early 1720s suggest the possibility of a G track parallel with that for St. Christopher. Part A of Table 6.1 joins Figures 6.1 and 6.2 in showing how G curves for Barbados, Antigua, and Montserrat followed along subsequently, with t_0's at more like 1650 than in the 1610s. Trinidad, a much later British acquisition, seems also to have gained women within her white population via a G trend (though the evidence covers a very short span of time).[2] Generally, these inter-colonial movements carried the percentage of women among white adults to about half (what the biology of reproduction would eventually dictate), though on Barbados, Bermuda, the Virgins, and perhaps Nevis the level visibly exceeded 50 percent while in the fishing base of Newfoundland females failed to achieve that high a proportion of the total, even just in the more permanent winter population.

By the 1720s, however, the share of women in the adult white populations of Bermuda, Nevis, and the British Virgins had begun to adjust back in D fashion. New York shared this movement, and, as scattered observations indicate, parallel declines might be possible in Figure 6.1 for Antigua and Montserrat. Barbados, St. Christopher (up to 1756 at least), and Newfoundland, however, seem to have avoided such a reversal in trend. What lay beneath the downward D movements that are observed is probably indicated by the way that they tended to bring women from a higher proportion back to about half of white adults. "Overshoots" (or perhaps biased counting that missed men living in certain kinds of settings) were being corrected.

In Bermuda, heavily engaged in fishing, losses of men (or poor recording while they were at sea) for a while pushed women to well over 50 percent of adults. Hence, the D trend seems to have involved a different *level* of normalization than found elsewhere. New York during the second half of the 1700s poised herself to soon surpass Philadelphia as the main point of intake for European immigrants. That heavy concentration, and the frontier expansion and military development based upon New York that drew it, probably encouraged a temporary accumulation of relatively more men than normal.

It is also possible to follow the accumulating significance of *children* within these New World populations of European origin. Figure 6.3 graphs the apparent G-related trends involved. Part B of Table 6.1 summarizes and compares them.

First of all, it is evident how the proportion of young individuals in most of these colonial populations rose via G trajectories from the 1600s into the early

Figure 6.2
Demographic Change in Colonial Newfoundland, 1675–1775

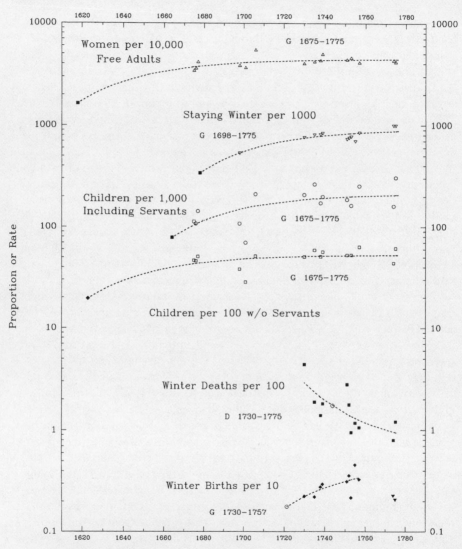

Source: Wells 1975, 47, 50, 52, 59.

Table 6.1
Trends in the Sex and Age of Some Early American Populations of European Origin

A. Proportion Women among Adults

St. Christopher	1678-1734	G	1611			
Newfoundland (winter)	1675-1775	G	1618			
New York	1698-1731	G	1614	1731-1771	D	1653
Barbados	1673-1783	G	1642			
Antigua	1678-1756	G	1652			
Montserrat	1678-1729	G	1653			
Bermuda				1721-1774	D	1657
Nevis				1720-1756	D	1664
Virgins				1717-1756	D	1681
Trinidad	1808-1822	G	1783			

B. Proportion Children

Newfoundland (w/o svts.)	1675-1775	G	1623			
Montserrat	1678-1756	G	1614			
New York				1703-1771	D	1629
Nevis	1678-1729	G	1631			
St. Christopher	1678-1720	G	1643	1720-1734	C	1802
Bermuda				1698-1774	D	1661
Barbados	1673-1712	G'	1707	1712-1747	D	1656
"				1734-1783	C	1840
Antigua	1678-1729	G	1669			
Newfoundland (w. svts.)	1675-1775	G	1664			
Surinam				1710-1744	D	1680
Trinidad	1808-1822	G	1794			

Sources: Figures 6.1, 6.2, and 6.3.

1700s or later. The earliest curves are for Montserrat and Newfoundland (Figure 6.2), followed by Nevis and St. Christopher (with t_0's at 1631 and 1643) and then Antigua (1664). The Newfoundland computation uses for its base only the free white population, excluding largely seasonal servants. Figure 6.2 shows how with time more and more of the residents of this fishing outpost stayed on through the winter. That trend made children as part of the *total* population, including servants, rise more steeply—along a G based at 1664 rather than 1619 (Wells 1975, 50). Tardily acquired Trinidad, as with regard to her proportion of females, accumulated children within her white population along a much later G, with t_0 only at 1794. The rising weight of colored persons among free people

Figure 6.3
The Accumulation of Children in White Colonial Populations

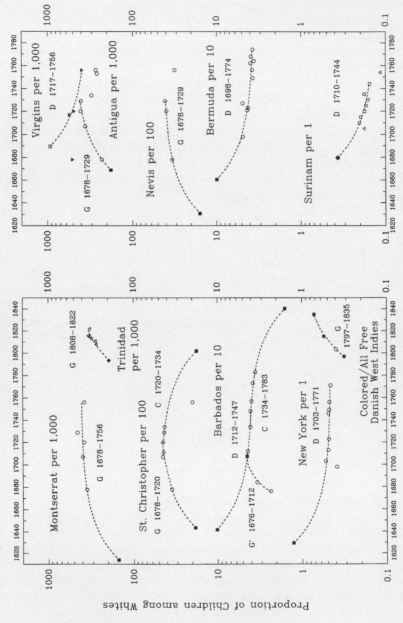

Sources: Wells 1975, 116, 176–77, 216, 219, 242; Pitman 1917, 373, 380; John 1988, 41–42; N. Hall 1992, 180; Postma 1990, 185.

in the Danish West Indies, meanwhile, would seem to serve as a surrogate for increase of children of mixed race. This development took G shape from 1797 through 1835, as is shown at the bottom of the left panel of Figure 6.3 (N. Hall 1992, 180).

On Barbados, something rather different seems to have happened. From 1676 through 1712 the increase of children among whites rose in G' rather than G form. In New York, meanwhile—if the data are accurate—the percentage of children may have for some reason jumped significantly between 1698 and 1703. In the British Virgins, furthermore, very gentle increase between 1678 and 1717, though there is too little information with which to apply a curve, seems to conform to the kind of flat segment of the G pattern found in Montserrat, on the left side of Figure 6.3. It will take further investigation, however, to confirm these patterns and establish the reason for the few exceptions to the more general G-type movements.

As a result of these increases in varying form, children represented a little over 40 percent of the white populations of Barbados, St. Christopher, Antigua, Nevis, and Montserrat in the early 1700s and around 50 percent or slightly higher in Bermuda, the British Virgins, New York, and Newfoundland (not counting servants).[3] Then, however, in most of these recorded colonial populations of European origin for at least a while during the 18th century the weight of the young *declined*. Usually this atrophy took D form, as in New York 1703–1771, Barbados 1712–1747, the British Virgins 1717–1756 (probably accompanied by nearby Antigua), Bermuda, and Dutch Surinam (where just children under 12 are recorded, giving the D trend a considerably lower level). Figure 6.3 and part B of Table 6.1 indicate, however, that beginning on St. Christopher in the 1720s and Barbados in the 1730s, the percentage of children among whites declined instead in the less usual, accelerating *C* form (though on St. Christopher by 1756 the proportion, if correctly recorded, had dropped off afresh more abruptly). What might have been making children start progressively to "go out of fashion" in the European populations of these places in that pattern? Did birth rates begin to decline this C way, as they did among blacks in Cuba from 1774 to 1877 (Figure 5.8b)? Figure 6.2 indicates, meanwhile, that after climbing in G manner, the birth rate for the year-round population on Newfoundland dropped by the 1770s; but no trend is evident. The death rate there probably improved (fell) in D shape from 1730 through 1775.

During the period examined, these white populations of the New World continued to be fed by significant flows of additional Europeans. What happened to the compositions of those in-migrations? Did they alter in G-connected ways as has been observed for the sex and age of imported slaves?

Apparently they did. Figure 6.4 presents some evidence on the age, sex, and legal status of migrants to British North America, those coming just to the Chesapeake or to the West Indies, and convicts and servants separately.

Menard (1975, 194) blended data from lists of immigrants, from headrights

Figure 6.4
The Composition of Migrations to Early British North America

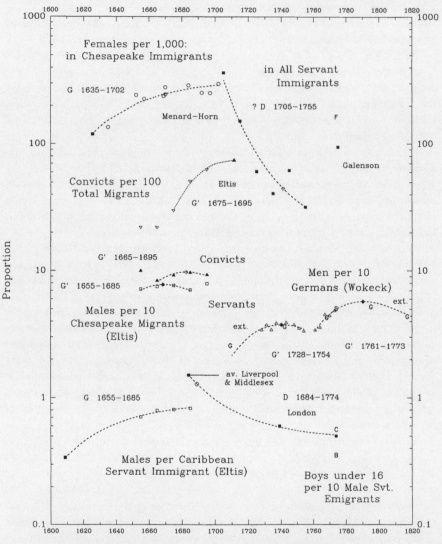

F = English females 1773–1776; S = Scots 1773–1776; G = Grubb; C = children; B = boys.

Sources: Menard 1975, 194; Horn 1979, 63; Galenson 1981, 25, 27; Eltis 2000, 50, 98; Wokeck 1999, 240–76; Wokeck files; Bailyn 1986, 128, 131–33; Grubb 1990, 420.

used to claim land in Virginia and Maryland (which was given out for bringing people to the colony), and from servants recorded in probate inventories to calculate the sex distribution among adult arrivals. Horn (1979, 63) added to this analysis a few immigrants from London for the years 1634–1635 and 1682–1687 and Liverpool for 1697–1707. The top plot in Figure 6.4 restates the composition of the enlarged group in terms of proportion of females, which rose from 1635 through 1702 generally around an underlying G curve with a base year at 1626 to attain approximately 30 percent by the turn of the century.

Thereafter, however, the weight of women among servants coming to the Chesapeake—and among servants migrating from England to all British America, according to the data of Galenson (1981, 25)—dropped away markedly into the 1750s, perhaps via the kind of D trend suggested. Galenson, it should be noted, covered only servants who had *indentures*. According to Chesapeake data, most particularly for Charles County, Maryland, these individuals constituted less than half of all servant migrants, the majority of whom came on terms to be decided only in America, according to "custom of the country."[4] The "F" symbol that accompanies the plot with solid squares for Galenson at the top of Figure 6.4 represents the 16 percent of females among all English migrants found by Bailyn in the lists of the years 1773–1776 (1986, 131). This is a considerably higher proportion than what the data of Galenson produce in the 1770s, though it should be noted that the Bailyn group includes free migrants and servants-to-be without indentures, not just those agreeing to terms of servitude before leaving England. There may be the kind of D tendency of decline indicated through the 1750s. It is unlikely to be so steep.

In the middle area of Figure 6.4 the servant data of Eltis (2000, 98—from his "Coldham's Emigrants" database) instead take a G' pattern for the proportion of *males* among servants going to Virginia and Maryland from the 1650s through the 1680s. It is not clear what mix of migrants is included in this source. The differences will have to be worked out in local Chesapeake analysis that is continuing, though it should be noted that to include the 1690s and to consider 1685 as an aberrant low average produce a trend not so different from that of Menard and Horn.[5]

Among the *convicts* of Eltis, meanwhile, a later G' pattern for maleness also appears, with t_0 at 1683 (rather than the possible 1669 for servants) and one with a projected maximum of 97 rather than 78 percent. The proportion of convicts among all immigrants to the Chesapeake, as he indicates (the downward-pointing hollow triangles of the second level of plotting in Figure 6.4), may also have climbed in G' fashion, toward a peak of about 75 percent near 1712. Taken together, these patterns would seem to signal a shift to convicts in an effort to replace free and servant men, who were becoming less available—in number and in proportion to the alternative offered by prisoners.

One reason for these changes was that, even as the absolute number faded away, the planters of the *Caribbean* were able to draw a male *proportion* of servants that from 1650 through 1690 rose steadily along a G path (from a base year at 1609, according to the bottom left plot in Figure 6.4). This male weighting from 1660 to the end of the century regularly exceeded the percentage among servants going to the Chesapeake (Eltis 2000, 98). The rich colonies of the West Indies were in a better position to bid for what they desired; and as local populations of European origin matured, for further immigration that they desired: extra men to perform skilled work and to supervise slaves. Their agents could pick over the most useful persons willing to sign indentures, a pool of people who to begin with were generally older and more talented than the other half or so of eventual servant migrants.

The G' type of swing in sex composition appears again, however, a century later among German immigrants who came to the mainland British colonies through the Delaware River. From 1728 through 1754 the weight of men among all entrants rose from about 35 percent to 40 percent and then dropped back to 33 percent (Wokeck 1999, 240–76, and her research files).[6] Then, as the number of German arrivals dwindled, the proportion of men among them rose sharply from the postwar renewal of Atlantic (and Rhineland) travel in the early 1760s to the American Revolution. Along something like the G' path offered in Figure 6.4, it reached 50 percent. Wokeck's narrative shows how these later males were now younger and more likely to be travelling alone, less often men who were bringing their families with them, a fact subsequently recognized in analysis by Grubb (1990, 420). His conclusions for 1709 and for the periods 1727–1756, 1761–1775, 1785–1804, and 1815–1820—denoted as "G"—are for comparison superimposed upon the more finely timed data of Wokeck and the two successive G' curves fitted to them. Grubb's additions to the argument demonstrate how the early, one-shot shipment of Palatines to New York in 1709 and dwindling German immigration following the Revolution mostly hug projected extensions of the G' trends indicated by the findings of Wokeck but usefully expand these patterns.

The "S" at 1774 in this plot denotes the 50 percent for adult men among *Scots* in the 1773–1776 lists studied by Bailyn (1986, 132). This closely resembles the current level among Germans. In marked contrast, among *English* emigrants of 1773–1776 no less than 80 percent were men (ibid.)—a proportion confirmed by Grubb from the lists employed by Bailyn and from independent records for English arriving in Philadelphia 1774–1776 (1990, 420).

Mirroring the way that Caribbean colonies along a G path steadily relied progressively more upon males among servants as the shift to slavery took place across the later 1600s, the weight of those *under 16* among servant emigrants leaving England seems to have eroded in long-term D rather than down-and-up 1/G' form. The bottom right plot in Figure 6.4 indicates how the percentage of boys among males leaving from London declined via a D curve from 15 in the mid-1680s to 6 percent between 1718 and 1759 and 5 percent by the mid-1770s (Galenson 1981, 27). Whereas the proportion for Middlesex departures around 1684 is low (just 3 percent) and that for Liverpool near 1702 is high (27 percent), the average for these two sources of male servants across those years comes to 15 percent boys, not unlike the level of the hypothetical curve for London at this time. More data would be helpful, especially for understanding regional variations better; but it appears that the decline of the young among male servants leaving England for America took the kind of long-term D path proposed.

As a check, the "C" at 1774 represents the 5.6 percent under 15 (not 16) among Bailyn's 1773–1776 English emigrants of both sexes. The "B" stands for just the 3.5 percent boys under 15 among males. Among Scottish emigrants on the 1773–1776 lists, in contrast, some 20 percent of males and 30 percent of females were under 15 (Bailyn 1986, 132). The Scottish migration of the 1770s, as Bailyn emphasizes, as a reaction to hardship and various kinds of pressure was quite a different kind of movement from the contemporary English flow. It included more families, as many people were in effect pushed out of their homeland, and not so many relatively young, unattached men pulled to further their fortunes in the New World as were present in the long-established migration of English to the colonies.

Chapter 5 indicates that among slaves, too, the weight of children was more likely to alter in lasting G or D fashion, less often via the G' pattern found here and there in the frequency of males or men. The proportion of males in both free and forced migration, it seems, was more likely to be affected by shorter-term shifts in what moved people from one place to another. Change in age distribution was more driven by underlying demographic dynamics. The distinction offers further perspective on how G and G' shapes are embedded in many developments in the makeup of populations and on reasons that such movements in demographic composition or structure may have taken those patterns.

Some further and more detailed insight into how such underlying demographic processes worked emerges from three other diverse migrations to the mainland of the Americas. Something is known of Spanish relocation to the New World from as far back as the 1500s and of how certain local colonial populations of this Iberian power subsequently evolved. French 17th-century arrivals to the St. Lawrence settlements of Canada, long regarded as the fountainhead of regional tradition and culture, have been much and fruitfully studied. The composition of these "pioneers" and the impact of their descendants informatively contribute to the present discussion. Finally, though the direct demographic records are generally not as good, in the end much can be determined one way or another about how local European populations in British colonial settlements of the Chesapeake evolved during the 17th and 18th centuries.

Figure 6.5, in the second plot from the top, first of all trends the proportion of females present among emigrants from all parts of Spain to the New World from 1506 (1493–1519) through 1570 (1560–1579) according to the research of Peter Boyd-Bowman (1976, 599). From 1530 through 1570 (incorporating grouped data from 1520 through 1579) this share rose from 6.3 to 28.5 percent

Figure 6.5
The Composition of Spanish Emigrants to America, 1506–1595

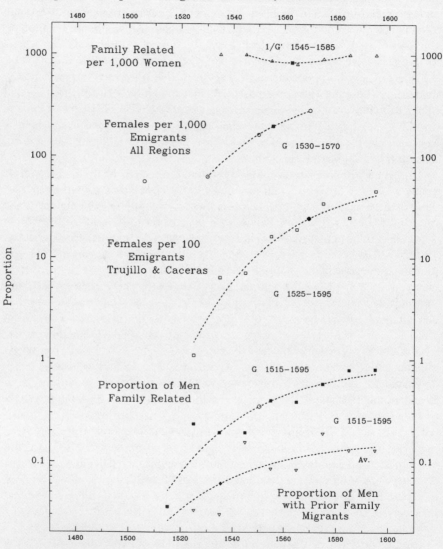

Sources: Boyd-Bowman 1976, 599; Altman 1989, 172–73.

along a G trend based at 1556. With a level of 19.9 percent at t_0 at that date, this curve rose about two-thirds higher than that for the English Chesapeake (Figure 6.4) three-quarters of a century later. (For that later, more male intake, t_0 came at 11.9 percent at 1625.) In each case, however—Spanish as well as English—G was the pattern according to which immigration became more female as early settlement matured.

The other information graphed in Figure 6.5 comes from a study by Ida Altman of emigration to America out of the two Spanish locales of Trujillo and Cáceres in the Extremadura region (1989, 172–73). The proportion of females in this particular group of emigrants climbed along a rather later G path than the one for all known Spanish people coming to America (the Boyd-Bowman evidence). The t_0 for the curve falls at 1570 rather than 1556. The percentage of females is also rather higher at the base year: 24.6 instead of 19.9. Yet the not only later but longer and more regular series for this local area confirms how the G shape characterized the balancing of the sexes within the early transatlantic migration of Iberians to America.

Altman also provides information about the connection of these Spanish migrants with each other and with those who had come to the New World before them. The second plot from the bottom in Figure 6.5 (with solid squares) indicates that from 1515 through 1595 more and more men in the flow traveled with relatives or joined relatives already in the New World. In the adventurous 1510s, the level was just 3.6 percent; by the 1590s it had climbed all the way to 80.4 percent. The underlying trajectory for this change was a G curve with base year at 1551. The very bottom plot of the figure shows that, beyond more often taking family (wives, parents, children, siblings) along with them, the percentage of men who were joining relatives *already* in America increased along a slightly flatter G path with t_0 at 6.1 percent at 1535 (the hollow downward triangles). By the 1580s and 1590s, on average, 12.9 percent of men immigrating to Spanish America were following relatives who had preceded them.

Among documented women from the Extremadura, all who came to the New World in the 1530s and 1540s traveled with or joined a relative. The top plot of Figure 6.5 shows how this percentage then dipped close to 80 in the 1560s, only to rise again to 100 in 1/G' fashion after the crest of the migration wave had passed (Figure 1.21 in Chapter 1). Unlike English servants coming to the Chesapeake in the 17th century (Menard 1975, 1988) or German immigrants to the Delaware Valley in the 18th (Wokeck 1999), there was not a steady flow of young European women who bet their futures and their quality of life upon prospects of the New World independent of their closest family ties. This phenomenon had significant consequences for ethnic and racial interaction in the Spanish settlements of the Americas. More non-European women became involved in the reproductive life of the colonies.

Something is known about that process of intergroup adjustment within the populations of the Spanish sector of New World settlement during the 17th and 18th centuries. Evidence exists, for example, concerning demographic composition in the northern frontier zone of Mexico and around the Guatemalan center of Santiago.

Figure 6.6a plots, first of all, the proportion of the population that was "Spanish" in New Mexico between 1760 and 1842 (Gutiérrez 1991, 167). This rose along a G path from about 40 to almost 75 percent. That trend, if projected backward in time, cuts between widely variant observations for 1746, on the one hand, and 1749 and 1750 on the other. In the sources employed by Gutiérrez, the number of Indians in the area doubles between 1746 and 1749. Comparable, though not identical, estimates provided by Thomas D. Hall (1989, 145) are labeled "Spanish and Caste." Apparently residents of mixed origin are included in these series. Hall, in addition, offers a few calculations for the El Paso District downriver from New Mexico. Here, it seems that the proportion of "Spanish" probably also rose in a G trajectory—at least between 1750 and 1790. This curve, however, ran at a level noticeably higher than that for New Mexico and advanced from a t_0 at 1731 rather than 1746. Settlers of whole or partial European origin had moved sooner and farther in permeating the population of El Paso than was the case in the more distant northern settlements of the Rio Grande.

Gutiérrez (1991, 288) also reports for New Mexico the extent to which people married across racial boundaries. The bottom plot in Figure 6.6a shows how a surge or shock of such exogamous unions appeared between the 1720s and the 1760s and then, after reaching 20 percent of all marriages around 1770, virtually disappeared by 1810. The rising phase of this phenomenon might fit a G trend with base year at 1747, simultaneous with that for the percentage of "Spanish" within the population of New Mexico. Perhaps insight is offered into how that proportion may have increased. The subsequent "crash" in racially exogamous marriage more clearly takes C shape from 1775 through 1810. In other historical circumstances such a downwardly accelerating pattern, headed for extinction, has been observed in the size of populations that have lost their niche or for practices that have gone out of style (Harris 2001). Did the church turn against intermarriage around 1770? Did the reduction of unions to those who were not "Spanish" to a smaller and smaller minority of marriages exacerbate racism? Experts on this region for this time period will have to sift out the various possibilities; but the G-based patterns of Figure 6.6a would seem to reveal much about the nature of certain demographic changes that took place along the northern frontier of Spanish America across the 18th and early 19th centuries.

Figure 6.6b focuses on quite a different part of the Spanish New World: the Mayan highlands of Guatemala. Santiago de Guatemala constituted the central place for this region. Christopher H. Lutz (1994, 87) has presented data on the number of marriages taking place according to "socioracial" group. These can be employed to obtain at least a general sense of how the proportions of persons with different heritage in this locality changed between the 1590s and the 1760s.

The Spanish share (solid squares near the top of the graph) probably fell along two D-shape trends. The first of these was relatively flat. From the 1590s for-

Figure 6.6a
Some Demographic Changes in Colonial Spanish America: "Spanish" Population and Exogamous Marriage in Northern Mexico, 1697–1842

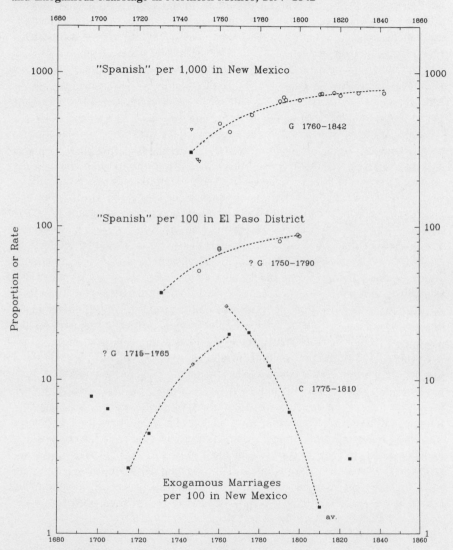

Sources: Gutiérrez 1991, 167, 288; T. D. Hall 1989, 145.

ward, it carried the proportion of those with European origin (at least in marriages that were *recorded*) only from the low 50s to more like 45 percent. Then, from the 1660s into the 1760s, the representation of Spanish marriages dropped off more severely, all the way down to 22 percent of the total—along a D curve with t_0 at 1659. Though the proportion of all recorded unions that took place among Indians rose from 1665 through 1725 in a G that vertically mirrored the bend of the Spanish D, Indian numbers were small (rising from 8 to 16 percent of all weddings in this period, before falling away into the 1750s). It was mestizo and mulatto marriages that expanded most consequentially for the composition of the population in the century after 1665. The first tripled from 9.3 to 27.8 percent along a G trend with base year at 1668; the second climbed from 23.0 to 38.5 percent along a G with t_0 at 1642.[7] By the 1770s, two-thirds of the recorded marriages of Santiago de Guatemala were of individuals whose European origin mingled with native or African heritage.

Earlier, from the 1590s through the 1660s, the proportion of mulatto marriages within the total for Santiago de Guatemala grew vigorously from 6.3 to 23.0 percent via a G trajectory based at 1608. Meanwhile the mestizo share of the whole seems also to have increased—from something like 4.5 percent to slightly over 10 percent. This change possibly took place along the kind of unusual accelerating E path indicated, but why it might have done so is unclear. The first fitted curve in the top plot of Figure 6.6b, however, shows the way that Indian marriages declined offsettingly ever faster via a C trend from 1595 to 1645 or later as unions involving Indian-Europeans (mestizos) accelerated upward. Recorded unions among blacks also shrank in relative significance during this period. A C trend likewise captures this downward movement from 1605 through 1675, as the bottom plot of Figure 6.6b indicates.[8] This relatively gentle change, however, as of the 1670s was followed by a sharper D-shaped drop that carried the weight of black marriages in the total from 10 percent to as low as 2 percent as the proportion of mulatto unions rose. Did blacks become a less distinct, perhaps smaller element of the community? Were their unions simply not being recorded as fully as before?

Together, data from the northern frontier of colonization amid the pueblos of the upper Rio Grande Valley and from Santiago de Guatemala, to the south of Mexico in Mayan Central America, demonstrate how change in the composition of populations in Spanish America in the 1600s, 1700s, and early 1800s unfolded in G-based forms just as much as the makeup of the migration flow from Iberia to the New World in the 1500s. Something kept steering demographic change along these few related paths as regularly as has been observed in the British colonies of the Caribbean and North America.

It is also possible to follow the evolving number and character of French emigrants during the 1600s and their impact upon the demographic development of the settlements of the St. Lawrence. Figures 6.7a and 6.7b plot some trends identified in the findings of Hubert Charbonneau and his associates.

Figure 6.6b
Some Demographic Changes in Colonial Spanish America: Weight of Racial Groups in Marriages at Santiago de Guatemala, 1595–1765

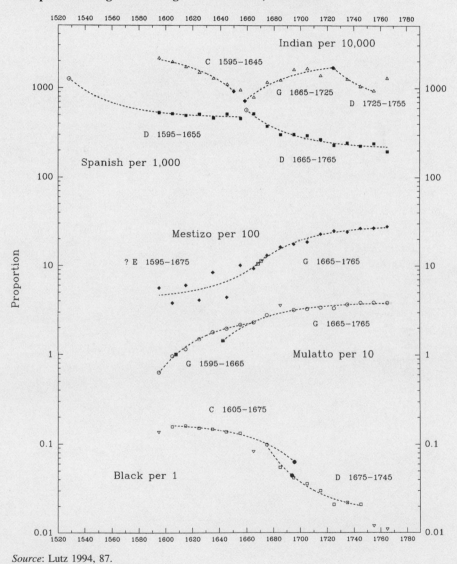

Source: Lutz 1994, 87.

Figure 6.7a
The Demographic Structure of French Canadian Settlement: Immigration

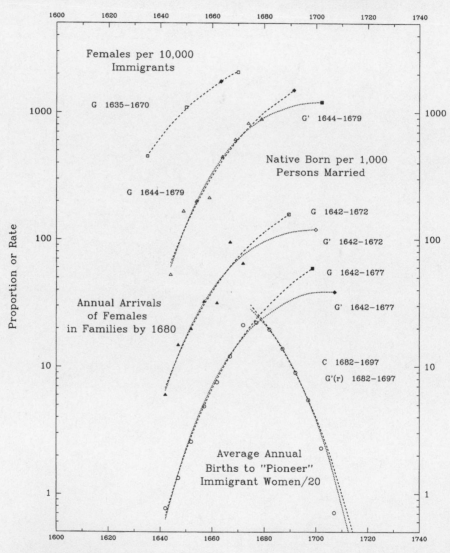

Source: Charbonneau et al. 1987, 15, 62, 19, 84.

Figure 6.7b

The Demographic Structure of French Canadian Settlement: The Impact of "Pioneer" Immigration upon the Population

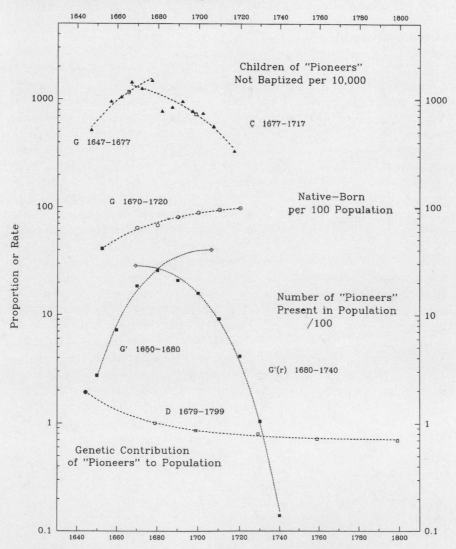

Sources: Charbonneau et al. 1987, 84, Table 22 (pocket), 124; Harris 2001, 65.

First, among all recorded immigrants from the 1630s through the 1670s females probably increased from 4.5 to 20.7 percent—if the assumption is correct that those of unknown sex were almost all men (Charbonneau et al. 1987, 15).[9] They did so along a G curve with base year at 1663 (the top plot of Figure 6.7a). Similarly, the proportion of *native-born* persons among Canadians of European stock probably rose from 1670 through 1720 via a G curve with t_0 at 1653 (the second plot of Figure 6.7b, with hollow circles). By mid-century, perhaps 40 percent of the population had been born in Canada, a proportion that exceeded 90 percent by the early 1700s. This series of calculations subtracts the number of "pioneers" alive and present in the colony at the time (ibid., back pocket, Table 22) from the curve used to fit Charbonneau's previously published numbers for population in the St. Lawrence settlements (Harris 2001, 65, which is based upon Charbonneau 1975, 30, 40). It overestimates the percentage of natives in the population to the extent that European immigrants other than "pioneers" and their families were present at the time. Given the conventional image of relative encapsulation for the French settlers of Canada and the well-established difficulty of administrators in securing a continuing supply of new colonists (Diamond 1961), however, the trend proposed should give a reasonable impression of the shape of change for the proportion of native-born in this colonial population even if the *level* may need to be adjusted. Into the 1720s that proportion, like the role of women among immigrants as far as 1680, took G form.

The absolute *number* of "pioneers" resident in the Canadian population, in contrast—as Figure 6.7b shows—first rose in G' fashion, like so many other migrations, then fell away markedly as this group of early settlers—defined so as to have no replacements—died off (Charbonneau et al. 1987, Table 22). The downward pattern for this disappearance from 1680 all the way through 1740 took the form of G' reversed with regard to time or G'(r), which is in effect C'. The G' rise from 1650 through 1680 not surprisingly paralleled (with t_0's at 1706 and 1707, respectively) G' increase in the average annual births to "pioneer" immigrant women from 1642 through 1677 (the bottom plot of Figure 6.7a). Females situated in families by 1680 had arrived in the colony according to a slightly earlier G' trajectory (t_0 at 1700). The children whom they produced became a larger and larger portion of persons who were married, also according to a G' pattern—with t_0 at 1702, shows the second plot of Figure 6.7a (with hollow triangles).

On the other hand, for these marriages, for the arrival times of women situated in families by 1680, and for annual births to "pioneer" women, alternative trendings in G (and C) shape are possible, as Figures 6.7a and 6.7b indicate. Illustrated for each of these three data series is how closely the G and G' curves run together for certain decades before the zero year of each curve. This degree of approximation in many different historical contexts can help in-migration in G' fashion foster demographic change of G shape in the population that receives the arrivals.

The reason for a possible G trend from 1647 through 1677 in the percentage of children of "pioneers" who were not baptized (top plot of Figure 6.7b), however, would seem to lie in another direction. Under the control of the commercial Hundred Associates, who operated St. Lawrence colonization in its early decades, agricultural and artisanal settlers began to leak out extensively into the more lucrative fur trade. Meanwhile, societal institutions—including the church—did not take root as firmly as the Crown desired. These deficiencies motivated a royal takeover in 1663, an initiative intent upon strengthening the European character of the settlements in the face of challenges posed by life in the New World "wilderness" (Diamond 1961). It appears, for reasons of scattered residence, limitations to religious resources or effectiveness, and perhaps intermarriage with the native American population, that the proportion of children who were not baptized rose across something like three decades of early settlement to about 14 percent. After the royal administration took over in the 1660s, however, the share of children not baptized then accelerated downward to 3 percent or less (Charbonneau et al. 1987, 84). Especially if the data for the late 1670s and the early 1680s are averaged, this decline very closely follows a C curve, the shape of trend that hastens toward oblivion. Non-baptized children virtually disappeared—at least from the records. The campaign to Christianize came to allow (or perhaps just to admit) no exceptions.

If one looks, finally, at the proportion of the European population of Canada that had paternal genetic roots in the "pioneer" families of the 17th century, a G-based pattern of change also emerges. The percentage fell from 100 at 1679 to 70 at 1799 as later arrivals left their mark on the population. The curve graphed at the bottom of Figure 6.7b actually extends all the way to fit findings of 69 percent at 1899 and 68 percent at 1949 for the population of the region that is now the province of Quebec (Charbonneau et al. 1987, 124). In sum, for one of the most carefully studied and best-documented groups of early modern European settlers in the New World, G-family curves represent very well changes that took place in the sex of immigrants, the emergence of a native-born nucleus of people of European stock, the impact of the earliest arrivers upon the demographic composition of Quebec, and perhaps even their early drift toward, then decisive rejection of, the kinds of connections with the native population that so prominently characterized the colonists of early Spanish America. (This last applies to the settlements of the St. Lawrence, not to the hinterlands of the fur trade, in which personal ties with Indian suppliers continued to form a crucial element of successful business.)

Another early regional settlement of the New World that throws further light upon particular processes through which immigrants are digested by a population is the Chesapeake of the 17th and 18th centuries. Figures 6.8a, 6.8b, and 6.8c draw upon work that several researchers have done on that region.

The top plot of Figure 6.8a begins by showing how the proportion of the Chesapeake population that was composed of non-taxable persons (young Europeans and Africans and white women) increased across the first century of

Figure 6.8a
Local Demographic Composition in the Chesapeake: Dependency, Sex, and Age

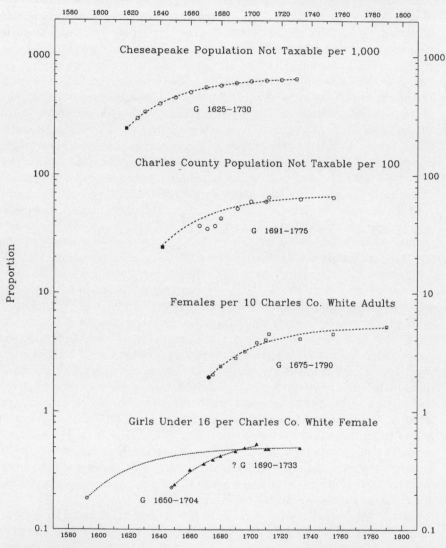

Sources: Harris 1992, 60; Menard 1977a, 96; 1980, 157–61; data supplied by Walsh.

settlement in G form (Menard 1977a, 96; fitted in Harris 1992, 60). This curve for 1625–1730 had its zero year at 1618 and carried the weight of non-taxables from about 30 to more like 65 percent by the second quarter of the 18th century as white women more evenly matched white men and as both black and white children became more numerous.

For Charles County, Maryland (whose data, originally supplied by Lorena S. Walsh, were fitted in Harris 1992, 60), estimates for non-taxables swing substantially before 1691. In this period young freed servants moved inland to Charles from earlier settlements looking for available land with which to establish themselves as planters and seeking bound male workers of their own for the heavy work that this process entailed. But from there through 1775 the proportion of non-taxables in the local population settled down to climb toward about 65 percent along a G trend with base year at 1642. First settlement took place in Maryland only in 1634 compared with the 1607 landing at Jamestown that started off English colonization in the Chesapeake. Thus, for Charles, the adjustment to have more women and children, which lagged behind the region-wide pattern by 23 years, essentially echoed a delayed Maryland settlement that commenced 27 years after the first James River toehold for the region.

One element in this change toward more non-taxables in Charles County was an increasing representation of women among white adults. The local estimates wobble somewhat (Walsh data; Harris 1992, 60); but this proportion rose from about 20 percent in the early 1670s to a shade over 50 percent as of 1790, approximately along a G path with base year at 1672. Another component in generating additional non-taxables was the emergence of children. The bottom plot in Figure 6.8a indicates how the proportion of white females in the county who were under 16 years of age increased from 1650 through 1704 via a G curve with t_0 at 1648. As of about 1700, however, the share of girls among white females in Charles essentially flattened out across the early 1700s. Except briefly with the 1704 census, those under 16 would not exceed 50 percent of white females. Perhaps the way that Charles County in its turn fed other, more inland areas with settlers has something to do with this change of trend that appears around 1700. More generally, though, there was a limit to how much reproduction the demographic regime for whites in the colony would sustain.

Data on decedents from other counties of Maryland[10] reveal other ways in which the composition of this regional British colonial population shifted along G-based lines. Figure 6.8b provides some illustrations. On the one hand, the proportion of probated men in certain contemporaneously developed areas of Somerset County who died without having been married dropped from 80 to under 20 percent between the 1670s and the 1770s along a D path with zero year at 1694. On the other, the proportion of native-born men among decedents rose everywhere we studied in G trends. In Anne Arundel County, around Annapolis, the curve from 1667 through 1768 has its t_0 at 1692. For decedents in Somerset, across the bay, the base year for the 1690–1775 curve comes rather later, at 1714. The bottom plot in Figure 6.8b indicates how the percentage of

Figure 6.8b

Local Demographic Composition in the Chesapeake: Never-Married Decedents and Generations of Native-Born

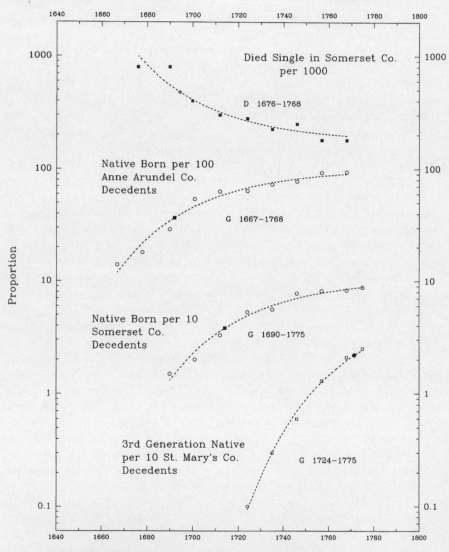

Sources: Harris 1992, 60; St. Mary's City Commission probate files.

decedents who can be identified as *third-generation* native rose in the initial county of Maryland settlement, St. Mary's, from under 1 percent in the 1720s to about 25 percent in the 1770s in a G trajectory anchored at 1771. Not just local birth but various depths of family history in the area expanded in G fashion.

From relatively late-developing Prince George's County, finally—up the Potomac River from Charles and inland behind Anne Arundel—come still other perspectives on how settler population was transformed in time by processes that took G-connected paths. Figure 6.8c draws upon Kulikoff's research (1986) for insights.

First of all, as the native population built up, the presence of white men who were not householders or their sons dropped away. The ratio sank from 1.00 per householder in 1704 to 0.33 by 1755, a level retained into the 1770s. The change took D form with base year at 1715. Anchored shortly thereafter, at 1722, was the G curve according to which an increasing proportion of Prince George's marriages linked blood relatives. This percentage rose from 10 in the unions of 1700–1730 to 28 among marriages of 1760–1790 (Kulikoff 1986, 254) as more and more of the young men and women of the county were locally born. Meanwhile, as the top plot in Figure 6.8c indicates, the average *duration* of unions in Prince George's and neighboring Charles Counties increased from 12.3 years in the 1658–1689 period (midpoint at 1674) to 25.3 in the marriages of 1750–1775. This implies that life expectancy increased in G form, a finding that is important to follow through where possible in other types of data.

One more perspective on the demographic changes taking place as settler populations matured or normalized reveals itself through customs of naming children (Kulikoff 1986, 247). The proportion of first sons who were named after a grandfather increased in Prince George's County from 1690 through 1810 around a G path with base year at 1692, reaching approximately 50 percent by the early 19th century. Up until about 1750, meanwhile, the proportion of first boy babies named after their fathers fell from about 65 to under 30 percent very much as an upside-down mirror image of the grand-paternal movement, via a declining D with t_0 at 1690. Longer life more often presented parents of the newborn with grandfathers to please, especially grandfathers who held onto the reins of family property. Then from 1730 or 1750 through 1790 the percentage of first sons named after fathers fell off even further in accelerating C form, dropping to 18 percent without marked additional increase in grandfather-pleasing. Such a pattern suggests that naming practices now simply opened up at the expense of fathers, though in the early 19th century (where a literature has constructed "patriarchy" *ad nauseam*) this decline was reversed somewhat.

The European populations of English, French, Dutch, and Spanish colonies in America all display the kinds of G-based developments in their sex and age structure, and in the composition of the migrations feeding them, that have been observed in the African slave trade (Chapter 5). Their histories, furthermore,

Figure 6.8c
Local Demographic Composition in the Chesapeake: Concomitant Social Changes in Prince George's County

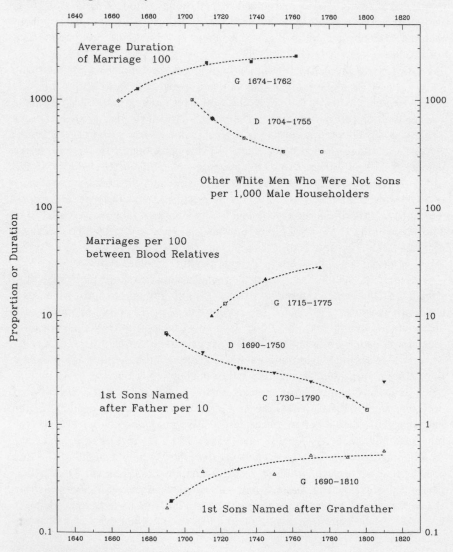

Source: Kulikoff 1986, 169, 66, 254, 247.

reveal several kinds of other, related demographic adjustments in G-connected form that have not been recorded for slave populations.

The migration of settlers from Europe—to 16th-century Spanish America, to French Canada in the 17th century, to the British colonies of Newfoundland, New York and Pennsylvania, the Chesapeake, and the West Indies down through the 18th century and into the early 19th—has been seen to evolve consistently in G-based patterns. The sex and especially the age of those coming to America altered primarily according to G itself and D (1/G), rarely via other members of the little G set of curves.

In G form also rose the degree to which migrants were family members of travelers who had preceded them or who accompanied them. Thus—if the Spanish evidence is at all typical, and the German and Irish experiences of the 18th century indicate that it is[11]—the emergence of the networks that in free migrations so importantly spread the word of conditions in the New World, informed others how to relocate, and encouraged them to do so and to commit loved ones to accompany them can be seen to have built up in G fashion. We begin to understand better how the "pull" out of source populations might so regularly take a G-connected shape.

Another dynamic that turned on then closed off the tap of migration was, of course, how change in the composition of the *receiving* population rendered relocation first more then less attractive. Increases in the proportions of women and children along G paths in the beginning made relocation seem more "civilized" and secure to prospective migrants. But such demographic change soon led in G trajectories to a higher proportion of native-born in the colonial population. The favored competition of these natives for land, work, credit, and spouses made satisfying establishment in the new society more and more difficult to attain for fresh arrivals. Presumably, this fact was known before long at the European sources of migration, cutting back the flow of those willing to move and changing the nature of who deemed the risk of relocation still worthwhile. Bound servants and convicts—not to mention slaves—could be pushed in where free migrants no longer liked to go.

Mostly, colonial populations of European stock (unlike slaves) started out heavily male and then included more women and girls. The change took G form in various colonies of the British West Indies, New York, the Chesapeake, and Newfoundland. As during the later 1600s and early 1700s a few dominant capitalists squeezed out smaller planters in the shift to sugar, the labor force swung toward slavery, and European men were imported for particular roles in this unusual economy, the white populations of several British islands shifted back in D form to become more male, accompanied by New York, where further immigration, too, stressed men—though for rather different reasons. Probably more typical for the mainland colonies as a whole, however, in Maryland white males who were not sons of householders dropped away markedly in D form from local tax lists.

From Newfoundland to Trinidad and Surinam the weight of children in settler populations also first rose along G paths. Then, like the proportion of females, among whites in the islands, Surinam, and New York the percentage of children shrank somewhat in D fashion to make room for a rebounding presence of men.

Increasing numbers of women and children allowed more men to marry and to procreate and produced a rising proportion of the native-born in colonial populations. In French Canada and in several localities of the Chesapeake such trends can be observed directly to take G paths. In related demographic dynamics, mulatto and mestizo proportions in populations increased in G fashion in Guatemala as Spanish individuals took partners among blacks and native Americans—another way that the population normalized or balanced out by sex and age. This was a practice apparently first spreading then suppressed in the 17th-century French settlements of the St. Lawrence, if the rise and fall of unbaptized children is an appropriate surrogate measure. A G-shape rise in the percentage of marriages that took place between blood relatives, as in 18th-century Prince George's County, Maryland, reflects in still another way how the native-born came to dominate colonial society in such patterns.

A lengthening of the duration of marriage in Maryland via the G curve, meanwhile, reflects increasing longevity among settlers. So does a G-shape trend to name first sons after grandfathers in lieu of fathers. Good direct estimates of crude vital rates for colonial populations are rare. But data from Newfoundland in the 1700s join evidence from the black populations of Cuba (Figure 5.8b) and Bahia (Figure 5.13d) in indicating that crude death rates and crude birth rates themselves took G-based patterns. The suspicion strengthens that it is something fundamental about the interplay of births and deaths in the "renewal" of populations that gives so many demographic trends their G-connected form.

BEYOND THE COLONIES OF THE AMERICAS: OTHER SETTLER SOCIETIES AND SOME LONG-ESTABLISHED POPULATIONS

To see the sex and age and ethnic or racial structure of European and mixed populations in British, Dutch, French, and Spanish settlements of the New World—and also the migration flows that did so much to feed them—normalize or stabilize in the same few G-based patterns as the slave populations and slave trades examined in Chapter 5 indicates that quite fundamental dynamics of how populations adjust underlie these forms of demographic change. All such combined evidence so far, nevertheless, still overwhelmingly concerns the bound or free colonizers of the Americas before about 1800. Just how far did the processes at work extend beyond the demographic transformation of the Western Hemisphere in the early modern age of European expansion? Data both from other settler societies and from long-established European populations begin to provide answers to this question for eras that are distinct from the epoch explored so far and for populations that developed in other parts of the globe.

The first intimation of a more general applicability of these movements for the structure of populations has already appeared in an examination of the Old Northwest of the United States in the 19th century. There, in Figure 1.11 of Chapter 1, while net in-migration surged in up-and-down G' fashion across the 19th century—and probably again through the first half of the 20th—and white foreign-born immigrants also peaked (roughly contemporaneously) via G' between the 1870s and the 1910s, the *rate* of in-migration relative to the size of the current population declined in successive D trends: first across the antebellum era and then from the 1850s into the 1950s. That is, the accumulative, long-term nativization of the region took 1/G (D) form, as has been found to be general among the slave populations of Chapter 5.

As this interior region of the United States after 1800 was being penetrated by migrants from east of the Alleghenies and from Europe, other new settler societies were being formed all the way around the globe—in Australia and New Zealand. Figures 6.9a and 6.9b depict patterns of change found in the population of New Zealand (Bloomfield 1984; *New Zealand Official Yearbook 1998*).

First of all, the proportion of females in both the European and the Maori segments of the population rose in G paths from about 1860 to the end of the 20th century.[12] Among Europeans, the 43 percent level of the 1850s dropped into the high 30s before starting to rise. A similar initial swing back and forth has been observed for the non-taxable (dependent) share of the population of Charles County, Maryland, in its early years (Figure 6.8a). As in the slave societies of Chapter 5, after the first foothold was established, men to exploit the opening economically could be at a premium for a while locally before demographic normalization took over.

The weight of children under 15 years of age in New Zealand (not including Maori until 1951) has followed a more complex historical patterning (the up-and-down second plot in Figure 6.9a). The several sequential movements, however, may have a simpler interpretation than at first appears. It is clear that relatively more children came onto the scene in the 1860s and 1870s (presumably, via a trend commencing rather earlier) as the population began to stabilize. (The recorded increase is actually from 34 percent at 1864 to 42 percent at 1878; Figure 6.9a plots the proportion per 500 simply in order to fit the graph.) The main feature thereafter is the repetition of three successive downwardly accelerating thrusts of C form 1878–1906, 1916–1936, and 1961–1976 (or later). The last two are separated by a rise from 1945 through 1961 that obviously reflects the "baby boom" that followed World War II in many countries around the globe. That this temporary surge in fertility probably was smoothed out into G shape for all current individuals aged 0 through 14 in New Zealand indicates in a further thought-provoking way how the internal dynamics of populations keep imprinting that form upon demographic change. The shorter, lesser jump in the 1910s may have something to do with the temporary spurt in immigration from British Commonwealth countries between 1891 and 1911 that shows up

Figure 6.9a
The Changing Composition of New Zealand's Population: Sex, Age, and Ethnicity

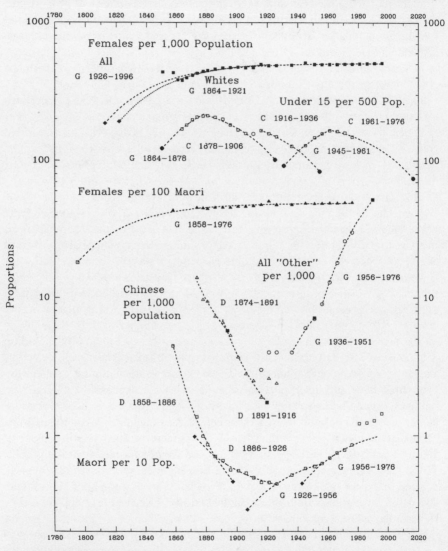

"Other" = Chinese, Fijian, Indian, Pacific Island Polynesian.

Sources: Bloomfield 1984, 29, 42, 47–53; *New Zealand Yearbook 1998*, 99, 103.

in Figure 6.9b. What the three successive C trends evident in the proportion of the population under 15 suggest, furthermore, is that the *birth rate* for New Zealand has tended repeatedly to fall in this C fashion since the 1870s, a hypothesis first raised in Chapter 5 with regard to data on Cuban blacks and perhaps other slave peoples (Figures 5.8b and 5.13d). This is a proposition that Volume III of this study evaluates systematically across several dozen societies that possess historically adequate demographic records. The small G family of curves, in short, may also characterize the trends of vital rates as populations change.

The bottom part of Figure 6.9a diplays some features of historical change in the ethnic composition of New Zealand society. That the proportion of residents who were Maori might fall in D fashion, as is shown at the bottom of the figure twice—from 1858 through 1886 and then from 1886 through 1926—has been presaged by the D-shape decline for several decades after 1858 in the *numbers* of these native New Zealanders discussed in the first volume of this study (Harris 2001, 86). Only fairly flat increase followed for them before the 1920s, although the population of the country swelled robustly, a difference that generated a second D decline in the proportion of Maori. Such D-type loss of native population, meanwhile, was all too common across the islands of the Pacific as previously isolated peoples came into contact with the dangers of the rest of the world, principally unfamiliar diseases (ibid., 131, 133, 375). Since 1926, though, the Maori share of New Zealand's people has increased twice in G form, first into the 1950s, then across the later 20th century. The sudden jump after 1976 seems to involve at least in part a change in ethnic classification to self-specification (*New Zealand Yearbook 1998*, 103) and a rising pride in native heritage. It is possible that the data since 1981 continue to follow the G-type bending of the 1956–1976 curve but at a higher level.

Others not of European stock, meanwhile, also lost weight in New Zealand's population precipitously via D-type declines as European settlement surged. Before the 20th century these persons were overwhelmingly Chinese. The proportion represented by this small ethnic community dropped from 1.40 percent at 1874 to 0.66 at 1891 and merely 0.19 by 1921 as neighbors of European origin multiplied vigorously. Thereafter, the array of non-European peoples became more diverse, including Indians, Fijians, and Pacific Island Polynesians who, along with Chinese, multiplied in strong G trends across the later 20th century (Harris 2001, 86) with the consequence that their small but visible and much-discussed proportion within the population of New Zealand was approaching a disturbing 3 percent in the 1970s.

Meanwhile, more and more New Zealanders were native-born. The top plot of Figure 6.9b shows how they became so via a trend of G shape from the 1870s to the 1950s that raised their weight to 86 percent from about 48 percent in the later 1870s. Earlier, around 1860, about 30 percent of New Zealand's modern group of European settlers were native-born. A backward extension of the 1878–1951 G curve runs through this level at that time, across a dip in the

Figure 6.9b
The Changing Composition of New Zealand's Population: Place of Birth

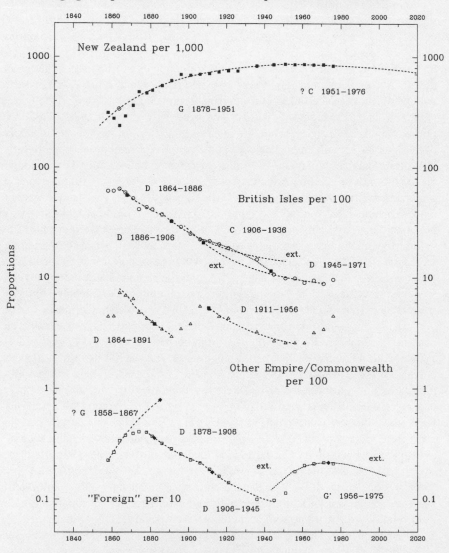

"Foreign" = not British Isles or Empire/Commonwealth.

Source: Bloomfield 1984, 78.

1860s and early 1870s that reflects the brief heavy influx of men already noted via the top plot of Figure 6.9a. Across the later 20th century, in the face of more robust immigration, the proportion of home-grown New Zealanders may have begun to fall, perhaps in C fashion. But further data and analysis are needed for any such conclusion.

As more and more New Zealanders had been born within the country, the weight of immigrants within the population fell, from all major sources, repeatedly in D form. Figure 6.9b shows this. Most visibly and simply, those who had been born not in the British Isles but in other parts of the British Empire or Commonwealth dropped away in D fashion between 1864 and 1891, then again between 1911 and the 1950s. In contrast, the role of in-migrants from these sources expanded sharply between 1858 and 1864, between 1891 and 1906, and after 1961.

Even at the peaks in the 1860s and the early 1900s, however, only 5 to 7 percent of the inhabitants of New Zealand had been born in these places. On the other hand, around 1860 some 62 percent of New Zealanders had come from the British Isles (including Ireland). As nativization proceeded, this proportion also sank in D fashion to 38 percent by 1886, then to 22 percent by 1906 along a second D trend. Tendencies thereafter, however, are open to multiple interpretation. One possibility is that the 1886–1906 D trend continued into the 1920s or early 1930s, as an extension of this curve in the figure indicates. Then the Depression knocked the level down to the third D track shown for 1945–1971, which now carried the British-born proportion under 10 percent. Alternatively, however, the data from 1906 through 1936 fit a C curve. What might temporarily have reversed the mode of decline that way, from deceleration to acceleration?

"Foreign" immigrants from all sources other than the British Isles or the Empire/Commonwealth, meanwhile, after an initial surge to about 4 percent of the non-Maori population, also shrank in relative significance via two successive D trends, from 1878 to 1906 and from 1906 to 1945, as shown in the last plot of Figure 9.6b. Then as the proportions of Chinese, Fijian, Indian, and Pacific Island Polynesian New Zealanders surged (the next to bottom plot of Figure 6.9a), these "foreign" percentages seem to have crested in the exceptional G' form from the 1950s forward. In assessing this apparent trend, like other movements of Figure 6.9b, further exploration of the data since the 1970s would be of interest.

This evidence for New Zealand looks at developments from the middle of the 19th century down to the present. Without trying to cover the same more modern span for Australia, some data on the early development of that far larger neighbor of New Zealand—from the 1790s to 1850—offer additional and different insight into the demographic evolution of British colonization in the Antipodes.

As is well known, the European invasion of Australia was for some time manned principally by convicts. The resulting size of the population surged from about 2,500 at 1790 to 334,000 by 1850 along three successive G curves.[13]

N. G. Butlin has computed the contributions of various kinds of free and forced settlers to this robust early demographic growth (1994, 34, 37–38).[14] Figure 6.10 plots some trends of demographic change that emerge from this analysis of the early population of Australia.

As displayed by the top plot in the left panel of the figure, by 1800 the percentage of convicts and ex-convicts (all current survivors of transportation, in other words) was falling as Australian-born children appeared on the scene. From 1795 through 1830 the D-shaped decline was relatively gentle: from 87 to 71 percent. Free immigrants were few at this time and actually declining in significance from 10 to more like 5 percent once the staffing of the penal colony was established. Colonial-born Australians of European descent rose by 1810, along a G path, to about 20 percent of the population; but then they ceased for a quarter of a century to expand proportionally as convicts poured into New South Wales and Van Diemen's Land up to the point where the practice of transportation began to collapse around 1840 (Figure 1.22).

The long G surge of expansion in the Australian population that began near 1830 and lasted until the eve of World War I (Harris 2001, 80, 82) was powered by the colonial-born and free immigrants at the expense of the collapsing supply of convicts. The proportion of each group in the population up to 1850 or later probably grew via a G trend that had its t_0 in the 1850s, as the left panel of Figure 6.10 indicates.[15] For the native-born, the 1835–1850 data take a G path that is generally parallel with, though much lower than, the early 1790–1810 G trend that had been interrupted by a surge in transportation. Meanwhile the proportion of convicts and ex-convicts dove downward in D form from 71 percent at 1830 to just 29 percent by 1850. It is known that complaints about further influxes of convicts, first from New South Wales and then from other parts of Australia, figured prominently in the demise of the system of transportation. Here it seems, in proportional terms, that the welcome wore out quite precisely inverse to the way that colonial births increased and the demographically normalizing colony attracted more free as opposed to forced immigration.

Among those who came to Australia on their own accord instead of arriving as guests of the British penal system, between 1790 and 1850—fairly consistently along a G path based at 1800—females formed a larger and larger proportion, rising from 17 to 49 percent, as the top plot in the central panel of Figure 6.10 shows. On the one hand, men from the early immigrant flows wanted a normal life as soon as they were free and had resources. On the other, Australia became relatively more attractive for free females as the society stabilized demographically. At a lower (less female) level, this G-shaped transition is also what happened to immigration to the Chesapeake between 1634 and 1702 (Figure 6.4), to emigration for Spanish America out of Extremadura between 1525 and 1595 and from all Spain between 1530 and 1570 (Figure 6.5), and to French arrivals in Canada between 1635 and 1670 (Figure 6.7a)—new societies of earlier eras. Very widely, it appears, the migration of free individuals (including those voluntarily bound in temporary service to pay for their transpor-

Figure 6.10
Composition of the Early European Population of Australia, 1790–1850

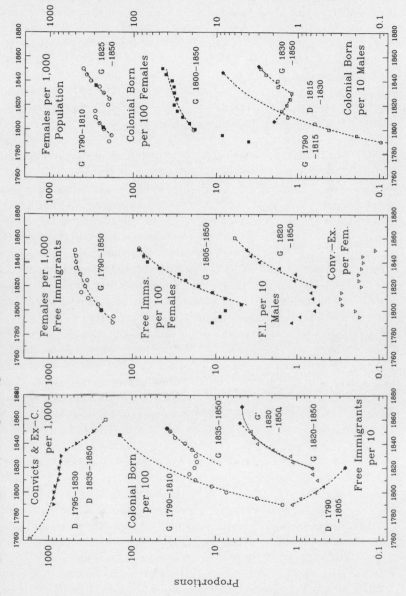

Source: Butlin 1994, 37–38.

tation) started heavily male but then balanced out via the G formula. What underlying demographic dynamics might keep generating this phenomenon?

As a consequence of these altering prospects, the proportion of resident (surviving) females who had come as free immigrants (the plot with solid squares in the middle panel), which had fallen by more than half from the opening years of settlement as prisoners arrived in force (the maximum presence of female convicts was attained about 1810), from 1805 through 1850 climbed from 5 to 85 percent—probably along a G trajectory with t_0 at 1851.[16] A comparable G trend characterized the changing weight of former free immigrants among Australian males (the plot with solid, upward triangles). This began later, however—after 1820—and reached only 42 percent by 1850, just half the proportion of erstwhile free immigrants found among women by that time.

The percentage of colonial-born persons among females, as the rightmost panel of Figure 6.10 indicates, by 1800 began to approximate a G trend from there until 1850 that showed just a little effect of the temporary break in expansion of native Australians of European stock evident in the left panel of the figure. In contrast, decline in the proportion of males who were native-born sank more clearly (in a D-type path?) between 1815 and 1830 than the percentage of colonial-born for both sexes together (in the left panel of Figure 6.10). The reason for the difference between the sexes was that between 1815 and 1820 alone the number of male convicts and ex-convicts multiplied almost 2.5 times from 8,600 to 20,700 as the amount of shipping available for transportation soared with the defeat of Napoleon and the British economy soured with peace (Butlin 1994, 40, 17). In contrast, in this same short period the number of female convicts and ex-convicts present is estimated to have increased only from 3,300 to 4,000 (ibid., 38). This is how the percentage of women in the settler population as a whole (the top plot in the right panel of the figure) was knocked back temporarily around 1820, only to start increasing via a new G curve to 1850 or later. One of the useful things that Figure 6.10 demonstrates is how even this postwar shock from shipping supply (and rising British convictions with sudden peacetime unemployment) was digested into the population of Australia in G-based form.

Of course, Australia was not exactly empty of *homo sapiens* when Europeans started to move in. The recent estimate of Butlin calculates some 670,000 native people as of 1800. As noted elsewhere (Harris 2001, 84, 132–33), their number was disastrously cut back by unfamiliar disease, inroads of European agriculture, and outright extermination (particularly in Tasmania). By 1850, Butlin says that some 290,000 were left. As their own number increased, meanwhile, Europeans grew from 0.3 percent of the population of the continent at 1800 to 58.6 percent at 1850—apparently along a G trend with its t_0 in the 1860s.

While the experience of Australia during her first six, transportation-impacted decades throws one kind of new and unusual light upon how the underlying dynamics of populations shape many kinds of change involving migration, a limited insight into the experience of immigrants in South Africa between 1701 and 1795 provides still another. Something can be established in general about the composition of the European population of this Dutch colony of the 18th century, situated about halfway between Australasia and the Americas. More specifically, one can see how immigrants married into it.

Figure 6.11, based upon the work of Robert Ross, first of all (top of left graph) demonstrates how the proportion of women among adults in the "white" population of South Africa rose in G form across the first three-quarters of the 1800s (Ross 1975, 221). The colony had been established at Capetown in 1652. The t_0 for the G curve lies back at about that time, implying that women constituted some 15 percent of the adult population at or soon after the start, rising to 41 percent in the 1750s and 1760s. Though its level was somewhat lower for South Africa, a major base for Dutch military and commercial operations in Asia, the timing of this G path relative to settlement resembles what has been found in the European populations of New York (originally another Dutch colonial venture), St. Christopher, Barbados, Antigua, Montserrat, Newfoundland, and Charles County, Maryland (Figures 6.1, 6.2, and 6.8a) as well as New Zealand and Australia (Figures 6.9a and 6.10). Right around the globe, the bias toward men in early free settlement has adjusted itself in G form toward the biological level of about 50 percent.

The number of women in "white" South African society for some reason did not grow at all between 1773 and 1778 (Ross 1975, 221), pushing down their proportion in the population as men multiplied by 13 percent over the quinquennium. The result might turn out to be just a temporary dip for the top plot in Figure 6.11. Or, new G-shaped increase, headed toward the internationally more usual higher level of 50 percent, may have been initiated, as the figure suggests. Some later data should readily settle the matter.

Like females among adults, the percentage of children in the South African population of European origin (the second plot in the left graph) rose in G form from 1701 into the 1770s, reaching over 50 before perhaps backing down a little 1778–1795 in D fashion, a kind of retrenchment previously encountered in New York and the West Indies (Figure 6.3). The long climb upward around the underlying G trend fluctuated more, with high observations near 1705 and 1740; but the summary curve seems appropriate. Its G form echoes what has been found for the expansion of the young native-born in European populations of Newfoundland, New York, several colonies of the British West Indies, Charles County, Maryland, and—more briefly—New Zealand and Australia (Figures 6.2, 6.3, 6.8a, 6.9a, and 6.10). Very generally, G seems to have been the pattern according to which the age structures of settler populations normalized, whether in the 17th, 18th, or 19th centuries.

Ross also provides information on immigrants who married into the "white" population of South Africa during the 18th century (1975, 222). From 1673 through 1733 (1657–1687, 1688–1717, and 1718–1747 are his chronological groupings), their *number*—shown in the middle plot in the left panel of Figure 6.11—probably rose and then started to fall off in the G' pattern that is so

Figure 6.11
Changes in the "White" Population of South Africa, 1673–1795: Sex, Age, and In-Marrying Immigrants

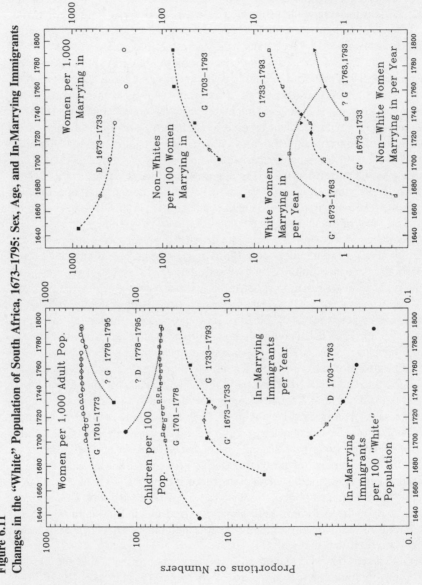

Source: Ross 1975, 221–22.

generally characteristic of migration flows. If the curve correctly interpolates the widely spaced data, the crest was reached at 1718. Then, from 1733 to 1793 (1718–1747 to 1778–1807) the number of immigrants recorded to have married in rose in approximate G form, settling down to constitute a continuing, long-term process rather than what is probably a reflection of the surge of arrivals—many of them military—who created the colony as a major settlement in the late 1600s.

These immigrants who are identified as forming families with members of the existing "white" population were few in number: 18 per year at 1718 and 34 at 1793. But if those who established themselves socially this way remained a fairly steady proportion of the total immigrant share of the population, what happened to the *rate of immigration* for the South African colony can be hypothesized: it fell from 1703 through 1763 in D fashion, the way that continuing immigration has been seen to become a smaller and smaller factor in the growth of other settler and slave populations.[17] Though only 1.40 immigrants per year married into the population per 100 resident persons of European stock around 1703, falling after the opening D trend to 0.24 by 1793, it should be remembered that the numerator for this ratio concerns marriage events, not men or women alive at any particular time who had already married in. Thus, the proportion of in-migrant individuals alive who *at some time or other* formed unions with the resident "white" population will be much higher, according to how long they survived after their nuptials.

Apparently, the European population of South Africa became more endogamous in 1/D or G fashion from the 1680s through the 1770s. That process is analogous to how the residents of Prince George's County, Maryland, more and more often married blood relatives between 1715 and 1775 (Figure 6.8c) along a G trend with t_0 at 1722. (The base year for the D decline in the weight of in-marrying South African migrants in the left panel of Figure 6.11 comes at 1714.) These trends are quite the opposite of what Figure 6.6a presents for Spanish New Mexico between 1715 and 1765 or 1775. There, *exogamous* marriages became a larger portion of the whole before virtually disappearing over the next three decades. In Guatemala, too, G-shape rises in mestizo and mulatto marriages indicate previous relationships between Spanish settlers and Indians or slaves that had extended rather than restricted exogamy (Figure 6.6.a). One can only wonder at what the history of South Africa (or the southeastern United States) might have been if the "Spanish" colonial model had prevailed instead. In Quebec, too, the G-form increase in unbaptized children up until the 1670s hints at expanding exogamy until the new, state-controlled regime after 1663 apparently closed that door.

The right-hand panel of Figure 6.11 examines change in the *composition* of the group of migrants who married into South Africa's "white" population (Ross 1975, 222). Notable is the soon increasing scarcity of white immigrant women which, among other things, dragged the proportion of females among all in-marrying immigrants from 49 down to 26 percent mostly along a D path between the late 1600s and the middle 1700s (the top plot in the graph). Their number (second plot from the bottom in the graph with solid downward triangles) probably surged in G' form between the 1650s and the 1740s but passed its peak around 1708. In-marrying *non-white* immigrant females, presumably mostly Asians pulled to South Africa from the far-flung operations of the Dutch East India Company (VOC), first multiplied along a somewhat later G' wave, which crested at 1725. Their number, however, was only one-seventh of that for their white competitors between 1657 and 1687 and about one-third at the turn of the century; but it kept rising toward parity in the second quarter of the 1700s. Then between 1733 (1718–1747) and 1793 (1787–1807) non-white females who married into the European population of South Africa expanded anew, now in persistently increasing G mode, generally outnumbering in-marrying immigrant white women three to one across the second half of the 18th century and the first years of the 19th, even though the latter may have increased in roughly parallel G form between 1748 and 1807 (midpoints 1763 and 1793). With these changes, the proportion of non-whites among all immigrant women who married into the European population of South Africa climbed from 24 to 75 percent over the 18th century, as the solid squares across the middle of the right graph of Figure 6.11 demonstrate. In South African society, racial exogamy as much as the incorporation of immigrants through marriage seems to have expanded via a G path during the Dutch colonial era.

These findings from other settler societies demonstrate that the colonization of the Americas was not the only context in which change in demographic composition repeatedly has taken G-based forms historically. Some basic evidence from four European nations illustrates how the structures of more than just new settlements have altered in G-based form—both in the era before 1800 mostly studied so far and down into very modern times, as presaged by Figures 6.9a and 6.9b for New Zealand.

Early age structure is elusive for the *Netherlands*. Calculations of the significance of migration for change in the Dutch population, however, reach back into the 16th century. Figure 6.12 trends some of these computations of one way in which the composition of long-established European populations altered historically.

Jan Lucassen and Rinus Penninx employed data from Amsterdam between the 1530s and the 1790s and from the Netherlands between 1849 and 1990 to estimate the weight of what they called "newcomers" in the Dutch population across four and a half centuries. Their conclusions are represented by the continuous dotted line from 1535 through 1990 across the middle of Figure 6.12. The proportion of those originating from outside the country, they estimate, starting from less than 2 percent in the 1530s and 1540s, surged to peak at about 11 percent in the early 1600s, the "Golden Age" of early modern economic development in the Netherlands that followed independence from Spain. (This compares, for example, with about 14 percent foreign-born in the United States

Figure 6.12

Migrants in the Netherlands, the Dutch East India Company, and Germany between 1535 and 1990

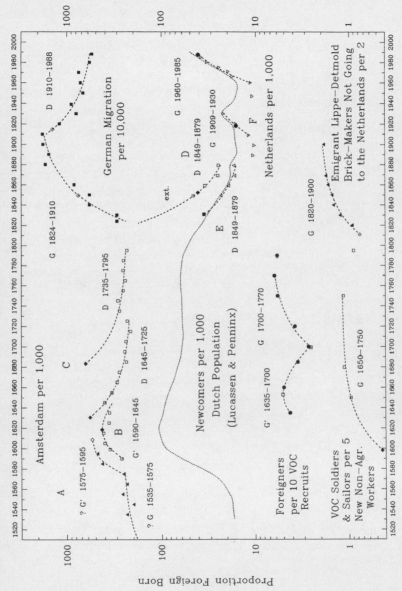

A = New Freemen; B = Men Marrying; C = Persons Marrying; D = Amsterdam Residents Foreign-Born; E = Netherlands
Residents Foreign-Born; F = Aliens in Netherlands.

Sources: Lucassen and Penninx 1985, 162–65; 1997, 29; Lucassen 1987, 157–58, 277; de Vries and van der Woude 1997, 644;
Hochstadt 1999, 277.

across the famous immigration era of the 19th and early 20th centuries.) Refugees from the southern Low Countries (now Belgium) flooded in along with other Europeans less drastically propelled who just wanted to share the booming life of the new country. Then, as the luster left the Golden Age, those of foreign origin shrank to level out at more like 6 percent from the 1690s through the 1790s, only to drop still further to just 1.6 percent or so for the period from the 1880s into the 1960s. Recently the proportion has been rising again.

This curve represents the smoothed estimations of Lucassen and Penninx (1997, 29), which adjust Amsterdam levels before 1849 to national proportions thereafter. Their data, though, which are available in the earlier Dutch edition (1985, 162–65), permit further analysis of movements in Amsterdam and in the country at large. These various underlying series of evidence are trended across the upper portion of Figure 6.12.

To begin, the percentage of new freemen or *poorters* (males admitted to urban citizenship) in Amsterdam who were of foreign birth—the A series of solid triangles in the figure—rose only very slowly between 1535 and 1575, possibly along the kind of G path fitted. From 1575 through 1595, however, as Amsterdam surged demographically while becoming the leading trading center for Europe (Harris 2001, 304) and war with Spain pushed people north, this proportion climbed—perhaps in the G' path suggested—from 25 to 47 percent (Lucassen and Penninx 1985, 162). Data for men born abroad among males publishing banns for intentions to marry in Amsterdam—the B series of hollow squares through 1600—indicates that this surge in persons of foreign origin indeed did take G' shape and peaked at about 43 percent at 1618 among men who married in the city as compared with 54 percent for new *poorters* near 1608. It seems likely that, in the male life cycle, admission to citizenship on average somewhat preceded marriage, which tended to call for even more economic stability and promise. Thus, a lag of a decade or so between the two curves is appropropriate in patterning the proportional impact of migration upon the population of the city.

From 1605 through 1795 the component being calculated shifts to both men and women foreign-born among all persons publishing banns for marriage in Amsterdam: the C series. How much the dip in the 1620s and 1630s below the G' curve that is suggested between 1590 and 1645 and the jump that followed in the 1640s derive from the addition of females to the calculation—or instead from swings in the general environment of the city or ups and downs in its particular way of life—will have to be sorted out by those with local expertise. From the 1640s into the 1720s, however, shrinkage in the role of the foreign-born among persons getting married in Amsterdam dropped away in a D-shape trend, declining from 40 to 22 percent. Over the next decade something kicked this level back up to 29 percent, only to atrophy once more to 24 percent as of the 1790s, apparently along a second D-shape path (Lucassen and Pennix 1985, 162–63).

There follows a gap in evidence until the middle of the 19th century. Then, from 1849 through 1879 the proportion of residents who were foreign-born is known both for Amsterdam and for the Netherlands as a whole (Lucassen and Pennix 1985, 164). Each series (D and E on the graph, respectively) declines in D shape across the period, that for Amsterdam rather more steeply. Interestingly, the data of Hochstadt (1999, 277) indicate that, during this period of rapid industrialization and urbanization for the neighboring country of *Germany*, the significance of migration rose in a G path that was nearly vertically symmetrical to the atrophying D shape for Amsterdam (solid squares in the top right corner of Figure 6.12). Finally, Dutch proportions from 1889 through 1985 (series F) concern aliens within the population of the Netherlands (ibid., 164–65). This share fell still further, to about 1 percent around 1900, before rising in what seem to be two G trends: first from 1909 through 1930 and then, after falling back with the Depression and World War II, from 1960 through the 1980s. Once again, for a while—between 1909 and 1930—change in the weight of foreigners in the Netherlands was accompanied by a mirroring movement for migration as a whole among Germans following World War I (here a G vs. a D trend, respectively). From about 1930 to the 1960s, in contrast, the proportion of aliens in the Netherlands seems to have declined (according to the calculations of Lucassen and Penninx, 1994, 29) very much *parallel* to the longer D-shaped lessening of migration in Germany that ran from 1910 through 1988. Do other international relationships like these show up when the G-based patterns of migrations are recognized?

Refinement of this analysis by those who know the sources better may change some of the patterning offered in Figure 6.12. The impression, nevertheless, is that migration swelled and shrank in significance for Dutch and German society, even in quite recent times, along the same kinds of paths observed in this and previous chapters for both the free and the bound populations of early modern colonies. The trend types were international, Old World as well as New, and pertained across several centuries of demographic record.

Another pespective on migration available from the history of the Netherlands comes into focus through the lens of recruitment for the Dutch East India Company (VOC), perhaps the world's first international business corporation. The organization needed a constant supply of fresh manpower for its operations in Asia, mostly in places where Europeans confronted poor life expectancy.

By the middle of the 1600s the proportion of recruits who were not Dutch (mainly Germans and other nearby Europeans) had climbed to 50 percent among the 4,000 or so men whom the company attracted annually (Lucassen 1987, 157). To secure manpower during the Golden Age, when many Dutch businesses and forms of agriculture thrived, the VOC had to employ a higher share of aliens in a G' pattern. But as the maritime cities of the Netherlands stagnated under the impact of international competition across the later 17th century and much Dutch wealth shifted from employment-producing manufacture and trade to less manpower-intensive financial services (Harris 2001, 304–5; de Vries and van der Woude 1997, chs. 6, 7, 8, 10), the annual intake of Netherlanders signing up for VOC employment more than doubled at the same time that the number of foreigners working for the company significantly declined. This shift drove the proportion of those who were not Dutch nationals as low as 27 percent by 1720 along the same G' curve that had crested around 1653. Yet as the VOC kept needing more and more men for its far-flung but deadly operations in the 18th century (total annual recruitments doubled from the 1690s to the 1760s), the share of foreigners in the intake climbed back as high as 63 percent by 1770 before dipping slightly as the VOC approached collapse through the last years of the century (Lucassen 1987, 157). This sustained increase, however, now took G form from 1700 through 1770, a trend that mostly just echoed the total numbers sent out to work for the company, which expanded in their own G trend 1695–1765 (Figure 1.22). More recruiting meant proportionally fewer Dutch. In virtually parallel movement, the t_0 for all recruitment came just a few years earlier than that for the foreign share within this total.

If, meanwhile, one examines the annual number of soldiers and sailors hired by the VOC from the maritime provinces of the Netherlands at 1650, 1680, and 1750 as a proportion of all new annual arrivals on the non-agrarian labor market in Holland and Friesland, the curve at the bottom left of Figure 6.12 results.[18] It takes the G form with base year at 1598. In other words, for the century after 1650 recruitment for the East India Company grew stonger and stronger this way relative to the total non-farm migrant labor pool as commerce and industry declined in Holland and Friesland with the passing of the Golden Age of the Netherlands.

In a considerably later era, too, change in a flow of migrants took similar G shape. Between 1820 and 1900, the proportion of brick-makers leaving Lippe-Detmold in northwestern Germany, not far from the Netherlands, who went to the Netherlands or the neighboring German North Sea area of Ostfriesland dwindled markedly (Lucassen 1987, 277). The change happened not because the Dutch number declined (at least not until after the 1860s) but because more and more Lippe-Detmold persons in the business were drawn to *other* destinations: from about 500 in 1820 to more like 14,000 as of 1900. This made the percentage *not* going to the Netherlands or Ostfriesland rise from 49 to 99 percent along the kind of G path shown in the bottom right corner of Figure 6.12. Thus, the channeling of migrant workers in a particular industry such as northwestern European brick-making, like the role of the great East India Company in providing international employment, altered in G fashion similar to the weight of migrants more generally within the Dutch and German economies. As is the case with many other demographic findings of this study, these discoveries present fundamental implications for the history of economic change.

Such trends in the relative number and composition of Europeans migrating to Asia through the VOC conduit in the 17th and 18th centuries, drawn to industrial regions like the Ruhr or Wupperthal, or seeking work in a regional 19th-century industry such as brick-making, altered—like the role of the foreign-born in the Netherlands as a whole—in the same G-based patterns that have been observed in the black and white composition of Caribbean colonies in Chapter 5, the interaction of European and native peoples of Spanish America in Figures 6.6a and 6.6b, or the absorption of various kinds of migrants into the populations of New Zealand, Australia, and South Africa in Figures 6.9a, 6.9b, 6.10, and 6.11. Such trends were not simply New World phenomena.

Nor were other changes in the compositions of populations that have first been noted in a colonial context. Whereas the settler societies in which shifts in sex and age have been examined so far often had as little as a few thousand— sometimes even a few hundred—inhabitants across segments of their history that have been studied, the population of *England* had reached 3 *million* by the middle of the 16th century and expanded to 20 million by the middle of the 19th. The boundaries of England, furthermore, remained constant across this era—unlike those of settler societies, which often expanded readily into continental interiors. Under these very different, much more stable conditions, do G-based trends in demographic structure have any significance?

Figures 6.13a and 6.13b indicate that they have. Drawing upon the monumental *Population History of England* (Wrigley and Schofield 1981, 528–29), they plot the changing weights of various age groups between 1541 and 1871. Table 6.2 summarizes the trends for comparison. Over and over again the movements take G-based forms.

First of all, the proportion of the young in the English population, for all three groups under 25, fell in slowly starting but accelerating C form between 1541 and the third quarter of the 17th century. For each successively older category, the C trend lasted a little longer (1661, 1671, then 1681) as the phenomenon climbed up the age ladder. In the early 1560s, however, the percentage of young children 0 to 4 dipped markedly, as the growth of the population was set back noticeably between 1556 and 1561 (Harris 2001, 150; Wrigley and Schofield 1981, 528).[19] Figure 6.13a demonstates how a short, sharp shock like this passes up the age structure, spreading out across the 1560s among those 5–14 and affecting those 15–24 in the 1570s. By the 1580s, however, all three age groups had settled quite tightly back into C trends that would last into the late 1600s and carry the proportion of the population under 25 from 54 percent of the English population down to more like 46 percent (from 36 down to 30 percent under 15 as of the Restoration). As Figure 6.13b and Table 6.2 show, these changes understandably involved relative gains among adults in roughly reciprocal, *upwardly* accelerating E fashion, though the weight of persons 60 and over apparently increased in two such trends, first 1561–1611 then 1626– 1666. Volume III will show how both birth and death rates for England altered in G-based movements that contributed to this change across the long era from the last years of Henry VIII through the reign of Charles II.

From the 1660s or 1670s into the middle of the next century, the proportion of the young in the English population swelled back again among those 0–4, 5–14, and 15–24—all in trends of G shape. By the 1750s about 51 percent of

Figure 6.13a
Changing Age Structure in the Population of England, 1541–1871: The Weights of Younger Age Groups

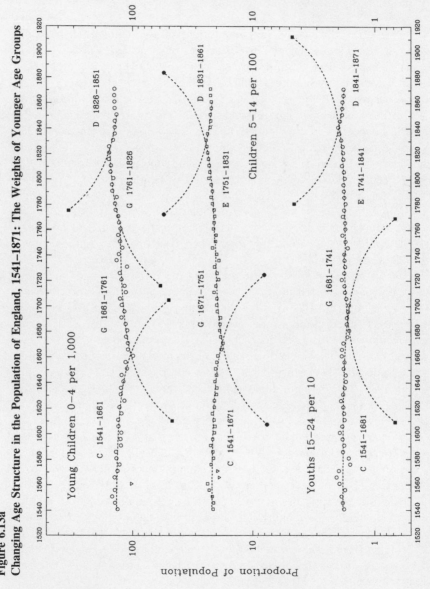

Source: Wrigley and Schofield 1981, 528–29.

Figure 6.13b
Changing Age Structure in the Population of England, 1541–1871: Proportions of Adults and the Elderly

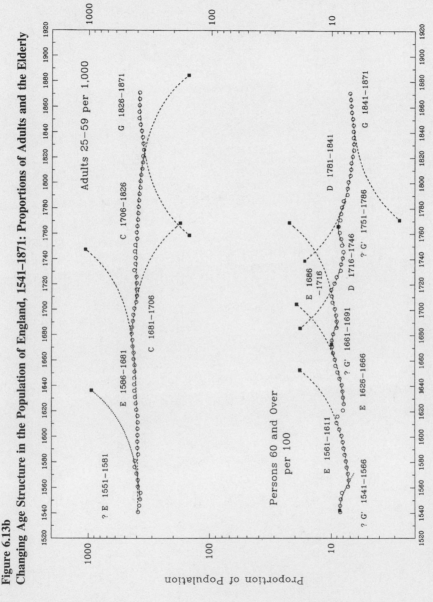

Source: Wrigley and Schofield 1981, 528–29.

Table 6.2
Movements in the Age Structure of England's Population, 1541–1871 (trends for the percentage in each age group)

0-4	5-14	15-24	25-59	60+
			1551-1586 ?E 1636	1541-1665 ?G' 1542
				1561-1611 E 1653
			1586-1681 E 1748	1626-1666 E 1705
				1661-1691 ?G' 1673
1541-1661 C 1705	1541-1671 C 1725	1541-1681 C 1769	1681-1706 C 1768	1686-1716 E 1769
1661-1761 G 1610	1671-1751 G 1608	1681-1741 G 1612		1716-1746 D 1686
				1751-1786 G' 1766
1761-1826 G 1716	1751-1831 E 1884	1741-1841 E 1912	1706-1826 C 1885	1781-1841 D 1739
1825-1851 D 1775	1831-1861 D 1772	1841-1871 D 1781	1826-1871 G 1759	1841-1871 G 1771

Source: Wrigley and Schofield 1981, 528–29.

England's people were again under 25. This time, the three movements for young, younger, and youngest were parallel in timing rather than lagged, each with t_0 near 1610. Between 1686 and 1706, meanwhile, the 25–59 group of adults seems to have acquired, for the time being at least, the C decline that had been moving up the age scale. Then, however, from 1706 all the way through 1826 this part of the population shrank in relative significance via a new and longer-lasting C trend, which—from the 1740s forward—was accompanied by comparably timed offsetting, E-type movements for the weights of those 5–14 and 15–24. In this era, though, the very young between 1761 and 1826 and the eldest element of the population (60+) between 1781 and 1841 took different and offsetting trends. These were of G and D shape instead: decelerating from their initial rate of change rather than accelerating. Finally, into the middle of the 19th century (or later) the proportion of all three younger age groups declined together in D trends with parallel timing; and those 25–59 and 60 or older became relatively more evident via complementary G paths. The proportion of England's population under 25, which had reached 58.1 percent in the 1820s, dropped back to 54.6 percent by 1871.

Before the 1780s, the comparatively small proportion of the population who were 60 or older (Figure 6.13b) generally rose and fell (within a range of 7.2 to 10.1 percent) in trends that are shorter than those evident for all the other age groupings. These patterns sometimes were also of distinctive shape. At three points in time—between 1541 and 1566, 1661 and 1691, and 1751 and 1786, as Figure 6.13b indicates—surges of G' shape form a possible trending. The indication is that, before the modern era, mortality among the elderly—perhaps adults rather more generally—shifted up and down in this more wavy way. Across the last century or so covered by the *Population History*, the trends became more enduring, and the proportion over 60 declined to as low as 6.5 percent as the youthfulness of England's population increased. A tendency for death rates to settle down and follow longer trends is a well-known feature of population history around the beginning of the modern era (Livi-Bacci 1992, 107).

Generally the trends discussed for this long-established European society did not involve big changes in the percentage for any one age group, but they sufficed to turn on and off the growth patterns of the English population that have been observed from the 1500s through the 1800s (Harris 2001, 148–51). Repeatedly, furthermore, they took G-based forms. Did the birth rates and death rates that swelled or trimmed the ranks of the young, the elderly, and those in between also then follow G-related shapes through time? That is implied by the movements that we have seen. The next volume of this study is thus devoted to delving into the behavior of these vital rates, their long-discussed relationships with age structure, and the processes of demographic replacement or renewal in which fertility and mortality principally participate.

Another example of how the structures of long-established populations, not just new settlements, alter in G-based forms is provided by the valuable histor-

ical data for *Sweden*. These series begin some two centuries later than the estimates for England; but from the start they are based upon contemporary counts
rather than backward reconstructions. Figure 6.14 presents trends for selected
age groups: the young, the old, and those in their 20s and 30s—the cohorts
forming most families and having most children (*Historisk statistik för Sverige*
1969, 1: 68; *Statistik årsbok för Sverige* 1979, 41; 1984, 29; 1991, 33).

The first thing to note is how the proportion of young children in the population fell between 1750 and 1800 in C fashion. That happened as the weight
of this age group *rose* significantly in England between 1761 and 1826. On the
one hand, the demographic regime of Sweden was moving in a different direction from that of England. From 1570 through 1720 the Swedish population had
probably swelled along an H path closely resembling the trends for England
between 1561 and 1656 and, after a break in the era of the Civil War and the
Restoration, again between 1686 and 1726. Then, from 1720 into the 1840s,
Swedish demographic expansion had taken a series of decelerating G paths,
while the people of England underwent what in modern circumstances has been
labeled "population explosion"—*accelerating* E-type multiplication (Harris
2001, 148–51). Here the difference in momentum for growth in the two countries that was available from the young stands out.

On the other hand, however, as children under 5 became a smaller proportion
of the Swedish population between 1750 and 1800, they did so in the same
pattern according to which the weight of those 0–4 (and 0–14) had shrunk in
England between the 1540s and the 1660s. In other words, the age groups most
affected by recent births in two different countries in two distinct eras of contraction narrowed according to the same C shape of trend. This finding implies
that *birth rates* may repeatedly fall in this manner, a hint that is strengthened
by the way that those 0–4 and 0–14 lost weight again later on in Sweden,
between 1890 and 1940, a time during which we know that birth rates plummeted in many countries during what has been called modern "demographic
transition." Volume III of this study carries this proposition to the birth rates of
several dozen nations for extensive testing of the trend, its causes, and its consequences.

In between, across the 19th century the young became a heftier portion of
the Swedish population. The G pattern for this era is most clear for the whole
segment under 15 (the second plot in Figure 6.14). There may have been a
temporary G' spurt for the very young (0–4) in the early 1800s. As in the C
trends of the later 1700s and early 1900s, however, as the consequences of the
birth rate moved up into the age structure—even just within the first 15 years—
wavering around the underlying trend was smoothed out. The particular mechanism that keeps steering demographic change into G-based paths this way is
what this study pursues.

For the years since World War II, one could say that a G' hump cresting at
1952 captures the proportional rise and fall of children 0–4 within the Swedish
population. Also possible, though, is a C curve from 1950 through 1982, also

Figure 6.14
The Weights of Selected Age Groups in the Population of Sweden, 1750–2000

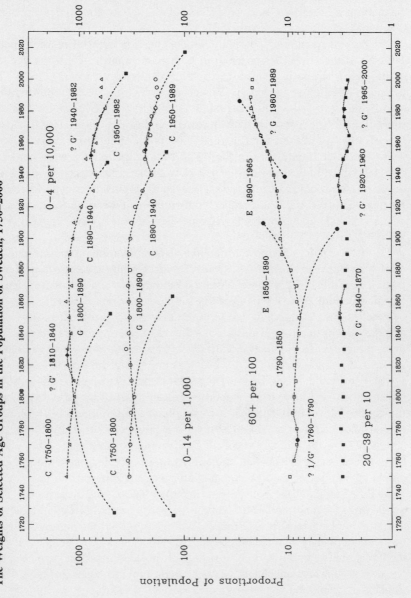

Sources: Historisk statistik för Sverige 1969, 1: 68; Statistik årsbok för Sverige 1979, 41; 1984, 29; 1991, 33.

shown in Figure 6.14. This latter trending characterizes the postwar "baby boom" as more of a quick jump in level before further downward movement of C shape took over, rather than a protracted surge. The merit of this alternative best shows up for all persons under 15. Here the fit to a C pattern looks quite tight, further illustrating how progress though the age structure keeps guiding demographic change into G-based forms.

The presence of those 60 or older in the population of Sweden, after a possible 1/G' dip in the late 1700s (what kind of illness might have cut the aged back at this time?) shrank in C fashion to about 1850 (from 9.1 to 7.7 percent). Then, as people lived longer and birth rates began to fall, it increased via two successive E trends to attain 11.5 percent by 1890 and 18.4 percent by 1965. A G trend through the 1980s perhaps followed, taking the level to 22.9 percent— though 1991 projections for 1995 and 2000 fall noticeably below such a curve. Comparatively, E-type rises in the proportion of the elderly were common in England historically (Figure 6.12b), but from the 1500s into the early 1700s only. After that point, quite different patterning applies from what is found for Sweden—distinctions at the upper end of the age scale that are once again consonant with contrasting national histories of demographic growth for the period (Harris 2001, 148–50).

The bottom plot in Figure 6.14 (solid squares) is for the proportion of Swedes who were between 20 and 40, the age group making most of the marriages, establishing most of the households, and having most of the children. The outstanding feature of this series is how stable it is: from 1750 through 1950 it clung closely to 30 percent, whatever impulses were being fed into the demographic system by changes in the rates for births and deaths. An occasional G' hump for relatively slight temporary change about every 30 years (1790, 1820, 1850) is possible here and there, but not compelling. In the 1950s the effects of the baby boom dragged down the relative weight of those 20 through 39 rather more, only to have the proportion regain most of its losses by the 1980s. In England, in contrast, the shares of people 25–59 and also 20–24 (the 20–39 data are not readily available) did not vary greatly, either, between the 1540s and the 1770s; but, unlike the Swedish record, quite clear and lasting trends of C, E, and G shape are evident (Figure 6.13b and 6.13a). Here, too, the demographic dynamics of the two countries appear to be different in spite of many generalizations that have been advanced about modern "demographic transition."

The prize for long-term stability, however, goes to the proportion in the 20–39 age group among females in *France*. As the bottom plot of Figure 6.15 shows, this clung to a level of about 30 percent from 1740 right through to 1936 without the occasional swings visible in Figure 6.14 for the comparable age category in Sweden or the distinguishable G-based trends for those 15–24 and 25–59 in England (Figures 6.13a and 6.13b). For French males, meanwhile, the long period of warfare between the Revolution and the final fall of Napoleon at Waterloo visibly depressed the weight of those 20–39, apparently in 1/G' fashion, between 1790 and 1830. World Wars I and II likewise cut back the per-

Figure 6.15
Stability and Change in the Age Structure of France, 1740–1951

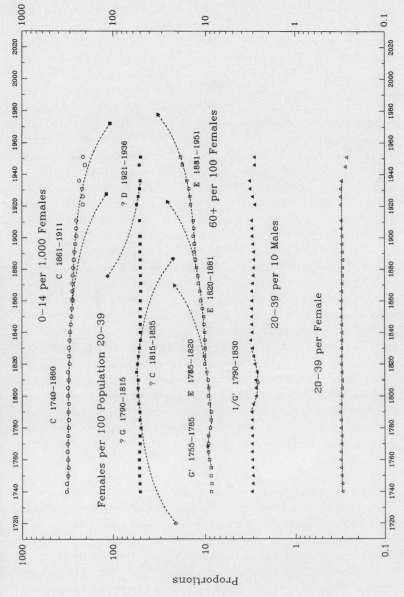

Sources: Henry and Blayo 1975, 92–93; Bourgeois-Pichat 1975, 502–3.

centage of males to be found within this age range; but they did so more abruptly and temporarily, without the accumulative effect of 1789–1815.

The impact of these movements among younger adult males upon sex ratios for those between 20 and 40 in France is graphed in the second plot from the top of Figure 6.15. The percentage of females in this age group rose via G from 1790 through 1815, then fell via C from there to 1835. These trends were not just a G' reflection of the 1/G' shrinking of the age category among males. Instead, it appears as though the impact of that dip was smoothed out even further. Later, having shot up with the losses of World War I, from 1921 through 1936 the proportion of females among French persons 20 to 39 dropped back in D fashion, once again smoothing out consequences of the more abrupt loss and recovery of young adults among men.

The general stability evident in the weight of young adults, in spite of some military consequences, did not keep significant change in the French population from happening. The top plot in Figure 6.15 demonstrates how the proportion under 15 contracted very steadily along a slowly but surely accelerating C curve from 32 percent in the 1740s to 28 percent by 1860. Then from 1861 through 1911 the share who were children atrophied still further in C form—from 28 to 25 percent, dropping further to just 22 percent in the 1920s following the war. In marked contrast, the role of the young in England built *up* in accelerating E fashion between 1750 and the 1830s (Figure 6.13a) and then contracted—at least for a while—in D rather than C form. In Sweden, far steeper C decline from 1890 through 1940 followed what had probably generally been G-type expansion for the young across the 19th century, though this had from 1750 through 1800 been preceded by C-form atrophy that was, again, steeper than the similar shape of trending for France. The French population has long had a reputation for historical fertility control. These comparisons of the role of youth in the three national age structures indicate that the movements of birth rates and more precise fertility measures are going to verify such national behavior. The relevant demographic developments, however, will probably take the same G-based trends evident for varying periods of time in other countries, not patterns exceptional to France. Only the mix, sequencing, and timing of movements will be different.

Those 60 and older, meanwhile, from the 1780s to the 1950s became a larger proportion of the French population according to three successive upwardly accelerating trends of E shape: 1785–1820, 1820–1881, and 1881–1951 or later. For females, graphed in Figure 6.15, this raised the proportion of the elderly from 8.6 to 18.8 percent. Earlier, between 1755 and 1785 a temporary G' hump of gain appears in the weight of those 60 and over. A similar movement has been encountered for the elderly in England between 1751 and 1786 (Figure 6.13b), though in Sweden (Figure 6.14) just the reverse—a 1/G' sag—appears between 1760 and 1790. Since comparable movements do not previously emerge in younger groups and march their way up the age structure past 60, it would seem that some temporary improvement in mortality, particularly relevant for older adults, occurred in England and France in the second half of the 18th century, but just the opposite—a $1/G'$ dip—for the same period in Sweden. What developments in health and disease might have caused these swings? Chapter 2 of Volume III explores such international contrasts and comparisons of trends in death rate considerably further.

It is possible, finally, to illustrate how movements in demographic composition resulting from migration and other sources could take the same limited set of G-based shapes historically in populations that were neither New World nor European. Figures 6.16a and 6.16b, drawing upon a recent study by James Z. Lee and Cameron D. Campbell, plot some trends from rural Liaoning Province in Manchuria between 1774 and 1873. The basis of their demographic analysis was the "Household and Population Registers of the Eight Banner Army Han Chinese Army" for the Daoyi area of Fengtian Prefecture just north of Shenyang (Lee and Campbell 1997, 1–4, 16).

The left panel of Figure 6.16a begins by indicating how the rates of male immigration into and out of this particular rural area (the former slightly surpassed the latter), while they could fluctuate substantially from one recorded period to another, generally both declined around underlying D-shape tracks (Lee and Campbell 1997, 37).[20] In these movements, the t_0 for the D of immigation for males came at 1826 and that for the D of emigration at 1823. In contrast, *internal* migration within the vicinity of Daoyi dropped off in accelerating C form between 1793 and 1863, as the bottom plot of the left panel of Figure 6.16a indicates.

In other words, the rate of more than very local migration for this part of Manchuria during the economic growth and change of the later 18th century and the majority of the 19th century probably compressed in the same D pattern found for slave imports as several colonies of the Western Hemisphere matured during the two centuries before (Chapter 5). This is likewise the type of movement through time that is implied by the G $(1/D)$ rise of the native-born in European settler populations from French Canada and the Chesapeake in the 17th and 18th centuries to New Zealand, Australia, and South Africa in the 18th and 19th (Figures 6.7b, 6.8b, 6.9b, 6.10, 6.11). Local demographic stability and discouragement for further migration seem to have built up the same way in China as in other parts of the world.

The right panel of Figure 6.16a then demonstrates how other dimensions of the rural Manchurian population, not just the proportional impact of migration, also changed in G-related ways that have previously been encountered elsewhere. On the one hand, the percentage of men 36 to 40 *sui* of age who had never been married (top plot in the graph) tended to decline in D fashion: first from 1777 through 1807 and then—after a sharp setback—from 1814 through 1854, each with base year for the curve around 1770 (Lee and Campbell 1997, 41). This is the kind of downward trend in bachelorhood that has been observed among settlers of European origin in Somerset County, Maryland, between 1676 and 1768 (Figure 6.8b). The difference in rural Liaoning Province was that in

Figure 6.16a

Changing Demographic Composition in Rural Liaoning Province, 1774–1873: Migration, Marriage, Extended Family in Household

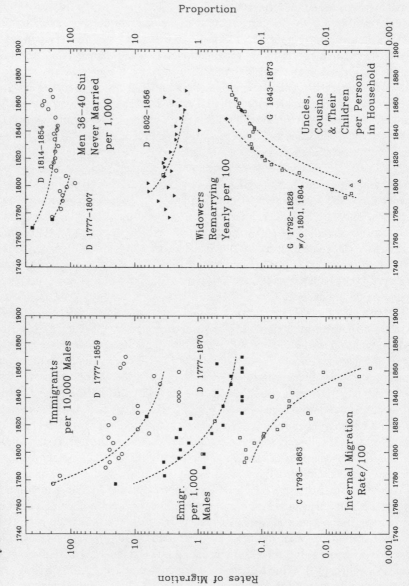

Source: Lee and Campbell 1997, 37, 41, 52.

the early 1800s for some reason the chances to marry for men worsened abruptly from 10 to more like 20 percent in a few years. Then, after steady D-shape decline had resumed for several decades, in the 1850s the proportion never married jumped once more, reaching close to 30 percent. The data run out before it can be determined whether or not D-form improvement in marital chances again resumed after this uward shift. As to the reasons for these interruptions, the 1850s were clearly a turbulent time for China.[21] Just how rural Liaoning was affected and whether similar or dissimilar causes worsened chances for men to marry in the early 1800s will have to be determined by historians of the area. The rate at which widowers remarried likewise fell away in D form, from 1802 through 1856 before rising quite steeply as it had done previously during the last years of the 1700s (ibid.). The *worsening* of marriage opportunity for widowers followed the same D shape as *improvement* in the chances for single men, but with distinct timing. How were these two patterns of change perhaps related?

Between the 1790s and the 1870s, meanwhile, the structure of households in rural Liaoning became appreciably more complex as more and more family members resided with others. A higher and higher proportion of extended relations—brothers, uncles, and their families—appeared in the mix. The bottom plot in the right panel of Figure 6.16a trends the rising share of uncles of the household head, their children (cousins of the head), and the families of their children (Lee and Campbell 1997, 52). These increasingly removed relatives resident in households not of their own climbed from about 2 to 15 percent of the rural population in this part of Manchuria between 1792 and 1828. After a brief setback in the 1830s, the proportion surged again from 1843 through 1873 to attain 31 percent of the total residents registered. The G curve for this second expansion closely paralleled, at a rather lower level, the trend of the same shape for earlier increase, with t_0's at 1856 and 1850, respectively. This rising proportion of uncles and their families gradually pushed down the weight of brothers of the head and their families from 31 to 20 percent—along the C trends shown at the bottom of Figure 6.16b (ibid.). Did fertility decline in C form give household heads fewer siblings and simultaneously reduce the number of children that their brothers had? Jointly, however, the proportion of households composed of the families of brothers and of uncles of the head, which had stayed level around 30 percent from 1792 through 1810, then rose to 44 percent by 1855 via one G surge and to 51 percent by 1873 via another (not graphed). Extended family structure expanded in rural Liaoning across the middle of the 19th century as population growth stagnated (ibid., 54; Harris 2001, 371). This expansion of interlocking family ties is reminiscent of G-shaped increases in marriage between blood relatives and naming of sons after grandfathers as the tobacco economy of Prince George's County, Maryland, became more fully developed and more densely populated a century before (Figure 6.8c).

The top plot in Figure 6.16b shows how the children of heads—and their spouses and their children and other descendants—between 1792 and 1858 at first slowly, but then progressively faster, became a smaller proportion of the

Figure 6.16b
Changing Demographic Composition in Rural Liaoning Province, 1774–1873:
Age, Sex, Generation, and Families of Brothers

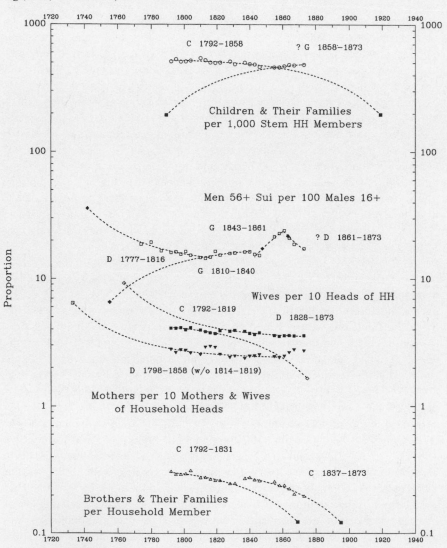

Source: Lee and Campbell 1997, 45–46, 52.

resident total direct line of descent for the household head (including head, wife, and mother). Beginning about 51 percent, this C curve declines to 46 percent by the late 1850s before rising somewhat again through 1873 or later, via a G path, it would seem. This measure can serve as a rough surrogate for age distribution across the generations of the householder's own stem family (excluding brothers, uncles, and their families). The C shape again suggests that fertility was falling in this form.

The proportion of the old in the rural population of Liaoning can be trended directly. Men of 56 or more *sui* as a proportion of all males 16 *sui* or older (Lee and Campbell 1997, 45–46) first fell from 1777 through 1816 in D form (from 19.0 to 14.5 percent), then climbed back slowly to 16.4 percent by 1840 before a short, second, and steeper G rise to 1861, where the percentage reached 24.0 before falling, perhaps in D fashion, to 1873 or later. As for the elderly in the population of England in the 17th and 18th centuries (Figure 6.13.b), the weight of this age group within the rural population of Liaoning fluctuated more than the role of the young. Still, also as in England, the shifts seem to have taken G-based forms. Age structure, both at the top and at the bottom of the range, altered in such trends in China as in Europe.

As to sex ratio, the wives of household heads for some reason declined as a proportion of the total of heads and spouses across the period studied. From 1828 through 1873 this decrease took D shape; but previously, from 1792 through 1819, the percentage appears to have atrophied in C form. Historical demographers of the locale will have to assess these proffered trends and probe the reasons for them (or more insightful modelings). Notable is how wives constituted only 41 to 35 percent of the pivotal conjugal pair. Most of this low level derives from the fact that when a head died, a new male head replaced him automatically, whereas a deceased wife might not be replaced for some time—if ever.

Turning finally to that demon of literature and cinematography, the Chinese mother-in-law, for most of the time mothers of the householder tended to shrink as a proportion of mothers and wives combined—in D trajectory from about 28 percent at 1792 to 24 percent at 1858. For the 1810s and perhaps again the 1860s, however, a short-term, temporary jump of about 4 percent appears. What caused this? The determinative shift for the time being at these points seems to have been having more mothers of the head rather than fewer wives (Lee and Campbell 1997, 52). If heads of household were for some reason markedly younger for a while, that might cause such a shift in the composition of recorded women. A trend toward older household heads as the result of improving longevity, on the other hand, might underlie the long-term decline in the weight of mothers as opposed to wives.

In several ways this example from northeastern China between the 1790s and the 1870s demonstrates how changes in the stucture of populations that have been seen to take G-based forms in other parts of the world probably did so in

Asia as well. Some very basic, ubiquitous guidance system has been at work to keep generating such globally shared demographic trends.

MORE RECENT MOVEMENTS IN DEMOGRAPHIC STRUCTURE

As presaged by later evidence observed from New Zealand, the Netherlands, Germany, England, Sweden, and France—and also China—G-based developments in the composition of populations, whether emanating from migration or from other dynamics, have comparably characterized generally better-documented populations in the more modern era of the 19th and 20th centuries. To confirm and extend this historically closer perspective, some further recent illustrations demonstrate the relevance of G-connected trends in how migrations fit into and interact with receiving populations, how the participants in migration flows change, and how their departure shapes sending populations as well as receiving ones. Examples come from a variety of immigrant groups attracted to the much-discussed "magnet" of the United States, from the demographic structure of settlement areas within that same migration-fed continental country, and from three international contexts: German industrialization during the 19th century; the relocation of Russian peasants in the era of legal and economic change from the 1860s to World War I; and the global dissemination of indentured laborers, from India and other sources, and their offspring between the 1840s and the 1950s.

Figure 6.17 begins by plotting how a dozen national groups of immigrants to the United States naturalized into the population of their new land. Graphed in each case are the proportions of those with recent roots in a given home country—the total "stock" of that nationality within America, as E. P. Hutchinson called them (1956, 5–6)—who were by successive dates between 1900 and 1950 now native-born: for example, those who had one or more Irish parents but had not come from Ireland themselves. Progressively, those born in America became a larger and larger share of the total from abroad or having parents from abroad. Such proportional change over and over took the shape of the G curve, just the way predominantly English decedents of Anne Arundel and Somerset Counties of Maryland more and more frequently between the 1670s and the 1770s had been born in the Chesapeake region (Figure 6.8b) or French colonists of Canada between 1670 and 1720 (Figure 6.7b) became increasingly creole.

Table 6.3 presents the spans of time involved in the G trends and their t_0's. In the cases of Austrian, Hungarian, Italian, and Russian immigrants, as the central panel of Figure 6.17 indicates, Kuznetsian long-swing spikes of new arrivals in the early 1900s temporarily knocked back the proportion of these groups currently joining the ranks of the native-born. The four curves are fitted without 1910. Scottish, French, and non-French Canadian data do not follow an underlying G pattern, bouncing around instead. For Mexican and Greek peoples

Figure 6.17
The Native-Born Share of Various Immigrant Groups in the United States, 1900–1950

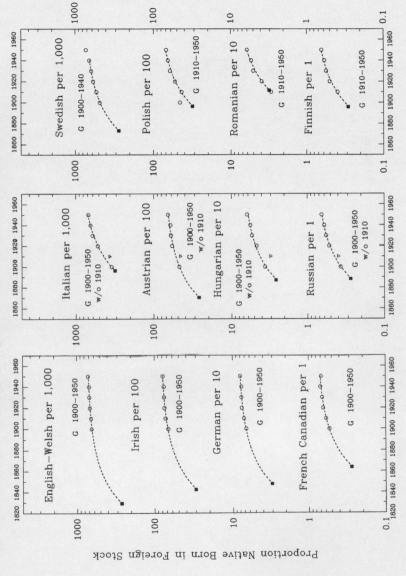

Source: Hutchinson 1956, 5–6.

Table 6.3
The Expansion of the Native-Born in Various Foreign Stock Groups in the United States, 1900–1950

A. Curve Fitted

English and Welsh	1900-1950	G	1829
Irish	1900-1950	G	1843
German	1900-1950	G	1849
French Canadian	1900-1950	G	1864
Austrian	1900-1950a	G	1870
Swedish	1900-1940	G	1873
Hungarian	1900-1950a	G	1887
Russian	1900-1950a	G	1888
Italian	1900-1950a	G	1895
Finnish	1910-1950	G	1896
Polish	1910-1950	G	1897
Romanian	1910-1950	G	1912

B. Trend Estimated

Other American	1900-1950	?G	1850
Swiss	1900-1940	G	1860
Dutch	1910-1950	G	1873
Danish	1910-1950	G	1874
Norwegian	1910-1950	G	1878
Portuguese	1920-1950	G	1897
Spanishb	1920-1950	G	1903

C. No Apparent G-Related Form

Scottish
French
Non-French Canadian

D. Possible G' Trends

Mexican	1920-1950	G'	1953
Greek	1910-1950	G'	1857

a = without 1910; b = 2nd-generation native proportion of 1st + 2nd.

Source: Hutchinson 1956, 5, 6, 14.

(also not graphed), G' trends with peaks in the 1950s seem to apply. The implication is that those last two groups came and stayed in spurts, perhaps fitting in between other flows when these were cut back by legislative restriction or international circumstances, a complementary behavior discussed with regard to incoming numbers in Chapter 1.[22] It would be interesting to see what form Mexican and Greek data then took across the second half of the 20th century. For Spanish immigrants, the curve represents second-generation native-born persons of Spanish descent as a proportion of first and second generation together.[23] The G shape for an even greater generational depth of integration into the American population has already been encountered for 18th-century St. Mary's County, Maryland, in Figure 6.8b. Hutchinson's data (1956, 14) allow the interested reader to follow the continuing generation-by-generation process for other immigrant groups from 1920 through 1950. More recent census data, of course, permit still further pursuit of the topic.

The fitted and estimated G trends from Table 6.3 together also indicate how the kind of succession of G'-shape immigrant waves to the United States noted in Chapter 1 (Table 1.1 and Figures 1.1 through 1.7) were subsequently integrated into native population in a similar sequence of G-type adjustments that display about the same clustering and typical Kuznetsian interval between surges. The cresting then breaking G' arrival of a group of immigrants repeatedly generated a G-shaped trend of generational replacement for those people and their descendants in America. What mechanism might so regularly shape replacement this way?

Figure 6.18 shows how this process played out in aggregate within the population of the United States. A now familiar type of succession from immigrants to their children took the G shape between 1870 and 1920 and then between 1920 and 1970 within the white population of the country (Hutchinson 1956, 2–3; *Historical Statistics*, 1: 16–19, Series A 119, 135–42). The first trend (for the top plot of the figure) lifted the native-born with one or more foreign parents from 49 to 62 percent of this new generation taken together with their foreign-born parents (what Hutchinson call the foreign-born "stock"). Then, between 1920 and 1970 even as further legal immigration was curtailed, the second G-shape transition carried the proportion up to 73 percent.

The current weight of just the foreign-born within the American population, however—the second plot in Figure 6.18—behaved rather differently. From 1850 through 1910, the proportion rose from just under 10 percent to just under 15 percent, swinging around a G trend parallel to that for the native-born among all of foreign stock. Then a D shape captures well the decline to 4.7 percent by 1970. The two successive G' trends also sketched out in this part of the figure, however, rather more tightly represent the movements between 1850 and 1960. Figure 1.7 in Chapter 1 demonstrates how a G' curve with crest at 1884 could be said to underlie the *number* of immigrants arriving in the United States between 1820 and 1900 (also part A of Table 1.2). The two G' humps for *proportion* of foreign-born persons in the population in Figure 6.18 apparently

Figure 6.18
Incorporating People of Foreign Birth and Foreign Parentage into the Population of the United States, 1850–1970

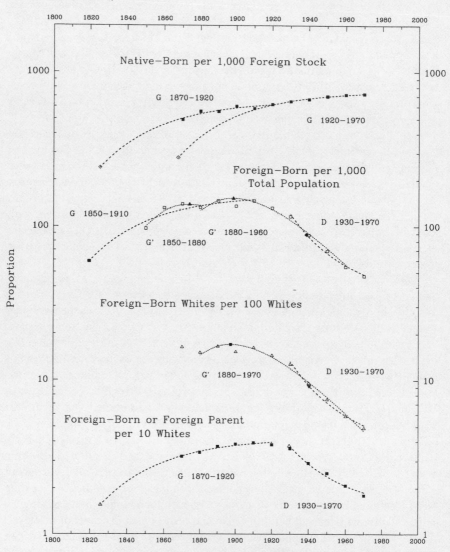

Sources: Hutchinson 1956, 2–3; *Historical Statistics* 1: 16–19, Series A 119, 135–42.

represent an echo of this intake, perhaps split by the "long-swing" nature of immigration into bracketing G' trends with crests at 1874 and 1899. On the other hand, the relatively steady tendency between 1850 and 1910 captures the consequences of the way that numbers of arrivals between 1847 and 1912 persistently rose, cutting through familar Kuznets cycles (Figure 1.7). Figure 6.18 shows how the *proportion* of living U.S. residents who had been born outside the country reflects the way that the flow of immigrants had been digested into the population.

The G' form with peak at 1897 not unexpectedly shows up as a possibility for the weight of foreign-born persons among all U.S. whites (the third plot of Figure 6.18), echoing the G' surge of fresh arrivals with crest at 1884 in Figure 1.7. Still, from 1870 (where these data begin) through 1910 or 1920 the proportion hovers near level; and the D shape fits decline from 1930 through 1970.

Once the children of immigrants are added to constitute a foreign "stock" (the bottom plot of the figure), however, then the percentage of the total white U.S. population in that category rises quite smoothly in G fashion from 1870 through 1920 in a curve based at 1826 compared with a t_0 of 1825 for the weight of the second generation within total foreign "stock" as Hutchinson defined it (the top plot of Figure 6.18). Then as immigration was cut back after the 1920s, persons of foreign "stock" contracted as a proportion of the white population in a D shape resembling the pattern for those actually born elsewhere. The often-feared child-bearing performance of immigrants no longer carried the potential to override recent trends of immigration.[24]

Trends in the age composition of the population of the United States and some of its sub-populations, meanwhile, consolidate impressions from England (Figures 6.13a and 6.13b), Sweden (6.14), and France (6.15) concerning the nature of modern movements in that dimension of demographic structure. Figure 6.19a first of all shows how the proportion of white females who were under age 15 from 1830 through 1890 declined in the accelerating C form with t_0 at 1932. Data for 1800, 1810, and 1820, furthermore, suggest—relative to a backward extension of this curve—parallel movement earlier, but for some reason at a rather higher level. Then, from 1890 to 1940 a second C trend with base year at 1966—about a generation later—captures the next phase of decline. (The data for 1950, 1960, and 1970 of course reflect the postwar baby boom and need to be trended with observations for the remainder of the century.) For black U.S. females, meanwhile, the proportion under 16 similarly declined in C form, toward a zero year at 1967—almost exactly parallel to the white trend for 1890–1940 but reaching back to start by 1850. For African Americans, no *prior* trend of decline occurred between 1850 and 1890. Also, the *level* of movement after 1890 for blacks was noticeably higher, headed toward 16.5 percent at 1967 rather than 14.5 percent at 1966. Greater longevity and reduction of fertility that appeared among U.S. whites before 1890 did not, for fairly obvious reasons, affect blacks comparably until the end of the 19th century.

On the broader international scene, the proportion of French females under

Figure 6.19a

The Young and the Old in the U.S. Population, 1800–1970: White and Black Females Nationally

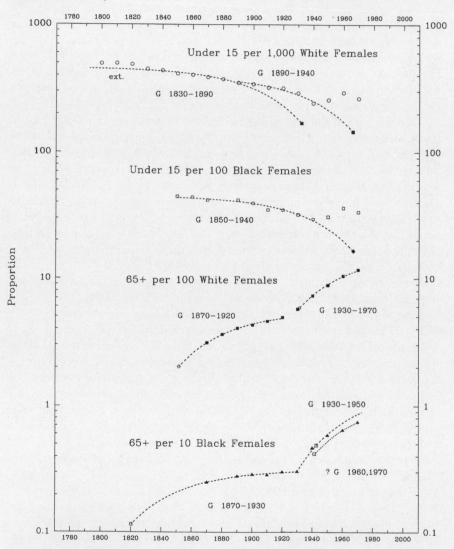

Source: *Historical Statistics* 1: 16–18, Series A 119–22, 133.

15 (Figure 6.15) has been seen to fall from 1740 through 1860 via a C trend with t_0 at 1928. This means that white U.S. females became less frequently young between 1830 (or earlier) and 1890 in almost exactly parallel fashion. The difference, however, was that in France—known for early reduction in fertility—the *level* of the C curve at its zero year was 11.8 rather than the 16.9 percent for American white females at 1932. Then, from 1861 through 1911, a further C trend in France headed toward a base year at 1972 compared with 1966 for U.S. white females from 1890 to 1940 and 1967 for U.S. black females from 1850 to 1940. Again, however, the French *level* was appreciably lower: toward 10.7 rather than 14.5 for whites and 16.5 for blacks in the United States. The movements of the national trends were very similar. It was just that the French had a head start by the middle of the 1800s, a differential that was maintained through two periods of parallel change.

In Sweden, meanwhile, the proportion under 15 (both sexes in Figure 6.14) fell in C fashion from 1890 through 1940 toward a t_0 of 1955 with a level of 14.7 percent (somewhat sooner but equivalent to white females in the United States). In England, furthermore, for both sexes the share under 15 shrank from 1866 through 1931 in a C pattern with the same base year as in Sweden 1890–1940 toward a zero year level of about 14 percent—an almost identical curve.[25] Given these widely shared C-shape movements in the weight of the young in diverse populations, it seems highly likely that birth rates during the modern era of fertility reduction have internationally, perhaps very generally, declined also in the C mode. The concluding volume of this inquiry systematically explores this possibility and the reasons for such a phenomenon.

At the other end of the age scale, those 65 or older increased among both white and black U.S. females from 1870 into the 1920s in G form; but the trend for whites was substantially steeper than that for blacks, carrying the level to 4.9 rather than 3.0 percent. Still further health improvements following World War II took the proportion for white women up along another G track to 11.7 percent of all females by 1970. The fraction for black females also climbed in G fashion a second time, reaching 7.5 percent by 1970; but it seems as if the curve was set back somewhat between 1950 and 1960. Was this the result of a change in the recording of age? Or did some setback in health improvement shift the apparently continuing G bend to a lower level?

In contrast, Figures 6.15 and 6.14 have shown how the proportion of those 60 and older among French females and Swedes of both sexes increased via E rather than G trajectories between 1881 and 1951 and 1890 and 1965, respectively, with t_0's at 1978 and 1987. From 1960 through 1989, however, the next Swedish trend seems to have taken G shape, as did increase in the weight of the elderly in England between 1841 and 1871 (Figure 6.13b). Previously, however, three E-type increases for the percentage of English persons 60 and older appear in the 16th, 17th, and 18th centuries. The two distinct kinds of expansion, G and E, in the weight of older adults within a population seem to be common historically. What are the mechanisms—especially the movements in mortality and life expectancy—that generate one form rather than the other? This is another topic that Volume III takes up comparatively, beginning with a survey of the international history of death rates.

The left panel of Figure 6.19b, meanwhile, displays how C trends characterized the proportional decline of individuals under 15 across the first half of the 20th century in the foreign-born population of the United States, among those of foreign or mixed parentage, and those with foreign roots but now second-generation native by birth (Hutchinson 1956, 16). At the same time, however, the weight of persons 65 and over in these three groups (the right panel of the figure) increased in both G and E modes. For the foreign-born, the G trend came first; for those with foreign or mixed parentage and those who were second-generation native, from 1890 through 1930 the change took E shape, thereafter apparently switching to G. Presumably these differences were related to the way that immigration to the United States was choked back in the 1920s.

The populations of individual states within the United States similarly display changes in age structure according to G-based trends. Since about 1850, C patterns have predominated, as Table 6.4 demonstrates.[26] Exceptions since then are mostly G-shape increases in more recently settled states of the West along with a few D-type declines. Before the middle of the 19th century, a mixture of falling C's or D's and up-and-down G' patterns prevails.

In Figure 6.20 Massachusetts illustrates how in 10 northern states from Maine to New Jersey and Indiana the proportion of the population under 15 from when records begin until World War II did nothing but repeatedly decline in C form. The left column of Table 6.4 shows how there was some spread in the timing of the first observed round of C-shape declines: earlier in New England, later in New York and New Jersey, later still in Ohio and Indiana. Maine and Vermont display exceptional second decreases across mid-century parallel to the first C pattern for Indiana. Then from mid-century through 1890 all 10 of these northeastern states experienced further C-type reductions in the weight of the young in their populations. The t_0's of these later curves (in the third column of the table) all fell close to 1924. A final round of C-form contraction then took place between 1890 and 1940. In Massachusetts, Rhode Island, Connecticut, New York, New Jersey, Ohio, and Indiana the curves headed toward base years around 1970; in Maine and Vermont the change was slower, along C trends with t_0's more like 2002. In New Hampshire, the proportion of the population under 15 actually *rose* between 1890 and 1930, probably along the kind of G path proposed in the rightmost column of Table 6.4. In Massachusetts, Rhode Island, Connecticut, Maine, Vermont, New York, and New Jersey, the percentages under 15 at 1920 and 1930 tended to sit somewhat higher than the underlying curves for between 1890 and 1940. This would seem to be the consequence of heavy immigration to these states around the turn of the century. After 1940, of course, the famous postwar baby boom came to bear in most states. Analysis for the second half of the 20th century is left for treatment elsewhere.

Figure 6.19b

The Young and the Old in the U.S. Population, 1800–1970: The Age Structure of Native-Born and Foreign-Born Whites

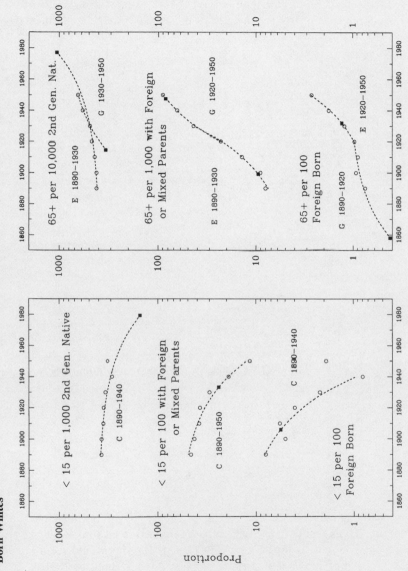

Source: Hutchinson 1956, 16.

Table 6.4
Apparent Trends in the Proportion of Population under 15 in 50 U.S. States, 1790–1940

Massachusetts*	1800-1840	C	1868				1840-1890	C	1931	1890-1940	C	1968[a]
Connecticut	1800-1830	C	1862				1830-1890	C	1925	1900-1940	C	1969[a]
Rhode Island	1800-1830	C	1860				1830-1890	C	1929	1890-1940	C	1978[a]
New Hampshire	1800-1840	C	1864				1850-1890	C	1920	1890-1930	G	1830
Maine	1800-1830	C	1866	1830-1870	C	1896	1870-1890	C	1928	1890-1940	C	2004[a]
Vermont	1800-1830	C	1864	1840-1860	C	1898	1860-1890	C	1928	1890-1940	C	2000[a]
New York	1800-1840	C	1874				1850-1890	C	1927	1890-1940	C	1967[a]
New Jersey	1800-1830	C	1875				1830-1890	C	1923	1890-1940	C	1960[a]
Ohio	1800-1840	C	1880				1840-1890	C	1918	1890-1940	C	1966
Indiana	1820-1850	C	1892				1850-1890	C	1923	1890-1940	C	1970
Pennsylvania*	1800-1830	G'	1809				1830-1890	C	1930	1890-1940	C	1974[a]
Delaware	1800-1830	G'	1806				1860-1890	C	1921	1890-1940	C	1966
Maryland	1800-1830	G'	1807				1850-1900	C	1941	1900-1940	C	1967
West Virginia							1870-1910	C	1950	1910-1940	C	1978
Kentucky	1800-1830	G'	1802				1850-1890	C	1938	1890-1940	C	1972
North Carolina	1800-1830	G'	1805				1850-1890	C	1938	1850-1940	C	1942
Virginia	1800-1830	D	1734							1880-1940	C	1966
Georgia*	1800-1840	D	1753							1850-1940	C	1968
South Carolina	1800-1840	D	1780	1850-1870	C	1905				1880-1940	C	1976
Alabama	1820-1840	D	1792							1850-1940	C	1968
Mississippi	1810-1840	D	1795							1850-1940	C	1974
Florida										1850-1940	C	1955
Arkansas	1820-1840	D	1796							1850-1940	C	1966
Texas										1850-1940	C	1960
Oklahoma										1900-1940	C	1964
Tennessee	1800-1840	D	1764				1850-1910	C	1949	1910-1940	C	1970
Missouri	1810-1840	?D	1758				1850-1910	C	1934	1910-1940	C	1966
Louisiana	1810-1840	?D	1758				1850-1890	G	1800	1880-1940	C	1968

Illinois	1810-1840	G'	1821	1840-1890	C	1922	1890-1940	C	1982
Wisconsin*	1840-1880	G'	1860				1890-1940	C	1965
Michigan	1820-1860	G'	1842				1870-1930	D	1835
Minnesota	1850-1890	G'	1869				1870-1930	D	1842
Iowa				1860-1890	C	1924	1890-1940	C	1975
Kansas				1860-1910	C	1941	1910-1940	C	1965
Nebraska				1880-1910	C	1940	1910-1940	C	1968
South Dakota							1900-1940	C	1969
Utah				1860-1890	C	1924	1890-1940	C	1975
New Mexico				1850-1890	C	1934	1900-1940	C	1987
Colorado				1880-1910	G'	1898	1900-1940	C	1988
North Dakota							1890-1920	G	1830
Montana				1870-1910	?G'	1902	1870-1930	G	1862
Idaho							1880-1920	G	1833
Wyoming							1870-1930	G	1838
Arizona*							1870-1930	G	1856
Nevada							1870-1970	?G	1838
Alaska							1900-1970	?G	1890
Hawaii							1900-1920	G	1899
California							1870-1930	D	1840
Oregon							1860-1930	D	1845
Washington							1870-1930	D	1837

*Fitted in Figure 6.20; ª 1920 and 1930 fall above curve.

Figure 6.20
Types of Change in the Proportion under 15 in the Populations of U.S. States, 1790–1970

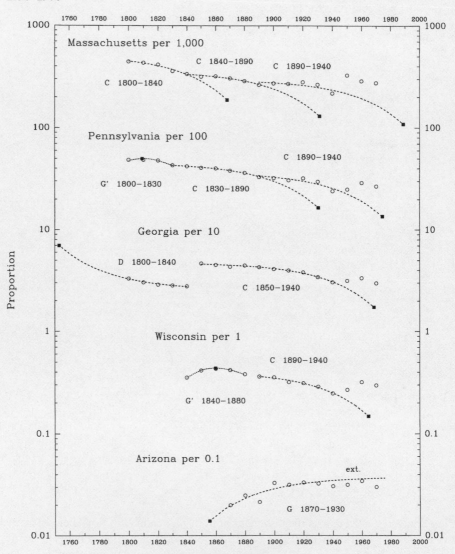

Source: *Historical Statistics* 1: 24–37, Series A 195, 204–5.

Pennsylvania (the second plot in Figure 6.20) shared along with Delaware the 1890–1940 C trend typical of more northern states of the East; unlike Delaware, it also displays values at 1920 and 1930 above the trend line. Maryland, West Virginia, and Kentucky, meanwhile, join these two Mid-Atlantic states both in typical timing of C decline following the 1890s and in preceding C-type proportional atrophy of the young in their populations between the middle of the 19th century and its end. For North Carolina, just one C trend (aimed at a zero year around 1942, like the next-to-last C movements elsewhere) lowered the percentage under 15 steadily between 1850 and 1940. In Pennsylvania, Delaware, Maryland, Kentucky, and North Carolina, however, between 1800 and 1830 it looks as though the proportion of the young may have gone up then down in G' fashion, in each case with a t_0 in the early 1800s. What this appears to be is the reflection of fresh settlement in Kentucky and in previously less developed areas within the other four states, an interpretation that is strengthened by information from states created later as slave-free settlement moved westward.

In most slave states of the American South, in contrast, up to about 1840 the youthful portion of the local population *shrank* in D fashion—earliest in Virginia, Georgia, Tennessee, Missouri, and Louisiana; later in South Carolina, Alabama, Mississippi, and Arkansas. Over this period, from the national census only the age distribution of whites is known. Thus, it was this portion of the population that was becoming less frequently young. To start including slaves in the calculation in later years made the percentage who were young jump, abruptly between 1840 and 1850 in all 14 currently recorded slave areas, as Figure 6.20 illustrates for Georgia.[27]

Subsequently, considering whole populations, in Tennessee and Missouri the proportion under 15 next shrank across the second half of the 19th century via C trends with t_0's around 1940 (like the states of the Northeast), South Carolina produced change between 1850 and 1870 in an even earlier trend of that shape, and Louisiana saw the weight of its youth *increase* via the kind of G trend proposed between 1850 and 1890. In most southern states, however, change in the fraction of the population under 15 between the middle 1800s and 1940 involved a single long C movement toward a base year between 1955 and 1976, as the last column of Table 6.4 indicates.

On slave-free frontiers, the kind of early G' hump in proportion under 15 that has been encountered previously in Pennsylvania, Delaware, and three northern states of the South appeared about two decades later in Illinois (t_0 at 1821), then Michigan (1842), then Wisconsin and Minnesota (1860 and 1869) as waves of settlement pushed across the continent in the 19th century. Illinois then displays the kind of C between 1840 and 1890 also found in Pennsylvania between 1830 and 1890. In Michigan and Minnesota, for some reason, D-type atrophy in the percentage under 15 then followed from 1870 through 1930, parallel in timing with similar change in California, Oregon, and Washington, the last group of states in Table 6.4, over the same period. Further research into why these five

areas experienced such a phenomenon might profitably focus on how intensely
their original settlement involved families (in spite of the Gold Rush?). In Wisconsin and Illinois, meanwhile, the share of the population under 15 fell away
from 1890 through 1940 in the type of C pattern found for most southern states.

The same kind of C trend appeared in seven states of the Plains and the
Rockies from about 1900 through 1940: first Iowa, Kansas, Nebraska, and South
Dakota, then Colorado, Utah, and New Mexico rather later. Previously, across
the second half of the 19th century, the share of the young in Iowa, Kansas,
Nebraska, Utah, and New Mexico had fallen via C trends timed like those of
Illinois and many eastern states. In Colorado, in contrast, the G' form appeared
between 1880 and 1910, as probably was the case simultaneously in Montana
between 1870 and 1910. Montana, however, was one of eight western states
(with North Dakota, Idaho, Wyoming, Arizona, Nevada, Hawaii, and Alaska)
in which the proportion of the population under 15 *rose* in G fashion across the
late 19th and early 20th centuries. The illustrative plot for Arizona in Figure
6.20 shows (as also found in Nevada) movement generally parallel with the
1870–1930 G curve for data from 1940 through 1970—though at a lower
level—in place of the baby-boom surges that were so general elsewhere.

In all, increase and decline in the weight of the young within local populations
for 50 U.S. states consistently rose and fell in G-related trends between 1800
and 1940. To pattern the movements this way clarifies what areas of the country
were sharing demographic changes and which in fact experienced quite divergent developments. It also helps point up the likely reasons (various settlement
histories and so forth) for which these structural alterations took place.

Change in sex ratios similarly took G-related shapes and set apart U.S. states
with certain historical conditions from others that lacked them. The most substantial and visible of these adjustments occurred in later-settled areas of the
West. Table 6.5 lists what seem to have been the trends in 15 such states; Figure
6.21 fits G and G' curves for 10 of these regions.

In North Dakota, Colorado, and Idaho, recorded percentages of females in
the population rose from the late 1800s to 1970 along a single G trend based
at a zero year level of 18.3 to 19.1 percent (i.e., with projected maxima between
49.7 and 51.9 percent). A similar height characterized the G curves for Michigan, Minnesota, and California from the 1910s to 1970; and these trends paralleled very closely in timing those for Colorado and Idaho, with t_0's also in the
1840s. In this second group of three states, however, there had visibly existed
also a previous G pattern of relative female increase from about mid-century to
1910 that ran about 1 percent lower in level than its succeeding G.

In the nine other states summarized in Table 6.5, G trends of comparable
level (except the low one for Alaska) since 1890 or later were also preceded by
stages of change in the composition of the population by sex; but this took G'
rather than G form (as the right panel of Figure 6.21 illustrates). In timing, the
base years of the eventual G curves for this group of states varied considerably—
from the 1814 for New Mexico (long settled by Europeans before its acquisition

Table 6.5
Trends in the Proportion of Females in the Populations of 15 Western U.S. States, 1840–1970

North Dakota				1880-1970	G	1826
Colorado				1890-1970	G	1841
Idaho				1880-1970	G	1849
Michigan	1840-1910	G	1737	1920-1970	G	1841
Minnesota	1860-1910	G	1777*	1920-1970	G	1840*
California	1870-1910	G	1824	1910-1970	G	1848
New Mexico	1850-1880	G'	1862*	1890-1960	G	1814*
Oregon	1850-1880	G'	1866	1880-1970	G	1833
Washington	1860-1890	?G'	1886	1890-1970	G	1850
Montana	1870-1910	G'	1904	1910-1970	G	1863
Arizona	1870-1910	?G'	1899*	1910-1970	G	1870*
Wyoming	1870-1910	G'	1899*	1910-1970	G	1878*
Nevada	1860-1910	G'	1897*	1910-1970	G	1879*
Hawaii	1900-1930	G'	1922	1940-1970	G	1889
Alaska	1910-1950	G'	1936	1950-1970	G	1920

*Trend estimated.

Source: Historical Statistics 1: 24–37, Series A 195, 198.

by the United States in the 1840s) to Alaska, whose t_0 probably came a century later. For the movement before these modern G changes, in contrast to Michigan, Minnesota, and California, the pattern was G' rather than G. Such a derivative curve capped out at from 37 to 43 percent female at the date that is fitted in Figure 6.21 or estimated for Table 6.5—except for 50 percent in New Mexico, with its extended history of Spanish occupation. The crests of these G' trends arrived anywhere from the 1860s to the 1930s. What the early trends seem to reflect are surges of early settlement by families—as with the conquest of New Mexico, in the exploitation of the Oregon Trail, or following the acquisition of Hawaii.

Interested readers can examine what are generally flatter patterns for earlier U.S. states or for settlements on other continental frontiers. The patterning of Figure 6.21 and Table 6.5, however, would seem to suggest that in the 19th and 20th centuries the kinds of temporary G' and more lasting G trends in sex composition that have been observed so generally among slave populations and in European colonial settlements of the 17th and 18th centuries (Chapter 5 and earlier in the present chapter) also have prevailed in much more modern adjustments of demographic structure. Four centuries of such evidence begins to accumulate.

Analysis of various slave trades and early modern migrations of Europeans has likewise indicated that the age and sex composition of *those who moved* also repeatedly altered in G-based forms as the flow from one place to another progressed. Does the same apply to the great modern international relocations that are more familiar to most readers?

Figure 6.21
Proportion of Females in the Populations of Some Western U.S. States

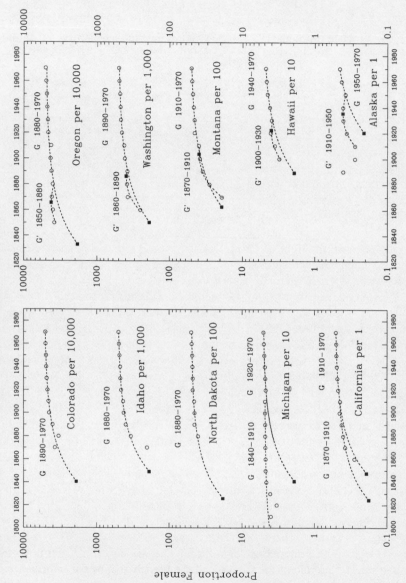

Proportion Female

Source: Historical Statistics, 1: 24–37, Series A 195, 198.

To begin to answer this question, Figure 6.22 trends the proportion of females in some well-known migrations of the 19th and early 20th centuries. Table 6.6 lists particulars of the movements that emerge from this analysis and adds estimates by eye and template for Norway, Switzerland, France, and Belgium. For most countries, two rather different kinds of data are involved, with trends spliced from one to the other. Where available, evidence from 1822 through 1853 (1820–1826 through 1851–1855) represents the proportion of females among passengers *arriving* in the United States who had been born in certain countries (Ferenczi and Willcox 1929, 401–17). For 1853 through 1922 the data concern the weight of females among all citizens who were recorded as *emigrating* from certain home countries (ibid., 303–9 with notes on page 354). Thus, after 1853 British persons going to Canada, Australia, New Zealand, and South Africa are included; before 1853 they are not. Generally, though, the transition of level from one series to the other seems relatively smooth and the combination of the two series appears to be justifiable.

In these international movements G has been the universal trend of feminization, except perhaps an alternative G' pattern in the rather special case of indentured servants leaving British India. D-type declines in the proportion of females appear after mid-century for the Low Countries and perhaps France. For emigration from Norway, there may have occurred a brief instance of C-shape reduction between 1883 and 1903 as the economy grew and independence from Sweden approached.

The *levels* of the noted G transitions toward a more female migration, however, varied considerably. For the first trends for Irish and for British (English, Welsh, Scottish) relocators of all ages the proportion at t_0 is such as to imply ultimate maxima of 52 to 54 percent female (47.3 actually reached by 1863 and 42.3 by 1853, respectively—with 43.2 attained by the 1878–1911 British trend for all ages and 42.1 by that for persons 15 and over only in the left panel of Figure 6.22).[28] In the second Irish trend of 1868–1903, the G curve for the Netherlands 1822–1853, and the Finnish pattern for 1883–1922, target levels of as much as 62 to 67 percent female are implied. This contrasts sharply with only 33 percent for the Italian curve of 1878–1922 (the right panel of Figure 6.22) and 39 to 43 percent for the Portuguese, Indian, and second Swiss (1903–1922) trends that are identified. Whatever the level, however, all these migrations most probably became proportionally more female with time in G form—though, as in Dutch migration, the tide could then turn back with time. The D trend for the Netherlands, it should be remembered, indicates increasing maleness among migrants in part because departures to the East Indies in the later 19th and early 20th centuries are significant. The downward Belgian flow may similarly reflect the role of the Congo and the French decline the importance of North Africa, other destinations not particularly attractive to European women or for men taking families. Further research should readily test these suggestions.

Figure 6.23 and Table 6.7 in turn deal with the weight of the young in these same migrations. The age categories vary considerably from country to coun-

Figure 6.22

Proportion of Females among Immigrants to America, 1804–1853, and Emigrants from Selected Countries, 1853–1922

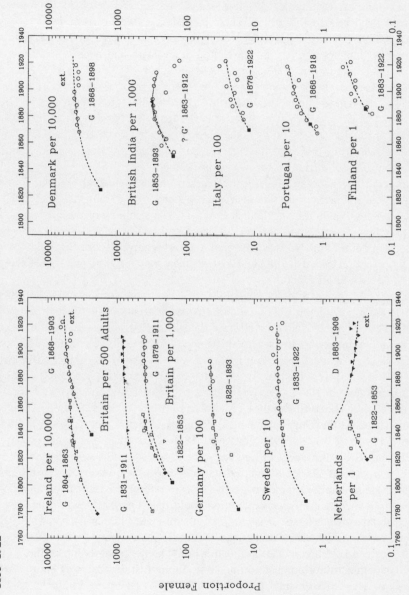

Sources: Ó Gráda 1986, 83, 88; Erickson 1989, 360–61; Ferenczi and Willcox 1929, 303–9 (see 354 for notes), 401–17.

Table 6.6
Trends in the Proportion of Females among Emigrants from Selected Countries or Their Immigrants to the United States, 1804–1922[a]

Ireland	1804-1863	G	1779	1868-1903	G	1838
Britain (adults)	1831-1911	G	1781			
Germany	1828-1893	G	1782			
Sweden	1833-1922	G	1786			
Norway	1833-1883	G	1792*	1883-1903	C	1934*
Britain (all)	1822-1853	G	1809	1831-1911	G	1802
Switzerland	1822-1853	G	1812*	1903-1922	G	1845*
France	1825-1853	G	1811*	1858-1878	?D	1808?*
Netherlands	1822-1853	G	1820	1863-1922	D	1843
Belgium				1888-1906	D	1848*
Denmark	1868-1898	G	1825			
British India	1853-1893	G	1850	1863-1912	G'	1891
Italy	1878-1922	G	1870			
Portugal	1868-1918	G	1875			
Finland	1883-1922	?G	1887			

* = Trend estimated; [a] Through 1853, passengers born in country who came to the United States; for 1853–1922, all emigrants recorded from country.

Sources: Ó Gráda 1986, 83, 88; Erickson 1989, 360–61; Ferenczi and Willcox, 1929, 303–9 (see 354 for notes), 401–17.

try.[29] Therefore, levels across the various recorded migrations are difficult to compare extensively. Yet it is clear that D-type decline quite generally occurred as these migrations matured. This is the form of decline noted in Figure 6.4 for boys under 16 among male English servant emigrants from the 1680s through the 1770s. As in the waning stages of 18th-century German relocation to colonial America (Wokeck 1999, 49), young adults became a larger and larger proportion of the flow in place of families that included children. Weighted averages for immigration to the United States from England, Wales, and Scotland at 1831, 1841, and 1886 (1873–1898) and comparable calculations for Ireland, both of which are from the detailed analysis of Charlotte Erickson (1989, 358), for several decades of the 19th century follow D paths with base years in the early 1810s. These sources had been sending people to America for some time. Presumably—though a satisfying direct record does not seem to exist—in that early era the proportion of the young among migrants had first grown, as observed in the G trends (Table 6.7) for later-burgeoning immigrations from Portugal, Italy, and Finland across the end of the 1800s and the beginning of the 1900s (and perhaps from Denmark until 1883). From Britain, the age group being measured alters significantly from the 1870s forward (except for Erickson's evidence around 1886—the hollow triangles above the hollow circles), and the proportion swings up and down markedly. In emigration from Ireland, however—to all destinations, not just the United States, it should be remembered—

Figure 6.23
Proportion of the Young among Emigrants from Certain Countries, 1831–1922

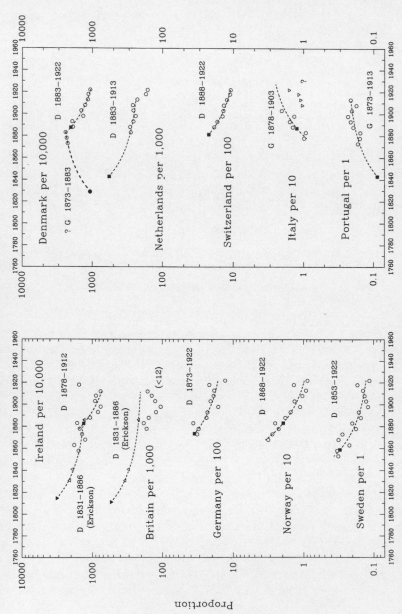

Sources: Erickson 1989, 358–59; Ferenczi and Willcox 1929, 303–9 (see 354 for notes on varying age groupings).

Table 6.7
Trends in the Proportion of the Young among Emigrants from Certain Countries

Britain	1831-1886	D	1811[e]				
Ireland I	1831-1886	D	1815[e]				
Netherlands	1883-1913	D	1843				
Sweden	1853-1922	D	1859				
Germany	1873-1922	D	1874[a]				
Ireland II	1878-1912	D	1883				
Norway	1868-1922	D	1883				
Switzerland	1888-1922	D	1887				
Denmark II	1883-1922	D	1888	Denmark I	1873-1883	G	1829
Belgium	1888-1913	D	1891*				
				Portugal	1878-1913	G	1862
				Italy	1878-1903	G	1887
				Finland	1883-1918	G	1886*

* Trend estimated; [e] from Erickson; [a] age adjusted for 1873–1883.

Sources: Erickson 1989, 358; Ferenczi and Willcox 1929, 303–9 (see 354 for notes on variations and changes in age groupings).

percentages of the young from 1858 into the 1880s (the hollow circles) first conform to the D trend from Erickson's calculations for the United States alone (the hollow triangles), then probably decline around a new D path from 1878 to 1912 with t_0 at 1883.

This second Irish D trend that is hypothesized resembles in timing those for Germany 1873–1922,[30] Norway 1868–1922, Switzerland 1888–1922, Denmark 1883–1922, and Belgium 1888–1913 (Figure 6.23 and Table 6.7)—with timing for the Netherlands 1883–1913 and Sweden 1853–1922 coming rather earlier (t_0's at 1843 and 1859). While one surge of Germans to America reached an early summit in the middle of the 1700s, a largely new influx across the Atlantic—by region and religion—came to its peak only in the middle 1800s, setting the stage for a typical turn with time to fewer families and children and more young adults. Danish emigration does not seem to have reached this point of transition until the 1880s, Portugal after 1913, and Italy also only in the early 20th century.[31]

In all, trends in the composition of those who moved—like the makeup of migrant populations across the years following arrival—display the same few G-related forms of change previously observed in settlements of the 17th and 18th centuries. Across four centuries very general shapes characterized structural change in migration to the New World as well as in the populations that benefited therefrom.

Three illustrations next demonstrate that in modern times it was not just settlement of the Western Hemisphere that drew and digested migrants in these same few G-based forms. Examples come from German industrialization, the mobility of Russian peasants after emancipation during an era of late-blooming national economic development there, and flows of workers from the Indian subcontinent to supply labor for regional economies previously fed by the slave trade.

Figure 6.24, first of all, depicts the annual rate of migration for the Düsseldorf region of Germany from the 1820s into the 1860s. In this area astride the northern Rhine between Köln and the Dutch border, the pace of relocation increased in G form from about 3 percent of the current population of the area annually to more like 10 percent (Hochstadt 1999, 62, 68).[32] The top plot in the figure averages in- and out-migration, which generally paralleled each other over the longer haul. Displayed, in other words, is an approximate trending of overall geographical mobility in this segment of the rapidly industrializing northern Rhineland. From the 1820s through the 1850s in-migration can be plotted separately for different kinds of zones within the Düsseldorf region (ibid., 74). The annual rate was flattest for five agricultural areas, rising from about 3 to about 5 percent. In the two heavily industrial zones of the region, Duisberg (the Ruhr) and Elberfeld (Wupperthal), and in six *Kreise* of mixed economic activity, which stretched from Kempen and Gladbach eastward across the Rhine through Krefeld and Düsseldorf to Solingen and Lennep, the ratio of current immigrants per existing population climbed more steeply: from 3.3 to 10.2 and from 2.5 to 8.0 percent, respectively, in each case via an underlying trend of G shape with t_0's at 1845 rather than the 1826 of the agricultural locales. The dip below the trend line that is evident in each series of Figure 6.24 at 1849 reflects the consequences of the European crisis of the 1840s upon migration. Interestingly, the annual data on immigration for single males, who had the highest rate of movement, plummeted from 1846 to 1848—*before* political tensions came to a head (ibid., 94). How did this apparent abrupt restriction of opportunity in industrializing Germany perhaps contribute to the revolutions that soon followed in several locations?

A country that developed modern economic institutions both less and later than Germany was tsarist Russia. Here, something is known about the proportion of the peasant population to whom passports (required for travel within Russia—including to work in the new businesses that were emerging) were issued during the several decades between the Edict of Emancipation for serfs by Alexander II in 1861 and World War I. Figure 6.25 presents the trends in these rates for eight major regions of the country (Burds 1998, 23).[33]

In most zones, the proportion of the peasant population who obtained passports increased via a G trajectory. Progressively more and more of the population moved, but at a steadily slowing change of rate of increase. In the Central Industrial and North and Northwest regions the proportion tripled from 5 or 6 percent in the 1860s to more like 15 to 22 percent 1906–1910.[34] Both lower and flatter in increase—with t_0's around 1860 rather than 1880—were the G trends for the Ural and Volga regions.[35] Here the proportion getting passports

Figure 6.24
Trends of In-Migration in the Düsseldorf District, 1824–1865

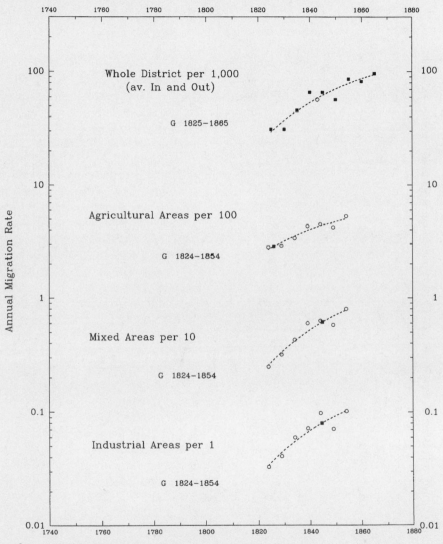

Source: Hochstadt 1999, 68, 74.

Figure 6.25

Passports Issued to Peasants as Proportion of Village Population in Regions of Russia, 1865–1908

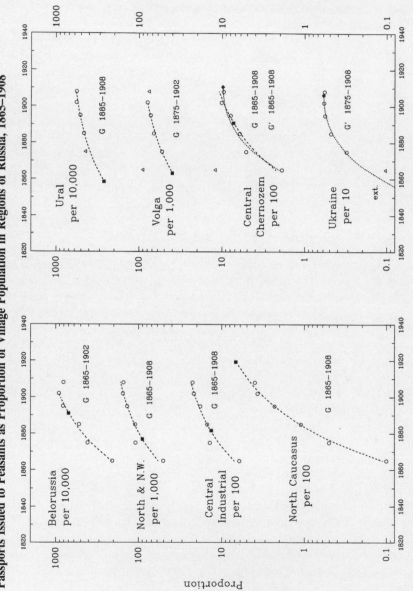

Source: Burds 1998, 23.

reached only 6 to 8 percent by the era of the 1905 Revolution. In Belorussia and probably the Central Chernozem (the provinces of Vitebsk, Minsk, and Mogilev and the "Black Earth" areas of Voronezh, Kursk, Orel, and Tambov) the apparent migration rate rose from about 2 to 8 or 10 percent along G paths with base years at 1891 but stopped their upward movement after 1902 (as was the case also in the Volga region). In the North Caucasus, a still later, steeper, G-shape rise in passport activity appeared, having its t_0 as late as 1919; but issued documents still went to only 4 percent of the peasant population there between 1906 and 1910. It was in the Ukraine that a G' rather than a G pattern clearly characterized the post-emancipation distribution of passports. This curve crested at 1906. A G' trend topping out at 1911 also constitutes a possible fit for the data of the Central Chernozem just above the Ukraine in the right-hand panel of Figure 6.25. These were the two prime breadbaskets of 19th-century Russia, doing much to feed the country's population and exporting to compete in world markets with Canada, the United States, Argentina, and Australia. What was it about these areas that, clearly in the Ukraine and possibly in the Central Chernozem, made peasant migration take a different shape between the 1860s and World War I than for other parts of Russia? The patterning through time raises matters that deserve further inquiry.

Figure 6.26, finally, shows some of the demographic change that took place as in the later 19th and early 20th centuries African slaves were replaced by indentured laborers recruited for canefields and other especially challenging work sites around the world. The largest group of these laborers came from India. The top plot in the figure shows how the proportion of these Indian migrants who were female (as known across time among those going to Mauritius and to British Guiana) probably rose and fell in G' form, peaking at 32 percent near 1883 (Northrup 1995, 75). Such movement suggests a more temporary change in the role of women than for other migrations examined in this chapter. It is reminiscent, however, of G' surges in the weight of women within Royal African Company *slave* deliveries to Barbados, Jamaica, and the Leewards between 1673 and 1723 (Figure 5.9 in Chapter 5), a G' pattern for women per 1,000 adults in the still primarily import-determined Chesapeake population of African origin between 1664 and 1695 (Figure 5.13a), and shipments to two parts of Brazil in the much later period 1813–1843 (Bahia and the South, stated upside down as a proportion of males in Figure 5.12c). In contrast to these local swings, for various regional slave trades as a whole the sex proportions in slave imports or exports more usually seem to have altered via longer-lasting G trends (Figure 5.12a). What might there have been about the 19th-century recruitment of Indian contract workers that resembled certain local slave imports of previous centuries more than free migrations or slave trades of broader and more composite nature?

The other four plots of Figure 6.26 examine declining death rates for populations of indentured laborers as an indicator of likely normalization by age and sex (Northrup 1995, 122; Shlomowitz 1997, 147). A rise in the weight of chil-

Figure 6.26
**Adjustment in Sex and Death Rate for Some Groups of Indentured Laborers,
1844–1950**

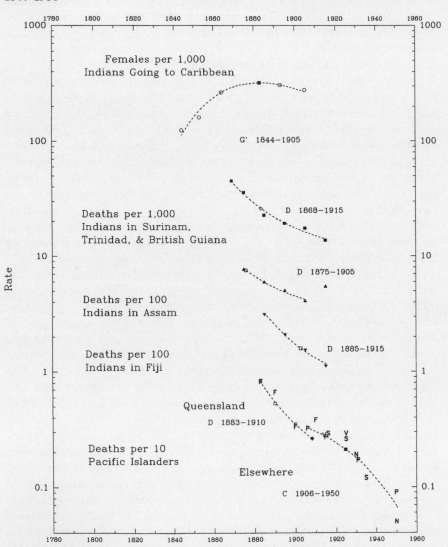

F = Fiji; N = New Guinea; P = Papua; S = Solomons; V = Vanatu.

Sources: Northrup 1995, 75, 122; Shlomowitz 1997, 147.

dren drives down the death rate; more women are necessary for more children to appear.

Among Indian workers in Surinam, British Guiana, and Trinidad the crude death rate (CDR) fell in D fashion from the 1860s to World War I.[36] Approximately parallel, but at a much higher level, the CDR for Indian workers in Assam contracted from a t_0 at 1876 compared with 1883 for the three Caribbean groups. Noticeably later adjustments, also in D shape, characterize declining death rates for Indian laborers in Fiji—thousands of miles away from northeastern India, let alone the Caribbean—and for Pacific Island workers in Australia's sugar-growing state of Queensland.

Imported Pacific Island workers resident on Fiji, up into the early 1900s at least, may have seen death rates decline in the same D type of trend as those in Queensland. Across the first half of the 20th century, however, populations on Papua, Vanatu, the Solomons, and New Guinea experienced declining CDR in quite another form: the accelerating C curve (bottom left corner of Figure 6.26, based on Shlomowitz 1997, 145). At first, one might think that for some reason the D path was taken by migrant workers and the C by their home populations across the Pacific. Figure 6.27, though, demonstrates the way that mortality on shipboard during travel to their new homes for contract workers from the Pacific Islands, India, China, and Africa all probably declined in C shape across the second half of the 19th century.[37] Data for the slave trade (the average for 1680–1807) and the first wave of British convicts sent to North America in the 18th century (1719–1736) suggest that such a C trend may have begun in the early 1700s.

That a C pattern of falling death rate on ocean voyages is not just an accidental product of the scattered global evidence invoked so far is demonstrated by the second trend of Figure 6.27. This lower C pattern captures declining mortality for *free* travelers on various ocean routes across time: Dutch passengers to Batavia, the main VOC base on Java, for the period 1620–1780; voyagers to Philadelphia in the later 1700s and to New York in the early 1800s; both convicts and free immigrants to Australia between 1788–1814 and 1854–1892, and persons going to South Africa between 1847 and 1864. By the years 1768–1775 the risk for North American convicts ("1"), which had resembled that for slaves in the early 1700s, had converged with the lower C trend for free persons. This had its t_0 at 5.1 per 1,000 per month at 1839, compared with 21.2 per 1,000 at 1863 for non-European workers. It seems that the difference between the health conditions of persons being loaded—European vs. non-European—most probably determined the level of trend unless the treatment of European convicts in passage was so significantly better than that for non-European contract workers. The possibilities merit further inquiry. Yet, with time, mortality on *both* kinds of passage markedly improved in C fashion. This form does not appear in most insights into mortality trends revealed so far: for early Newfoundland (Figure 6.2), Cuban blacks to 1900 (Figure 5.8b), and the contract worker populations before 1900 in Figure 6.26. Historical E-type trends for the

Figure 6.27
Mortality per Month on Certain Migrant Voyages

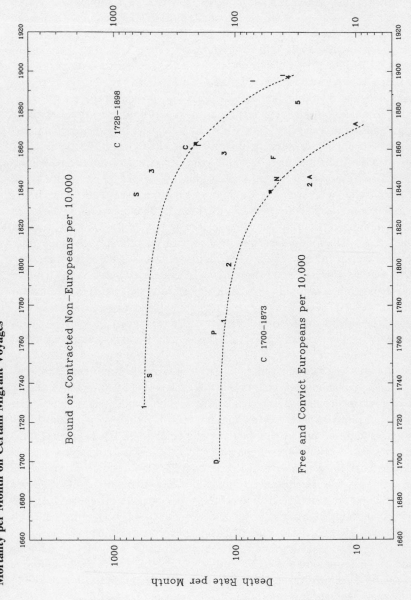

Sources: Shlomovitz 1997, 145; Klein et al. 2001, 112.

A = Australian; C = Chinese; D = Dutch; F = South Africa; I = Indian; N = New York; P = Philadelphia; S = Slaves; 1 = North American Convicts; 2 = Australian Convicts; 3 = Contracted Africans; 4 = Pacific Is. to Fiji; 5 = Pacific Is. to Queensland.

proportion of the elderly in the populations of England, France, and Sweden (Figures 6.13b, 6.14, and 6.15), on the one hand, and the United States (Figure 6.19b), on the other, nonetheless join the evidence of Figures 6.26 and 6.27 from 20th-century Pacific Island populations and the transport of various labor groups to suggest that lessening mortality in C (1/E) form is a likely international phenomenon, a possibility whose causes and consequences the third volume of this study probes systematically.

In general, however, until better direct measurements can be obtained, the trendable evidence from death rates up until about 1900 implies principally D and G (1/D) patterns for changes in the age and sex of world-ranging populations of modern indentured workers. In these respects they join what has been learned about free immigrants of all recorded eras in all parts of the world and the slaves, convicts, and bound servants of previous colonial centuries.

It is possible, finally, to obtain some insight into the relevance of G-based forms of change in demographic structure for current movements of population on a global scale. Figure 6.28 draws upon UN- and *Population Studies*–based material provided at a presentation by the late George Stolnitz (to the Population Institute for Research and Training, Indiana University-Bloomington, October 1992).

The left panel shows how the proportion of people under 15 has apparently been declining in C form within global population as a whole, in developed countries (without Russia), and in newly developing countries as well. This is a phenomenon already observed historically, sometimes more than once, in several different national populations. In recent examples, for instance, C trends for Sweden between 1950 and 1989 and starting in New Zealand between 1945 and 1961 (Figures 6.14 and 6.9a) follow timing resembling that for all developed countries between 1950 and 2000 in Figure 6.28. In earlier-developed nations, the proportion under 15 came down noticeably sooner, reaching about 20 percent by 2000 and then declining appreciably more slowly in projections from there to 2025. In more recently developing countries, meanwhile, though the t_0 for the C curve also sits at about 15 percent, it arrives appreciably later—at 2047 rather than 2029. Declining youthfulness has seemingly been taking comparable form and toward a similar level. It is just unfolding later.

On a global scale, proportions of the elderly (those 60 and over) are rising in paths of E shape, as the middle panel of Figure 6.28 indicates. In this second structural change, toward the upper end of the age pyramid, the populations of the world, of developed countries, and of newly developing ones all have been aging via E trends with very *parallel* timing, without noticeable lag according to economic history. The difference here is in the *level*. At its zero year, the curve for newly developing nations attains just 13.7 percent in Figure 6.28 compared with 36.6 percent, almost three times as much, in previously developed countries. Among those 60 or more, meanwhile, since 1975 the percentage who are 75 and over has also been rising in very parallel fashion for countries with older and more recent histories of development. Again, the *level* for the

Figure 6.28
Some Recent Global Trends in Age Structure

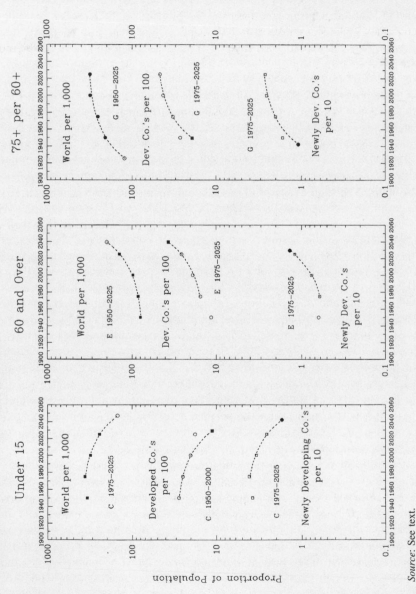

Source: See text.

former is markedly higher that that for the latter—19.0 at t_0 as opposed to 10.9 percent. For the old within the elderly, however, the shape of the trend is G rather than the E for all persons 60 or more. The changes progressively slow down because there is, after all, some limit on the human life span.

On the whole, though these proposed curves are based upon observations that are few and far between, the indication is that structural change in populations continues globally to take G-based shapes. More than just historical insight emerges from noting the presence of G and its related curves in demographic developments.

Following up and building upon insights from the slave trades and the development of African American populations in Chapter 5, evidence from many other kinds of migrations expands and strengthens a sense of how change in several different dimensions of demographic structure has historically taken G-related forms over and over again. Such patterns have notably prevailed both in colonial or other settler societies and in the flows of people that so significantly fed them. The same types of G-based trend, moreover, have also characterized changes in the composition of populations far less sensitive to the impact of migration—such as the European gold mines for historical demographers represented by England, France, and Sweden. These movements appear to apply also to global changes of the present and near future. The study of migrations, in short, unveils very general ways in which demographic structures alter. The set of processes that is revealed includes the consequences of migration but is not at all limited to the circumstances of migration.

To begin with a summary of what has been found with the makeup of migrations themselves, the sex and age of those relocating have repeatedly altered via G and D trends, though sometimes the typical G' movement of migration *numbers* has left upon the demographic composition of flows its up-and-down imprint, especially in economic circumstances craving an infusion of men. Evidence comes from the American colonies of Spain in the 1500s, settlements controlled by England in the 1600s and 1700s (the Chesapeake, the Caribbean, the Delaware Valley), Australia and South Africa, contract labor leaving India for the Caribbean, flows from several nations to that most notorious 19th- and early-20th-century "consumer" of the unsatisfied, the United States, and total *emigration* to all destinations from these same countries. Findings about the composition of special sub-populations such as convicts (North American as well as Australian), bound servants of the colonial era, 19th-century Indian and Oceanic indentured laborers, and those signing on with the Dutch East India Company in the 1600s and 1700s to seek their fortunes in Asia join Chapter 5's evidence for slaves in demonstrating how widely the fundamental patterns of change through time—in ethnic makeup and legal status along with sex and age—permeated quite different groups of movers.

A special insight comes from the way that Spanish migrants to America across the 1500s increasingly brought families with them and had connections with

those already established in the New World. Information and support from previous settlers—links considered to be so vital in the development of migration
flows—also evolved, it is suggested, in G-based patterns.

After providing virtually everybody at the start of settlement, the weight of
current and former migrants in receiving *populations*—as in the slave peoples
of Chapter 5—inevitably declined. It did this repeatedly in D form, like the rate
of slave imports relative to current slave populations in Chapter 5. This is shown
by evidence from New Zealand and Australia in the 19th century, South Africa
in the 18th, and the Chesapeake earlier still (Harris 1992, 62). Within longer-
settled societies, too, after a surge of arrivals the proportion of the population
that was composed of immigrants typically waned repeatedly in D fashion. Examples come from the Netherlands for three eras between 1645 and 1879, rural
Liaoning County in China's province of Manchuria between 1774 and 1873,
and the United States after the 1920s. In these same well-established populations
and in others such as industrializing Germany and Russia during the 19th century, when the significance of migration increased historically it took G or,
exceptionally, G' shape.

The counterpart of having migrants dwindle in importance in D trends—both
as current arrivals and as an accumulated element within the receiving population—was to have the weight of the native-born rise via G. Such trends appear
for French Canada and the British Chesapeake in the 1600s and 1700s, for early
Australia, New Zealand in the 1800s and first half of the 1900s, and for the
United States between 1870 and 1970. Meanwhile, across the period 1900–1950
percentages of first- and later-generation native-born persons rose in G fashion
among 19 of 24 migrant populations residing in the United States who had come
from various countries, as had been the case for British settlers in colonial
Maryland between the 1650s and the 1770s. Maryland data also illustrate particular consequences of having more and more native-born: chances for men to
marry, the naming of first sons after grandfathers rather than fathers, and marriage with blood relatives all increased proportionally in G fashion. Lest it be
thought that such adjustments applied only to New World settlements, it can be
seen that in rural Liaoning Province of China a period of declining immigration
between the 1770s and the 1870s saw extended family members constitute a
rising percentage of household residents along a G path, and G trends appear
for the proportion of men who could marry (bracketing an abrupt shift the other
way in the first decade of the 1800s). A special feature of the early Canadian
evidence is how with further immigration over the centuries the proportional
"genetic contribution" of the first wave of "pioneer" settlers of what is now
Quebec Province atrophied all the way from 1679 to 1949 via a single D curve
(i.e., the significance of those with other, later origins rose via G).

Similarly, the composition of *populations* as well as migrant groups has repeatedly altered in G-based trends. G and D patterns predominate, accompanied
by some exceptions from other G-related curves.

As found over and over again for the proportion of populations composed by slaves in Chapter 5, the ethnic or racial makeup of peoples historically has altered repeatedly via G and D trends. Shifts in the presence of Maori, Chinese, and other non-Europeans within the population of New Zealand between the 1850s and the 1970s have provided modern examples of such trends. Movements in the weights of Indian, Spanish, black, mestizo, and mulatto couples in marriages in Guatemala between 1595 and 1765 offer earlier illustrations, including a few less familiar C and E patterns. Exogamous unions as a proportion of all marriages, meanwhile, have been observed to rise via G then fall via C in New Mexico between 1715 and 1810 and, if the presence of unbaptized children implies out-marriage, in the St. Lawrence settlements of Canada between 1647 and 1717.

G-based trends for sex composition and age structure likewise emerge ubiquitously in data from colonial populations of the early modern era: all along the Atlantic littoral southward from Newfoundland and through the Caribbean to Trinidad and Surinam; in New Zealand, early Australia, and 18th-century South Africa; and among U.S. state populations as settlement spread westward. Typically, the proportion of females in the population increased via G until somewhat over 50 percent was achieved.[38] After also rising in G fashion, however, the share of the young then frequently contracted somewhat via D. In certain cases, it seems, the population simply aged, perhaps as the mortality of settlers declined and their life expectancy improved; in other situations, special circumstances—such as a shift to slavery that discouraged white family formation—could play a significant part. On the mainland of North America, U.S. states that attracted strong family settlement in the very first stages of their history could see their proportion of young and the share of females go up and down in G' form before settling into typical G-type increase.

Here and there, however, the less usual C pattern began to emerge. Barbados and perhaps St. Christopher provide rare colonial examples in which the percentage of the young in the non-slave population atrophied in this accelerating way. By the early 1800s, however, several older-settled U.S. states saw the percentage under 15 years of age in their populations atrophy similarly. In the late 19th and early 20th centuries, C had become the most common trend for the percentage of the young in the 50 scattered regions of America. For the whole United States, those under 15 among whites and among blacks and among the foreign-born, those with one or more foreign-born parents, and those with only native parents all became less significant in C fashion across the late 1800s and early 1900s. Repeated downward C movements likewise characterized the percentage of the young in New Zealand between the 1870s and the 1960s.

Data from rural Manchuria, furthermore, raise the prospect that the young shrank and expanded proportionally in C and G forms also in societies very different from New World settlements. Indeed, the much-analyzed demographic histories of England, France, and Sweden turn out to be replete with G-based trends in age structure. Modern C patterns for the young in these populations (along with New Zealand and the United States) bring to mind the type of general decline in birth rates that permeates discussions of modern "demographic transition." Yet the C shape, while characteristic of the impact of French fertility behavior upon the national age structure from the 1740s right through to World War II, also appears for a time in England as early as the 1500s and in Sweden between 1750 and 1800, as well as in several American states by 1790. It is neither initially French nor strictly modern.

Increases in the weight of the old in populations, meanwhile, have in Europe as in America (recently quite globally) at times taken the accelerating E shape. Still, under other conditions—from China's Liaoning Province 1810–1860 to England 1841–1871, Sweden 1960 to 1989, and black, white, foreign and native components of the United States population between 1870 and 1970—the G pattern of increase for the weight of the elderly has been evident. Like the very uncommon E-type pattern of increase for the percentage of children and youths in England between the 1740s and 1840s, or infrequent G' or 1/G' movements for age groups that are found here and there, the exceptional trends seem in their own way to throw light upon what was happening within certain societies at particular times: for instance, an accelerating youthfulness for the population of England as the country moved into industrialization.

Increase or decline in the role of the young in a population obviously reflects the recent birth rate and in turn influences the current or future one. Comparably, to have relatively more elderly persons in a population can be linked with changing rates of death as well as expansion and contraction among other age groups. Thus, the universally G-connected trends in age structure found here, along with those for slave populations identified in Chapter 5, strongly suggest that birth and death rates will be found also regularly to have followed G-based paths historically. Evidence from 18th-century Newfoundland in Figure 6.2 and from several 19th- and early-20th-century populations of indentured laborers from India and various Pacific Islands in Figure 6.26 add to examples from African slave groups (Cuban blacks 1774–1897 in Figure 5.8b; several national slave trades between the 1640s and the 1840s in Figure 5.11; Bahian slaves 1663–1873 in Figure 5.13d) in illustrating how this may be the case. To ascertain whether G-based patterns in vital rates have been the norm or not all across the international demographic record is the first task of the volume that follows this one. The second is to determine from where the distinctive curvature of G comes. Since Euler's work of 1760, rediscovered in the early 1900s, it has been known that birth and death rates interact constantly with age structure. But what element of this fundamental interaction so repeatedly produces the G shape and its related curves for so many types of demographic change and apparently much social and economic development as well?

NOTES

1. On Barbados, 17th-century percentages for females of all ages among whites (the hollow triangles) seem to splice smoothly with later weights for just women among adults (Wells 1975, 242—the hollow circles).

2. A D-type decline in the percentage of *men* in the total white population of Barbados from 1673 through 1712 that Gemery calculates (1980, 221) appears to have its base year at 1658, making this appropriately inverse trend closer in timing to changes on Antigua and Montserrat than the percentage of just women among adults in Table 6.1. For Virginia, Gemery's comparable calculations for men at 1616, 1625, and 1665 imply a D trend with t_0 near 1618, very much like what is indicated for the winter population of Newfoundland (or St. Christopher, New York, and perhaps Bermuda), while the weights at 1665 and 1715 then would fit a D trend with base year near 1652 as if by the later 1600s the normalization of the white population in Virginia shifted, as settlement in this mainland colony continued to expand in the later 17th century, to parallel the later (steeper) G trends of Barbados, Antigua, and Montserrat. Unfortunately, very little evidence exists for Jamaica. It can be said that the proportion of women among white adults there rose rapidly from 1661 through 1673, though it had reached only 33 percent by the latter date in contrast to about 40 percent on Barbados. In South Carolina (Menard 1989, Table 5), women at 1703 and 1708 composed 40 percent of white adults, about 10 percent less than at this time on Barbados, whence many settlers came.

3. In Jamaica a calculation of just 19.5 percent at 1730 is very low by comparison, especially since the portion reached 17.7 percent already by 1673 (Wells 1975, 200). In South Carolina, as of 1708 some 42 percent of the white population was under 16, up from 32 percent at 1703 (Menard 1989, Table 5). In Surinam, only children under 12 are known (Postma 1990, 185).

4. Dr. Lorena Walsh has kindly reminded the author, who should not have forgotten, of this aspect of her early research.

5. To complicate the picture still further, servants going to the Chesapeake according to Galenson (1981, 220–27) became proportionately less female between 1656 and 1672 (contrary to Menard) and then proportionately more female from 1672 through 1703 (parallel to Menard and contrary to Eltis). Part of the difference may arise from the fact that for significant periods of time Menard incorporated information on sex from head-rights in both Maryland and Virginia. These were claimed on behalf of free men and their families, not just servants. The "Coldham" data of Eltis record only 33 free migrants to the Chesapeake between 1650 and 1700, an implausibly low number. In a sample of Maryland headrights from 1634 through 1681, for example, Menard (1988, 120) identifies free immigrants as about 30 percent of the total, not the 0.3 percent in the "Coldham" data set employed by Eltis. On the whole, the Menard-Horn trending would seem preferable for all Europeans until positively proven otherwise.

6. For these calculations only passengers on vessels at least whose number of "freights" were known are employed. Beyond ships for which counts of women and children were actually specified, a quite regular ratio of children to women across the years in fully specifying passenger lists allows one to work reliably across time from known "freights" and known men to a passenger total and therefore a proportion for men on board, an insight that has not been recognized by other scholars citing the sources, who do not realize from their reading how the changing proportion could be, and was, worked out by Wokeck.

7. The hollow, downward triangle indicates that a briefly high mulatto proportion for the 1680s is not included in the latter curve-fitting.

8. The low percentage for 1665 is not included in the fit.

9. If, to the contrary, there were instead a significant number of females among the unknowns, did that proportion alter in a way that would affect the shape of trend proposed—or would it just raise the level? The time periods are 1608–1639, 1640–1659,

and 1660–1679. Females subsequently became a tiny portion of a dwindling 1680–1699 immigrant influx that was dominated by military personnel. The date of 1635 is employed for the first year group (rather than its midpoint) because finer data for what the research group calls the "pioneer" immigrants (Charbonneau et al. 1987, 19) show that 75 percent of those who came before 1640 arrived just from 1635 through 1639.

10. From the probate files of the St. Mary's City Commission.

11. Wokeck in several publications.

12. The curve for whites only from 1864 through 1921 is rather later and steeper than that for the Maori. Data for both together since 1926 project backward in a manner that splits the difference in timing.

13. Butlin's recent estimations commence from a higher level at 1790 and attain a somewhat smaller size by 1850 than what I culled some time ago from Knibbs (1915, 116) and Cameron (1982, 90). Those earlier calculations rose from about 2,000 to 400,000 (Harris 2001, 80–83). His data, nevertheless, generate three comparably timed G trends for 1790–1815, 1815–1830, and 1830–1850 (vs. my previous 1790–1815, 1810–1830, and 1830–1911 fittings).

14. I was introduced to Butlin's analysis through the privilege of reading a version in progress of a paper by Colin Forster (Eltis 2002, 259–91).

15. Though, as shown, a G' alternative might fit the rising percentage of former free immigrants from 1820 through 1850. Later data should readily determine the better model for those who study early Australia.

16. It is possible, however, that two G' trends more accurately capture the changes that this G trend generally represents.

17. Figures 6.7b, 6.8b, 6.9b, and 6.10 for free persons and voluntary servants, sometimes stated as percentage of native-born; and Figures 5.3, 5.4, 5.5, 5.6b, 5.6c, 5.6d, and 5.14, usually perceived as slave imports per current non-white population.

18. Lucassen 1987, 158. To fit the curve, the implications of his two maximum and minimum sets of estimates for 1650 are averaged (correcting the misprinted 4.2 percent of the "b" version to its true 20.4 value).

19. For an analysis of that event see Chapter 1 of the third volume of this study, which examines the birth and death rates estimated for England since the 1540s. As indicated by the different, triangular symbol, this extreme data point is not employed in fitting the 1541–1661 trend for the 0 through 4 population in the figure.

20. Both legal and illegal departures are counted for this analysis. At much lower rates, the immigration and emigration of women—legal and illegal—also tended to sag concavely before spiking up in the 1860s (Lee and Campbell 1997, 40).

21. For loss of population in several provinces, see Harris 2001, 258–61 and surrounding text. Substantial demographic contraction between 1812 and 1819 in Hebei, the province of Beijing, might signal migration into neighboring Liaoning of men who could not find mates; or perhaps the two contiguous northeastern provinces shared some demographic disaster at this time.

22. For instance, concerning migrants from the Americas in Figure 1.7.

23. That is all that Hutchinson gives for people of this origin (1956, 14).

24. It was a stronger reproduction by recent immigrants relative to those of more familiar northern and western European origin that especially traumatized prejudiced commentators in the late 1800s and early 1900s.

25. Graphed and discussed in the first chapter of Volume III of this study.

26. Trends offered for Massachusetts, Pennsylvania, Georgia, Wisconsin, and Arizona

were fitted for Figure 6.20. Others are approximated visually by template, just the first step in the usual process of fitting.

27. Texas is not reported for 1840; Oklahoma not until 1900. In South Carolina, the upward shift amounted to as much as 29 percent (from just 20 to 49). In Virginia, Mississippi, and Florida the increase was 23 percent. Georgia, Alabama, and Louisiana saw changes of 17 to 19 percent; North Carolina and Maryland 13 to 15 percent; Kentucky, Delaware, the District of Columbia, Tennessee, and Arkansas 8 to 10 percent; and Missouri 5 percent. Such was the effect of the difference in age structure between white and black parts of the population as the consequence of poorer life expectancy and perhaps some differences in fertility.

28. For adults, British estimates come from Erickson 1989, 360–61. English and Welsh are combined with Scots according to their number. The Irish calculations represented by hollow squares from 1804 through 1848 come from Cormac Ó Gráda (1986, 83). They draw upon data for several entry ports, while the hollow triangles are based upon New York alone (ibid., 88). The squares for 1858 and 1863 are from Ferenczi and Willcox, whose percentage of females drops off somewhat further than that of Ó Gráda as one looks backward before the 1840s. I use his more recent analysis.

29. Ferenczi and Willcox 1929, 354. For Germany, those under 10 for 1873–1883 have been divided by .714 in order to splice with those under 14 thereafter.

30. With adjustment of 1873–1883 for a narrower age group covered.

31. An apparent major shift in record-keeping at 1904 requires locally expert analysis to determine any Italian trend thereafter.

32. For simplicity of calculation, every fifth year from 1824 through 1854 is taken from his graphs.

33. Rough estimates for the regions are made here by averaging the rates for component provinces without regard to variations in number from province to province.

34. The provinces of Iaroslavl, Moscow, Vladimir, Kostroma, Kaluga, Nizhni Novgorod, Tula, and Riazin, on the one hand; and Arkhangel, Vologda, Olonets, St. Petersburg, Novgorod, Pskov, Smolensk, and Tver, on the other.

35. The provinces of Astrakhan, Saratov, Samara, Penza, Simbirsk, Kazan, Viatka, and Ufa and of Perm and Orenburg, respectively. Very low proportions for the 1860s (represented by hollow triangles in the figure) are not trended. Apparently migration was notably slow in starting in these regions.

36. Though the Jamaican evidence behaves differently.

37. Contracted African workers ("3") in three early years of their flow (1848–1850) were apparently affected by the elevated voyage mortality that was characteristic of the waning, increasingly illegal, and subvertive years of the Atlantic slave trade of the mid-19th century (Figure 5.11 in Chapter 5). Their death rate, however, quickly came into line with the trend for other non-European indentured workers. Indians leaving Madras between 1855 and 1866 suffered a death rate of 5.6 (not graphed), which is rather low relative to the underlying curve.

38. Though some pullback via D appeared here and there.

Summary and Implications

In the preceding volume of this study (Harris 2001), it was demonstrated how historically recorded human populations have increased or declined according to six closely related patterns. The most common, the G curve of constantly proportionally decelerating growth at the .03 rate, captures how populations usually expand to exploit some opportunity in their environment. This form of increase has been found to be virtually universal in small and local populations of all eras and for recorded regional or national populations before the 1500s as well.

Beginning in the 16th century three alternative but simply and closely G-related forms of demographic expansion began to appear here and there, each apparently in a typical historical context of its own. The log-linear F slope at the .03 exponential rate, discovered by Benjamin Franklin 250 years ago as doubling about every 23 years, is pretty much just what he said it was: the way that populations increase if there is some open end of resources for them. The F formula is nothing but the .03 exponential slope for G at its base year, extended backward and forward without deceleration. It shows up, beginning in the Americas in the 1600s, where there have been uncramped geographical frontiers of settlement or, in the 20th century, rolling peripheries of global economic systems.

In the H pattern, rather than being totally removed, the brake pressure that makes G decelerate is lightened—in effect roughly halved (more precisely, $1/e$ or $1/2.718$). This way populations, though their growth does slow down, sustain more robust increase longer. For that they must have lasting expansion in their resources. The H pattern of demographic growth has thus occurred in historical contexts of economic development. Evidence of this shape of trend begins in northwestern Europe in the 16th century. It spreads thereafter to much of the rest of the continent for some period or another before World War II and appears in a few leading European colonies of the Americas in the 18th century (but also in China). The form is clear in the United States (after the frontier was no longer so open), Mexico, Brazil, Argentina, and Chile in the 19th century (but also Dutch colonial Java). In the 20th century, the countries of Europe were no longer able to support such growth, but it appeared in many societies of Asia, including places like India where threatening population explosion was at last being slowed.

That third alternative to G-shape demographic increase, the E curve with accelerating rather than decelerating pace of expansion, is nothing but G^I (G inverse) or G reversed with respect to time and simultaneously turned upside down. There has been a tendency to think of such population explosion as a Third World phenomenon of the 20th century. It has indeed been common in that kind of historical context; but its roots go much further back. The population of England enlarged this way from the 1720s into the early 1800s, followed by a whole geographically spreading procession of European societies and regions—and also Japan—that show demographic increase of the E shape for some period or another between there and World War II. To last for any length of time, accelerating demographic increase must enjoy resources, not just impose hardship (though the latter has so evidently appeared). Historically, activities hungry for large quantities of cheap and pliable labor such as the early stage of factory development two centuries ago or more recently the global migration of textiles and other manufacturing, from toys to technology, seem to thrive with E-type demographic increase. Given insufficient economic opportunity, so of course does political unrest.

Populations have also declined. The demographic consequences of shocks like the intercontinental plague pandemic of the 14th century, the European invasion of the Americas (and then the southern Pacific), China's periodic monumental disasters across so much national history, and the famous 19th-century Irish famine have been absorbed in trends of D shape, first dropping fast but progressively levelling out. The D curve is nothing but G stood on its head. Demographic atrophy for less dramatic or massive causes also has repeatedly taken the decelerating shape of D but has followed flatter segments of the curve. D has in fact been more universally the shape of population loss than G, with its three alternatives, which has predominated among historically documented cases of demographic increase.

There is evident, however, one other form of sustained demographic decline. In this, atrophy often begins almost imperceptibly; but it picks up speed continually. This C curve is simply E upside down, accelerating contraction rather than ever faster expansion. The form is just G reversed according to time. Human populations (i.e., those that have left histories) show few instances of C-shape atrophy. It has occurred here and there, however, usually in societies losing their niche, such as failed, would-be sugar islands of the 18th-century West Indies or certain rural departments of France as that country "faced depopulation" in the late 19th and early 20th centuries.

SHARED PATTERNS IN FREE, FORCED, AND URBAN MIGRATIONS

What the present volume has done is to ask what can be learned about how these forms of demographic change occur by probing the histories of various forms of migration, one of the dynamics through which populations swell or shrink. In turn, what then can be better understood about migration itself from identifying movements of the same few G-related shapes that are involved in it? Various types of migration in the historical record have been examined: a wide range of intercontinental and interregional flows of free or partially free persons, the much-discussed, centuries-long Atlantic slave trade, and—the largest global movement of all—relocation to cities or urbanization.

To begin, it has been seen that all sorts of specific migrations have built up and tapered off in the shape of G', the first derivative of the G curve. This has been true of the great transoceanic relocations of 19th and early 20 centuries. For example, the number of Irish *coming* to America rose and fell this way from 1815 through 1927; and so, only in rather later patterns of G' shape, did all emigration *leaving* Norway 1847–1927 and Russia 1877–1912, total immigration to Brazil 1842–1962, and relocations to Australia and New Zealand for several decades after the 1930s. In previous historical eras, European flows to settle in America likewise took trends of G' form, from the time of first colonization forward. The pattern characterized Spanish migration in the 1500s, French and British in the 1600s (to the West Indies as well as to the North American mainland), and various flows of English, Southern Irish, Northern Irish, and German peoples to the area that became the United States—and to particular colonies within it.

Meanwhile, the number of persons leaving southwestern Germany—some of whom came west to America but even more of whom went east to Prussia, Austria, Hungary, and Russia—built up and then began to recede in G' fashion between 1700 and 1800. Subsequently, within the 19th-century United States flows of free settlers into the Old Northwest and of slaves with their masters into the New South between 1790 and 1860 as the Mississippi River watershed opened up both took G' shape, as did movements of people into the West North Central, Mountain, and Pacific regions across the *second* half of the 19th century. In other words, interregional as well as international migration typically took this form.

So did movements of those not always free to determine where they went. The annual number of bound servants delivered to the Chesapeake and to the British and French West Indies in the 17th century and the number of convicts arriving in colonial America or, later, shipped to New South Wales and Van

Diemen's Land rose and fell through time in G' manner. So, thereafter, did the transportation of a new torrent of indentured workers—mostly from India but also from Africa, China, and Polynesia—who, during the later 19th century and the early 20th, replaced now forbidden slaves and unwanted prisoners in the British and Dutch Caribbean, the Mascarenes and French Polynesia, Queensland, Fiji, and British Africa.

The most unfree migrants of all, of course, were African slaves. Their collection, transport, and disposal were even more of a business—and a far bigger business—than trades in free passengers, bound servants and redemptioners, and convicts. In such an environment of hard-nosed, often brutal concern for profit and cost, was there any way that demographically shaped trends such as those of the small G-based set of curves could be relevant?

Indeed there were. Below the aggregate level of the Atlantic slave trade as a whole, national branches of it that bought cargoes in several places along the African coast and delivered them to more than one region of consumption, or large mixed zones of supply or purchase such as West Central Africa or Brazil (whose participation expanded in accumulative G or H forms instead), the lop-sided up-and-down G' pattern was as ubiquitous in specific parts of the slave trade from the middle 1400s to the middle 1800s as it has been among particular flows of freer migration.

As African slavery was introduced into Europe, the Atlantic Islands, São Tomé, and various parts of the New World, on beachhead after beachhead starting in the 15th century, where the early pattern of local imports can be identified, it takes G' shape. In the 17th century the form appears in Dutch deliveries to their temporary toehold in Brazil and their islands that supplied mainland Spanish America, legally or illegally. Later shipments to particular areas of the Guiana coast that they colonized followed similar patterns. British sales to Barbados, Jamaica, the Leewards, and North American settlements likewise surged from the middle 1600s to 1800 or so repeatedly in G' shape as new markets were opened or familiar ones displayed heightened demand. French Caribbean colonies, even slave-hungry St. Domingue, consumed Africans over and over according to the G' pattern. And when parts of Brazil can be separated out from the whole, for the 1720s through the 1840s, furthermore, imports to Pernambuco, Bahia, and Rio de Janeiro all swelled and contracted in G' fashion.

If one looks at the acquisition of slaves in Africa, meanwhile, the first recorded exports from each area (except perhaps the uncertainly defined Windward Coast) all take the G' shape. Later phases of supply from Senegambia, Sierra Leone, and the Windward and Gold Coasts—not the largest sources—again crest in G' form. When one breaks down the huge area of West Central Africa into its leading zones of slave-loading, furthermore, exports from Loango or the North Coast, Luanda in the center, and Benguela to the south all rise and fall from era to era in G' manner. Within the much-bled Bight of Benin, meanwhile, from the 1650s into the 1860s the trades of Portuguese-Brazilian, Dutch, English, French, American, and Spanish vessels that competed to tap the black human riches of what was sometimes called the Slave Coast, the drain of specific regional peoples—Aja, various Voltaic groups, Hausa, Nupe, and Yoruba—to meet such demand, and the role of particular loading points such as Whydah, Bonny, Calabar, East Benin, and Southeast Biafra all took G' shape as specific sources of supply spurted and then fell back during successive phases of regional development that pushed the acquisition of slaves into new catchment areas.

Once the Atlantic slave trade was firmly under way, national groups of slavers as an aggregate drew their cargoes from several loading points and disposed of them in more than one New World area of consumption. In these circumstances the trends of expansion and contraction are G and D rather than G'. But if one looks at Dutch, British, French, and Portuguese-Brazilian aquisitions and sales place by place, the G' pattern pervades. It also shows up in how the slaving business of particular ports came and went. For the Dutch, the rise and fall of the West India Company monopoly from the 1630s through the 1730s and the traffic of free traders that displaced it both take G' form. For the French, two phases of jockeying between Nantes and her competitors produce two pairs of G' trends, one before and one after about 1770. In the British trade, not only the participation of the Royal African Company from the 1670s into the 1720s but the activity of merchants and captains based upon London, Bristol, and Liverpool across the 18th century are seen to have surged and ebbed in G' fashion. The slave trade, every bit as much as freer migration that has been historically documented, was a river fed by local streams of G' shape and emptied out through a New World estuary of many G' channels.

Over the past few centuries, however, far more people have moved to cities than even the millions who were forcibly transported by the slave trade or undertook freer forms of transoceanic relocation. While there is less evidence— and often less clear evidence—for individual cities, it seems that in this kind of migration, too, G' trends characterize the basic, lower-level building blocks out of which more general urbanizatlon has developed.

For example, 16th-century migrations to Amsterdam, Norwich, and London appear to have mounted in waves of G' shape. So did two surges of relocation to Nottingham between 1700 and 1800. Less definitive evidence suggests in-migration of the same shape for Barmen and Düsseldorf in Germany's booming 19th-century Rhineland—and perhaps also contemporary Berlin. The up-and-down presence of several minority groups in the population of Batavia on Java during the 18th century, meanwhile, indicates that they, too, had arrived in G' surges; and a succession of G' pulses from various European countries descended upon U.S. cities from the 1830s through the 1910s, as the immigration findings of Chapter 1—though indirect—almost surely imply.

At the local or bottom level—as opposed to broader and more diverse inter-national flows of migrants coming from several sources or going to several destinations, branches of the slave trade that loaded and delivered at more than one place, or patterns of urbanization resulting from movement to a group of cities rather than a single center—all kinds of migrations, forced and free, seem to have typically surged then tapered off in the G' form. (The conglomerate flows typically swelled and shrank via G and D instead.) This virtually universal G' patterning means that specific migrations very generally behave like additives that will accumulate in G shape, which is, Volume I has shown, the basic and most common form of historical population increase.

To date, the flow and ebb of migration has been mostly addressed in the literature in economic terms: poor conditions push people out, and better opportunities pull them in. Clearly such considerations are involved in the motivations that must be present to make people desire, at least accept, strange new neighbors or give up the familiar, travel to sometimes very distant new homes, and gamble their fortunes upon the largely unknown—though obviously other stimuli are also involved (such as religious tension, political oppression, or a specific practice like conscription). But those who would like to think that economics governs how the numbers who relocate change through time must explain how migrations of so many types over and over again take just the one G' form. What dynamics of an economic sort could be so general across so many and such diverse historical settings as are covered in this study? What, for instance, would apply equally to free and semi-free migration, the slave trade, and movement to cities as illustrated in Chapters 1, 2, and 3—in each context from pre-modern times to the present? The necessary general economic proof for that line of interpretation appears unattainable. The analysis of the *shape* of migrations through time (once *any* kind of stimulus sets them off) seems to have been on the wrong track. Instead, the determinative mechanism was demographic.

HOW THE COMPOSITIONS OF POPULATIONS HAVE ALTERED

While it is striking that ground-level migration so consistently takes the G' shape, the derivative of the G curve, the overwhelmingly general form for growth in local populations (Harris 2001, 382), which way does that relationship work? Though contributing migrations arriving in G' form will help a receiving population keep accumulating according to the integral of G' or G, what makes migrations so generally follow G' trends in the first place? Perhaps the emphasis in how the two widespread phenomena interact should be put the other way around.

Migration, whether one stresses "push" or "pull," begins with the impression (true or not) that opportunity at some other place is sufficiently better than where one is at present to justify the costs and risks of relocating (for the merchant providing transportation or the slaver, that the demand will be great enough to generate profits that will make being in the business worthwhile). How might these perceived opportunities collectively first expand to draw more and more people into the flow, then contract as the promise of the process fades—both via the G' curve?

The first insight has come from the way that certain simple changes in the *composition* of populations receiving migrants have unfolded. The proportion of those with African forebears in societies that adopted slavery quite universally increased in G trends as slavery took hold, from Maryland southward through the West Indies to French Guiana, and also on Mauritius in the Indian Ocean. The proportion of considerably freer immigrant groups within populations could also increase this way, as locally among apprentices in Norwich from the 1540s through the 1590s or, on a broader stage, the role of foreigners in recruitment to the Dutch East India Company in the 18th century or the percentage of people within the total population of Germany who in one way or another relocated during the period 1824–1910. Contemporaneously, in the United States from the 1870s into the 1920s the percentage of whites who were foreign-born or who had a foreign-born parent swelled in a G pattern. Looking, in contrast, at a population that *provided* migrants, the proportion of Russian peasants who were issued passports to allow them to relocate within the tsar's domains between Emancipation and World War I typically swelled via G trends in regions from Belorussia to the North Caucasus.

Changes in the *ethnic* composition of populations have also repeatedly followed G form. This was the case as between the 1750s and the 1840s a larger and larger proportion of the residents of New Mexico and the El Paso District claimed "Spanish" roots and, conversely, between the 1660s and the 1760s as the proportions of mulattos, mestizos, and Indians expanded among marriages in Santiago de Guatemala at the expense of unions for Spaniards and blacks. The proportional recovery of the Maori within the population of New Zealand also advanced via successive G paths starting in the 1920s. In such a fashion, too, local Javanese and Balinese began to multiply within the population of Batavia after about 1700 at the expense of the many and diverse external groups that had peopled this administrative and commercial center of Dutch colonization.

For understanding the dynamics of how G and G-based trends keep appearing, however, the next step was the most important one. This involved determining the way that migrant groups shrank within and naturalized into the populations that they entered: not the trip toward greater significance but the return journey.

Some of the clearest insight comes from the history of the slave trade. Here, in colony after colony from the Chesapeake south to Surinam, the rate for the continuing importation of Africans relative to the existing slave population began to fall in D shape. It did so as estimated net natural replacement in the local African American population improved, whether this meant a G trend of natural increase, as in the Chesapeake and South Carolina, or a D-shape *reduction* in the level of net natural *decrease* as in the sugar colonies of the West Indies. Whatever the level, as the local slave population became better at replacing itself, new Africans were less and less important.

Turning to how other kinds of migrants have nativized, among virtually all the familiar ethnic groups migrating to the United States during modern times, across the first half of the 20th century the proportion of the native-born in that particular foreign "stock" increased in G fashion. In an earlier era, the percentage of French Canadians in the settlements of the St. Lawrence who were native-born rose along a G path 1670–1720, while the genetic role of the "pioneer" settlers of the 17th century for this population declined in a closely reciprocal D trend that was to last all the way into the 1900s. The native-born likewise increased in G patterns among probated decedents in various Maryland counties between the 1660s and the 1770s, while in Prince George's County the proportion of marriages taking place between blood relatives also climbed in a G manner, along with the percentage of first sons named after their grandfathers, another indicator of increasing strength in family connections (and of improving longevity).

In a later era, from the 1870s through the 1940s, the proportion of New Zealand's people who were native-born also swelled along a G path, illustrating how a society of immigrants in another place and another time "naturalized" (one might say "took over") in its new home. The European population of Australia across its early years 1790–1850 similarly, right through successive waves of convict arrivals, generally became native in G fashion (as, also via G, all these intruders became a higher percentage of the *total* population of the continent at the expense of its former residents). Previously, in another settler society of the Southern Hemisphere, across the first several decades of the 1700s the rate at which immigrants married into the "white" population of Dutch South Africa contracted in D shape. In homeland contexts, meanwhile, the role of foreigners in Amsterdam marriages apparently repeatedly declined in D fashion between the 1640s and the 1790s, as the size of the city stagnated. More generally, the proportions of "newcomers" in the Netherlands as a whole in the later 1800s and likewise migrants within the German population between 1910 and 1988 both also atrophied via D trends. Far away in Asia, meanwhile, in rural Liaoning Province the weight of both immigrants and emigrants fell in D form between the 1770s and the middle of the 1800s in a cluster of local populations as new opportunity in Manchuria was used up more and more by resident families. Meanwhile, chances to marry and the weight of extended family in households in this part of northeastern China moved in G and G-based patterns that are reminiscent of the rise of "patriarchy" proposed for Prince George's County, Maryland, across the century before.

All these peoples, free or enslaved, became more native and less migrant because they began to *reproduce*. More women and children appeared in settler or slave or urban populations that originally were biased toward men.

As small groups of Europeans persisted in the British West Indies alongside the shift of the labor force to African slaves, the percentage of women among adults and the proportion of children in the total both swelled in trends of G shape (before dropping back somewhat via D or C paths in the 18th century). Similar movements occurred in northern colonies with few slaves, like Newfoundland and New York and in the economically intermediate Chesapeake between the 1620s and the 1790s. Later, as much larger flows of U.S. settlers pushed across the continent, the proportion of the population that was female in state after state rose in G fashion, sometimes preceded by a relatively brief G' hump of feminization as new settlement first took hold, sometimes not. From about 1860 through 1920 or later, meanwhile, in New Zealand the proportion of females both among whites and among Maori rose in G fashion, too, as may have been the case for Europeans in Australia between 1790 and 1850 (though this trend was split by a shock wave of male convict arrivals that followed the Napoleonic Wars). In South Africa rather earlier, across the first seven decades of the 18th century, the weights of women among adults and of children in the total settler population increased via G trends.

Historically, more change in age structure has followed G shape than just the appearance of children in new societies. In the United States between 1870 and 1970, for example, the proportions of white and black females who were 65 years of age and over both rose via two successive G curves, before and after 1930, as did the share of this age group in both sexes together among foreign-born whites up through 1920 and among their offspring thereafter. In rural Manchuria, meanwhile, the percentage of men who were 56 *sui* or older among all males of 16 *sui* or more climbed along one G path between 1810 and 1840 probably followed by another, steeper movement of that shape from there to 1861. Previously, from 1777 through about 1810—and subsequently, from 1861 into the 1870s or later—however, the weight of older men among all adult males in this part of rural Liaoning Province declined in D trends, G upside-down. Sometimes populations age; sometimes they become younger.

The historical movements in age structure with the most evidence come, as is so often the case, from the three "poster countries" of historical demography: England, Sweden, and France. In these long-running data sets between the middle 1500s and the end of the 1900s, not only G and D but E and C trends appear—all four positionings of G curvature on the Cartesian plane. The proportion of children, and younger age groups more generally, rose in G fashion in England from the 1660s into the middle 1700s, in Sweden from about 1800 to 1890. In France, noted for early fertility control, as soon as 1740 the weight of those under 15 was already lessening via a slow-starting, but ever downwardly accelerating C path. Evidence on completed family size and proportion of females married by age 25 produces trends of this shape for Rouen and Geneva between the 1630s and 1715 and again between 1715 and the early 1800s. Similar C-shape trending in the percentage of the young was adopted by Sweden after 1890—two such movements by the 1990s. In the United States, two C patterns also show up for white females between 1830 and 1940 and one for black females, while trends of this shape also characterize the dwindling presence of the young among the foreign-born and their first and second generations of offspring. C trends in the percentage of population under 15, furthermore, spread across this country between 1800 or earlier and the post–World War II baby boom, state by state, from New England to the Great Plains and some of the inter-mountain region (Colorado, Utah, New Mexico)—though not yet to the rest of it or to the Pacific coast and Hawaii and Alaska.

These C patterns at the younger end of the age spectrum—from Paris, France, to Paris, Indiana—clearly reflect the nature of the fertility decline that has, around the world, been a key element in modern "demographic transition." Increasing proportions of the elderly in populations similarly reflect the other part of the modern demographic equation: rising life expectancy. For the proportion of French females 60 and over, three upwardly accelerating E trends appear between the 1780s and the 1950s. In Sweden, two such patterns show themselves between the 1850s and the 1960s. The English data, with a series of perhaps three E trends for the increasing weight of the elderly between 1561 and 1716, indicate how rising life expectancy in this form could be a phenomenon of pre-modern societies, too. E-shape expansion of the proportion of the young, furthermore, does much to explain how the total population of England started to "explode" in such a manner between the 1720s and the early 1800s, demographic behavior that provided extra labor for increasingly large-scale farming and the new factories, a population pattern that spread across most of Europe during the next century and a half. Shrinkage of C shape in the percentage who were young in England, furthermore, shows up from the 1540s into the 1670s. Even considering findings for Rouen and the lower Seine Valley, this is well before the pattern can be documented for France, which has traditionally been regarded as the cultural "hearth" for modern fertility reduction. Meanwhile, the way that the weight of children and their families within the households of rural Manchuria began to fall off in a C manner from the 1790s into the 1850 (before rebounding somewhat) suggests that reproduction there, too, may have dropped away in the same accelerating manner observed in Europe.

These G-based trends of age structure—for the young, the old, and those in between—almost certainly signal that rates of birth and death, which, more than net migration, determine movements in the size and shape of all but the newest populations, themselves took G-related forms. To establish these vital patterns across extensive historical evidence, as the next volume of this study does, serves two kinds of purpose. On the one hand, it throws fresh light upon how various population changes and accompanying economic developments occurred historically, not always in the manner according to which they have so far been interpreted. Even more basically, though, it asks what there is about the way that birth rates or death rates are generated—the processes of fertility and mortality—that might imprint the shape of G and its simple transpositions so universally upon so many types of demographic and economic change.

Slave societies, it should be remembered, leave comparable impressions about the role of G-related movements in the inner workings of populations. Most directly, the intrinsic birth rate calculated for blacks in Cuba fell from 1774 through 1877 in C form, though the intrinsic death rate rose simultaneously via a G path 1816–1897. In the Bahia region of Brazil, meanwhile, the crude death rate for slaves seems likely to have declined in D fashion instead between the 1630s and the early 1800s. This is the shape of improvement that is probable for the year-round population of Newfoundland between 1730 and 1775 and for indentured laborers in the Caribbean, Assam, Fiji, and Queensland between the 1860s and World War I. Bettering odds against the grim reaper that follow a D path in mortality are likewise implied by G trends for the lengthening duration of marriages in Prince George's County, Maryland, between 1674 and 1762 and for increase in the proportion of first sons named for grandfathers between 1690 and 1810.

Meanwhile, where the composition of slave populations by age and sex can be followed, familar shapes of trend repeatedly occur. G patterns for the rising percentage of children emerge as slave groups "naturalize" demographically in their new surroundings: in the Chesapeake, in South Carolina, on Bermuda, from the older British West Indies of Barbados and Jamaica to newer Caribbean colonies like Grenada and Trinidad, in Dutch Surinam, and in the Bahia region of Portuguese Brazil. The proportion of women among slaves established in the New World likewise increased via G trends in these colonies, along with Danish St. Croix, though the Chesapeake and South Carolina both display G' humps of feminization during the very first years of local slavery before settling into the general G path for gains in the demographic weight of women. It was these G trends toward more women and children that made net natural decrease improve in D form in one slave population after another and reduced via D the rate at which further Africans were imported.

How did such demographic changes in the societies receiving forced or free migrants in turn affect not only the number but the makeup of the people who continued to arrive? To begin, much has been said about sex and age in the slave trade.

Evidence synthesized from several national slave trades has indicated, first of all, that the proportion of males of any age among cargoes of the leading slaving powers increased in G fashion from the 1660s through the 1720s and again from the 1760s into the 1860s. In between, their share in cargoes probably contracted along a D path. For just adult males within the Dutch trade, comparable trends appear, with an appreciably steeper decline of D shape from the 1730s into the 1760s. Apparently there were regional differences along the African coast as well as variations among national trades. Loadings in the Bight of Biafra, for example, display the same successive G trends but apparently without the D-type atrophy in between.

Local patterns for deliveries in the New World also demonstrate variation. The proportion of adult males among all slaves sold by the Royal African Company in the British West Indies as a whole, and both Barbados and Jamaica separately, dipped in 1/G' patterns between the 1670s and the 1720s as the share of sales to the Leeward Islands that was composed of men rose and fell in G' fashion. Planters there for a while pulled extra men out of the market. During the twilight of the Atlantic slave trade, between 1792 and 1817, Cuba, too, attracted a G' surge of more frequently male imports, though from 1818 through 1858 what followed was a continually rising G trend toward a higher percentage of males. From 1813 through 1843, meanwhile, both Bahia and southern Brazil (deliveries via Rio de Janeiro) saw the proportion of their slave imports composed of members of that sex sag in 1/G' shape. Men were in special demand where heavy work was needed, as in the expansion of canefields when the Leewards took up sugar in the early 1700s or when, around the end of the 18th century, Cuba became the new American area where sugar production could be aggressively expanded.

The proportion of *children* among Africans delivered to the New World appears in general to have increased via two successive G trends between the 1660s and the 1780s. One of the ways to get more males was to take more boys. The Dutch West India Company seems to have transported relatively fewer children in D form between 1690 and 1730; but this nation's free traders who supplanted this failing organization in the business took more across the next several decades in G fashion like their competitors, and no widespread decline between the first and second increases of G form emerges. Vessels of several nations loading in the Bight of Biafra may have filled their cargoes with a higher percentage of children along single G trends from the 1660s into the 1770s. In the 1780s, however, as the Dutch and the English began to abandon the trade, the proportion of children dropped markedly—but only to rise once more via G to new heights by the 1840s, both in general and in the Bight of Biafra. In Royal African Company deliveries to the British West Indies as a whole, and to Barbados, Jamaica, and the Leewards separately, between the 1670s and the 1720s the weight of children in the total probably rose everywhere via G, as it did in slave shipments to Cuba from the 1790s through the 1830s, though in the last decades of the business the proportion of the young among Africans transported to Brazil out of Angola for some reason swung back and forth sharply.

Just what drove some of these trends in the parts played by women and children in the slave trade needs further investigation. It should be noted, though, that the G-type emphasis on males occurred as colonial slave populations normalized, including the presence of more women and children, and *fewer slaves of any kind* were being purchased relative to the size of current slave populations. What planters and processors could use was extra men for certain kinds of tasks. In contrast, the rising proportion of children in shipments—though what to do with the young in a slave labor system was increasingly familiar—may have had more to do with how slaves became harder and harder to get in Africa. Supply as well as demand seems to have followed G-related movements.

In all, one of the most extreme businesses of the 17th, 18th, and 19th centuries evolved in trends of G-related shape that were rooted in how populations on two sides of the Atlantic stamped their demographic movements upon the conditions and procedures of the trade. As later on—in the 19th and 20th centuries—waves of freer immigrants left Old World societies (in Asia and Latin America as well as Europe) for lives in places like the United States and Canada, or Brazil and Argentina, or Guyana, Fijii, and South Africa, should one expect the demonomic interactions to be so very different, the particulars of economic development to be any less sensitive to demographically shaped movements as the number and character of producers and consumers repeatedly altered in G-related forms?

Like the various streams of the slave trade, the demographic composition of freer migrations altered by sex and age in G-related patterns. Among the much-studied flows out of Europe during the 19th and early 20th centuries, in the relatively new migrations from Italy, Portugal, Denmark, and Finland the pro-portion of children increased via G paths from the 1870s onward. In older out-flows such as those from Britain, Ireland, Germany, and Sweden—and likewise later from Denmark between 1883 and 1922—the weight of children declined in D fashion. The percentage of females in these modern migrations, meanwhile, rose in G shape almost everywhere from the early 1800s onward, though from the Netherlands and Belgium (and probably France) the tide turned to ebb via D across the later decades of the 19th century. The role of single females ex-panded; the proportion of families shrank.

Comparable trends in the composition of earlier historical migrations have been identified. Among emigrants from Spain to the New World in the 1500s, the percentage who were females climbed for 70 years in G fashion. In the next century, the proportion of migrants to French Canada who were of that sex increased in G form from the 1630s into the 1670s as the settlements of the St. Lawrence began to look more civilized and successful *habitants* who had come earlier wanted wives and families. In the 17th-century Chesapeake, from the 1630s into the first years of the 1700s, females likewise progressively constituted more and more of the arrivals, servant or free—once again along a G path. Then, however, among *servant* immigrants their proportion fell drastically in D form to the 1750s. Among servants going to the British West Indies, in contrast, the proportion of *males* rose via G instead during the later 17th century as these far richer colonies could pull the skilled workers and potential managers of slaves that they wanted out of the labor pool emigrating from Britain. It quickly became known, too, that the Caribbean was not a particularly attractive place for unattached women, among other things because it lacked a small planter class that might provide husbands once the term of service was over.

Though in particular flows at particular times (as also among slave deliveries) colonial migrations of Europeans could display a G' wave of temporarily ele-vated maleness, in general the G and D patterns capture enduring changes in the composition of these transoceanic movements. Among free immigrants to Australia between 1790 and 1850 females increased in the general G way. In South Africa, on the other hand, among immigrants who married into the "white" population, the proportion who were women declined in D fashion from the 1670s into the 1730s. That happened as the percentage of immigrant women

who *did* marry in who were not white grew in G fashion. The implication is
that white women were becoming less and less common among immigrants in
a D pattern, a phenomenon found so readily elsewhere.

As to the weight of children, English data indicate that among male servants
who emigrated (to any recorded destination) boys under 16 composed a smaller
and smaller fraction between about 1680 and 1780, probably via a D trend. In
the 19th and early 20th centuries, much more ample evidence demonstrates such
D patterns for the significance of the young in mature emigration from Ireland,
Britain, Germany, Norway, Sweden, Denmark (after 1883), the Netherlands, and
Switzerland. In contrast, as Portugal and Italy *began* to supply large numbers
of emigrants from the 1870s forward, the proportion of children in these flows
rose in G form—as it perhaps did from Denmark before 1883. The G-shape
increase between 1515 and 1595 in the percentage of Spanish men who came
to the Americas with families also suggests an expanding role of children in the
G pattern during early migration, while evidence for German New World arrivals of the 18th century indicates a decline in the weight of children beginning
in the 1740s after a stronger presence in the earlier phase of this transatlantic
movement.

INTERACTING PATTERNS OF DEMOGRAPHIC AND ECONOMIC CHANGE

These trends in the composition of free migrations not only show the same
few G-connected shapes as among various flows of Africans. They also suggest
comparable ways, right down into modern times, in which the demographic
dynamics of the receiving population shaped how many additional people were
suitable and what sort, while the internal workings of the sending populations
left comparable G-related imprints upon how many and which kinds of persons
might still be available or attracted to relocate. With the supply and demand of
people who were at once both producers and consumers shaped in these few
closely connected ways, the economic implications are many and obvious.

To begin with one clear and striking context in which to illustrate such consequences for economic developments, slaving was most certainly a business.
As observed, many circumstances of its customers unfolded in G-based patterns.
So may have the operations of its suppliers, as it was African *populations* that
had to be stripped of people. These ran dry or became resistant after constant
tapping and had to be followed by new, often more remote sources with higher
costs of acquisition and transportation. In this intercontinental demonomic setting, the *price* of slaves not surprisingly tended to take G-related patterns.

In one American colony after another, prices for prime male Africans rose in
G form—both as slavery became established locally and as it, for one reason
or another, underwent subsequent expansions. As the rate of further importation
went down in D shape, the price for top-quality men rose reciprocally. Indeed,
colonists seem in general to have been willing to keep on paying about the same

amount for new labor relative to the size of their collective operations; fewer new slaves, more of them expensive men who with time cost more and more per additional worker.

Though prices in the New World for slaves from different parts of Africa also increased via G trends—twice or more between the 1670s and the early 19th century—they did not do so simultaneously or equally. In consequence, relative American prices for slaves from the leading African sources rose and fell against each other in G' fashion. These patterns seem to reflect more how the search for cargoes shifted along the African coast than preferences of buyers for workers of a particular origin, which the literature has tended to stress. After all, look how easy it is to sell a pink round pill to replace a square blue one or one brand of sports utility vehicle in lieu of another.

Prices among colonies rose and fell in the same G' manner. According to the currently available evidence, these shifts clearly derive from where expansion in much-desired tropical crops or new ways of processing and profiting from them was forging ahead at the time.

The price for slaves in the Americas (at least in the colonies of northern European powers—adequate Portuguese and Spanish series do not yet seem to exist) rose and tapered off in G' fashion during the early years of Dutch, English, and French colonization in the tropics. In the middle 1600s, they settled down to climb substantially but not markedly in three G trends between the 1680s and the early 1800s. This increase, it should again be noted, generally offset decline in the rate at which planters were adding new labor, with the result that total revenues to be obtained from selling Africans held to scale, only paralleling the growth of existing labor forces, not increasing with price. The cost of slaves in Africa, in contrast, multiplied by 8 between the 1670s and the 1740s, also in G shape but much more aggressively. Competition among buyers and the costs of going further and further into the continent for "product" drove the level up and up. As a consequence of these sets of G-based trends on the two sides of the Atlantic, crude profit margins for northern European slave traders crested in G' shape in the middle 1600s, then fell back via this trend into the 1740s. Thereafter—apparently thanks to new supply from West Central Africa, the Bight of Biafra, and Southeast Africa, regions more remote for Caribbean delivery than the various sections of the Guinea Coast—costs of acquiring slaves rose, again taking G form. They now, however, climbed more slowly than prices obtained in the New World (which also increased in G fashion) so that the gross profit margin to be had in the business now *rose* via G across the remainder of the 18th century.

Purchase costs and sale prices for Dutch traders as opposed to British ones seem to have taken rather different patterns, but also G-related ones. As a consequence of the two different sets of movements, what the British paid in Africa compared with the Dutch declined over the long term via two downward-stepped G' movements, while what they obtained in America, relatively speaking, *rose* in two other sequential G' pulses. As a result of these movements on the two sides of the Atlantic, profit margins for the English advanced against those achieved by the Dutch generally along a G path across the 18th century.

Other aspects of the slave trade besides comparative prices and previously summarized competition among zones of loading, ships of different home ports, and local markets for labor in the colonies have been seen to evolve in G-connected forms. Records here and there of how long the Atlantic voyage took, how much time was spent along the African coast in order to fill vessels, how many slaves were loaded per day, how many were carried per ship in the "middle passage," and how often those ships had been built in the colonies rather than the homeland all follow G-based trends.

As more slaves were loaded and more time was taken filling cargoes along the African coast because conditions of supply altered through the years, more strain built up in the system. The rate at which vessels experienced revolts increased via G from the 1680s or sooner into the 1760s, before more effective procedures apparently clamped down on such loss of profit and the incidence of these events accelerated downward in C form into the early 19th century, like a species going extinct.

The pace at which both slaves and the crews who manned the ships died during successive legs of the trade as slave voyages took longer and profit margins were squeezed also followed G-based trends. On the one hand, the death rate for French crews declined in D fashion across the 18th century, presumably as better practices were identified and applied. For slaves, on the other hand, the patterns are mostly repeated waves of G' shape. Losses while disposing of slaves after arriving in America crested this way around 1700, about the time when rates of sales relative to local African American populations began to fall, as pickier purchasers more often took men and paid higher prices for them, and reshipments out of Jamaica crested. Deaths while coasting from one African port to another acquiring cargo peaked in G' form near 1740. When Dutch, British, French, Portuguese, and Spanish branches of the trade faced new challenges, attracted inexperienced participants in boom eras, or perhaps cut new corners as business shifted along the African coast and from colony to colony in America and profit margins fell, G' surges in the death rate for this group of slavers appeared—the British and the Dutch in the middle 1600s, both of these and the French around 1730, the Portuguese near 1790 and again in the middle of the 1800s, the Spanish and French in between those points in time.

As a whole, however, mortality per month at sea for non-European bound or contract laborers of several sorts—slaves and indentured workers from Africa, India, China, and various islands of the Pacific—came down along a single C curve between the early 1700s and the early 1900s. This trend lagged slightly behind and stayed at a higher level than another C track that fits comparable death rates across the same era for various groups of free European migrants carried by sea and, after the early 1700s, even convicts shipped to America and Australia. Very generally, international health improvements seem to have taken this form, which is the reciprocal of the kinds of E trends along which higher proportions of the elderly appear across the 19th century in the populations of France and Sweden. This evidence from events at sea once again suggests that C is going to turn out to be the trajectory along which crude death rates improved as one part of what is called "demographic transition."

The operations of the Atlantic slave trade from the 1600s into the 1800s have provided one historical case through which some economic changes with G-related shapes and obvious ties to demographic movements could be followed. On an even grander global scale, across the half-millennium following 1500 in both the Old World and the New, it is similarly possible to develop some fresh perspective on another topic that has long fascinated economic, demographic, and social historians. This concerns the interactions among agricultural change, non-agricultural enterprise and employment, urbanization, and demographic movements. Indications have appeared here and there in this study that these processes, which have been so central to the emergence of modern life, have very generally worked themselves out along G-based trends.

To begin with some recent and regularly documented patterns, in the United States, Sweden, New Zealand, and Ireland the percentage of the population living in substantial towns or cities increased across long periods of the 19th and 20th centuries in trends of the slowly decelerating H shape. Though parallel total population growth in this form appeared only in the United States, and a considerably flatter H in Sweden, we are reminded that the H curve as a shape of population growth has been found in the global survey of Volume I to occur since the 16th century across Europe, the Americas, Asia, and even once in a while Africa in contexts of *economic growth*. Though it is sometimes necessary to rely upon infrequent data for trending, fresh perspectives on urbanization, other migration, and agricultural change begin to cast further light upon just what such development has involved and how it has unfolded through time.

City people, to begin, are sustained by food that is produced by somebody else. To have proportionally more urban dwellers in a population means, on the whole, that relatively fewer and fewer people must produce more and more food. In the United States, for example, in the originally farm-focused states of the Old Northwest, between 1830 and 1900 as settlement became more dense and urbanization expanded, the proportion of the labor force that was *not* engaged in agriculture rose also in H fashion. It, furthermore, seems possible that the whole labor force of the United States changed this way as well across the 19th century.

Meanwhile, the total amount of immigration to the United States followed an H path from 1847 to World War I that, with its base year at 1850, almost exactly paralleled the growth of the whole national population between 1850 and 1930. On the other hand, the settled area of this devastatingly land-hungry nation also expanded in H fashion between the War of 1812 and the Civil War, though this H trend was flatter than the curve segments of that type for total population increase, aggregate immigration, and urbanization in all centers of 10,000 or more residents. Still shallower segments of the H trend appear in the amount of settled land that was being added and for gain in the proportion of the labor force employed outside of agriculture as the "farmer's frontier" became less and less a factor in American life. While sometimes parallel and sometimes rather differently timed, nonetheless, the processes of occupying the continent, pulling in people from the Old World, urbanization, and developing economically beyond agriculture all—like population growth for the country as a whole after 1850—took H form in the United States.

The ingredients that were involved in a modern interlocking demonomic system like this, furthermore, are hardly unfamiliar to historians of an earlier era in Europe. The likely nature of the trends along which they evolved, however, has not yet been perceived in data that so far are mostly widely spaced through time, often available at just half-century intervals. The new discovery here is, first of all, that identical, G-based shapes of movement appear in such work on much earlier historical contexts and provide further insight into how the same elements of change interacted in Europe between about 1500 and 1800.

The demographic aspect of Wrigley's classic exposition of the rising significance of London within England, for example, can be quantified very precisely via H trends. The inhabitants of London as a percentage of the population of England enlarged in H form from the later 1500s into the 1730s. So between 1520 and 1670 did the fraction of all the urban population in England to be found in the metropolis alone. Then, when London became less dynamic than the thriving industrial cities of the country in the 18th century, the weight of these competitors within the total urban population of England in turn increased in H shape between 1700 and 1801. London, meanwhile, became a less proportionally significant part of the overall national population via a D path between the 1730s and the 1810s; and the demographic deficit of the metropolis, both in absolute numbers and as a percentage of the surplus of people produced by the remainder of the country, swung up and down in G' movements from the 1560s to the early 1800s. These fundamental patterns of early modern English urbanization all took H shape or followed contributing, G-related trends of other sorts.

When one looks at key components of the population of England between 1520 and 1800, furthermore, again a crucial role for changes in H form appears. These movements clarify what happened as England began to modernize and how this country developed differently from her chief competitors of the era, the Netherlands and France.

In the first place, across the 1600s and the 1700s the number of workers per farm in England seems to have risen via an H trend with t_0 in the 1540s. The improvements in agricultural production associated with this development in scale apparently were sufficient to allow the proportion of England's rural population that was not engaged in agriculture to expand along an almost exactly parallel H path between 1670 and 1800, and to allow the urban percentage of the country's total population to do likewise from 1670 through 1750, while the number of people supported per person in agriculture increased along a slightly flatter H path (with base year in the 1510s).

In contrast, though the agriculture of the Netherlands had become famously inventive and productive in the 16th century, and probably also already in the 1400s, after 1600 the number of people supported per person in agriculture there increased only a little more up to 1700 (via a flat segment of the more rapidly decelerating G shape), then actually shrank back in D fashion from there to 1800. Meanwhile, the percentage of the nation's rural population not engaged in agriculture remained virtually unchanged from the early 1600s to the opening of the 19th century. While urbanization in the Netherlands had advanced in strong, sustained H shape from about 1550 to 1700, making the country the most urban in Europe for this era, across the 18th century the percentage of the Dutch population living in cities actually atrophied in D manner. Data by province indicate that the absolute numbers living in cities increased in the interior from the 1670s forward, while in the maritime regions they declined via D. Proportionally, however, in *all* recorded parts of the country the Netherlands de-urbanized. Also contracting in D fashion was the number of people supported per person in agriculture. To what extent was the goose of the Golden Age killed by limitations upon the further development of Dutch agriculture, the number of whose participants stayed virtually unchanged from 1550 through 1750?

Sheer manpower was not the issue, however; the rural agricultural population of England, for example, actually became smaller in D mode between 1650 and 1750 as relatively more people lived in cities or engaged in non-agricultural pursuits in the countryside. The question was what rural people did. Relatively speaking, in the Netherlands they stopped swelling the populations of cities through migration or expanding the non-agricultural production of the countryside. Was the Dutch rural population perchance practicing significant family limitation this early, along with—say—the residents of the lower Seine Valley around Rouen? Has there been too much stress on French exceptionalism with regard to such early modern demographic behavior? A C-shape decline in the proportion of children in the population of England from the 1540s into the 1670s suggests that, too.

In France, the third and by far the largest challenger for preeminence in northwestern Europe between 1500 and 1800, the composition of the population according to its agricultural, rural non-agricultural, and urban components remained virtually unchanged across three centuries. Total population per person in agriculture hardly increased at all between 1500 and 1800. A just barely larger proportion of French people lived in cities a decade after the Revolution than had 300 years previously. Along a shallow H segment, however, rather more gain occurred across the 18th century in the proportion of the rural population not occupied in agriculture. These people manned the relatively small-scale, scattered enterprises that provided the luxuries and sinews of war that were so characteristic of France during this era. For the most part, however, the three sectors of the French population expanded along with each other, not producing much change in demographic composition or in economic activity except to scale, albeit a large and powerful continental scale compared with the Netherlands or England.

As these national shifts in the weight of major components took place, the English population grew in H form from the 1680s into the middle of the 18th century, a shape of trend also followed (rather more flatly) from the 1560s through the 1650s—before the intervening demographic losses of the later 1600s. No trend of total demographic expansion in this H pattern appears between 1500 and 1800 in the Netherlands or France (though it did in the Dutch maritime province of Holland between 1514 and 1680, where new agricultural practices—some involving industrial rather than edible crops—contributed to place the Netherlands for a while at the peak of the European economic development). In the era 1570–1720, when Sweden experienced H-type total demographic increase along with England, it is easy to imagine agricultural change combining with non-agricultural developments, often in conjunction with the Dutch, to provide the soldiers and the supplies for the armies of first Gustavus Adolphus and then three Charleses who followed. Later, for the United States in the 19th century, similar connections among H-shaped changes in population and economy have been noted. Though more and better data need to be developed and explored, the movements already observed seem to expand our understanding of the tie of H trends of total demographic expansion to economic growth, a connection suspected in modern times for *many* countries on more than one continent in Volume I.

In these 1500–1800 trendings—based primarily upon Wrigley's pathbreaking study (1985)—the H curve is the illuminating and interconnecting form. During the later years of the 18th century, in contrast, combinations among patterns of demographic growth, the weight of key sub-populations within the whole, and the role of agriculture hint at interrelated demonomic change in quite a different shape. This takes the upward accelerating transposition of G, the E curve. How do the relationships work when this other pattern of change occurs? International data provided by Paul Bairoch (1988, 1990) from the 1700s through the 1900s make it possible to carry forward some of this type of analysis via G-based trending into quite recent times.

In the middle of the 18th century, E-shape changes in total demographic expansion, numbers resident in cities, and proportion of the population that was urban began to diffuse across Europe. In at least several countries such movements were accompanied by improvements of crop yield and labor productivity in agriculture that took similar E form. In other words, considerable parallelism among various ingredients of interacting demonomic change continued; but the shared shape was now E rather than H. Generally, this new tidal wave of developments began in the north and west of Europe and progressively swept to the south and east. The contributing E movements were evident in England and Ireland already by the 1720s; showed up in Spain, Portugal, and Romania only several decades later; and lasted to or past World War II via repeated appearances in Germany, Switzerland, and Czechoslovakia and late entrances in Hungary and Albania. By fairly early in the 1800s, however, the first countries in this rolling geographical diffusion had gone back to experiencing H-type trends of population increase, urbanization, and agricultural change instead. Following World War II, though, most further advances for these historical leaders in demographic and economic development began visibly to decelerate more rapidly, in G rather than H manner.

The evidence of Bairoch, accompanied by the analysis of population growth presented in Volume I, makes it possible to see how these demographic and economic trends found in Europe played out on an even wider intercontinental stage. Parallels and divergences in the G-based shapes of crucial movements in population size, urbanization, and forms of economic change can be identified elsewhere, not only in the United States but in other countries like Australia, New Zealand, and South Africa or Japan, China, and India. Still broader groupings such as Asian market economies, Latin America, Africa, all "Third World" societies, and all more "advanced" nations likewise display the patterns of related demographic and economic change found to be central in modern developments since the 1500s. The observed G-based trendings and their relationships to each other seem to offer a fresh and fruitful framework for guiding further analysis of how some of the key ingredients of present life have evolved.

In all, movements that structure the topics of three large and lively historical literatures—on migration, on the slave trade and slave societies, and on urbanization—prove to have taken the G-related shapes first evident in the historical record of population growth and decline. In consequence of these findings, one agenda that this volume presents for further attention is this: How have such observed G-related trends of population growth, migration, and urbanization participated in the evolution of modern life in interaction with economic developments linked to them? As indicated by samples and references included in the present volume, the author is working on further publication (*deo volente*) that pursues a few historical cases in depth with more and better evidence. Others are challenged to join the chase.

The other meaty agenda, meanwhile, asks: From where might so many demographic and economic trends taking G-based shapes come? The universality of just a few, repeated G-connected trends in the growth and decline of the size of populations (Volume I), in the flow and ebb of migrations that have shifted people from one to another, in the weights of different kinds of persons involved in these movements, and in the composition of the populations receiving (and providing) movers strongly suggests that the sources of such trend shapes are not economic but demographic. Though one can readily recognize the role of economic stimuli in starting movements going, whether in population growth or in migration, it seems impossible to conceptualize economic laws that would steer demographic change so repeatedly and so regularly into a few G-based paths in such a wide variety of historical contexts as our two volumes have covered. There are doubtless going to be readers who will try to identify universal underlying dynamics of an economic nature to account for the repeated patterns observed. According to the canon of inquiry and verification it is healthy that they do so. Here, though, the wager—the challenge—is that such efforts will prove futile, that the answer lies in other directions.

What directions? Rates of births and deaths, it is generally understood, join (usually overwhelm) migration in determining trends in the size of populations, the place where our awareness of G forms first began (Volume I). Together, birth rates and death rates determine how populations renew or replace themselves with or without the help (or interference) of net migration. G-based patterns have already been observed in the way that net natural decrease declined or net natural increase appeared and strengthened as slaves and other in-migrant peoples who have been examined established themselves and normalized demographically. It has become evident, furthermore, that such stabilization set the pattern for further migration to the receiving population, not the other way around. What, then, repeatedly embeds G-type curvature of one form or another into the demographic renewal process?

Already a few trends of crude death rates and crude birth rates in G-connected shapes have emerged here and there from the historical literature on migration that has just been surveyed. How universal are such patterns for vital rates across time and culture and type of economy? Unfortunately, the reliable information that exists on birth and death rates in general, let alone specifics by age and sex or context of living, is mostly modern and predominantly European, though historical demographers have heroically generated some notable exceptions. In the end, however, enough evidence exists to permit as well as to require exploring fruitfully and extensively how one or another aspect of human fertility or mortality might constantly keep imprinting G-based trends upon demographic and related social and economic change. That is the task of the third volume of this study, which follows.

Bibliography

PRIMARY SOURCES

St. Mary's City Commission Files

GOVERNMENT DOCUMENTS

Australia

Cameron, R. J. 1982. *Year Book: Australia* 66. Canberra: Australian Bureau of Statistics.
Knibbs, G. H. 1915. *Official Yearbook of the Commonwealth of Australia* 8. Melbourne:
   Commonwealth Bureau of Census and Statistics.

New Zealand

Department of Statistics. 1998. *New Zealand Official 1998 Yearbook (Te Pukapuka
   Houanga Whaimana o Aotearoa)*. Auckland.

Sweden

Statistika Centralbyrån. 1969. *Historisk statistik för Sverige* (National Central Bureau of
   Statistics. *Historical Statistics of Sweden*). Part 1, *Population*, 2nd ed., 1720–
   1967. Stockholm: AB Allmänna Fölaget.
———. 1979, 1984, 1991. *Statistik årsbok för Sverige* (*Statistical Abstract of Sweden*).
   Stockholm: Statistika Centralbyrån.

United States

U.S. Bureau of the Census. 1975. *Historical Statistics of the United States, Colonial Times to 1970*. 2 vols. Washington, D.C.: U.S. Government Printing Office.

―――. 1998. *Statistical Abstracts*. Washington, D.C.: U.S. Department of Commerce.

SECONDARY SOURCES

Abel, W. 1962. *Geschichte der Deutschen Landwirtschaft*. Stuttgart: Ulmer.

Adams, William Forbes. 1932. *Ireland and Irish Emigration to the New World from 1815 to the Famine*. New Haven: Yale University Press.

Altman, Ida. 1989. *Emigrants and Society: Extremadura and America in the Sixteenth Century*. Berkeley: University of California Press.

Anstey, Roger. 1975. "The Volume and Profitability of the British Slave Trade, 1761–1807." In Engerman and Genovese, eds., 1975, 3–32.

Anstey, Roger, and P. E. H. Hair, eds. 1976. *Liverpool, the African Slave Trade, and Abolition: Essays to Illustrate Current Knowledge and Research*. Occasional Series 2. Bristol: Historic Society of Lancashire and Cheshire.

Austen, Ralph A. 1979. "The Trans-Saharan Slave Trade: A Tentative Census." In Gemery and Hogendorn, eds., 1979, 23–76.

Bade, Klaus J. 1992. "German Transatlantic Emigration on the Nineteenth and Twentieth Centuries." In Emmer and Mörner, eds., 1990, 121–56.

Bailyn, Bernard. 1955. *The New England Merchants in the Seventeenth Century*. Cambridge, Mass.: Harvard University Press.

―――. 1986. *Voyagers to the West: A Passage in the Peopling of America on the Eve of the American Revolution*. New York: Knopf.

Bairoch, Paul. 1988. *Cities and Economic Development: From the Dawn of History to the Present*. Chicago: University of Chicago Press. Trans. by Christopher Baider from *De Jéricho à Mexico: Villes et économie dans l'historie*. Paris: Editions Gallimard, 1985.

―――. 1990. "The Impact of Crop Yields, Agricultural Productivity, and Transport Costs on Urban Growth between 1800 and 1910." In van der Woude et al., eds., 1990, 134–51.

Bardet, Jean-Pierre. 1990. "Innovators and Immitators in the Practice of Contraception in Town and Country." In van der Woude et al., eds., 1990, 264–81.

Bardet, Jean-Pierre, and Jacques Dupâquier, eds. 1997. *Histoire des populations de l'Europe. I. Des origines aux prémices de la révolution démographique*. Paris: Fayard.

Beckles, Hilary McD. 1989. *White Servitude and Black Slavery in Barbados, 1627–1715*. Knoxville: University of Tennessee Press.

Beckles, Hilary McD., and A. Downes 1987. "The Economics of Transition to the Black Labor System in Barbados, 1630–1680." *Journal of Interdisciplinary History* 18: 225–47.

Behrendt, Stephen D. 1997. "Crew Mortality in the Transatlantic Slave Trade in the Eighteenth Century." In Eltis and Richardson, eds., 1997, 49–71.

―――. 2001. "Markets, Transaction Cycles, and Profits: Merchant Decision Making in the British Slave Trade." *William and Mary Quarterly*, 3rd ser., 58: 171–204.

Berlin, Ira. 1980. "Time, Space, and the Evolution of Afro-American Society on British Mainland North America." *American Historical Review* 85: 44–78.

Bernhard, Virginia. 1999. *Slaves and Slaveholders in Bermuda 1616–1782*. Columbia: University of Missouri Press.

Bloomfield, G. T. 1984. *New Zealand: A Handbook of Historical Statistics*. Boston: G. K. Hall & Co.

Boserup, Ester. 1965. *The Conditions of Agricultural Growth: The Economics of Agrarian Change under Population Pressure*. Chicago: Aldine Publishing Company.

Bourgeois-Pichat, J. 1965. "The General Development of the Population of France since the Eighteenth Century." In Glass and Eversley, eds., 1965, 474–506.

Boyd-Bowman, Peter. 1976. "Patterns of Spanish Emigration to the Indies until 1600." *Hispanic American Historical Review* 56: 580–604.

Braun, Rudolf. 1978. "Protoindustrialization and Demographic Changes in the Canton of Zürich." In Tilly, ed., 1978, 289–334.

Brumbaugh, Martin G. 1899. *A History of the German Baptist Brethren in Europe and America*. Morris, Ill.: Brethren Publishing House.

Bulst, Neithard, and Christian Pfister. 1997. "L'Allemagne." In Bardet and Dupâquier, eds., 1997, 509–26.

Burds, Jeffrey. 1998. *Peasant Dreams & Market Politics: Labor Management and the Russian Village, 1861–1905*. Pittsburgh: University of Pittsburgh Press.

Burkholder, Mark A., and Lyman L. Johnson. 1994. *Colonial Latin America*. 2nd ed. Oxford: Oxford University Press.

Burnard, Trevor, and Kenneth Morgan. 2001. "The Dynamics of the Slave Market and Slave Purchasing Patterns in Jamaica, 1655–1788." *William and Mary Quarterly*, 3rd ser., 58: 205–28.

Butlin, N. G. 1994. *Forming a Colonial Economy, Australia 1810–1850*. Cambridge: Cambridge University Press.

Canny, Nicholas. 1994a. "English Migration into and across the Atlantic during the Seventeenth and Eighteenth Centuries." In Canny, ed., 1994b, 39–75.

———, ed. 1994b. *Europeans on the Move: Studies on European Migration, 1500–1800*. Oxford: Clarendon Press.

Carr, Lois Green, Philip D. Morgan, and Jean B. Russo, eds. 1988. *Colonial Chesapeake Society*. Chapel Hill: University of North Carolina Press.

Chambers, J. D. 1965. "Population Change in a Provincial Town: Nottingham 1760–1800." In Glass and Eversley, eds., 1965, 334–53. First published in L. S. Presnell, ed., *Studies in the Industrial Revolution: Essays Presented to T. S. Ashton*. London: Athlone Press 1960.

Charbonneau, Hubert, Bertrand Desjardins, André Guillemette, Yves Landry, Jacques Légaré, and François Nault. 1987. *Naissance d'une Population: Les Français établis au Canada au XVIIe siècle*. Montréal: Presses de l'Université de Montréal.

Chaunu, Huguette, and Pierre Chaunu. 1955–1960. *Séville et l'Atlantique (1504–1650)*. 8 vols. Paris: S.E.V.P.E.N.

Clark, Gregory. 2001. "Farm Wages and Living Standards in the Industrial Revolution: England, 1670–1869." *Economic History Review* 54: 477–505.

Clark, Peter. 2000. "Small Towns 1700–1840." In Clark, ed., 2000, 733–73.

Clark, Peter, ed. 2000. *The Cambridge Urban History of Britain: II. 1540–1840*. Cambridge: Cambridge University Press.

Clark, Peter, and David Souden, eds. 1987. *Migration and Society in Early Modern England.* London: Hutchinson.

Clemens, Paul G. E., and Lucy Simler. 1988. "Rural Labor and the Farm Household in Chester County, Pennsylvania, 1720–1820." In Innes, ed., 1988, 1106–143.

Cook, Sherburne F., and Woodrow Wilson Borah. 1971, 1974, 1979. *Essays in Population History: Mexico and the Caribbean.* 3 vols. Berkeley: University of California Press.

Craton, Michael. 1971. "Jamaican Slave Mortality." *Journal of Caribbean History* 3: 1–27.

———. 1975. "Jamaican Slavery." In Engerman and Genovese, eds., 1975, 249–84.

Craven, Wesley Frank. 1971. *White, Red, and Black: The Seventeenth-Century Virginian.* Charlottesville: University Press of Virginia.

Cullen, L. M. 1994. "The Irish Diaspora of the Seventeenth and Eighteenth Centuries." In Canny, ed., 1994b, 113–49.

Curtin, Philip D. 1969. *The Atlantic Slave Trade: A Census.* Madison: University of Wisconsin Press.

———. 1975. "Measuring the Atlantic Slave Trade." In Engerman and Genovese, eds., 1975, 107–28.

———. 1981. "The Abolition of the Slave Trade from Senegambia." In Eltis and Walvin, eds., 1981, 83–97.

Daultry, Stuart, David Dickson, and Cormac Ó Gráda. 1981. "Eighteenth-Century Irish Population: New Perspective from Old Sources." *Journal of Economic History* 41: 601–28.

David, Paul, 1967. "The Growth of Real Product in the United States before 1840." *Journal of Economic History* 27: 151–97.

Davies, K. G. 1957. *The Royal African Company.* London: Longmans.

Debien, Gabriel. 1951. *Les engagés pour les Antilles, 1634–1715.* Abbeville: F. Paillart.

Deerr, Noel. 1949–1950. *The History of Sugar.* 2 vols. London: Chapman and Hall.

Deprez, Paul. 1965. "The Demographic Development of Flanders in the Eighteenth Century." In Glass and Eversley, eds., 1965, 608–30.

De Vries, Jan. 1974. *The Dutch Rural Economy in the Golden Age.* New Haven: Yale University Press.

———. 1984. *European Urbanization 1500–1800.* Cambridge, Mass.: Harvard University Press.

———. 1985. "The Population and Economy of the Preindustrial Netherlands." *Journal of Interdisciplinary History* 15: 661–82.

De Vries, Jan, and Ad van der Woude. 1997. *The First Modern Economy: Success, Failure, and Perseverance of the Dutch Economy, 1500–1815.* Cambridge: Cambridge University Press.

Diamond, Sigmund. 1961. "An Experiment in 'Feudalism': French Canada in the Seventeenth Century." *William and Mary Quarterly,* 3d ser., 18: 1–34.

Dickson, Robert J. 1988. *Ulster Emigration to Colonial America, 1718–1775.* London: W. and G. Bairds; first published 1966, London: Routledge and Kegan Paul.

Dunn, Richard S. 1972. *Sugar and Slaves: The Rise of the Planter Class in the English West Indies, 1624–1713.* Chapel Hill: University of North Carolina Press.

———. 1984. "Servants and Slaves: The Recruitment and Employment of Labor." In Greene and Pole, eds., 1984, 157–94.

Dupâquier, Jacques. 1997. "La France avant la transition démographique." In Bardet and Dupâquier, eds., 1997, 441–62.

Eblen, Jack Ericson. 1975. "On the Natural Increase of Slave Populations: The Example of the Cuban Black Population, 1775–1900." In Engerman and Genovese, eds., 1975, 211–47.

Ekirch, A. Roger. 1987. *Bound for America: The Transportation of British Convicts to the Colonies 1718–1775*. Oxford: Clarendon Press.

Eltis, David. 1986. "Fluctuations in the Age and Sex Ratios of Slaves in the Nineteenth-Century Transatlantic Slave Traffic." *Slavery and Abolition* 7: 257–72.

———. 1987. *Economic Growth and the Ending of the Transatlantic Slave Trade*. New York: Oxford University Press.

———. 1996. "The British Transatlantic Slave Trade before 1714: Annual Estimates of Volume and Direction." In Paquette and Engerman, eds., 1996, 182–205.

———. 2000. *The Rise of African Slavery in the Americas*. Cambridge: Cambridge University Press.

———. 2001. "The Volume and Structure of the Atlantic Slave Trade: A Reassessment." *William and Mary Quarterly*, 3rd ser., 58: 17–46.

Eltis, David, ed. 2002. *Coerced and Free Migration: Global Perspectives*. Stanford, Calif.: Stanford University Press.

Eltis, David, and James Walvin, eds. 1981. *The Abolition of the Atlantic Slave Trade: Origins and Effects in Europe, Africa, and the Americas*. Madison: University of Wisconsin Press.

Eltis, David, and Stanley L. Engerman. 1992. "Was the Slave Trade Dominated by Men?" *Journal of Interdisciplinary History* 23: 237–57.

Eltis, David, and David Richardson. 1997. "West Africa and the Transatlantic Slave Trade: New Evidence of Long-Run Trends." In Eltis and Richardson, eds., 1997, 16–35.

———. 2003. "Markets for Slaves Newly Arrived in the Americas: Price Patterns, 1673–1865." Forthcoming in Eltis et al., eds., *Slavery in the Development of the Americas*. Cambridge: Cambridge University Press.

Eltis, David, and David Richardson, eds. 1997. *Routes to Slavery: Direction, Ethnicity, and Mortality in the Transatlantic Slave Trade*. London: Frank Cass.

Eltis, David, Stephen D. Behrendt, David Richardson, and Herbert S. Klein, eds. 1999. *The Trans-Atlantic Slave Trade: A Database on CD-ROM*. Cambridge: Cambridge University Press.

Eltis, David, F. Lewis, and K. Sokoloff, eds. 2003. *Slavery in the Development of the Americas*. Forthcoming, Cambridge: Cambridge University Press.

Emmer, P. C., ed. 1986. *Colonialism and Migration; Indentured Labor before and after Slavery*. Dordrecht: Martinus Nijhoff.

Emmer, P. C., and Magnus Mörner, eds. 1992. *European Expansion and Migration: Essays on the Intercontinental Migration from Africa, Asia, and Europe*. New York: Berg.

Engerman, Stanley L., and Eugene D. Genovese, eds. 1975. *Race and Slavery in the Western Hemisphere: Quantitative Studies*. Princeton, N.J.: Princeton University Press.

Erickson, Charlotte J. 1981. "Emigration from the British Isles to the U.S.A. in 1831." *Population Studies* 35: 175–97.

———. 1989. "Emigration from the British Isles to the U.S.A. in 1841: Part I. Emigration from the British Isles." *Population Studies* 43: 347–67.

———. 1990. "Emigration from the British Isles to the U.S.A in 1841: Part II. Who Were the English Emigrants?" *Population Studies* 44: 21–40.

Euler, Leonhard. 1760. "Recherches générales sur la mortalité et la multiplication du genre humaine." *Memoires de l'Académie Royale des Sciences et Belle Lettres* (Berlin) 16: 144–64. Trans. by Nathan and Beatrice Keyfitz in Smith and Keyfitz, eds., 1977, 83–91.

Eversley, D. E. C. 1965. "A Survey of Population in an Area of Worcestershire from 1660 to 1850 on the Basis of Parish Registers." In Glass and Eversley, eds., 1965, 394–419. First published in *Population Studies* 10, 1957.

Ferenczi, Imre, and Walter F. Willcox. 1929. *International Migrations*, I. *Statistics*. New York: National Bureau of Economic Research.

Fertig, Georg. 1994. "Transatlantic Migration from the German-Speaking Parts of Central Europe, 1600–1800: Proportions, Structures, and Explanations." In Canny, ed., 1994b, 192–235.

Finlay, Roger. 1981. *Population and Metropolis: The Demography of London 1580–1650.* Cambridge: Cambridge University Press.

Fogel, Robert William, and Stanley L. Engerman. 1974. *Time on the Cross: The Economics of American Negro Slavery.* 2 vols. Boston: Little, Brown and Company.

Fogleman, Aaron Spencer. 1991. *Hopeful Journeys: German Immigration and Settlement in Greater Pennsylvania.* Ph.D. dissertation, University of Michigan.

———. 1992. "Migration to the Thirteen British North American Colonies, 1700–1775: New Estimates." *Interdisciplinary History* 22: 691–709.

———. 1996. *Hopeful Journeys: German Immigration, Settlement, and Political Culture in Colonial America.* Philadelphia: University of Pennsylvania Press.

———. 1998. "From Slaves, Convicts, and Servants to Free Passengers: The Transformation of Immigration in the Era of the American Revolution." *Journal of American History* 85: 43–76.

Forster, Colin. 2002. "Convicts: Unwilling Migrants from Britain and France." In Eltis, ed., 2002, 259–91.

Franklin, Benjamin. 1751. "OBSERVATIONS concerning the Increase of Mankind, Peopling of Countries, &c." In Leonard W. Labaree, ed., *The Papers of Benjamin Franklin* 4: 227–34. New Haven: Yale University Press, 1961.

Galenson, David W. 1981. *White Servitude in Colonial America.* Cambridge: Cambridge University Press.

———. 1986. *Traders, Planters, and Slaves: Market Behavior in Early English America.* Cambridge: Cambridge University Press.

Gallman, Robert E. 1975. "The Agricultural Sector and the Pace of Economic Growth: U.S. Experience in the Nineteenth Century." In Klingaman and Vedder, eds., 1975, 35–76.

Gates, Paul W. 1960. *The Farmer's Age: Agriculture 1815–1860*; Vol. 3, *The Economic History of the United States.* New York: Holt, Rinehart and Winston.

Geggus, David. 1989. "Sex Ratio, Age, and Ethnicity in the Atlantic Slave Trade: Data from French Shipping and Plantation Records." *Journal of African History* 30: 23–44.

———. 2001. "The French Slave Trade: An Overview." *William and Mary Quarterly*, 3rd ser., 58: 118–38.

Gemery, Henry A. 1980. "Emigration from the British Isles to the New World, 1630–1700: Inferences from Colonial Populations." *Research in Economic History* 5: 179–231.

———. 1984. "European Emigration to North America, 1700–1820: Numbers and Quasi-Numbers." *Perspectives in American History* n.s., 1: 283–342.

———. 1986. "Markets for Migrants: English Indentured Servitude and Emigration in the Seventeenth and Eighteenth Centuries." In Emmer, ed., 1986, 33–54.

Gemery, Henry A., and Jan S. Hogendorn, eds. 1979. *The Uncommon Market: Essays in the Economic History of the Slave Trade*. New York: Academic Press.

Glass, D. V., and D. E. C. Eversley, eds. 1965. *Population in History: Essays in Historical Demography*. Chicago: Aldine Publishing Company.

Glazier, Ira A., and Luigi de Rosa, eds. 1986. *Migration across Time and Nations: Population Mobility in Historical Contexts*. New York: Holmes and Meier.

Grabbe, Hans-Jürgen. 1989. "European Immigration to the United States in the Early National Period, 1783–1820." *Proceedings of the American Philosophical Society* 132: 190–218.

———. 1997. "Before the Great Tidal Waves: Patterns of Transatlantic Migration at the Beginning of the Nineteenth Century." *Amerikastudien/American Studies* 42: 377–89.

Graham, Ian C. C. 1956. *Colonists from Scotland: Emigration to North America, 1707–1783*. Ithaca: Cornell University Press.

Greene, Jack P., and J. R. Pole, eds. 1984. *Colonial British America: Essays in the New History of the Early Modern Era*. Baltimore: Johns Hopkins University Press.

Green-Pedersen, Svend E. 1981. "Slave Demography in the Danish West Indies and the Abolition of the Danish Slave Trade." In Eltis and Walvin, eds., 1981, 231–57.

Grubb, Farley. 1990. "German Immigration to Pennsylvania, 1709 to 1820." *Journal of Interdisciplinary History* 20: 417–36.

Gutiérrez, Ramón A. 1991. *When Jesus Came, the Corn Mothers Went Away: Marriage, Sexuality, and Power in New Mexico 1500–1846*. Stanford, Calif.: Stanford University Press.

Haines, Robin, and Ralph Shlomovitz. 2000. "Explaining the Mortality Decline in the Eighteenth-Century British Slave Trade." *Economic History Review* 53: 262–83.

Hall, Nevill A. T. 1992. *Slave Society in the Danish West Indies: St. Thomas, St. John, and St. Croix*. B. W. Higman, ed. Mona, Jamaica: University of the West Indies Press.

Hall, Thomas D. 1989. *Social Change in the Southwest, 1350–1880*. Lawrence: University Press of Kansas.

Handler, Jerome S., and Frederick W. Lange. 1978. *Plantation Slavery in Barbados: An Archaeological and Historical Investigation*. Cambridge, Mass.: Harvard University Press.

Handlin, Oscar. 1972. *Boston's Immigrants: A Study in Acculturation* (revised and enlarged edition, New York: Atheneum; first published 1941).

Harris, P. M. G. 1969. "The Social Origins of American Leaders: The Demographic Foundations." *Perspectives in American History* 3: 159–344.

———. 1978. "Integrating Interpretations of Local and Regionwide Change in the Study of Economic Development and Demographic Growth in the Colonial Chesapeake, 1630–1775." Regional Economic History Research Center, *Working Papers* 1 (3): 35–71.

————. 1983. "Settling the Chesapeake: The Growth, Spread, and Stabilization of a European Population." Paper for the seminar of the Philadelphia Center for Early American Studies. November 18.

————. 1984. "The Spread of Slavery in the Chesapeake." Paper presented to the Third Hall of Records Conference on Maryland History, St. Mary's City, May 17–20.

————. 1989. "The Demographic Development of Philadelphia in Some Comparative Perspective." *Proceedings of the American Philosophical Society* 133: 262–304.

————. 1992. "Economic Growth in Demographic Perspective: The Example of the Chesapeake, 1607–1775. In *Lois Green Carr: The Chesapeake and Beyond—A Celebration.* Crownsville: Maryland Historical and Cultural Publications, 55–92.

————. 1996. "Inflation and Deflation in Early America, 1634–1860." *Social Science History* 20: 469–505.

————. 1997. "Another Assessment of Demographic and Economic Interactions in England 1250–1860." Working paper #9697–15, Economic History Workshop, Indiana University, Bloomington, February 27.

————. 2001. *The History of Human Populations, I. Forms of Growth and Decline.* Westport, Conn.: Praeger Publishers.

Helin, Etienne, and Ad van der Woude. 1997. "Les Pays Bas." In Bardet and Dupâquier, eds., 1997, 411–40.

Henry, Louis, and Yves Blayo. 1975. "La population de la France de 1740 à 1860." *Population*, special issue: *Démographie Historique*, 71–122.

Heywood, Linda M., ed. 2002. *Central Africans and Cultural Transformation in the American Diaspora.* Cambridge: Cambridge University Press.

Higman, B. W. 1984. *Slave Populations of the British Caribbean 1807–1834.* Baltimore: The Johns Hopkins University Press.

————. 2000. "The Sugar Revolution." *Economic History Review* 53: 213–36.

Hochstadt, Steve. 1999. *Mobility and Modernity: Migration in Germany, 1820–1989.* Ann Arbor: University of Michigan Press.

Horn, James. 1979. "Servant Emigration to the Chesapeake in the Seventeenth Century." In Thad W. Tate and David Ammerman, eds., *The Chesapeake in the Seventeenth Century: Essays on Anglo-American Society and Politics.* New York: W. W. Norton and Company, 51–95.

Hutchinson, E. P. 1956. *Immigrants and Their Children, 1850–1950.* New York: John Wiley and Sons.

Inikori, Joseph E., ed. 1982. *Forced Migration: The Impact of the Export Slave Trade on African Societies.* New York: Africana Publishing Company.

Inikori, Joseph E., and Stanley L. Engerman, eds. 1992. *The Atlantic Slave Trade: Effects on Economies, Societies, and Peoples in Africa, the Americas, and Europe.* Durham, N.C.: Duke University Press.

Innes, Stephen, ed. 1988. *Work and Labor in Colonial America.* Chapel Hill: University of North Carolina Press.

Israel, Jonathan I. 1998. *The Dutch Republic: Its Rise, Greatness, and Fall 1477–1806.* Rev. ed. Oxford: Clarendon Press.

John, A. Meredith. 1988. *The Plantation Slaves of Trinidad, 1783–1816.* Cambridge: Cambridge University Press.

Klein, Herbert S. 1978. *The Middle Passage: Comparative Studies in the Atlantic Slave Trade.* Princeton, N.J.: Princeton University Press.

———. 1982. "The Portuguese Slave Trade from Angola in the Eighteenth Century." In Inikori, ed., 1982, 221–41.

———. 1999. *The Atlantic Slave Trade*. Cambridge: Cambridge University Press.

Klein, Herbert S., and Stanley L. Engerman. 1979. "A Note on Mortality in the French Slave Trade in the Eighteenth Century." In Gemery and Hogendorn, eds., 1979, 261–72.

Klein, Herbert S., Stanley L. Engerman, Robin Haines, and Ralph Shlomovitz. 2001. "Transoceanic Mortality: The Slave Trade in Comparative Perspective." *William and Mary Quarterly*, 3rd ser., 58: 93–118.

Klingaman, David C., and Richard K. Vedder, eds. 1975. *Essays in Nineteenth Century Economic History: The Old Northwest*. Athens: Ohio University Press.

———. 1987. *Essays in the Economy of the Old Northwest*. Athens: Ohio University Press.

Köllmann, W. 1965. "The Population of Barmen before and during the Period of Industrialization." In Glass and Eversley, eds., 1965, 588–607.

Kulikoff, Allan. 1975. "Black Society and the Economics of Slavery." *Maryland Historical Magazine* 70: 203–10.

———. 1976. *Tobacco and Slaves: Population, Economy, and Society in Prince Georges County, Maryland*. Ph.D. dissertation. Brandeis University.

———. 1977. "A 'Prolifik' People: Black Population Growth in the Chesapeake Colonies, 1700–1790." *Southern Studies* 16: 391–428.

———. 1986. *Tobacco and Slaves: The Development of Southern Cultures in the Chesapeake, 1680–1800*. Chapel Hill: University of North Carolina Press.

Kussmaul, Ann. 1981. *Servants in Husbandry in Early Modern England*. Cambridge: Cambridge University Press.

Kuznets, Simon. 1975. "Immigration of Russian Jews to the United States: Background and Structure." *Perspectives in American History* 9: 35–124.

Labaree, Benjamin W. 1962. *Patriots and Partisans: The Merchants of Newburyport, 1764–1815*. Cambridge, Mass.: Harvard University Press.

Lamb, D. P. 1976. "Volume and Tonnage of the Liverpool Slave Trade 1772–1807." In Anstey and Hair, eds., 1976, 91–112.

Land, Aubrey C., Lois Green Carr, and Edward C. Papenfuse, eds. 1977. *Law, Society, and Politics in Early Maryland*. Baltimore: The Johns Hopkins University Press.

Lee, James Z., and Cameron D. Campbell. 1997. *Fate and Fortune in Rural China: Social Organization and Population Behavior in Liaoning 1774–1873*. Cambridge: Cambridge University Press.

Le Veen, E. Philip. 1977. *British Slave Trade Suppressive Policies 1821–65*. New York: Arno Press.

Livi-Bacci, Massimo. 1992. *A Concise History of World Population*. Oxford: Blackwell Publishers; trans. by Carl Ipsen from *Storia minima della popolazione del mondo* (Turin: Loescher, 1989).

———. 2000. *The Population of Europe: A History*. Oxford: Blackwell Publishers; trans. by Cynthia De Nardi Ipsen and Carl Ipsen from *La popolazione nella storia d'Europa* (Rome: Gius. Laterza and Figlii, 1998).

Lockhart, Audrey. 1976. *Some Aspects of Emigration to the North American Colonies between 1660 and 1775*. New York: Arno Press.

Lotka, Alfred J. 1925. *Elements of Physical Biology*. Baltimore: Williams and Wilkins.

Lovejoy, Paul E. 1998. *Transformations in Slavery: A History of Slavery in Africa*.

African Studies Series 36. Cambridge: Cambridge University Press. First published 1983.

Lucassen, Jan. 1987. *Migrant Labour in Europe 1600–1900: The Drift to the North Sea.* London: Croom Helm.

———. 1994. "The Netherlands, the Dutch, and Long-Distance Migration in the Late Sixteenth to the Early Nineteenth Centuries." In Canny, ed., 1994b, 153–91.

Lucassen, Jan, and Leo Lucassen, eds. 1997. *Migration, Migration History, History: Old Paradigms and New Perspectives.* Bern: Peter Lang.

Lucassen, Jan, and Rinus Penninx. 1985. *Nieuwkomers: Immigranten en hun nakomelingen in Nederland 1550–1985.* Amsterdam: Meulenhoff Informatief.

———. 1997. *Newcomers: Immigrants and Their Descendants in the Netherlands 1550–1995.* Amsterdam: Het Spinhuis.

Lutz, Christopher H. 1994. *Santiago de Guatemala, 1541–1773: City, Caste, and Their Colonial Experience.* Norman: University of Oklahoma Press.

Magalhães Godinho, Vitorino. 1992. "Portugese Emigration from the Fifteenth to the Twentieth Century: Constants and Changes." In Emmer and Mörner eds., 1992, 13–48.

Malthus, Thomas Robert. 1798. *An Essay on the Principle of Population.* London: J. Johnson; reprinted New York: Augustus M. Kelley, 1965.

Mancall, Peter C., Joshua L. Rosenbloom, and Thomas Weiss. 2001. "Slave Prices and the South Carolina Economy." *Journal of Economic History* 61: 616–39.

Manning, Patrick. 1979. "The Slave Trade in the Bight of Benin, 1640–1890." In Gemery and Hogendorn, eds., 1979, 107–141.

———. 1982. *Slavery, Colonialism and Economic Growth in Dahomey, 1640–1960.* Cambridge: Cambridge University Press.

Martellone, Anna Maria. 1984. "Italian Mass Emigration to the United States, 1876–1930: A Historical Survey." *Perspectives in American History* n.s., 1: 378–423.

Mauro, Frédéric. 1986. "French Indentured Servants for America, 1500–1800." In Emmer, ed., 1986, 83–104.

McCusker, John J. 1970. *The Rum Trade and the Balance of Payments of the Thirteen Continental Colonies, 1650–1775.* 2 vols. Ph.D. dissertation, University of Pittsburgh.

———. 1978. *Money and Exchange in Europe and America, 1600–1775.* Chapel Hill: University of North Carolina Press.

McCusker, John J., and Russell R. Menard. 1991. *The Economy of British America, 1607–1789.* Chapel Hill: University of North Carolina Press.

Menard, Russell R. 1975. "The Maryland Slave Population, 1658 to 1730: A Demographic Profile of Blacks in Four Counties." *William and Mary Quarterly*, 3rd. ser., 32: 29–54.

———. 1977a. "Immigrants and Their Increase: The Process of Population Growth in Early Colonial Maryland." In Land et al., eds., 1977, 88–110.

———. 1977b. "From Servants to Slaves: The Transformation of the Chesapeake Labor System." *Southern Studies* 16: 355–90.

———. 1980. "The Tobacco Industry in the Chesapeake Colonies, 1617–1730: An Interpretation." *Research in Economic History* 5: 109–77.

———. 1988. "British Migration to the Chesapeake Colonies in the Seventeenth Century." In Carr, Morgan, and Russo, eds., 1988, 99–132.

———. 1989. "Slave Demography in the Low Country, 1670–1740: From Frontier Society to Plantation Regime." *Working Papers of the Social History Workshop*, University of Minnesota, Department of History.

Miller, Joseph C. 1988. *Way of Death: Merchant Capitalism and the Angolan Slave Trade 1730–1830*. Madison: University of Wisconsin Press.

———. 1992. "The Numbers, Origins, and Destinations of Slaves in the Eighteenth-Century Angolan Slave Trade." In Inikori and Engerman, eds., 1992, 77–115.

———. 2002. "Central Africa during the Era of the Slave Trade, c. 1490s–1850s." In Heywood, ed., 2002, 21–69.

Minchinton, W. E. 1976. "The Slave Trade of Bristol with the British Mainland Colonies in North America 1699–1770." In Anstey and Hair, eds., 1976, 39–59.

———. 1989. "Characteristics of British Slaving Vessels, 1698–1775." *Journal of Interdisciplinary History* 20: 53–81.

Mitchell, B(rian). R. 1992. *International Historical Statistics: Europe 1750–1988*. 3rd ed. New York: Stockton Press.

———. 1993. *International Historical Statistics: The Americas 1750–1988*. 2nd ed. New York: Stockton Press.

———. 1995. *International Historical Statistics: Africa, Asia, & Oceania 1750–1988*. 2nd rev. ed., New York: Stockton Press.

Morgan, Edmund S. 1975. *American Slavery, American Freedom: The Ordeal of Colonial Virginia*. New York: W. W. Norton & Company.

Morgan, Philip D. 1998. *Slave Counterpoint: Black Culture in the Eighteenth-Century Chesapeake and Low Country*. Chapel Hill: University of North Carolina Press.

Mörner, Magnus. 1992. "Immigration into Latin America, Especially Argentina and Chile." In Emmer and Mörner, eds., 1992, 211–43.

Nadal, Jordi. 1984. *La Población Española (Siglios XVI a XX)*, Edición corregida y aumentada. Barcelona: Editorial Ariel, S.A.; first published 1966.

Northrup, David. 1995. *Indentured Labor in the Age of Imperialism, 1834–1922*. Cambridge: Cambridge University Press.

Nwokeji, G. Ugo. 2001. "African Conceptions of Gender and the Slave Traffic." *William and Mary Quarterly*, 3rd ser., 58: 47–68.

Ó Gráda, Cormac. 1986. "Across the Briny Ocean: Some Thoughts on Irish Migration to America." In Glazier and de Rosa, eds., 1986, 79–94.

Otterstrom, Samuel M., and Carville Earle. 2002. "The Settlement of the United States from 1790 to 1990: Divergent Rates of Growth and the End of the Frontier." *Journal of Interdisciplinary History* 33: 59–81.

Paquette, Robert L., and Stanley L. Engerman, eds. 1996. *The Lesser Antilles in the Age of European Expansion*. Gainesville: University Press of Florida.

Parker, William N. 1987. "Native Origins of Modern Industry: Heavy Industrialization in the Old Northwest before 1900." In Klingaman and Vedder, eds., 1987, 243–74.

Patten, John. 1987. "Patterns of Migration and Movement of Labour to Three Pre-Industrial East Anglian Towns." In Clark and Souden, eds., 1987, 77–106.

Pearl, Raymond A., and Lowell J. Reed. 1920. "The Rate of Population Growth in the United States since 1970 and Its Mathematical Representation." *Proceedings of the National Academy of Sciences* 6: 275–88.

Perrenoud, Alfred. 1990. "Aspects of Fertility Decline in an Urban Setting: Rouen and Geneva." In van der Woude et al., eds., 1990, 243–63.

Pitman, Frank Wesley. 1917. *The Development of the British West Indies 1700–1763.* New Haven: Yale University Press.

Postma, Johannes Menne. 1990. *The Dutch in the Atlantic Slave Trade 1600–1815.* Cambridge: Cambridge University Press.

Pounds, N. J. G. 1994. *An Economic History of Medieval Europe.* 2nd ed. London: Longman.

Poussou, Jean-Perre. 1997. "Migrations et mobilitée de la population en Europe à l'époque moderne." In Bardet and Dupâquier, eds., 1997, 262–88.

Price, Jacob M. 1973. *France and the Chesapeake: A History of the French Tobacco Monopoly, 1674–1791, and of Its Relationship to the British and American Tobacco Trades.* 2 vols. Ann Arbor: University of Michigan Press.

Purvis, Thomas L. 1984. "The European Ancestry of the United States Population 1790." *William and Mary Quarterly*, 3rd ser., 41: 84–101.

Reher, David Sven. 1990. *Town and Country in Pre-Industrial Spain: Cuenca, 1550–1870.* Cambridge: Cambridge University Press.

Richardson, David. 1989. "Slave Exports from West and West-Central Africa, 1700–1810: New Estimates of Volume and Distribution." *Journal of African History* 30: 1–22.

———. 2001. "Shipboard Revolts, African Authority, and the Atlantic Slave Trade." *William and Mary Quarterly*, 3rd ser., 58: 69–92.

Ross, Robert. 1975. "The 'White' Population of South Africa in the Eighteenth Century." *Population Studies* 29: 217–30.

Russell, Josiah Cox. 1948. *British Medieval Population.* Albuquerque: University of New Mexico Press.

Sachse, Julius F. 1970. *The German Pietists of Provincial Pennsylvania.* New York: AMS Press. First published 1895.

Saito, Osamu. 1990. "The Changing Structure of Urban Employment and Its Effects on Migration Patterns in Eighteenth- and Nineteenth-Century Japan." In van der Woude et al., eds., 1990, 205–19.

Samuelson, Paul A. 1977. "Resolving a Historical Confusion in Population Analysis." In D. Smith and Keyfitz, eds., 1977, 109–29.

Schwartz, Stuart B. 1985. *Sugar Plantations in the Formation of Brazilian Society: Bahia 1550–1835.* Cambridge Latin American Studies 52. Cambridge: Cambridge University Press.

Schwarz, Leonard. 2000. "London 1700–1840." In Clark, ed., 2000, 641–71.

Sheridan, Richard B. 1974. *Sugar and Slavery: An Economic History of the British West Indies, 1623–1775.* Baltimore: Johns Hopkins University Press.

———. 1975. "Mortality and the Medical Treatment of Slaves in the British West Indies." In Engerman and Genovese, eds., 1975, 285–310.

Shlomowitz, Ralph. 1997. "Coerced and Free Migration from the United Kingdom to Australia, and Indentured Labour Migration from India and the Pacific Islands to Various Destinations: Issues, Debates, and New Evidence." In Lucassen and Lucassen, eds., 1997, 131–50.

Smallwood, Stephanie E. 2001. Review of Eltis, *Rise of African Slavery* and Eltis et al., *The Trans-Atlantic Slave Trade: A Database. William and Mary Quarterly*, 3rd ser., 58: 253–61.

Smith, David, and Nathan Keyfitz, eds. 1977. *Mathematical Demography: Selected Papers.* Berlin: Springer Verlag.

Smout, T. C., N. C. Landsman, and T. M. Devine. 1994. "Scottish Emigration in the Seventeenth and Eighteenth Centuries." In Canny, ed., 1994b, 76–112.

Smyth, William J. 1992. "Irish Emigration, 1700–1920." In Emmer and Mörner, eds., 1992, 49–78.

Souden, David. 1979, "Seventeenth-Century Indentured Servants Seen within a General English Migration System." Paper presented to the annual meeting of the Organization of American Historians, New Orleans, La., April 1979.

Spengler, Joseph J. 1938. *France Faces Depopulation*. Durham, N.C.: Duke University Press.

Spooner, Frank. 1986. "Batavia, 1673–1790: A City of Colonial Growth and Migration." In Glazier and de Rosa, eds., 1986, 58–78.

Stein, Robert Louis. 1979. *The French Slave Trade in the Eighteenth Century: An Old Regime Business*. Madison: University of Wisconsin Press.

Stone, Lawrence. 1947. "State Control in Sixteenth-Century England." *Economic History Review* 17: 103–20.

Strassburger, Ralph B., and William J. Hinke, eds. 1934. *Pennsylvania German Pioneers: A Publication of the Original Lists of Arrivals in the Port of Philadelphia from 1727–1808*. 3 vols. Norristown: Pennsylvania German Society.

Thernstrom, Stephan. 1964. *Poverty and Progress: Social Mobility in a Nineteenth Century City*. Cambridge, Mass.: Harvard University Press.

Thirsk, Joan. 1978. *Economic Policies and Projects: The Development of a Consumer Society in Early Modern England*. Oxford: Clarendon Press.

Tilly, Charles, ed. 1978. *Historical Studies of Changing Fertility*. Princeton: Princeton University Press.

Vamplew, W., ed. 1987. *Australians: Historical Statistics*. Broadway, NSW: Fairfax, Syme and Weldon.

Van den Boogaart, Ernst. 1986. "The Servant Migration to New Netherland, 1624–1664." In Emmer, ed., 1986, 55–81.

Van den Boogaart, Ernst, and Pieter C. Emmer. 1979. "The Dutch Participation in the Atlantic Slave Trade, 1596–1650." In Gemery and Hogendorn, eds., 1979, 353–75.

Van der Woude, Ad, Akira Hayami, and Jan de Vries, eds. 1990. *Urbanization in History: A Process of Dynamic Interactions*. Oxford: Clarendon Press.

Vedder, Richard K., and Lowell E. Gallaway. 1975. "Migration and the Old Northwest." In Klingaman and Vedder, eds., 1975, 159–76.

———. 1987. "Economic Growth and Decline in the Old Northwest." In Klingaman and Vedder, eds., 1987, 299–318.

Verhulst, Pierre-François. 1838. "Notice sur la loi que la population suit dans son accroissment." *Correspondence Mathématique et Physique* 10: 113–17. Brussels: A. Quetelet; trans. by David Smith in Smith and Keyfitz, eds., 1977, 333–37.

———. 1845. "Recherches mathématique sur la loi d'acroissement de la population." *Nouveaux Mémoires de l'Académie Royales des Sciences* (Brussels) 18: 3–40.

———. 1847. "Deuxième mémoire sur la loi d'accroissement de la population." *Nouveaux Mémoires de l'Académie Royales des Sciences* (Brussels) 20: 1–32.

Vila Vilar, Enriqueta. 1977. *Hispanoamérica y el comercio de esclavos*. Sevilla: Escuelo de Estudios Hispano-Americanos.

Von Ende, Eleanor, and Thomas Weiss. 1987. "Labor Force Changes in the Old Northwest." In Klingaman and Vedder, eds., 1987, 103–30.

Von Hippel, Wolfgang. 1984. *Auswanderung aus Südwestdeutschland: Studien zur württembergischen Auswanderung und Auswanderungspolitik im 18. und 19. Jahrhundert*. Stuttgart: Klett-Cotta.

Wallerstein, Immanuel. 1974. *The Modern World-System I: Capitalist Agriculture and the Origins of the European World-Economy in the Sixteenth Century*. San Diego: Academic Press.

―――. 1980. *The Modern World-System II: Mercantilism and the Consolidation of the European World-Economy*. New York: Academic Press.

Walsh, Lorena S. 2001. "The Chesapeake Slave Trade: Regional Patterns, African Origins, and Some Implications." *William and Mary Quarterly*, 3rd ser., 58: 139–70.

Wells, Robert V. 1975. *The Population of the British Colonies in America before 1776*. Princeton: Princeton University Press.

Williams, Eric E. 1944. *Capitalism and Slavery*. Chapel Hill: University of North Carolina Press.

Wokeck, Marianne S. 1981. "The Flow and Composition of German Immigration to Philadelphia, 1727–1775." *Pennsylvania Magazine of History and Biography* 105: 245–78.

―――. 1983. *Tide of Alien Tongues: The Flow and Ebb of German Immigration to Pennsylvania, 1683–1775*. Ph.D. dissertation, Temple University.

―――. 1986. "German Immigration to Colonial America: Prototype of a Transatlantic Mass Migration." In Frank Trommler and Joseph McVeigh, eds., *American and the Germans: An Assessment of a Three-Hundred-Year History*. 2 vols. Philadelphia: University of Pennsylvania Press, 1: 3–13.

―――. 1991. "Harnessing the Lure of 'the Best Poor Man's Country': The Dynamics of German-Speaking Immigration to British North America, 1683–1783." In Ida Altman and James Horn, eds., *To Make America: European Emigration in the Early Modern Period*. Berkeley: University of California Press, 104–43.

―――. 1996. "Irish Immigration to the Delaware Valley before the American Revolution." *Proceedings of the Royal Irish Academy* 96, C: 103–35.

―――. 1999. *Trade in Strangers: The Beginnings of Mass Migration to North America*. University Park: Pennsylvania State University Press.

―――. 2002. "Irish and German Migration to Eighteenth-Century North America." In Eltis, ed., 2002, 152–75.

Wood, Peter H. 1974. *Black Majority: Negroes in South Carolina from 1670 through the Stono Rebellion*. New York: Knopf.

Woodruff, William. 1966. *Impact of Western Man: A Study of Europe's Role in the World Economy 1750–1960*. London: Macmillan.

Wrigley, E. A. 1967. "A Simple Model of London's Importance in Changing English Society and Economy 1650–1750." *Past and Present* 37: 44–70.

―――. 1985. "Urban Growth and Agricultural Change: England and the Continent in the Early Modern Period." *Journal of Interdisciplinary History* 15: 683–728.

Wrigley, E A., and R. S. Schofield. 1981. *The Population History of England, 1541–1871: A Reconstruction*. Cambridge, Mass.: Harvard University Press.

Index

Africa: H curve of population, 246–47; indentured workers, 84, 85; urbanization, 286–87, 297. *See also* Slaves/slaving; *specific countries*

Age: C curve, 497–99; U.S. population, 473–82. *See also* Children; *specific countries*

Agriculture, 290–98; labor productivity, 290–95; rural development and urbanization, 229–40, 285; U.S. move away from, 214–15

Aja people, 124–28, 149–50, 364

Alabama: African Americans, 314–15, 319, 320; internal U.S. migration, 43, 47; population age, 478, 481

Alaska, 479, 482–83, 484

Albania, 286–87

Alost, 206, 207, 208

Amboinese, 199–203

American colonies. *See* Colonial America

Amsterdam: foreign-born, 448–50, 514; geographic potential, 263–65; migration to, 184–85; population size, 254, 272, 273; urbanization, 219, 221, 223, 227, 244

Angola: slaves/slaving, 143–46, 152, 153, 159; slaves/slaving, children, 366, 367–68; slaves/slaving, treatment/mortality, 399. *See also specific regions*

Anne Arundel County, decedents, 431–33

Antigua: Africanization, 3–7, 309, 310, 312; European children, 413, 414, 415; European women, 410, 411, 413; immigration, 53–56; slaves/slaving, 158, 161; slaves/slaving, age/gender proportions, 353; slaves/slaving, prices, 375–76, 377, 389; slaves/slaving, self-replacement, 330, 339

Antwerp, geographic potential, 262–63, 272, 273

Argentina: migration, 32, 37, 38; population growth, 246, 508

Arizona: population age, 479, 480, 482; women in population, 482–83, 484

Arkansas: African Americans, 314, 317, 319, 320; population age, 478, 481; U.S. internal migration, 43

Asia: slaves/slaving, 114, 117, 119; urbanization, 286–87, 294, 296. *See also specific countries*

Atlantic Islands, 95, 96, 97, 100

Atlantic slave trade. *See* Slaves/slaving

About the Author

P. M. G. HARRIS is Professor Emeritus of History from Temple University, currently an independent scholar adjunct in History at Indiana University Purdue University Indianapolis. He has published essays and articles on the historical social origins of American leaders, the relationship of local and regional settlement in early America, the demographic expansions of the Chesapeake and the Delaware Valley in the colonial era, connections between population change and economic development in early Maryland and Virginia, and the trends of prices in the American colonies.